HANKEY

Man of Secrets

Volume II 1919-1931

*by the same author*

THE WAR AT SEA (3 vols. in 4 parts. HMSO)

H.M.S. WARSPITE

THE SECRET CAPTURE

THE NAVY AT WAR 1939-1945

THE STRATEGY OF SEA POWER

A MERCHANT FLEET IN WAR 1939-1945

THE ART OF LEADERSHIP

NAVAL POLICY BETWEEN THE WARS
VOL. I 1919-1929

(Ed.) DOCUMENTS RELATING TO THE NAVAL AIR SERVICE
VOL. I 1908-1918 (NAVY RECORDS SOCIETY)

HANKEY MAN OF SECRETS
VOL. I 1877-1918

# HANKEY
## Man of Secrets
### Volume II 1919-1931

STEPHEN ROSKILL

COLLINS
*St James's Place London*
1972

William Collins Sons & Co Ltd
London · Glasgow · Sydney · Auckland
Toronto · Johannesburg



First published 1972

ISBN 0 00 211330 9
Set in Monotype Garamond
Made and Printed in Great Britain by
William Collins Sons & Co Ltd Glasgow

# Contents

FOREWORD AND ACKNOWLEDGEMENTS 11

1 The First Steps to Peace. November-December 1918 19
2 The Hard Road to Peace. January-February 1919 43
3 The Council of Four. March-May 1919 68
4 The Treaties Signed. June-August 1919 94
5 The End of the War Cabinet. September-December 1919 114
6 Europe in Disarray. January-April 1920 140
7 The Era of Conferences I. May-December 1920 164
8 The Era of Conferences II. January-October 1921 213
9 The Washington and Genoa Conferences. November 1921-May 1922 238
10 The Near East Crisis and the Fall of Lloyd George. June-October 1922 279
11 Under Bonar Law. The fight for the Cabinet Secretariat. October-December 1922 304
12 From Bonar Law to Baldwin. January-December 1923 330
13 The First Labour Government. January-October 1924 353
14 Back to Baldwin. November 1924-December 1925 387
15 The Essentials of Defence. January 1926-May 1929 417
16 The Second Labour Government. June-December 1929 475
17 A Year of Conferences. 1930 502
18 Crisis. 1931 535

INDEX 577

# Illustrations


President Wilson's note *page* 59

Hankey at the Peace Conference *between pages* 80-81

Lloyd George and his family visit the battlefields

The Paris Peace Conference—a panorama of personalities (*Illustrated London News*)

Curzon's doodles

Curzon and Hankey

*Ordre du Jour* for the signature of the Peace Treaty *page* 93

Will Dyson's prophetic cartoon 102

Lloyd George's doodles *facing page* 192

The First Lympne Conference May 1920 193

The Third Lympne Conference August 1920 193

Hankey, Lloyd George and Giolitti 224

Lloyd George and Hankey 224

Hankey and Chelmsford (*Sport and General Press Agency*) 225

Balfour's notes for his Washington speech *page* 243

Hankey's draft letter to Lloyd George (*Crown Copyright*) 247

Exchange of notes between Hankey and Lloyd George at Genoa 275

The Imperial Conference of 1926 *facing page* 480 (*Illustrated London News*)

At ease at Highstead 480

Sir Warden Chilcott at Deauville (*The Tatler*) 481

The 'Dolphin' at Cowes (*Beken of Cowes*) 481

The Order of the Bath procession *facing page* 512
The Imperial Conference of 1930 (*The Tatler*) 512
The London Naval Conference: 513
King George at the opening
(*Illustrated London News*)
Empire and Commonwealth Delegates
(*Illustrated London News*)
Hankey's draft 'Manifesto' August 1931 *page* 549
MacDonald's amended note on financial measures 551

*MAP*

The Dardanelles in 1922 *page* 278

# Abbreviations

| | |
|---|---|
| Adm. | Admiralty document in P.R.O. |
| Air | Air Ministry document in P.R.O. |
| A.R.P. | Air Raid Precautions (also Sub-Committee of C.I.D. on same). |
| B.E.D. | British Empire Delegation (to International Conferences). |
| B.M. | British Museum. |
| B.R. | Belligerent Rights (also Sub-Committee of C.I.D. on same). |
| Cab. | (Followed by suffix indicating series and number) Cabinet Minute or Memorandum in P.R.O. |
| C.A.S. | Chief of the Air Staff. |
| C.C.R. | Committee of Civil Research. |
| Cd. and Cmd. | Command Papers. |
| C.F. | Council of Four (at Paris Peace Conference). |
| C.I.D. | Committee of Imperial Defence (followed by symbols indicating series). |
| C.I.G.S. | Chief of Imperial General Staff. |
| C-in-C. | Commander-in-Chief. |
| C.N.S. | Chief of Naval Staff. |
| C.O.S. | Chiefs of Staff Sub-Committee of C.I.D. |
| C.P. | Cabinet Memorandum of series indicated. |
| D.B.F.P. | Documents on British Foreign Policy. |
| D.M.O. | Director of Military Operations. |
| D.P.C. | Disarmament Policy Committee of 1931. |
| D.R.C. | Defence Requirements Committee of 1933-35. |
| E.A.C. | Economic Advisory Council of 1929-30. |
| F.O. | Foreign Office document in P.R.O. |
| F.S. | Fighting Services' Committee of 1929-30. |
| G.H.Q. | General Headquarters. |
| G.O.C. | General Officer Commanding. |

| | |
|---|---|
| G.T. | Cabinet Memorandum in series indicated. |
| H.A.C. | Home Affairs Sub-Committee of C.I.D. |
| H.P.D.C. | Home Ports Defence Sub-Committee of C.I.D. |
| I.C. | International Conference series in P.R.O. |
| I.I.C. | Industrial Intelligence Centre. |
| I.R.A. | Irish Republican Army. |
| I.W.C. | Imperial War Cabinet series in P.R.O. |
| L.N.C. | London Naval Conference 1930. |
| N.M.M. | National Maritime Museum. |
| O.D.C. | Overseas Defence Sub-Committee of C.I.D. |
| Parl. Deb. | Parliamentary Debates (*Hansard*, Lords or Commons as indicated). All in 5th series. |
| P.M. | Prime Minister (British). |
| Premier | Correspondence of Prime Ministers in P.R.O. |
| P.R.O. | Public Record Office. |
| R.A. | Royal Archives, Windsor Castle. |
| R.G. | Record Group, U.S. National Archives. |
| R.I.C. | Royal Irish Constabulary. |
| S.W.C. | Supreme War Council of Allies. |
| U.P. | University Press. |
| W.O. | War Office document in P.R.O. |

# Foreword and Acknowledgements

SEVERAL considerations have contributed to the decision to end this second volume of the biography of Lord Hankey at the political and economic crisis of 1931, and to devote a third volume to the final phase of his career. In the first place a number of important private collections of papers, which undoubtedly contain much Hankey material covering the years 1932–42, are not yet available for research. It seems very undesirable to attempt to describe authoritatively his work and influence during that period without having studied his correspondence with, for example, Mr. Neville Chamberlain and Lord Avon. Secondly the official archives for the years 1939–42, when Lord Hankey was a member of Neville Chamberlain's War Cabinet and of Churchill's administration, will not be wholly open until 1972. Thirdly when I had completed the story as far as the end of 1931 I realised that a vast amount of important material dealing with the next decade existed in Lord Hankey's papers and in other collections made available to me; and that if I adhered to my original intention of completing my task in two volumes I would have to cut down drastically or totally omit much that the historically minded reader would wish to have presented to him. And, lastly, I hope it will not be considered immodest if I admit that the very generous reception accorded to my first volume encouraged hopes that the general reader would prefer me to continue to give Hankey's life and work the same full scope. His position at the centre of British politics lasted so long, and his encounters with the statesmen, politicians and service men of foreign countries, as well as those of the British Empire and Commonwealth, were so numerous and frequent that I make no apology for the fact that his biography is in some degree a history of the period. Indeed I cannot see in what other manner his life and work can be given adequate treatment.

Publication of my first volume brought me a very large correspondence from men and women who may reasonably be said to represent a broad spectrum of British and Commonwealth politics and public affairs during the first half of this century. Most of my correspondents had known Hankey personally, or had dealings with him in one or other of the many fields of his official activities. Their letters contributed greatly to my understanding of the subject of this biography, and to my knowledge of the events of the period. The majority of my correspondents may justly be described as admirers of Hankey, who believed that, even though he was certainly not always right, his judgement was generally so sound, and based on such wide experience, that the history of this country would have taken a happier course had his advice been followed more often. A few were critical of his attitude to particular issues in which he was involved, and a still smaller minority were in some degree critical of him as a person. For example the 'self praise' to which he gave voice in his diary evidently aroused the distaste of some readers. To those critics I would reply that such a trait is by no means uncommon among political diarists, and that even Samuel Pepys indulged in it quite frequently. Moreover Hankey was far too astute not to realise that publication of such remarks would lay him open to criticism. Yet, unlike Charles Fulke Greville, he left his diary untouched, knowing full well that it would some day be published exactly as he wrote it. I could of course easily have omitted such passages; but I have throughout this work been deeply conscious of the danger that besets every biographer – namely to allow himself to be seduced into what Iris Origo has so aptly stigmatised as 'the smoothing-out and the touching up', with the result that 'in the end a portrait is built up: slick, vivid, convincing – and false'.[1] Instead I have tried, as I am sure Hankey himself would have wished, to combine what Virginia Woolf called 'the granite-like solidity of truth' with 'the rainbow-like intangibility of personality'. If in Hankey's case the personality as here revealed does not appeal to some readers I can only express the hope that he or she will accept that there is a good deal in Dr. Johnson's remark that 'If nothing but the bright side of characters should be shown, we should sit in despondency, and think it utterly impossible to imitate them in *anything*'.

I would like to take this opportunity to thank all my correspondents for their letters, and to assure the few who have corrected me on matters of fact that I have noted their corrections for use when the

[1]From a lecture *Biography – True and False*. Quoted in *Images and Shadows* (Murray, 1970) p. 4.

first volume is reprinted. To those who have disagreed with me on matters of historical interpretation I would say that I fully accept their entitlement to do so, and lay no claim whatever to having said the final word on my subject.

Having received such universal kindness and consideration from all those whom I have pestered for information it may seem invidious to single out a few for special mention. But I must particularly thank The Right Hon. the Earl of Avon, The Right Hon. the Earl of Swinton, The Right Hon. the Baron Casey, Frances, Countess Lloyd George, Wing-Commander Sir Archibald James, Sir Graham Vincent, Sir Colin Coote, Sir Harry Batterbee, Sir Keith Officer, J. Burgon Bickersteth, Dr. A. L. Rowse, Montgomery Belgion and Ronald Wells for the trouble they took to answer my importunities, for the hospitality many of them have shown me in their homes, and for the letters and papers they have lent or given to me. The Right Hon. the Viscount Simon and The Right Hon. the Viscount Trenchard have provided me with much valuable material from their fathers' papers, and I have been particularly fortunate in my contacts with a number of Hankey's erstwhile assistants in the offices of the Cabinet and C.I.D. In particular Lord Casey, Air Chief-Marshal Sir William Elliot, Wing-Commander Sir John Hodsoll, Vice-Admiral A. D. Nichol and Captain A. W. Clarke, R.N., all of whom worked in Whitehall Gardens in between the wars, have allowed me to exploit their memories.

My research has brought me into contact with a large number of historians who have been working on some particular aspect of the same period, and I must acknowledge my debt to Mr. Christopher Thorne and Mr. Keith Middlemas, both of the University of Sussex, Dr. David Carlton of the North-Western Polytechnic, Mr. Larry Pratt of the London School of Economics and Mrs. Rosemary Righter, formerly of the University of Warwick. I hope that in all these cases the information I have been able to give has been as helpful as that which I have received. The debt for research I owe to Commander Geoffrey Hare, and to my daughter-in-law Mrs. Nicholas Roskill increases with the passage of every year and the production of every book, as does my dependence on Miss Edith Eales for her devoted and careful secretarial work. Once again Mr. Richard Ollard, of Collins & Co. has given me far more than any writer is entitled to expect of his Publisher's editor. Not only is his historical training and experience far superior to my own, but his encouragement and friendship have constantly helped me through the periods from which I suppose all writers suffer – when nothing seems to go right and even the grasshopper has become a burden. Without the encouragement of his frequent company and the uncomplaining support of my wife I am quite sure this work would never have seen the light of day.

I must thank my colleagues at Churchill College, Cambridge most warmly for their generosity and understanding in providing me over so many years with exceptionally favourable conditions under which to work, and with the constant stimulus of their company. And when at last I passed the age at which the University of Cambridge regards one as superannuated my college greatly eased the change by electing me into a Life Fellowship. I must also acknowledge my debt to the Trustees of the Leverhulme Foundation for their generous grant of an Emeritus Fellowship for the year 1970–71 and to the American Philosophical Society for support which enabled me to pay a visit to the United States in 1969 to search for Hankey material in the official archives and the numerous private collections of papers held in that country.

In addition to the Libraries, Universities, museums and individuals to whom I acknowledged my debt for access to papers in their charge in my first volume I would add the following:—

The University of Cambridge Library – Papers of 1st Earl Baldwin and 1st Viscount Templewood.

The British Museum – Papers of 1st Viscount D'Abernon.

The Right Hon. Malcolm MacDonald and Mr. David Marquand – Papers of Mr. Ramsay MacDonald.

The Right Hon. the Viscount Bridgeman – Papers of 1st Viscount Bridgeman.

The Right Hon. the Earl Beatty – Papers of Admiral of the Fleet Earl Beatty.

The Right Hon. the Viscount Trenchard – Papers of Marshal of the Royal Air Force Viscount Trenchard.

For permission to publish copyright material I am indebted to the following:—

H.M. The Queen – Papers of King George V and official papers of Lord Stamfordham as Private Secretary to King George V.

Sir Michael Adeane – Private papers of Lord Stamfordham.

The First Beaverbrook Foundation – Papers of 1st Earl Lloyd George and of Mr. A. Bonar Law held by the Beaverbrook Library.

The First Beaverbrook Foundation and the National Library of Wales

jointly – Papers of 1st Earl Lloyd George not held by the Beaverbrook Library.
The Right Hon. the Viscount Scarsdale – Papers of Marquess Curzon.
The Right Hon. the Earl Balfour – Papers of 1st Earl Balfour.
C. and T. Publications and Mr. Winston Churchill – Papers of Sir Winston Churchill.
The Right Hon. the Viscount Esher – Papers of 2nd Viscount Esher.
A. R. B. Haldane, Esq. – Papers of Viscount Haldane.
Baroness White and Mr. Tristan Jones – Papers of Dr. Thomas Jones and, where published in Mr. Keith Middlemas's *Whitehall Diary* (Oxford U.P., 2 Vols., 1969) to the editor and publisher.
The Right Hon. Malcolm MacDonald – Papers of Mr. Ramsay MacDonald.
The Warden and Fellows, New College, Oxford – Papers of Viscount Milner.
The Right Hon. the Earl Baldwin – Papers of 1st Earl Baldwin.
The Right Hon. the Viscount Bridgeman – Papers of 1st Viscount Bridgeman.
Henry Borden, Esq. – Papers of Sir Robert Borden.
Sir Geoffrey Keynes – Papers of 1st Baron Keynes.
Paul E. Paget, Esq. – Papers of 1st Viscount Templewood.
The Right Hon. the Earl of Birkenhead – Papers of 1st Earl of Birkenhead.
The Right Hon. the Viscount Trenchard – Papers of Marshal of the Royal Air Force Viscount Trenchard.
Mrs. William T. Gossett – Papers of Chief Justice Charles Evans Hughes.
Lawrence Burgis, Esq. – His own letters to Lord Hankey.

All quotations from British official documents held in the Public Record Office are Crown Copyright and are reproduced by kind permission of The Controller, Her Majesty's Stationery Office. I must also acknowledge the constant help received from Mr. T. J. Donovan of the Public Record Office and his staff, who have piloted my course through the vast collection of British Cabinet papers and have constantly helped me to find what I need.

Perhaps I should here add a note on the system I have followed in my source references to Cabinet papers. Wherever in the footnotes two figures are shown separated by a diagonal stroke thus Cab. 21/212 or Cab. 2/5 the reference is to the Public Record Office's numeration. But I have thought it advantageous to the student to give in most cases the original Cabinet Office references as well, since otherwise he or she may have to search through a large amount of paper in order to find the document in question. Under Hankey's system Cabinet Minutes were numbered seriatim in every year, and the number indicating the meeting had the last two figures of the year printed after it in round brackets. Thus 'Cabinet 28(20)' refers to the Minutes (after August 1919 called the Conclusions) of the 28th Cabinet meeting held in 1920.[1] The original C.P. series of Cabinet Memoranda started in November 1919 and ended with C.P. 4379 of 30th December 1922. Thereafter Hankey started the C.P. series afresh at the beginning of every year. Thus C.P. 1(23) is the first memorandum of 1923; C.P. 181(31) the 181st memorandum of 1931 and so on. The memoranda submitted to the C.I.D. retain throughout the period covered by this volume the numbers in the (A), (B), (C) and (D) series with which the reader of my first volume will be familiar.[2] And the memoranda submitted to the numerous sub-committees of the C.I.D. and the Cabinet, and those prepared for Imperial and International conferences, are still given self-evident symbols, such as C.O.S. for Chiefs of Staff Committee, and are numbered consecutively on the well-tried system which dates to the early days of the C.I.D. When a C.I.D. memorandum was brought before the Cabinet for consideration or decision, as happened in a great many cases, it would be reprinted with a C.P. number. Thus C.I.D. 388D also became C.P. 22(23). In the case of C.I.D. and Cabinet memoranda in these special series I have also usually given the original C.I.D. or Cabinet Office reference, as well as that given to the document in question by the Public Record Office. My object has been to try and make it as easy as possible to trace the documents to which I refer in the text. As in my first volume all documents not given source references are in the Hankey papers.

One other point must be explained. Very early in my study of the Hankey diaries and papers I realised that much of his correspondence and many memoranda written by him had been placed in special files which he always referred to as his 'Magnum Opus'.[3] These files were not to be found among the Cabinet papers transferred to the Public Record Office and opened under the new 'Thirty Year Rule'. As they were obviously of prime importance to Hankey's biographer I enquired of the Cabinet office in 1967 whether the 'Magnum Opus' still existed. In reply I was told that investigation would be made to see whether any more material held in that office could be released. As nothing

[1]In the headings to Cabinet Minutes or Conclusions Hankey always wrote the word 'Cabinet' in full. The same practice has been followed here – partly to avoid confusion with P.R.O. references in which the abbreviation 'Cab.' is always used.
[2]See Vol. I, pp. 91–2. [3]See Vol. I, p. 140, *note* 2.

further was heard I assumed that either the 'Magnum Opus' had been destroyed during the process known as 'weeding' to which all official records are subjected, or that it was classed among those papers which were to remain closed under the Public Record Act for longer periods than 30 years. To my great surprise I discovered in November 1970 that the 'Magnum Opus' files, or 191 of them, had turned up in the Public Record Office and been given P.R.O. numbers Cab. 63/1–191. Unfortunately this volume was by that time already typed; but I have been through this new collection as quickly as possible and have made additions and insertions at various points. Fortunately copies of a great many of the papers in the 'Magnum Opus' exist in one or other of the series of Cabinet documents which I had already studied.

Finally I must once again acknowledge my gratitude to the Rev. S. B.-R. Poole for the great trouble he has taken over compiling the Index.

STEPHEN ROSKILL

Blounce, South Warnborough, Hants.
Churchill College, Cambridge.
1969–71.

*Chapter* 1

# The First Steps to Peace. November-December 1918

HANKEY did not fully recover from the attack of influenza which had laid him low throughout the critical days of the Armistice negotiations until 19th November. His first action on returning to the office after a fortnight's absence was to assemble the whole staff of the Cabinet Secretariat, from his assistant secretaries down to the humblest typist, in order to thank them for their contribution to the Allied victory. He told them about the many tributes he had recently received, and how the U.S.A., France and Italy had all paid them the compliment of copying the British system; which confirmed his own 'heartfelt pride in the efficiency of this office'. He specially praised their discretion in the past, and strongly stressed the importance of 'observation of secrecy in the future'. Colonel Dally Jones, the senior Assistant Secretary, replied to this encomium by recalling 'the extraordinary way' Hankey had applied himself to any task set before him, and his 'unflagging energy'. If he had worked the staff hard, Jones concluded, he had worked himself much harder – all of which was certainly no exaggeration.[1]

Here it may be appropriate to record an incident which, although it occurred before the end of the war, demonstrates very clearly how and why Hankey obtained such loyal and devoted service from his staff. Lawrence Burgis, his private secretary from 1921–37, recalls that when he joined the War Cabinet Secretariat early in 1918 he was highly apprehensive about having to take some of the minutes – having had no experience at all of such work. As the discussion progressed Burgis found himself more and more out of his depth, and when it ended he had only 'a few indecipherable scrawls' on his pad. When he got up to leave the Cabinet room Hankey beckoned Burgis to come over to where he was sitting next to Lloyd George, and handed him a sheet of

[1]Cab. 21/128.

paper with the remark 'This may help you with your minute'. On the paper was a complete summary of the Cabinet's discussion and the Conclusion reached. 'That takes a bit of beating' is Burgis's retrospective comment.[1]

Immediately after the exchange of compliments with his staff Hankey turned his attention to the arrears of business which had piled up during his absence; and the most urgent matter was that the third and final session of the Imperial War Conference was to begin next day.[2] He had already heard from Sir Robert Borden that the Dominion representatives were getting restive over their exclusion from the current discussions in the War Cabinet; but the pressure on British Ministers was so heavy that he was able to do little except warn Lloyd George and Walter Long regarding the unwisdom of keeping the Commonwealth statesmen ignorant of what was happening.[3] Rather oddly the trial of the Kaiser, to which Lloyd George had unwisely committed himself, figured prominently in these deliberations. Many years later, when Hankey was campaigning against the 'War Crimes' trials which followed the end of World War II, he recalled hearing Bonar Law call out to the Prime Minister 'George! If you take my advice you will not touch it! [i.e. the trial and possible execution of the Kaiser]. If you do, believe me you will always regret it'.[4] Hankey's view was exactly the same; but Lloyd George did not abandon the proposal until, in January 1920, the Dutch government delivered what Hankey described as a 'well-deserved snub' by refusing to admit the validity of the claim of the Allies to extradite and try the Kaiser.[5]

At this early stage, before the militarist elements in Germany had shown their determination to do all they could to evade the Armistice terms, and the inability of the weak Weimar government to control those elements had not yet become apparent, the revictualling of Germany, where distress was acute, stood high on the Cabinet's agenda. On 21st November Hankey, on Lloyd George's instructions, approached Lord Reading, who had temporarily returned from the

[1]Burgis to the author 11th April 1970. [2]I.W.C. series. Cab. 23.

[3]See Lord Hankey, *The Supreme Control at the Paris Peace Conference 1919* (Chatto and Windus, 1963) p. 13. Henceforth cited as *Supreme Control*.

[4]Lord Hankey, *Politics, Trials and Errors* (Pen-in-Hand, Oxford, 1950) p. 1.

[5]For Lloyd George's case regarding the trial of the Kaiser see *The Truth about the Peace Treaties*, Vol. I, pp. 94–114 and 136–45. This source is henceforth cited as Lloyd George, *Peace Treaties*. The Dutch government's decisive rejection of the Allies' demand took place on 23rd Jan. 1920. *Supreme Control*, p. 195.

Washington embassy, to press him to accept the post of 'High Commissioner in charge of the relief and revictualling of allied, enemy and neutral countries'.[1] This was an extremely onerous and complicated task, involving the Ministries of Food and of Shipping, Austen Chamberlain's Economic Defence and Development Commission, and many other British and Allied authorities. But within a few days Hankey had obtained the necessary departmental agreement, and had persuaded the reluctant Reading to take on the job.[2]

The representation of the self-governing Dominions at the Peace Conference quickly became an important issue; since the great contribution they had made to the Allied war effort, taken with their new-found determination to run their own affairs in complete independence of the Mother Country, made it certain that they would not be content to be represented solely by a unified British Empire delegation. Lloyd George and Hankey were both alive to the problem from the beginning, and were determined that the Dominions' views should be met. Hankey's preference was for a 'Panel' of British, Empire and Dominion representatives; and, as we saw earlier, he wanted a place to be made for Asquith on the panel. But that did not fully meet Dominion aspirations. We will return later to the solution arrived at.

Almost simultaneously with the first move in the campaign for contraction and economy in government departments Hankey circulated a memorandum urging 'that the experience of the present war should be available in a practical form for any future war in which, at however distant a date, this country may have the misfortune to be involved'.[3] This was his first step towards revising and bringing up to date the famous War Book of 1914.

*Diary 22nd November 1918*

The meeting of the War Cabinet arranged for noon was cancelled at the last moment, as Ll. G., who had said he was not coming up, turned up and wanted the room. He is in a most excited and irritable condition owing to the General Election, and it is very difficult to get any serious work out of him. Bonar Law is said to be little better, though I have not found him so. A. J. Balfour came in at noon and stayed some time, talking over a number of matters. He agreed with me that the best method of delegates for the peace conference is to have a panel from which the agreed number can be drawn. This is the only way I can see of working in the Dominion repre-

[1]Diary 21st Nov. 1918. [2]See Vol. I, pp. 240 and 616, *notes*.
[3]G.T. 6338 of 21st Nov. 1918. Cab. 24/70.

sentatives at all, as they would never agree to appoint one of their number to represent them. Moreover Asquith could be fitted in on this plan. Later Smuts came to see me and agreed about the 'panel' plan for the peace conference. Then I went to see Lord Hardinge at the Foreign Office and arranged with him our relations at the peace conference, viz. I would look after the meetings of British delegates outside the conference, while he should be in charge of all conference arrangements. This of course depends on the P.M., who doesn't much like Hardinge. I lunched alone with Sir Eric Geddes who wanted to consult me about his own future. He is reluctant to leave the Adty. until he has placed the War Staff on a more permanent footing and effected certain measures of re-organisation.[1] The P.M. gives him the choice of remaining as First Lord or becoming Minister of Transportation. He has a burning enthusiasm, and plans for the latter, on which he expounded to me at great length. One difficulty is that he is actually drawing a salary of £10,000 a year from the N.E. Rlwy. with a pension of £4,000 a year at 60, and he will be sacrificing this by remaining in the Ministry, without any certainty of continuing long in office. My advice was – to leave the Admiralty, which will become a sideshow in 3 months, but to try and select his successor and inculcate him with sound ideas, enabling him to resist the reactionary and muddly tendencies of the naval officer; and to take up the Transportation problem, for which he has an obvious 'call', trusting to get directorships, if Ll. G. should fail politically. We had much interesting talk on other subjects, and he told me that everyone had been singing my praises while I was away. Long talk with Tom Jones and Professor Adams about the desirability of linking the Universities and their professors and academic studies more closely to the practical work of Govt. Depts. This discussion arose out of a Memo. I have put to the War Cabinet advocating that all Depts. shall record their experiences etc. with a view to our preparation for future wars. . .[2]

*November 23rd*

. . . When I arrived at the office I found the King had sent for me. I went to him at 12.15 and stayed about an hour. I noticed a deference among the flunkeys at the door, and a cordiality and respect among the A.D.Cs and the Gentlemen-in-Waiting, which seemed to show that my position at the palace was a strong one. The King has aged since I saw him last some two years ago, and his beard is now partly grey. He began by explaining that he had not sent for me since the present Govt. has come into office, partly because he knew I was so busy, but also because he did not wish it to be thought that

[1]See Stephen Roskill, *Naval Policy between the Wars* (Collins, 1968), Vol. I, p. 30 regarding Geddes's departure from the Admiralty. This source is henceforth cited as Roskill, *Naval Policy*.

[2]G.T. 6338. See above.

he was trying to influence matters or interfere through my instrumentality. He then reminded me that early in the war he had warned me that, if I confined myself to my job, and avoided all temptation to make suggestions and get power into my hands, I should be a great force in the war.[1] He said I had followed his advice, with the result that, in his opinion, I had done more than any other person towards winning the war. He added that Asquith and Lloyd George had independently said this. He therefore had sent for me to express his appreciation and thanks. I did my best to make a suitable reply to this very kind and gracious speech, though I was constantly interrupted. I then spoke up for my office and asked if His Majesty would give me a message for all the staff of both sexes. He gladly did so, and I prepared it for circulation immediately on my return. Next, the King, after cautioning me to keep the matter secret, asked me to do my best to get Asquith to go to the peace conference and consulted me as to the best way in which he should tackle Ll. G. on the subject, when he saw him on Monday. I advised him to urge the adoption of the 'panel' system, which would enable Asquith or anyone else to be fitted in. . . . He said 'Lloyd George will say that the King wants Asquith to go to the peace conference, because he is his friend. But the truth is I want him to go for the good of the nation, for the good of Lloyd George himself, and to make for unity.' He hardly concealed his own personal mistrust of Lloyd George, and his liking for Asquith. He thinks that, if Ll. G. wins the election he will not last more than 18 months; that, Labour is not ready to form a Govt.; and that Asquith is certain to get back before long. He asked me to do all I could to further this,[2] which of course I promised to do, as I am keen on it myself. . . . On my way out I called on Lord Stamfordham, who spoke in the most complimentary terms of my work. He consulted me as to the advisability of introducing a Labour man into the King's secretariat, and I promised to consult Tom Jones. Stamfordham, clearly, does not like or trust Ll. G. He spoke bitterly of Ll. G.'s absence last Tuesday from the King's message to parlt., but I assured him that Ll. G. had really been seedy and I think got him right. He said 'Well, I suppose one suspects Lloyd George of things, which one would not suspect in another man.' Ll. G. has no opinion of him either.

The message which Hankey extracted from the King was issued as an Office Note.[3]

[1]See Vol. I, p. 250.
[2]Hankey obviously here meant getting a place for Asquith at the Peace Conference. As written it might be taken to mean that the King was enlisting Hankey's support to accomplish Asquith's return to political power.
[3]Lloyd George papers F/23/3/20.

*2 Whitehall Gardens. 23rd November 1918*

I have to-day received a personal command from The King to express to all the Members of the War Cabinet Secretariat and Staff his high appreciation of the expeditious handling of business in this Office, and particularly of the prompt reproduction and circulation of War Cabinet Minutes and other documents. His Majesty authorised me to state that, in his opinion, the work of this Office had been an important element in the winning of the War.

Hankey's diary entry for 22nd November throws interesting light on his handling of the tricky matter of who should be head of the administrative and secretarial arrangements for the British delegation to the Paris conference. Now that the guns had ceased firing, and the chief issue would be the resettlement of war-torn Europe, the Foreign Office clearly had a prior claim to the top post; and the obvious man to fill it was Lord Hardinge, the Permanent Under-Secretary. On the other hand Hardinge had, as we saw earlier, come under heavy fire from the Mesopotamia Commission[1]; and doubts were probably felt whether a former Viceroy of India and an intimate friend of Edward VII was the right man to carry the novel responsibilities which were bound to arise. Such misgivings certainly found expression inside the walls of the Foreign Office; for an unsigned marginal note on a document in which representation at the Paris Conference was discussed reads 'Better Hankey than Hardinge'.[2] It is hard to believe that such a comment could have been made by an underling. Moreover the view it expressed receives support from a writer, also anonymous, of comparatively modern times who has stated that 'Hardinge lacked altogether the adaptability, the technical competence, the patience and the devotion which Hankey so abundantly displayed'.[3] We will return shortly to the typically astute way in which Hankey secured for himself the position which his knowledge and experience justified – yet avoided giving offence to Hardinge.

*Diary November 24th*

No War Cabinet, but at noon I was sent for by Ll. G., who had summoned an impromptu conference of the President of the Board of Trade, Coal

[1]See Volume I, pp. 408–9.

[2]I am indebted to Mrs. Zara Steiner, Fellow of New Hall, Cambridge, for drawing my attention to this note.

[3]*Times Literary Supplement*, 2nd Jan. 1969. Lead review of R. Ullman, *Britain and the Russian Civil War*, November 1918–February 1919 (Princeton and Oxford, 1968).

Controller, Milner, and the Adjutant-General to insist on the rapid return of coal miners from the front. It was arranged that Lord Milner should at once go to G.H.Q. and speed things up. Afterwards Milner, the P.M., and I had some conversation about our representation at the peace conference and I strongly urged the panel system. The P.M. was very hostile about Asquith, and annoyed with the King for wanting him to be at the peace conference. The P.M. was at first rather hostile to the panel system, but eventually became more friendly to the idea of having three permanent members and two variable ones. On my initiative I was instructed to telegraph to Orlando and House asking them to come to the conference in London next week, and to Clemenceau, asking him to bring Foch. The P.M. wants to have a big public reception next Sunday [1st December]. There was also some conversation about Northcliffe, who is becoming hostile. The P.M. discussed the alternatives of keeping him quiet by bringing him to the peace conference (justifying it by the fact that Clemenceau is said to intend to bring in Tardieu); of taking no notice of him; or of attacking him. Milner and I were strongly opposed to the first course; but thought the second was all right for the moment; while, if he continued to attack, it would be good electioneering tactics to counter-attack him. I lunched with Lord Grey and Lady Glenconner,[1] with whom he is staying. We had a great quack about the League of Nations and he agreed with all my views, viz. . . . the concentration there of all international conferences and bureaux such as the Agricultural, Postal, Telegraph, Wireless bureaux etc.; and the importance of not trying to make the League of Nations run before it could walk i.e. making it at first a consultative and not an executive instrument. Afterwards we discussed Freedom of Seas. He had had interviews with one or two leading Americans here, who had admitted what we know – that the Americans are jealous of our naval supremacy and are building for all they are worth.[2] The suggestion had arisen in the course of the conversation that we should make a declaration that we did not insist on the British Navy being larger than [their] own, and Grey had qualified this by saying that we could not limit our effort against European competitors, although, in the future as in the past we would not build against the U.S.A. The Americans had then said 'If you would make this declaration, it would probably stop American building of warships altogether.' This is very important, but Grey said he had reported it to Hardinge. . . . Later on I saw Reading about the proposal that he should be

[1]Wife of Sir Edward P. Tennant, 1st Baron Glenconner 1911. (1859–1920) Politician (Lib.) and great landowner in Scotland.

[2]This must refer to the enormous naval building programme put forward in the summer of 1918. It comprised 156 warships of all classes, including 16 capital ships, and was in all essentials a repetition of the 1916 programme. All ships were again to be completed within 3 years. See Roskill, *Naval Policy*, I, p. 212.

in charge of the revictualling of Germany and other enemy and allied countries. I found him very pulled down by influenza, which he contracted the same night as I did, and in need of a change, which made him reluctant to take on this heavy job. Also, in his debilitated condition, he was upset about attacks on him in the *Morning Post*, to which, as Lord Chief Justice, he was not in a position to reply, and was apprehensive as to its effect on the minds of Americans. Finally, he did not want to be too much tied to this new job, so as to prevent him from going back to America with President Wilson on his return in order to wind up his affairs as Ambassador there. I urged that with such competent assistants as Sir John Beale[1] and Salter he could easily take leave until the end of the year; that the *Morning Post*, for the moment was negligible and discredited; and that, having got the revictualling job on its legs, he could hand it to someone else. I saw that, though reluctant, he had really committed himself to it. It is a matter of real importance that he should take it on, as there is a danger that we may be at loggerheads with the Americans over it. We want the negotiations to be in London, where the Allied machinery for food and shipping is situated, – personally I want to use this machinery as the beginning of the League of Nations. Hoover,[2] however, wants the negotiations to be at Brussels. The French and Italians will back us over it, but this is just the situation we want to avoid, viz. a combination of Great Britain, France, and Italy against America; for, next day, we might find America, France, and Italy, against Great Britain. As Hoover, the American Food Controller, and Hurley,[3] the American shipping man are off to France, Lord Reading can easily slip in his holiday. Eventually we arranged that he should place his difficulties before the P.M. personally.

On 28th November Milner wrote very dejectedly to Esher about what he called the 'Post-Bellum Army'. Plainly the Secretary of State for War was not only tired out and longing to be 'relegated to private

[1]Sir John F. Beale (1874–1935). Business man. Chairman, Wheat Executive during World War I. Worked with Lord Reading on Allied Supreme Council of Shipping and Relief 1919. Director, L.M.S. Railway; Midland Bank; Guest, Keen and Nettlefold and of other companies.

[2]Herbert C. Hoover (1874–1964). American mining engineer and politician (Repub.). In charge of American Relief Committee, London 1914–15. U.S. Commissioner for relief to Belgium 1915–19 and U.S. Food Administrator 1917–19. Secretary of Commerce 1921–28. Elected 31st President of U.S.A. 1928. Initiated London Naval Conference 1930 but signally failed to deal effectively with economic crisis of 1930-31. Co-ordinator, European Food Programme 1947.

[3]Edward N. Hurley (1864–1933). Chairman, U.S. Shipping Board and President, Emergency Fleet Corporation 1917–19. Member, World War Funding Commission 1924 and of President Hoover's Advisory Shipping Commission.

life', but was '*thoroughly out of sympathy with the spirit of the times*' (his italics). He believed that a satisfactory military system could not be established without continuing 'compulsory service of a kind' – as he expected both France and Germany to do. But what he called 'end of war and League of Nations flapdoodle' made any such policy totally unacceptable to the Government and to the nation as a whole. At the end of this depressing epistle Milner wrote 'About Hankey, I entirely agree with you. He is invaluable and I don't think that *in his case* there is any fear of his extraordinary services not being fully recognised, and it not being made worth his while to remain in the service of the State'.[1] Although, as we will see shortly, Hankey himself was both pressed, and for a time tempted, to transfer his allegiance to the League of Nations, Milner's prophecy was to be fulfilled. Rather oddly Hankey wrote to Esher on the same day discussing what form the army of the future should take. They were in agreement that 'the question of demobilisation could not be considered without that of remobilisation'; and Hankey fully accepted that 'the old army conception of universal training [by which he must have meant Lord Roberts's pre-war scheme[2]] will not meet the case'. The army of the future, he continued, 'cannot be as large as the army of the present, but it must be much larger than the army of the past'. He believed, however, that under modern conditions overseas commitments could be met 'with relatively short service troops', though 'some system of voluntary extension [of the enlistment period] will be necessary for the army abroad'. Though he correctly foresaw that 'the political difficulties are going to be prodigious', and that 'it will be more difficult than ever to get money for armaments', he plainly underestimated both the effects of the nation's decline in economic strength and the popular revulsion against military service in any form. He ended with an attack on the outlook and methods of the Treasury, which foreshadowed the fight he was to have with that department over the whole question of the future of the Cabinet Secretariat.[3]

At this time Hankey had another of his periodical brushes with Stamfordham over the King being kept properly informed about Cabinet deliberations and decisions. It seems that Stamfordham was still hankering for the personal letters from the Prime Minister which, as

[1]Milner to Esher, 28th November 1918. Holograph. Esher papers.

[2] See Vol. I, pp. 94–5.

[3]Hankey to Esher, 28th November 1918. Esher papers.

we saw earlier, were dropped at the time of the institution of the War Cabinet in December 1916.[1] At any rate Stamfordham now claimed that neither the King nor he himself 'have any recollection of the decision to grant self local government to Malta'. This time Hankey stood on firm ground, and he recapitulated the whole story, giving the dates when the various minutes and memoranda on the subject had been sent to the King. By way of rubbing a little salt into the wound he enclosed duplicates of all the relevant papers – obviously suggesting that the Palace had lost the originals! His victory was complete, and on 28th Stamfordham made a handsome apology.[2]

On Sunday 1st December Hankey reluctantly left Highstead for London to meet the French and Italian delegations. Then he was at once involved in conferences between the three Prime Ministers.

*Diary 4th December 1918*

Alas, I have been too busy to write my diary for more than a week, a not uneventful period. The last days of last week were occupied with preparations for the visit of Clemenceau, Foch, Orlando, and Sonnino. [J. T.] Davies, who generally does these things was away with the P.M. electioneering and a good deal fell on me. I will draw a veil over it; trouble with the Court over the use of State Carriages; questions of precedence – should the Duke of Connaught, who was coming to the station to meet Foch, go in front of Ll. G. and Clemenceau in the procession?; the protests of the Italian ambassador against Orlando going behind Clemenceau etc. etc. The German war was a trifle compared with this! On Sunday [1st Dec.] I had to go to town (no holiday) and attend at the station to meet our guests. All went well and they all had a magnificent reception. Afterwards I saw Ll. G. at 10 Downing St. He said Clemenceau had been really affected by his welcome. Ll. G. had seized the opportunity to demand first Mosul and then Jerusalem in the peace terms. Clemenceau, in his malleable state, had agreed, but had said 'But Pichon will make difficulties about Mosul.' [Here Hankey inserted a note referring to his diary for 11th December 1920 'for further details of this episode'. The entry in question reads as follows:—

Clemenceau and Foch had come over after the armistice and were given a great military and public reception. Ll. G. and Clemenceau had driven to the French embassy . . . When they were alone . . . Clemenceau said 'Well, what are we to discuss?' 'Mesopotamia and Palestine' replied Ll. G. 'Tell me what you want' asked Clemenceau. 'I want Mosul', said Ll. G. 'You shall have it'

[1]See Vol. I, p. 340.

[2]Hankey to Stamfordham 27th Nov. 1919 and reply by letter of 28th. RA GV L1519/4 and L1519/6.

said Clemenceau. 'Anything else?' 'Yes, I want Jerusalem too' continued Ll. G. 'You shall have it' said Clemenceau 'but Pichon will make difficulties about Mosul'. There was absolutely no record or memorandum made at the time, and I believe my diary of Dec. 4th 1918 contains the only record ... and that was only secondhand from Ll. G. for I was not present. Nevertheless, and in spite of great pressure from his colleagues and from all kinds of interested parties Clemenceau, who was always straight as a die, never went back on his word, and I am bound to say Ll. G. never gave him a chance. Thus and thus is history made!]

Later we had an important conference – P.M., Henry Wilson, Bonar Law, Foch and Weygand in which Foch outlined a plan for a defensive alliance of France (including Alsace-Lorraine), Luxemburg, Belgium, and a new state or states constituted out of the German territory west of the Rhine, with Great Britain. Without the barrier of the Rhine, and without the organised defensive alliance, ensuring the proper training and disposition of the Belgian and Luxemburg forces, he saw no hope of preventing the repetition of the onslaught of 1914, which would take the form of the occupation of the Channel ports and the virtual separation of France and G.B. . . . On Monday [2nd Dec.] I had two conferences with the three P.Ms and other ministers, and dined in the evening with the Round Table group at F. S. Oliver's. Tuesday was a really terrible day – Imperial War Cabinet at 10.30; meeting of the I.W.C. with the Allied Ministers at 11.15 to 1.30; meeting of Allied Ministers at 4.15; I.W.C. and Allied Ministers at 5.30 p.m. Four meetings in one day. Nevertheless I got all the conclusions circulated Tuesday night. Luckily I had brought over Caccia[1] and some of the Versailles staff to help out my over-worked office. To-day Borden asked to see me early, and I went to his room at once. He was full of grievances, and rather formidable. First he had a grievance about a decision taken by the Allied Prime Ministers on Monday to try the Kaiser. He said there had been an understanding that the question should not be decided without a further discussion at the Imperial War Cabinet. . . . Then he had a worse grievance about a decision that, when questions specially affecting them were being discussed at the peace conference, the Dominions should be entitled to special representation. He said that Canada was not 'specially affected' by any one question but had come into the war on the broadest grounds like the U.S.A.; and he implied that she had the fullest right to representation at the conference. He said that, if this decision was published there would be nothing left for him to do but to pack his trunks, return to Canada, summon Parliament, and put the whole

[1]Anthony M. F. Caccia (1869–1962). Indian Forests Service 1889–1914. Assistant Director, Timber Supplies, War Office 1917. A Secretary to Supreme War Council, Versailles 1918 and to Paris Peace Conference 1919. Director of Forest Studies in England 1911–1926. Father of Harold, 1st Baron Caccia. Diplomat.

thing before them. I pointed out that the Dominions had been put on the same footing as the smaller powers, and that in addition there was nothing to prevent their being represented on the British delegation of 5 members. However, I promised to do what I could to prevent publication. I also telephoned to the Colonial Secretary asking him not to communicate this decision to Canada until he heard from me. Before the Cabinet I went to see the P.M. and told him the whole story. He told me he meant to put Borden on the British delegation. I had barely time to warn him, as I had done before, that he could not have Borden without Hughes, as Australia had made the same sacrifices as Canada. But the warning seemed to fall on deaf ears. After the Cabinet I went straight to see Long. Borden was with him, and, as I didn't want to see Borden, I had to secrete myself until he had gone. He had told Long the same yarn as he told me. I then begged Long to see the P.M. at once and warn him at his interview in the afternoon not to commit himself to giving Borden a place in the British delegation without Hughes. He did so, and, as his private secretary told me in the afternoon, the P.M. told him that he had already offered Borden a place 'if he could secure the consent of the other Dominions' (not a fair condition, as the Dominions are as jealous of each other as cats). Late in the afternoon Borden came to see me. His whole attitude had changed. Ll. G. had 'wangled' him and, he said, had promised him some representation on the panel system. He was satisfied, but begged there should be no announcement. I fear leakage rather than an announcement. I had another difficulty to-day. Balfour, in spite of my objection, had, on the previous evening at the end of the conference carried a motion rendering all the decisions of the conference provisional, pending fresh discussion with President Wilson, who starts to-day for Europe. This was owing to the absence of Col. House, ostensibly through illness, but, according to Ll. G. for other reasons. The only exceptions were cases where immediate action was concerned, or where the U.S.A. was not affected, and it had been left to the secretaries (practically to me, as the others were 'duds') to select the exceptions. Sonnino had at once insisted that a decision for an international commission of 4 Admirals (British, French, Italian, and U.S.A.) to examine affairs on the Austrian Adriatic coast should be reserved for further discussion with U.S.A., and I had been obliged to include it.[1] But this decision had been reached in order to avert bloodshed and fighting between the Italians and Jugo-Slavs, and was of great urgency. I had to see Balfour and point out this and other serious consequences of his ill-timed resolution. He saw the point and sent a telegram to House asking him to

[1]See Roskill, *Naval Policy*, I, p. 76. The Italian Admiral Mola was chairman of this body, but the strife in the commission over Italian claims to the Austrian warships and to possession of Fiume and the Dalmatian coast became so acute that the united front of the other three members finally achieved his removal.

express agreement in as many of the resolutions as possible. They would really get in a great mess without me! Borden would still be sulking and the Italians and Jugo-Slavs would be fighting. Yet these were only two of several similar matters into which I had to butt to-day.

*5th December 1918*
No War Cabinet, the P.M. being at Walton Heath preparing a speech and Bonar Law ill. Sir Albert Stanley[1] rang me up and demanded a Cabinet, as the Govt. are threatened with an immediate general strike on the railways, if they do not at once concede an 8 hour day. I rang up the P.M. at Walton Heath, but he replied he would neither come to town nor see Stanley at Walton Heath. As Curzon and Smuts were the only members of the War Cabinet in town I had to tell Stanley to try and get 24 hours' postponement. Then Lord Stamfordham came to see me to consult me about Haig's honour. He has been offered a Viscountcy, but has declined until his soldiers get their rewards, better money etc. The people round the King are clamouring for a Dukedom on the precedent of the Duke of Wellington, whose army was not one-tenth the size of Haig's. I replied that I was certain Lloyd George would never agree, and suggested to work for an Earldom. You must give Beatty pretty much the same as Haig, and you cannot give him a Dukedom. Stamfordham was also wholly opposed to a Dukedom and agreed to work for an Earldom. Apparently Henry Wilson and Allenby are to have peerages and I said that, in this case, Admiral Wemyss ought also to have a peerage. The P.M. apparently wants Allenby to get the same as Haig. Longhurst asked if he had said anything about *my* peerage!! – But I really don't care a rap about these things, and don't care a hang if I get anything or nothing. I motored home early, as I am taking Adeline to Torquay to-morrow.

For the next week Hankey and Adeline were at Torquay staying with some of his relations; for Adeline was badly in need of a rest and a change after her serious illness. Hankey spent his leisure hours reading Disraeli's *Endymion*, from which he culled for his files some revealing quotations. 'The most powerful men are not public men . . . A public man is responsible, and a responsible man is a slave. It is private life that governs the world . . . The world talks much of powerful sovereigns and great ministers; and if being talked about made one powerful, they would be irresistible. But the fact is, the more you are talked about the less powerful you are . . .'; and again 'the first requisite in the successful conduct of public affairs is a personal acquaintance with the statesmen engaged . . .'. Obviously Hankey was applying

[1]See Vol. I, p. 582, *note*.

Disraeli's views to his own position and prospects. He sent the foregoing quotations to Esher in amplification of his refusal of political office, saying that he believed Lloyd George had 'cast me for the Whips' office, but I dare say I could have had the Admiralty, or, if Milner goes, the War Office, or the reversion of Bob Cecil's job'. But he had remembered Esher's advice, and Lloyd George was, he felt, 'relieved and commended my decision.'[1] In fact Milner turned over the War Office to Churchill in the middle of January 1919, and the former plainly never visualised Hankey as his successor. At the same time Churchill also became Secretary of State for the R.A.F.[2]; and the placing of the two offices under the same Minister inevitably opened the question of creating a Ministry of Defence which would be responsible for all three fighting services. On grounds of economy this measure appeared attractive, and Churchill undoubtedly saw himself as the first incumbent. But such developments aroused strong opposition in the recently created Air Ministry, which saw in them a first step towards the division of the R.A.F. between the Navy and Army and a return to the pre-1918 state of affairs. In February the redoubtable Trenchard became Chief of the Air Staff again, and at once went into action. He found a ready ally in Hankey, who was also strongly opposed to the concept of a Defence Ministry; and, if one was created, to Churchill becoming its head.[3] When Esher wrote asking for Hankey's opinion, and expressed the view that the Prime Minister was the only person who could reasonably hold the suggested new office Hankey replied fully agreeing with him.[4] Thus began Hankey's long fight against the placing of all three fighting services under one Minister.

When Hankey returned to the office in mid-December from Torquay, where he had left Adeline to recuperate her strength fully, he found 'everyone away on election business', and no Cabinets or Imperial War Cabinets being held. Polling Day in the 'khaki (or "Coupon") Election' which Lloyd George had so skilfully engineered had been fixed for 14th December. Hankey seized the opportunity to send Lloyd George his views about 'the best machinery of government during the period of reconstruction'. After considering various alternatives, including

[1]Hankey to Esher 10th Dec. 1918 from Torquay. Esher papers.

[2]The title was changed to Secretary of State for War and Air in March.

[3]A. Boyle, *Trenchard* (Collins, 1962) pp. 346–8. This source is henceforth cited as Boyle, *Trenchard*.

[4]Esher to Hankey 4th March 1919.

reversion to 'a large Cabinet of the pre-war type', he came down heavily in favour of 'the War Cabinet system', which 'in spite of its well-known objections' (by which he presumably meant the concentration of power in few hands) he none the less considered 'by far the best system'. He proposed that it should be called the Reconstruction Cabinet; and, to mitigate the opposition which he anticipated this proposal would arouse, he suggested that formal meetings of all Ministers who were heads of Departments should be held, additional to Cabinet meetings, at frequent intervals. If continuation of the War Cabinet was impossible he preferred to revert to a large Cabinet 'of the pre-war type', because this would eliminate the complaints of Ministers, of which he had much experience, about their being excluded from discussions in which their department had an interest. He then reviewed the question of which Cabinet Committees should be continued; and as Lloyd George was 'committed to an Imperial Cabinet' he considered that such a body might 'absorb the work done by the C.I.D. before the war'. The Demobilisation Committee under Smuts and the Home Affairs Committee under the Home Secretary would have to carry on, though a replacement for Smuts, preferably a Minister without Portfolio, would be required if the General was to play a large part in the Peace Conference. The Eastern Committee (Curzon) would also probably have to continue, unless Lloyd George envisaged a new Department for Eastern Affairs; but Hankey was doubtful whether Austen Chamberlain's Economic Defence and Development Committee would be required for long.[1] Next day he wrote again to say that, as Smuts had resigned from the Demobilisation Committee, the appointment of a replacement was 'of the first importance'. Doubtless he was aware that the demobilisation scheme had come under very severe, and wholly justifiable criticism in the fighting services because of the grossly inequitable principles on which priorities had been worked out. Men in 'reserved occupations', who had been the last to be called up, were now urgently needed back in industries such as the coal mines. Thus the effect of the scheme was that those with the shortest service were often the first to be discharged – to the fury of men who had endured several years of war.[2] Hankey also warned Lloyd

[1]Hankey to Lloyd George 13th Dec. 1918. Lloyd George papers F/23/3/25.

[2]See Roskill, *Naval Policy*, I, pp. 102–3. Boyle, *Trenchard*, pp. 317–24 describes the mutinies in the Army in 1919 which the inequities in the demobilisation scheme provoked. For a moving account of how the soldiers actually felt, by a fine writer

George that there was 'a very heavy programme' for the Imperial War Cabinet, which he gave in outline; and, he added in his own hand, 'we ought to have at least two days to clear the arrears'.[1] Thus did Hankey try to smooth the transformation of the machinery of government from a war to a peace basis, and at the same time get the most important issues, which had been gestating and accumulating while Lloyd George had been electioneering, settled. About a fortnight later Esher, whom Hankey had consulted on these matters, wrote that 'I only pray he [Lloyd George] may not revert to the old forms of government but stick to the principle of the War Cabinet and an Imperial ditto'. To do otherwise would, in Esher's view, mean reverting to the 'Party System', which he stigmatised as 'childish'. If Lloyd George did so Esher foretold his downfall. Hankey at once sent this letter on to Lloyd George[2]; but the Prime Minister probably paid little attention to it – because he was already clear about the form of government he would have if he was returned to power.

Though the spell at Torquay helped to restore Adeline's health all was not yet well. The Hankeys, like all other middle-class families at that time, were beset by what was called 'the servant problem'. Running Highstead and looking after four lively and growing children without staff was beyond Adeline's strength. To make things easier for her Hankey seriously considered moving to London, where servants were more easily found. Moreover as he was almost certain to have to spend a lot of time in Paris in the near future, he felt that a London base might be better for both of them. Meanwhile he was 'trying to get the Ministry of Labour to take up the question of directing female munitions workers to domestic service'.[3] In the event Adeline's health improved faster than her husband had expected, some home help was finally obtained, and the family never did move from Highstead.

*Diary December 16th 1918*
War Cabinet cancelled. Went to see Bonar Law to urge the claims to office of Amery and Leslie Wilson, who have done good work in my office during the war. Lloyd George came in while we were talking, 'Well, Sir', I said,

---

who had been through the war in the Royal Fusiliers, see Guy Chapman, *A Passionate Prodigality* (reprinted MacGibbon and Kee, 1965) pp. 274–81.

[1]Hankey to Lloyd George 14th Dec. 1918. Lloyd George papers F/23/3/28.

[2]Esher to Hankey 29th Dec. 1918. *ibid.* F/23/3/34.

[3]To Lady Hankey 16th Dec. 1918.

'what majority have I to congratulate you on?' 'All I have to say', he replied 'is that your new chief is Mr. Arthur Henderson. I am going away to an island in the Pacific for 6 months, after which I shall come back and make it hot for my successor.' 'If that were true', said Bonar Law, who always pretends he doesn't want office, 'I would give you £1,000, George.' They then discussed new appointments to the Ministry, Bonar Law urging Chamberlain's claims to be Chancellor of the Exchequer, and Lloyd George absolutely refusing, because of the newspaper attacks when Chamberlain was appointed.[1] Ll. G. wants Auckland Geddes to take charge of demobilisation, vice Smuts, who has resigned, but Geddes has the influenza, which is embarrassing.[2] . . . In the afternoon I took the chair at a conference to stop the Ministry of Shipping and Admiralty from writing histories of the Mercantile Marine to clash with our official histories. Complete success.[3] Then General Maynard,[4] who commands at Murmansk (in N. Russia) called to explain his troubles. A good man . . .

Lloyd George's remark about Labour winning the election was not of course meant to be taken seriously. But it probably reflected the strain and anxiety he felt during the fortnight which elapsed between Polling Day and the count, in order to allow time for the votes of men serving overseas to come in.

*Diary December 17th 1918*

War Cabinet at noon. P.M. rather over-wrought after the election and a bit difficult. Lunched with the P.M., Gen. and Mrs. Botha, Gen. Smuts, and

[1]In fact Austen Chamberlain did become Chancellor of the Exchequer, and held that office until April 1921.

[2]Smuts's Demobilisation Committee was dissolved on 19th December and its work taken over by the Co-ordination of Demobilisation Section of the War Cabinet under Sir Eric Geddes, not his brother Auckland. Cab. 27/41, /42 and /49.

[3]This is misleading. The volumes of the official history by C. E. Fayle, *Seaborne Trade* (3 Vols. Murray, 1920–24) were first sponsored by the Garton Foundation, whose Trustees later approved that a member of their staff should undertake the work 'in co-operation with the Historical Section of the C.I.D.'. The volumes of the same history by A. Hurd, *The Merchant Navy* (3 Vols., Murray, 1921–29) had originally been suggested by the Board of Trade. They were actually produced under the aegis of the Historical Section of the C.I.D. 'with the cordial support of the Admiralty and the Ministry of Shipping'. It would thus be more accurate to say that Hankey took the histories in question under his own wing, rather than claim that he prevented the interested departments getting them written.

[4]Later Major-General Sir Charles C. M. Maynard (1870–1945). Brigade Commander 1915–17. G.O. C-in-C, Allied Forces, Murmansk 1918–19.

Philip Kerr. Botha has got rather fat, but looked better than I expected, and has aged very little. The talk was mainly retrospective about the S. African rebellion and the expedition against German S.W. Africa. Ll. G. alarmed me by saying that Borden was to have one of the places in our peace conference team of five. I at once chipped in that Australia had made as great a military effort on land as Canada, and a considerable naval effort as well. Ll. G. seems to me to be wilfully blind to the inflammatory state of public opinion in Australia. In the afternoon I had to see Lord R. Cecil to put the hat on a proposal he has made to the P.M. to go to Paris to see Col. House about the League of Nations. I told him from the P.M. that he could go as long as his visit does not coincide with the visit the P.M. and Balfour are making to Paris this weekend. If the P.M. takes any British Minister or ex-Minister the Dominions' representatives will be on their hind legs at once. Later Sir Robert Borden called and stayed for some time, to consult me about Imperial War Cabinet business. He and some of the other Dominions' representatives are a bit restive at being given so little to do, and having so few Imperial War Cabinet meetings. But the election has blocked business terribly.

*December 18th*

A very long Imperial War Cabinet at 11.30. Chamberlain came to me in the afternoon to say that he thought it had been 'flapdoodle' and [a] fearful waste of time, and implored me to try and do something to crystallise the discussion at the next meeting. I promised to try and get the P.M. to propose some specific resolutions. Curiously, however, Borden rang me up later to say what a satisfactory meeting it had been. I had a rather amusing telephone conversation during the meeting with Lord Stamfordham. I could hear the King, who was in the room with him, grumbling about the action of the War Cabinet in closing with an offer by President Wilson to come to London just after Xmas, as this would interrupt and clash with the King's much needed and well earned holiday at Sandringham. I asked the Prime Minister whether he would not see the King. He said, however, that the King's objections had been put before the Imperial War Cabinet by Mr. Balfour, who had come to the meeting straight from Buckingham Palace, and that 'the Imperial War Cabinet had over-ruled the King.' The utmost concession I could get was that the telegram in reply to President Wilson's offer should be shown to the King. Late in the evening I received a message asking me to go to 10 Downing St. 'as quick as I could or quicker'. I found the P.M., Bonar Law, Eric and Auckland Geddes and Dr. Addison there. Eric Geddes had just accepted an invitation to become a member of the War Cabinet in charge of Demobilisation and the reconstruction of industry. Geddes had told me in the morning that he would not take it on, but must have been 'wangled' by the P.M. I was asked how to manage War Cabinet approval, and I there and then drafted a Minute to be approved on the morrow at a special meeting of the War Cabinet . . .

*December 19th 1918*

Short War Cabinet at 11.45 to fix up the appointment of Sir Eric Geddes as principal demobiliser. Churchill sulky and hostile. Went to Charing Cross at 1 a.m. [?] to meet Sir Douglas Haig.

That day Hankey sent Lloyd George his proposals for the forthcoming discussion in the Imperial War Cabinet on the disposal of the captured German colonies. The most interesting points he brought up were, firstly, the likelihood of Hughes of Australia opposing the cession to Japan of the islands in the Pacific north of the equator. 'But', commented Hankey, 'we are irrevocably committed by the pact of 1917 and discussion should not be permitted.' Secondly the French claim to a large part of the Cameroons might raise objections from the Colonial Office; but Hankey considered it would be 'an extremely ungracious task and an ungenerous act' to go back on the arrangements agreed during the war. German East Africa was, he continued, 'the main contentious issue', and as the British were already in occupation he considered that the attitude to be adopted should be '*J'y suis, j'y reste*'. Lastly he foresaw trouble over the carve up of the former Turkish provinces of Mesopotamia, Syria and Palestine, regarding which Curzon had put forward resolutions which in effect involved cancelling the Sykes-Picot agreement.[1] Over this tricky problem he thought it best for Lloyd George and Curzon to seek a free hand to reach a satisfactory arrangement with the French.[2]

*Diary December 20th 1918*

Imperial War Cabinet at 11 a.m. on the disposal of the captured German colonies and Turkish territory. Very long meeting, and rather strong differences of opinion. It was left to me to try and draft a Memorandum of conclusions for consideration at the next meeting. Busy afternoon drafting these. Milner called and stayed an hour. He asked if I was going to become a Minister, and expressed satisfaction when I told him I had refused and was going on with my present job. 'This,' he said, 'will make for that continuity in administration which I have always hoped for, and no-one will realise it.'

*December 21st*

Spent most of the day lobbying for my conclusions *re* the captured colonies,

[1]See Vol. I, pp. 270, *note*, 607 and 609. [2]Lloyd George papers F/23/3/30.

seeing Botha, Borden, Balfour, and sending Amery to Hughes. We succeeded in [reaching] a concordat based on the idea of mandatory powers, nominated by the League of Nations, for the administration of this territory, German S.W. Africa and the Pacific Islands being excluded. It required extraordinarily nice drafting to reconcile Borden, who doesn't want to grab territory, and Botha, Smuts and Hughes, who do. They all congratulated me very warmly.

Hankey's optimism, and the congratulations he received, were both quickly proved premature, since next day, a Sunday which he was spending quietly at home, he received a telephone message from Lloyd George refusing to allow his draft conclusions on the question of the former German colonies to be circulated.[1] His reasons became apparent at the next meeting of the Imperial War Cabinet.

*Diary 23rd December 1918*
Imperial War Cabinet from 3 to 6 p.m. The P.M. flatly declined even to discuss the question of the German colonies. The fact is that he didn't mean to be bound in any sort or kind of a way in his conversation with President Wilson. He has told me plainly that he means to try and get President Wilson into German East Africa in order to ride him off Palestine. I think he will get in a great mess with his colleagues if he does this . . . Ll. G. was in a most irritable frame of mind.

*24th December*
Imperial War Cabinet 11 to 1.30 or later on the League of Nations. Good and satisfactory discussion, trending in the direction I have always advocated. I lunched in the office 'vetting' the draft minute the while, and dictated the P.M.'s important summing up. The I.W.C. resumed its meeting from 3 p.m. to 5 p.m. In these three meetings we have covered, if somewhat sparsely, all the subjects likely to be discussed with President Wilson at the end of the week. Hughes had got up his case quite well for once, and his repartee was admirable. Balfour made a very able and amusing statement as *advocatus diaboli* for the Freedom of the Seas. . . . After the morning meeting the P.M. asked me to accompany him next Tuesday [31st Dec.] to Wales, to help him reconstruct his Government. He apparently wants more business men.

Hankey's Christmas break amounted to no more than a day – and that was marred by such severe toothache, that he spent part of it in a dentist's chair. In the evening he ruminated in his diary on the difficulties he was encountering in his dealings with Lloyd George. With the knowledge we now possess regarding the events of the years to come it seems that Hankey was not far wrong in accusing him of a

[1]Diary 22nd Dec. 1918.

'lust for power'. But at the same time one must make allowances for the vast weight and scope of the problems which the Prime Minister knew must fall largely on his shoulders – in handling the statesmen of the Allied nations, the Americans and the Dominions, all of whose aims and outlook were widely divergent. In such circumstances the first need surely was to receive a firm mandate from the electorate; and one can well understand the strain felt by Lloyd George until that vital matter was settled.

*Diary 25th December 1918*
. . . This is the first peace Xmas for five years, and one's thoughts wander backwards. Ll. G. has brought the country through the war, but is very anxious lest he should not get the big majority in the election on which his supporters count. Consequently he is in a nervous, irritable, and difficult frame of mind. The mistake he is making is to try and absorb too much into his hands. He seems to have a sort of lust for power; ignores his colleagues, or tolerates them in an almost disdainful way, and seems more and more to assume the attitude of a dictator. He takes but little advice, and even Philip Kerr and I have few opportunities to coach him.

*26th December 1918*
To London in the morning, as I had to be on the platform to meet President Wilson. A very fine reception. After his arrival I had a conference with Ll. G., Bonar Law, and Balfour about the subjects to be discussed. On return to the office Borden asked to see me. He was in a towering rage, as he had not been able to get on to the platform, having mislaid his ticket (through his private secretary's fault as it afterwards transpired). I did my best to soothe him and undertook to probe the matter to the bottom – though it is no affair of mine. . . .

On the morning of 27th Hankey drove with Lloyd George to Buckingham Palace for the first of the conferences with President Wilson; but as the President wanted no records kept he was not admitted to the session. That evening he attended the State Banquet – which he described as 'a superb function, beautiful and impressive'. He was flattered when the King introduced him to Wilson as 'a very important person, the Secretary of the War Cabinet', and by the Queen's 'graceful greeting' – which left him 'absurdly tongue-tied'. Later on he got himself 'put on the list' to talk with the President, to whom he wanted to give his experiences of the Allied war conferences and the Imperial War Cabinet, because of their relevance to Wilson's favourite project for a League of Nations. But to Hankey's annoyance Curzon jumped in ahead of him in the queue and deprived him of his chance.[1] None the less he 'talked to a very large number of interesting people' from the Archbishop of Canterbury, Randall Davidson,[2] who wanted to bring before the peace conference 'the restoration of St. Sophia to the Christian religion', to Lord Bryce a former and very successful ambassador to U.S.A.[3] Plainly it was an occasion which appealed deeply to Hankey's sense of tradition and of dignity, as well as to his enjoyment of being at the centre of affairs.

Next day Hankey was again involved in the formal entertainment of the President – this time at the Guildhall lunch to receive the Freedom of the City of London.[4] In the afternoon the election results began to come in, and, according to Hankey, the full extent of the Coalition victory left Lloyd George 'almost stunned' and 'really upset by Asquith's defeat'.[5] In fact candidates who had fought under the Coalition 'Coupon' won 478 seats, as against 229 by all other parties. The Asquith Liberals slumped to only 28 seats, and their leader was heavily defeated by a Conservative in the East Fife constituency, which had returned him for no less than 32 years. Lloyd George certainly showed little charity or magnanimity towards anyone who had voted for the Select Committee in the Maurice Debate of the previous May.[6]

[1]Diary 27th Dec. 1918.

[2]Baron Davidson 1928 (1848–1930). Archbishop of Canterbury 1903, resigning 1928 after rejection by Parliament of the revised Prayer Book.

[3]See Vol. I, p. 568, *note*. [4]Diary 28th Dec. 1918. [5]*ibid.*

[6]The reviewer of the first volume of this biography in the *Times Literary Supplement* (23rd April 1970) deplored the lack of any study of the conduct of Members of Parliament during the years 1916–18, especially over the crucial Maurice Debate of May 1918 (see Vol. I, pp. 539–45). Such a study has now been supplied by Edward David in *The Historical Journal*, XIII, 3 (1970) pp. 509–33 under the title *The Liberal Party Divided 1916–18*. The author analyses very fully the voting record of Liberal M.P.s, and shows that the view expressed by Dr. Trevor Wilson in *The Downfall of the Liberal Party* (London, 1966) – namely that the way M.P.s voted in the Maurice Debate did *not* decide whether they should be 'couponed' or not in the December 1918 election – requires substantial modification. Furthermore Mr. David convincingly refutes the view expressed by Mr. A. J. P. Taylor in *English History 1914–1945* (O.U.P., 1965, p. 159) that there were marked social and class differences between the Asquithian and Lloyd Georgian Liberals. Mr. Taylor's statement in his Raleigh Lecture of 1959 (reprinted in *Politics in Wartime*, 1964) that 'none of these [Lloyd George] Liberals was a banker, merchant or financial magnate' is described by Mr. David, with a supporting analytical table, as 'quite inaccurate'. It now seems beyond doubt that, contrary to Mr. Taylor's letter in the *T.L.S.* (30th April 1970) in which he supported Dr. Trevor Wilson, the way M.P.s

*Hankey to Asquith. 2 Whitehall Gardens, 28th Dec. 1918.* Holograph[1]

Dear Mr. Asquith,

I am most awfully sorry to hear the bad news about your election. It is nothing less than a national misfortune. To-day however is not the time to take short views of the future. Who knows what the next turn of the wheel of fortune may bring?

When times are less breathless and the public perspective is restored, the people will learn what those who were with you at the time know well – the tremendous burden you carried through the first half of the war, and that it was you that saved the Empire from absolute disaster.

With unabated confidence in you

Yours very sincerely

Balfour now did his utmost to persuade Lloyd George to accompany him to the French Riviera; and the Prime Minister declared that he had 'requisitioned Hankey' to go with him wherever he went.[2] So Hankey went home and packed his bags preparatory to enjoying a real rest in a pleasant climate. But, as so often with Lloyd George, Hankey had to forego an attractive prospect in order to meet his exacting master's wishes; and he actually spent the last day of the old year and most of the first week of the new one at Criccieth, where he and Philip Kerr had 'long talks about the membership of the new Cabinet'. Lloyd George's first and greatest anxiety now being out of the way his mood changed abruptly, and Hankey described him as 'always gay and cheery'. Hankey, who never repined for what was lost beyond recall, soon forgot the sunshine of the Riviera and found instead in Wales 'a very delightful interlude'.[3]

Here we may retrace our steps for a few days to survey briefly the outcome of the preliminary discussions between Lloyd George and Balfour on the British side and President Wilson, supported by Auchincloss, on the American side. Lloyd George has himself made clear how 'chilly' Wilson was towards the countries which had borne the main burden of the war, and how 'ungenerous' he was in speeches made in Paris as well as in London[4]; and he has himself printed the

---

voted in the Maurice Debate, and on other crucial issues such as conscription for Ireland, was decisive in the award or withholding of the 'coupon'.

[1]Asquith papers, Vol. 33. Nos. 27/8.

[2]Diary 28th Dec. 1918. Part reproduced in *Supreme Control*, p. 20.

[3]Diary 31st Dec. 1918–5th Jan. 1919. *Supreme Control*, p. 20.

[4]Lloyd George, *Peace Treaties*, I, pp. 156 and 182.

report he made to the War Cabinet after the Buckingham Palace meeting.[1] Hankey wrote some notes on the conversation long afterwards, in which he remarked that the talks revealed 'more agreement in principle than we had expected' – a statement that seems surprising observing that on the cardinal issue of Freedom of the Seas there was total disagreement; and wide differences of opinion soon became apparent on such matters as Indemnities and the future of the German colonies. Hankey was, however, absolutely right in noting that the talks 'revealed pretty clearly the direction the [Peace] Conference would take, and its main features'.

Hankey and Lloyd George returned from Criccieth to London on 5th January. We do not know exactly what part Hankey played in the Cabinet-making talks in Wales; but the very fact that he made no criticisms of, or even mild comments on the new appointments must surely signify that he and his master were in close accord. Hankey knew that Asquith had been offered, but had declined the Lord Chancellorship[2]; and although he deeply regretted Asquith's exclusion from office he was still hoping to find a place for him at the Peace Conference. On 11th January Hankey left for Paris, where two large hotels, the Majestic and the Astoria, had been taken over to accommodate the British missions. He himself lived in an annexe to the former called the Villa Majestic, and it was from there that he sent Adeline regular accounts of the new task which had fallen to his lot. On the day before he left London Hankey sent Tom Jones a memorandum telling him that the Prime Minister had selected him to act as Secretary of the Cabinet during his absence in Paris. Curzon would act as Chairman when neither Lloyd George nor Bonar Law was present, and the Prime Minister had decided that 'the Cabinet shall be worked on the same system as the War Cabinet'. Hankey made various other suggestions with regard to the conduct of business, but stressed that he did not wish to fetter Jones in any way, and left him 'the fullest authority to deal with all matters in the office'.[3]

[1] *ibid.*, pp. 184–202.
[2] Roy Jenkins, *Asquith* (Collins, 1964) pp. 476–7. This source is henceforth cited as *Jenkins*. Lloyd George, *Peace Treaties*, I, pp. 174–6.
[3] Memo. of 10th Jan. 1919. Cab. 21/124.

*Chapter 2*

# The Hard Road to Peace. January-February 1919

HANKEY's arrival in Paris late on Saturday 11th January left him very little time to get the next day's meetings organised. Moreover he at once realised that difficulties would arise if the military questions which lay within the province of the Supreme War Council became entangled with the wider and more complex issues which the Peace Conference would have to settle. Therein lay the chance to get his secretarial system, which had been created for the Supreme Council, adopted by the Conference. As there were some military questions to be disposed of, Hankey got Clemenceau to hold the first part of the afternoon's meeting as one of the Supreme War Council. At its end the military representatives were asked to withdraw, and the meeting continued as a preliminary session of the Peace Conference – still with Clemenceau in the chair. That evening Hankey sat up late to dictate the two sets of minutes, and when Rawlins his chief clerk asked what title the second minutes should carry Hankey replied at once 'The Council of Ten' – because ten representatives, namely the Prime Ministers and Foreign Secretaries of the five principal powers, would normally be present.[1] In this rather haphazard way there came into being the body which was to play a very large part in the Peace Conference; and the Council of Ten, like the British Empire Delegation (B.E.D.), was served by the secretariat established by Hankey at the Villa Majestic. By the admission of the Generals and Admirals it could, and quite often did, revert to its earlier form of the Supreme War Council – just as the B.E.D. was in effect a continuation and extension of the Imperial War Cabinet. On 14th Hankey sent Milner a long and enthusiastic description of his secretarial arrangements, which included the assistance of one of the staff of the Dominion Prime Ministers at all the meetings of the B.E.D. This, he said, achieved

[1] *Supreme Control*, pp. 23–4.

a purpose towards which he had been working 'for at least six years'; and he regarded it, somewhat exaggeratedly, as being 'of tremendous importance to the development of the British Empire'. He was confident of Milner's 'sympathy and approval' over his having made the B.E.D. secretariat 'completely Imperial', and looked forward to the next development – namely the creating of 'a real Imperial Cabinet Office'. Altogether he considered the outcome of these first deliberations 'a most splendid day for the Empire'.[1]

When the representatives of the five great powers met on 15th M. Pichon read out a draft agreement on the organisation of the Secretariat for the Peace Conference. The British record states that 'Mr. Lloyd George said that . . . the Secretariat should be organised on exactly the same lines as had been followed in the case of the Supreme War Council . . . That organisation had always worked very well'.[2] It is a fair deduction that, although the words quoted were Lloyd George's the spirit and intention behind them were Hankey's. Sir Harold Nicolson probably had in mind Hankey's rapid and effective action to place the secretarial side on a firm and efficient footing when he wrote that 'Before the Conference opened the whole machinery of the Majestic, the Astoria, the Villa Majestic and the Rue Nitot [Lloyd George's flat] hummed with the frictionless efficiency of a British Department of State'.[3]

*To Lady Hankey. British War Cabinet Offices, Villa Majestic. 16th Jan. 1919*
. . . Ll. G. wanted to make me British Secretary of the conference, but I pointed out to him that in this case I should no longer be *his* man, and could not continue for the time as Secretary of the War Cabinet. Further I see plainly that the real work will all be done in the 'hush' meetings, which are a veritable 'Cabinet of Nations'. I asked him to make me Secretary-General of the British Delegation so that I could continue my work at the 'hush' meetings. I cannot get a final decision from him, though I think he agrees. In the meantime I can make no final personal arrangements. He must settle before to-morrow though.

I have been frightfully busy, as I have had to attend two 'hush' meetings a day, and in addition I am on a committee drawing up the Rules of Procedure of the conference – a very heavy job. But we have nearly finished. I am also, for my sins, on the committee which draws up the press communiqué at the end of each meeting . . .

[1]Hankey to Milner 14th Jan. 1919. [2]Cab. 21/141.
[3]*Peacemaking 1919* (Constable, 1933) p. 46.

The principal subject discussed at the first meeting of the Council of Ten was what countries should be invited to take part in the conference proper, and how many delegates should be provided by each. We have already seen how the British Dominions were demanding separate representation; and that was the cause of the first brush between Lloyd George and President Wilson, who, not unreasonably, held that it would increase the overall 'British' representation to an excessive extent. Next day a compromise was reached whereby the U.S.A., France, Italy, Japan and the British *Empire* were each to have five delegates; Canada, Australia, India and South Africa two each, and New Zealand one. This satisfied everyone except New Zealand; but it raised the number of delegates to a grand total of no less than 70, which was a very unwieldy body for the Chairman (Clemenceau) and the secretariat to handle.[1] An outstanding feature was the total exclusion of Soviet Russia, which had of course been compelled by Germany to sign a separate and humiliating peace at Brest-Litovsk in March 1918, was not yet recognised by any of the Allied powers, and was still rent by civil strife. Towards the end of the month the Council of Ten considered a proposal to bring all the warring factions in Russia to the conference table; but it proved abortive.[2]

The British Empire Delegation also held its first meeting on 13th January, with Lloyd George in the chair and Hankey acting as secretary. The Prime Minister explained the attitude of Wilson and Lansing[3] to the question of separate Dominion representation, and argued for it 'with considerable force'. Policy towards Russia was also discussed, and Lloyd George favoured non-interference in the large and growing areas under Bolshevik control.[4] The B.E.D. then adjourned for a week, while discussions moved on to a higher level.

[1]The 'Secretary's Notes' of Council of Ten and Supreme War Council meetings are printed in *Foreign Relations of the United States: The Paris Peace Conference 1919*, (4 Vols, Govt. Printing Office, Washington 1943–46). Henceforth cited as *Foreign Relations, U.S.A.* The notes of the meetings on 12th and 13th January 1919 are in Vol. III, pp. 482–94 and 531–38. For the sake of simplicity all references to minutes of Supreme War Council and Council of Ten meetings will here be taken from this source. But the same minutes will be found in the I.C. series in Cab. 28.

[2]Council of Ten meeting on 22nd Jan. 1919. *Foreign Relations, U.S.A.*, III, pp. 676–92. See also *Supreme Control*, p. 54, and Roskill, *Naval Policy*, I, p. 139.

[3]Robert Lansing (1864–1928). American lawyer and politician (Dem.). Secretary of State 1915–20. Member of U.S. Commission to negotiate peace 1918–19.

[4]Cab. 29/28/1.

*To Lady Hankey. British War Cabinet Offices, Villa Majestic, Paris. 13th Jan. 1919*
I was too busy to write yesterday, as I was doing *all* the work of the Conference. At yesterday's rate it will take about 7 years! . . . Yesterday, owing to bad French organisation, I had to take single-handed, first a Supreme War Council and then a 'hush-frock' [Council of Ten] conference – 5 hours on end. I was working until past midnight dictating 30 pages of Minutes. Today I have an Imperial War Cabinet at 11 a.m., a Supreme War Council at 2.30, to be followed by a 'hush-frock' meeting.[1] But I have warning and can mobilise assistance. I am bringing in one of Borden's people to help me today – laying the foundations of converting the Imperial War Cabinet office into an Imperial Staff. Hush! No-one suspects!

. . . keep these letters – I have no time for a diary and you shall be my diary . . .

*To the same. 14th Jan. 1919*
My mind is chock full of a great scheme of Imperial development, which I have actually carried out; that is to say that I have got [it] approved that I shall have an Assistant Secretary from each Dominion for the work of the British Imperial Delegation. As this body is for all practical purposes the Imperial War Cabinet it means that when I return home I shall continue the same procedure with the I.W.C. In short I have actually started a great Imperial office . . . I have tried to do this for 6 years, but circumstances have always blocked it – mainly the Colonial Office. But I know that Milner favours it. I got the P.M. to agree on the plea that I was overworked. The Canadians and Australians absolutely jumped at it, and at my meeting yesterday I had a Canadian Asst. Secy. I am filling them all with my own enthusiasm, and shall just make things hum.

Besides the [B.E.] Delegation meeting I had two Allied Conference meetings, but I had assistants, so I was not overworked.

Last night, just as I had settled down to dinner . . . with Smuts I got a message from the P.M. that I must dine with him even if I was half way through dinner! So off I had to go. He is in great form and very pleased with me I can see. . . . Things are going better as regards the conference. I am hatching a scheme for bringing you to Paris . . .

To return to London for a moment, it was on 15th January that Churchill assumed responsibility for both the War Office and Air Ministry. According to Churchill's account Lloyd George had first told him that he could have either the Admiralty or the War Office, and said 'You can take the Air with you in either case; I am not going to keep it as a separate department.'[2] Trenchard's biographer quotes

[1] *Foreign Relations, U.S.A.,* III, pp. 508–30 and 531–42.
[2] *The Aftermath* (Macmillan, 1929) p. 52.

Hankey's explanation of Lloyd George's decision to wind up the Air Ministry as having arisen from his total immersion in the Peace Conference.[1] Be that as it may, the government soon changed its mind – under pressure from Lord Weir, the previous Secretary of State for Air. At any rate Churchill soon recalled Trenchard as Chief of the Air Staff; and that made it certain that the Royal Air Force would preserve its identity. Hankey at this stage seems to have preserved a strictly neutral attitude with regard to what was soon to become the greatest inter-service squabble of the century.

Meanwhile Tom Jones was keeping Hankey fully informed about Cabinet business in London. On 17th January he wrote that Churchill was pressing for 'an army of 1 million on a compulsory basis' – which would make a Bill for the continuation of compulsory service necessary. The Geddes brothers and Sir Robert Horne were, according to Jones, in favour of Churchill's proposal – which was obviously framed with the war of intervention in Russia in mind. Hankey endorsed Jones's letter 'Very important', and sent it straight on to Lloyd George[2]; but the Prime Minister was taking a very different view about Russia from Churchill's, and was most averse to maintaining a huge peace time army. That same day Hankey replied to Jones thanking him warmly for the warning about Churchill's proposal. 'The P.M. was much annoyed', he wrote, 'and has written to him to stop it.'[3]

On 17th Lloyd George duly made up his mind about Hankey's position. He wrote to Adeline 'I have been appointed British secretary to the Peace Conference. It is very awkward, as it ought to have been Lord Hardinge's job, and he has brought over a huge organisation. However, he has been most charming about it, and I think I can fit in without friction, as I generally can.' The prospect of Adeline joining him in Paris was now improved, and as his salary would be £3,000–£4,000 a year he told her that they would be 'justified in taking a relatively expensive flat here'. Hankey had put the invaluable

[1]Boyle, *Trenchard*, p. 326.

[2]Lloyd George papers F/23/4/4. Also K. *Middlemas* (Ed), *Whitehall Diary*, Vol. I of 2 Vols. (Oxford U.P., 1969) p. 72. This source is henceforth cited as *Middlemas*, I or II.

[3]Hankey to Jones 18th January 1919. *Middlemas*, *loc. cit.* and Lloyd George, *Peace Treaties*, I, pp. 371–2. In his letter to Tom Jones Hankey described his functions as three-fold, namely Secretary of the British Empire Delegation, British Secretary of the Peace Conference and British Secretary of the Cabinet of Nations; but in fact Clement Jones soon took over full responsibility for the B.E.D.

Sylvester on to investigating the problem of passages and accommodation; but there were, he said, 'still one or two "Ifs" ' – the chief of which was that the post of secretary to the B.E.D. must now be transferred to someone else. Hankey hoped to get Captain Clement Jones[1] out quickly to take that work off his hands.[2]

The actual decision regarding the position of Hardinge and of Hankey was recorded as follows:—

'The following arrangements have been approved provisionally by the Prime Minister:

1. Lord Hardinge as Organising Ambassador is in charge of the Administrative organisation of the whole Departmental mission.

2. Lt. Col. Sir M. P. A. Hankey has been nominated by the Prime Minister as British Secretary to the Peace Conference . . . His secretariat is arranged to meet the secretarial needs of the Peace Conference as it is now functioning, that is to say for the following two distinct but connected organisations:—

(a) A Series of Conversations between the Prime Ministers and Foreign Secretaries of the Five Great Powers [i.e. the Council of Ten].

(b) The main conference at which the proposals of the Great Powers will be discussed'.[3] The memorandum then listed the Assistant Secretaries whom, as we have seen, Hankey had been so carefully assembling.[4]

Though Balfour's latest biographer has recorded the Foreign Secretary's satisfaction at 'his old friend Maurice Hankey' becoming British Secretary of the Conference, and states that he was invaluable 'in maintaining close liaison between the Foreign Minister and his chief',[5]

[1]See Vol. I, p. 344, *note*. [2]To Lady Hankey 17th Jan. 1919.

[3]Memo. of 22nd Jan. 1919. Cab. 21/141. Also *Supreme Control*, pp. 27–9 and Lloyd George, *Peace Treaties*, pp. 132–3.

[4]The Assistant Secretaries were:

Major H. A. Caccia and Captain E. Abraham from the S.W.C. staff at Versailles. They were responsible, under Hankey, for recording the 'Conversations' of the Prime Ministers and Foreign Secretaries of the Allies.

Mr. H. C. Norman and Mr. E. C. E. (later Sir Eric) Phipps were responsible for the secretarial arrangements of the main Peace Conference. They were joined later by Mr. T. A. Spring-Rice of the Foreign Office; Mr. C. J. B. (later Sir Cecil) Hurst, legal adviser to the Foreign Office, as member of the Drafting Committee, and Captain (later Sir Clement) Jones as Secretary of the B.E.D. under Hankey's 'general direction'. In addition 'a panel to assist' Jones was to be provided by three nominees of Australia, two of Canada, two of South Africa and one each from New Zealand and India.

[5]K. Young, *Arthur James Balfour* (Bell, 1963) p. 407.

at least one member of Hardinge's 'huge organisation' did not take Hankey's appointment well. J. W. Headlam-Morley of the Foreign Office complained in his diary that 'He [Hankey] is an admirable secretary but with no diplomatic experience and no knowledge of Europe [sic], and it is apparently regarded as a grave slight to the Foreign Office and to Lord Hardinge, and may lead to his going back to London'.[1] In fact Hankey's celebrated tact proved fully equal to the occasion, and Hardinge accepted his relegation to a high-sounding but unimportant position on the sidelines of the conference without demur.

All was now clear, and the first Plenary Session of the preliminary conference took place at 3 p.m. on 18th January.[2] But, as Hankey described to his wife, the preparatory processes had not gone at all smoothly.

*To Lady Hankey. British War Cabinet Office, Villa Majestic. 18th January 1919*
The great Peace Conference has at last met. The great game of Blind Man's Buff has begun – for such it is . . . The week has been a dreadful one for me. We have been mainly engaged on thrashing out the machinery of the conference. The process has been a gruelling one. From 10.30 to 5.30, with an interval for lunch, I have usually been in the secret meetings, which may fairly be termed the 'Cabinet of Nations'. After this I have to attend a committee to draft a press notice, and a committee drawing up the rules of the big conference . . ., which may fairly be termed 'The Legislature of Nations'. You cannot believe the petty jealousies that are shown . . . I believe that Venizelos did not come to the meeting to-day because Bulgaria and Serbia had three representatives and Greece only two. Our own Dominions are as bad as anyone. Borden declined to come to the opening meeting to-day because Newfoundland, which has no separate representation, was for this one meeting included in the British Empire Delegation – a generous act on the part of Lloyd George to a tiny self-governing State. There has also been a terrible fuss about the Indian constitutional position. All these troubles fall automatically on my unfortunate head.

[1]Headlam-Morley diary, 19th June 1919. Young, *op. cit.* pp. 411–12 describes the part played by Hankey and Balfour in refuting the attack by Headlam-Morley of 1922 on Lloyd George's good faith over reparations during the Paris Conference. The paper in question (F.O. 11984) entitled 'A Chapter of a History of the Peace Conference' did not reach Hankey until July 1924. He then described it as 'a partisan pamphlet or tract in which a case is built up against Mr. Lloyd George and his government', and as 'If not pro-German . . . at any rate strongly anti-Ally'. Cab. 63/36.

[2]*Foreign Relations, U.S.A.*, III, pp. 157–75.

What is to be born from these rather sordid birth-pangs and throes? I think I see a splendid child with a solid constitution and a sound brain growing up. The brain is the Cabinet of Nations – men such as Lloyd George, Clemenceau, Wilson (whom I now know quite well); the constitution is the Parliament of Nations, of which I have spoken . . . [Hankey then went on to describe the social life at the Astoria and Majestic Hotels, where 'all the most beautiful and well dressed society ladies', brought over by the various missions, engaged in dancing, bridge and gossip. He himself took no part in such activities, because he was 'in tremendous demand for lunch and dinner for business purposes'.]

Despite the prolonged nature of the preliminary discussions on the Peace Conference, and the jealousies and antagonisms which they revealed, Hankey later rebutted the charge of undue dilatoriness.[1] The impatience voiced at the time derived, of course, chiefly from the strong and natural public desire to get the treaty signed as soon as possible and to return to something like normal peace time conditions; but such views did take too little account of the many conflicting interests which had to be resolved before the conference could really get down to business. To give only one example of those difficulties, the question of the official language to be used at the conference had not been decided by the time the first Plenary Session of the Preliminary Conference took place; and it took the Council of Ten and Hankey another week of hard lobbying before French and English were accepted as having equal status.[2] French pride was mollified by the appointment as Secretary-General of Paul Dutasta, whom Sir Harold Nicolson has described as 'a weak, flustered, surprised but not unamiable man'. The same acute observer remarks that 'the defect . . . was gradually remedied by the hearty British efficiency of Sir Maurice Hankey'. But Nicolson considered that Dutasta's appointment constituted 'a serious drawback', and resulted in the waste of the first six weeks in discussing subjects 'in their order of temporal urgency, not in their order of actual importance'. Study of the records of the conference does indeed lend much support to this criticism, and to Nicolson's attribution of it to the absence of 'secretarial strategy'.[3] It is hard to escape the conclusion that things would have gone faster had Hankey been put in complete charge. At any rate Paul Mantoux, his old friend and colleague of many wartime Inter-Allied meetings, acted

[1] *Supreme Control,* p. 40. [2] *ibid.* pp. 30–1.
[3] *Peacemaking 1919*, pp. 119–20.

as interpreter[1]; and he and Hankey between them produced the French and English *procès verbaux* and 'Secretary's Notes' in intimate cordiality.

*To Lady Hankey. British War Cabinet Offices, Villa Majestic. 20th January 1919*
I am very busy re-organising office arrangements to suit my new position as British Secretary of the Peace Conference. I was at it all day Sunday [19th] save for a short interval for church. In the end I got in despair and went for a four mile walk, at the end of which I saw daylight. . . . I have found a tendency on the part of the French secretaries to be overbearing and insolent, so I wrote an effusively polite but fundamentally stiff letter to Dutasta . . . warning him that I would not put up with his bringing 4 French secretaries to the meeting when I had only one. He took it very well and gave in, so I invited him to dinner to-morrow and we are the best of friends again. *But* I find the whole demeanour of the French F.O. officials has changed as a result, and the American and Italian secretaries have both been to me to thank me for my action. It is not pleasant, but with Frenchmen it always has to be done . . .

Next day Clement Jones arrived from London and took over from Hankey the responsibility for the B.E.D. Secretariat. He carried this heavy burden right to the end of the peace conference, and acquitted himself admirably. After it was all over Clement Jones wrote the history of the Delegation, and Hankey went to immense pains to get it cleared for publication by the Historical Section of the C.I.D. Early in 1921 he wrote personally to all the British Ministers concerned, and also to the Prime Ministers of the Dominions. Favourable replies were received from everyone – except 'Billy' Hughes of Australia, who had always been the *enfant terrible* of the Paris conference. After two hasteners had been sent Hughes finally wrote (26th October 1921) that he was 'not in agreement with many of the statements made' and 'feared that the publication will call forth undesirable comment': he could not therefore approve publication. Hankey made one more effort – in a telegram from Lloyd George to the Governor-General; but it was of no avail and the book never was published. The typescript remains in the Cabinet files to this day as a mine of information about the conduct of the business of the B.E.D. and the characters of its members.[2]

[1]See Vol. I, pp. 348, *note*, 386, etc.,

[2]Cab. 21/217. Clement Jones also wrote an extremely perceptive and witty study of W. M. Hughes at the Paris Conference – presumably for the confidential information of the Cabinet Office. Hankey kept a copy of the typescript in his papers.

Meanwhile the Council of Ten had begun discussions on the very thorny question of the future of the former German colonies.[1] This was an issue over which the B.E.D. itself was divided. Whereas Canada had no annexationist ambitions, South Africa, Australia and New Zealand had strong desires to acquire outright German South-West Africa, German New Guinea and Samoa respectively – which of course ran directly counter to President Wilson's anti-colonialism. Lloyd George on the other hand was prepared to accept the mandatory principle on behalf of Britain, as was Clemenceau on behalf of France. This obviously left Smuts, Hughes and Massey in danger of isolation, and so began the search for a compromise – initially in the B.E.D., and then before the Council of Ten – which would satisfy all parties. It was fortunate that, just when this major issue came to a head Hankey had got his organisation 'humming like a top'.[2] With the administrative machinery running smoothly he increased the pressure for Adeline to come out and join him.

*To Lady Hankey. British War Cabinet Offices, Villa Majestic. 24th January 1919*
Another two meeting day, so don't expect much of a letter . . . In spite of all my hard work I am gloriously fit. Paris is extraordinarily stimulating just now. That is why I want you to come. Here is my average day. Get up 7.45: Müller [i.e. physical exercises]: beautiful hot bath: breakfast in my sitting room with Clement Jones and Sylvester at 8.30, but very often with the P.M. at his flat. If I don't go to the P.M. I try to get a short walk: then to the office. At 9.45 I have all my staff to my room, and I give them a whole mass of instructions on all the innumerable points which have occurred to me . . . These staff meetings are a great feature of my system. I send them out all over our own Delegation, to the Secretary-General of the conference [Dutasta], the French Foreign Office and all the missions. By these means I am gradually establishing my grip over the whole machine. At 10.30 there is usually a Conference. Immediately after it I go on to a committee to draft the press communiqué . . . I very often have to lunch either with the P.M., the Ambassador or someone else. At 2.30 or 3.0 p.m. the 'conversations' at the Quai d'Orsay [begin], and they last until about 5.30 when some very nasty tea comes in and we adjourn. Then another press communiqué . . . Next I come back here and write to you while my assistants do the Minutes. After that I generally get a little walk before dinner . . . Mr. Balfour says he cannot understand how I do it, and that the whole place would stop if I was not there . . .

[1]Council of Ten meeting on 24th, 27th and 28th January 1919. *Foreign Relations, U.S.A.*, III, pp. 716–71.

[2]To Lady Hankey 22nd Jan. 1919.

On 25th, a Saturday, the second Plenary Session of the Preliminary Conference took place.[1] Hankey was 'bored stiff' by the protracted proceedings, which he regarded as 'sheer camouflage' – all the important decisions having already been taken in the 'hush frock' (that is the Council of Ten) meetings. So he whiled away the time by writing to Adeline while 'sitting on the official secretary's bench', and described to her a brush with Dutasta over his having issued the *procès verbal* of the previous conference in French only. In general he was satisfied with the progress made on the highest level, but regarded the 'insistent demand of the press for publicity in regard to the most delicate questions' as a serious handicap.[2]

The next day, Sunday 26th, brought him a break through visiting Rheims and the neighbouring battlefields with Smuts. Then the grinding routine of long daily meetings was resumed, and the next letter to Adeline was written in the 'hush frock' meeting at which General Botha made 'a most moving speech, spoken straight from the heart, to the effect that all his work for the unity of the two races in South Africa will be undone unless the Union gets German S.W. Africa'. Botha's English, however, was not very fluent and he ended by saying that 'If this Council decides against us it will do more harm than it ever meant to do'![3] Meanwhile, with Sylvester's help, Hankey made good progress with finding suitable accommodation for Adeline to join him – possibly with Ursula.

*To Lady Hankey. Quai d'Orsay. 29th January 1919*

[Written during a 'Council of Ten' meeting]

... We have been greatly agitated this week by the difficult questions raised by the disposal of the conquered German colonies. It has been extremely difficult to reconcile the views of President Wilson and some of our Dominions. It has involved many meetings of the British Empire Delegation, and an infinity of delicate negotiation.[4] I have had to have nearly all my meals with the Prime Minister in order to help him in squaring this or that party. Hughes

[1] *Foreign Relations, U.S.A.*, III, pp. 176–207.

[2] To Lady Hankey 25th January 1919.

[3] To the same 27th January 1919. See also *Supreme Control*, p. 59 and *Foreign Relations, U.S.A.*, III, pp. 738–48. Botha's slip of the tongue does not, however, appear in the official *procès-verbal* (*loc. cit.* p. 744) where he is stated to have said that 'if this [i.e. union with South-West Africa] is rejected then there would be constant agitation.'

[4] See Minutes of 3rd and 4th Meetings of the B.E.D. Cab. 29/28/1 and Secretary's

and Massey, who insist on annexation of the German islands in the South Pacific, are our principal difficulty, but President Wilson, in his insistence on the affiliation of these colonies, in some form or another, to the League of Nations, is even more obstinate. . . . However I am hopeful that we are now on the way to an accommodation.

Smuts and I have been comparing notes, and I think we are both agreed that, if this League of Nations is to have half a chance, it is almost essential that he and I should be associated with it in one form or another – he in a political and I in a secretarial capacity. It is too early to say more on this at present.

I have succeeded in getting together a very efficient office here. Here is an instance of their admirable spirit. This week they have been dreadfully overworked, three meetings a day . . . they have been working from 9 a.m. until midnight. As we have been doing the minutes for the Americans, Japanese and Italians, as well as for ourselves, I proposed . . . to arrange that the Americans should reproduce the minutes alternately with ourselves. The whole office at once asked to continue to do the work! Pretty good, I thought!

Also my scheme for organising a staff of Assistants from the Dominions is working most admirably. In fact to-day I have a South African taking the notes at a 'hush-frock' meeting. . . .

In fact it was at the meeting of the B.E.D. on 29th January that Hankey, supported by Smuts and J. G. Latham,[1] invented the device of the 'Class C' League of Nations mandates whereby territories whose people were regarded as too sparse and 'remote from the centres of civilisation' for self-government should be 'administered under the laws of the mandatory' – an arrangement which in effect differed but little from direct colonial rule. This ultimately overcame the serious stumbling block produced by the intransigence of Billy Hughes of Australia over the future of the former German part of New Guinea and other islands to the north of Australia.[2] But before that came to pass Hankey had to exercise all his renowned tact towards Hughes,

---

Notes of Council of Ten meetings on 28th January. *Foreign Relations, U.S.A.*, III, pp. 749–71.

[1]Later Sir John G. Latham (1877–1964). Australian lawyer and politician. Attorney-General 1925–29. Deputy Prime Minister, Attorney-General and Minister for Industry and for External Affairs 1932–34. Minister to Japan 1940–41. Chief Justice of Australia 1935–52. Represented Australia at League of Nations and many international conferences 1919–32.

[2]5th Meeting of B.E.D. Cab. 29/28/1. The discussion in the Council of Ten had

who had written direct to President Wilson, without any reference to Balfour or to any of his colleagues on the B.E.D., urging Australia's claims to the Pacific islands. Hankey at once took the matter up with Sir Robert Garran, the Solicitor-General of Australia, pointing out that Hughes had done exactly what the Dominions had so often complained of the British government doing – namely 'to discuss matters of Policy affecting them without consulting them'. Though one may feel that the parallel produced by Hankey was not very exact Garran was evidently impressed. He took the usually intractable and ebullient Hughes to task so successfully that he promised not to repeat the offence. After it was all over Hankey described the incident in a letter to Lloyd George, which ended with the comforting assurance that 'Lord Milner thinks that the question may be left at that'.[1]

*To Lady Hankey. British Delegation, Paris. 31st January 1919*

[Again written during a Council of Ten meeting.[2]]

. . . Yesterday we had a very difficult day at the conference, trying to reconcile the differences of the President of the U.S.A. and our Dominions.[3]

The President made an extraordinary speech in which he said that he . . . would like to be able to say that religion was a good working proposition, but he regretted that this was not the case. In the case of the League of Nations he did not want to make the mistake that had been made in regard to religion. It was almost tantamount to saying that he did not intend to make the mistake Jesus Christ had made! It drew some rather nicely veiled comments from our Dominions' people, particularly Borden and Massey. . . .

That day, 31st January, serious industrial unrest broke out on Clyde-

---

started on 23rd January. See *Foreign Relations, U.S.A.*, III, pp. 718–22, 749 and 763–71. For an admirable summary see L. F. Fitzhardinge, *W. M. Hughes and the Treaty of Versailles, 1919*. Journal of Commonwealth Studies, Vol. V, No. 2 (July 1967) pp. 130–42. Though Sir James Butler in *Lord Lothian* (London, 1960) p. 75 records Philip Kerr's claims to have drafted the clause about Class C. Mandates, and Kerr and Hankey certainly worked in close accord at this time, Mr. Fitzhardinge agrees with this biographer in attributing it to Smuts, Latham and Hankey.

[1]Hankey to Lloyd George 21st February 1919. Lloyd George papers F/25/4/18.

[2]*Foreign Relations, U.S.A.*, III, pp. 818–34.

[3]*ibid.* pp. 785–817. It was at the meeting on the afternoon of 30th that Hughes had his famous passage of arms with President Wilson, answering the enquiry by the latter whether 'Australia is prepared to defy the appeal of the whole civilized world' to agree to a mandate with 'That's about the size of it, Mr. President'. See Fitzhardinge, *op. cit.* p. 137.

side[1]; and signs were not lacking that the trouble would spread. Lloyd George had to hurry home to deal with a House of Commons which was showing justifiable anxiety about the industrial situation, and becoming increasingly restive about the slow progress being made in Paris. This of course ruined Hankey's plans for Adeline to join him, as he had no idea whether Lloyd George would want him in London or be prepared to leave him in Paris. So ended a month full of disappointments. It is easy to see now that if only Wilson had, in Churchill's words, 'locked himself up with Clemenceau and Lloyd George, with only Maurice Hankey to record and give precise shape to the decisions'[2] – as he was forced to do three months later – the long-drawn agony of Europe would have been shortened. Small wonder that Hankey chafed at having to listen to the claims and aspirations of minor nations. At the end of January he complained to his wife about the Poles and Czecho-Slovaks 'droning out their interminable *revendications* [claims]', which were 'only remotely a British interest'. Lloyd George was also, according to Hankey, getting restless, and interrupted the proceedings to try and prevent 'the most infernal waste of time'.[3] Early in the following month Hankey told Adeline that 'The conference goes on much the same as ever – not so fast as I should like. All the small powers insist on presenting their case at interminable length. It is a great bore, but everyone agrees that, so long as they are allowed their say, they will accept the decision of the Great Powers and that otherwise they will not.' The principle therefore followed was to listen – even if it meant allowing Bratianu, Prime Minister of Roumania, to 'drone out his case for two days', and then to 'remit the questions to experts for advice'. He hoped that 'when we get the experts' reports we shall reach decisions'; but he was obviously impatient about the time taken over such processes.[4]

*To Lady Hankey. Palais Murat, Paris, 5th February 1919*

I am writing this in President Wilson's residence . . . The P.M. is having a heart-to-heart talk with President Wilson about some of the most delicate

[1] 31st January 1919 is sometimes referred to as 'Red Friday'. But that appellation is more correctly applied to 31st July 1925, when Baldwin gave way to the coal miners and introduced the subsidy in order to preserve peace temporarily. See p. 411.

[2] *The Aftermath* (1929) p. 144. [3] To Lady Hankey, 29th and 31st Jan. 1919.

[4] To the same, 3rd Feb. 1919.

questions before the Peace Conference.[1] I have been sent for several times to produce documents and have been in [the conference room] for some time. They asked for two documents of 1915, and I feared I was done – but luckily I had put them in the box.

Yesterday ... the P.M. had a long conference in the afternoon and I was continuously busy thereafter ... The fact is that we are entering upon the most delicate ground. The result is that there are fewer formal meetings and more exchanges of views outside ...

Meanwhile a number of Commissions are in full swing and seem to be going all right. I had a meeting of secretaries of Commissions this morning at 9.15 in order to introduce common action and co-ordination of method ...

The P.M. returns on Saturday [8th] to England and says he will be back in 9 or 10 days – but I have my doubts. I rather dread being left here with A. J. B. [Balfour] who though delightful as ever, has aged a good deal and will be difficult to 'run' effectively. It will throw a good deal more responsibility on to me for keeping the thing moving ... [Hankey then went on to discuss the reasons why a move from Highstead to London had much to commend it]. We must wait, though, until this show is through. It is quite on the cards that I may become the British Secretary to the League of Nations ... At the present moment the League of Nations inquiry is not proceeding on sound lines and, as I have warned the P.M., may produce an acutely difficult situation.[2] I could not possibly undertake to run the League on the lines now contemplated. It would inevitably break down, and I should be involved in the smash. But it may straighten out, and I regard it as by no means improbable that I may undertake it ...

The foregoing letter is revealing on several counts. In the first place it shows how reluctant Wilson still was to admit Hankey to the very secret, top-level discussions – of which no record was therefore kept. Secondly Hankey's remarkable prescience in always having in his 'box' the exact papers needed at any meeting has frequently been remarked on. With Sylvester's help he invariably prepared the contents of the box with the utmost care before any meeting, and no example exists of his ever being unable to produce the right paper when called for. This capacity, which repeatedly amazed those who observed it, in-

[1]No record exists of this conversation, but the 'delicate questions' must surely have included the future of the German colonies and Italian claims in the Adriatic and in Asia Minor. The 'documents of 1915' referred to by Hankey almost certainly concerned the Secret Treaty of London by which Italy had been bribed to enter the war.

[2]President Wilson was Chairman of the Commission on the League of Nations. The British representatives were Smuts and Lord Robert Cecil.

cluding President Wilson, derived of course from his remarkable memory, his long experience and his systematically thorough methods. Thirdly the letter shows that, at this early stage, Hankey was by no means unwilling to hitch his wagon to the star of the League of Nations – provided he was sure it was soundly organised. His aversion to accepting any connection with a conference which he considered to be based on wrong principles, or whose failure he foresaw, was remarked on earlier.[1]

By the end of the first week in February it was clear that the conference was going to suffer further delays. Not only had Lloyd George to return home, but the opposition aroused by Italy's claims and conditions – especially towards the new Yugo-Slav state – caused Orlando to withdraw temporarily from the conference, infuriated by Wilson having addressed himself direct to the Italian people over his own head. A clear indication of the tension aroused at those meetings is provided by a manuscript note which Wilson probably passed to Lloyd George at the Council of Four on 10th February, and which Hankey preserved. 'We have lost all control (indeed we have never exercised any control) over our own business', wrote the President. 'Have we no recourse? I would very much value your thought about this.' It was in those depressing circumstances that Wilson himself left for America on the 15th – there to learn about the rising opposition to the League of Nations in the Senate. With only the second eleven – House and Lansing for U.S.A., Sonnino for Italy and Balfour for Britain – left in charge of their delegations trouble was all too likely and real progress improbable. Small wonder that Hankey's next letters home show frustration and fatigue. Only Clemenceau kept up his spirits. '*Restez jeune, mon Colonel, aussi longtemps que vous pouvez*' he remarked to Hankey on 6th February; to which the latter replied 'If I can remain young half as long as you I shall be content'. Two days later Clemenceau demonstrated his vigour by provoking such a serious quarrel with Foch that the Marshal 'picked up his papers and walked out of the room in a huff'.[2]

Hankey's unsettlement was aggravated by a message from Esher to the effect that he was making a grave mistake by not returning to London with Lloyd George. Sylvester thought that Esher might be referring to Hankey's personal position. 'Is it possible', Hankey asked his wife, 'that Tom Jones is trying to cut me out? I thought my posi-

[1]See Vol. I, p. 18. [2]To Lady Hankey, 7th and 9th February 1919.

We have lost all control (indeed we have never exercised any control) over our own business.
Have we no recourse?
I could very much value your thought about this.

W W

(President Wilson's initials, 10 Feb. 1919)

Sheer waste of time

A note passed by President Wilson at the Paris Peace Conference, 10th February 1919

tion was too strong for that. Anyhow I have always said that only the best man available ought to have my job, and if he is better than me [sic] he shall have it!' He went on to say that he knew that Tom Jones was better at dealing with industrial problems, and when he got home he intended to split the secretariat into two branches, with Jones at the head of one and Brigadier-General 'Sammy' Wilson of the other,[1] he himself 'being in general charge of the two'. 'My soul is a little disquieted within me', he confided to Adeline; 'but I mean to take the big view of principle and stick to that'.[2] In fact there were no grounds

[1]See Vol. I, p. 601, *note*.
[2]To Lady Hankey 10th Feb. 1919.

for Hankey's disquiet, for on the same day that he gave vent to his misgivings Jones wrote to him at length about the prevailing industrial troubles, and how Lloyd George was handling them. He ended in humorous vein, assuring his 'Chief' that he was 'endeavouring to behave more or less with the serious dignity appropriate to an Acting Secretary'.[1] It seems unlikely that any idea of displacing Hankey ever entered Jones's head. Next day Hankey wrote to him saying that he considered 'the time has now come when we ought to get a move on about the War Book' – that is to say bringing it up to date from the experiences of the recent conflict – and enclosing a draft instruction to Departments to do so. Jones replied a week later that Lloyd George 'was not very definite one way or the other about the War Book'; but he was 'satisfied that the letter could go out as a direction from him [i.e. Lloyd George]', and he would 'probably take an opportunity of mentioning the matter to B.L. [Bonar Law] and others'. Obviously he was determined to carry out his 'Chief's' wishes without any qualifications.[2]

On 10th February Hankey wrote at length to Esher in justification of his decision not to return to London with Lloyd George. He described all that he had accomplished, and was accomplishing in Paris, with which the reader is familiar, and then turned his shrewd and practical eye on the prospects for the League of Nations.

*Hankey to Esher. Villa Majestic, 10th February 1919*
. . . I should like to think that the League of Nations with all the high principles that are behind it, was going to be the great constructive work for this conference, but I am very sceptical. On the one hand there is the idealism (combined with the shrewd instinct of President Wilson for his home politics, which makes him very obstinate); on the other hand there is the gross materialism of the Italians and the complete scepticism of the French. We stand somewhere between with a good deal of idealism but with an eye always on the practical side. The trouble is that the men who represent us on the League of Nations Commission, Lord Robert Cecil and Smuts, are both idealists, and the former at any rate [is] not very practical on this particular question. I am afraid their scheme will prove unworkable for two reasons,

[1]Jones to Hankey 10th Feb. 1919. *Middlemas*, I, pp. 75–6.
[2]Hankey to Jones 11th Feb. and reply by latter of 18th Feb. 1919. *ibid.* pp. 75–6 and 78.

first, that it attempts too much, and second, that not enough attention is given to the machine. . . . So long as the League of Nations is merely a place to which the nations are accustomed to come to concert their policy in common, I think it might be built up into a great international constitutional instrument. The inclusion, however, of clauses compelling nations, in certain circumstances, to boycott an offender, or to make war on him, will I believe defeat the very objects that the promoters have in view. Then, I do not like their Secretariat. They have a person called a Chancellor. I asked Lord Robert Cecil what it meant. He replied 'Oh, he is only a Secretary'. Now, if you had had a Chancellor instead of a Secretary of the Committee of Imperial Defence, and had treated him as 'only a Secretary' you would have busted long ago. What you want is a person who is in name only a Secretary, but in fact is a Chancellor. Thus he causes no jealousies. They have inverted the order, and I cannot get them to see the mistake of this. The Secretariat will be the only permanent element in the League of Nations and must be kept free from all jealousy, etc. Between a very doubtful fundamental basis . . . and the badly constituted machine I am not very hopeful for it, but we shall have to do our best. . . .

*To Lady Hankey. Villa Majestic, 11th February 1919*
[Written during a Council of Ten Meeting]

I hope I did not depress you with the hurried scrawl I sent you yesterday. I believe my position to be absolutely secure, and if Ll. G. ever wants some-one else he will see me well provided for. . .

At present we are only having one meeting a day. I am busy all the morning though, on work of different kinds, and then I lunch with Mr. Balfour and Lord Milner to discuss what line they are to take at the afternoon meeting. Still the work is much less strenuous and exciting without the P.M.

Personally I don't think the P.M. will get back here for two or three weeks, as he has so much to do in England, and I dare say it will be March before he comes over. Of course, it is always on the cards that he may send for me . . .

We have had rather difficult relations lately with the French about Syria, and there were some rather sharp passages yesterday[1] . . . However Milner has been seeing Clemenceau and Sonnino this morning, and I think the difficulty is laid for the moment . . .

I have been dining out a good deal lately. . . . On Sunday I dined with Botha, who was very flattering to me, and said that my action with the Dominions was resounding throughout the Empire. He is a good friend to me. I must stop now, as the 'hush frock' meeting at which I am writing is suddenly getting interesting . . .

[1]Council of Ten meeting on 10th February 1919. *Foreign Relations, U.S.A.,* III, pp. 945–56.

P.S. Lord Justice Sumner,[1] who has arrived here for a commission,[2] was introduced to me yesterday, and at once said 'I hear everywhere that you are the mainspring of the whole thing here'.

Next day, 12th, the Supreme War Council met to consider the report of the commission set up to review the 'preliminaries' for peace, and also the terms on which the Armistice, which was about to lapse, might be renewed.[3] For Hankey these protracted sessions were lightened by the news that Adeline had at last found it possible to come out and join him. He made the most careful domestic arrangements for her reception and comfort; and the clouds of tedium which had loomed over the interminable meetings he was forced to attend at once lifted. But another, and to Hankey a less welcome visitor – in the person of Winston Churchill – actually reached Paris first. He attended Council of Ten meetings on 14th, 15th and 17th to press for full military intervention in Russia.[4] Hankey later described this episode as 'Churchill at his worst'.[5] Fortunately Lloyd George had left Philip Kerr in Paris; and his report quickly provoked what Hankey called 'a very hot telegram' from the Prime Minister totally repudiating the measures for which his ardent Secretary of State for War was pressing.[6] President Wilson, who had left Paris for his own country on 14th, took a very similar line with Colonel House[7]; and the whole Churchill intervention finally came to nothing. But it was not of course exactly helpful in furthering the purposes for which the Paris Conference had been convened – namely the preparation of a Treaty of Peace between the Allies and the Central Powers. As Lloyd George has written 'at bottom [it] merely meant the setting up of a great army for the eventual invasion of Russia'.[8]

At this difficult and frustrating time a proposal reached Hankey from

[1]1859–1934. 1st Viscount Sumner 1927. A Lord Justice of Appeal 1912–13 and Lord of Appeal in Ordinary 1913–30. Chairman of many commissions and committees appointed by the government 1918–26.

[2]This was the Commission on Reparations. In addition to Lord Sumner, Lord Cunliffe and Mr. W. M. Hughes of Australia were the British Empire representatives on it.

[3]*Foreign Relations, U.S.A.*, III, pp. 970–1012.

[4]*Supreme Control*, pp. 66–73.

[5]Hankey to Sir James Butler. Undated letter *c.* 21st May 1958 about Philip Kerr's part in the Versailles Conference.

[6]*Supreme Control*, p. 71. Lloyd George, *Peace Treaties*, I, pp. 367–83.

[7]House, *Intimate Papers,* IV, pp. 358–9. [8]Quoted *Supreme Control*, p. 73.

Auckland Geddes, who was temporarily out of office, which caused him alarm. Geddes wanted a new department added to the Cabinet Secretariat 'to which the public may turn in cases where they have complaints against the administrative nets of a Department of State' – in effect the equivalent of the modern 'Ombudsman'.[1] Hankey sent the proposal on to Tom Jones, who showed it to Lloyd George; and the Prime Minister was rather taken with the idea of having a department which could handle the 400–1,000 complaints which reached him daily. Jones, however, at once saw the dangers of the Secretariat being landed with this enormous and thankless task. In what he described to Hankey as 'a preliminary skirmish' he made it plain that, as responsibility for action on complaints must be taken in the Prime Minister's name, 'we could not take it [on] as a Secretariat or Department'.[2] Hankey agreed with Jones, and told Lloyd George so; and so the matter was dropped – for nearly half a century.

On 19th February an anarchist who had concealed himself in a 'Vespasienne' at the corner of the Rue Franklin, where Clemenceau lived, and the Boulevard Delessert attempted to assassinate the old Tiger while on his way to his office.[3] Though nine shots were fired into his car Clemenceau was only wounded in the shoulder, and was never in danger; but the last of the 'Big Four' was now out of action, and it was more difficult than ever to speed up the deliberations of the conference.

A few days after the attempted assassination Hankey sent Lloyd George a long letter describing Balfour's efforts to get things moving, and the difficulties which were being encountered with the Italians. As regards the former he suggested that, on his return to Paris, Lloyd George's main tasks should be, firstly, 'to settle the question whether naval and military and air conditions of peace are to be imposed as an advance instalment on Germany'; and, secondly, to stimulate the senior British Empire delegates on the more important commissions

[1] Hankey to Lloyd George, 14th Feb. 1919. Lloyd George papers F/23/4/16.

[2] Jones to Hankey 18th Feb. 1919. *Middlemas*, I, p. 78.

[3] Lloyd George, *Peace Treaties*, I, p. 396 says the attempted assassination took place on 18th, but on p. 490 it is correctly given as 19th. 'Vespasienne' (or Pisotière) are the Parisian's names for the iron public urinals which, as *The Times* (20th Feb. 1919) rather smugly remarked 'disfigure the streets of Paris'. The name is derived from the (actually false) belief that the Emperor Vespasian equipped Rome with public urinals. See *Les Vespasiennes de Paris ou les Précieux Edicules* (Paris 1968) for a history of these fast disappearing relics of 19th century Paris.

into improving the progress made by those bodies.[1] This was a formidable undertaking since, six weeks after the start of the conference, nineteen commissions had been set up to study detailed questions and report to the Plenary Conference or the Council of Ten; and they had given birth to no less than twenty-seven sub-commissions. The main obstacle to speeding up the conference was, said Hankey, the deliberately obstructive attitude of the Italians – particularly with regard to their territorial claims in Asia Minor; nor was it yet known what the American attitude was towards accepting a mandate in that part of the world. Thus it was impossible to improve progress 'until we get the Italians in a better frame of mind'; and to accomplish that purpose he thought it might be necessary 'to expose the fact that the Italians are blocking us in the Council of Ten' in order to bring the pressure of public opinion to bear on them. He gave Lloyd George various examples of the deliberate, deceitful and obstructive practices adopted by Italian delegates on certain commissions.[2]

Balfour was the mainspring of the effort to get things moving in the absence of the 'Big Four', and on 24th the Council of Ten, which was of course temporarily reduced to a Foreign Ministers' conference, approved a Resolution that 'the necessary investigations' for producing preliminary peace terms for each of the ex-enemy countries should be pressed ahead 'with all possible speed'.[3] It is difficult not to feel that the public impatience aroused by the time taken to reach even this preparatory stage was fully justified; and Hankey was surely too complimentary when he later wrote that the Foreign Ministers had, by the end of February, 'done a fine job in speeding up the work'.[4]

Meanwhile Hankey had been giving a good deal of thought to his own future, since the time was obviously approaching when he would have to make his mind up whether to accept the post of Secretary-General to the League of Nations. One of those whom he consulted was, very naturally, Esher; and on 19th February he received a long and affectionate letter of advice from him. Esher suggested that, as a result of the long years of strain and overwork, and of his absence in Paris, Hankey had got his perspective about future trends wrong. The analogy which Hankey had suggested between the C.I.D. and the

[1]Hankey to Lloyd George 23rd Feb. 1919. Lloyd George papers F/23/4/22. Part reproduced in *Middlemas*, I, pp. 78–9.

[2]Lloyd George papers F/23/4/22. [3]*Foreign Relations, U.S.A.*, IV, pp. 104–11.

[4]*Supreme Control*, p. 81.

League Covenant was, in Esher's opinion, wholly false. Whereas there had never been any doubt about the functions of the pre-war C.I.D., which Hankey had 'helped to fashion' and had 'wielded with skill', the future of the League was entirely nebulous; and if Hankey joined it he would be 'a wasted force for England'. At the best the League 'must be a plant of slow growth', and while it was developing great events would be happening at home. Esher fully recognised that 'the old England' which he had 'known and loved' was changing, and that entirely new forces 'of dynamic power' were at work. If those forces were properly guided he considered that they 'may make our country happier and greater than ever'; but if they were not restrained 'they may break England'. He pleaded with Hankey to play the part of which he was capable in 'controlling and directing' the new forces. Furthermore, he went on, 'the Empire has now come of age', and 'infinite tact, sympathetic treatment, profound understanding and exemplary patience' would be essential in the coming years if the Commonwealth was 'to stand the test'. The Prime Minister of England would in his opinion still be the chief power, and Esher was sure that Hankey's proper place 'for the next ten years is at the right hand of the Prime Minister of the day', acting as the catalyst between the British and Commonwealth Cabinets. Those two bodies were, he concluded, 'the only League of Nations in which you and I can be primarily interested'.[1]

At about the same time Hankey evidently consulted Curzon on the same matter, and the reply he received is revealing with regard to the attitude of the future Foreign Secretary towards the embryo League of Nations.

*Curzon to Hankey. 1 Carlton House Terrace. Undated, but probably early April 1919.* Holograph

PRIVATE

My dear Hankey,

I was very much flattered at your paying me the compliment of asking my advice on the question of your future career, and I have thought carefully over the problem which you submitted to me.

My own opinion is clear, but I am not certain that it is wholly unprejudiced – at least to this extent. I am very doubtful whether the League of Nations is going to be the great and potent and world-pacifying instrument that its creators desire, and further I shrink from any decision that wd. turn you

[1]Esher to Hankey 19th February 1919. Holograph. Part printed in *Journals*, IV, pp. 226–8 but is there misdated 18th February.

into an international official instead of being one of the most valued and influential servants of your own country.

These are my prejudices and prepossessions. But they incline me to an opinion which I think I should have arrived at independently of them.

Should you become the first Secy. General of the League of Nations, I quite grant that you are more likely to make a success of it than any living man. But you will be away at Geneva. You will be serving a multitude of masters. The League will experience many and great disappointments. It may even fail of much of its objects. I do not like to think of you giving all your time and talents to the service of anything so impersonal and soulless [heartless deleted] as an international bureau. On the other hand if you remain in England you will be mainly responsible for converting the War Cabinet into a Peace Cabinet, for constituting the Imperial Cabinet of the future, and for moulding the future organisation of the British Empire. There are great, imminent and inevitable problems that cannot be shirked, and that with reasonable prudence and patriotism cannot fail of solution. These solutions will be a signpost in the history of the Empire and the progress of the world.

All the while you will be associated with the men who know and trust you, and whom you like; for you are equally respected and confided in by both parties – or rather by all parties in this country. Then whenever you are tired of this work or regard it as done, there will be nothing to prevent you from securing some big post – should you care for it – like a Governorship abroad or some important office at home.

Your life will be full and fruitful. There will be no severance of ties or disappointment. You may achieve great things.

Therefore if I am qualified to give an opinion I give it in favour of your remaining at home and declining the gilded chair at Geneva.

Ever sincerely

No doubt Hankey had in mind the advice he had received from Esher when, on the last day of February, he wrote to Lloyd George on the subject. He said that he was being subjected to a good deal of pressure, especially by Colonel House, to accept the Secretary-Generalship. Much depended, however, 'on the feeling that you and your government have towards the League'. He would be prepared to serve wherever he would be 'most useful', and if the Government wanted to make the League 'into a factor of great importance in future world politics' his best services might well be rendered to the new organisation. On the other hand Esher had pressed the view 'that I should be able to help you make the League of Nations a success better by remaining as Secretary of the Cabinet'. As 'a poor man' he could not afford entirely to disregard 'the financial consideration'; and the Secretary-General's salary would presumably 'be higher than ever could be given to the Secretary of the Cabinet'. But he placed such considerations second to the issue of principle. Finally he summed up the pros and cons, and admitted that he felt 'rather a strong attraction towards the post', provided that the British Government wanted an Englishman to become Secretary-General. But, he farsightedly added, it would be unwise to decide the matter 'until we know whether President Wilson is able to carry his policy in America'; since 'if he fails the League will probably fail also'.[1]

As we shall see Hankey did not make up his mind on what must have been a very difficult decision until early in April – by which time the difficulties President Wilson was encountering in gaining acceptance of his policy by his own countrymen had become a good deal clearer.

[1]Hankey to Lloyd George 28th February 1919. Lloyd George papers F/23/4/27.

*Chapter 3*

# The Council of Four. March-May 1919

DESPITE his earlier dissatisfaction with the progress of the conference on 1st March Hankey was able to give Lloyd George a favourable report. 'The speeding up of Resolutions . . . passed a week or so ago', he wrote, 'had the most admirable effect', and the various commissions were now 'going ahead very fast indeed'. The only exceptions were the Economic and Financial Commissions, which he stigmatised as 'the bottle neck'. To save more time the British secretaries of the Commissions had been told to attach to their reports 'draft articles for incorporation in the Terms of Peace'. In general Hankey was hopeful that by the time the heads of Delegations returned 'matters will be in a relatively advanced stage', though various differences between the Allies, notably over the distribution of mandates for the former German Colonies, still remained to be settled. There were, he concluded, four main issues, awaiting Lloyd George's own return. These were the Naval, Military and Air conditions of Peace, which might be presented before the other preliminary steps; the western frontier of Germany; the division of mandates in Turkey, in which country he was hopeful of American participation; and, lastly, the speeding up of the Reparations Commission. All in all he was confident that Lloyd George 'could now do very useful work here'.[1] In fact the Naval, Military and Air conditions for peace came before the Supreme War Council on 3rd, but were held over at Balfour's request – ostensibly to await Lloyd George's return but actually because he was well aware that Foch's draconian proposals would not be acceptable to the British government.[2]

Meanwhile Hankey was also keeping a grip on events in London. On 5th he wrote to Tom Jones stressing the need for him to get the conclusions of the important ministerial conferences then in train

[1] Hankey to Lloyd George 1st March 1919. Lloyd George papers F/23/4/28.
[2] *Foreign Relations, U.S.A.,* IV, pp. 182–92. *Supreme Control*, pp. 84–6.

incorporated in the index of Cabinet Minutes – as had always been his own practice. 'Otherwise when you or I are turned to at short notice', he wrote, 'we may not be able to lay our hands on it'.[1] On the same day he sent Jones a description of progress in Paris – in very much the same terms as he had just given Lloyd George.[2]

During the first half of March the 'Big Four' gradually reassembled in Paris. Clemenceau, though barely recovered from his wound, returned to the conference table on 1st; Lloyd George arrived back on 6th; and on 11th he was followed by Orlando – still in a very intransigent mood over Italian territorial claims. Finally on 14th President Wilson rejoined his colleagues after a month's absence which should have made it plain to him that the Senate would not accept his proposals for a League of Nations – at any rate without incorporating a great many 'reservations'.

On Lloyd George's very first day back at the conference table he gave the Supreme War Council his criticisms of the military conditions of peace proposed by the French. His chief objection was to the Germans being allowed to recruit 200,000 men annually, because with the passage of time this would provide them with an enormous reserve of at any rate partially trained soldiers. The naval conditions had a much easier passage, though the French and Americans wanted the interned German warships to be broken up instead of being divided among the Allies. Next day, 7th, the discussion was resumed and Lloyd George put forward a draft resolution the most important points of which were that the German fighting services were in future to be raised only from volunteers serving for a minimum of twelve years, that the total strength of the German army and air force was not to exceed 200,000 men, and that of their navy 10,000.[3] That day's discussion in effect decided the military, naval and air terms for peace, and Hankey considered this 'a big triumph' for Lloyd George. Ten days later he had to scotch another attempt by Foch and his supporters to launch an anti-Bolshevik crusade – this time by employing Polish troops from Odessa, supported by the Roumanian army. Hankey has very reasonably described the Prime Minister's comments on this proposal as 'scorching'.[4]

Lloyd George's first step to speed up the conference was to stop the

[1]Hankey to Jones 5th March 1919. *Middlemas*, I, p. 80. [2]*ibid.* pp. 80–1.
[3]*Foreign Relations, U.S.A.*, IV, pp. 212–51. *Supreme Control*, pp. 87–91.
[4]*Supreme Control*, p. 95.

constant, and generally garbled 'leakages' to the Press which embarrassed the delegates and infuriated Hankey by repeatedly injecting grit into the machinery. The danger of leakage was vastly increased by the large number of Commissions and Sub-Commissions which had been set up – and to that extent Hankey's system may be said to have produced the results he complained of. Lloyd George's second, and more important purpose was to replace the Council of Ten, and the still more unwieldy Supreme War Council, with a much smaller body armed with executive authority. The analogy between this concept and his replacement of Asquith's large Cabinet Committees by a small War Cabinet in December 1916 is plain.[1] It was this purpose that caused Lloyd George to decide on 21st to withdraw with Smuts, Henry Wilson, Philip Kerr and Hankey 'to the seclusion of the forest of Fontainebleau, to work out definite proposals for the kind of treaty of peace to which alone we were prepared to append our signature'.[2] In fact, however, two days earlier Hankey had sent Lloyd George a long paper describing his 'vague and indefinite uneasiness as to whether the Peace Treaty was developing on sound lines of policy'; and he went on to describe in some detail the grounds for his uneasiness. The chief reason for his concern was the need to contain the spread of 'Bolshevism'; and he considered that 'a barrier' should be provided in the treaty against this threat. The overriding concern of the Paris Conference with preventing the extension of the Russian revolutionary movement has often been remarked on[3]; but nowhere is that phenomenon made clearer than in Hankey's memorandum to Lloyd George of 19th March 1919.[4] To quote his own words, his 'general thesis was that in the coming years Bolshevism was the greatest danger to Europe'.[5] The fact that the communist rising under Bela Kun in Hungary coincided exactly with the Fontainebleau discussions must surely have strengthened the fears he expressed.

As Hankey has himself printed the first paragraph of his memorandum, and its broad outline has already been made plain, there is no need to

[1]See Vol. I, pp. 334–48.

[2]Lloyd George, *Peace Treaties*, I, p. 266.

[3]See for example *Times Literary Supplement*, 6th June 1968 in lead review of Arno J. Mayer *Politics and Diplomacy of Peacemaking*.

[4]Original in Lloyd George papers F/23/4/39. Another copy in Smuts Archive, folio 72.

[5]*Supreme Control*, p. 98.

reproduce it in full here; but it is worth remarking that he later endorsed his own copy with the words 'The original of this paper is believed to have influenced Mr. Lloyd George in his decision to hold the Fontainebleau Conference of March 22nd–23rd'.[1] There is however in the Hankey papers another memorandum which throws interesting light on that occasion, and on his own views. It is dated 23rd March (the Sunday spent at Fontainebleau), and Hankey later wrote on it an endorsement that he believed 'it was drafted to assist Philip Kerr in writing up the results of our talk', and that its contents were 'a summary of my remarks at the Fontainebleau Conference of March 22nd–23rd'.[2] As this paper shows very clearly Hankey's own ideas on the form the peace treaty should take we will summarise the main points in it. Under 'British Interests' the limitation of German naval strength came first, and he wanted an agreement with the U.S.A. on future warship construction. The British government's signature of the League Covenant should, he held, be made conditional on such an agreement being reached; and it would be a first step towards general limitation of armaments. He stressed the need, and the right, for the British Empire 'to get as large an indemnity out of Germany as possible', and in a later paragraph where he discussed Reparations he put forward a total figure of £500 millions annually to be distributed: 50% to France, 30% to the British Empire and 20% to other nations. He emphasised that 'Germany's indebtedness to-day is less than that of Great Britain, and less than that of France when the devastation of her territory is taken into account'. Obviously he felt it very unfair that victorious Britain should emerge from the war burdened by a vastly greater debt than defeated Germany; but the latter was to be granted 'a period of grace for the first years after the war during which payments should be reduced.' A permanent Reparations Commission was to be set up as the authority for dealing with all problems arising out of the exaction of the payments from Germany. Hankey wanted the British Empire to become the mandatory power for Palestine, Mesopotamia, East Africa, South-West Africa and the South Pacific Islands,

[1]Endorsement dated 15th November (?) 1958. However the editor of Henry Wilson's diaries General Sir C. E. Callwell remarks (Vol. II, p. 175) that Wilson gave Hankey 'a strategical lecture', which Lloyd George heard of. Callwell claims that this led to Lloyd George's decision to go to Fontainebleau; but no evidence to support that claim – except Wilson's inclusion in the party – has come to light.
[2]Endorsements dated 15th and 16th November 1958.

and hoped for 'the consolidation of the British Empire as the outcome of the war'. At home he looked forward to reforms aiming at all classes sharing 'in the national well-being'; but he was unspecific about how this was to be achieved.

Turning to the terms of peace, he was strongly opposed to the imposition of 'penal terms on Germany', which would be likely to drive her 'to make common cause with Bolshevism'. For this reason he opposed the incorporation of large minorities of Germans in other states. He accepted, however, the need for Poland to be given a 'corridor' to Danzig to provide her with an outlet to the sea. The Rhineland should not, in his view, be separated from Germany but might be demilitarised. The Saar should be under French control for about ten years until their own coal mines had been restored.

A cardinal point was that the British Empire and the U.S.A. should give a 'joint guarantee to come to the immediate assistance of France ... in the event of German aggression'. Germany was also 'to be given a fresh start by allowing her full access to raw materials etc.'; and the Allies should show 'willingness to help Germany to get on her legs again'.

After developing further his scheme for Reparations payments he concluded with a number of principles which should be incorporated in the treaty, such as the limitation of German armaments and the trial of the Kaiser and of 'all individuals responsible for inhuman breaches of the laws of war'. Finally he proposed that 'the League of Nations [should] be set up to deal with international quarrels, especially in their opening stages, and generally to keep small states in order'.

Hankey also outlined terms for a settlement with Turkey, which included the incorporation of Smyrna and Thrace in Greece; and he assumed that the U.S.A. would accept a mandate for Constantinople and parts of Asia Minor. Taking account of the circumstances prevailing at the time Hankey wrote this paper his proposals for Germany seem in the main both far-sighted and statesmanlike; but his ideas on the treatment of Turkey certainly contained the seeds of future strife – because they took no account of the centuries-old hatred of Turk for Greek. One wonders whether Hankey's strong Phil-Hellenism, remarked on earlier, did not warp his judgement in this matter.

The outcome of the talks in the sylvan peace at Fontainebleau was the paper entitled 'Some Considerations for the Peace Conference before they finally draft their terms', of which Philip Kerr was the chief author and which Lloyd George has reproduced almost in full.[1] Predictably it aroused the indignation and resentment of the French, because much of it ran counter to their ideas on security and reparations.

On the Monday following the return from Fontainebleau the Council of Ten met for the last time until the middle of April. The Council of Four (Wilson, Clemenceau, Lloyd George and Orlando) now became the supreme directing authority of the conference. It met twice a day, but – to Hankey's indignation – without a secretary at first. Though Paul Mantoux, the interpreter, was present and took notes of the discussions, which were published in 1955, Hankey knew nothing about this at the time – or indeed until he received copies of the volumes.[2] Henry Wilson recorded in his diary 'I think the Frocks have gone mad. They sit and talk all day; but as no secretary attends no records are kept, and Hankey is [driven?] crazy'.[3] Almost as an afterthought the Council of Five (Foreign Ministers) was set up on 27th, and that took a considerable load off the Big Four.[4] Possibly because of his discontent with the prevailing procedure, or possibly to ensure that such records as were possible were kept, Hankey restarted his diary at this time; but the entries are irregular, and to students interested in the proceedings of the Council of Four, Mantoux's 'Notes' are far more valuable.[5] On 30th, however, Hankey recorded 'I am being pressed to decide whether I will take the post of Secretary-General of the League of Nations. I am very doubtful about it'; and on that day he made his 'début at the Council of Four' – though not yet as its secretary.[6] The diary then lapses into silence until mid-April.

During these days of fundamental change in the procedure at the conference Tom Jones kept in constant touch with Hankey about the current discussions in London – whether they concerned Chamber-

[1] *Peace Treaties*, I, pp. 404–16.

[2] *Les Délibérations du Conseil des Quatre, 24 Mars–28 Juin 1919* (Centre National de la Recherche Scientifique, 1955). Henceforth cited as *Mantoux,* Notes. In his Preface Mantoux pays a warm tribute to Hankey as 'a high official of exceptional merit and experience'.

[3] C. E. Callwell, *Field-Marshal Sir Henry Wilson*, Vol. II, p. 177. Henceforth cited as Callwell, *Wilson.*

[4] The Council of Five held 28 meetings between 27th March and 25th June 1919.

[5] Most of the diary entries for 26th and 30th March 1919 are in *Supreme Control*, pp. 112–13.

[6] *Supreme Control*, pp. 112–13.

lain's proposals for import duties, Churchill's and Curzon's prophecy of 'vast and immediate disaster' if the Roumanian armies were not at once equipped to fight the Bolsheviks, or the growing danger of a coal strike. In a series of letters written in the middle of March Jones described how public sympathy towards the miners and against the coal owners was increasing. On 17th and 18th he wrote urgently that 'We *must* avert a strike', and that Lloyd George should return before publication of the report of the Coal Commission,[1] because the miners' leaders had declared that if national ownership of the mines was not conceded a strike was certain.[2] Hankey passed all these letters at once to Lloyd George, and one feels that both of them were extremely fortunate in having so skilled and patient a negotiator on the spot to handle these tricky problems at such a time of crisis. Furthermore Jones's letters and diary show him in a most favourable light in the matter of loyalty to his 'Chief' while acting as his *locum tenens*.[3]

Despite his increasing doubts about accepting the post of Secretary-General of the League, Hankey found time to draw up a 'Sketch Plan' of its organisation, and sent it to Smuts on the last day of March. It was, expectedly, based on his experience of the organisation and working of the C.I.D., the Imperial War Cabinet and the Inter-Allied conferences in which he had played so large a part. Its general tone was cautiously optimistic, and it contained some idealistic suggestions, such as the creation of a special League university to provide 'a nursery for the creation of a civil service, not only for the League of Nations but, if it is not too much to hope, for the diplomatic and Foreign Office services of the world'. He then went on to suggest in some detail the general organisation (Permanent Naval and Military Commission, Court of International Justice, Mandatory Commission, Permanent Bureau of Labour etc.), the duties of the Secretary-General and his assistants, and the organisation of the Finance, Treaties and Establishment Departments. The Registry and Indexing Departments were to follow the system which he had so successfully built up and applied in Whitehall

[1]The Interim and Second Stage Reports, dated 20th March and 20th June 1919, of the Commission set up under Mr. Justice Sankey (1886–1948, 1st Viscount Sankey 1932) to frame recommendations on the future of the coal industry. The nationalisation of coal royalties was recommended, and accepted by the government. Hours of work were to be reduced and wages increased. See Cmd. 359.

[2]Jones to Hankey 14th, 17th and 18th March 1919. Lloyd George papers F/23/4/34 and 36.

[3]*Middlemas,* I, pp. 83–5.

Gardens; nor did he forget the need for a properly staffed Reference Library.[1] Though Hankey was to play no part in it, the reader will remark that a great many of his administrative proposals were in fact adopted at Geneva. As he also sent a copy to Lord Robert Cecil, one of the leading advocates of the League, it seems reasonable to claim that it was Hankey who first began to put flesh on the bare bones of the draft Charter. In May 1920 Hankey reverted to his 'Sketch Plan' for the League in a letter to Lloyd George, pointing out that the Supreme War Council was still a far more influential body than the League Council and suggesting that the two should gradually be merged into a single organisation.[2]

On 1st April 1919, Hankey's 41st birthday, he sent Smuts instructions from the Council of Four regarding a mission to Hungary which the General had agreed to undertake in an effort to resolve the acute crisis which had arisen in the neutral zone in Transylvania between Hungarian and Roumanian troops as a consequence of Bela Kun's seizure of power.[3] From Buda-Pest Smuts was to go on to Prague to discuss Dr. Beneš's proposal for a corridor linking Czecho-Slovakia with Jugo-Slavia – which Lloyd George has described as 'audacious and indefensible'.[4] These problems were inextricably linked with the fate of the minority populations in central Europe, and with the territorial claims of the succession states to the defunct Austro-Hungarian empire. With the official instructions to Smuts Hankey enclosed private letters in which he described the chief characters the General would encounter, and the history of the armistice and other agreements affecting the situation. He also gave Smuts introductions designed to smooth what was bound to prove a very difficult task.[5]

That same day, 1st April, Lloyd George and Josephus Daniels the American Secretary of the Navy met over breakfast to try and resolve the impasse which had arisen between the Admiralty and the U.S. Navy Department over the American claim to 'a navy second to none', and over British objections to President Wilson's insistence on

[1]Hankey to Smuts 31st March 1919. Hankey's final 'Sketch Plan' for the League became F.O. 608/242 of 6th May 1919. Copy also in Cab. 63/25.

[2]Hankey to Lloyd George 12th May 1920. Cab. 63/27.

[3]Hankey to Smuts 1st April 1919. The instructions were slightly amended next day. Smuts Archive, folios 80 and 81. See also W. K. Hancock, *Smuts*, I, pp. 515–18. Smuts did not in the event go on from Buda-Pest to Prague.

[4]*Peace Treaties*, II, p. 940.

[5]Hankey to Smuts, 1st and 2nd April 1919. Smuts Archive, folios 81 and 82.

'Freedom of the Seas' (the second of his famous Fourteen points) being incorporated in the League Charter. Lloyd George strongly supported the Admiralty view, and by threatening to withhold British support for the League he secured the exclusion of Freedom of the Seas from the Charter – to the great satisfaction of Hankey, who had always been strongly antagonistic towards that concept.[1] So ended 'the Naval Battle of Paris'.[2]

Up to the beginning of April the Council of Four had held 17 meetings of which no records had been kept – except of course Mantoux's 'Notes', of whose existence Hankey was unaware. He communicated his anxiety about the consequences of this unbusinesslike procedure to Henry Wilson, who recorded it in his diary.[3] On 5th April however, President Wilson fell ill – possibly suffering a slight stroke which was to prove the harbinger of his complete physical breakdown in the following September. At any rate this produced 'a lapse from the usual exclusiveness' by the admission of secretaries to the arcanum – though at first without any official status.[4] During the succeeding days Hankey again attended the Council's meetings, but when on the afternoon of 8th President Wilson returned he was once more excluded.[5]

That same day Foch's committee was invited to frame proposals regarding the action to be taken if Germany refused to sign the treaty. At about the same time Esher sent Hankey a long letter describing the trend of public opinion at home with regard to the imposition of a harsh treaty, as desired by the French, or a moderate one such as had emerged from the Fontainebleau discussions. He was anxious about the gulf between those who really governed France and the British and American delegations, and feared that if Lloyd George's policy prevailed 'he will have aroused in France and in this country a mass of antagonism that will bear evil fruit in the future'. Esher's claim to know and understand the French far better than most British politicians

[1]See *Supreme Command*, II, pp. 857–63.

[2]For a full account of this clash see Roskill, *Naval Policy*, I, pp. 53–4 and 80–3; also H. and M. Sprout *Toward a New Order of Sea Power* (Princeton U.P., 1946) pp. 62–72.

[3]Callwell, *Wilson*, II, p. 180.

[4]The British record of 21st meeting of Council of Four on 5th April shows Hankey present as a British *delegate* (Cab. 27/37/1. I.C.21). *Mantoux,* Notes, I, pp. 151 and 159 makes no mention of his presence.

[5]*Supreme Control,* p. 116. Hankey was present at the meeting at Lloyd George's residence on the morning of 8th April. I.C.170L. Cab. 29/37/1.

was well founded; and his pessimistic forecast about Anglo-French relations was to prove all too true. But, as he also remarked, the British people were 'thoroughly tired of the war', were determined not 'to embark again on extensive military operations . . . in Russia', and were showing increasing impatience over the slow progress made with the peace treaty.[1]

Hankey has written that between 10th and 19th April he paid his first visit to England since the beginning of the conference;[2] but although Adeline evidently returned home on or about 10th her husband was still in Paris for at least two more days – since he wrote to her regularly until 12th.

*To Lady Hankey 10th April 1919*

Paris is mourning your departure by a very *triste* demeanour . . . The P.M. still says he is coming home on Tuesday [15th] and that he will insist on the Big Four working all day Sunday [13th] in order to enable him to do so. But of course he is very changeable . . . The P.M. talks of getting the Germans here the week after next! I don't believe, myself, that this is practical politics, but I don't see why they should delay much longer. Unfortunately at the most critical point of the conference Malkin,[3] Hurst's understudy as our principal draughtsman has broken down . . .

*To the same 11th April 1919*

. . . Yesterday afternoon I was 'in' at the Council of Four, which meant that, until a late hour, I was dictating minutes . . . I really believe that I may be able to come over next week. The P.M. . . . is working on the speech he means to make, for which I have collected a good deal of material . . . The Big Four have reached some more conclusions, but I horrified them yesterday by pointing out that their conclusion on Breaches of Laws of War would involve rather difficult legislation in our country and America at any rate. It rather amused me to pose as a lawyer, but as it was a question of military and naval law I was all right . . .

*To the same 12th April 1919*

Yesterday was another of my terrific days, as I had a 4 hour conference in the morning, beginning at breakfast! The trouble [was] Hughes, who refuses to agree to the Prime Minister's 'reparations' scheme. He obviously means to reap all the benefit he can from it, and then to damn it in public. I spent an hour or two after the meeting trying for an accommodation, but could

[1] Esher to Hankey 7th April 1919. *Journals*, IV, pp. 228–30.

[2] *Supreme Control*, p. 116.

[3] Later Sir H. William Malkin (1883–1945). Assistant Legal Adviser to Foreign Office 1914–25 and Second Legal Adviser 1925–29.

get nothing from Hughes that Ll. G. would take. I only had a snatch of lunch ... after which I was dictating until the Plenary Conference at 3 p.m.[1] The latter was dull, and I was able to work off all my papers. Then dictating until 8.45 p.m. Rather slavery!

Last night Col. Kisch[2] introduced me to his wife, who is Swiss. Both of them say that the place selected by the Swiss Govt. for the League of Nations is a most gorgeous site, with some lovely houses already there which will be available ...

But, despite the allurements of Geneva, the decisive moment for Hankey had in fact almost arrived.

Lloyd George's anxiety to return home arose from the urgent need for him to reply to the growing volume of criticism of his government, which Bonar Law had altogether failed to allay. A telegram of protest for which an M.P. named Kennedy Jones[3] collected 233 signatures decided him to face the music in person, and on 14th he and Hankey crossed the Channel to London.[4] As always when a crisis arose Lloyd George showed his mastery of the House, and Hankey recorded that in face of his lucid explanation of the government's policy and purposes with regard to the peace treaty 'the Opposition collapsed utterly'.

Meanwhile on the day Lloyd George left Paris Wilson had a 'very tempestuous' confrontation with Orlando about Italian claims[5]; and it was that issue which was to produce what Hankey has called 'the most acute, distressing and prolonged crisis' of the conference. As, however, the reader of our first volume will already be fully familiar with the broad outline of Italian claims to Fiume and the Dalmatian coast, as agreed in the Secret Treaty of London of 1915, and with the allocation to Italy of a vast sphere of interest in Asia Minor under the Sykes–Picot agreement of May 1916, they will not be repeated here.[6]

[1]*Foreign Relations, U.S.A.,* III, pp. 240–84. This was the 4th Plenary Session of the Preliminary Peace Conference.

[2]Later Brigadier-General F. H. Kisch (1888–1943). Member of team of British Military Experts at Paris Conference 1919. Chairman, Palestine Zionist Executive 1922–31.

[3]1865–1921. Journalist and politician (Ind.). Editor, *Evening News* 1894–1900. Chairman Select Committee on Transport 1919 and Advisory Committee, Ministry of Transport 1920.

[4]*Peace Treaties,* I, pp. 560–77.

[5]There are no 'Notes' on this conversation in *Mantoux*. The sole record of it is in Aldrovandi's diary. See *Supreme Control*, p. 119.

[6]See Vol. I, pp. 270 and 446, *notes*.

On 15th April, while Lloyd George and Hankey were in London, the Greeks, aided and abetted by the Italians, landed at Smyrna; and so began the prolonged and lamentable Allied intervention in Asia Minor, which was to bring Britain to the brink of the war with resurgent, nationalist Turkey and contributed greatly to the fall of Lloyd George.

Hankey returned to Paris on 17th, and quickly sensed that 'his status was in some way altered'.[1] The reason soon became apparent. Next day, Good Friday, he took the decision which was to shape his whole future career.

*Hankey to Lord Robert Cecil. 18th April 1919*
*Strictly Personal and Confidential*
Dear Lord Robert,

It is only this afternoon that I have had the full talk with the Prime Minister on the subject of the Secretary-Generalship of the League of Nations, which I always insisted was an indispensable condition to a decision as to whether I would formally offer myself as a candidate for the post.

The result of the conversation, following on a most earnest and anxious consideration of the question in all its bearings (including as you know the elaboration of a partial scheme of organisation of the Secretariat) has brought me to the decision that my duty is to remain in the post I now occupy.

In these circumstances I must ask that my name will not be put forward officially as a candidate.

I very much regret this decision because I realise the delay in reaching it may cause you great inconvenience. Yet, on so important a subject I would not give an affirmative decision until I had all the necessary data before me. These included, on the one hand, some general idea as to what my position would be, under peace conditions, if I remained where I am and, on the other hand, a clear perception of the duties and responsibilities which would fall to the Secretary-General of the League of Nations, and of the conditions under which he would work. These latter could not be ascertained until the Covenant had been revised; until the seat of the League was fixed; and until the Treaties of Peace had reached an advanced stage of development. Most of these factors were indeterminate until within the last few days, while some are still unsettled, including perhaps what, rightly or wrongly, I always regarded as an essential condition, namely the certainty of the acceptance of the Covenant by the United States of America.

The development of all these questions has, on the whole, been steadily in a direction contrary to my conception.

[1] *Supreme Control,* p.105.

I wish to thank you personally for considering me as a possible candidate, and for your forbearance in the uncertainty in which I have kept you.

I need hardly say, in conclusion, that, if I can render any assistance to you in finding a British candidate, I will do my utmost, and that, if he should be selected, he will have not only my interest and sympathy, but all the practical assistance that I can give him.

Sylvester sent Adeline a copy of the above letter, and on the same day her husband wrote to her that, on the way back to Paris, he had a long talk with the P.M. about the League of Nations, and 'he agrees in my chucking it'.[1] To his diary he confided what he had not told Cecil – namely that his visit to London had convinced him 'that the British Empire is worth a thousand Leagues of Nations. They are a sane, sound nation over there – the sheet anchor of the world. I can do more for the peace of the world there than in Geneva'. But a note of melancholy in the letter – a rare event with Hankey – suggests that the decision was more of a renunciation than he admitted even to his wife. Moreover he was at the time oppressed by the difficulties which he knew lay ahead in Paris, where the Italians were expected 'to present an ultimatum about Fiume'.[2] However he forced himself to face the troubles, and when called into the Council of Four on 19th he told them bluntly that their sitting without secretaries caused 'an infinity of chaos and confusion', and only a week remained to get the treaty ready for presentation to the Germans.

Hankey's 'ultimatum' brought greater profit than the one the Italians intended to present, and next day he actually 'functioned as Secretary at a meeting of the [Council of] Four'.[3] Sure enough there was 'a terrible scene with the Italians about their claims.'[4] The discussion continued on Easter Sunday (20th), when, according to the English record, Wilson said that it was 'incredible to him that the representatives of Italy should take up this position', and castigated their 'imperialistic ambitions'.[5]

Hankey's diary entry for 20th April reflects his anger and despair. 'The Italians', he wrote, 'now agree to give up Fiume if they get Dalmatia, but Wilson has stuck his toes in and refuses to agree . . .

[1]To Lady Hankey 18th April 1919. [2]Diary 18th April 1919.
[3]*ibid.* 19th April 1919. *Supreme Control*, pp. 106 and 116.
[4]Diary 19th April 1919. In *Supreme Control*, p. 105 Hankey omitted this terse and accurate description. See *Mantoux,* Notes, I, pp. 277–99.
[5]Cab. 29/37/1, No. 40.

Hankey (left) with Vice-Admiral E. F. B. Charlton, President Naval Inter-Allied Control Commission. Probably at the Paris Peace Conference 1919

Lloyd George and family with French officers on a visit to the battlefields 1919. Mrs Carey Evans (Olwen Lloyd George) on extreme right, Hankey next to her. Foch on left of Lloyd George, Weygand behind his right shoulder. Megan Lloyd George the centre of the three ladies on left. Sir William Sutherland behind her

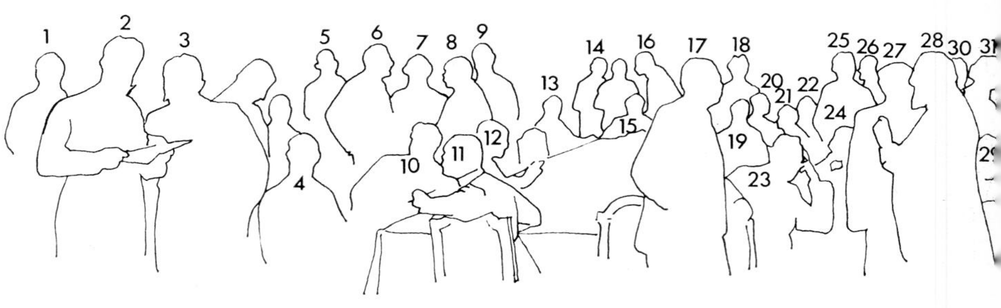


1. M. Dutasta (General Secretary).
2. M. Ph. Berthelot (France).
3. M. Pichon (France).
4. Col. E. M. House (United States).
5. Lieut.-Col. Hankey (Great Britain).
6. President Wilson (United States).
7. Mr. Lloyd George (Great Britain).
8. M. Clemenceau, President (France).
9. Mr. A. J. Balfour (Great Britain).
10. Mr. H. White (United States).
11. General Bliss (United States).
12. Mr. R. Lansing (United States).
13. Lord Milner (Great Britain).
14. Mr. A. Bonar Law (Great Britain).
15. Mr. G. N. Barnes (Great Britain).
16. Lord Robert Cecil (Great Britain).
17. M. A. Tardieu (France).
18. Sir Robert Borden (Canada).
19. Prince Charoon (Siam).
20. Sir J. Ward (New Zealand).
21. M. Phya Bibadh Kosha (Siam).
22. Mr. W. M. Hughes (Australia).
23. M. L. L. Klotz (France).
24. M. Beněs (Czecho-Slovak Republic).
25. M. Bratiano (Roumania).
26. General Botha (South Africa).
27. M. Cambon (France).
28. M. Bourgeois (France).
29. M. Vesnič (Serbia).
30. M. Dmowski (Poland).
31. M. Paderewski (Poland).
32. Lieut.-Gen. Smuts (South Africa).
33. Mr. W. F. Massey (New Zealand).
34. M. Burgos (Panama).

The Paris Peace Conference 1919

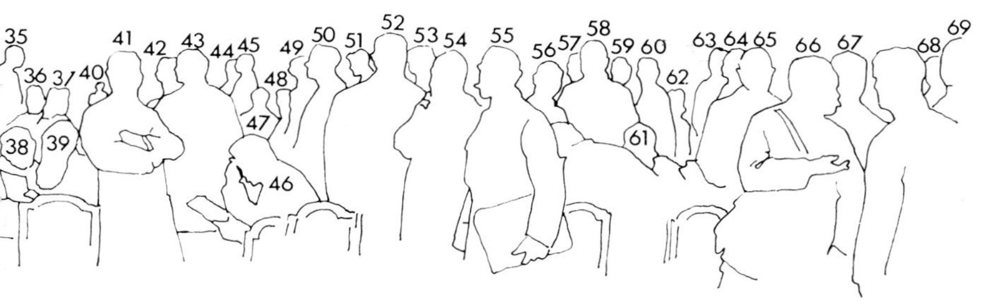


35. The Maharajah of Bikanir (India).
36. Lord Sinha (India).
37. The Emir Faisul (Hedjaz).
38. M. Trumbič (Serbia).
39. M. Pasic (Serbia).
40. M. Haidar (Hedjaz).
41. Signor Orlando (Italy).
42. Dr. Monitz (Portugal).
43. Dr. Villela (Portugal).
44. M. Matsui (Japan).
45. Baron Makino (Japan).
46. Baron Sonnino (Italy).
47. Marquis Saionji (Japan).
48. M. Dorn y de Alsua (Ecuador).
49. Mr. C. D. B. King (Liberia).
50. M. Calderon (Peru).
51. M. Mantoux (Interpreter).
52. Marquis Salvago Raggi (Italy).
53. M. Guilbaud (Haiti).
54. M. Barzilaï (Italy).
55. Marshal Foch (France).
56. M. Politis (Greece).
57. M. Blanco (Uruguay).
58. M. Venizelos (Greece).
59. M. Lou Tseng Tsiang (China).
60. M. Sao Ke Alfred Sze (China).
61. M. de Bustamante (Cuba).
62. M. Montes (Bolivia).
63. M. Mendes (Guatemala).
64. M. O. de Magalhaes (Brazil).
65. M. Vandervelde (Belgium).
66. General Weygand (France).
67. M. Hymans (Belgium).
68. President E. Pessoa (Brazil).
69. M. van den Heuvel (Belgium).

Lord Curzon's doodles at the San Remo Conference 1920

Lord Curzon and Hankey disembarking at Marseille on their way to the San Remo Conference 1920

Meanwhile the Germans are due next Friday, the Peace Treaty [is] not half ready and we have wasted two whole days over a question quite unrelated with the German Peace [Treaty]. God help us!'

To the foregoing he added, probably later in the day, a graphic account of the effects of Lloyd George's final effort to prevent a breakdown.

*Diary 20th April 1919.* Addendum

Lloyd George had made an eloquent appeal to Orlando on the subject of Fiume. In words I could not attempt to emulate he had recalled all that he and Orlando had been through together. Scarcely had Orlando taken office when there had come the frightful catastrophe of Caporetto. At the Rapallo conference to discuss the situation Orlando had declared that Italy would never yield. Inch by inch her armies would if necessary retire to the toe of Italy – nay into Sicily itself. No sacrifice was too great for the sacred cause of the Allies. Could not Italy make one more sacrifice for peace, the Prime Minister asked? As he continued in this strain Orlando, who could more or less follow the English, was more and more moved. First he sniffed; then he wiped his eyes; then he broke down and went into the window sobbing aloud. Lloyd George sat in embarrassed silence at the surprising effect of his eloquence. Clemenceau stared with a stony and cynical look on his hard old face. President Wilson got up and shook Orlando by the hand in sympathy. Aldrovandi, Mantoux and I exchanged embarrassed glances. After the meeting Orlando spoke to me of his '*peu d'émotion*' as though it were an ordinary incident. Outside, the incident did not altogether escape notice. Newnham, Lloyd George's valet, from the flat at Rue Nitot, the other side of the street, happened to glance across at the window of President Wilson's room, where we were sitting. There he spied Orlando in tears. Calling to Lord Riddell, who happened to be in the flat, he cried 'Why, if that isn't M. Orlando in the window crying! What have they been doing to the poor old gentleman?' It only remains to record the remarks of Mr. Balfour, to whom I related the incident later. 'I have heard of nations winning their way to Empire', he said, 'by bribery, cajolery, by threats and by war, but this is the first attempt I have heard of by any statesman to sob his way to Empire!'

On Easter Monday (21st) the signatories of the Treaty of London of April 1915 met to try and find a compromise, after which the scene moved to President Wilson's flat to report progress – or rather lack of progress. From there Hankey was sent round to ask Orlando and Sonnino 'if they thought it worth while to come and discuss on the basis of their getting the islands off the Dalmatian coast but not Fiume'

– which was Lloyd George's proposal.[1] He rejoined the Big Three while they were still in session, and could only report that the Italians had 'declined'.[2]

The meeting on the afternoon of 21st had another, and less expected result for Hankey, since it produced what he later called the 'Yap imbroglio' with the Americans. The island of Yap was one of the formerly German Caroline Islands, which had been promised to the Japanese. It enjoyed a special importance because the trans-Pacific submarine telegraph cables passed through it. The British record states that President Wilson 'reminded the Japanese Delegates that it had been understood that Japan was to have a mandate for the islands in the North Pacific, *although he had made reserve in the case of the island of Yap, which he himself considered should be international*' (italics supplied).[3] In April 1921 Auckland Geddes, the ambassador in Washington, telegraphed home that the U.S. State Department had alleged that the allocation of Yap to the Japanese had been through 'a trick' by Hankey. On learning this Hankey's reaction was 'intense indignation and affront', and he at once searched out the relevant records.[4] The result was that he was able to show that, although Wilson had made 'a reserve' about Yap on 21st April, he had not repeated it when the Council of Four recorded its final conclusion on 6th May. The minutes of that meeting stated that with regard to 'German Islands north of the Equator, the Mandate shall be held by Japan'. Hankey at once sent Wilson and Dutasta, the Secretary-General of the Paris Conference, copies of the agreement, and followed them up with the full notes of the meeting. He pointed out that he still held Wilson's receipt for the documents in question, that no corrections had ever been requested, and that the text was published on 9th May. Thus Wilson's statement of 3rd March 1921 that 'I did not agree on 7th May 1919, *or at any other time* (italics supplied) that the island of Yap should be included in the assignment of mandates to Japan' was quite untrue. One has to remember, however, that by March 1921 Wilson was a very sick man; but the 'imbroglio' provides an interesting example of the essential need to keep and circulate precise records of high-level discussions, on

[1]Diary 21st April 1919. *Mantoux*, Notes, I, pp. 300–17.
[2]*Supreme Control*, pp. 126–8.
[3]No. 42, Item 2. Cab. 29/37/1. See also *Foreign Relations, U.S.A.*, V, p. 109.
[4]Cab. 63/31. Hankey to Curzon 15th April 1921 gives the whole story of the 'Yap imbroglio' – written of course from Hankey's point of view.

which Hankey was always so insistent; and also how the possession of such records enabled the British government to refute on at least one occasion a very unpleasant insinuation made against themselves and their servant.[1]

To return from the Yap imbroglio of 1921 to the Paris crisis of 1919, on 22nd April Lloyd George made yet another effort to heal the breach with the Italians; but it was of no avail, as they merely put up what Hankey called 'totally unacceptable' counter-proposals.[2] Two days later Orlando and most of the Italian delegation left Paris. Hankey bade a sincerely regretful farewell to Aldrovandi, his Italian opposite number, with whom he had long enjoyed a warm friendship, which was obviously reciprocated.

*To Lady Hankey. British Delegation, Paris 25th April 1919*

... It has been a shocking week ... The pressure on a secretary, working single-handed, of 2 meetings a day is simply incredible. Of course things have been very strained with the Italians, which has made the work harder. They have now gone home to consult the Italian Parliament. Personally I think they are bluffing and will come back, but they will always be very sore against the U.S.A., and this will be a terrific stab at the League of Nations. I rather expect a Japanese crisis this afternoon, and I shouldn't be a bit surprised if they left the conference too. President Wilson, with his wretched, hypocritical Fourteen Points, has already alienated the Italians, and is now about to alienate the Japs. I don't mind his alienating them from the League of Nations, but I do mind his driving a wedge between them and us ...

In fact the meetings with the Japanese did not produce the dire results forecast by Hankey – because their claims were not seriously disputed. In retrospect it seems odd that Wilson should have fought so hard against Italian territorial ambitions yet have agreed to Japan gaining control (through a League mandate) of islands which assured them of domination over the western Pacific, as well as conceding their claims to a special status in the indisputably Chinese province of Shantung. Harold Nicolson's view was that the Japanese 'timed their stand upon the Shantung settlement with exquisite cunning'. With the Italians already gone Wilson could not afford a further defection; and, finding himself 'in a minority of one he surrendered'.[3] This viola-

[1]Hankey to Curzon 15th January 1921. Lloyd George papers F/25/1/25.
[2]*Supreme Control*, pp. 128–9. [3]*Peacemaking 1919*, p. 146.

tion of his own oft-repeated principles gave Japan virtually all she claimed; and the price ultimately exacted from the U.S.A. was not light.

At the end of that 'shocking week' Hankey brought the Council of Three back to realities by 'bluntly but quietly' telling Lloyd George and Wilson that, with the arrival of the German delegates only five days off, no decision had yet been reached about the 'official language of the treaty'. The withdrawal of the Italians probably made it easier to get it accepted that English and French should be the official languages; and Hankey quickly followed up that decision by getting a number of other outstanding points settled. 'This is the first week that I have really gripped the conference', he told his wife – with justifiable self-satisfaction; for at last he could record that 'the bulk of the Treaty is now settled'.[1] Furthermore on 28th April the conference approved the revised League Covenant – with all mention of Freedom of the Seas excluded.

Despite the success of Hankey's efforts to force the pace he still had to cope with a large number of changes in the draft treaty proposed by various commissions; and all the time the pressure was rising, because the German delegates were expected to arrive on 1st May. The Council of Three continued to meet at least once a day to discuss various abstruse issues such as the future of the Kiel Canal and of the former German port of Kiaochow in China. And only a strong protest from Hankey frustrated Lloyd George's idea of inviting the Austro-Hungarian delegates also to come to Paris at the beginning of May to receive their treaty.

The confused nature of the discussions in the Council of Three is nicely illustrated by a parody of the minutes of one of its meetings which has survived in Hankey's papers. It is inscribed in a hand which is unmistakably that of John Maynard Keynes[2] (who was present) 'Sir Maurice Hankey. This report of the meeting of April 29th is, as distinct from yours, *really* confidential. J.M.K.'; and Hankey endorsed it 'The above is an absolutely correct record of what took place'. One must surely assume that the whole paper is the work of Keynes. It is worth reproducing in full.

[1]Diary 26th April 1919.
[2]See Vol. I, p. 445, *note*.

## COUNCIL OF THREE[1]

### 29th April 1919

(*What actually happened*)

The question before the Council was whether Belgium should have priority in Indemnity payments and should receive from Germany the 'costs of the war'.

Three Belgian Delegates addressed the Council, each in a set speech.

M. Hymans[2] read a number of letters to which nobody paid attention. M. Clemenceau slept. President Wilson read the paper. Mr. Lloyd George kept up a running fire of comments, to the effect that M. Hymans was in his best form, was a poseur of the old type, and was attempting blackmail.

M. Van den Heuvel[3] delivered his oration in a falsetto voice which attracted the attention of the British Prime Minister, who compared it to a number of other voices, human and animal, that he remembered to have heard – the comparison being in each case to the disadvantage of M. Van den Heuvel. Mr. Lloyd George remarked that M. Van den Heuvel was obviously enjoying himself immensely. M. Clemenceau slept. President Wilson read the paper.

M. Vandervelde very nearly lost the chance of speaking at all as M. Clemenceau at this stage of the proceedings woke up and was inclined to interrupt. M. Vandervelde insisted however on delivering the speech which he had prepared. M. Clemenceau went to sleep again. President Wilson read the paper. Mr. Lloyd George remarked that this fellow was really very good: but that he talked a good deal more about Belgium's right than about Belgium's fight. The Belgians, in point of fact, never fought at all. They refused to fight. And now they were trying to bully. Mr. Lloyd George would not endure being bullied. How many dead had Belgium in comparison with Australia?

The Belgian Delegates having delivered their speeches, M. Clemenceau was woken up. President Wilson put down the paper, and remembering the Fourteen Points reminded the assembly that his conscience could not allow Belgium to claim the costs of the war.

The Belgian Delegates thereupon left the room with the subordinate representatives of the Allies, to see if there was really anything doing in the way of business.

The interval was fortunately filled up by the arrival of a telegram giving the text of Signor Orlando's speech in Rome. This speech was translated to the Council. President Wilson made two comments, one on a passage refer-

[1]cf. *Foreign Relations, U.S.A.,* V, pp. 344–51 and *Mantoux,* Notes, I, pp. 409–20.

[2]See Vol. I, p. 626, *note.*

[3]Van den Heuvel and Vandervelde were the other Belgian representatives at this meeting.

ring to the efforts made by Orlando to arrive at an arrangement with President Wilson. The President's comment was 'You bet he did'. His second remark, referring to one of the more rhetorical passages in Signor Orlando's speech, was brief and to the point. (Textually 'Rats'.)

At this stage the Belgian Delegates returned, but were unable to obtain a hearing on account of the exclusive attention devoted to the news from Rome. They consequently withdrew, and repudiated all the agreements which had been informally reached in discussion in the interval.

Signor Orlando's speech having been translated, M. Clemenceau enquired whether the Belgians had run away. He said he would kill M. Hymans for his bad manners and his bad diplomacy, and exhorted everybody else to do the same.

M. Hymans returned and made a further speech to the effect that Belgium adhered to her demands. M. Clemenceau muttered 'kill him'. Mr. Lloyd George winked to himself. President Wilson read the paper.

The meeting now broke up into two parts; one part, including the Belgians and the subordinate representatives of the Allies, attempted to come to terms. The other part, including the Council of Three, listened to the anecdotes which Mr. Lloyd George had to relate about the behaviour of Belgian troops at Nieuport in 1917.

It was then discovered that the French Delegates were attempting to fix up with the Belgians an arrangement that would be considerably to the advantage of the French. Mr. Lloyd George was warned and immediately protested. This woke up everybody. There was a general mêlée in the middle of the room, where explanations and protests, avowals and disavowals, were tossed about in noisy confusion. Nothing of what was said could be clearly distinguished above the storm except the cries of M. Clemenceau who wailed continuously 'Kill them, kill them'. Suddenly Mr. Lloyd George emerged from the tumult and flounced out of the room in a passion, winking to himself.

The upshot of it all was that M. Klotz[1] realised that he had been detected, and, with instinctive and hereditary compliancy, hoped Mr. Lloyd George was not really very angry. President Wilson once more took up the paper. M. Clemenceau composed himself to sleep.

*It was agreed* that Belgium should be released from the debt which she would in any event never have paid to the Allies; and that the Allies should require Germany to pay that debt. But nobody ever supposed for a moment that any addition had been made or had ever been contemplated to the total German Indemnity, and it was understood among the interested parties that whatever advantage Belgium derived from this arrangement (if any)

[1] A French representative at this meeting.

should be deducted subsequently by reducing the percentage of her reparation allotment. The Belgians were apparently satisfied.

On 3rd May the first feelers from the Italians about returning to the conference reached Hankey. Obviously they were determined not to be excluded from the final scenes; and to that extent Hankey's view that their withdrawal was a bluff proved correct. They actually arrived back in Paris on 7th, the day when the first Plenary Session of the Peace Conference (as opposed to the preliminary conference) took place in the Trianon Palace at Versailles, and the peace terms were presented to the German delegates.[1] At the eleventh hour, when the Council of Four met to consider the guarantee of assistance to France by the United States and Britain in the event of a new German aggression, Hankey expressed his 'uneasiness' over the fact that all President Wilson promised was to seek the 'advice and consent' of the U.S. Senate to such a treaty.[2] His misgivings were reinforced when at a Plenary Session of the Preliminary Conference convened on the same day, 6th May, to review the draft treaty Foch made what Hankey called 'a devastating and . . . prophetic criticism' of the settlement of the western frontiers of Germany.[3] Hankey seems to have been the only person, apart from Foch, who appreciated that France was being asked to base her future security on the flimsiest of promissory notes.

On 5th, while driving in his car with Hankey, Lloyd George asked him if he would like to have a peerage. He told Adeline that he had 'replied straight away' that he 'could not afford to saddle Robin with it', but that 'if Life Peerages were introduced he would accept one'. Lloyd George replied that 'there ought to be such things'; but many years were to elapse before they were introduced. Hankey told Lloyd George that he 'would like an O.M. [Order of Merit] but realised they were usually given to old buffers'. Lloyd George, however, 'seemed rather to like the notion'.[4] In his next letter Hankey told his wife that Sir Eric Drummond was to receive a salary of £4,000 a year and £6,000 a year entertainment allowance as Secretary-General of the League of

[1] *Foreign Relations, U.S.A.*, V, pp. 413–20. On the reception of the Italians see *Supreme Control*, p. 148.

[2] Council of Four meeting of 6th May 1919. *Foreign Relations, U.S.A.*, V, pp. 491–5.

[3] *Supreme Control*, pp. 146–7. *Foreign Relations, U.S.A.*, III, pp. 384–8.

[4] To Lady Hankey 5th May 1919. Hankey's diary for the same day contains an almost identical account of this conversation.

Nations. 'Do you realise,' he remarked, 'that I have refused £10,000 a year and a peerage in the last month? Looked at that way it seems serious, but honestly I cannot bring myself to regret it. The P.M. and everyone else says I was right to refuse the League of Nations. The more we look at the famous Covenant the less we like it! It is not a workable machine. The real League of Nations will be the present Council of Three (or Four) and I shall always be its secretary. Make no mistake about that!' In fact Hankey received no honour or pecuniary reward for all his labours at Paris and Versailles.

The treaty was presented to the German delegates at the Trianon Palace at 4.0 p.m. on 7th May, and they were given 15 days in which to reply.[1] Hankey, like Lloyd George, gained the worst possible impression of Count Brockdorff-Rantzau,[2] the chief German delegate, whom he described as 'a sinister looking rascal and a typical Junker'.[3] But it is at least possible that the German's apparent rudeness and arrogance stemmed from sheer nervousness.[4] One of those present, Lord Riddell, for whom Hankey arranged a special seat, paid him a very warm tribute for his work at this exacting time. 'The truth is', wrote Riddell, 'that Hankey is one of the best-tempered, most agreeable, kindest men I have ever met – a real Christian in every sense of the word – as well as one of the most efficient'.[5]

The conclusion of the first stage of the protracted process of treaty making brought no easing of the strain on Hankey. As always his mind was ranging far beyond the narrow horizon of his immediate duties; and on the very evening that the Germans received the treaty he wrote to Lloyd George to protest against the Greek occupation of

[1]Much confusion has been caused by Lloyd George (*Peace Treaties*, I, p. 674), Sir Harold Nicolson (*Peacemaking 1919*, p. 328) and Lord Riddell (*Intimate Diary*, p. 70) all stating that the presentation of the treaty took place at the *Trianon Palace Hotel* at Versailles. This was undoubtedly incorrect, but the Council of Four did meet briefly at that hotel immediately after the presentation of the treaty. Hankey forestalled the same mistake appearing in Sir James Butler's biography of Philip Kerr, Lord Lothian. Enclosure to Hankey to Butler undated but *c.* 22nd Sept. 1958.

[2]Ulrich von Brockdorff-Rantzau (1869–1928). German diplomat and politician. Foreign Minister 1918–19. Ambassador at Moscow 1922.

[3]Diary 7th May 1919. Lloyd George, *Peace Treaties*, I, pp. 675–7.

[4]Dr. Stern-Rubarth, a friend of Brockdorff-Rantzau and his biographer, later claimed that his attitude was 'intentional and deliberate' (see *Daily Telegraph*, 10th August 1938). However as that statement was made when the Nazis had made arrogance a prime virtue it is, at the very least, suspect.

[5]Riddell, *Intimate Diary*, p. 69.

Smyrna – from which he foresaw nothing but trouble. Lloyd George, however, viewed the situation in Asia Minor with such complacency that he merely passed Hankey's letter to Venizelos – the person least likely to heed such a warning; and Venizelos at once 'pocketed' the letter. It has never been seen since.[1] Nor did the Greek action arouse any hostile comment from President Wilson. What Hankey sarcastically described as his 'very elastic mind' allowed him completely to 'shut his eyes to the passage in the League of Nations Covenant which says that the wishes of the inhabitants should be a factor in mandates'.[2] Though Wilson regarded Greek ambitions in Asia Minor with some complacency his hostility to Italian territorial avarice remained unabated. On 11th, after Hankey had explained that the agreement made with the Italians at St. Jean-de-Maurienne in April 1917[3] was 'by no means clear', and Balfour had said that it had provided for Smyrna to be given to Italy, Wilson was so provoked that he described himself as 'on the point of explosion'.[4] Hankey too was evidently worried by the inconsistency between the Treaty of London of 1915 and the League Covenant. Towards the end of May he wrote to Lloyd George that the Italian attempt to occupy Dalmatia was entirely contrary to Article 20 of the Covenant, but was based on the London Treaty of 1915. He urged that Britain and France 'should take immediate steps to procure their release from obligations inconsistent with the terms of the Covenant'.[5] But he did not describe how that could be done, and Lloyd George was evidently not prepared to repudiate the ill-famed treaty. It was probably these entanglements that caused Balfour to remark bitterly at this time on 'These three all-powerful, all-ignorant men sitting there and carving up continents, with only a child to lead them'. Harold Nicolson thought at first that the 'child' might be himself, but finally told his wife 'Perhaps he meant Hankey . . . After all Hankey is younger by 35 years than A.J.B.' It seems likely that Nicolson's second thoughts correctly expressed what was in Balfour's mind.[6]

As soon as the German delegates had departed the conference turned to the preparation of the Austro-Hungarian treaty, as their

[1]*Supreme Control*, p. 163. [2]Diary 8th May 1919. [3]See Vol. I, pp. 177-8.
[4]*Mantoux*, Notes, II, p. 43. There is no record of this meeting in *Foreign Relations, U.S.A.*, but Mantoux's record is confirmed by Cab. 29/37 No. 91.
[5]Hankey to Lloyd George 27th May 1919. Lloyd George papers F/23/4/71.
[6]Letter to Victoria Sackville-West of 17th May 1919. Quoted *Peacemaking 1919*, pp. 341–2.

delegates were expected at St. Germain in the middle of the month. This task proved a good deal easier than the German treaty – from Hankey's point of view. For the deadlock with Italy remained unbroken; and trouble was also brewing between the British and French over the frontier between Syria and Palestine. And the Council of Four had to consider what military and naval measures should be put in hand in the event of the ex-enemy powers refusing to sign the treaties.[1]

With 'things moving rather fast', and the end of the conference likely to be reached in June, Hankey hoped to get Adeline over to Paris again; but domestic affairs, and especially the responsibility of getting Robin to Rugby School for his first term, made it impossible for her to come until nearly the end of May. Her husband was also still worried about his future, which he described as 'a disturbing factor'. He believed that there was 'no job the Government would refuse me if I asked for it' – such as the Washington or Paris embassy, or the governorship of Mesopotamia or of East Africa; but such posts generally marked the end of their holder's careers. He therefore believed that he was right to keep his hand 'on the helm at London, which is the real directing centre of world politics', where he would be 'in an absolutely unique position to give our policy just a push in one direction or another'. With all his 'accumulated knowledge and experience' he was sure he ought not 'to relinquish that position'.[2]

Much later, when in the House of Lords Hankey was criticising the methods and procedures of the large international conferences which followed on World War II, he commended the informality of the Council of Four, and recalled how they had sat at ease in armchairs, and when maps were needed they had got down on their knees to study them. His diary entry for 14th May, when the future of Asia Minor was being discussed, describes one such occasion very precisely. 'They all sat on the floor looking at maps', he wrote, 'which I dished out to them. They looked very funny, especially Clemenceau lying on his tummy'. But the next diary entry (21st May) shows that things by no means always went smoothly in the Council. British and French interests in Syria and Mosul and the Sykes–Picot agreement were being discussed and, recorded Hankey, 'Clemenceau and Lloyd George

[1]*Foreign Relations, U.S.A.*, V, pp. 532–6. Also in Cab. 29/37 Nos. 85 and 86 of 9th and 10th May 1919.

[2]To Lady Hankey 9th May 1919.

had a most frightful row . . . Both lost their tempers violently and made the most absurd accusations. Clemenceau tried hard to recover his temper at the end, and when they parted said "You are the very badest boy" '.[1] Evidently Hankey remembered 25 years later the friendly informality of some meetings but forgot those at which tempers became ruffled.

By the middle of May the pressure had noticeably eased, and Hankey was able to refresh himself by a visit with Balfour to Barbizon, and a two-day trip around the battlefields with Lloyd George. On 18th old Jacky Fisher turned up in Paris with 'his duchess',[2] and was 'in the most uproarious form' keeping 'all Paris roaring at the funny stories he tells'. Running true to form the Admiral was 'wangling for all he is worth to get sent to Washington as Ambassador'. With the President and Mrs. Wilson, Lloyd George and his daughter Megan, the Admiral and his Duchess, Hankey went to a Presbyterian church to hear a sermon by Dr. Black, an American preacher, who described Donald Hankey's *Student in Arms* and its author as 'that splendid English boy who wrote the greatest book on the war'.[3] Hankey was evidently much moved by the sermon, and asked Adeline to bring out a copy of Donald's book as Lloyd George had not read it.[4]

By the end of the month Adeline had arrived in Paris, and her husband's contentment over their reunion was enhanced by the 'great relief' he felt when the Council of Four managed to agree on the Austro-Italian frontier. But Fiume and Dalmatia continued to plague the conference right up to the signature of the German treaty – even after Orlando's government had been replaced by one under Nitti in June.

It was at this time that Hankey resolved the difficulties produced by the Supreme Control sometimes consisting of three, sometimes of four and occasionally of five members by treating each subject discussed as though it had been a separate meeting. This vastly simplified the distribution of the relevant minutes and papers; but it is simplest to follow the practice of the American editors of their record of the conference and to refer to all meetings as those of the Council of Four. At the same time Hankey dropped the word 'Supreme' from the title 'Supreme

[1] *Mantoux,* Notes, II, pp. 159–64 describes this fracas in suitably diplomatic language.
[2] Nina, Duchess of Hamilton, with whom Fisher had long enjoyed an intimate but possibly platonic friendship. See Richard Hough, *First Sea Lord* (Allen and Unwin, 1969).
[3] See Vol. I, p. 308. [4] To Lady Hankey 18th and 20th May 1919.

Council of the Principal Allied and Associated Powers', which was a sensible rationalisation of a fluid and fluctuating organisation.

With the end obviously approaching Hankey received a large number of laudatory letters about the contribution he and his staff had made to the running of the conference. Two which he probably appreciated especially – the first because it came from the representative of one of the Dominions, and the second because Lloyd George never set pen to paper if he could avoid doing so – are reproduced below.

*Sir Robert Borden to Hankey. British Delegation. Hotel Majestic, Paris, 13th May 1919*

Dear Sir Maurice Hankey,

You have carried a tremendous burden of duties during the past five years, which has perhaps been greater during the past five months than ever before. I venture to send a word of warm congratulation upon the remarkable ability, tact and courtesy which, throughout the proceedings of the Peace Conference, have distinguished your work, attended as it has been with difficulties and perplexities that only a few are able to realize.

With every good wish, believe me,

Yours faithfully,

*Lloyd George to Hankey. British Delegation, Paris, 30th May 1919.* Last paragraph Holograph.

My dear Hankey,

At a moment when Mr. Balfour and I are thanking the Staff of the British Delegation for the prompt and extraordinarily efficient manner in which they have translated the German Reply, I should like to say how much we all owe to your staff. I know that they have been working day in and day out for long hours and often far into the night. The work of the Conference would never have been accomplished at all had it not been for the accuracy, rapidity and extraordinary efficiency with which the Minutes and Decisions of the Council of Four were recorded and circulated. Though the work of the Peace Conference is not yet over I should like all those who have already contributed so much towards its success to know how much we appreciate their work.

You know what I think of your share in this conference. Your work has been beyond the praise of words.

Ever sincerely,

28 JUNE
1919

PEACE
CONGRESS

VERSAILLES 1919

SESSION
OF 28 JUNE 1919

AGENDA

SIGNATURE OF THE TREATY
OF PEACE BETWEEN THE
ALLIED AND ASSOCIATED POWERS
AND GERMANY

*Ordre du Jour* for the Signature of the Treaty of Peace 28th June, 1919

*Chapter 4*

# The Treaties Signed. June-August 1919

AT the beginning of June the British Empire Delegation devoted a good deal of time to considering the draft treaty with Germany. Smuts described it as 'an impossible document', and other members expressed uneasiness about the reparations clauses, the new eastern frontiers, the exclusion of Germany from the League, the occupation terms, and in general the more draconian measures. The proposed Anglo-American guarantee to France was also unpopular.[1] The final decision was to authorise Lloyd George to inform the Council of Four that unless the treaty was modified the British army would take no part in the advance into Germany in the event of a German refusal to sign, nor would the British navy reimpose the blockade. Lloyd George reported these views on 2nd, and thereby produced what Hankey described as 'an extemporized outburst from Clemenceau'.[2] However with time running out, since the Armistice expired on 23rd, and Wilson adopting 'a conciliatory and understanding rôle' the decision was finally taken to allow the Germans seven more days' grace to sign – that is until 22nd. Meanwhile the military measures which would be taken if the Germans remained obdurate were discussed. Despite the atmosphere of gloom and crisis in Paris Hankey managed to fit in a visit to Verdun and the southern battlefields with Lloyd George on 18th–19th. On their return there took place what he called 'a kind of Council of War' on the enforcement of the treaty, at which Foch's plan for an advance into Germany was accepted – despite the misgivings of the B.E.D.[3]

On 21st, while the Council of Four was in session to consider the German reply to the peace terms, a message came from the Admiralty

[1]33rd and 34th Meetings of B.E.D. Cab. 29/28/1.
[2]C.F.43A of 2nd June 1919. Cab. 29/38. *Foreign Relations, U.S.A.*, VI, pp. 138–46. *Supreme Control*, pp. 172–3.
[3]Meeting of 20th June 1919. Cab. 29/39.

that the warships of the High Seas Fleet interned at Scapa Flow had scuttled themselves. This action not only aroused great indignation in British circles – especially in the Navy – but caused President Wilson to remark that 'the case for the bad faith of the Germans was . . . overwhelming'.[1] It undoubtedly strengthened the hands of those who favoured taking a hard line towards Germany. Next day the Council of Four considered the German reply that they were ready to sign 'without recognising the responsibility of the German people for the war' or for delivering up the persons named by the Allies for trial. Wilson's proposed answer was that the Allies 'can accept no exception or reservation', and that the German representatives were required to give 'an unequivocal decision as to their purpose to sign and accept as a whole, or not to sign and accept the Treaty as finally formulated'. Hankey was instructed to act with Balfour in drafting a letter to the German delegates placing responsibility for the scuttling of the fleet on the German government.[2] Meanwhile on 21st the German government had resigned and a new one was formed under Gustav Bauer,[3] whose request for a 48-hour extension of the armistice was refused.[4] That evening, 23rd, a meeting of the Council of Four was interrupted by Dutasta entering the room with a note that the German delegates were prepared 'to sign under compulsion a dishonourable peace'. 'Orders were given', the minutes state, 'for guns to be fired. No further discussion took place'.[5] Only 1½ hours remained before the Armistice expired – at which time Foch's plan for an advance into Germany would presumably have been put into action. Henry Wilson wrote prophetically in his diary 'So, after five years of war, here comes peace at last. And yet I am as certain as I can be that the Boches have no

[1]*Foreign Relations U.S.A.*, VI, p. 614. See Roskill, *Naval Policy*, I, pp. 92–4 for a full account of the scuttling. The inclusion of the Japanese delegate Baron Makino actually made the Council of Four into a Council of Five at this time, but its former title has here been retained to avoid confusion with the earlier Council of Five (Foreign Ministers). The official minutes follow the same practice.

[2]No. 183 of 22nd June 1919. Cab. 29/39. We now know that the German government was entirely in the dark about the scuttling, which was in effect ordered by Admiral von Trotha, the head of the German Admiralty. Roskill, *Naval Policy*, I, p. 93.

[3]1870–1944. German politician. Reichstag Deputy (Soc.) 1912–18 and 1920–28. As first Chancellor of German Republic 1919 signed Treaty of Versailles. Resigned after 'Kapp Putsch' of 1920.

[4]No. 185 of 23rd June 1919. Cab. 29/39.

[5]No. 190 of 23rd June 1919. Cab. 29/39. *Supreme Control*, pp. 180–1.

intention of carrying out our Peace Terms, and in my judgement this ending is a disaster.'[1]

The German decision to sign brought no immediate easement of the pressure on Hankey, since the Council of Four continued to meet several times daily to consider retaliatory measures for the scuttling of the fleet and the trial of 'war criminals' including the Kaiser (which Hankey later stigmatised as 'an outrage'); and of course the old issue of Italian territorial claims in Istria and Asia Minor still remained unresolved. On 27th the Council of Ten was resurrected to handle post-treaty problems, and a special committee was formed to put the treaty into effect.

The actual signing of the treaty in the Galerie des Glaces at Versailles has often been described, and Hankey has recounted his own part in that momentous ceremony – including the ingenious way in which he overcame the last-minute crisis, when it was discovered that some of the British Empire signatories had brought no seals with them. The Paris curio shops were rapidly scoured for substitutes, and 'in at least one case a brass uniform button of a Dominion soldier was mounted on a holder and used'.[2] He even managed to find time to send his daughter Ursula a letter written at the conference table; and, unlike Harold Nicolson, who ended his account of that day with the words 'To bed, sick of life',[3] Hankey left the room 'in a spirit of optimism'. Another associate of Hankey's in the long-drawn negotiations who was bitterly disappointed over the outcome was Maynard Keynes. A few months later he told Austen Chamberlain, the Chancellor of the Exchequer, that Britain 'did not keep faith' at the conference, and that it was grossly unfair to blame the Reparations clauses on President Wilson, since the formula adopted had been of British not American origin.[4] No doubt it was the knowledge that about six months of very arduous work had ended that caused Hankey to take a less realistic view of the treaty than Nicolson, Henry Wilson or Keynes.

On 2nd July, Hankey's last day in Paris, he made a long entry in the diary which he had neglected for some weeks, summing up all his experiences. After recapitulating the story of how the Council of Four came into existence, and had tried at first to work without a secretary – with very unfortunate results – he wrote that 'For two and a half months I have organised every meeting, mobilising a succession of

[1]Callwell, *Wilson*, II, p. 201. [2]*Supreme Control*, p. 185. [3]*Peacemaking 1919*.
[4]Keynes to Chamberlain 28th Dec. 1919. Austen Chamberlain papers AC35/1/10.

experts of all the nations as each subject came up', and keeping 'very full minutes' of every discussion. 'As time went on', he wrote, 'and the Big Four got more and more tired, they left more and more to me' – until at the end he was 'almost making their decisions for them'. In addition he had to spend much time 'coaxing, cajoling and threatening the chairmen and secretaries [of the various Commissions] whose business was lagging'. 'At the Council of Four', he continued, 'there was no regular and formal Agenda . . . but every day I brought to the meeting a long slip of paper on which I wrote down all the subjects on which decisions were wanted. At first it was difficult for me to get in a word edgeways, but gradually they became more tolerant, and finally tame, and would let me sit in the middle of the circle and bring up one point after another for decision. Before the meetings I had to pack my two famous black despatch boxes with great care. They would contain envelopes containing spare copies of all the Memoranda and Reports for consideration – for one of the peculiarities of great men is that they can never bring the right paper to a meeting. President Wilson was the one exception. My boxes contained many other things; for example files of certain documents often required, such as the Treaties on which the peace was being based, President Wilson's Fourteen Points, the Armistice Conventions, indexes to the Minutes and files . . . according to the subjects for discussion. It is my boast that during nearly six months I never failed to produce the right paper at the right moment, and it became a regular joke . . .' Probably Frances Stevenson (later Lady Lloyd George) had this period in mind when she wrote that 'Sir Maurice Hankey was an exceptional personality . . . The serenity – the gaiety almost – of his character was phenomenal. I do not remember him angry or put out. Clemenceau became very much attached to Hankey, and when a point was in question would say affectionately: "I am sure Hankey can find the answer in that little bag of his" '.[1] And another shrewd observer of those times who later achieved high office recalled that 'The more I saw of negotiation the more I marvelled at Hankey's capacity for taking pains'.[2] So much for his methods of work, and how he was viewed by others who were present. In his recapitulatory diary entry he went on to describe his secretarial system in detail, and gave high praise to 'my famous Villa [Majestic] staff . . . Day and night they worked without complaint . . . and I never had a grumble or

[1]*The Years that are Passed* (Hutchinson, 1967), p. 100.

[2]Lord Vansittart, *The Mist Procession* (Hutchinson, 1958), p. 263.

a difficulty about a paper. Men and women were equally zealous and devoted to me'. Then he went on to record his impression of the Big Four – and their idiosyncracies. President Wilson, he recalled, 'had a knack of beginning his statements with the words "My dear Friend". One day Clemenceau turned to Lloyd George and said . . . "I do wish he wouldn't begin like that. I always know something horrible is coming" '. After that, recorded Hankey, 'Wilson used to begin "My associates and colleagues" which generally produced a laugh'. 'Clemenceau', he continued, 'was always quizzing Wilson about his Fourteen Points and having sly digs. He was asked by a friend how he got on after the withdrawal of Orlando . . . and replied "I sit between two lunatics. One imagines himself Jesus Christ and the other Napoleon" '. However Wilson too, he recalled, 'seemed to have an inexhaustible fund of amusing anecdotes'. Hankey also remarked how Lloyd George 'gradually established an increasing ascendancy, and in the end always got his way . . . but President Wilson was always suggestive and has a more practical though less brilliant mind than Lloyd George'. Clemenceau Hankey regarded as chiefly distinguished for his scintillating, if often mordant wit. He 'did not contribute much to the common stock of ideas', wrote Hankey, 'though his judgement was generally good. Orlando contributed little, though at times he had a knack of smoothing out a difficulty'. 'My relations with all', Hankey concluded, 'have always been of the happiest. I completely won their confidence and regard. They all showed extraordinary confidence in my impartiality and sense of fair play. I often had in my hands cipher telegrams which I could have used to get the key, but I was scrupulously careful never to abuse their confidence in this or in any other matter'. He had noticed that Mantoux 'assiduously took notes', and believed that 'he contemplates a great and monumental book of memoirs in which all the proceedings will appear'; and that in fact was fulfilled when Mantoux's 'Notes' were published in 1955. After describing the final sessions of the Council of Four, and the signing of the Treaty, Hankey wrote that 'the final parting then came. It was unceremonious and they all spoke the kindest words to me'. He presented Woodrow Wilson with a bound and indexed copy of the final minutes, and a few minutes later 'a beautiful basket of flowers arrived for Adeline from him'. Other presents and presentations followed, and at President Poincaré's banquet at the Elysée Hankey was 'overwhelmed with congratulations'. Finally on 1st July he himself gave a dinner 'to the secretaries of all the

Great Powers and as many of their wives as I could collect'. So ended his account of an experience which he described as having been 'Secretary of the Cabinet of the world'.

Hardly had Hankey completed his diary when Philip Kerr rang up from London to ask whether a decision had been taken that the Kaiser should be tried in England, as Lloyd George wanted to announce it in his speech to the House next day. After enquiring of Clemenceau through Mandel, his Chef-de-Cabinet, Hankey was able to telephone an affirmative reply.[1] But that decision produced a strong protest from Stamfordham, who pointed out on behalf of the King that President Wilson had said that 'the trial should not take place in any great city', and that on 25th and 26th June Clemenceau had 'withheld assent' from the trial being held in England. Obviously the King was very much averse to his cousin being arraigned in his own capital city; and Stamfordham's statement that 'the King feels aggrieved that . . . a decision of such supreme importance, and one so especially affecting His Majesty personally, was not communicated to him in some other way than through the medium of the Press'. This was perhaps the sharpest reprimand Hankey ever received; and one feels that he – or possibly Tom Jones who was deputising for him in London – was at fault in not ensuring that the Palace was told of the decision reached on 2nd July. Hankey expressed 'the utmost regret that the King did not receive some notification'; and it was therefore doubly fortunate for him that the Dutch government firmly refused to permit the extradition of the Kaiser.[2]

In his own retrospective account of the Paris Conference and the treaty which resulted from it Hankey was very critical of the 'Penalties' section (Part VII) of the Treaty, and made four points in mitigation of the failure to secure an enduring peace. These were, firstly, the rejection of the League Covenant, and so of the treaty of which it formed a part, by the Senate of the United States; secondly the chaos that prevailed in Russia and the prevailing fear about the spread of what he called 'the contagion' of Bolshevism; thirdly the clash between Wilson's idealistic purposes, as exemplified by his Fourteen Points, and the prior commitments, such as the Treaty of London of 1915, entered into by the Allies; and, lastly, the inevitable preoccupation of the con-

[1]Diary 2nd July 1919.

[2]Hankey to Stamfordham 8th July 1919. Stamfordham to Hankey 11th July and Hankey to Stamfordham 12th July. RA GV Q1560/13, 17 and 19.

ference with diversions from the main issue – such as Greek ambitions in Anatolia and Italian claims in the Adriatic. As against the unfavourable results he claimed (rather obviously) that the treaty ended the war; that it was followed by rapid demobilisation and the relief of the starving people of Europe; that it led to the creation of the International Labour Office, and to the building up of 'a machinery for later international conferences, and to treaties of peace with Austria, Bulgaria and (ultimately) Turkey'.[1] To-day the impartial historian must surely conclude that Hankey's 'mitigations' provide an inadequate explanation for all that was wrong in the treaty, that his balance sheet of profit and loss exaggerated the profits and minimised the losses, and that Sir Harold Nicolson's pessimistic view was all too well justified. For the truth surely is that Clemenceau and Foch alone believed that Germany could be permanently crushed, and held in a state of subjection by France creating a bulwark of military alliances. Only in regard to the need to contain 'Bolshevism' were the Allies united; and that purpose always loomed large in their councils. The inescapable conclusion is that the seeds of national and international democracy were not sown at the Paris conference. On the other hand some historians have recently argued that the evil growths of Fascism and Nazism sprang from the failures at Paris in 1919[2]; but that view seems at the very least questionable, since Fascism did not become overtly aggressive until the 1930s, and the Weimar Republic was reasonably stable and widely respected in the late 1920s. Furthermore in the 1928 German elections, which were genuinely free, only twelve Nazis were elected; yet within five years that party had achieved complete control. This rapid and disastrous deterioration must surely be attributed to the great depression of the early 1930s rather than to the deficiencies in the Versailles Treaty – serious though these may now appear.

One statement by Hankey can, however, be accepted without qualification; and that is his view that 'without a highly trained and tested staff specialising in the top secret work of the Council of Four, the Council of Five and, incidentally, of the British Empire Delegation,

[1] *Supreme Control,* pp. 196–7.

[2] Arno J. Mayer in *The Politics and Diplomacy of Peacemaking at Versailles 1918–19* (Weidenfeld and Nicolson, 1968) takes this view and Richard Watt, *The Kings Depart* (Weidenfeld and Nicolson, 1969) is highly critical of the policies of the Allies. His view was, however, strongly challenged by Elizabeth Wiskemann (*The Times,* 11th October 1969).

the Paris Conference would probably have failed . . .'.[1] And the chief credit for that accomplishment is accorded to Hankey himself in the memoirs of all the statesmen and officials who took part.[2] But he was on less firm ground when he compared the Paris organisation of 1919 with that employed at international conferences after World War II, and claimed that the latter failed because 'they were run for the most part on totally different and hastily improvised lines'. Late in his life Hankey repeated that view in speeches in the House of Lords[3]; which suggests that he looked back too nostalgically to the time of his greatest power and influence, and took too little regard of the totally different circumstances which prevailed after the surrender of Germany and Japan in 1945.

The rapid break-up of the Paris conference prevented Hankey saying goodbye to Smuts, but on 21st July he wrote from Whitehall Gardens in reply to the warm letter of farewell which the General had sent him. Hankey recalled their happy association in many fields during the war, and expressed his appreciation of Smuts's readiness at any time to take on arduous and difficult tasks. He hoped that their collaboration would continue in peace, and that he himself would one day visit South Africa again. Both wishes were to be fulfilled. Five weeks later he heard of Botha's death 'with great sorrow',[4] and recalled in his diary how he had been 'a great friend and supporter' at the time of the Paris conference and 'one of the biggest men' in that assembly. Botha was, according to Hankey, a very good raconteur, and he recorded in his diary two stories about President Kruger which Botha had told at a birthday party when Lloyd George was one of his guests. 'Kruger used to receive the people and hear their complaints sitting on his stoep from 4 a.m. in the morning. One day there came a deputation of Uitlanders after the Jameson raid, who talked for a long time. At the end Kruger took his pipe out of his mouth and said "You remind me of a little baboon that I once caught out hunting and tamed. One night as I sat by the fire the baboon got his tail in the fire and he bit me in the leg!" Another Kruger story he told was of two brothers who had inherited a farm and had quarrelled about its division. They asked Kruger to settle the dispute for them. His reply was "Let Piet divide the farm in

[1] *Supreme Control*, p. 171.
[2] See for example Lloyd George, *Peace Treaties*, I, pp. 132–3 and 371.
[3] Speech of 14th March 1956. Parl. Deb., Lords, Vol. 196, Cols. 413–19.
[4] General Botha died suddenly at midnight on 27th–28th August 1919.

**PEACE AND FUTURE CANNON FODDER**

***The Tiger: "Curious! I seem to hear a child weeping!"***

A prophetic cartoon of June 1919 by Will Dyson. Published in *Daily Herald*

two and let Jan choose which half he will have" ' – a true Judgement of Solomon.

*Diary July 27th* [*Sunday*]

. . . Most of the week has been spent in dealing with a coal strike, and for the first time I attended the negotiations. First Lloyd George met the owners, and next day the Miners' Federation with the redoubtable Smillie[1] at its head. The second man [Hodges[2]] impressed me most, with his fine head, pronounced jaw, intellectual forehead, classic features, and deep-set dreamy eyes. He had great power of expression and complete command of temper. They were a very formidable lot of men, quite equal to holding their own with these experienced politicians – Lloyd George, Bonar Law, Hoare, and Auckland Geddes – and vastly superior to the coal-owners, who were a very ordinary set. The business was settled all right, but I took no part, as I am only out to learn the business – an essential part of the equipment of the 'compleat statesman'. I also heard a tarriff reform deputation, an indifferent lot of men.[3] Lloyd George handled them with extraordinary skill, hardly touching tariff reform, which he doesn't want, and drawing out of them facts and figures to fit in with the Criccieth policy. I am gradually forming my views on all these questions. Coal is the root of everything, and I feel sure that we have to free ourselves of the domination of the miners, who have the nation's 'head in chancery'. I shall try and persuade Lloyd George to get the scientists going on every alternative form of power – tides and water power, wind, heat, oil, electrical storage etc. . . .

At the end of July Hankey received a message from Captain Abraham, his representative in Paris, that a copy of the secret minutes of the Council of Four had got into the hands of a press agent of the Quai d'Orsay, and that Wickham Steed,[4] the editor of *The Times* and former editor of the Paris *Daily Mail* had reportedly been involved in the leak. This set the alarm bells ringing loudly for Hankey, since he feared that a member of his own staff might have committed a grave breach of confidence. He showed Abraham's letter to Lloyd George, who agreed

[1]See Vol. I, p. 614, *note*.

[2]Frank Hodges (1887–1947). Trade Unionist and politician (Lab.). General Secretary, Miners' Federation of Great Britain 1918–24. Civil Lord of Admiralty 1924.

[3]Hankey's habitual mis-spelling of 'tariff' as 'tarriff' has hereafter been corrected.

[4]H. Wickham Steed (1871–1956). Journalist and historian. Foreign Editor, *The Times* 1914–19 and Editor 1919–22. On death of Lord Northcliffe and purchase of *The Times* by J. J. Astor (1886–1971), 1st Baron Astor of Hever 1956, younger son of 1st Viscount Astor, Steed was replaced by Geoffrey Dawson who had been Editor 1912–19 (see Vol. I, p. 270, *note*). Under Dawson *The Times* was very influential in the cause of 'appeasement' in the 1930s.

that he should leave for Paris at once, taking with him 'the best lawyer I could find'. This was a member of the firm of solicitors of which Sir George Lewis[1] was the head, and which had for many years handled London's most notorious *causes célèbres*. The choice of adviser strongly suggests that Lloyd George, or Hankey, saw in the leak a possible case for the prosecution of Steed and the discrediting of Northcliffe, who in Lloyd George's words had become 'the inveterate and implacable enemy of the administration' and 'the leading spirit in the intrigues that had stirred up trouble for the government'.[2] On reaching Paris Hankey conducted 'a most minute examination into the procedure at the Villa [Majestic]' without 'awakening suspicions among the staff'; but the only result was that he was convinced that no secret papers had got into wrong hands through the agency of any member of the secretariat.[3] Indeed he described the whole episode as 'a mare's nest', and it is only of interest in showing the hostility felt, not without reason, by Lloyd George towards Northcliffe and Steed at this time.

Three years later Hankey was sorely troubled by what appeared to be a more serious leak of the proceedings of the Council of Four in articles which Ray Stannard Baker,[4] who had been director of President Wilson's Press Bureau at the time of the Paris Conference, published in the *New York Times*. Baker made out that Balfour had been 'the arch conspirator' against Wilson during the conference, and Hankey at once went into action to refute the American journalist's charges.[5] Hankey was in the U.S.A. for the Washington Conference at the time, and investigated the matter closely. He was in the end able to show that when Wilson, by that time a very sick man, handed over to Baker the keys of the strong-box containing the minutes of the Council of Four in order that he might write an account of the conference he had not 'refreshed his memory' regarding its contents, and did not recall the 'limitations on publicity' which had been agreed. Long afterwards Hankey admitted that Baker was therefore 'justified in quoting the

[1]1868–1927. Son of 1st Baronet who built up the firm of Lewis and Lewis to great prominence in late Victorian times. See Theo Lang, *My Darling Daisy* (Michael Joseph, 1966) for Lewis's part in advising Edward, Prince of Wales (later Edward VII) over the attempted use by Lady Warwick of his love letters for blackmail.

[2]*Peace Treaties*, I, pp. 270, 371 and 575.

[3]Diary 25th August 1919.

[4]1870–1946. Author. Sometimes wrote under pseudonym of 'David Grayson'. The first editor of President Wilson's papers and author of the authorised biography.

[5]Hankey to Balfour 10th July 1922. B.M. Add. MSS. 49704.

minutes'[1]; but at the time his articles caused Hankey great annoyance.

With the Treaty of Versailles signed, and the treaties with the other Central Powers well on the way to completion, Hankey realised that the days of the War Cabinet were numbered, and that reversion to a conventional peacetime system could not be long deferred. He therefore set about putting his own house in order. On 12th July he wrote to Tom Jones from Criccieth, where he had evidently been discussing the matter with Lloyd George, enclosing two memoranda he had written on the subject and asking Jones for his opinion on them. Lloyd George, he said, wanted to have a Cabinet of only fifteen; but Hankey thought he would 'find it very difficult' to keep it so small. As regards the Secretariat he was sure that 'we must sooner or later revert to the employment of Civil Servants' as Assistant Secretaries; but in fact his prediction was only fulfilled to a limited extent, and on the C.I.D. side serving officers continued to fill such appointments.[2]

The more important of the two papers Hankey sent to Jones, dated 11th July from Criccieth, began with a historical review of the circumstances which had led to the formation of the Cabinet Secretariat, and an analysis of its present staff and their duties. He then went on to say that the continued existence of the Secretariat was a matter of policy 'which is outside the scope of this paper'; but 'for the immediate present' certain services must none the less 'continue to be provided'. These were 'the secretarial service' of the Cabinet itself and of its branch in Paris, the Imperial Cabinet, the C.I.D. and its 'affiliated committees', any permanent Cabinet committees which might be continued, and 'the large number of *ad hoc* committees which exist at the present time'; also the Supreme War Council, and possibly the League of Nations – 'unless it is preferred to establish this in the Foreign Office'. Hankey then went on to survey the staff needed to fulfil those requirements. The implication of the whole paper obviously was that the Secretariat should carry on exactly as it had been doing since 1916. Jones's remarks on this logically argued paper have not survived; nor does it seem ever to have reached Lloyd George, let alone the Cabinet. But in fact the only important change made was that in April 1921, on the initiative of Baldwin, the Financial Secretary of the Treasury, the cost of the Secretariat was shifted from the 'Treasury and Subordinate Departments' Vote' to a separate Parliamentary Vote. Hankey opposed

[1]*Supreme Control,* pp. 191–2. [2]Hankey to Jones 12th July 1919.

the change strongly, and later described it as a bad mistake. It was actually reversed late in the following year.

A month after Hankey had tried to establish a firm and enduring basis for his office he was in trouble with Lloyd George over the form and length of Cabinet minutes. He admitted that while he had been away they had become 'inordinately long', and proposed that instead of circulating a record of what each member said only the Conclusions should be sent to Ministers. He himself would retain a single copy of the full 'Secretary's Notes' for reference purposes. This, he said, 'would obviate all risk of what individual Ministers said being repeated outside'; but it 'would not obviate the risk of *decisions* leaking out'. That depended entirely 'on the discretion of the persons to whom the decisions are sent'.[1] At about the same time he circularised his staff about cutting down the distribution of both the draft minutes and the final version; and only Dally Jones, Tom Jones and Longhurst were to be allowed to keep 'permanent files' of the minutes. Obviously he was anxious to reduce the risk of leakages.[2] In fact, however, another two months were to elapse before the demise of the War Cabinet; and it was nearly the end of the year before Hankey got approval for the revised instructions to the Secretariat. Nor, as we shall see later, was he by any means successful in stopping the leakages about which he had always been so sensitive.

It was at this time that Lloyd George left Walton Heath and went to live at a house called The Firs on the London–Portsmouth road between Esher and Cobham. Here, recorded Hankey, they could escape the 'prying eyes which make Walton Heath and Criccieth so public'.[3] Lloyd George's love affair with Frances Stevenson, which had apparently begun as long ago as 1913, probably gave him greater reason

[1]Hankey to Lloyd George 15th Aug. 1919. Lloyd George papers F/24/1/9. Also in Cab. 21/100. From this date the title 'Minutes' disappears from the headings of Hankey's records of discussions in Cabinet and is replaced by 'Conclusions'. The Conclusion reached on each item on the Cabinet's agenda was thereafter recorded serially e.g. 'Cabinet 12(22) Conclusion 3' refers to the 3rd item of the 12th meeting of the Cabinet held in 1922.

[2]Office Minute of 15th and Office Notice of 16th August 1919. Cab. 21/100.

[3]Diary 25th Aug. 1919. Frances, Countess Lloyd George writes (to the author 20th Dec. 1970) that The Firs at Cobham was actually bought by Lloyd George's son Richard during the Paris Peace Conference as a residence for his father on his return. Its acquisition had nothing to do with her, but neither she nor Lloyd George liked it and it was sold after a short time.

than Hankey to wish to avoid 'prying eyes'. During August Hankey spent most weekends at The Firs, since his family had gone to Norfolk and Lloyd George wanted his help to 'work up a speech on trade, coal, labour and economic policy' – which Lloyd George actually delivered on 18th.[1] At various times they were joined and helped by Auckland Geddes, now President of the Board of Trade, Professor Chapman[2] of the same office, Sir Robert Horne the Minister of Labour,[3] and of course the inevitable Riddell. A more surprising visitor was J. H. Thomas, General Secretary of the Railwaymen's Union – who vainly 'tried to tempt' Hankey 'to go into politics' – presumably in the Labour Party's interest.

It was during these discussions that the notorious 'Ten Year Rule', directing that the service departments were to plan their budgets on the assumption that there would be no major war for ten years, was adumbrated.[4] Hankey noted that 'Churchill obviously does not care to be War Minister without a war in prospect, and finds the task of curtailing expenditure distasteful'. But Hankey himself accepted that it was 'absolutely vital to cut down expenditure'; and he had 'urged Lloyd George . . . to abolish the Air Ministry, Ministry of Munitions, Ministry of Shipping and Ministry of Food as soon as it can be done'. 'Other wise', he concluded, 'bankruptcy stares us in the face'.[5] This was o course the orthodox economic view of the period, and Hankey was by no means alone in believing that economy alone marked the road to solvency and prosperity. But his inclusion of the Air Ministry in the departments to be expunged contributed to one of the greatest controversies of the inter-war years – the conflict between the Admiralty and Air Ministry over the control of naval aviation.

At the end of August Hankey managed to join his family at Hunstanton for a holiday; but the weather was miserable, and the fact that he seized the opportunity to bring his neglected diary up to date suggests that it was not a very great success. Moreover he was still anxious about Adeline's health, as she was far from fully recovered from the

[1]Parl. Deb., Commons, Vol. 119, Cols. 1979–2022. Lloyd George's speech included most of the points raised by Hankey in his paper 'Towards a National Policy'.

[2]Later Sir Sydney J. Chapman (1871–1951). Economist and civil servant. Permanent Secretary, Board of Trade 1920–27. Chief economic adviser to government 1927–32. Member of Economic Consultative Committee, League of Nations 1928–32.

[3]See Vol. I, p. 585, *note*.

[4]The Ten Year Rule was actually approved by the Cabinet on 15th August 1919.

[5]Diary 25th August 1919.

severe bout of influenza which had struck her at the time of the Armistice.

When the end of the Peace Conference was plainly approaching the government considered what honours and money grants should be made to those who had contributed most to the success of the Allied cause. As to the soldiers, Churchill proposed to Lloyd George that Haig should receive £100,000, Robertson £10,000 and Henry Wilson only a Field-Marshal's baton. He then added 'It is not my duty to make recommendations about Hankey, but I am most strongly of the opinion that his brilliant services deserve exceptional recognition; and since you have talked the matter over with me I would suggest to you that he should be made a Privy Counsellor and receive a grant of £20,000 but that this should be announced in a separate part of the list to the military honours'.[1] Hankey had actually learnt what was in the wind when he lunched with Lloyd George on his last day in Paris and had declined the offer of a peerage. Lloyd George then said he would recommend his being raised to Grand Commander of the Bath, but a telephone enquiry came from London to ask whether he would prefer a baronetcy. That title Hankey described as 'a poor sort of thing', and so he again declined.[2]

Early in the following month the Cabinet considered the question of the money awards, and Lloyd George later told Hankey that they had agreed to £25,000 for him 'without a dissentient voice'. Yet he hesitated to accept. 'On principle', he wrote in his diary, 'I am rather against grants. But I am a poor man and have my wife and family to think of. It places me beyond reach of want, and provides for old age and relieves my mind of anxiety as regards Adeline and the children'. He then justified his acceptance by recapitulating at some length his contribution to winning the war – which he described as having been 'as much as any of the admirals and generals'. But he was distressed that Lloyd George, 'the man who really won the war' had refused to accept a grant, despite the fact that 'he has spoken to me rather pathetically about it. He is poor. He has been able to make but little provision for his family. And when he leaves office he will have to earn his own living. But he thinks his position with democracy would be jeopardised if he accepted a grant, or the subscription which his friends in the city are clamouring to raise for him'. Rather did he prefer what Hankey described

[1] Churchill to Lloyd George 23rd June 1919. Lloyd George papers F/8/3/65.
[2] Diary 25th August 1919.

as 'a noble poverty'.[1] He was therefore all the more delighted to learn a few weeks later that Andrew Carnegie[2] had provided in his Will a £2,000 annuity for Lloyd George.[3]

On 5th August the money awards were announced in the House, and when they were debated next day Lloyd George said that 'If Sir Maurice Hankey's name were left out of this list I should feel ashamed of it'.[4] He then read Asquith's tribute to Hankey written shortly after the Armistice.[5] In the event Hankey received the money grant recommended by the Cabinet, and was promoted Knight Grand Cross of the Order of the Bath – in the list of Army honours. But one does wonder why, he being a Marine, it was the Secretary of State for War and not the First Lord who first proposed a grant to him. Could the Admiralty still have harboured resentment towards him because of his strong line over the introduction of convoy in 1917?

The money award to Hankey was not well received by the Press. *The Times* found it 'not easy to justify the grant of £25,000 to Sir Maurice Hankey when Sir Henry Wilson, Sir William Robertson and Sir Hugh Trenchard receive £10,000 each'[6]; but the House agreed with the Prime Minister that Hankey's services had been in a different class from those of any of the soldiers, sailors and airmen named. He did not attend the debate himself ('modesty forbade'!), but Adeline did and reported that the grant to her husband 'was well received' by the House. However Hankey certainly played down the criticisms it aroused when he wrote in his diary that 'on the whole it got a good Press, except for a few second-rate weeklies'.[7] Despite the newspaper criticisms letters of congratulations poured in on him from wartime political and military colleagues – including Curzon, Derby and Henry Wilson; and in the same week he was summoned to Buckingham Palace at very short notice to receive his Knight's Grand Cross from the hands of the King at a private investiture.[8] Hankey described to his

[1]*ibid.*

[2]1835–1919. Steel and railway promoter and industrialist. Philanthropist on very large scale, especially to public libraries.

[3]Diary 28th August 1919.

[4]Parl. Deb. Commons, Vol. 119, Cols. 183–5 and 415–448.

[5]See Vol. I, pp. 631–2. [6]Editorial 6th August 1919.

[7]The *Morning Post* and *Birmingham Post* of 6th August and the *Saturday Review* were all critical of the award to Hankey.

[8]Hankey's banner was not actually hung over Stall No. 4 South in the Henry VII Chapel, Westminster Abbey, until about 15th July 1926, according to the bill made

wife how, after investing him, the King 'burst out into a violent tirade against trying the Kaiser in England, a subject on which he was moved to vehement eloquence'. After the Monarch had 'continued this on and off for half an hour', wrote Hankey, he 'had to quit' – probably thankful to escape further manifestations of Royal displeasure which he was in no position to mollify.[1]

On 7th July, after being allowed no more than a weekend at home, Hankey was summoned by Lloyd George to Criccieth. He found the Prime Minister 'dead beat', and admitted that he was 'a bit tired' himself. For the first week they therefore relaxed, and did little except read the Cabinet papers sent down to them and draft various telegrams and letters. Then Churchill and Henry Wilson joined the party, both of them depressed – Hankey thought by the collapse of Admiral Kolchak's anti-Bolshevik movement in Siberia. Lloyd George, who had always been opposed to the war of intervention, 'twitted Winston a good deal' about the failure of his pet project. Then the conversation turned to the creation of a Ministry of Defence and to Cabinet reorganisation, and it became apparent that Churchill was 'very anxious to take on' the former job.[2] Lloyd George, however, was non-committal; and with a débâcle in prospect in Russia it was not perhaps a well-chosen moment for Churchill to press his claims to supreme authority over the fighting services. Moreover Esher wrote to Hankey at about this time to say, prophetically, that 'only the P.M. of the day can be Minister of Defence *in War*'; and that he could not 'believe that Winston is a good administrator in so-called time of peace'.[3] The future of the Cabinet Secretariat likewise came under review at this time.

*Diary 22nd July 1919*

... Winston, formerly hostile to a Cabinet Secretariat, now favours it. His scheme tallies with mine – a large Cabinet, a small executive committee worked on War Cabinet lines; a Home Affairs Ctee. of the Cabinet and a Committee of Imperial Defence. The P.M. to be *ex-officio* chairman of all these committees with a vice-chairman. I worked out for the P.M. a scheme on these lines and a secretariat scheme to match. On the 15th Auckland

out by the Banner maker. He was installed during the Bath Service on 20th May 1928. Information from Major-General P. B. Gillett, Deputy Secretary, Order of the Bath, 4th May 1970.

[1]To Lady Hankey 12th August 1919 – the day of her husband's investiture.

[2]Diary 7th July 1919. [3]Esher to Hankey 8th August 1919. Esher papers.

Geddes,[1] Llewellyn Smith[2] and Professor Chapman arrived and on the 16th Sir Robert Horne. We had great conferences on the Trade Policy to be adopted and worked out a complete scheme, which did *not* include Tariff Reform! We also worked out a coal policy – with most difficult questions. I wrote a big paper entitled 'Towards a national policy' which the P.M. was very pleased with.

Hankey's 'big paper'[3] was in effect a continuation of the reviews of the world situation which he had produced periodically for the War Cabinet or its various sub-committees ever since 1917. He began by surveying the changed economic and financial circumstances of the country, and laid great stress on the need to stimulate exports and increase industrial efficiency by 'utilising mechanical methods to their fullest extent'. Recovery would be impossible unless 'non-productive employment of man-power' was 'reduced within the narrowest limits consistent with national safety'; and that meant heavy cuts in the fighting services. Hankey also emphasised the need to make good 'building deficiencies', and to improve the health and education of the people – all of which would of course cost money which, in real terms, could only be earned by exports. Having recommended that the chief economies should fall on the armed forces he went on to survey 'Foreign and Defence Policy' in order to try and establish the limits to which they should be reduced. The League of Nations he regarded as 'an experiment on the success of which we cannot yet afford to base our national security'. He was sceptical about its ability 'to enforce its decisions', and anxious about the consequences which would stem from failure to do so. As to possible enemies, France, Italy, Germany and Austria were 'too exhausted to become really dangerous for a long time'; but he feared that Italy might endeavour to achieve 'her greedy ends by force' at some future date. He expected 'Bolshevism' to prevail in Russia, and recommended gradually 'disinteresting ourselves in the civil war'. Thereafter Hankey favoured taking the first steps to re-establish trade with Russia.[4] At the end of the month he enlarged on the question of putting an end to the War of Intervention in a letter to

[1]See Vol. I, p. 344, *note*.

[2]Later Sir Hubert Llewellyn Smith (1864–1945). Economist and Civil Servant. Permanent Secretary, Board of Trade 1907–19. Chief Economic Adviser to government 1919–27. Member, Economic Committee, League of Nations 1920–27.

[3]The paper is actually dated 17th July 1919.

[4]In the draft Hankey sidelined the passage referring to trade with Russia with 'omit for the present'; but it appears in the printed version. Cab. 21/159.

Lloyd George proposing that all forces should be withdrawn by the autumn, and a date fixed after which no more war material would be supplied to 'the anti-Bolshevist groups'. British policy should, he proposed, then be one of 'benevolent neutrality' towards them.[1] Plainly Hankey had, for all his strong dislike of 'Bolshevism', come to the conclusion that further military intervention was futile.

In his 'National Policy' paper Hankey recognised that the United States was now the most powerful nation in the world – financially and economically as well as militarily. War with her was, he wrote, 'unthinkable', and would in any case lead to disaster. None the less 'our fleet should not be allowed to sink below the level of the United States fleet'. It is likely that Hankey's view of the perils of a naval building race with America derived at any rate in part from a warning he had just received from Tom Jones about the building programme put forward by the Admiralty. 'The crux of the matter', wrote Jones, 'is, having squashed Germany are we now going to start building against America? . . . I know your love for the Navy but I think even you will hesitate to endorse the new estimates'.[2] The nation about which Hankey expressed most concern was actually Japan, which he described as 'a country of some potential danger'; but he believed we could maintain the friendly relations which had been very evident at the Peace Conference. It appears that Hankey envisaged an extension of the Anglo-Japanese alliance, which was due to expire in 1921. In his view military forces necessary to maintain order in India, Egypt, Palestine and Mesopotamia were essential; but he thought that recent technical developments (aircraft, tanks etc.) might enable economies to be achieved. Hankey ended the first part of his survey with the proposal that the C.I.D. or a sub-committee of it should 'draw up a basis of policy' on which the service departments 'should work out their estimates'. This suggestion probably marks the genesis of the 'Ten Year Rule', which the government enunciated exactly a month after Hankey showed his paper to Lloyd George. Internal evidence suggests that Hankey's paper also played a part in the government's decision to ask Lord Grey to undertake a mission to U.S.A. in August 1919, and in the preparation of his instructions; since the principal matters to be discussed – the League of Nations, British financial and economic problems, the Irish imbroglio and the evidence of a naval building race

[1]Hankey to Lloyd George 28th July 1919. Lloyd George papers F/24/1/4.
[2]Jones to Hankey 11th July 1919. *Middlemas*, I, pp. 89–90.

– were all stressed by Hankey.[1] Unhappily the breakdown of President Wilson's health made the Grey mission completely abortive. The second part of Hankey's paper was mostly produced by Professor Chapman, and dealt in great detail with trade and industrial policy. The most remarkable feature of Hankey's survey is the applicability of nearly everything he wrote to the problems which faced his country half a century later. Indeed it might well have emanated from a Cabinet Committee of the late 1960s.

Towards the end of August Hankey tried to get away to join his family at Hunstanton on the Norfolk coast. But with the German treaty out of the way and a multitude of difficult problems at home demanding his attention, Lloyd George increased the pressure. 'The P.M. expects everything to be done in a week' grumbled Austen Chamberlain to Walter Long on 30th[2]; and Hankey was of course the chief sufferer from his master's relentless energy. In fact Lloyd George was planning another of the informal Cabinet sessions, held in seclusion and at a distance from Whitehall, which had become a speciality of his at times of crisis during the war. The discussions were to take place at Hennequeville near Trouville on the Normandy coast, where the assiduously attentive Riddell had taken a large house – doubtless with the object of ensuring his own presence at the conclave. So Hankey's holiday was once again interrupted, and he had to leave Adeline and the children in Norfolk.

[1]Grey to Curzon. Enclosure to letter of 5th August 1919. Lloyd George papers F/12/1/35 and Long to Lloyd George 8th August 1919. *ibid.* F/33/2/69. Also Admiralty Memo. G.T. 7975 of 12th August 1919, Cab. 24/86 and G. M. Trevelyan, *Grey of Fallodon* (Longmans, Green, 1938) pp. 351–2. I am grateful to Dr. J. K. McDonald of Yale and Oxford Universities for drawing my attention to the similarities between Hankey's paper and Grey's instructions.
[2]Austen Chamberlain papers AC. 25/2/32.

*Chapter 5*

# The End of the War Cabinet. September-December 1919

HANKEY joined Lloyd George at Hennequeville on 4th September. The principal items to be discussed at the informal Cabinet were, firstly, ways and means of bringing intervention in Russia to an end without causing excessive suffering to those whom we had supported in the anti-Bolshevik crusade; secondly Arab aspirations regarding the former Turkish provinces in the Middle East, which the Paris Conference had left unsettled; thirdly the perennial Irish question, which was obviously coming to a head again, with the threat of full-scale civil war; fourthly the increasing industrial unrest at home; and, lastly, the continuation of the Coalition Government, in which the right-wing Conservatives were showing increasing discontent and a desire to gain power for themselves.

Apart from Lloyd George, accompanied as usual by Frances Stevenson and Lord Riddell their host, the party consisted initially of Sir Hamar Greenwood, Under-Secretary in the Home Office, who was soon to become Chief Secretary for Ireland, and his wife; the Waldorf Astors, F. E. Guest, the Chief Government Whip and Hankey's invaluable Sylvester. Hankey sent Adeline amusing descriptions of his fellow guests (Nancy Astor 'very vivacious but constantly asserting "the mother of six"'); and he quickly noticed that no love was lost between her and the Greenwoods.[1] These incompatibilities made the house party a good deal less than a social success; moreover Hankey himself was far from being fully fit, and was resentful at being separated yet again from his family.

On the first day at Hennequeville Hankey 'had several talks with the P.M. about Armenia, where the renewal of massacres [by the Turks] was threatening'. He at once set down on paper his views on what should be done. 'The only nation which can intervene in time to save

[1]To Lady Hankey 4th Sept. 1919.

the situation', he wrote, 'is Great Britain'. But the decision to withdraw from the Caucasus had been taken 'in response to an overwhelming desire to get quit of Russia and of all territory formerly belonging to Russia'. The troops employed in the intervention were, he said 'restless' – which was a considerable understatement; and a new intervention must therefore be 'an *Allied* one in the fullest sense'. He proposed to slow down the evacuation of the Caucasus region, form a 'flying column, if possible of volunteers', and prepare French and Italian contingents to move to Batum. He also suggested the formation of a local gendarmerie 'on the lines of the Macedonian gendarmerie' – which he himself had nearly joined in 1903.[1] Finally he urged the prompt settlement of Turkey's new boundaries at the Peace Conference, and strongly held that Constantinople should remain Turkish 'for the present'.[2] The last part of Hankey's paper was more likely to appeal to Lloyd George than the suggestion of renewed entanglement in the remote Caucasus theatre; and the unfortunate Armenians were in fact left to the not very tender mercy of the Red Army, which conquered the country early in 1920. Churchill remained, however, enthusiastic for more intervention, and when Hankey dined with him and Seely in Paris at this time he lectured them until the small hours 'at enormous length and [with] great brilliancy about Russia'. 'He is quite barmy in his enthusiasm for the anti-Bolshevists' was Hankey's truthful if somewhat juvenile description of Churchill's obsession.[3]

During the next ten days Bonar Law, Eric Geddes and Horne – all Conservative members of the Coalition – joined the house party, and a series of conferences on the political situation at home and in the Middle East took place. Lord Allenby, the 'popular and liberal-minded Field-Marshal',[4] whom Lloyd George had sent out in March to replace Sir Reginald Wingate as High Commissioner in Egypt, also arrived. Allenby's purposes were, firstly, to represent the troubles which were arising through British vacillations over the future status of Egypt, whereby the Nationalist movement was encouraged;[5] and, secondly, to

[1] See Vol. I, pp. 62–3. [2] Lloyd George papers F/24/1/10.

[3] Diary 14th Sept. 1919.

[4] Harold Nicolson, *Curzon: the Last Phase* (Constable, 1934) pp. 173 and 181. Henceforth cited as Nicolson, *Curzon.*

[5] Allenby had urged that under the peace treaty with Turkey the Sultan's suzerainty over Egypt (which had for a long time been no more than nominal) should be transferred to Britain, thereby regularising the anomalies produced by our having only declared a Protectorate over that country in December 1914. However Lloyd

try and resolve the *impasse* which had come to pass through the alleged contradictions between the Sykes–Picot agreement of 1915 and later pronouncements by the British government regarding Arab and Zionist aspirations.[1] These problems had brought us into serious conflict with the French, who were determined to establish themselves in Syria, and had also laid claim to the oil bearing territories of Mosul in northern Mesopotamia, which the British regarded as coming within their sphere of influence. Clemenceau, it will be recalled, had readily accepted the British claim to Mosul when he came to London in December 1918.[2] On 9th September Hankey wrote to Tom Jones from Normandy stressing the British need for a railway and an oil pipeline from Mosul to the Mediterranean, probably terminating at Haifa, and asking him to find out whether construction of the pipeline really was a practicable proposition.[3] The French, though they were more ready than the British to employ force to attain their ends and to disregard Arab aspirations, were certainly not alone in entertaining imperialistic aspirations in the Middle East.

Hankey had met T. E. Lawrence during the Paris Peace Conference, when he acted as interpreter to Faisal, son of Hussein the Sherif of Mecca, and had pleaded the Arab cause. But Hankey seems to have

---

George hesitated to take so drastic a step, since under the Hague Convention a belligerent was forbidden to annex 'occupied enemy territory' while hostilities continued. For a succinct account of the consequences see Nicolson, *op. cit.* Ch. VI.

[1]See Vol. I, p. 270, *note*. However, the most recent research into this complicated story strongly supports the view that, despite the lack of clarity of Sir Henry McMahon's letter of 24th October 1915 to the Sherif Hussein, no British pledge was given then or later to set up an independent Arab state or federation after the war. It was Hussein who promised military assistance to the British, not *vice versâ*. Furthermore Lebanon and the whole of Palestine west of the Jordan were specifically excluded from McMahon's loose phrase about 'Arab independence' – as both Hussein and Faisal his son well understood. It was the rapid collapse of the Sherifian revolt that forced the British to give the military and financial assistance which they had not promised – to the final tune of £11 millions in gold. And it was not until after Faisal's expulsion from Damascus in 1921 that accusations 'of betrayal and double dealing were hurled at the British'. See Isaiah Friedman, *The McMahon–Hussein Correspondence and the Question of Palestine. Journal of Contemporary History*, Vol. 5, No. 2 (1970). Also Arnold Toynbee's 'Reply', *loc. cit.* No 4 (1970). On 14th Oct. 1925 Hankey sent Birkenhead, then Secretary of State for India, a long paper giving the whole tangled story. Though it does not entirely accord with Mr. Friedman's views, quoted above, it is an admirable synopsis. Cab. 63/37.

[2]See pp. 28-9. [3]*Middlemas*, I, p. 93.

been unimpressed by Lawrence – possibly because he was much too astute to be taken in by Lawrence's unreliability as a witness. They found common ground only in the desire to extend British influence in the Middle East. They were not even in accord over Syria, since whereas Lawrence was working to thwart French ambitions in that country, Hankey realised that we were too deeply committed to our ally to be able to deny her the promised share of the plunder. Many years later Liddell Hart, who was working on his biography of Lawrence, consulted Hankey about whether there was any truth in Richard Aldington's accusation that Lawrence had lied in saying that he had been approached about succeeding Allenby as High Commissioner for Egypt,[1] and also whether his statement that he had been sounded about becoming Hankey's deputy in 1935 was true. To the first question Hankey answered that there was 'nothing inherently improbable in the story that he was *sounded* on the subject'. Hankey pointed out that he himself had, as we have seen, been considered for several different posts, including 'becoming a "Satrap" in Mesopotamia or even some more extensive area in the Middle East'. But so far as he knew no definite offer of that nature had ever been made to Lawrence.[2] To Liddell Hart's second question he replied that 'The suggestion . . . never came to my notice at the time', and that Lawrence 'was too much of a specialist' to have been seriously considered for such an appointment.[3] In his memoirs Lord Vansittart has flatly denied that either offer was ever made[4]; and one surely must conclude that in both cases Lawrence let his imagination run riot.

The discussions about what Hankey called 'the difficult Syrian question' at Hennequeville were prolonged. 'But', he continued, 'we eventually thrashed out a policy (after I had prepared at least 6 editions) to take to Paris. The scheme announces our withdrawal from Cilicia and Syria; the handing over of Damascus, Homs, Hamah and Aleppo to the French; the withdrawal of the British army into Palestine behind the boundary we claim; and the submission of the permanent boundaries of Syria with Palestine and Mesopotamia to American arbitration if we cannot agree with the French; the right to construct a British railway and oil pipe line through the French zone, and to use it in time

[1]See Richard Aldington, *Lawrence of Arabia: a Biographical Enquiry* (Collins, 1955) pp. 385–6.
[2]Hankey to Liddell Hart 20th Feb. 1954. Liddell Hart papers.
[3]Same to same 9th Jan. 1955. [4]*The Mist Procession* (Hutchinson, 1958) p. 327.

of war without infringing French or Arab neutrality. The French to be responsible for protection of the Armenians [presumably those deported to Syria by the Turks in 1915] and to be allowed to land immediately at Alexandretta and Mersin'.[1] Most of this was, of course, anathema to Faisal and to Lawrence. When on 12th Hankey and Lloyd George motored to Paris and the latter put the proposals to Clemenceau he 'did not much like it and was rather annoyed at our having invited Faisal here, though we had told him we were doing so . . . Clemenceau wants a mandate for the remaining Turkish Empire (Anatolia and perhaps including Constantinople)'. That evening Hankey and Lloyd George entertained Frank L. Polk,[2] now chief American delegate to the peace conference, and he was shown the proposals. Polk felt that the French occupation of Alexandretta and Mersin 'hits at the American mandate for Armenia', which, according to Polk, President Wilson had 'tabled in the American Senate'.[3] But, of course, the Senate's rejection of the Versailles Treaty, shortly followed by President Wilson's complete breakdown, killed all schemes for American participation in the restoration of the war-torn Near East.

Some years later Hankey recalled an amusing clash between Clemenceau and the American representative in Paris, which must have taken place at about the time when President Wilson's illness had brought his country's administration and diplomacy to a complete standstill. Clemenceau was particularly irritated by American indecision over accepting a mandate in the Near East, and pressed the ambassador hard for a definite reply; but the unhappy envoy 'could only talk of the difficulties of the American constitution', recorded Hankey. Finally the French Premier 'could contain himself no longer. Rising from his chair he placed himself in front of the American ambassador in a characteristic pose with his hands behind his back and his shoulders slightly hunched, and delivered a speech *at* the Ambassador with tigerish vehemence. "We have heard a great deal of the beauties of the American Constitution", he said, "We are told that if the President dies, the Vice-President takes his place, and all goes on as before. But there is no provision for the contingency of the President being ill. I wish that if your President must die, he would die without being

[1]Diary 14th Sept. 1919. See also Hankey to Jones, 9th Sept. 1919. *Middlemas*, I, p. 93.
[2]American lawyer and businessman (1871–1943). Acting Secretary of State 1918–19. Head of American delegation to Peace Conference July–December 1919.
[3]Diary 14th Sept. 1919.

ill!" ' 'The Ambassador', Hankey went on, 'was always rather tongue-tied and could not find speech, but Clemenceau relieved a tense situation by bursting into laughter'.[1]

At the end of September, by which time the French were encountering serious difficulties in Syria, Lawrence accompanied Faisal to London for another conference. Lloyd George then tried his hand at what Hankey called 'oriental diplomacy with great skill'. So Lawrence was 'turned on' to try to persuade the Emir 'to fall in with our scheme' – a manoeuvre which the leader of the Arab Revolt must have found highly distasteful. Hankey described Faisal as 'an attractive creature with a very pleasant smile. He is given to uttering such expressions as "My ancestors were civilised when those of every other man in this room were savages" '. But at first he had merely 'indicated his intention to kill every Frenchman in Syria' as soon as the British withdrew.[2] Finally, however, Hankey was able to write 'We persuaded him to meet the French at a military conference in London, but he made it a condition that an American should be present. We proposed this by personal telegram from the P.M. to Clemenceau, who replied yesterday [October 15th] by an exceedingly rude refusal, suggesting bad faith on our part, to discuss [the matter] anywhere except in Paris or to admit an American. Curzon tells me that he hears privately this is due to personal animus on Clemenceau's part against Lloyd George'.[3] In fact Faisal had already come to terms with Clemenceau, who had offered to recognise the independence of Syria on condition that he supported French interests. At the Paris conference and afterwards Faisal – supported by Lawrence – tried to further his aims by playing off the British and French against each other; but the fundamental weakness and falsity of his claim to be king of a united Arab nation were soon exposed. The end of the story is well known. The mandate for Syria went to France, who relinquished her claim to Mosul, while those for Palestine and Mesopotamia went to Britain. Asia Minor, excluding Armenia, remained Turkish. But the widespread propagation of the view that Britain had committed a breach of faith towards the Arabs, and that the Sykes–Picot agreement of 1916 was an iniquity – notably in Lloyd George's *War Memoirs* – contributed to the loss of

[1]Diary 7th Jan. 1923. Sir Eyre Crowe reminded Hankey of this incident at the Paris Conference of that time, which Hankey was attending under Bonar Law's government.

[2]Diary 28th Sept. 1919. [3]*ibid.*, 16th Oct. 1919.

confidence in Britain by the Arabs, and so ultimately to the destruction of the whole British position in the Middle East after World War II.[1]

To retrace our steps to mid-September, while in Paris Hankey made a retrospective entry in his diary about the political discussions held at Hennequeville.

*Diary 14th September 1919*

. . . The P.M's idea is that the coalition must go, and a genuine amalgamation must be formed under some such title as the National Democratic Party. There is no enthusiasm for this coalition. The two party machines do not really co-operate. Consequently there are few organised public meetings, and the political field is left clear for the Bolshevists, Independent Labour party, and the Labour Party. A genuine national movement is essential to combat extremists of all kinds. I was not present at the final meeting with Bonar Law, as I was otherwise engaged, but I think they will probably bring matters to a head before Parliament meets. It has been in the air for a long time, but the scheme is only now taking permanent shape. Freddy Guest (Chief Whip) threw a fly over me to see if I would take on the job of Chief Whip, but I did not rise . . .

On the very day that Hankey outlined Lloyd George's ideas regarding the future shape of the government Esher wrote to the former prophesying the failure of the League, with consequential public disillusion; also that the Prime Minister's 'following [would] crumble away before the repeated blows of Smillie and Co.' unless he could provide a renewed 'moral stimulant' as he had done in 1917.[2] But to Esher, as to many others of the upper class, the Labour movement was barely distinguishable from the dreaded 'Bolshevists'. Hankey's old friend Jack Seely, with whom he dined in Paris at this time, was also nervous that the prevailing industrial unrest would lead to revolution. Even Lloyd George apparently thought it 'not remotely improbable';

[1]See Elie Kedourie, *Cairo and Khartoum on the Arab Question 1915–18* (*The Historical Journal*, VII, 2 (1964), pp. 280–97). The author makes a strong case that the description of the Sykes–Picot agreement of 1916 as 'a shameful and dishonourable thing' was propagated by the Arabophil British officials in Cairo and Khartoum, and soon 'acquired the venerable sheen of orthodoxy'. In fact the British never promised the Arabs anything except liberation from the Turks. King Hussein, Faisal's father, was shown the Sykes–Picot agreement in the spring of 1917, and never raised any objection to it. The same author's *England and the Middle East* (Bowes & Bowes, 1956) deals more fully with the whole story. For Lawrence's side see B. H. Liddell Hart, *T. E. Lawrence* (Cape, 1934), esp. pp. 383–97.

[2]Esher to Hankey 14th Sept. 1919. Part printed in *Journals*, IV, pp. 243–4.

but Hankey 'took the line that as long as there is a decent government in England the people are too sensible'.[1]

Hankey seized the opportunity of the September visit to Paris to close down the office he had established at the Villa Majestic for the Peace Conference. Not only was its work more or less completed but the staff was badly needed at home, where the pressure was increasing all the time. Moreover Hankey knew that his own position was secure – at any rate while Lloyd George remained Prime Minister; for when he wrote from Hennequeville to Smuts to offer his condolences on the death of Botha he ended by saying that he was 'going on as Secretary of the Cabinet'.[2]

On his return to London Hankey was involved in further discussions with Faisal, and in the Cabinet decision not to send more military supplies to the Baltic states to help them in their struggle for freedom from Russian or German domination. Furthermore a Cabinet Committee under Lloyd George's chairmanship was set up to review ways and means of reducing government expenditure. Then on 23rd 'the Railwaymen's Union pointed a pistol at the Government, and after two days' most hectic discussions suddenly broke off negotiations and declared a strike'. 'J. H. Thomas', continued Hankey, 'tried his utmost to effect a settlement, but since his trip to America he has been losing ground to his deputy Cramp,[3] a sinister looking fellow reported to be a Bolshevist'. Hankey was amused to witness the negotiations between Thomas and Lloyd George 'both Welshmen and full of cunning, and in private life good friends'. He considered that Thomas played his part 'with skill and dignity', but when the Prime Minister made his final concession and offered 'to leave the room for the men's representatives to consider it some of the men at the back called out "We have made up our minds" or words to that effect'.[4]

For the next week, during which the government were 'fighting the strike hard', Hankey stayed in London and was 'inseparable from the Prime Minister'. 'The harder the times the more he leans on me', he

[1]Diary 14th Sept. 1919.

[2]Hankey to Smuts 9th Sept. 1919. Smuts Archive.

[3]Concemore T. Cramp (1876–1933). General Secretary, National Union of Railwaymen 1920. Chairman, Labour Party 1925. President, International Transport Workers' Federation, 1926. Served on many Committees of Inquiry and Royal Commissions in 1920s.

[4]Diary 28th Sept. 1919.

declared; and Hankey himself seems to have regarded the fight against the railwaymen in terms of a military operation.[1]

*Diary 29th September 1919*

. . . We are meeting the strike with a very powerful organisation. Eric Geddes is the Commander-in-Chief. To help him he has a strong Cabinet Committee for which I supply the Secretariat, though I do not attend it myself. Defensively our policy is to get the railways going gradually with non-strikers and volunteers, increasing from the few trains now running to a respectable total within a few weeks. Also to utilise motor lorries etc. to the utmost possible extent for the purpose of maintaining and replenishing the not-inconsiderable supplies of food and petrol. We are further organising coastal shipping and canal transport, and we have also made considerable provision for the maintenance of order in the event of sabotage or disturbances. Aircraft are being used for mails and urgent journeys, and an emergency communication by wireless, aircraft, and pigeons has been organised in case, later on, the telegraph and telephone wires are cut. Offensively we are relying for the present on an intensive newspaper barrage. This has so far upset the strikers that they have been endeavouring to call out the compositors, and in other ways to interrupt the service of publicity. It is very significant that the strikers' Committee meets in the headquarters of the Herald League (Gough Square), practically a revolutionary organisation. Yesterday I prepared for the Prime Minister a paper on the consequences of the strike, to make clear to the public how serious they would be,[2] but, so far, he has not utilised it. I think he is reserving it for a speech. . . .

The strike actually continued until 5th October, and a week later Hankey made another retrospective entry in his diary recording his satisfaction over how 'the Government's organisation fairly knocked the strikers endways'. He also made some interesting comments on the characters of the principal Trade Unionists involved. Thus Harry Gosling,[3] leader of the Transport Workers, who worked assiduously for conciliation with the railwaymen, he described as 'a decent old fellow'; but Tom Williams, his deputy, he regarded as 'a Bolshevist'. The most helpful person on the workers' side was his 'old friend Arthur Henderson' – about whom Hankey had in fact said some harsh things at the time of his mission to Russia in 1917 and his support of the proposal to send delegates to the International Socialist Conference at Stockholm, which brought about his dismissal from the War

[1] *ibid.* [2] Original in Lloyd George papers F/24/1/12.

[3] 1861–1930. Politician (Lab.) and Trade Unionist. President, Transport and General Workers' Union. Minister of Transport and Paymaster-General 1924.

Cabinet.[1] On 4th, a Saturday, Lloyd George 'felt tired' of the prolonged but seemingly futile attempts to achieve a settlement, and 'went off to the country'. Hankey 'followed suit', only to be summoned back to London for a meeting between Bonar Law and the workers' representatives, which had been fixed for Sunday morning the 5th. 'The conference', he wrote, 'gradually led to a rapprochement. Thomas was playing a curious game. He had arranged to address the railwaymen at the Albert Hall in the evening, and he was very anxious to prolong the negotiations so that his full announcement should be made then. If it appeared in the Sunday evening papers the men would have time to study the terms and would realise that they had been given away . . .'; which makes it appear that Thomas was not exactly loyal to those whose interests he was supposed to be representing. Hankey drafted the terms of settlement 'during lunch', had copies reproduced at once, and then organised the Ministers concerned to meet in Bonar Law's study at 11 Downing Street to approve them. That done the terms were put to the men, who 'accepted them without amendment'. The meeting ended 'amid mutual congratulations', and Lloyd George at once went off to Cobham, insisting on Hankey accompanying him. He summed up his chief's handling of the strike in very laudatory terms, praising his 'absolute firmness and fairness, and [his] most conciliatory, frank and persuasive manner'. On the men's side Hankey wrote that Thomas tried several times to frighten Lloyd George with 'hints of the men getting out of hand'; but 'he refused to be bluffed'. There was, he declared, 'continuous liaison between the Prime Minister and Thomas throughout the whole strike'. This 'was conducted partly through Tom Jones, my assistant' – a somewhat backhanded and inadequate tribute to Jones's work as conciliator in industrial disputes. Thomas, most surprisingly, apparently summoned Lord Astor (Under-Secretary for Health) to London from Sandwich, and arrived at the Astors' house in St. James's Square 'in a very highly strung condition'. Nancy Astor 'a woman of great force of character' – at once sent him up 'to have a bath and go to bed', and on Thomas's protesting she replied ' "Oh no! You may be able to manage your executive committee, but you cannot manage me!" '. What made Thomas's night at the Astors even more incongruous was that Auckland Geddes, the President of the Board of Trade, was also staying in the house; but their hostess successfully avoided a confrontation between them – knowing Thomas's antipathy

[1]See Vol. I, pp. 416–21.

towards the Geddes brothers. Hankey recorded Thomas's remark to J. T. Davies at this time '"Jesus Christ! J. T., them Geddes brothers is bloody duds"' – a view with which Hankey apparently felt some sympathy, since when he and Thomas were motoring to Cobham, and Thomas 'abused Eric Geddes all the way', Hankey apparently did not feel obliged to defend the Minister of Transport.

Hankey also recorded a number of other amusing incidents which took place during the last two days of the strike. On 4th the principal Ministers concerned, including Birkenhead, the Lord Chancellor, were summoned to No. 10. For some reason 'they were all very hilarious', and Lloyd George remarked '"Well, I know why the Lord Chancellor is so happy – it is because the milk supply is assured!"' Birkenhead apparently took the oblique reference to his addiction to the bottle 'in good part'.

Next day the railwaymen were left alone in the Cabinet room to consider the terms drafted by Hankey and approved by the Cabinet, while the Transport Workers' Conciliation Committee, which had played a pacificatory part throughout the dispute, were 'turned out into the hall'. As Lloyd George and Hankey passed through the hall the former called out '"You must not keep your friends on the door-mat, Henderson"' – a reminder of how Henderson had made a great fuss about being kept waiting 'on the self-same spot' while the Cabinet considered his actions with regard to the Stockholm conference of 1917. After a long wait the Conciliation Committee decided to relieve their boredom by singing; and the strains of 'Cockles and Mussels' and 'The Red Flag' were wafted out to the waiting crowds in Downing Street. So ended the railway strike of 1919 in an atmosphere not far removed from *opéra bouffe*. Hankey's final summing up was that 'the strike was beaten by the overwhelming good sense of the British people, and by good organisation by the government'. From enquiries which reached them from Washington and Paris it seems that the admiration, even envy, of the Americans and French had been aroused.[1] After it was all over Hankey sent Lloyd George a warm commendation of the work of his two assistants Launcelot Storr and G. M. Evans, who had been joint secretaries of the Cabinet Strike Committee.[2] It was this

[1]All these incidents are recorded in Hankey's diary for 12th Oct. 1919. The original of the agreement, drafted by Hankey, which ended the Railway Strike is in Lloyd George papers F/24/1/13.

[2]Hankey to Lloyd George 9th Oct. 1919. Lloyd George papers F/24/1/14.

loyalty to his staff which gained for Hankey their respect and devotion.

Towards the end of November Hankey recorded that he was 'having a harassing time working out the establishment of the Cabinet Office'. His main difficulty was 'to reconcile the good of the public service' – presumably by cutting down staff – 'with the interests of those who have served me faithfully and well during the war'.[1] One of the few persons whom Hankey took completely into his confidence about his troubles over the future of the secretariat was his old friend Esher. He regarded 'a permanent and expert Cabinet Secretariat' as a 'sheet anchor' of the country, and urged Hankey not 'to weaken' – as though there was the slightest likelihood of his doing so on such a matter.[2] Hankey replied at length outlining the plans he was presenting to the Treasury to keep 'the C.I.D. staff practically intact', though giving no guarantee 'to keep it always engaged on C.I.D. work'. He was also scheming to provide 'the nucleus of a real Imperial Office', a Home Branch and a League of Nations branch; and he was optimistic of getting what he wanted despite opposition 'in certain quarters' – notably the Asquith liberal Press – to the idea of a Cabinet Secretariat.[3] That his optimism was fully justified is shown by a letter he sent to Lloyd George early in the following year enclosing the agreement approved by the Treasury 'after prolonged and frequent discussion'. The secretariat was to be placed 'on a permanent and established basis', and its branches were to be organised exactly as he had written to Esher three months earlier. Though Hankey was to have an even harder fight to preserve the secretariat after the fall of Lloyd George this was a substantial victory for him.[4]

With the railway strike over Hankey tackled Lloyd George about future Cabinet business, enclosing the minutes of three meetings held while the Prime Minister had been away. The most important issues were, he wrote, the reduction of our forces in Mesopotamia, and the desire of the Admiralty and War Office to censor or suppress the second report of the Dardanelles Commission. The latter proposal, Hankey pointed out, must be rejected – because Bonar Law had made a categorical promise in the House that it should be published.[5] In

[1]Diary 23rd Nov. 1919. [2]Esher to Hankey 25th Nov. 1919. Esher papers.
[3]Hankey to Esher 27th Nov. 1919. *ibid.*
[4]Hankey to Lloyd George 28th Feb. 1920 enclosing Hankey to Secretary of Treasury of same date. Lloyd George papers F/24/2/12.
[5]Hankey to Lloyd George 17th Oct. 1919. Lloyd George papers F/24/1/17.

fact when it did appear it aroused little comment – no doubt because the public was no longer interested in wartime controversies.[1] Hankey was also deeply involved at this time in the arguments which arose out of the writing of both the military and naval official histories. On 28th October he circulated a note on the dismissal of John Fortescue as official military historian – because he had published a controversial article entitled 'Lord French 1914' in the *Quarterly Review*. The Cabinet had approved Fortescue's dismissal on the grounds that 'the official history, when published, should be considered as thoroughly impartial', and Hankey was given the distasteful job of getting rid of a distinguished scholar whom he liked and respected.[2] Then trouble blew up between the Admiralty and Sir Julian Corbett, and between the Admiralty and Churchill over the first volume of 'Naval Operations'; but although Hankey circulated a long paper on the subject we cannot here go into the details of these historical dissensions.[3]

Stimulated by its busy secretary the Cabinet now settled down to deal with matters which had been thrust aside during the railway strike – especially Finance. The most troublesome issue was the reduction of military expenditure on overseas commitments – notably Mesopotamia; and concrete action was made much more difficult by President Wilson's illness. 'We cannot get on with the Turkish treaty', complained Hankey in his diary, 'until we know whether the Americans will accept a mandate in Turkey; and although all Americans tell us privately that the Senate will never agree to do so, no-one can say so officially'. Meanwhile the rise of the Nationalist movement in Turkey under Kemal Pasha was 'growing apace', and the British government felt obliged to retain large forces in that country as well as in Palestine, Mesopotamia and Egypt. This of course ran totally counter to the government's search for economies. Moreover, as Hankey far-sightedly remarked, an 'incident in Anatolia' with the Nationalists 'might plunge us into renewed hostilities'. He seems to have been almost alone in appreciating the very real dangers developing in Turkey at this time; and he was of course justified in attributing British troubles, at any rate in part, to the paralysis of the executive authority in America.

[1]Cmd. 371 (1919). [2]C.P. 5 of 28th Oct. 1919. Cab. 24/92.
[3]For the benefit of scholars who may wish to follow up this matter C.P. 9 of 28th Oct. and C.P. 202 of 26th Nov. 1919 (both in Cab. 24/92) mark the initial stages of what proved a very prolonged controversy over the official naval history.

On 23rd October Lloyd George, Bonar Law, Churchill and Hankey conferred on the size of the future Cabinet, and they agreed that the War Cabinet should come to an end on 27th and should be replaced by a body of twenty members. When it was proposed to have only twelve Hankey 'made an appeal for the larger number' on the ground that with only a dozen Cabinet Ministers 'all those left out would be discontented, and the Coalition would be weakened'.[1] He thought that his advocacy of the larger number 'came at the right moment', and that 'the reasons for it were overwhelming', since people like the Geddes brothers and Horne would never continue to support the Coalition unless they were in the Cabinet. Many years later, when Leo Amery was writing his memoirs, Hankey told him that 'there was talk of [having] both Empire and Home Sections . . . and a Cabinet of twelve', a proposal which arose out of the report of Haldane's committee on the machinery of government of 1918. But 'with a Coalition Government Ll. G. could not see his way to satisfy personal ambitions with less than twenty'[2] – which had in fact been his own contemporary argument in favour of the larger body.

One change made when the War Cabinet was abolished was to cause Hankey a great deal of trouble. The rule that when a Minister resigned he 'was charged with the duty of recovering their [Cabinet] papers' was, he wrote some five years later, 'deliberately waived . . . and the old pre-war rule was restored – [namely] that Cabinet documents (other than those of the C.I.D.) were the personal property of Ministers'.[3] It is a fair deduction that Lloyd George himself, and probably Churchill as well, insisted on this change with an eye on the histories of the period they would one day write or were already engaged on.

As the War Cabinet now passes out of our story it may interest the reader to have a few statistics concerning it. Hankey evidently had these prepared by the Cabinet Office Registry for his own use many years later. Between 8th December 1916 and 27th October 1919 the War Cabinet met 625 times, excluding all the Paris Peace Conference sessions. Between August 1914 and February 1920 Hankey himself

[1]Diary 26th Oct. 1919. The twelve were to have been Lloyd George, Bonar Law, Balfour, Curzon, Milner, Churchill, Shortt, Long, Montagu, Chamberlain, Barnes and Birkenhead.

[2]Hankey to Amery 11th Sept. 1946.

[3]Hankey to MacDonald 4th Oct. 1924. MacDonald papers 1/195.

attended 600 Cabinet and War Cabinet meetings, excluding those whose minutes were recorded in the 'A' and 'X' series.[1] But if one includes the meetings of all the other committees on high level policy (War Council, Dardanelles Committee, War Policy Committee etc.), the Inter-Allied Conferences held during the war, and the meetings of the various bodies concerned with the Peace Conference (British Empire Delegation, Council of Four etc.) the grand total attended by Hankey during the same period reaches the staggering figure of 1,240. How many millions of words were recorded by him in the minutes and *procès-verbaux* of all those meetings can only be guessed, but study of many specimens suggests that it cannot have been less than five million and probably was far higher.

On the very evening that the decision regarding the future Cabinet was taken the government was defeated on a comparatively minor issue – the Aliens Restriction Bill.[2] Lloyd George was 'less upset' than Hankey expected, and after Law had dropped in at No. 10 to explain how the defeat had come to pass he and Hankey joined the Churchills at Covent Garden opera house to hear the American Lowell Thomas give one of his highly embellished, and very profitable, 'travelogues' on Allenby's campaign and Lawrence's part in the Arab revolt.[3] On arrival Lloyd George received what Hankey called 'a real popular ovation'. But what probably gave Hankey greater satisfaction than either this evidence of Lloyd George's continued hold on the public or the American lecturer's pretentious histrionics was Churchill's expression of the opinion that he 'should be the only secretary at the new Cabinet, with no assistants'; and that he should 'be made a Privy Counsellor in order to restore the old principles of secrecy'.[4]

The crisis over the government's defeat was successfully surmounted next day, when the leading critics of the Bill in question were invited

[1]See Vol. I, pp. 354 and 547 ff.

[2]Parl. Deb., Commons, Vol. 120, Cols. 183–242 and 1349–1419.

[3]Lowell Thomas used an opera set for the Moonlight-on-the-Nile scene from 'Joseph and his Brethren' for the *mise-en-scène* of his lecture, which was preceded by a prologue including a Dance of the Seven Veils. A musical setting for the Mahomedan call to prayer, composed by Mrs. Thomas, was sung off stage to herald her husband's entry, and the band of the Welsh Guards provided incidental music of appropriate atmosphere. This exotic performance, advertised as 'America's Tribute to British Valour', attracted huge audiences and after a fortnight at Covent Garden was transferred to the Albert Hall. *The Times*, 10th and 23rd Oct. 1919.

[4]Diary 26th Oct. 1919.

to meet Lloyd George and other Ministers. According to Hankey they soon 'came to terms'.

With the main issues out of the way Hankey at once set about reorganising his own office to meet the new conditions. He proposed to Lloyd George that, in addition to normal Cabinet meetings, daily conferences should be held to deal with routine business. The minutes of those conferences would be circulated to Ministers, and 'taken note' of in the next Cabinet minutes. 'I have been steering Cabinet business in this direction for a long time', he remarked in his diary; and it is a fact that he had always rebelled against Cabinet time being taken up by matters of minor importance.

In the same diary entry Hankey recorded that Balfour had consulted him about whether 'he should do as the King wants and take a peerage'. Hankey's reply was that Lloyd George had already asked him whether Balfour would accept such an honour, and that he had given an emphatic opinion that it would be declined. Balfour replied 'that this was his own instinct', and he was 'very anxious not to be burdened with the heavy task of leading the House of Lords'. In fact he remained a commoner until 1922.

The revised instructions to the Secretary of the Cabinet were approved at the first meeting of the new Cabinet on 4th November with only slight amendments to Hankey's draft.[1] Next day he circulated those instructions as the first of a new series of Cabinet papers – the C.P. Series, which rapidly assumed vast proportions.[2] But instead of quoting the official instructions, which can readily be looked up, we will here reproduce Hankey's diary entry, which gives a more intimate picture of the new system and how it actually worked.

*Diary 9th November 1919*

We have now reverted to the old Cabinet of 20 with a Secretary. . . . I am not permitted to have an Assistant Secretary in the room with me, and I am only supposed to record Conclusions and nothing of the discussion. According to Lloyd George the Cabinet is only intended to meet about once a week. It has already met four times [in] the first week. This makes the work very hard for me, and has compelled me entirely to reorganise my office. It is, of course, impossible to write down Conclusions only, because what actually

[1]Cabinet 1(19) Conclusion 3 of 4th Nov. 1919. Cab. 23/18.

[2]C.P. 1 of 5th Nov. 1919. Cab. 24/92. By the end of 1922 the C.P. Series had reached No. 4,379 and Hankey then restarted the series at the beginning of every year.

happens in a Cabinet of 20 is that someone drops a suggestion, later on someone reverts to it and perhaps amplifies it, and then it becomes the Conclusion. No-one knows exactly what the Conclusion is, and the Secretary only discovers it by piecing together the bits. Churchill attacked me for taking full notes the other day, and I had to explain this to him, but I told him I would destroy my pencil notes, which is now being done. As a matter of fact I work the whole of the important points of the discussion into the Conclusion. I cannot bear a bald Conclusion such as 'the Cabinet approved the proposals of the First Lord of the Admiralty in regard to the Baltic', and, although I am limited by the rules under which I have to work, I take very great pains to make the Conclusions intelligible and dignified. We took the actual decision about the Cabinet on Tuesday Nov. 4th. They decided that the Conclusions should be sent only to those who have to act on them, or are departmentally concerned, and not to the Cabinet generally, nor to those who have played the most important part in the discussion. All this week we have been discussing the unemployment donation – rather a dull subject, but difficult. I am sure the decision not to continue it, except for sailors and soldiers is a right one, but I don't know if Labour will stand it. Luckily there is very little unemployment. . . . I only succeeded in getting home 2 nights last week, and Adeline and I mean seriously to start house-hunting in London.

Observing that the new instructions to Hankey were in fact framed with the object of reducing the likelihood of leakages regarding Cabinet discussions it is ironical that one day after they came into force the Press should have reported the proceedings of the Cabinet Committee on Ireland. Hankey at once wrote to Lloyd George that, as no Minutes had been produced on the evening of the discussion, the leak must have come from someone present at the meeting. He therefore enclosed the draft of a letter for the Prime Minister to send to the Ministers concerned (Long, Birkenhead, Auckland Geddes,[1] Worthington-Evans[2] and Hewart[3] the Attorney-General) impressing on them 'the serious results which may ensue from the premature divulgence of the Committee's deliberations'. But Lloyd George seems to have been understandably averse to taking his colleagues to task like naughty schoolboys, and not

[1]See respectively Vol. I, pp. 349, 237 and 480, *notes*.

[2]Sir Laming Worthington-Evans (1868–1931). Politician (Cons.). Parliamentary Secretary to Ministry of Munitions 1916–18. Minister of Blockade 1918 and of Pensions 1919–20. Secretary of State for War 1921–22 and 1924–29. Postmaster-General 1923–24.

[3]Gordon Hewart, 1st Viscount 1940 (1870–1943). Lawyer and politician (Lib.). Solicitor-General 1916–19. Attorney-General 1919-22; Lord Chief Justice 1922-40.

to have sent the letter.[1] Such troubles none the less continued. On 8th December the *Daily Mail* published verbatim a letter dated 20th November which Hankey had sent to all government departments on the subject of reductions of staff; and when early in the following year the *Daily Express* published the conclusions of the draft declaration on Economic Conditions, a secret document approved by the Supreme Council of the Allies, Tom Jones in Hankey's absence proposed that the Law Officers should force the paper to reveal its source.[2] Although such drastic action was not taken these leakages caused the government to set up an inter-departmental committee to investigate and report on the matter. It was that body's report which led to the passing of the Official Secrets Act, 1920, which revised and strengthened the Act of 1911 but did not replace it. Those two Acts, as amended again in 1939, still remain in force – despite the fact that they have constantly been infringed by politicians, from Churchill in the 1930s to Anthony Nutting in 1967.[3] The Cabinet Office Registry evidently kept a careful record of the more important leakages. In 1919 there were five, and the following two years each produced six; and so it went on right to the end of Hankey's time as Secretary. Some were, of course, more serious than others; and in a few instances they were conclusively attributed to Ministers themselves. But in only one case, and that a seemingly trivial one – Edgar Lansbury's use in 1934 of some Cabinet documents in his biography of his father George Lansbury – was a prosecution initiated.[4]

[1]Hankey to Lloyd George 5th Nov. 1919. Lloyd George papers F/24/1/33.

[2]Jones to Lloyd George 8th March 1920. *ibid.* F/24/2/15.

[3]For an admirable summary of the history of the Official Secrets Acts, and of their working see leading article by Professor Hugh Thomas in *The Times* (Saturday Review) of 17th Feb. 1968.

[4]A schedule of leakages from 1919 to end of 1933 is in Cab. 21/457 (another copy in Cab. 21/391). Cab. 21/443 contains correspondence on leakages. Examples of Ministers leaking information to the Press are Bonar Law's letter to *The Times* of 30th Jan. 1923 about the American debt settlement (signed 'Colonial'). See Robert Rhodes James, *Memoirs of a Conservative* (Weidenfeld and Nicolson, 1969), p. 142, about what the author calls 'this extraordinary episode'. This source is henceforth cited as James, *Davidson.* Also on 21st Jan. 1926 *The Times* carried an article based on information supplied by Neville Chamberlain. Though the King expressed 'much concern', and Stamfordham sought Hankey's advice on the matter, it was never pursued because Chamberlain declared there had been 'no leakage'. (Cab. 21/443). Perhaps the worst case of all arose in 1931, when the *Daily Herald* for 24th August carried details of how Cabinet members had actually voted on the proposed

At the time when Hankey was plagued by leakages of secret information to the Press he was also being pestered by Lord Riddell to relax war time restrictions on the release of government papers marked 'not to be published before a certain date'. He brought the matter before the Cabinet, which finally agreed to the proposal of the powerful chairman of the Newspaper Proprietors' Association – who had of course long been an intimate friend of Lloyd George's.[1]

The new Cabinet had not been long in existence before Hankey was involved in another of his periodic brushes with Stamfordham, who wrote to protest at 'the inordinate length' of the King's speech for the Prorogation of Parliament, and at the delay in getting it to the Monarch. Hankey replied that this was the first time his office had anything to do with such a speech, and that he himself had merely acted as a Post Office for the departments. Nor had he anything to do with its composition, which had been the work of a Cabinet Committee under Balfour. Finally he had 'never heard of His Majesty's command that the speech should be as short as possible'.[2] Hankey was always very quick with his ripostes to the Private Secretary's complaints. In the following year, when Hankey forwarded the draft of the speech for the same occasion, Stamfordham requested alterations and again protested about it reaching him so late. Hankey replied, patiently, that as it was the practice not to forward the speech until all Ministers' comments had been received he was 'in the Ministers' hands'; but if Stamfordham desired it he would ask the Prime Minister's permission to forward the first draft – a proposal which was accepted by both parties.[3]

*Diary 16th November 1919*

The new Cabinet system is now in full working order. We had three meetings this week, as well as a great number of conferences. Both Lloyd George and I were very exhausted at the end, but I had to go to town all the same yesterday as I am engaged on my new organisation and estimates and Saturday

---

cut in unemployment benefit. MacDonald apparently knew who the culprit was, but again the matter was not pursued. Rupert Howorth, Hankey's deputy, was 'doubtful whether so flagrant a case will ever recur'. This leakage and the prosecution of Edgar Lansbury are described in Cab. 21/443.

[1]C.P. 163 of 29th Nov. 1919. Cab. 24/93.

[2]RA GV K692/36 of 20th Dec. 1919.

[3]RA GV K692/44 of 22nd Nov. 1920 and K692/83 and /84 of 13th and 14th Dec. 1920. Also K692/85.

is the only day for such matters. The Cabinet has dealt with the interminable Russian question, Irish policy (approving in principle the Cabinet Committee's scheme for two parliaments, for Ulster and the rest of Ireland respectively, and a common Council with limited powers). Housing, Unemployment Insurance (adopted in principle), renewal of restrictions on whiskey and other important matters. The writing of the Minutes covering such a wide ground is a very exacting job. To make a mere summarised record of what each person said is very easy. But this I am not allowed to do. To write intelligent Conclusions, which will convey to those who were not present, and to posterity, some idea of the questions at issue is not easy. The discussion with 20 people present is very diffuse and every minute someone raises some new departmental aspect cutting across the whole discussion. What I actually do is to write notes of everything that is said, mark in the margin anything of importance, or which is likely to lead to a Conclusion, and mark in double lines anything which I feel sure is a Conclusion. No-one ever knows what the Conclusions were until they get my minutes. I interpret very widely my instructions to record Conclusions only, and really give a summary of all the arguments leading to the Conclusion. I have been congratulated by several Ministers on the value of my Minutes. It seems to have been decided not to make me a Privy Counsellor, as a question has been answered in the House of Commons last week to the effect that the Secretary of the Cabinet is trusted exactly as was the Secretary to the C.I.D. Of course I shall respect this confidence, in or out of office, so long as necessary for the safety of the country, or for the stability of the Government, but I do not regard myself or my heirs to be bound by an oath that I have never been asked to take, and my memoirs will be the more interesting for my not having taken the Privy Counsellor's oath.[1] Otherwise I am not sure that I should feel free to keep this diary. Rather a scandalous circumstance arose in connection with the Channel Tunnel. A parliamentary deputation had been promised an interview on the subject, but, as it was on the Agenda, the P.M. brought it up at the fag end of an exhausting and exceptionally long Cabinet meeting on Ireland, just as everyone was getting up to go to the Guildhall to the lunch to Poincaré. Although this question has at least 14 times been turned down by Parliament, and has been rejected 6 times by Committees after prolonged inquiry, including the Committee of Imperial Defence in 1907 and 1914, the P.M. thought fit, without any discussion, and without hearing the views of a single expert, to take opinions. To my

[1]Here Hankey added, evidently at a later date, 'But if ever I write them they will be discreet, and I hope no-one will publish this diary for 50 years at least.' In the shaky hand of his very old age is written 'No publication for 60 years or so'.

surprise the Cabinet were . . . almost unanimously in favour, Balfour alone saying that his opinion was shaken by a letter I had written to him. This, and a few rather hedging utterances by other Ministers about agreeing, provided there was no risk to national safety, enabled me to record a very feeble support in the official Conclusion.[1] The P.M. and Bonar Law both thought they had secured complete agreement, but I saw them both before the deputation on the following day and convinced them that it would be unsafe to agree without much fuller inquiry into the project. Mr. Balfour, Sir Eric Geddes, and Dr. Addison all came to me to say they hoped I had not recorded a decision in favour of the Channel tunnel. What power lies in the draftsman's hands! I could easily, had I been a Channel tunnel man, have rushed the situation, recorded a decision, and induced the P.M. to sell the fact to the deputation. In fact he told me afterwards that I only had induced him not to do so. As matters stand I may be able to block the whole thing, . . . I will stop at nothing to prevent what I believe to be a danger to this country. People have forgotten that 21 years ago our Mediterranean fleet was cleared for action against France; that 18 years ago during the Boer War there was real danger of a Continental coalition against us; that 18 months ago we were seriously discussing the evacuation of the Channel ports. France may become hostile, Germany or a Bolshevist state may get the other side of the Channel, or the League of Nations may become a mere coalition against us. How should we like the Channel tunnel then? The increased range of modern guns which can fire across the Channel, aircraft, and the possibility of using 'tanks' walking out of barges as intended in the landing on the coast of Flanders have infinitely increased the risk of a raid – always considered possible. And a successful raid on the British end of the tunnel converts a raid into an invasion . . .

On 23rd Hankey recorded that the Home Ports Defence Committee, of which he was chairman, had held a meeting to consider the measures to safeguard the country 'if the tunnel is built'. He then put up strong arguments against the project, and was 'hoping to kill the tunnel in spite of the bias in favour of it.' All his life, both as an official and after his retirement, Hankey remained resolutely opposed to the idea of a Channel tunnel; and each time the matter came before the C.I.D. or the Cabinet he resurrected the opinions which he had expressed against it in years gone by.[2] There seems to have been no issue except the

[1]C.P. 88 of 10th Nov. 1919 merely circulates the report of the C.I.D. of October 1916. Cab. 24/92.

[2]Hankey's 'Magnum Opus' contains many papers written by him every time the Channel Tunnel question was raised e.g. his 'Note' of 10th Nov. 1919 in Cab. 63/25; his Memo. of 28th Jan. 1920 in Cab. 63/26; his summary of the history of the

preservation of Maritime Belligerent Rights by Britain, of which more later, over which he felt more strongly.

We have seen how Hankey corresponded with Esher about the future of the Cabinet and its secretariat. On 29th November Esher sent him a long and woolly letter about current problems and future policies, much of it in critical vein. This stimulated Hankey to set out his own views on many issues, including the League of Nations – 'an impossible conception' which would 'never have worked even if it had passed the [U.S.] Senate' because of the rigid obligations it imposed on its members. Had it been made a purely consultative body like the C.I.D., and its business conducted on lines analagous to those employed between Britain and the Dominions, Hankey would, he said, 'probably have been Secretary-General'. But the 'theorists' like Lord Robert Cecil, President Wilson, House and Smuts had been determined to adopt 'the rigid constitution'. Wilson's principle of 'self-determination' had, Hankey pointed out, produced serious problems for Britain and her allies in many areas – notably the Adriatic, where it conflicted directly with the promises made to Italy in the secret Treaty of London of 1915. Nor could he understand what Esher wanted done in the Middle East. We could not 'leave the Turks' in Mesopotamia and Palestine, and he himself hoped to see created 'a strong, autonomous Arab state or group of states'. Though he 'loathed military commitments' such as had fallen to us in those countries, the refusal of the Americans to accept a mandate, and the alleged desire of the inhabitants that Britain should be the mandatory, made the commitments unavoidable – at any rate for a time. And he foresaw, correctly, that 'we may have a pretty kettle of fish with the French in Syria'. Esher's somewhat surprising attack on the Cabinet and C.I.D. secretariat, among whom he had declared that there was 'no tradition, no continuity, no loyalty and no *esprit de corps*', provoked an angry refutation from Hankey, who pointed out how well he had been served in the past and how he was trying to secure equally good service for the future. As regards the machinery of government his strong preference was for a large Cabinet 'which does not meet often' but would be served by 'intermediate conferences' such as the C.I.D. which would carry out all the detailed work for the Cabinet. This would ensure that all Ministers, whether in

---

project of 10th June 1920 in Cab. 63/28; his 'Observations' of 21st June 1924 in Cab. 63/36; and later references in Cab. 63/42 and 43.

the Cabinet or not, were kept properly informed on matters which concerned their departments. Only on the proposal to keep an Imperial Cabinet in being was Hankey in accord with his erstwhile supporter, whom he described as being 'crabbing without being constructive'.[1]

Esher took the foregoing explosion in good part, rejoicing that his protégé of many years standing was evidently 'as keen as ever after the wear and tear of the past five years'. He proposed among other things that 'all idea of a Minister of Defence' – which Hankey had no intention of pressing – should be 'put aside'; and that the Cabinet Secretariat should be freed 'once and for all . . . from Treasury control and regulation' – which, however much Hankey might have liked it, was of course quite impracticable for constitutional reasons.[2] Hankey did not continue the argument, but he took one piece of advice given by Esher – namely to keep Smuts informed of what was happening at home. His next letter to the General accordingly described the reorganisation of the Cabinet and its Secretariat and expressed the hope that for the next Imperial Conference each Dominion Prime Minister would bring 'an official who will be associated with me in the secretarial work of the Imperial Cabinet'. If a Resident Minister were appointed to London he proposed he should have under him an official who would be given 'the run of the Cabinet Office'. Turning to the future of the Coalition government he contradicted reports of 'internal bickering and difficulty', and expressed the belief that 'they are quite firm for years to come' – a rare example of Hankey twisting facts and making a rash prophecy. As regards America he correctly reported that President Wilson 'is worse than is generally admitted', and his collapse had stultified all prospect of 'decisive action' – notably about the League of Nations. Finally he summed up the political situation in France ('almost reactionary'), Germany ('in much sounder condition than she was'), Italy ('a very serious situation' caused by 'the failure of the Army and Navy to obey the Government'), and Russia ('in course of time a moderate Government . . . will spring up'). Progress with the Turkish treaty was not yet clear enough for him to write about it, so he promised a separate letter on that subject.[3] A fortnight later he

[1]Hankey to Esher 1st Dec. 1919. Parts holograph Esher Papers.

[2]Esher to Hankey 7th Dec. 1919. Esher papers. Part printed in *Journals*, IV, pp. 250–1.

[3]Hankey to Smuts 18th Dec. 1919. Smuts Archive.

circulated a note to the Cabinet proposing to regularise the constitutional position with regard to communications between the League of Nations and the self-governing Dominions.[1]

Hankey marked the close of a very busy year with a long diary entry recapitulating the events of the previous month.

*Diary 29th December 1919*

The last month before Xmas was too busy for me to write my diary. . . . The Cabinet was meeting 3 times a week, and, under the new régime, this keeps me very busy. The main subject was the Irish Bill. I have not had much to do with the fashioning of this, which was done by a Cabinet Ctee. under Walter Long. Philip Kerr was the originator of the general scheme and has piloted it through its preliminary stages. It is a very ingenious scheme, but, as I anticipated, has not been well received in Ireland, nor as well as had been expected in U.S.A. In these circumstances I doubt if any good will come of it, and I adhere to my original view that it was premature to bring it up so soon. The next most important event of the last month has been the visit of Clemenceau to London shortly before Xmas [11th–14th Dec.]. I accompanied Lloyd George to meet him at the station and the old boy seized me by the hand and said 'This is a great friend of mine'. He was in great form all through the conference, saying witty things every moment, in spite of the fact that he had had a bad fall on board a destroyer on passage, and, as it subsequently transpired, had broken a rib. He discussed French politicians very frankly with Lloyd George. 'Barthou'[2] he said 'would murder his own mother. Briand would not murder his own mother, but he would murder someone else's mother!' Berthelot,[3] who is now much in the ascendant in France, came with him, and was particularly civil to me. . . . The main lines of the Turkish Treaty were remitted to him and Lord Curzon to work out for consideration, and he came over to London again at the beginning of Xmas week for this purpose. The Turkish Treaty is another

[1]C.P. 393 of 6th Jan. 1920. Cab. 24/95.

[2]Louis Barthou. French lawyer and politician (1862–1934). Member of Clemenceau's cabinet 1906–9 and of Briand's 1909–10. Prime Minister 1913. War Minister under Briand 1920 and Minister for Justice under Poincaré 1922 and again 1926. Senator 1922. Foreign Minister under Doumergue 1934. Victim of the assassination of Alexander I of Yugoslavia, whom he had gone to meet at Marseilles 9th Oct. 1934.

[3]Philippe Berthelot. French diplomat (1866–1934). Director of political affairs and a principal counsellor of Briand during World War I. As Secretary-General, Foreign Ministry 1920 he played a large part in post-treaty negotiations, notably over Reparations. A supporter of Briand's attempted rapprochement with Germany. Resigned because of involvement with his brother in collapse of Industrial Bank of Indo-China. Secretary-General again in left-wing coalition 1924–32.

subject that has engaged very close attention. Just before Clemenceau's visit . . . Lloyd George, or rather Bonar Law, gave a lunch party at which, besides the two mentioned, Mr. Balfour, Lord Curzon, Lord Milner (on the eve of his departure on the Egyptian Commission[1]), Philip Kerr and myself were present. The general view was in favour of internationalisation of the Straits; the Turks to be turned out of Constantinople, except perhaps for a 'Vatican' for the Sultan; some system of placing the Turks under tutelage, either by means of concessions to the various Powers, which might either be territorial or in respect of specific services such as Customs, finance, army, gendarmerie, railways etc.; Armenia to be looked after by the French who will have Cilicia and Syria; while we have the mandates for Palestine and Mesopotamia. Clemenceau however was now advocating the Turks remaining in Constantinople, though he did not press it, and the proceedings were perfectly amicable. We also discussed the Adriatic question with Scialoja,[2] the Italian foreign minister, a mere nonentity, who was on a visit to London. No serious progress was made as Scialoja could not speak with authority. In addition we secured the adoption by our allies of a Russian policy practically identical with that which we have ourselves already adopted – i.e. to keep the Bolshevists in a ring fence; not to send further support in troops, supplies, or money to Denikin and the other anti-Bolshevists, beyond what is already promised. Clemenceau induced us to agree in principle to a strong Poland, as a safeguard against Germany. Personally I doubt if Poland is of much value, as her people is [are?] unstable. If the policy is to be carried through I incline to the view adumbrated by Loraine,[3] one of my foreign office staff in Paris, who came to see me on Dec. 23rd on his return from a mission to Buda Pesth with George Clerk and advocated the formation of a great block of states – Poland, Czecho-Slovakia, Hungary, Roumania, Jugo-Slavia, and Greece (probably also Bulgaria as a counterpoise to Germany). Ll. G. has taken a most violent objection to Sir Eyre

[1]Milner, as Colonial Secretary, was in Egypt November 1919–March 1920 to study and recommend on the future relations of that country with Britain. After prolonged negotiations with the Nationalist leaders he reported in favour of independence for Egypt, subject to certain safeguards, and an alliance with Britain; but the proposal was rejected by the Cabinet in 1920, though subsequently accepted without the guarantee Milner considered essential.

[2]Vittorio Scialoja. Italian lawyer and politician (1856–1933). Senator 1904. Minister of Justice 1909–10; Foreign Minister 1919–20. Delegate at Peace Conference 1919 and at League of Nations 1921–32.

[3]Later Sir Percy Loraine (1880–1961). Diplomat. Minister to Persia 1921–26, and at Athens 1926–29. High Commissioner for Egypt and Sudan 1929–33. Ambassador in Turkey 1933–39 and in Rome 1939–40.

Crowe,[1] who has represented us at the Peace Conference since September. This is most unjustifiable as Crowe, who is after all only an official and lacks the responsibility of a Minister, has represented us with great dignity and ability. The ostensible cause of Ll. G's objection is the harshness of some of the notes sent to Germany. In fact Ll. G. was very excited and (quite unnecessarily) jumped to the conclusion that Germany was going to refuse to ratify the Treaty. One Saturday night [Dec. 6th], after he had been speaking at Manchester in the afternoon, he insisted on holding a Cabinet conference at 9.30 p.m. and Balfour, Curzon, Churchill and Bonar Law with Kerr and myself, had to stay in town. Kerr had to leave after midnight by special train, destroyer, and motor car for Paris – luckily Ll. G. pitched on him and not me, as it was a fearful night! . . .

Hankey ended the entry by recapitulating his opposition to the Channel Tunnel, the trouble he had with his 'old enemy the Official History of the War', and the effects of the reorganisation of his office on the staff which had served him so loyally throughout the war; but the reader is already familiar with all these matters.

[1] 1864–1925. Diplomat. Assistant Under-Secretary of State 1912. Minister Plenipotentiary for Peace Conference 1919. Permanent Under-Secretary for Foreign Affairs 1920. A strong advocate for intervention with France and Russia in 1914 and always a powerful supporter of British imperial interests.

*Chapter 6*

# Europe in Disarray. January-April 1920

At the beginning of 1920 the British government was faced by six major problems of foreign policy, in all of which Hankey was involved. The first was the ratification of the peace treaty with Germany and the achievement of agreement on the sum to be paid by way of Reparations. Second came the peace treaty with Turkey, which had been gestating ever since the armistice with that country was signed at Mudros on 30th October 1918. Third stood the need for Britain to maintain a united front with France and Italy – despite the fact that the Paris Conference had revealed the full extent of the disagreements between them. Then there was the long-standing question of extricating ourselves from intervention in Russia, and of initiating the first steps towards the resumption of normal relations with the Soviets – probably by way of a trade agreement. This problem was intimately linked with future relations with Persia, the key to which lay of course in the British government's interest in her oil, and in fear of Russian penetration reviving 19th century apprehensions of a threat to India. Finally we had yet to come to terms with the rising tide of nationalism in Egypt, which had been governed under martial law ever since the riots of March 1919, and the consequential deportation of the nationalist leaders.

In addition to the problems of foreign policy the Cabinet had to devote much time to the civil strife in Ireland, and to the prevailing industrial unrest at home; while its Finance Committee was concurrently seeking ways and means of reducing government expenditure, especially on overseas commitments such as Mesopotamia. And in most cases the search for economy conflicted directly with the issues of foreign policy, which generally necessitated a British 'military presence' designed to secure special interests such as Mesopotamian and Persian oil and the uninterrupted use of the Suez Canal, or even to oversee the voting in the plebiscites in disputed areas designated in the Versailles Treaty.

We will first review Hankey's part in the attempted solution of the problems of foreign policy outlined above. The method adopted became known as 'Diplomacy by Conference' – a description which Hankey himself seems to have coined.[1] No less than 23 international conferences took place between the beginning of 1920 and the end of 1922. They were held to an accompaniment of resounding publicity; and they aroused expectations which were most unlikely to be fulfilled. Furthermore they produced a clash with the advocates of the 'old diplomacy'. These men were trained in the tradition of secret approaches and negotiations between the British envoys in foreign capitals, working to the broad directives issued by the Foreign Office, and the diplomats and politicians of the countries to which they were accredited. On the other hand historical precedents for the settlement by conference of international problems following on great wars existed in the meetings held in 1713–14 after the Treaty of Utrecht, and still more in those that took place in 1814–15 after the Congress of Vienna; and Lloyd George was, of course, a great believer in personal contact. That he was not unaware of the disadvantages of such methods is shown by his statement at one of the meetings to be discussed in this chapter that 'the real danger in conferences was that they lived in a world of illusions, and did not face facts. Conferences were inclined to think [that] when they had framed resolutions and adopted clauses they had solved difficulties'.[2] Hankey's support of Diplomacy by Conference plainly derived from the experience he had gained at the many inter-Allied meetings held during the war and at the Paris Peace Conference; and to him, as to Lloyd George, the extension of the same principles and practices into the first years of peace evidently appeared both logical and natural. Yet we can now see that this method of conducting foreign affairs possessed many disadvantages – not least of which was the strain it imposed on the statesmen involved and their personal advisers. Even Hankey, for all his abundant energy and remarkable stamina, soon began to experience exhaustion; and physically and mentally exhausted statesmen and administrators are not the best

[1]He used it as the title of the lecture he delivered at the British (now Royal) Institute of International Affairs in November 1920, which he later expanded in the book of the same title (Benn, 1946).

[2]D.B.F.P. 1st Series, Vol. VII, Document 13 Minute 3.

agents to find enduring solutions to intractable problems. Furthermore Curzon, who replaced Balfour as Foreign Secretary in October 1919 after having held the same office in an acting capacity since the previous January, was fundamentally uninterested in, and ignorant of current European problems such as the establishment of Poland's frontiers, the future of the Rhineland, Italian claims in the Adriatic and the eastern Mediterranean, and Reparations – all of which, as we have seen, were prominent in the deliberations of the Peace Conference. On the other hand Curzon was very knowledgeable and experienced in the affairs of the Orient, and it was he and Hankey who first foresaw the likelihood of a revivified Turkey contesting harsh peace terms, and appreciated the dangers inherent in the carve-up of Asia Minor between the victorious powers.[1] It thus came to pass that negotiations on the European problems devolved chiefly on Lloyd George himself, who frequently acted as his own Foreign Secretary; and he depended greatly on the advice of his closest associates such as Hankey and Philip Kerr. Though Hankey always maintained good personal relations with the officials of the department on whom the responsibility for foreign policy rested, the new diplomacy was unlikely to appeal to them.

On 8th January Hankey set off once again with Lloyd George and his usual entourage for Paris, where the Peace Conference was to be resumed. Hankey described the British delegation's main purposes as 'to settle once and for all the Adriatic question', and 'to settle the bases of the treaty of peace with Turkey'. After it was all over he added, despondently 'We have accomplished neither'.[2] Shortly before leaving London the Cabinet had considered the future ownership of Constantinople. At what Hankey described as 'a dramatic meeting' the decision was taken not 'to turn the Turks out' – despite Balfour having recently circulated a paper in favour of doing so.[3] Hankey attributed this decision which he deplored, to 'the back-stairs work' of Edwin Montagu, the Secretary of State for India, who 'through his cowardice has allowed Indian opinion to become seriously moved about it, and who got Henry Wilson to express some extraordinary military views'.[4] Lloyd George and Curzon had both been in favour of placing the

[1]Nicolson, *Curzon*, pp. 72–81, especially Curzon's minutes of 25th March and 18th April 1919 (p. 78).

[2]Diary 24th Jan. 1920. [3]C.P. 390 of 6th Jan. 1920. Cab. 24/95.

[4]Diary 24th Jan. 1920.

disputed city under international control, exercised through the League of Nations; but Montagu had argued that the expulsion of the Turks would have disastrous effects on the Moslem population in India. Hankey was sure that 'to keep the Sultan in Constantinople . . . will cause endless trouble', and considered that the stream of letters with which Montagu bombarded him on the subject were intended primarily for the eyes of 'Indians who make complaints about the [Turkish] treaty'. 'He may have a great deal to answer for one of these days', he prophesied; and in fact Montagu's attitude on this issue, and the clash it provoked with Curzon, culminated in his resignation from the government.[1] Lloyd George was of course greatly influenced by his long-standing Turkophobia, and by the spell which the plausible and persuasive Venizelos had cast over him; nor did Hankey escape the influence of the Greek patriot-politician. In retrospect it does however seem that if the plan for international control of Constantinople which Curzon had first adumbrated in November 1918, and resurrected early in 1920, had been accepted many later troubles would have been avoided.[2] As it was the Paris Conference made no progress at all with regard to the Turkish treaty, which never got beyond informal discussions with the French.

As to the Adriatic question, Hankey believed that, had it not been for Clemenceau's early departure from the conference, agreement would have been reached; for the new Italian Prime Minister, Nitti,[3] proved a good deal less intransigent than Orlando. 'After prolonged negotiations', wrote Hankey, 'we had persuaded Nitti . . . to accept a solution giving Fiume independence under the guarantee of the League of Nations'; and he went on to outline the various concessions offered to satisfy Italian claims. However 'at the very last session of the conference', he continued, 'the Jugo-Slav delegates[4] . . . under instruction

[1]Nicolson, *Curzon*, pp. 111–12 makes out a strong case to this effect, and confirms Hankey's view of Montagu's influence.

[2]The Curzon plan was rejected by the Cabinet on 6th Jan. 1920.

[3]Francesco S. Nitti (1868–1953). Politician (Dem.) and economist. Minister for Agriculture 1911–14 and for Finance 1917–19. Prime Minister 1919–20. Fled from Fascist Italy to France 1924. Arrested by Germans 1943 and deported. Senator 1948.

[4]These were N. Pasitch (see Vol. I, p. 259, *note*) and A. Trumbitch Yugo-Slav politician (1864–1938). Fled Austrian Empire before 1914 and set up Yugo-Slav Committee in London. Foreign Minister and delegate to Paris Peace Conference 1919. Resigned after Treaty of Rapallo Nov. 1920.

from their government, declined some of these terms'; whereupon Clemenceau told them that the only alternative was the enforcement of the Treaty of London of 1915 – which would of course, have been much less favourable to Yugo-Slavia. 'It was very unfortunate', concluded Hankey. 'We had established good relations with both sides, and in a day or two more could have effected an adjustment.'[1]

The only results accomplished in Paris were the ratification of the German treaty, at which Hankey was present; the forwarding to the Dutch government of a demand for the extradition of the Kaiser, which was rejected; and the compilation of a list of 888 Germans ('much too large a number' was Hankey's comment) whom the Allies proposed to bring to trial as 'war criminals'. The first steps towards establishing 'commercial relations with Russia' were also approved, and the decision was taken to supply arms to the Caucasian states, to whom formal recognition was to be accorded, 'as part of a policy of supporting the whole of the Border States from Finland to the Caucasus against Bolshevist aggression'.[2] One curious development was that Eric Geddes and Henry Wilson came specially to Paris with the object of frightening the government over the paucity of the military forces available at home (a mere 28 regular battalions) to cope with the anticipated industrial strife. Wilson privately told Hankey that even 'some of the Guards battalions are unreliable'; but the latter was 'unimpressed' by such alarmist views, and considered that the two visitors 'fairly had the "wind up"'. The Secret Service reports, he recorded, 'did not indicate an increase in the number of revolutionaries, or in the increase of the efficiency of their organisation'. Though aware of the unrest produced by shortage of housing and rising prices Hankey did not 'anticipate red revolution', because he had 'too much confidence in the collective good sense of my fellow countrymen'. None the less he felt obliged to recommend to Lloyd George that the troops to be sent to the plebiscitary areas should be reduced, and half a dozen battalions destined for Egypt, Palestine or India held at home. Tom Jones once again kept Hankey fully informed regarding industrial developments, and when the latter wrote from Paris describing the state of 'dreadful nerves' of the C.I.G.S. and suggesting various precautionary measures, Jones replied that he 'entirely agreed' with his Chief's view of the industrial outlook. It was fortunate that at such a time two such steady pairs of hands should have been holding the reins

[1]Diary 24th Jan. 1920. [2]*ibid.*

in Whitehall and Paris.[1] None the less the Supply and Transport Sub-Committee of the Cabinet, which had been formed early in 1919 with the object of organising the maintenance of essential services during a strike, continued its preparations; and Hankey's office, with its unrivalled knowledge of departmental responsibilities, placed all the experience gained in compiling and keeping up to date the War Book at the disposal of the Committee.

One other interesting point arises from Hankey's notes on the Paris discussions, namely that the agreement on Middle East oil, which had been accepted by the British and French departments concerned, failed for the second time to receive the approval of Clemenceau and Lloyd George.[2] Hankey wrote that the agreement 'would have put the whole of Mesopotamian and Persian oil into hotchpot with the various oil deposits under the Shell company'. France was to get an 18% share, but Hankey none the less liked the agreement because 'it brought about 50% of the oil production of the world under British control compared with 4% at present'. Lloyd George, however, 'felt an instinctive distrust of the whole thing. His points were that the oil of Mesopotamia ought to go to pay for Mesopotamia [presumably meaning the British occupation forces], . . . and not go into the bulging pockets of Marcus Samuel[3] and the shareholders of the Shell Company.' One feels that on this issue at least Lloyd George's instincts were sound.

While the Paris Conference was in session Paul Deschanel[4] was preferred to Clemenceau in the Presidential elections. Though the old Tiger took his fall with good humour ('How can I go to the Elysée without a wife?' he asked Lloyd George, adding with his customary witty cynicism, 'unless Poincaré will leave Henriette'). Hankey was deeply distressed at the French people's 'ingratitude', and considered their choice 'a rabbit' compared to his rival. He regarded Briand as largely responsible for the fall of the man who had saved France.[5] But,

[1] *Middlemas*, I, pp. 96–99. Also Jones to Hankey 15th Jan. and Hankey to Jones 17th Jan. 1920 from Claridge's Hotel, Paris. Jones papers.

[2] This was the Long-Bérenger Agreement of April 8th 1919. See D.B.F.P., First Series, Vol. IV, pp. 1089–95 regarding its signature and first withdrawal.

[3] 1853–1927. 1st Viscount Bearsted 1925. Joint founder of Shell Transport and Trading Company 1897.

[4] 1855–1922. French politician (Progressive Rep.) President of Chamber 1898–1902 and 1912–20. Elected President of Republic Feb. 1920 but resigned in Sept. on account of ill health.

[5] To Lady Hankey 18th and 19th Jan. 1920.

as an English statesman of comparable stature and achievement was to learn after another war, the electors in a liberal democracy do not willingly extend into peacetime the exceptional powers they are prepared to accord for the prosecution of a war. Hankey's final parting with Clemenceau when he left Paris on 21st January was affecting. 'You mustn't go without shaking me by the hand . . . I want you to remain my friend' said Clemenceau.[1] Obviously Hankey's affection and admiration were reciprocated.

On returning to London Hankey at once raised the question of reopening trade with Russia. The naval blockade in the Baltic had already been lifted, and he sought an early decision regarding whether the same steps were to be taken in the Black Sea – despite Admiralty objections on the grounds that Soviet arms and equipment would then certainly reach the Turkish nationalists.[2] But it was not until the San Remo conference of the following April that the decision 'to remove obstacles to trade with Russia' was actually taken.[3]

In February a very large week-end party at Cliveden, to which Adeline was invited as well as her husband and the Lloyd Georges, proved anything but enjoyable to two men whose most urgent need was rest. Hankey was irritated by 'a lot of silly women'; while Lloyd George, after worsting J. L. Garvin of *The Observer*, who made a strong attack on the Versailles Treaty, 'slipped off home' after generously offering to extricate Hankey by saying he needed his services. Hankey, however, refused to abandon his wife in strange and not very congenial society, and therefore reluctantly stayed on until the Monday morning.[4] We may here remark that Hankey never felt at ease in the magnificent setting provided by the Astors, as did Tom Jones; and that generally speaking he disliked the people he met there.

After a very busy week preparing for the start of the Parliamentary Session on 10th February, and taking a hand in drafting the King's speech, Hankey was once again immersed in international negotiations when the Peace Conference reopened in London on 12th, and he had to act 'to all intents and purposes as Secretary-General'. As however many of its Commissions remained in Paris he was faced by what he called 'mechanical difficulties' in producing orderly agendas and conclusions. The chief subjects were, once again, the Adriatic problem

[1]Diary 24th Jan. 1920.
[2]C.P. 499 of 23rd Jan. and C.P. 550 of 4th Feb. 1920. Cab. 24/96 and 24/97.
[3]Diary 30th May 1920. [4]*ibid.* 15th Feb. 1920.

and the Turkish treaty. He now missed 'the scintillating wit and liveliness of Clemenceau', and found Millerand[1] 'rather heavy' but 'not nearly as obstinate as I expected'. Solution of the Adriatic question was not made easier by what Hankey called 'a violent and terrifically long message of protest' from President Wilson refusing to accept the agreement reached between Lloyd George and Clemenceau in Paris, and threatening 'to disinterest himself in European affairs'.[2] Lloyd George described Wilson's conduct as 'trying to slip out through the back door' – in which there was at least an element of truth.[3] In the following week no less than 12 meetings of the Supreme Allied Council took place,[4] and better progress was made with the Turkish treaty. Hankey attributed this to the fact that he was now 'driving the conference'.

*Diary 22nd February 1920* [Sunday]
. . . The strain on my office is very heavy, and I have brought in as reinforcements Caccia and Abraham, who were with me at Versailles and Paris, both very good men . . . Last Wednesday [18th] after the evening meeting at about 7.30 p.m. Lloyd George turned to me and said 'Before to-morrow's meeting you might draft some Conclusions showing how we are as regards the Turkish Treaty'. 'All right' I said . . . and I carried off my private secretary [A. J. Sylvester] to dinner. We then returned and worked until midnight. In this time, with the aid of some notes given me by Philip Kerr, I dictated a synopsis of the whole treaty, inventing Conclusions where they had not already been reached. I sent it that night to Lord Curzon, who let me have it back with his suggestions first thing in the morning, and I had a second edition out by 11.30 a.m. This formed the basis of discussion until the end of the week, and last night [21st] I was able to send an approved version to the drafting Committee . . . This week we had to do without Millerand, who has gone back to Paris. Berthelot made a most efficient substitute. Nitti is still here. We all like him . . . In fact the friendly spirit of the conference has been most remarkable, in spite of the rivalries and conflicting ambitions of the Powers in Constantinople, Asia Minor and Syria . . .

[1]See Vol. I, p. 166, *note*.
[2]This telegram is not printed in *Foreign Relations, U.S.A.,* 1920 I, but on 9th February Lansing the Secretary of State telegraphed to Davis, Ambassador in London 'The President does not wish you to attend London meeting of Premiers in any capacity even if you should be invited'. *op. cit.*, p. 1.
[3]Diary 15th Feb. 1920.
[4]See D.B.F.P., 1st Series, Vol. VII, Ch. 1 for details of these meetings.

*29th February*
The Supreme Council of the Peace Conference has continued to meet all the week . . . We are making steady progress with the Turkish Treaty, though not as fast as I should like, and we have got Nitti and the Serbs to meet and discuss the Adriatic question together. They met by stealth at 10 Downing Street at my suggestion, since they cannot meet at a hotel without setting the Press speculating. [Hankey went on to complain about the conduct of the Press, and especially of *The Times*. Finding that the French were no longer 'leaking' information to them, as in Paris, they 'invented' the news. Hankey had 'to talk rather straight to Lord Riddell' about this.]

At the beginning of March Hankey was ordered ten days' 'rest cure', during which he received no papers. He was suffering again from abscesses in his gums, but under Adeline's care he made a quick recovery. The children being at the seaside he had her, for once, entirely to himself. 'Gardening and primrosing were our only diversions', he wrote; 'but we are always perfectly happy in each other's company'. In the middle of the month he wrote down his impressions of the recent negotiations.

*Diary 14th March 1920*
. . . Reviewing, as I can now do, our work at the Supreme Council from a detached point of view I can see that it has been spasmodic and badly organised. Lloyd George insisted on meetings of the Supreme Council twice a day. Often I had to invent work for them to do! But, most of these meetings had to be attended by experts, who were consequently unable to get on with the detailed work on the various Commissions, which provide the greater part of the Treaty. Day after day, for example, there were endless discussions on a great manifesto about the economic condition of Europe. This contained nothing which every well-informed person does not know, and nothing of permanent value. But, in order to secure agreement in every phase it took 4 or 5 days' work, and absorbed the energies of the experts who ought to have been giving all their time to the financial and economic clauses of the Turkish Treaty. Consequently, we are all behind-hand. The fact is that Lloyd George's erratic, inconsequent, and hasty methods are the negation of organisation. Owing to his personal habits (sleeping after lunch for instance) involving late evening meetings and very discursive talk on every question, he exhausts to an extraordinary degree not only his own colleagues and his immediate subordinates, but the whole executive of the state. He centralises far too much in himself, and thus cannot get through the work. What a difference it would make, if he would keep regular, consistent hours and work to a programme!

Plainly Hankey was becoming increasingly disturbed about the consequences of Lloyd George's method of conducting diplomacy – with scant regard for traditional usages, often without adequate preparatory groundwork, and in disregard of the accumulated knowledge and experience of the Foreign Office. His next diary entry shows that the slow progress made with the Turkish treaty, combined with increasing difficulties with the French, were steadily strengthening his misgivings.

*Diary 27th March 1920*

... [The French] have never in their hearts admitted the validity of the London Conference, and are perpetually taking the attitude that each decision is *ad referendum* to Paris. Only yesterday Malkin [Assistant Legal Adviser to the Foreign Office[1]] ... came over to tell me that Millerand had ordered the French member of the drafting Committee not to work on the Turkish treaty, as the London decisions were all likely to be upset by a report from Marshal Foch as to the means available for enforcing the treaty. This of course means that he intends to have Smyrna taken away from the Greeks. This is a very delicate point. Lord Curzon is as anti-Greek as he is anti-Turk, and does not want the Greeks in Smyrna any more than the French do. The Foreign Office, though on the whole phil-Hellene, does not want the Greeks in Smyrna. Our military people are all traditionally Turco-phile (God only knows why!) and anti-Greek. Lloyd George however is violently phil-Hellene and has committed himself deeply to Venizelos on the question of Smyrna. He takes the view that the Turks are moribund, and the Greeks the nation of the future. Even now, with their geographical position and control of their islands, their friendship in case of war may be valuable to a maritime power whose communications in the eastern Mediterranean are peculiarly open to attack from submarines lurking in the islands. As he puts it 'You never know when this little mouse may not serve to gnaw the rope that binds the British Empire.' But later he thinks that Greece, whose population increases rapidly, will become a great nation, and it will be a great thing for it to be known that it was Britain that founded her greatness in the Peace Conference of 1920. This seems sound to me, but I may be biassed, having always been phil-Hellene.

This is not the only question on which we are at loggerheads with the French. They never seem able to see eye to eye with us anywhere. We are perpetually having rows with [them] about the execution of the German treaty. The fact is that they wanted a stiffer treaty and we wanted an easier one. Moreover, from the first we always intended to ease up the execution

[1]See p. 77, *note*.

of the treaty if the Germans played the game. With the French, the exact opposite is the case. They are always trying to stiffen the treaty. Thus, last week, the Germans, after Kapp's revolution had failed,[1] wanted to send troops into the neutral zone to suppress a communist revolution in the Ruhr valley, though this was forbidden by the Treaty. We wanted to let them [do so]. The French first wanted to send in Allied troops to suppress the revolution and occupy the zone (their real reason was to get the coal!), and, when we refused, only agreed to let the Germans go in on condition that the Allies occupied Frankfurt and Stuttgart! Of course we refused this, as utterly provocative and tending to weaken the present German Government, which is a decent one . . . Still, the situation is difficult. What with our continual rows with the French; the entire withdrawal of the Americans from European affairs; the mechanical difficulties of conducting a Peace Conference with a Supreme Council under Lloyd George in London; a Foreign Ministers' Conference under Lord Curzon in London; an Ambassadors' Conference under Millerand in Paris (a jealous rival of the London Conference); Commissions of the Peace Conference some in London and some in Paris, with exasperated experts dashing from one to the other; a League of Nations meeting at odd times, though no-one has any steam left to drive it along; – what with all this, international affairs are not easy to conduct!

I am doing my best to maintain good personal relations with the French. [Hankey here described the sight-seeing expeditions and social engagements which he arranged for the Berthelots. He described Berthelot as 'a brilliant, much travelled and interesting man', who did not suffer from the Anglophobia which prevailed among many of his colleagues.]

To enlarge a little on the reference in Hankey's diary to the trouble in Germany, on 18th March he wrote to Lloyd George about the German request to send troops into the Ruhr neutral zone 'to deal with Communists'. The request had first been made on behalf of Kapp's transient régime, and had been rejected. Now the lawful and restored government under President Ebert had made a similar request

[1]German army officers, supported by nationalist and militarist factions, had organised themselves into armed bands known as *Freikorps*. The attempt to disarm one of these bodies, led by Wolfgang Kapp (1858–1922) and General von Lüttwitz (1859–1942) resulted in the Socialist government of Gustav Bauer, the first Chancellor of the German Republic (1870–1944) under President Ebert, being temporarily ejected from Berlin. The *Freikorps* then demanded a General Election, in the hope of obtaining a monarchist majority. However the workers' response was quick and effective. A General Strike was called, Kapp's so-called 'Government of Technicians' was routed in five days, and he fled to Sweden. A new democratic government with Hermann Müller (1876–1931) as Chancellor then took office.

in order to cope with the 'Spartacist' movement.[1] Hankey told the Prime Minister that the real purposes of the French proposal to advance into the Ruhr, where according to Brussels everything was in fact quiet, were, firstly, 'their general desire to trample on Germany', and, secondly, to secure for their own benefit the coal fields.[2] He also noted in his diary that Henry Wilson had told him that the true proportion of the French coloured troops in the Rhineland was 72%, and not 60% as officially rumoured; and that their presence gravely exacerbated German feelings and gained support for the extreme militarist elements.[3] An interesting point is that much of Hankey's knowledge of events in Germany at this time came from Violet Markham,[4] a close friend of Tom Jones, who was travelling in the country and sent Jones a series of acutely perceptive reports on conditions and politics. Hankey passed these letters on to Lloyd George, who can have been left in no doubt regarding the dangers which were developing.[5] In fact on 3rd April the Ebert government sent 20,000 troops into the Ruhr demilitarised zone, which was far in excess of the permitted strength; and the French retaliated by occupying Frankfurt and Darmstadt – in spite of what Hankey called 'a most explicit refusal by our government to agree to it'.[6]

*Diary 7th April 1920*

It is the first time since the outbreak of war that our Ally has acted not merely independently of but in defiance of the views of others. I had a long talk with Bonar Law and Lord Curzon about it. Bonar says he gave [Paul]

[1]This comprised the left wing of the Social Democrats. Formed soon after the Armistice they tried to stop the elections to the National Assembly in Jan. 1919 but were put down by Gustav Noske the Minister of Defence (1868–1946) after severe street fighting in Berlin. He thereupon made the grave error of recruiting the *Freikorps* to deal with similar outbreaks, and that led to the Kapp Putsch. Spartacus was the leader of the slave revolt against Rome (73–71 B.C.).

[2]Lloyd George papers F/24/2/19.

[3]The author of this biography, who was in Germany during the early 1920s as a language officer, and so learnt a good deal about German sentiments, can fully confirm Hankey's remarks on the consequences of the presence of the French colonial troops.

[4]Violet R. Markham (Mrs. Carruthers) (1872–1959). Social Welfare worker and author. Chairman or member of many government-appointed bodies concerned with women's work and status, notably the Assistance Board. Founder-President of Chesterfield Settlement. Her book *A Woman's Watch on the Rhine* (1921) tells the story of her travels in Germany at this time.

[5]Lloyd George papers F/24/2. [6]Diary 7th April 1920.

Cambon, the French ambassador, a pretty straight talking to on the subject yesterday. He is now apprehensive that the P.M. will want to do something ultra-drastic about it. I pointed out what a relief it would be if we could withdraw our force from Cologne, as this horrible continental entanglement is always a nightmare to me. Moreover this incident shows the danger of being dragged at the heels of the French, who are a very provocative people, into a new war. Of course, though, we cannot afford to allow the Germans to take advantage of our dilemma. It is an awkward situation which needs statesmanship. Everyone agrees that the old 'Tiger' would never have allowed such a situation to develop, and that Millerand is being led by the nose by Foch.

An interesting point in the foregoing diary entry is that according to Hankey it was Bonar Law and not Curzon the Foreign Secretary who gave Cambon the dressing down about French military activities. This was doubtless a reflection of Curzon's lack of interest in European affairs, already remarked on. In Harold Nicolson's words, he was 'a bad European', and could produce no policy to satisfy the French search for security once the Anglo-American guarantee had collapsed through the rejection of the Versailles Treaty by the U.S. Senate.[1] In fact the crisis of the spring of 1920 was resolved – temporarily – by the withdrawal of the German troops in mid May; but the ill effects of this first failure of the Coalition government to produce a consistent, firm and fair European policy were to be very serious.

While the London Conference was making little progress with the Turkish treaty, the threat of a coal strike, supported by the railwaymen and transport workers, arose. Hankey recorded that he 'personally never thought they [the miners] meant to strike'; and he left the secretarial and advisory side of the negotiations almost entirely in the capable hands of Tom Jones. In fact the miners did come out in October, but they were not supported by the other unions, and a settlement was achieved which conceded the principle that profits and wages should be governed by a national agreement, as opposed to district settlements.[2]

The week before Easter, which fell on 4th April, was a fairly quiet period for Hankey, because 'neither Lloyd George nor his Cabinet could think of anything except the debate on the second reading of the [Irish] Home Rule Bill.' The debate actually ended on 31st March, 'the necessary majority was secured'; and, continued Hankey with exces-

[1]Nicolson, *Curzon*, p. 192. [2]See *Middlemas*, I, p. 104.

sive optimism, 'sanity was more or less re-established'.[1] As with the negotiations over industrial troubles Hankey left the Irish negotiations mainly in Jones's hands; but on 30th April he recorded that Lloyd George 'had a long conference with Lord French, the Lord Lieutenant, and Hamar Greenwood the new Chief Secretary, about the state of Ireland. French made it quite clear that the Sinn Feiners regarded themselves as being in a state of war, and the continual murders merely as acts of war. Curiously enough he was not without hope that an arrangement might be reached. According to Hankey Greenwood 'talked the most awful tosh about shooting Sinn Feiners at sight, and without evidence, and [about] frightfulness generally. He has not been to Ireland yet, and will no doubt be sobered by responsibility'.[2] A fortnight later he wrote that 'General [Sir Nevil] Macready[3] the new G.O.C. Ireland had come over on behalf of the Irish Govt. to demand all kinds of assistance. Macready now seems to be *the* man there'. Lloyd George had insisted on Macready and not Robertson being appointed to that very difficult post, 'and now they seem to trust him more than the Viceroy or the new Chief Secretary. He [Macready] went down to Lympne [Sir Philip Sassoon's house] to see Lloyd George, and next morning the Cabinet gave him all he asked for – existing battalions in Ireland to be completed up to war strength; 8 more battalions at call . . .; masses of motor transport to render the troops mobile; and a special gendarmerie was approved in principle though later it was altered to 8 garrison battalions. Macready told us the Dublin Metropolitan police's morale had been destroyed by the murders, and the R.I.C.'s is threatened. He was full of courage and heart, though his own life is threatened. His plan is to render the troops so mobile that . . . they may from time to time surprise the Sinn Fein bands. I don't think that will be much use, but his Secret Service may be better. Henry Wilson thinks Macready's plan useless. He wants to collect the names of Sinn Feiners by districts; proclaim them on the church doors all over the country; and, whenever a policeman is murdered, pick 5 by lot and shoot them! My view is that somehow or other terror must be met by greater terror'.[4] The last sentence shows how far Hankey had moved from his earlier opposition to coercion in Ireland.[5]

[1]Diary 5th April 1920. The Dominion of Ireland Bill was circulated on 28th June 1920. C.P. 1539. Cab. 24/108.
[2]Diary 8th May 1920. [3]See Vol. I, p. 469, *note*.
[4]Diary 23rd May 1920. [5]See Vol. I, pp. 517–18, 521, etc.

On 24th May Macready submitted his 'blue print' for a new era in that unhappy country. It comprised the granting of Dominion Home Rule with Ulster excluded; and Warren Fisher came out strongly in support of that solution. Austen Chamberlain circulated Macready's report and Fisher's remarks to the Cabinet, and minuted 'Tell Hankey I think there ought to be a very early discussion'.[1] On the last day of that month Lloyd George met the Viceroy and the Irish government, and further measures of repression were discussed, with Churchill as their extreme advocate.[2] Towards the end of July Jones sent Lloyd George a note on the deteriorating situation, about which he and Hankey were becoming increasingly perturbed. The alternatives, wrote Jones, were either to get tough, impose martial law and suspend the civil government, or to try and reach an agreement with Sinn Fein. He suggested Lloyd George should make a speech threatening to adopt the first alternative, but should offer Ireland Dominion Home Rule with self-determination for Ulster and defence a 'reserved' issue before adopting severe measures.[3] We will return later to the agonies of the final failure of repression in Ireland.

Meanwhile Hankey was agitating for the revival of the Committee of Imperial Defence in its pre-war form. Late in 1919 and early in the following year Parliamentary Questions were asked on the subject,[4] and Hankey himself took a hand in drafting the replies.[5] Then in March 1920 the matter came up again in speeches made in Parliament during the debate on the Army Estimates.[6] It was probably the interest shown in the subject on those occasions by M.P.s that caused Hankey to press on Lloyd George his view that 'the time has come for bringing the C.I.D. once more into operation'. He added that 'the movement for a Joint Staff and Ministry of Defence [which had always been one of his bugbears] will be much easier to deal with once the C.I.D. is again on its legs', and appended a long list 'of questions requiring consideration'.[7] Two days later he told Walter Long, the First Lord, that Lloyd George

[1]Austen Chamberlain papers AC 25/4/16 and 25/4/19 of 15th and 24th May.
[2]*Middlemas*, I, p. 114.
[3]Jones to Lloyd George 24th July 1920. Lloyd George papers F/24/3/3.
[4]Parl. Deb., Commons, Vol. 120, Col. 1666 and Vol. 125, Cols. 1287–8.
[5]Cab. 21/468.
[6]Parl. Deb., Commons, Vol. 126, Cols. 780 ff. and Vol. 127, Cols. 81 ff.
[7]Hankey to Lloyd George 17th March 1920. Lloyd George papers F/24/3/3. Copy in Cab. 21/468.

had agreed to hold a meeting on 26th March;[1] but it did not take place – because the Prime Minister was unwell, or perhaps, more realistically, because he had many problems on his hands which he regarded as having a higher priority than Hankey's beloved C.I.D. Two months later Hankey returned to the charge, giving complete proposals for the conduct of Cabinet business up to the Whitsun recess, stressing the issues that demanded early attention, and asking again for a meeting of the C.I.D. in the near future.[2] Once again he was frustrated, and complained to Tom Jones that he had 'not had much luck about business', chiefly because the Prime Minister was 'looking old and not very fit'.[3] However in that same month he found, or perhaps procured, an ally in Admiral Beatty, the First Sea Lord, who wrote pressing for action on the lines that Hankey himself had been so assiduously propagating. They agreed that if the Prime Minister could not take the chair it would be far better to have a deputy to act for him than prolong the prevailing inactivity; and that was Hankey's next line of attack.[4]

While the future of the C.I.D. hung in the balance Hankey busied himself with revising and bringing up to date the War Book – which had of course always been a responsibility of the Committee and one of his most favoured scions. In his diary he wrote 'I am trying to push on the preparations for the next war, which I hope will not happen in my time'.[5] Though he was never a 'militarist' in the chauvinistic sense Hankey always believed that war might be forced on his country, and that it was merely common sense to make such preparations as could be undertaken in peace time at negligible cost.

At the end of June Hankey's pressure on Lloyd George did bear some fruit, and the C.I.D. actually met – for the first time since February 1915.[6] A Sub-Committee was then set up to carry out a complete survey of the nation's defence commitments, and that body became the Standing Defence Sub-Committee which in effect conducted the C.I.D.'s business until after the fall of the Coalition government.[7] The

[1]Hankey to Long 19th March 1920.
[2]Hankey to Lloyd George 13th May 1920. Lloyd George papers F/24/2/36.
[3]*Middlemas*, I, p. 113.
[4]Beatty to Hankey 22nd May 1920 and reply by letter of same day. Cab. 21/468.
[5]Diary 8th May 1920.
[6]133rd meeting. Cab. 2/3. The 132nd meeting took place on 23rd Feb. 1915.
[7]Diary 30th June 1920. Even Hankey seems to have got rather entangled over the minutes of the C.I.D. proper and of its Standing Sub-Committee. For example the minutes of the 136th and 137th meetings of the former (2nd and 6th May 1921)

Prime Minister remained *ex-officio* Chairman, but in fact he generally delegated the responsibility to a senior Minister such as Balfour, Churchill or, later, Lord Salisbury. Though this decision marked some progress in the direction desired by Hankey, all did not go smoothly. In October Hankey had a long correspondence with Churchill and Long about what he called 'the serious and complete stagnation as regards the business of the C.I.D.', and the difficulty of finding a Minister who was willing and able to act regularly as Chairman of the Standing Sub-Committee.[1] As so often in the past he opened his heart to Esher, who fully shared his views, but was not surprised at his 'failure to galvanize the C.I.D. back to life.'[2] Milner was Hankey's first choice for the chairmanship of the Standing Sub-Committee; but he turned the job down because he 'had too much work . . . [and] intended to leave the Government soon for "private reasons" '. Hankey at once showed Milner's letter to Lloyd George, who was 'very excited . . . and felt sure it confirmed a theory he had long held that Milner had for some years had a mysterious and clandestine love affair which is going to get him into trouble! He was fairly bursting with it', recorded Hankey.[3] Possibly Lloyd George was judging Milner by his own standards of 'clandestine love affairs'. On the other hand the reader will recollect that a surprise visit paid to Milner's country home in 1918 raised somewhat similar thoughts in Hankey's mind.[4]

Though it breaches chronology we may conveniently here carry on the story of Hankey's efforts to get the C.I.D. restarted. By April 1921, he was still dissatisfied, and on 1st of that month he again tackled Lloyd George, saying that 'not unnaturally in view of the pressure of other business' progress had been 'very slow'; but 'the time has now come when we can go ahead faster'. He placed his demand at no more than 'one meeting of the full committee a month, or even one in six weeks provided we can get some sub-committees started'; and as he 'despaired of Mr. Balfour', because he was away so much and his

---

are endorsed 'Originally issued as minutes of the First [Second] meeting of the Standing Defence Sub-Committee'; and from that time onwards the Sub-Committee's minutes were incorporated in those of the C.I.D. proper. This necessitated renumbering some minutes of the latter body.

[1]Hankey to Churchill 21st and 22nd Oct. 1920, and replies by latter of 22nd and 24th Oct. Long to Hankey 25th Oct. 1920. Cab. 21/468.

[2]Esher to Hankey. Undated but *c.* 13th Oct. 1920.

[3]Diary 23rd Oct. 1920. [4]See Vol. I, p. 575.

health was uncertain, he urged that Lloyd George himself or Austen Chamberlain should take the chair. He attached what he called 'a short note' on the business that called for attention (which actually comprised 11 pages of typescript), and ended by suggesting that 'a sharply worded instruction to the Co-ordination Committee to push on with the War Book would be a great help to me' – a good example of his method of stimulating to greater activity a body which he regarded as sluggish.[1]

Nearly a year later he was still at it, and in preparing some notes for use by Churchill in the debate on the Air Estimates he proposed that 'the opportunity should be taken to make a general statement on what the C.I.D. is doing, and referred to Churchill's 'exceptional qualifications to take Mr. Balfour's place as Chairman of the Standing Sub-Committee'. The weak point was, he said, that the C.I.D. itself had only met three times since the Armistice, and in consequence all real work had devolved on the Standing Sub-Committee.[2] Obviously he wanted to harness Churchill's great energy to the chariot of his favourite organisation. On 5th July 1922 he finally got his way and the full committee met once again, with Lloyd George himself in the chair.

To return to 1920, at the end of March Hankey recorded, rather despairingly, that 'we have been plugging on with the Turkish Peace Treaty'; but in truth little real progress was made at the London Conference – chiefly because of the deliberately dilatory attitude of the French. The whole matter was therefore deferred until the Inter-Allied meeting at San Remo in April. The composition of the British delegation brought Hankey once again into conflict with Edwin Montagu, the Secretary of State for India, who considered that he should be present, and that the Indian representatives should state their country's case. In reply Hankey wrote that 'The Prime Minister's view was that it was for him [Lloyd George], as the senior British representative, to represent the British case as a whole'; that 'it would not be in order for the Indian Delegation to address the Peace Conference direct'; also that Curzon, the Foreign Secretary, would be the only Minister to accompany Lloyd George to San Remo. Montagu

[1]Hankey to Lloyd George 1st April 1921. Cab. 21/468. The 11 page memo., of which Hankey sent a copy to Chamberlain, is in Cab. 21/209 as well.

[2]Hankey to Churchill 20th March 1922. Cab. 21/468. The secretary of the Standing Sub-Committee was Brigadier S. H. Wilson until Sir John Chancellor (1870–1952) took over from him in November 1921.

riposted with objections – 'surely a very unwise letter' comments his biographer with good reason.[1] In fact Lloyd George took with him his daughter Megan, Frances Stevenson, J. T. Davies, Philip Kerr, Hankey and the inevitable Riddell.[2] Just before they left London on 10th a new French note arrived 'rather truculent in tone, and upholding their point of view over the German occupation [of the Ruhr]' and a reply had to be concocted in haste. Hankey 'managed to induce them [Lloyd George, Milner, Eyre Crowe and Kerr] to soften rather a harsh passage', although he was 'much jeered at especially by the P.M. as though I was rather a milksop'.[3] After that delay the party left to catch the P. and O. liner *Naldera*, which was on her maiden voyage, to Marseilles. In the Bay of Biscay they were struck by a severe storm which prostrated most of the party – including Hankey. Newnham, Lloyd George's valet, who was always something of a Mrs. Malaprop, amused Hankey by answering his enquiry as to the likelihood of the Prime Minister's appearance on deck 'No; he prefers the *perpendicular* position to-day'.[4]

As soon as calm waters were reached off the Straits Hankey settled down to organise the documents relating to the Turkish treaty; and a brief call at Gibraltar gave him the chance to produce for Lloyd George a paper on the value of that base in war.[5] While in port Lloyd George, who had been in a difficult mood and at first 'absolutely declined to call on the Governor Sir Horace Smith-Dorrien',[6] revived when news of Coalition successes in two by-elections (Camberwell and Basingstoke) came in. Lord Riddell has recorded that he had many interesting talks with Hankey during this voyage, including a discussion on why Bulgaria sued for peace and so initiated the collapse of the Central Powers. According to Riddell Hankey said that this was one of the most interesting historical problems of the war, and 'the reputation of the "Easterners" [who of course included himself] depends in some

[1] Hankey to Montagu 9th April 1920 and reply by letter of 15th. S. D. Waley, *Edwin Montagu: a Memoir* (Asia Publishing House, 1964), p. 244.
[2] Lloyd George Papers F/24/2/23.
[3] To Lady Hankey 11th April 1920.
[4] To the same 15th April 1920.
[5] Hankey to Lloyd George 15th April 1920. Lloyd George papers F/24/2/26.
[6] General Sir H. L. Smith-Dorrien (1858–1930). C-in-C, Aldershot Command 1907–12 and Southern Command 1912–14. Commanded 2nd Army Corps, and then 2nd Army, B.E.F. 1914–15. C-in-C, East Africa 1915–16. Governor of Gibraltar 1918–23.

measure upon the answer to that question'. He was therefore having it 'carefully investigated and dealt with in the official history'.[1]

From Marseilles the party split up between two motor cars to drive to San Remo via San Raphael, Cannes and Nice. Hankey noted with amusement how 'Lloyd George, who is always very nervous, especially in France, of being seen in public with Miss Stevenson', insisted on her starting off with him and Riddell. Once the open country was reached 'he stopped and Miss Stevenson was transferred to his car'. They called for lunch at Lord Rothermere's beautiful villa on Cap Martin, and once again Miss Stevenson had to be whisked away into obscurity. 'He lives in a perfect terror of gossip' was Hankey's justifiable conclusion.[2] On reaching San Remo the party put up at the Royal Hotel, where they were joined by Curzon and the rest of the delegation who had come out overland.

The first talks between Lloyd George and Millerand took place on Sunday 18th April – 'still under the shadow of the Ruhr incident, and the interview was the reverse of cordial' remarked Hankey. Then began the preliminary conference at the Castello de Vachan 'a beautiful villa high up in the hills'. But difficulties with the Press and something of a crisis with the French and Italians quickly clouded the beauty of the Riviera scenery. As regards the former, on Lloyd George's initiative the decision was taken that no announcements would be made about the conference except for a daily *communiqué*. This was highly unsatisfactory to Riddell, who threatened to boycott the conference. Lloyd George thereupon capitulated, causing Hankey to remark in Riddell's presence 'L. G. made the proposal and now he is the first to break it'.[3] Not for the first time did Lloyd George's close association with magnates of the Press prove a two edged weapon. The political crisis is well described in Hankey's diary.

*Diary 18th April 1920* [Written on 1st May]

. . . As I had nothing arranged for the afternoon I assumed that, being Sunday, we were to have a half holiday. Having dictated my notes of the morning meeting, and having taken the precaution to ask Ll. G. if he wanted me, I went off for a tramp with Field-Marshal Wilson with a clear conscience. Returning at 5.30 p.m. I found the whole of San Remo in a state of hue and cry after me. It seems that at about 4.50 p.m. Ll. G. suddenly remembered

[1]Riddell, *Intimate Diary* p. 182.

[2]Diary 17th April 1820 (written on 1st May).

[3]Riddell, *Intimate Diary*, pp. 187–8.

he had promised to meet Nitti and Millerand at the former's hotel at 5 p.m., but he had forgotten to tell anyone else and there was no car and no Secretary. I hurried off there, and arrived about 5.45 p.m. I found the three P.M.s in a state of considerable heat. Ll. G. and Nitti wanted the Allies to meet the Germans face to face. Ll. G. in the morning, as a concession to Millerand, had proposed Paris. Nitti, at a short subsequent interview with Ll. G. at which I was present, had urged San Remo or anywhere but Paris, where he was convinced the French would never behave decently. Ll. G. had agreed and said he had only proposed Paris as a 'thin end of the wedge' to get Millerand at all! When I arrived at the afternoon discussion the proposal of the meeting (which was not at all agreeable to Millerand) had led to a discussion of the topics to be raised, and at the moment of my appearance on the scene a heated discussion was in progress on the subject of Reparations. Millerand wanted the Germans to pay an instalment on account, in order to relieve the embarrassed French exchequer. Ll. G. was urging that the Germans could not pay anything on account, and no-one would give them credit until the sum total of their obligations was known. He therefore wanted to get the Germans to make an offer of a total lump sum, as contemplated in the Protocol to the Peace Treaty. Millerand was urging that it was quite unnecessary, in order to raise a sum on account, for Germany to know her total indebtedness, in which he was obviously wrong. He had never heard of the Protocol, but luckily I had it in my box. The moment he saw it, being above all things a lawyer, his attitude changed and he promised to consider it. Thus a very stormy interview, in which the genial Nitti had done his best to avoid an overt quarrel, ended almost, but not quite, in an *impasse*, at any rate in the worst possible atmosphere, all of which was immediately reflected in the French Press. The next few days were spent in settling the outstanding details of the Turkish Treaty. They ought not to have been difficult, but the atmosphere was so bad that every point was most bitterly contested. Berthelot, who, as second French representative, took a leading part in obstruction, told me privately that he was acting under instructions, that he hated it, intended to get out of it and go for a long tour of the world. . . . The Italians used to give us a most sumptuous tea with delicious cakes and all sorts of fruits – strawberries, oranges, green figs etc., and, on reassembly after this pleasant interlude on a verandah with an exquisite view, we generally managed to reach an agreement. Meantime the German question was not again broached. On Wednesday the 21st, Camerlynck, the admirable French interpreter, a diplomatist and a gentleman,[1] came to me and hinted that in his view we were not getting on. 'Mr. Ll. G. has a daughter here and M. Millerand has a son', he said, 'could we not

[1]Described in Riddell, *Intimate Diary*, p. 189 as being in the general opinion of the conference 'as good as Mantoux'. See Vol. I, p. 348, *note*.

arrange some social amenities?' I said I would do my best. I found next day was Megan's birthday, so I suggested a dinner and a dance. Ll. G. changed this to rather a formal dinner to Millerand, his son, and Berthelot on Thursday evening. It was an enormous success. An immense number of amusing stories were told. Everyone was at the top of his form. Ll. G. had just received the news of two successful by-elections at Edinburgh, including Runciman's defeat, and someone had pasted the figures up in huge letters on the looking glass. This was the seventh consecutive [coalition] victory in a by-election. Millerand, who had been led by *The Times* articles to believe that Ll. G. had lost the confidence of the country was impressed. From that moment the whole atmosphere of the conference changed. Next evening [23rd April] Foch and Weygand came to dinner and this again was a huge success and innumerable stories were told of the war. . . . Weygand told me the young men of France were refusing to take up a military career, as all France was 'fed up' with war, and even his own sons were becoming engineers. Foch, however, glorious old reactionary that he is, extolled patriotism as the supreme virtue, and gave more than a hint that, now the war was over, it was the business of each of the Allies to look after its own interests, which were not any longer necessarily identical. He said that Germany was so exhausted that she could not pay reparations, and the only thing to be done was to take what we could. This accounts for the French attitude in the Ruhr affair, I suspect. On the Saturday [24th] we dined with the French, and the entente was again fully re-established . . . [Here Hankey enlarged on the current intrigues and clashes of personalities between the French and Italians.] However, no Frenchman has a good word for any Italian these days, and *vice-versâ*, so one must not believe too much. As some French lady who married an Italian said 'The French and English don't get on because they don't know each other; the French and Italians don't get on because they know each other too well.' So much for Anglo-French relations. They continued most intimate and cordial to the end, and all the difficulties at private conversations between Ll. G. and Millerand at which I was present on the morning of 23rd April were easily surmounted. Millerand specially thanked me for my share in bringing this about . . .

Anglo-Italian relations remained undisturbed throughout. We all liked the Italian officials. Nitti himself was a genial and courteous chairman with a useful sense of humour. His pronounced pro-Germanism, however, greatly offended the French, and Millerand on at least one occasion, alluded to 'the brilliant speech of the President [of the Conference] on behalf of Germany'. In his conversations with Ll. G. Nitti showed himself profoundly distrustful of the French. He declared they were stirring up socialist trouble for him in Italy. He considered that, as a nation, France was absolutely degenerate and done. She was short of 5 million men, Italy, with a large and increasing population, would soon out-distance her. France would not submit to the same taxes and sacrifices as Italy. He was quite openly sceptical as to the possibility of getting any reparations out of Germany. I was sent by Ll. G. to ask him to authorise his financial expert to collaborate with the British, French, and Belgian experts in a new reparations scheme. 'They are both lunatics' he said, referring to Ll. G. and Millerand 'if they think they can get a penny. Germany is starving.' One day he turned to me and pointed to two donkeys on the top of a bookshelf. 'Experts', he said! This was after a discussion with the military advisers! Still, he is a man of good judgment, not carried away either by sentiment or by vanity, as Orlando was, or by national avarice and jingoism, as was Sonnino. He sees Fiume in its true perspective, and wants to get out of the difficulty without discredit.[1] He does not conceal his political difficulties, which depend on steering his way without a real parliamentary majority by manipulating now the Socialists, now the Catholics. In this he is very adroit.

Personally I got some kudos at the conference. Of course I was not the Secretary-General and had to comport myself with tact. On the first day, after no less than three Italians had introduced themselves to me as *the* secretary of the conference and had asked [for] the benefit of my experience, Nitti introduced a stranger, M. Garbasso, as *the* secretary. . . . Anyhow I got on with him quite well. Storr and Abraham helped me with the *procès-verbaux*. Soon we were days ahead of the Italians, and the French and other delegations accepted ours as authoritative. I fancy the Italians even waited for ours before writing theirs. . . . Fromageot, the chairman of the drafting Committee, came to me at the end to present the *hommage* of the drafting Ctee. (who prepare the actual articles for the Treaty) and to say that without me they would have broken down. Foch told me that he regarded me as 'the Chancellor of the Conference.' At the end, Ll. G. moved a vote of thanks to Garbasso, on which Berthelot burst in with '*et à Sir Hankey, le roi des Secretaires*'. Weygand, whom I informed that my telephone had broken down said 'Then the conference will break down'. [Here Hankey described the social life in which he had been involved.]

Anyhow it was one of the most successful and agreeable conferences I ever attended. I spent most of the journey home preparing a brief for Ll. G.'s speech in the House of Commons.

Hankey's daily letters to his wife, written during the conference, generally repeat and confirm the long entry he made in his diary after it was over; but they sometimes add interesting details. Thus on 24th

[1]That is to say the illegal occupation of Fiume by the forces under the Italian nationalist and poet Gabriele D'Annunzio (1863–1938) in 1919. He was expelled by regular Italian forces in December 1920.

the American ambassador at Rome,[1] who had actually been staying at the same hotel as the British delegates, suddenly appeared and 'stated he had instructions to attend'. 'Of course he was admitted', wrote Hankey; but he promptly blocked a suggestion that the ambassador should be given all the *procès-verbaux* – because President Wilson 'was at times rather criticised' in them.[2]

The fruits of the San Remo Conference were certainly not negligible. The Treaty of Peace with Turkey and Greece, signed at Sèvres on 10th August 1920, was at last drawn up; but in fact by that time the Turkish nationalist movement under Kemal Pasha was in control, and the treaty was quickly rendered obsolete.[3] The Syrian, Palestine and Iraq mandates were allocated, the first to France and the other two to Britain, and the Anglo–French agreement on Middle East oil interests was also confirmed.[4] As regards Germany, the request to double the strength of her army, put forward as a result of the Kapp putsch, was refused, and a discreet veil was drawn over the French occupation of Frankfurt and Darmstadt. Germany was also charged with default on Reparations; and that issue was to prove a veritable Pandora's box of trouble during the next decade.

On 28th April Hankey reached his home, and after a brief rest he took up again the heavy burden of his office duties on the last day of the month.

[1]Robert U. Johnson (1853–1937). Author and diplomat. A lover of Italy and originator of memorial to Keats and Shelley in Rome. President, New York Committee for Italian War Relief 1918–19. Ambassador to Italy Feb. 1920–July 1921.

[2]See Cab. 29/85, 86A and 87 for Minutes of San Remo Conference. No reports from Ambassador Johnson to Washington are printed in *Foreign Relations, U.S.A.*, 1920.

[3]See Nicolson, *Curzon*, and Richard M. Watt, *The Kings Depart* (Weidenfeld and Nicolson, 1969) for succinct surveys of the Turkish Treaty negotiations, and their outcome. D.B.F.P., 1st Series, Vol. VII, Ch. I contains a number of important documents on the subject.

[4]The Cadman-Berthelot Agreement of 24th April, 1920, confirmed by Lloyd George and Millerand next day. Cmd. 675. Misc. No. 11 (1920). For American protests about this agreement, and their attempts to assert the rights of U.S. interests, notably Standard Oil, in Mesopotamia see *Foreign Relations, U.S.A., 1920*, Vol. II, pp. 649–67.

*Chapter 7*

# The Era of Conferences I. May-December 1920

On Hankey's return from San Remo he was at once immersed in preparations for the next conference, which was to be held at Spa and was to deal mainly with Reparations and Disarmament. His difficulties were exacerbated by Lloyd George falling ill and going off to Folkestone to recuperate until the middle of May. 'He is really suffering from nervous exhaustion' was Hankey's reasonable diagnosis. 'He jeered at Montagu, Eric Geddes and myself when we were advised by our doctors to take a rest, but this is about the fourth time I have known him beaten to a frazzle himself. This week (8th May) I have had to shove along the Cabinet under Bonar Law'.[1]

In addition to preparing for Spa, which involved long consultations with Sir John Bradbury[2] and other financial and economic experts, Hankey involved himself with Sir Eric Drummond, the Secretary-General of the League, 'to try and get the League of Nations linked up with the Supreme Council at Spa'.[3] In fact it was in this month that the League Council set up the 'Permanent Advisory Commission on Military, Naval and Air Questions' under Article IX of the Covenant – a body whose deliberations were to become a matter of close concern to Hankey.[4] On 12th he wrote at some length to Lloyd George expressing his hopes for the League and his misgivings with regard to the direction in which it was developing. He first reverted to his memorandum of 12th January 1918 as the basis on which the League should be

[1]Diary 8th May 1920.

[2]1872–1950. 1st Baron Bradbury 1925. Joint Permanent Secretary, Treasury 1913–19. Principal British delegate on Reparations Commission 1919–25. President, British Bankers' Association 1929–30 and 1935–36.

[3]Diary 8th May 1920.

[4]See J. W. Wheeler Bennett, *Information on the Reduction of Armaments* (Allen and Unwin, 1925), p. 19.

organised,[1] and then continued by claiming that the developments he had foretold – that the Supreme War Council would become the directing body at the peace conference – had in fact come to pass. The next step was, again as he had foreseen, 'the bringing of the enemy into council', which would take place at Spa; but the deliberative body would be the Supreme Council of the Allies and not the Council of the League. 'Unless some closer liaison than at present exists', he went on, 'is established between the League and the Supreme Council there is the gravest danger that the great developments on which so many hopes have been based may miscarry . . .'; and he described how this peril could best be avoided by the League's business being conducted on lines analogous to those practised by the British Cabinet. As a first step he wanted the League 'to be encouraged to ask for permission to send a liaison officer to Spa', and he urged Lloyd George to get Millerand's support for this proposal.[2] Lloyd George, however, does not seem to have been taken by the idea. At any rate the next round of conferences took place largely in isolation from the League.

A month later Hankey's apprehensions had increased, and he tried to persuade Lloyd George to attend a meeting of the League Council himself. In his diary he repeated his earlier strictures on the whole basis of the Covenant, especially the 'sanctions' clauses, and on the machinery of the Secretariat set up by Drummond. 'At present the Secretariat-General is merely an international Foreign Office', he complained, 'and presents most of the ideas for the Council, instead of making the Council do the work and [the secretariat] confining itself to secretarial functions. The results are fatal. The tail is wagging the dog. Our Foreign Office is very jealous and refuses to have anything to do with the League. Harold Nicolson, the best F.O. man in the Secretariat-General has deserted and come back to the Foreign Office. Finally the Secretariat-General is so overworked that it cannot properly handle even the few second-rate questions referred to it. The League is as yet a poor thing, but if I can get Lloyd George to go there I will make something of it.'[3] It does not seem to have occurred to Hankey that there was any contradiction between his urging that the League should be modelled on the British Cabinet system, under which the Secretary (himself) certainly 'presented many of the ideas',

[1]See Vol. I, p. 482.
[2]Hankey to Lloyd George 12th May 1920. Lloyd George papers F/24/2/32.
[3]Diary 13th June 1920.

and his criticism of the League's Secretariat for doing exactly the same.

In the same month Hankey sent Lloyd George notes of a conversation he had with Colonel House over lunch with him, Balfour and Wiseman. House had optimistically declared that within twelve months the United States would join the League, and that the Republican Party, if successful in the forthcoming elections, would favour such a development – though with reservations. Hankey said that House considered the Covenant 'too rigid'; which of course accorded with his own view. House also spoke favourably of Senator Harding,[1] and Hankey 'got the impression that, from a British point of view' Harding 'would not make a bad President'.[2] Hankey's informant could hardly have been more wrong; for Harding's Presidency proved disastrous, and culminated in one of the greatest scandals in American history – the notorious 'Teapot Dome' case over the sale of the U.S. Navy's leases of oil-bearing lands.

On 14th May Hankey set off with Philip Kerr, Sylvester and Owen (his 'best stenographer') for Sir Philip Sassoon's luxurious house 'Belcaire' near Lympne where he found the host and Frances Stevenson 'looking after the P.M.', who 'looked old and ill'. He also commented harshly on Churchill's drinking habits, and thought he looked 'bloated and bleary'. The luxury of the Sassoon household he described as 'a positive surfeit', and he 'had rather a disagreeable feeling that the P.M. is getting too fond of high-living and luxury' – a view with which Kerr apparently agreed. Lloyd George's doctor had ordered him to take another fortnight's rest; which Hankey described as 'a terrible nuisance', as he had set out an elaborate programme with the object of the Cabinet clearing up 'a mass of urgent business' before Whitsun.[3] The main purposes of this meeting, generally called the First Hythe Conference, were in Lloyd George's words 'to mend an Alliance that has been nearly ruptured', and to prepare for a meeting with the Germans on their failure to execute the disarmament clauses of the Versailles Treaty, pay reparations and deliver coal to France and Belgium.[4]

[1]Warren Gamaliel Harding (1865–1923). American journalist and politician (Rep.). Senator from Ohio 1915–21. 29th President of U.S.A. Nov. 1920. Died while in office August 1923.

[2]Hankey to Lloyd George 25th June 1920. Lloyd George papers F/24/2/40. Also Cab. 63/28.

[3] Diary 23rd May 1920 [4] D.B.F.P. 1st Series, Vol. VII, Ch. II.

On 23rd Austen Chamberlain turned up with Bradbury and Basil Blackett of the Treasury[1]; but Chamberlain left almost at once to meet Millerand and François Marsal, the French Minister of Finance, at Folkestone.

*Diary 23rd May 1920*

. . The postponement of the Spa Conference was early decided on. It was also agreed that disarmament should be the first question at Spa. Ll. G., who had heard that the French wanted to treat the Germans very coolly at Spa and to show them that they were regarded merely as criminals at the bar, made rather a provocative statement in favour of a proper discussion there. He later put the situation rather well by comparing the position of the Allies to that of a litigant, who has secured a judgment in his favour, and afterwards agrees to meet the other party, not with a view to altering the judgment but to discussing how it can best be carried out. Millerand accepted this. Then began a great tussle on finance, which lasted until the end of the conference. The French were out to get an alteration in their favour of the arrangement whereby France gets £55 and the British Empire £25 of every £100 paid by Germany. They supported it by piteous appeals on behalf of the devastated regions. We wouldn't agree. The arrangement had taken nearly a year to complete; was considered by us as very generous to France; and had only been accepted by the Dominions with the utmost reluctance. After that there followed an endless succession of proposals and counter-proposals, each involving an adjournment to enable the opposite party to consider it. This went on until the end of the conference, about mid-day Sunday [16th], when these projects were all referred to the experts and the conference was adjourned. My task was a stiff one, as I was the only secretary, but the constant adjournments enabled me to keep dictating my *procès-verbal* in instalments. The subject however was terribly technical. Marsal was so woolly that, even with the aid of the interpreter I could not make out what he meant to say. Ll. G., Millerand, and Chamberlain were all clear and in good form. . . . I had a few talks with Lord Derby, who told me he would like a G.C.B. I will get it for him.[2] The P.M., in spite of his recent indisposition, was in splendid form. . . .

[1] Later Sir Basil P. Blackett (1882-1935). Treasury official. Secretary, Indian Currency and Finance Commission 1913-14 and Capital Issues Committee 1915. Member of Anglo-French financial mission to U.S.A. 1915, and represented British Treasury in U.S.A. 1917-19. Controller of Finance, Treasury 1919-22. Finance Member of Executive Council, India 1922-28.

[2] Hankey was evidently as good as his word, and Derby's G.C.B. was gazetted on 8th Dec. 1920. He wrote gratefully to Hankey on the following 22nd Jan. 'It was an honour I very much wanted because my father had it.' Lloyd George papers F/25/1/16

I motored to town with Chamberlain, leaving the P.M. and Miss Stevenson at Lympne. Chamberlain asked me to arrange a financial committee to go into the question of the Treasury's finance in the war with a view to the future Treasury War Book . . .

So ended the First Lympne (or Hythe) conference, which Hankey accurately described as 'thoroughly unsatisfactory'.[1] No progress at all had been made in settling Germany's total liability under Reparations, and the Allies were still squabbling about the proportions each should receive of a pay-out which was becoming increasingly problematic. The fantastic sum of £24,000 millions payable in annual instalments of £1,200 millions put forward by the Hughes–Cunliffe Committee in 1918 still remained the target of the Allies, though the Americans had estimated the total payable at the more reasonable figure of £13,000 millions.

Hankey arranged to enjoy a short holiday with his family over Whitsun (23rd May); but he had 'reckoned without Ll. G.' who, after declaring his intention of spending the recess at Criccieth suddenly telephoned for Hankey to organise a Cabinet on the Friday. Curzon and Chamberlain both 'had to rise from a bed of sickness for the meeting'; but the Cabinet none the less sat all the morning, and then continued in the afternoon until 5 p.m. 'It really seemed perversity', protested Hankey. 'I never minded this in war time . . . But in peace time it is intolerable. There was he [Lloyd George], fresh from 3 weeks' rest, detaining all his colleagues, exhausted and tired from a long parliamentary session, for a whole day'. And Hankey of course had to go back to the office on the Saturday to finalise the minutes. He admitted that the main subjects dealt with – Inter-Allied debts and the situation in north Persia – were important; but 'they could have waited or been dealt with the day before.'[2] Yet such was Lloyd George's magnetism that none of his secretaries or advisers ever seem to have revolted against his inconsiderateness. In the end Hankey did get a few days' rest; but he spent them 'reading a great number of old letters and writing two chapters of my Memoirs dealing with the Owen Committee and the Committee of 1906 on Naval War Plans'.[3] Presumably these ultimately became the first four chapters of *The Supreme Command*, though that work was not to see the light of day for another

[1]See C.P. 1297 of 17th May 1920 for Hankey's 'Note on the Conversations at Hythe' for the Cabinet. Cab. 24/105.

[2]Diary 23rd May 1920. [3]*ibid.* 30th May 1920. See Vol. I, pp. 65–79.

forty years. What Adeline thought of her husband's recreational activities during the holiday we are not told.

Lloyd George came back to town on 29th May, to find Hankey ready with a great deal of business. The previous day he had produced a paper on the 'ingenious proposals' of Churchill, now Secretary of State for War and Air, 'for controlling Mesopotamia by aircraft', and so enabling the occupying forces to be reduced.[1] This was a favourite project of Sir Hugh Trenchard, who had resumed office as Chief of the Air Staff in March 1919. Hankey surveyed all recent experience of civil disturbances – in Somaliland, Egypt, Palestine, the North-West frontier of India and Ireland, and came broadly speaking to the conclusion that although aircraft could be valuable in improving the mobility of ground forces, to try and control rebellious tribes or factions by bombing was not promising. He thought that an experiment in using aircraft to stop Bedouin raids on Palestine should be carried out before 'entrusting Mesopotamia to the Royal Air Force'. Though Mesopotamia was in fact handed over to the R.A.F. later, and Trenchard's biographer makes far-reaching claims for the success of 'air control', they have recently been disputed[2]; and Hankey's sober, logical approach to an issue which had moral as well as strategic and political overtones now seems to have been remarkably statesmanlike. After all 'air control' was merely a polite euphemism for the bombing of villages, some of whose inhabitants were certainly innocent of any crime; and it was the first stage in the escalation of 'strategic bombing', which culminated in the Dresden raid of World War II, and in Hiroshima and Nagasaki. But in 1920, and for many years later, the pressure to save money was so heavy that all British governments were glad to snatch at any straw that appeared to promise a saving – especially in the Service Estimates.

High on the Cabinet's agenda after Whitsun stood the negotiations for a trade agreement with the U.S.S.R., whose representatives, led by Krassin,[3] were expected in London very shortly.

[1]Hankey to Lloyd George 28th May 1920. Lloyd George papers F/24/2/37.

[2]Boyle, *Trenchard*, pp. 365–9, 376–86, 533, 570 etc. For the refutation of such views see letters by Lord Ismay, Sir Geoffrey Archer and others in *Daily Telegraph* of 13th, 24th and 27th April and 14th May 1962.

[3]Leonid B. Krassin (1870–1926). Engineer and diplomat. Organised supply of Red Army in civil war. Commissar for Trade and Industry 1920. Ambassador to Britain 1925–6.

*Diary 30th May 1920*

. . . Lloyd George returned [from Lympne to London] yesterday and we had prolonged conferences in the morning on the visit of Krassin the Bolshevist Minister and the way in which he is to be treated, and in the afternoon on the Irish sitn. The Cabinet have decided to take the opportunity of Krassin's visit to insist, as a condition of trade relations, on an all-round settlement in regard to British prisoners [of war], Afghanistan, N. Persia, Caucasus, Denikin's remnant in the Crimea and perhaps Poland. The decision at San Remo was a meeting 'to remove obstacles to trade' or words to that effect. Lloyd George says that our difficulties with the Bolshevist Govt. referred to above are all 'obstacles to trade'; but there was another decision that there were to be no diplomatic relations with the Bolshevists, and if these are not diplomatic relations I don't know what they are! We may therefore have trouble with the French, who loathe the idea of any relations with the Soviets, but I think the Prime Minister is right. . . . I was very shocked at a proposal by Ll. G. to accept gold in payment of rolling stock to be sent to the Soviets and to deny the right of the holders of Russian bonds to the gold. It may be possible by some legal quibble to do this, but it will be very sharp practice to use the only tangible assets of the Russians without the consent of the old creditors. Of course some arrangement ought to be made . . .

*31st May 1920*

. . . [After lunch] I 'grasped the hairy paw of the baboon' to use Winston Churchill's picturesque phrase. In other words, in company with Lloyd George, Curzon, Horne, Bonar Law and Harmsworth[1] I took part in a conference with the Bolshevists – Krassin and Klishko.[2] Both had the appearance of men who have lived for long under great strain. Klishko merely acted as interpreter and Krassin conducted the negotiations. He is an intelligent looking, alert man of between 50 and 60 with a close-cut beard, rather a good eye and with a slightly defiant look. His hands moved nervously all the time, but his voice was firm and rather sympathetic and he stated his case in a masterly manner. As Lloyd George remarked to me afterwards 'He is the first Russian whom we have ever heard state his case with real ability'. He was under the impression that the Poles had acted with the support of the

[1]Probably Cecil B. H. Harmsworth, 1st Baron Harmsworth 1929 (1869–1948). Politician (Lib.). Under-Secretary of State, Home Office 1915. Member of Prime Minister's Secretariat 1917–19. Under-Secretary for Foreign Affairs 1919–22. British Member of Council of League of Nations 1922.

[2]Klishko was secretary to the Russian delegation. See *The Times*, 17th May 1920. Also D.B.F.P., 1st Series, VII, Ch. III regarding the negotiations with the Russian Trade Delegation 31st May–7th June 1920.

Allies in attacking the Bolshevists. At this point I passed a note to Lloyd George that I thought Krassin was trying to 'draw' him as to how far the Poles had the Allies behind them. And he did draw him too, for the P.M. told him in the greatest detail how he had warned Pathek,[1] the Polish Foreign minister, sitting in the same room and the same chair as Krassin, that he would not support them in an attack on Russia. Krassin said that the principal result of the Polish attack had been to rally all Russia to the Bolshevists, and that thousands of ex-officers were volunteering for service under them against the Poles. This was exactly what Lloyd George had warned the Poles would happen. Each side formulated the points it wanted to have cleared up preliminary to trading relations and the meeting adjourned. . . .

*June 13th 1920*

. . . We had another interview with Krassin last Monday [7th]. It was fairly satisfactory, but he revealed a somewhat truculent attitude. He made a very important statement about Persia viz. that the Soviet had ordered their forces to withdraw from Enzeli, and were prepared to enter into friendly discussions with Persia. At my suggestion this was communicated to the League of Nations, who are meeting to-morrow at Persia's request to discuss the Russian occupation. This, I recalled, required Krassin's consent, as it had been agreed to publish nothing without mutual agreement. This was obtained through Mr. Wise[2] of the Ministry of Food. I gave up the whole of Wednesday [9th] afternoon (when I had intended to have a half-holiday for once) to this Persian business, going to and fro between Lord Curzon, Mr. Balfour and Sir Eric Drummond.

Towards the end of June Hankey sent Lloyd George his suggestions regarding the attitude to be adopted towards the Germans at the Spa Conference. He took account of the discussions recently held at Hythe and Boulogne, and urged that at Spa the Allies must impress on the Germans that they were 'absolutely united on the necessity for disarmament'. At Hythe it had been agreed that the speed of the German execution of the disarmament clauses of the Versailles Treaty was 'profoundly unsatisfactory', and on 22nd June a note had been sent to their government protesting against their 'slowness and lack of good will' in this matter. He urged that 'absolutely no relaxation' of the

[1]Stanislaw Patek (or Pathek) (1866–1945). Polish lawyer and diplomat. Minister for Foreign Affairs in Skrelski government 1919. Minister in Tokyo 1922. Ambassador in Moscow 1926 and in Washington 1933–35. Senator 1936–39.

[2]Edward F. Wise (1855–1933). Civil Servant. Principal Assistant Secretary, Ministry of Food 1917. Member of Food Council 1918. A delegate on Supreme Economic Council and Chairman of Sub-Committee on Germany 1919. M.P. (Lab.) 1929–31.

relevant clauses of the treaty should be accepted; nor were his misgivings on this issue by any means exaggerated.[1]

Early in July, during the Spa Conference – of which more later – news came through 'that Krassin and the Soviet accept the conditions we laid down as a preliminary to trade negotiations'. Lloyd George was delighted, and Hankey told his wife thankfully 'It means peace with Russia – a very great factor in the peace of the world'.[2] Towards the end of that month Krassin returned to London, this time accompanied by Kamenev[3]; but the British government's troubles were by no means at an end – largely because of the intransigence of the right-wing Conservatives in the Cabinet. Discussion on the proposed Anglo-Russian trade treaty continued almost to the end of the year.

*Diary 17th November 1920*

Cabinet at 11.30 to consider the reopening of trading relations with Russia. Very warm discussion, Curzon making a strong plea against reopening the negotiations . . . until all the conditions of the July basis had been agreed to i.e. return of prisoners, cessation of propaganda, cancellation of the Soviets' treaty with Afghanistan. Lord Birkenhead however knocked the bottom out of this by pointing out that the July basis did not become operative until the trading agreement was actually signed. Curzon was on stronger ground when quoting intercepted correspondence proving that the Soviets had no intention of keeping this agreement on the points mentioned above. Bonar Law and Ll. George both made powerful statements in favour of the agreement, which was essential, they said, for British trade, or at least to convince the workers that the Govt. had interposed no obstacle to Russian orders, if these can be obtained. As a matter of fact a big diamond syndicate is buying £10 million worth of diamonds from Russia, which are at this moment in sacks at Riga. Their object is to prevent the continued depreciation of diamonds due to Bolshevist selling, but they will insist that the money shall be spent in England, provided the agreement goes through . . .

*18th November*

Continuation of discussion on Russia. A frantic appeal from Churchill against the agreement. He said the diamonds were all stolen, many from the dead bodies of the Russian aristocracy. The decision was taken by vote, subject to the return of all prisoners, [and] was in favour of continuing the

[1]Hankey's 'Notes' of 23rd June 1920. Cab. 63/28. Became C.P. 1526.

[2]To Lady Hankey. From Conférence de Spa, 8th July 1920.

[3]Lev. B. R. Kamenev (1883–1936). President of Moscow Soviet 1918–22. Expelled from the Party 1927. Re-admitted, then expelled again and finally executed in the great Stalinist 'purge' of the 1930s.

negotiations. Curzon, Churchill, and Milner voting against. Walter Long, who is ill, had sent word he was also against. Churchill asked it might be recorded in the Cabinet Minutes that no Cabinet Minister was fettered as regards making anti-Bolshevist speeches – and went down that night to the Oxford Union, where he delivered a violently anti-Bolshevist speech.[1] He was so upset by the decision that he declared himself unequal to discussing other items on the Agenda affecting the army. He was quite pale, and did not speak again during the meeting. In fact I had to undertake the exposition of one of his questions, too urgent to be left, in regard to the arrangements for seeing that Germany does not create fresh armaments after the withdrawal of the Commissions of Control. . . .

*November 19th*

Yet another Cabinet meeting to clear up certain details. The P.M. has got the wind up about one of my Cabinet conclusions on the Russian question viz. that Curzon, Churchill and Montagu are to lay down certain interpretations of the political conditions laid down in July for inclusion in the trading agreement – e.g. no co-operation with Mustapha Kemal, and no propaganda. He fears that Curzon and Churchill may include such stipulations as to render the agreement unacceptable to the Soviets. . . . The result is that I have to go to town to-morrow (Saturday) . . . to see Horne, who was away to-day, and who is to conduct the negotiations, and to rub into him that, if Curzon and Churchill are obstructive, he must bring the matter to Lloyd George, who is determined to put the agreement through.

At the end of November there was another 'short but sharp Cabinet' on the political conditions to be inserted in the Russian trade agreement. Curzon, Churchill, Austen Chamberlain and Milner again registered a protest against the decision, 'but there was not much in it' recorded Hankey.

To go back to June, on 19th–20th a second conference took place in the luxurious setting of Sir Philip Sassoon's house at Lympne. The main subject considered was the Turkish nationalist army's threat to Constantinople. Millerand came over again, with Foch and Weygand to advise him; and in face of the crisis which had arisen Anglo-French relations took a marked turn for the better – despite Lloyd George keeping Millerand waiting for 1½ hours in the golf club house while he finished his round![2] It was now that Lloyd George's refusal to heed Hankey's repeated suggestions that the C.I.D. should be revived had most unhappy consequences. For, as Hankey very well knew, that body had been constituted with the object of presenting accurate and

[1]See *The Times*, 19th Nov. 1920. [2]To Lady Hankey 20th June 1920.

co-ordinated reports on difficult international problems. But instead of the situation being properly investigated by the C.I.D. in conjunction with the Foreign Office and the Service departments Lloyd George's pronounced Phil-Hellenism, on which even Hankey, who to some extent shared it, had recently commented with concern, carried the day. 'The Middle East situation is very serious', he wrote in his diary, 'and we are threatened with critical situations in the Constantinople area, Persia and Mesopotamia. Venizelos came to the meeting [at Lympne], and without making any bargain offered practically to place at our disposal the whole of the Greek resources. C.I.G.S. very despondent'.[1]

On 20th Hankey wrote to Adeline from Lympne 'We are rather gloomy today, as we have had all sorts of bad news. The Turkish nationalists have actually reached the Dardanelles, the one thing I have dreaded and been warning the P.M. and Bonar Law about. Unless they are soon cleared out the Allied forces up at Constantinople, both naval and military, will be bottled up, which . . . has appalling possibilities. Say nothing of this until it is published'. Lloyd George of course committed a bad blunder in accepting Venizelos's offer of the Greek army; and Hankey himself evidently did not at first fully appreciate the consequences. On the last day of June he wrote in his diary 'so far they [the Greeks] are doing well, which is a triumph for Lloyd George who concerted the measure with Venizelos notwithstanding that the C.I.G.S., though consenting, was not at all sanguine that the Greeks could bring it off'.[2]

From Lympne Hankey went to Boulogne, where a meeting of experts had been called to review the problem of Reparations, preparatory to putting the Allies' proposals to the Germans at the Spa conference. Hankey remarked in his diary that 'our reception at Boulogne was extraordinarily cordial, proving what I have always found that Paris (where we are not overpopular) does not represent France'. As always he observed closely the characters of the participants, and Count Sforza,[3] the new Italian Foreign Minister, made a favourable impression – partly because he was the only member of the conference besides himself to indulge in sea bathing! The Allies

[1]Diary 19th June 1920. [2]Diary 30th June 1920.

[3]1872–1952. Italian Diplomat and politician. Minister in Serbia 1915–18. Minister for Foreign Affairs 1920–21. Ambassador at Paris 1922. Left Italy on establishment of Fascist government and did not return until 1943 when he declared for a Republic. Again Foreign Minister 1947–51.

now estimated Germany's capacity to pay Reparations at the enormous figure of £13,450 millions – which was slightly above the American estimate of 1919 but only a little over half the figure produced by the Hughes-Cunliffe committee of 1918.

Before both the Boulogne and the Spa conferences (21st–22nd June and 5th–16th July respectively) the British Empire Delegation met in London 'in order that the Dominions may have a voice in Reparations and other questions to be discussed'; but Australia was unrepresented because 'Billy' Hughes, ever 'truculent and difficult. . . has not answered our telegram inviting him to nominate someone in lieu of Watt[1] [who has] resigned'.[2] On the last day of June Hankey left London with Lloyd George, Curzon, Worthington-Evans[3] and Henry Wilson ('rather a jolly party') for Brussels, where the preliminaries to the Spa conference were to take place.

*To Lady Hankey. Palace Hotel, Brussels, 2nd July 1920 (evening)*

. . . We had a very uneventful conference in the morning . . . the afternoon meeting was cancelled, as Lloyd George has been conducting the business of the conference in a series of private conversations with the various Prime Ministers, one after the other. This was a very good plan, which I myself advised, as the question of Reparations is a most awfully delicate one, in which the greed of the various nations seems to be in inverse proportion to their war effort. First Millerand came; then Delacroix the Belgian Prime Minister.[4] Then Millerand again, and now Count Sforza the Italian Foreign Minister with him. I knew Ll. G. meant to talk very straight to the greedy people, who are all fighting for the prime cut off the skinny German goose and won't even wait for it to be fattened up a bit. Ll. G. wanted to say things which are better unrecorded! I am afraid, though, that not much progress has been made. Still, Ll. G. has a wonderful knack of pulling things off at the last moment, and I expect that before we go to Spa he will have secured agreement . . .

[1]William A. Watt (1871–1946). Australian politician. Premier and Treasurer of Victoria 1909–14. Commonwealth Treasurer 1918–20. Acting Prime Minister 1918–19. Speaker of House of Representatives 1923–26.

[2]Diary 30th June 1920. Sir George Perly represented Canada (see Vol. I, p. 599). New Zealand's representative was Sir James Allen, New Zealand politician (1855–1942). Minister of Finance and Education 1912–15, of Defence 1912–20 and of External Affairs and Defence 1919–20. High Commissioner in London 1920–26. Member of Legislative Council 1927–41.

[3]See Vol. I, p. 423, *note*.

[4]L. Delacroix, not de la Croix as written by Hankey, (1867–1929). Belgian politician. Prime Minister and Minister of Finance 1920.

Next day he wrote that 'the game of haggling is still going on', and told Adeline how they all longed to get out of the heat of Brussels up into the cool climate and lovely scenery of the Ardennes. He had dined at the Palace, and was flattered when, on being presented to King Albert,[1] the latter said 'Oh yes! I remember. You are the Secretary I have heard so much of!'

Though Hankey's part in the Soviet–Polish imbroglio of 1920 will be told later the crisis was blowing up at the time of the Brussels–Spa meetings. On 30th June he wrote in his diary that 'the Poles . . . are getting a hiding from the Bolshevists as Lloyd George solemnly warned them would occur if they attacked [Russia]'. Two days later, writing from Brussels, he told Adeline how after a dinner given by the Belgian Prime Minister 'Foch and Henry Wilson came to me and said they wanted to talk to Ll. G. So I managed to shepherd them with Millerand behind a table in a corner, and they had a very important talk about Poland – which may even settle the fate of that country. It was rather a dramatic incident, this informal conference of some of the greatest men in Europe whispered in the corner of the great reception room. Not far off was standing M. Patek the Polish Foreign Minister. Last time I met him was in January or February in Paris at breakfast with Ll. G. who talked to him like a Dutch uncle, warning him of the frightful retribution which would follow if Poland attacked the Bolshevists . . . And so it has come to pass, for the warning was neglected. Patek looks 10 years older, poor devil . . .'.

On 4th Hankey motored to Spa with Lloyd George, stopping at Waterloo 'where General Sackville-West[2] explained the battlefield'. The first meeting took place next day and, wrote Hankey, was 'short and formal, as the Allies refused to discuss disarmament . . . with the Germans unless Gessler, the Minister of War, is present.[3] . . . Gessler is notoriously a resister to disarmament, and Ll. G. who is to state the disarmament case for the Allies, absolutely refused to go on without

[1]Albert I, King of the Belgians (1875–1934). Succeeded to throne 1909. He and Queen Elisabeth remained with the Belgian army throughout World War I and re-entered Brussels amid great enthusiasm on 22nd Nov. 1918.

[2]Major-General Sir Charles Sackville-West, 4th Baron Sackville 1928 (1870–1962). British military representative at Supreme War Council 1918–19. Military attaché, Paris 1920–24.

[3]Otto Gessler. German lawyer and politician (1875–1955). Minister for Reconstruction 1919 and for War 1920–28. Dismissed 1928. Arrested at end of Hitler régime. President of German Red Cross 1950–52.

him. I spent a couple of hours in bed in the morning just before we left Brussels making a brief for Ll. G. [on German disarmament], and it is a pretty hot one. I believe he means to stick pretty close to it . . . Fehrenbach[1] the German Chancellor made a good impression this morning. He seemed sincerely desirous of carrying out the treaty, but I doubt if he has the strength to impose himself . . .'.[2]

*To Lady Hankey. Hotel Britannique, Spa. 6th July 1920*

. . . The meeting with the Germans was a highly dramatic one. They kept reiterating their intention to execute the treaty loyally, but the moment they were pinned down to anything definite they fell back on vague generalisations and excuses. At last Lloyd George, who was conducting the Allied case, got tired of it and told them plainly that if they did not come up to-morrow with a proper plan for the rapid execution of the disarmament clauses of the treaty he for one would not be a party to the conference, which would be broken up. Fehrenbach . . . said that all his life he had been an honest man, and he hoped to meet his Eternal Judge as an honest man; he had promised to fulfil the treaty, and this ought to be good enough for the Allies. It looked as though the conference might break up there and then, but Dr. Simons,[3] the German Foreign Minister, burst in with a declaration that they would bring a plan tomorrow, and this was accepted. [Hankey went on to describe the appearance and characters of the German delegates. Fehrenbach 'rather an attractive figure – a heavy, stoutly built man with a drooping moustache', who bore some resemblance to General Botha. Gessler 'a truculent, bullet-headed Bosch'. Simons 'quiet and clever looking'.] My impression was that, as politicians, they were a set of inexperienced amateurs, floundering about when pitted against some of the acutest political minds in the world. I asked Foch afterwards what he thought about it. 'Oh, Lloyd George did very well', he said, 'and he was right not to break off to-day. But to-morrow all that they will offer will be *that*' [and Foch made a gesture with thumb and forefinger indicating 'nought'] . . .

On 8th Hankey found himself acting again more or less as secretary to a new 'Council of Four' at whose 'hush meeting' he was amused to watch Millerand, 'who always wants to bully the Germans', and Lloyd George, 'who wants to treat them reasonably', manoeuvre towards

[1]Konstantin Fehrenbach (1852–1926). German politician (Centre). President of Reichstag and of first National Assembly at Weimar 1918–19. Charged by President Ebert with forming a Centre-coalition government 1920, but dismissed 1921 over non-settlement of war debts.

[2]To Lady Hankey. Conférence de Spa. 8th July 1920.

[3]Walther Simons, not Simon as written by Hankey (1861–1937). German lawyer and politician. Foreign Minister 1920–21.

agreement. When the German delegates were called in Lloyd George eased the tension by getting what Hankey described as 'a real laugh out of old Fehrenbach by chaffingly remarking that he might use some of the unemployed in Berlin to execute the treaty quicker'.[1]

Two days later Hankey was able to tell Adeline that Lloyd George had achieved 'a magnificent series of successes at the conference', but had 'gone to bed with bad tummy ache'. He had brought with him to Spa 'a famous Manchester surgeon' – in reality to give him a holiday[2]; but Hankey regarded him 'as the wrong man for the P.M. with no understanding of his psychology'. He wrote that the surgeon 'always frightens the P.M. who is timid about his health', and entertained apprehensions that he was 'itching to cut him open'.[3] Certainly Hankey understood his master better than anyone else in his entourage – except possibly Frances Stevenson. Then Millerand declared that he had to return to Paris to take the salute at the annual review to mark the 'Quatorze Juillet', and it was with some difficulty that Lloyd George, to the vast amusement of the conference, dissuaded him on the grounds that 'standing in the sun for four hours with his hat off' was to risk an attack of sunstroke.[4]

Despite all Lloyd George's persistence and persuasiveness by 13th it seemed that an *impasse* had been reached.

*To Lady Hankey. Hotel Britannique, Spa. 13th July 1920*

... At the moment the conference appears to be on the eve of breaking. The Germans have refused this afternoon to make an offer which we can accept in deliveries of coal under the treaty, and [? we] won't go ahead with Reparations until coal is settled. Stinnes,[5] a capitalist of enormous wealth, who owns more than 70 newspapers, a most sinister figure with a black beard and hideous sensual face, appears master of the situation and to have got Fehrenbach and Simons, who are reasonable men, in his grip. The only reason why we have not broken off – and this is secret – is that we want to

[1]To Lady Hankey. From Hotel Britannique, Spa. 5th July 1920.

[2]Apparently Sir William Milligan (1864–1929). Consultant surgeon, aurist and laryngologist to many hospitals in Manchester and the north-west.

[3]To Lady Hankey 10th July 1920. [4]To Lady Hankey 13th July 1920.

[5]Hugo Stinnes (1870–1924). German industrialist who during and after World War I created a huge empire in the fields of transport, newspapers, coal mines and factories of the Ruhr etc. etc. Elected a Deputy 1920–24 as Nationalist. Amassed a vast fortune through the inflation of the 1920s. For a time economic dictator of Germany, he has much to answer for in stimulating French apprehensions and so preventing a fair revision of the Versailles Treaty.

know whether the Bolshevists are going to accept our invitation to them to make an armistice with Poland before we break with the Huns. If we break now the Bolshevists may say that this is their opportunity to ally with the Germans, and we shall be face to face with a very grave situation, as the Germans may be driven into their arms ... Meanwhile we have sent for Foch and Henry Wilson to advise on military measures [against Germany] ...

Hankey's strictures on Stinnes's character and conduct were fully justified; but there is nothing in his papers to show that, despite the presence at Spa of representatives of the Control Commission, he was as yet aware of the strength of the unholy alliance formed between the German militarist factions and the industrialists to evade the disarmament clauses in the Versailles Treaty.[1]

*To Lady Hankey. Spa. 16th July 1920*
... The Allied agreement on the difficult coal question was only reached late yesterday afternoon, and was handed immediately to the Bosch. They, we hear, are having desperate wrangles about it ... If they refuse we shall come home to-morrow, but if they accept, or if they accept subject to conditions, we shall not get away ...

The fact is that there has been an infinity of wrangling about points which, though not quite of the greatest intrinsic importance, have in a way become test questions. Principal among these has been the coal price question ... The Treaty provided that France should pay Germany for coal she had to deliver, at a price which, owing to the fall in the German exchange and other causes, has become a ridiculously low one. Germany, as a condition of agreeing to supply certain quantities of coal we are insisting on, stipulated for a higher price. We British took the German view that conditions had changed and the price ought to be raised.[2] ... The French stood out for the Treaty price on the ground that they ought not to pay more for the German coal than the Germans themselves pay. The result was a complete *impasse*. [Hankey here enlarged on the compromise solution reached – a slightly higher price to be paid and a loan guaranteed by the Allies to be granted to Germany in order to buy food abroad] ... Part of the secret history is that Lloyd George saw Dr. Simons and more or less encouraged him to put in this condition [i.e. about the loan]. Then of course Lloyd George was more or less committed, and had to take a very intransigent line. He was rather brutal and rude to the French whom he compared to Shylock ... We learn

[1]See Roskill, *Naval Policy*, I, pp. 97–8.

[2]Lloyd George, according to Hankey, represented that the French government would make £30–40 millions yearly by selling the coal to the French people at a far higher price than they had paid the Germans for it. D.B.F.P., 1st Series, Vol. VII, Ch. VIII has a number of important documents on the Spa Conference.

that Stinnes and the capitalistic elements want us to occupy the Ruhr, as they think the Rhine provinces, being then no longer dependent for coal on Prussia, the masters of the Ruhr, would break away [with the result, noted Hankey, that Stinnes would pay less tax on his Rhenish properties!] Bavaria would probably break away also in this case, and the German empire would be smashed. This would suit the French, and is probably at the back of their intense desire to occupy the Ruhr . . . It would not suit us so well though, as France would be left the only great military power on the continent . . . You will see that we are caught up in the very vortex of European continental politics, which in my view we ought to try and steer clear of. . . . From the secretarial point of view this conference has been appalling – mainly owing to the P.M.'s extraordinary habits [Here Hankey described how Lloyd George constantly 'slipped in' Ministers or advisers whom he wanted present, regardless of 'the rules', with the result that other nations did the same and up to 50 people would be crammed into the small room he insisted on using. The climax came when Lloyd George held 'a veritable conference seated in a basket chair with an enormous ring of people standing round three deep.' The secretaries then 'unanimously agreed to "chuck their hands in" and none of us recorded a word all day']. At the very last moment (9 p.m.) the Huns have climbed down, so I shall put this letter in my diary instead of posting it.

Hankey finally got home from Spa, very tired and out of humour, on 17th. That day Lord Derby wrote to him from the Paris Embassy saying that 'As George Curzon seems rather to resent my writing to you, although I write to him at the same time, I am altering the form and send you under cover of this letter a letter to the Prime Minister'.[1] He wanted Hankey to 'dictate something' giving his views on the results of the Spa Conference – as though the overworked secretary had nothing better to do than pass to the Ambassador information which should have been provided by the Foreign Office. Presumably the request arose from Derby's bad relations with Curzon. More tiresome than Derby's importunities was the new and onerous demand Lloyd George now suddenly made of Hankey.

*Diary 20th July 1920*

. . . On the way back on Saturday [17th] Lloyd George asked me if I would go on a special mission to Poland with Lord D'Abernon,[2] our ambassador in

[1]Derby to Hankey 17th July 1920.

[2]Edgar V. D'Abernon, 1st Baron 1914, Viscount 1926. (1857–1941). Expert on Middle East, diplomat and politician (Cons.). Financial adviser to Egyptian government 1883–90. Governor of Ottoman Bank, Constantinople 1889–97. Ambassador at Berlin 1920–26.

Berlin, and General P. de B. Radcliffe.[1] I am due to start this evening and have my passport and railway ticket, although Lloyd George, with whom I spent most of yesterday at Cobham, still refuses to say finally whether I am to go. All he says is that I must be ready to start – so I have had to pack in a frightful hurry late last night and make all preparations. I do not at all appreciate the job and hereby put it on record . . .

All this I have told Lloyd George. He knows that I have both a dislike and contempt for the Poles, and that I don't believe, in the long run, anything can be done to save them, and finally that I am doubtful if they are worth saving. He knows that in my view it is inevitable sooner or later that Russia gets a coterminous frontier with Germany, and that . . . we ought to orientate our policy so as to make Germany and not Poland the barrier between eastern and western civilisation. Finally he knows that I want a holiday with my family after all these years of work. Yet he insists on my going off on this ridiculous and vague mission.

The Polish frontier dispute in which Hankey was so unwillingly involved, had actually taken up quite a lot of the time of the Spa Conference – as indeed it had at the Paris Peace Conference. The re-creation of an independent Poland was one consequence of the break-up of the Habsburg Empire; but the settlement of the new nation's frontiers proved an extremely intractable problem, and the aggressive nationalism of the Polish government under Marshal Pilsudski, the Head of State and Commander-in-Chief of the army,[2] nearly proved their undoing. Very rashly, and as we have seen in total contradiction to British advice, they set out in the spring of 1920 to conquer and annex the Ukraine. Soviet Russia, at last free from foreign intervention and civil strife, at once turned unitedly on the Poles, and in June smote them so heavily that it seemed likely that Warsaw itself would fall. The chief purpose of the D'Abernon mission was to press the Polish government to seek an armistice. But the presence of military advisers, together with the fact that on 23rd Hankey passed a message to the War Office to prepare 'a list of 200 suitable officers for service with the Poles' shows that active assistance was certainly envisaged as a possibility.

[1]See Vol. I, p. 529, *note*.

[2]Jozef Pilsudski (1867–1935). Polish nationalist leader who, after taking part in plots against Russia, became Head of State and C-in-C of Army with dictatorial powers 1919–22. Resumed power 1926 as result of military *coup d'état*. As head of government and Minister of War was the effective head of Polish state until his death.

Hankey and his invaluable Sylvester left London for Paris on 20th July, accompanied by D'Abernon and Radcliffe. By the time they reached Paris Hankey's ill humour had evaporated, and he told Adeline, who had evidently taken this new separation from her husband hardly, that he was 'in this "*con amore*" ' and would do his 'level best to put it through'.[1] After calling on Lord Derby at the British Embassy, D'Abernon and Hankey went to the Quai d'Orsay for talks with Millerand, Berthelot, Paléologue[2] and General Weygand, which Hankey described as 'most satisfactory and cordial'.[3] Meanwhile M. Paderewski[4] had arrived in Paris 'as a special commissioner with wide powers to represent Poland'. He dined with the British mission that evening and, according to Hankey, gave 'a most disturbing account' of affairs in his country. But when the need to ask for an armistice was mentioned he was at first 'rather truculent'.[5] Hankey, who was as usual keeping Tom Jones *au courant* with his contacts and discussions, told him that he must on no account let Adeline know anything about Paderewski's 'rather disquieting information'.[6] If his mission was to involve him in danger he was evidently determined that his wife should not be caused avoidable anxiety. Typically Lord Derby took advantage of Hankey's presence in Paris to further his own interests – namely the extension of his appointment – while keeping Curzon in ignorance of his request. Hankey passed this on to the Prime Minister saying, very naturally, that he did not want 'to mix himself up in this business'.[7] As Lord Hardinge did not take over the Paris embassy until September it seems that Derby did gain a brief extension. An interesting development which arose out of Hardinge's departure from the Foreign Office is that Hankey was apparently considered for the post of Permanent Secretary. At any rate on 7th September Esher wrote to him 'It may interest you to hear that at Balmoral there came a rumour . . . that you

[1]To Lady Hankey. Ritz Hotel, Paris. 21st July 1920.

[2]Maurice Paléologue (1859–1944). French diplomat and author. Ambassador at Sofia 1907 and in Russia 1914–17. Secretary-General for Foreign Affairs 1920.

[3]Diary 21st July 1920.

[4]Ignace Paderewski (1860–1941). Polish politician and world-famous pianist. Visited U.S.A. 1915 and obtained from President Wilson the promise of a free and independent Poland. Prime Minister and Foreign Minister 1919. Signed Treaty of Versailles. Retired from public life 1921.

[5]Diary 21st July 1920.

[6]Hankey to Jones 22nd July 1920 from Ritz Hotel, Paris.

[7]Hankey to Lloyd George from same.

were to succeed Hardinge at the F.O. The King flew into a fury, and said that you were the most important and useful public servant of the Crown and State, that you were the only possible link between this Government and any possible successor Government, and the Guardian of the traditions of Government . . . He added that . . . he would die in the last ditch or go on hunger strike rather than allow you to accept such a post. So there. And I certainly entirely agree with H.M.'[1] . . . Obviously George V's admiration for and confidence in Hankey had in no way weakened with the coming of peace.

In Paris the mission was soon engaged in more talks, including a long session with Dr. Beneš, the Czecho-Slovak Foreign Minister. Like Paderewski he feared 'an outbreak of Bolshevism' in Poland; and to provide against such an eventuality the French government provided the mission with a special train 'provisioned and prepared for them to live in for some time'. The French members, led by M. Jusserand,[2] joined their British colleagues at the Gare de l'Est, and late on 22nd the train left for Prague. Almost continuous conferences took place en route, and Hankey made extensive notes on the condition of the inhabitants of the towns through which they passed, on the quality of the harvest and on anything else that caught his observant eye.[3] Early on 24th they arrived at Prague, and were met by Hankey's 'old friend Sir George Clerk', the British Minister.[4] Clerk at once took them to visit Masaryk,[5] The President, whom Hankey described as 'a very remarkable man with a very big view of the situation'. Obviously he was gratified to find that the President's opinions on the Polish problem

[1]Esher to Hankey 7th Sept. 1920.

[2]Jules Jusserand (1855–1932). Diplomat and writer on English literature and history. Ambassador to Denmark 1898 and to Washington 1902–20.

[3]Diary 22nd–23rd July 1920. Lord D'Abernon included in the mission Lord Colum Crichton-Stuart (not Stewart as written by Hankey) (1886–1957) a brother of 5th Marquess of Bute and a Mr. Eagles whose name Hankey suspected had originally been Adler. As the former was 'an ardent Roman Catholic' and the latter 'isn't a Jew according to his own account but looks like one' D'Abernon evidently thought they would be useful in handling the religious and minority problems in Poland. To Lady Hankey 22nd July 1920.

[4]See Vol. I, p. 348, *note*.

[5]Tomáš G. Masaryk. (1850–1937) Czech academic and statesman. Professor at Vienna 1879 and at Prague 1882. Emigrated 1914 and conducted vigorous Czech nationalist campaign. President of Provisional Government 1917. President 1918, re-elected 1927 and 1934. A supporter of alliance with France. Father of Jan Masaryk, ambassador at London 1921–38.

'were in almost every detail' the same as his own – namely that 'Polish resistance had collapsed beyond possibility of repair'. Masaryk was emphatic that in no event would Czecho-Slovakia involve herself in support for the Poles. He even went further, and declared that if such support were provided it would 'inevitably fail', and that the Allies would as a result sacrifice their 'power and prestige to influence the situation'. That same day Hankey wrote in his diary that he was 'trying gradually to force the idea' on his colleagues that 'the main object of our mission is an armistice and a general peace, and that the military side viz. support to Poland, though important, is only an alternative and a bad one.' He went on to declare that 'Bolshevism could not be beaten by bayonets', that an anti-Bolshevist barrier such as Foch wanted to create with Poland, Czecho-Slovakia and Roumania [an accurate forecast of the 'Little Entente' of 1920–21, except that Yugo-Slavia was substituted for Poland[1]] was futile'; and that 'the only way to combat Bolshevism was by propaganda and by trade.' With evident approval he quoted Masaryk's saying that 'one locomotive is worth more than the capture of a Bolshevist battalion'.[2]

On the evening of 24th the mission's train entered Poland, and on reaching Warsaw next morning they were met by the British Minister Sir Horace Rumbold, another old friend of Hankey's.[3] Talks with members of the Polish government began at once – and as always Hankey jotted down shrewd comments on their appearance and personalities. By 27th he was able to write that 'a tremendous change has come over the situation', that peace negotiations would probably take place in London, that a Russian advance on Warsaw was now unlikely, and that his presence was therefore no longer necessary. Though he still regarded the mission as 'a waste of time' he told Adeline that he was 'picking up a lot of information about Polish, Central European, Russian and Baltic politics which cannot fail to be useful hereafter'. 'Knowledge, according to my experience', he went on, 'is always useful, and one should never lose an opportunity to acquire it'. Certainly he consistently lived up to that maxim.[4]

[1]See E. H. Carr, *International Relations since the Peace Treaties* (Macmillan, 1940), pp. 38–43 regarding the French treaties with the Little Entente, which were based on their support for the enforcement of the Versailles Treaty, in return for which France would support their national claims and interests.

[2]Diary 24th July 1920. [3]See Vol. I, p. 507, *note*.

[4]To Lady Hankey, British Legation, Warsaw, 27th July 1920.

Hankey actually left Warsaw on 30th and travelled home via Danzig, where the dockers were refusing to unload arms for the Poles, and Berlin. During the journey he dictated a long report to the Cabinet, in which he was highly critical of the Poles and of their expansionist aims. It covered 40 pages of foolscap typescript, but as the most important parts of it have been published there is no need to summarise it here.[1] Hankey's efforts drew very warm praise from D'Abernon who, on the last day of July wrote to Curzon drawing his attention to 'the remarkable services rendered by Sir Maurice Hankey', and stressing 'that he is deserving of special thanks from His Majesty's Government'.[2] In truth Hankey had made a firm friend of D'Abernon who, for the rest of his career, regularly sent him extracts from his diary and copies of his reports to the Foreign Office.[3]

Contrary to Hankey's pessimistic prognostications about Polish military prospects, in August the situation was transformed by their total defeat of the Red Army – justly described by General Radcliffe as 'a victory as complete and dramatic as any in the annals of war'. Weygand, with more than a touch of genius, at once appreciated the opportunity afforded by the large gap which separated the army under Tukachevsky (Soviet Chief of Staff), who aimed to capture Warsaw, and that under Generals Yegorov and Budienny, which was advancing through eastern Galicia towards Lemberg. Weygand urged the Poles to strike into the gap, and within a few days the Red Army was in full retreat. As Trotsky, the Commissar for War, was Tukachevsky's superior and patron, and Joseph Stalin was political Commissar attached to Yegorov and Budienny these events had profound effects on the struggle for power as successor to Lenin – and so probably on the entire history of the 20th century.[4]

Hankey made no entry in his diary between the day he reached Warsaw and 18th September, by which time he was of course well

[1] D.B.F.P., 1st Series, Vol. XI, pp. 429–34. The complete report is C.P. 1724 dated 3rd Aug. 1920 Cab. 24/110. Another copy in D'Abernon papers B.M. Add. MSS. 48923.

[2] B.M. Add. MSS. 48923.

[3] Add. MSS. 48924 contain despatches, diary extracts and letters sent by D'Abernon to Hankey during his embassy to Germany 1920–26.

[4] See H. J. Elcock, *Britain and the Russo-Polish Frontier 1919–21*. The Historical Journal, XII, 1 (1969), pp. 137-54 for an admirable account of these events. Lord D'Abernon's *The Eighteenth Decisive Battle of the World – Warsaw 1920* (Hodder & Stoughton, 1931) has his version,

aware that, although his criticisms of Polish territorial greed were justified, much of what he had foretold had proved erroneous. That misjudgment no doubt explains the unusual note of defensiveness in his next entry.

*Diary 18th September 1920*
My visit to Poland will be found described in my letters and official reports.[1] I was about 6 days in Warsaw. By that time I felt there was not much more to be done. We had compelled the Polish Government to employ the French officers and to take Weygand's advice. My main preoccupation had been that the Poles would not make peace and that Lord D'Abernon and M. Jusserand would not put sufficient pressure on them and would support them in taking up an intransigent attitude. But, by this time, I felt satisfied as regards Lord D'Abernon and my farewell interviews with Prince Sapieha[2] and M. Grabski[3] were of a reassuring character as regards the Poles. Lord D'Abernon and M. Jusserand were quite sufficient for keeping the Poles up to the mark, and Rumbold, the British Minister, with whom I stayed at Warsaw, was a tower of strength. ... Before leaving the subject of Poland I should mention that I found England in general and Lloyd George in particular very unpopular there. ... They considered that Ll. G. had thwarted Polish aspirations in Danzig, Upper Silesia, and Eastern Galicia; but a few, including a wise Under-Secretary for Foreign Affairs, realised that Ll. G. was really their friend by refusing to them at the peace conferences large blocks of alien populations whom they could never have assimilated, and by warning them against the Kiev offensive ... I received a very warm welcome – quite a touching welcome – from Lloyd George and the Cabinet, a meeting of which I attended within an hour of my arrival in London. The subsequent recovery of the Poles was unexpected by me. I thought they were absolutely done and a hopeless people altogether. Still I had the satisfaction of knowing that their recovery was entirely due to our mission's insistence on the employment of Weygand and the French officers on the spot, and that the plan eventually carried out was one which I had outlined to Gen. Radcliffe before I left

[1]C.P. 1724 of 3rd Aug. 1920. Copy in Cab. 63/29.

[2]Prince Eustache Sapieha, a member of a famous and influential family, originally Lithuanian, was Polish ambassador in London July 1919–June 1920, when he became Foreign Minister in M. Grabski's government.

[3]Stanislaw Grabski (1871–1949) and his brother Wladislaw (1874–1938) were both active in Polish politics at this time, but Hankey is here probably referring to the latter, who was a Polish delegate at the Paris Peace Conference and President of the Council at the time of the Bolshevist invasion of 1920. It was however Stanislaw who signed the Treaty of Riga in 1921. Both held many Ministerial offices and played a large part in Polish politics in between the wars.

Poland . . . After all, it was the proper and only reasonable plan in the circumstances, and the Russians played into our hands by their foolhardy advance along the frontier of East Prussia. On my return I found, as I had anticipated, that Lloyd George had altogether underrated the hostility of British public opinion to the Poles and was running away from it. He never gave any public recognition to the value of the work of our mission . . . for fear of letting the public see he had helped the Poles.

To carry the story of Poland on to the end, peace talks started at Minsk in August, when Kamenev, who was in London, gave the Foreign Office a copy of what purported to be the Russian terms. These provided for the eastern frontier to be the 'Curzon Line' which had been accepted by the Supreme Council in December 1919,[1] and the British Government urged the Poles to accept the terms. In fact however the Russian proposals put forward at Minsk differed markedly from those handed in by Kamenev – which produced from Hankey an explosion about his 'treachery', and a stormy interview between the Soviet envoy and Lloyd George. Pressure was next put on the Poles to moderate their demands; but in the flush of victory they continued to insist on further aggrandisement. Britain refused to recognise the final frontier, which lay far to the east of the Curzon Line; but it was incorporated in the Treaty of Riga, signed on 8th March 1921. Though peace had come at last the implacable hatred of Poles and Russians had been aggravated, and the harvest sown in 1920–21 was to be reaped in the disaster of 1939.

Early in August Hankey had to attend 'a perfectly hectic' conference with the French at Lympne, at which Polish problems, and in particular the trouble with Kamenev over the peace terms, took priority.[2] His chief concern was to prepare for Lloyd George the very difficult statement which he was to make in the House on 10th.[3] Then Hankey had a brief holiday with his family at Eastbourne 'much interrupted by journeys to town and papers'.[4] On 18th he left, most unusually in company with Adeline and Robin, for Lucerne, where Lloyd George was to discuss the Polish situation and the execution of the Spa agree-

[1]Nicolson, *Curzon*, pp. 202–8.
[2]To Lady Hankey 9th Aug. 1920. This was the Third Lympne (or Hythe) Conference. See D.B.F.P., 1st Series, Vol. VII, Ch. XI.
[3]On the Consolidated Fund Bill. Parl. Deb., Commons, Vol. 133, Cols. 253–72.
[4]Diary 18th Sept., 1920.

ments with Giolitti the new Italian Prime Minister.[1] But Lucerne was a place Hankey had 'never cared for'; and the constant pressure of telegrams from Balfour who 'had been left in charge of the British Government' (which Hankey often had to decipher because J. T. Davies 'was in a rather lazy frame of mind'), combined with the need to produce *procès-verbaux* of the meetings, prevented him enjoying much of his family's company. Furthermore Lloyd George ('a gregarious creature') always 'wanted the whole party to go about with him'; and, as with all of Lloyd George's parties, some of his friends – in this case Mrs. Rupert Beckett 'a regular society woman with few ideas beyond dress and extravagance'[2] – were not to Hankey's taste. On the other hand Megan Lloyd George's friend Thelma Cazalet he described as 'a charming girl'.[3] Later on Sir Hamar and Lady Greenwood turned up 'and were an acquisition'. So was Oliver Locker-Lampson[4]; but Freddy Guest 'was more in Mrs. Beckett's line'. However, right at the end the Hankeys and Lloyd George managed to get up to the Riffel-Alp, Zermatt, for two nights; which gave Robin the chance to show that in the mountains he was now fully a match for his father's prodigious energy.

During the Lucerne Conference the question of the expulsion of Kamenev and Krassin caused a great deal of telegraphing to and from London. Lloyd George was at first reluctant to approve so drastic a step, but after the evidence regarding political propaganda, the subsidy paid to the *Daily Herald*, attempts to influence British foreign policy

[1]Giovanni Giolitti (1842–1928) Italian politician, sometimes Right Wing, sometimes Left. Minister of Finance 1889–90. Prime Minister 1892–3, resigning as a result of leak scandals. Minister of Interior 1901–3. Prime Minister 1903–5, 1906–9 and 1911–14 – 11 years often called 'The Dictatorship of Giolitti'. A supporter of war against Turkey 1911 but opponent of Italy's entry into World War I 1915. Prime Minister again 1920–21. At first a supporter of Mussolini, then (1928) one of the few politicians to oppose the suspension of Parliamentary government by him.

[2]Muriel, daughter of Lord Berkeley Paget and wife of Hon. Rupert E. Beckett (1870–1955). She died in 1941.

[3]Now (1970) Mrs. Thelma Cazalet-Keir. Entered politics (Cons.) 1931. Parliamentary Secretary to Ministry of Education 1945. Member of many government committees and inquiries on status of women.

[4]Commander Oliver S. Locker-Lampson (1880–1954). Politician (Cons.) and pioneer of naval aviation. Served with naval armoured cars all over Europe, including Russia, in World War I. Parliamentary Secretary to Leader of House of Commons and to Lord Privy Seal 1921.

and Russian deceit over the Polish peace terms had been produced he came into line with Balfour in a long telegram to Law which, he said, 'Hankey is doing his best to make intelligible'.[1] The original proposal was, according to Hankey, 'to publish the whole of the evidence'; but as this 'would have compromised a most valuable and trustworthy source of secret information' he tried to persuade Lloyd George that an adequate case could be made out in a *communiqué*; and in the end that recommendation was approved. The exact nature of the source of our secret information is made plain in another memorandum by Hankey. 'This particular cypher [i.e. the Russian one]', he wrote, 'is a very ingenious one which was discovered [? deciphered] by great cleverness and hard work. The key is changed daily and sometimes as often as three times in one message. Hence if it becomes known that we decoded the messages all the Governments of the world will probably soon discover that no messages are safe'.[2]

The other matter which caused lengthy discussions at this time was the hunger strike by Terence McSwiney, the Lord Mayor of Cork, which was now in its sixth week. Lloyd George stood out firmly against his release, on the grounds that it would 'completely disintegrate and dishearten the Police Force in Ireland and the Military'. 'We might as well give up attempting to maintain law and order in Ireland' he told Bonar Law.[3] But everyone else was anxious that McSwiney should not be allowed to die. Hankey believed that arrangements had been made to feed him surreptitiously 'with his aperient doses and by other imperceptible means'; or that he was being 'secretly fed through the Mass'. Tom Jones's diary reveals that it was probably Sir George Newman, Chief Medical Officer at the Board of Education and Ministry of Health, who at Lloyd George's instigation kept the Lord Mayor alive for the astounding period of 72 (or by some accounts 74) days of hunger strike.[4]

[1]Lloyd George to Law from Lucerne 4th Sept. 1920. Cab. 63/29.

[2]Memo. of 8th Sept. 1920. Cab. 63/29. None the less some of the deciphered messages were apparently published, since in the following year Hankey drew Lloyd George's attention to the 'remarkable drop' in deciphered Russian telegrams, which he attributed to that action. The head of the Secret Service, Admiral Sinclair, had pointed out that 'if intelligence is used for publicity it will be lost to us'. Hankey to Lloyd George 22nd March 1921. Lloyd George Papers F/25/1/20.

[3]Lloyd George to Law 4th Sept. 1920. Cab. 63/29.

[4]*Middlemas*, I, p. 279. James, *Davidson*, p. 98. McSwiney was already in frail health when imprisoned in Brixton gaol as an I.R.A. leader. He died on 25th October.

Lloyd George's policy towards Ireland, wrote Hankey at this time, 'is to pass the Irish Bill, establish a parliament in Ulster; and, if Southern Ireland refuses to establish a parliament, withdraw from the interior, occupying the ports only and collecting there the customs and excise duties'.[1] Threats to the lives of Ministers were now flying around freely, and at Lucerne 'detectives of several nationalities' were called in to protect them. Whereas Greenwood was, according to Hankey, 'quite unshaken by his recent nerve-racking experience as Chief Secretary' Lloyd George went in terror for his life; and on returning from Lucerne he constantly moved about between various houses, whilst giving out that he was at Cobham for weekends.

Throughout the summer threats of a coal strike also loomed large in the Cabinet's deliberations. On 22nd September Hankey joined a meeting of 'the Triple Alliance' (miners, railwaymen and dock workers) late in the evening at No. 10, and after the Union leaders had withdrawn to discuss the government's offer among themselves he told Adeline that he was 'afraid this means a strike'. The miners actually stopped work on 16th October, and six days later 'the P.M. held a surreptitious meeting with Smillie and Hodges', Bonar Law also being present. Most incongruously it apparently took place at Philip Sassoon's luxurious Park Lane house. Meanwhile the railwaymen had declared that if no settlement with the miners was in sight by the end of the week they too would come out[2]; but Hankey foretold, correctly, that the leadership of J. H. Thomas, 'a moderate', would prevent that threat being carried out.

On 24th, a Sunday, Hankey came up early from Highstead to be present at a full-scale meeting called to try and settle the strike. William Brace[3] and Vernon Hartshorn[4], two Welsh miners' M.P.s, had put forward some proposals which 'provided a very useful starting point for discussions'. Lloyd George, Bonar Law, Horne, Bridgeman and A. R. Duncan[5] the Coal Controller represented the government; while

[1]Diary 18th Sept. 1920. [2]Diary 22nd Oct. 1920.

[3]1865–1947. Politician (Lab.) and Trade Union leader. President, South Wales Miners' Federation. Parliamentary Under-Secretary, Home Office 1915–18. Chief Labour Adviser to Department of Mines 1920–27.

[4]1872–1931. Politician (Lab.) and Trade Union leader. Postmaster-General 1924. Member, Indian Reforms Commission 1927–30. President, South Wales Miners' Federation.

[5]Later Sir Andrew Duncan (1884–1952). Industrialist and politician (Cons.). Coal Controller 1919–20. Chairman, Advisory Committee of Coal Mines Department

Smillie, Hodges, Herbert Smith and William Straker represented the miners. In Hankey's view the railwaymen's uninvited intervention, and Northcliffe's change of front 'with his usual inconsistency' from advocating 'no surrender' to urging concessions, made things more difficult. None the less good progress was made 'in an admirable atmosphere' – until the issues were passed to the full Miners' Federation. Then 'the same intimacy and cordiality became impossible; time after time when we seemed on the verge of an agreement some extremist would queer the pitch', wrote Hankey. He considered that many of the later troubles which beset the coal industry would have been avoided had the conference not ignored his proposal that a drafting committee should be formed to set out with complete clarity the terms agreed on. They were circulated on 28th, prior to placing them before Parliament; but they were so complicated that, according to Hankey, neither Herbert Smith nor Brace understood them properly.[1] The strike ended on 4th November after a ballot in which some 685,000 votes were cast; but the majority in favour of returning to work was under 8,500.

This seems to have been the only occasion when Hankey rather than Tom Jones acted as principal official and adviser to the government in an industrial dispute. For the remainder of the year industrial relations remained comparatively quiet – if ominously so. For the post-war boom had ended, and unemployment was rising rapidly. Hankey considered that the continued employment of thousands of women in jobs which could and should be done by men, at a time when there was an acute shortage of women for domestic service, was a big contributory factor in the rising number of unemployed men. He reverted to this theme again and again at this time, pressing his view on Lloyd George, Chamberlain, Worthington-Evans and other Ministers.[2]

Exactly a week after the end of the coal strike the ceremonies of the unveiling of the Cenotaph and the burial of the Unknown Soldier in Westminster Abbey took place. Hankey did not attend them because he disliked such occasions, and disapproved of the random selection

---

1920–29. Chairman, Executive Committee, Iron and Steel Federation 1935–40 and from 1945. President, Board of Trade 1940 and 1941. Minister of Supply 1940–41 and 1942-45.

[1]Diary 30th Oct. 1920. C.P. 2018 of 28th Oct. 1920 has the proposals for the coal settlement. Cab. 24/114.

[2]Hankey to Worthington-Evans 14th Dec. 1920 (Jones papers) and to Lloyd George 5th Oct. 1921. Lloyd George papers F/25/2/27. Also Cab. 63/20.

of a body from the battlefields to represent the fallen thousands of the British Empire. But he watched the ceremony at the Cenotaph from his office, and admitted that the two minutes' silence, 'the wonderful pealing of the Abbey bells, each being answered by a muffled peal which sounded like an echo', and 'the immense queue of quiet humble people bringing their wreaths' moved him deeply. A point of interest mentioned in his diary is that the idea of the Unknown Soldier being buried in the Abbey apparently came from the Dean of Westminster (Dr. Herbert E. Ryle). He suggested it to the King who at once told him to go to Hankey in order to ensure that 'it was not dropped'. Hankey brought the matter up in Cabinet that same afternoon, the proposal was approved, and a committee under Curzon, with Hankey's assistant Colonel Storr as secretary, was appointed to work out the details.[1]

The Cabinet met immediately after the ceremonies of 11th November, and the discussion was mainly about 'whether railway workers are to be on the Boards of Directors of the Amalgamated Railway Companies'. Hankey considered that 'we are absolutely pledged to it', and was astonished at the amount of hostility the proposal evoked.[2] Nor was such a measure ever implemented.

In the autumn of 1920 the League of Nations also demanded much of Hankey's attention, and on 9th September he circulated a note asking for the nomination of the British representatives to the first Assembly, which was to meet on 11th November.[3] A short time later he wrote to Lloyd George that the Cabinet had decided that their secretariat should be the distributing office for all League business, but should have no executive or advisory authority. Such a principle, he declared, simply would not work, because initiatives often had to be taken with the departments concerned. As things were one of his staff was already engaged chiefly on League work, and the Foreign Office had an official similarly employed. He therefore proposed to take over the latter; and, careful as ever to gain the necessary backing, he had already obtained the agreement of Balfour and Hardinge to his doing so. He now sought the Prime Minister's approval.[4] A Cabinet paper of the following month records that Mr. G. S. Spicer had been

[1]Diary 13th Nov. 1920. C.P. 2008 and 2064 of 28th Oct. and 8th Nov. 1920 are the reports of the committee on the ceremonies of 11th November. Cab. 24/114.
[2]Diary 13th Nov. 1920. [3]C.P. 1841 of 9th Sept. 1920. Cab. 24/111.
[4]Hankey to Lloyd George 27th Sept. 1920. Lloyd George papers F/24/3/3.

Lloyd George's doodles at the San Remo Conference 1920

The First Lympne Conference May 1920
Austen Chamberlain, M. Millerand, Lloyd George, M. Marsal, Lady Rocksavage (sister of Sir Philip Sassoon), Hankey, M. Paul Cambon, Sir Philip Sassoon, (?) M. Camerlynck (interpreter), Lord Derby

The Third Lympne Conference August 1920
Ralph Wigram, Lord Riddell, Sir Philip Sassoon, – ? –, Hankey, Lloyd George, Robert Vansittart, Lady Rocksavage, (?) M. Camerlynck (interpreter), M. Philippe Berthelot, M. Aristide Briand, – ? –, – ? –

transferred from the Foreign Office to the Cabinet Secretariat[1]. In his diary Hankey claimed that he thereby secured 'a great increase in efficiency', since there was no longer any doubt about where responsibility for League affairs rested. He also claimed that the change secured 'the goodwill of the Foreign Office', which now had 'their own man at the head of the organisation'. As this had all been accomplished without additional expenditure 'everyone was pleased'.[2] It certainly provides an excellent example of Hankey's astuteness in getting what he wanted.

His next piece of manipulation was less successful. While at Cobham he 'got the P.M. and Balfour into a corner' and showed them his proposal to substitute for 'the long and complicated mandates' which the Foreign Office intended the League to issue, a simple 'one clause provisional mandate' merely stating that the powers concerned would administer their mandates in accordance with Article 22 of the Charter. This he claimed would save 'another row with the French', who disliked the draft formula prepared in London; it also gave us 'time to look around and get experience before the permanent mandates are issued'. But the real purpose behind Hankey's proposal, as revealed in his diary, was that it 'saves us from the idiotic provision included in the Foreign Office draft that the forces raised locally can only be used for the preservation of order, or possibly for defence'. Hankey was sure that 'we should certainly break' this provision if another great war broke out, or if serious trouble arose in India or Egypt. He had been 'brought to make this proposal by a wild enthusiast from Eric Drummond's staff Philip [Noel-] Baker' who had 'annoyed him intensely' with a proposal for the Council 'to force on us mandates of a kind we do not want.' 'These cranks will bust the League if given their head' he concluded[3]; but Noel-Baker, as we will see later, had in his turn some harsh things to say about Hankey's attitude towards the League. Though the Cabinet did not accept Hankey's proposal *in toto* they did amend the Foreign Office draft to permit troops raised in mandated territories being used outside them in certain circumstances. 'This meets my main objection' remarked Hankey with satisfaction.[4] Although, as we saw earlier, Hankey had not opposed the principle of allocating mandates over the former enemy colonial territories to the victors – and indeed had a considerable hand in executing that novel

[1]C.P. 1952 of 12th Oct. 1920. Cab. 24/112. [2]Diary 22nd Oct. 1920.
[3]Diary 17th Oct. 1920. [4]*ibid.* 22nd Oct. 1920.

idea – at this time he realistically foretold that 'more kicks than ha'pence' would be the lot of the mandatory power for Mesopotamia and Palestine.[1] And early in the following year he told Balfour that he had 'the strongest objections to Mandates in any shape or form', and regarded them as 'an evil legacy of President Wilson's'.[2] His second thoughts were to prove nearer the mark than his initial acceptance of the principle, unenthusiastic though it had been.

Meanwhile Lloyd George had made strenuous efforts to persuade Lord Grey to go to Geneva as one of the British representatives at the forthcoming Assembly. But Grey 'would have none of it', and expressed strong dissatisfaction with the government's policy towards the League – notably over the Persian oil agreement, Ireland and Poland. And when Lloyd George rebutted those criticisms 'to a certain extent' the elder statesman fell back on the plea that his increasing blindness made the task impossible. Incidentally the discussion revealed – to Lloyd George's vast amusement – a wide disagreement between Grey and his leader Asquith over policy towards Ireland.[3]

From 7th–9th October Hankey was at home working on the lecture which he was to give at the newly-founded Institute of International Affairs on 'Diplomacy by Conference', with Balfour in the chair. 'I don't want to weaken the League of Nations', he wrote dubiously in his diary, 'but I dislike the Covenant and should like to see it amended'.[4] A few days later he sent Bonar Law his typescript for comment and criticism. The Lord Privy Seal made only one suggestion – that Hankey should emphasise more heavily 'that unless the League of Nations is prepared to undertake the enforcement of treaties the Supreme Council [of the Allies] must remain in being'.[5] This accorded precisely with Hankey's view, and he strengthened the proviso accordingly.

The lecture took place on 3rd November before 'about 400 High Brows', and Hankey recorded that 'it was very well received', though 'part of the audience did not relish a defence I made of the Supreme Council.' The audience, he concluded, was mainly 'Cecilian and Asquithian'; and Lord Robert Cecil's subsequent attack on the Supreme Council 'drew a good deal of applause' – despite Balfour's rebuttal in the final summing up. Hankey's account of the discussion which

[1]Memo. of 12th Oct. 1920. Cab. 63/30.
[2]Hankey to Balfour 12th Jan. 1921. Cab. 63/31.
[3]Diary 5th Oct. 1920. [4]Diary 7th, 8th, 9th Oct. 1920.
[5]Law to Hankey 1st Nov. 1920. Bonar Law papers BL 99/6/8.

followed his lecture highlights the fundamental cleavage between those who, like Cecil and Noel-Baker, believed that British foreign policy should be wholly based on the League – despite its complete lack of power to enforce its decisions – and those who agreed with Hankey that the strength of the British Empire and its Allies was a far surer foundation on which to build world peace.[1] This cleavage was of course to continue throughout the 1920s, and indeed endured almost to the day when Britain was unwillingly forced to go to war a second time against Germany.

The British Empire Delegation to the first League Assembly began its meetings in London on 6th November under Curzon's chairmanship, and Hankey 'arranged to run it with a staff of Dominion Secretaries'. He evidently regarded this as a valuable step towards full integration of the Dominions in the C.I.D. secretariat – towards which he had been working ever since the formation of the Imperial War Cabinet.[2] He was, however, embarrassed by Smuts nominating Lord Robert Cecil as one of the South African representatives, because he was 'a violent opponent of the Government', and 'almost demurred to the B.E.D. meeting being held' because the Americans, who had always strongly disliked 'the solid block of 6 British votes' which it represented, might 'make capital out of it'. 'Personally', wrote Hankey, 'I regard the B.E.D. as a more important element in the preservation of peace than the League of Nations and the Yankees combined'.[3] In fact it was soon decided, on the Canadians' initiative, to drop the title 'British Empire Delegation' out of deference to American and Dominion susceptibilities[4] – despite the fact that, as the Dominion delegates were deeply divided among themselves on fundamental issues such as the admission of Germany to the League, the Americans had 'little to fear from our bloc vote'. Nor did the British delegates display more unanimity than their Dominion colleagues, since Balfour and H. A. L. Fisher were determined 'to avoid a quarrel with France', while George Barnes[5] (an unofficial representative) 'made it a condition of his going that he should be free to express his views'. Hankey was disappointed also over the poor quality of some of the Dominions'

[1]Diary 25th and 29th Nov. 1920. [2]See Vol. I, pp. 365–6.
[3]Diary 7th Nov. 1920.
[4]The title was however used again at the Washington Conference of 1921–22. (See pp. 238–58).
[5]See Vol. I, p. 409, *note*.

representatives, and agreed with H. A. L. Fisher's description of them as 'like fourth-rate municipal councillors'. Summing up his impressions of the B.E.D.'s meetings Hankey found the Greek proverb 'with your relatives eat and drink but do no business' apt. As he wrote it in his diary in Greek script he had evidently not forgotten the language he had studied so assiduously at the beginning of his career![1] His final conclusion was that 'If they don't smash up the League of Nations and the British Empire we shall do well'.[2] Ten days later he was warning Lloyd George and Curzon against holding a meeting of the Supreme Council in London during the League Assembly at Geneva. 'Neither of them paid much attention', he recorded, 'and I don't think they realise how strong the feeling is against the Supreme Council'.[3]

In fact the first League Assembly was not very productive, the chief result being the setting up of the Temporary Mixed Commission on the Reduction of Armaments,[4] a body on which Hankey helped the Service Departments to select their 'expert' representatives. Towards the end of the year he had a long talk with Balfour about his experiences at Geneva. 'He is annoyed with Lord Robert Cecil', wrote Hankey, 'who bids fair to kill the League by excess of enthusiasm.'[5] Obviously his relations with 'Lord Bob' were becoming increasingly strained.

Here we must revert to the troubles in Ireland. Lloyd George and his government were by this time under heavy fire about the reprisals exacted for the murder of police and soldiers. In his talk with Grey on 5th October Lloyd George, whilst condemning the burning of houses – sometimes of innocent people – 'strongly defended the murder reprisals'. 'He showed', Hankey went on, 'that these had from time immemorial been resorted to in difficult times in Ireland; he gave numerous instances where they had been effective in checking crimes; he quoted two eminent [Irish] nationalists who had told him in confidence that the Irish quite understood such reprisals, and that they ought not to be stopped . . . The truth is that these reprisals are more or less winked at by the Government'[6] – as had become apparent at a conference on 1st between Lloyd George and Bonar Law and the Irish Executive (Greenwood, Anderson, General Macready and General

[1]See Vol. I, Ch. 2.
[2]Diary 13th Nov. 1920. Actually Balfour did not attend the first meetings of the League Assembly due to illness, but went out later.
[3]Diary 24th Nov. 1920. [4]Roskill, *Naval Policy*, I, p. 99.
[5]Diary 20th Dec. 1920. [6]Diary 26th Sept. 1920.

Tudor). But the fact was that public opinion was moving strongly against repression, and especially against the savagery of the notorious 'Black and Tans'.

On 10th November Hankey attended a 'very Hush-Hush meeting' on the subject with only Lloyd George, Law, Churchill, Shortt[1] and Greenwood present, to consider a proposal by Churchill 'advocating the substitution of regular, authorised and legalised reprisals for the unauthorised reprisals by the police and soldiers'. 'No decision was taken' recorded Hankey laconically.[2] Then on Sunday 21st fourteen army officers were murdered – in some cases in front of their wives – in Dublin. The result was something not far short of panic in London, where attacks 'by desperadoes' on government buildings, and even on the House of Commons, were expected hourly. A committee was at once set up under Shortt, the Home Secretary, some of the plain-clothes police were armed, a military guard was established near to St. Stephen's, and alarm signals were installed at various key points. 'All my household are armed' declared Greenwood at the Cabinet conference on 25th, 'my valet, my butler and my cook. So if you have any complaints about the soup you may know what to expect'. Even the usually phlegmatic Hankey conferred with his staff on 'the security of the office in the event of a raid'[3]; while Lloyd George himself, as always when he was frightened, was 'nervous and irritable'. He even found in the dead Kitchener a handy whipping-boy for the current troubles, on the grounds of 'his treatment of Redmond and the Irish regiments'. 'He [Kitchener] would allow no nationalist officers except a few and under pressure', declared Lloyd George; 'and he actually had burned an Irish banner that some ladies had worked for some Irish regiment'.[4] All of which reads as incoherently as the badly rattled Prime Minister probably declaimed it.

Early in December there were 'some nibblings by the Sinn Feiners for a settlement, including a telegram from Father O'Flannagan [a Vice-President of Sinn Fein] and a declaration by the Galway County Council'. Greenwood's statements in Parliament (notably on 24th November)[5] 'reveal a much stiffer attitude towards the Sinn Feiners

[1]Edward Shortt (1862–1935). Politician (Lib.) and lawyer. Chief Secretary for Ireland 1918–19. Home Secretary 1919–22.

[2]Diary 25th Nov. 1920. [3]Diary 30th Nov. 1920.

[4]Diary 8th Dec. 1920.

[5]Parl. Deb., Commons, Vol. 135, Cols. 494–512. The debate was on a motion by

than most of his colleagues', remarked Hankey. The majority view was in favour of a meeting of the Dail Eireann and granting an amnesty to 'all except the notorious murder gang'. But Hankey admitted, a little ruefully, that he was 'not completely in the P.M's confidence about Ireland . . . Neither is any member of the Cabinet except Bonar Law.' Hankey's deputy Tom Jones was, however, rapidly achieving that very special status.[1] The government's reply to the tentative Sinn Fein feelers was that 'we would allow Dail Eireann to meet but not [grant] an amnesty to serious law breakers, nor desist from seeking them out.'[2]

In mid-December the Government of Ireland Bill had been returned from the Lords with some amendments,[3] which the Cabinet promptly considered. The Bill became law just before Christmas, and Hankey was at least able to close the year's diary on the hopeful note that 'it was decided to make all preparations for bringing the Government of Ireland Act into operation next May', by which time 'the Generals calculate [that] order will have been restored'[4] – a calculation which was to be completely falsified.

While the second Lympne and Boulogne conferences were in progress in June 1920 the Greco-Turkish imbroglio steadily worsened; for the terms of the Treaty of Sèvres were now known, and had stimulated Turkish nationalism as effectively as they encouraged Hellenic greed. Hankey, like the Prime Minister, took a Phil-Hellenic line, and on 17th he sent Lloyd George a memorandum setting out a 'basis for discussion' on the whole issue. Greek 'co-operation' should in his view include an advance into the disputed province of eastern Thrace and 'freedom of manoeuvre in the Smyrna area with preparations to advance if rendered necessary by the situation on the Ismid peninsula [on the Asia Minor side of the Bosphorus]'. He also envisaged 'the despatch of Greek forces to the eastern side of the Dardanelles'. Here indeed was a total, if rare, misreading of the situation by Hankey.[5] We have already seen how he had developed a warm

---

Mr. Asquith condemning reprisals for the murders by Sinn Fein, and Greenwood made a very strong defence of the actions of the British military forces.

[1]See *Middlemas*, I, *passim*. [2]Diary 9th Dec. 1920.

[3]C.P. 2305 of 16th Dec. 1920. Cab. 24/117. [4]Diary 17th and 31st Dec. 1920.

[5]Hankey to Lloyd George 17th June 1920. Lloyd George papers F/24/2/38. See map p. 278.

admiration for Venizelos, and when on 12th August an attempt was made on the Greek Prime Minister's life in Paris he immediately sent him a letter of sympathy. Venizelos replied thanking him for his 'very touching letter' about what he courageously dismissed as 'the unhappy incident'.[1] But the truth was that Venizelos had completely lost touch with his politically volatile countrymen, and when in October King Alexander died as a result of a bite by a pet monkey matters quickly came to a head. In the November elections Venizelos sustained a heavy defeat and left the country. The elder statesman Demetrios Rhallis became Prime Minister,[2] the Dowager Queen Olga briefly became Regent, and on 5th December a large majority voted for the return of Constantine. Meanwhile Hankey noted in his diary that 'Lloyd George had come to much the same conclusion as I . . ., namely that it would be inexpedient on our part to prohibit the return of Constantine, if the Greeks want him. Now that the war is over it is no business of ours to interfere with the Greek people in their choice of a ruler. Our policy should be to try and work with them . . . Bonar Law on the other hand was all for coming to terms with the Turks'.[3] Hankey wanted Lloyd George to send Philip Kerr to Nice to discuss the whole matter with Venizelos; but Lloyd George preferred a friend of Venizelos, Sir John Stavridi,[4] to undertake the mission. He briefed his envoy on the dire effects on Greece which would probably result from a refusal to recognise Constantine.[5]

But even before the cataclysmic changes in Greece had taken place Hankey had evidently begun to have misgivings – partly as a result of talks with Commodore Fitzmaurice,[6] who had recently been serving as Senior Naval Officer, Smyrna, and had realistic views on Greek

[1]Venizelos to Hankey 22nd Aug. 1920. The assassination attempt was made by two ex-officers who had been supporters of King Constantine at the Gare de Lyon on the evening of 12th August. Seven revolver shots were fired, but only two of them hit the target and Venizelos was not seriously hurt.

[2]Or Rallis or Ralli (1844–1921). Minister of Justice 1882, of Interior 1893, and Prime Minister 1897, 1901–3, 1905–9 and 1920–21.

[3]Diary 22nd Nov. 1920.

[4]1867–1948. Middle East banker. Chairman, Ionian Bank and Hellenic and General Trust. Consul-General for Greece in Britain 1903–16. and again 1917–20. A strong supporter of Venizelist policies in World War I and employed as an agent by the British government.

[5]Diary 23rd Nov. 1920.

[6]Later Admiral Sir Herbert Fitzmaurice (1885–1958). Commanded R.N. Signal School, Portsmouth 1932–34, and Royal Indian Navy 1937–43.

prospects. On 23rd November Hankey passed the Commodore's views on to Lloyd George, and soon followed them up with a letter saying that he regarded the situation as 'disquieting'.[1] On 8th December the Allies had protested to Athens about the restoration of Constantine and had stopped financial aid. Deprived of that support Greece could not, wrote Hankey, keep her armies mobilised, and Kemal might attack the Smyrna area. If the Greeks withdrew troops from the Ismid Peninsula, Constantinople and the Straits would be 'at Kemal's mercy and our small garrisons threatened'.[2] Obviously Hankey had overcome his Phil-Hellenic instincts and was again exhibiting his customary grasp of the realities of a highly complicated situation. At the end of the month he recorded a discussion on Greece held at the House of Commons between Lloyd George, Bonar Law and Curzon, who were to meet Leygues and Berthelot that afternoon. Bonar Law had 'gone back to the old Tory fondness for the Turks', and wanted to revise the Treaty of Sèvres in their favour; but the Prime Minister and Curzon considered this would be 'a victory for agitation and a sign of weakness'. Meanwhile the reply had come in from Stavridi. It was that Venizelos considered that 'the heir apparent should become King; but that, failing this, we should not interfere with Constantine's return.'[3]

At the beginning of December Hankey was engaged in 'almost incessant conferences' with the French and Italians about the Greek situation. He recorded that the meetings were 'a great success', and went far 'to remove the ill feeling between France and ourselves'.[4] On 19th Constantine returned to Athens; but the final *dénouement* of the Greco-Turkish tangle was not to come until the autumn of 1922.

Future policy in Palestine and Mesopotamia was of course inextricably linked with Greco-Turkish antagonisms, and did in fact come up for discussion at the Inter-Allied conference of early December. Lloyd George, typically, engaged in conversations with Berthelot on the northern boundary of Palestine during completely informal talks at

[1]Hankey to Lloyd George 23rd Nov. 1920. Lloyd George papers F/24/3/25. Also Cab. 63/30.

[2]Hankey to Lloyd George 8th and 10th Dec. 1920. Lloyd George papers F/24/3/28 and 30.

[3]Diary 28th Nov. 1920. Constantine's younger brother Prince Paul having refused the vacant throne the 'heir apparent' became Constantine's eldest son George (1890–1947) who became King George II of Greece in September 1922.

[4]*ibid.* 4th Dec. 1920. This was the Second London Conference, held 26th Nov.–4th Dec. 1920. See D.B.F.P., 1st Series, Vol. VII, Ch. XIV.

No. 10. Hankey noticed what was going on, and at once infiltrated one of his assistants to eavesdrop on the conversation – which produced agreement to set up a joint boundary commission on the spot. But no one heard whether Berthelot had definitely agreed that the French government would treat 'the needs of Palestine in the matter of water in the most favourable spirit'; and it was only after some hectic telegraphing to Paris that Hankey was able to make sure that such a clause could safely be included in the final draft of the *procès-verbal*. 'It was a near thing', he wrote, '. . . and is a good illustration of Ll. G's methods of doing business – to produce a maximum of informality; to get a snap decision at the fag end of a long meeting on a difficult subject; and possibly to have no record. It is most distracting for the Secretaries, unless one is very wide-awake . . .'.[1] Happily Hankey knew his master's methods too well to be caught napping.

At a Cabinet meeting on 13th December a proposal by Churchill, strongly supported by Lloyd George, to withdraw from the Mosul and Baghdad villayets to a line covering Basra and the Persian oil field was nearly adopted – in order to save some £50 millions a year. Such an idea of course appealed greatly to the Treasury, where Sir Warren Fisher had just been asked by Hankey on behalf of the Prime Minister to produce a memorandum aiming to cut total expenditure in the next financial year to £800 millions.[2] But Hankey, though keen enough on economy, pointed out that by the withdrawal 'we should have to sacrifice our mandate and our oil prospects, the latter of which is serious'. The discussion continued in the evening, when 'the Cabinet heard Sir Arnold Wilson, until lately administrator in Mesopotamia'.[3] 'This remarkable man', wrote Hankey, 'who is only 36 years of age, made a most favourable impression . . . He was very pessimistic; thought that there was no real desire in Mesopotamia for an Arab government, that the Arabs would appreciate British rule, but if we cleared out would not be sorry to have the Turks back.' Wilson expected that the extra expenditure would ultimately be recouped from the Mosul oil wells, but that if Britain really could not afford it 'he seemed to favour with-

[1]Diary 11th Dec. 1920.
[2]*ibid*. 4th Dec. 1920.
[3]1884–1940. Joined Indian Political Department 1909. Resident in the Persian Gulf 1904–14. Deputy Chief Political Officer, Mesopotamia Expeditionary Force 1914. Acting Civil Commissioner, Baghdad 1918–20. M.P. (Cons.) 1933. Killed while serving as an Air Gunner in R.A.F. 1940.

drawal'. No decision was taken at that meeting, but in fact the withdrawal, so nearly accepted at the beginning, did not take place.[1]

Nor was the administration of the Palestine and Mesopotamia mandates easily decided. On the last day of the year Hankey recorded the unusual way the issue was settled by the Cabinet.

*Diary 31st December 1920*

... To-day there was a very important discussion on Mesopotamia and the Middle East. The upshot was a decision that the administration of Palestine and Mesopotamia will be concentrated in the Colonial Office, which will receive some such new title as the Department for Colonies and Mandated Territories. Everyone agreed that the responsibility for all civil and military action in these regions, now divided between Foreign Office, India Office, and War Office with great consequential waste, must be concentrated in a single department, which should bear the whole of the cost on its votes. There was, however, a great struggle between the partisans of the Foreign Office and Colonial Office. Curzon made a most powerful plea for the F.O., pointing out that the affairs of the two mandated territories are inextricably bound up with those of Egypt, Persia, Turkey, Syria, and Arabia; that Egypt in particular ought to be administered by the same Dept. as Palestine and Mesopotamia, that if Egypt were put under the Colonial Office it would lead to a mutiny in Egypt. The P.M. however urged that the F.O. had never succeeded as an administering Dept. – in Egypt, Somaliland, or anywhere. Moreover it distorted the perspective of the office, and induced them to attach too much importance to those regions which they were administering. He had a sly thrust at Curzon over Persia, where – thanks almost entirely to Curzon – we have responsibilities, both civil and military, we ought never to have assumed, and which have cost us tremendous sums, and militated against the Russian trade agreement. The question [of departmental responsibility for Mandated Territories] was eventually settled by resort to the unusual expedient of a vote, which resulted in 8 votes for Colonial Office and 5 for Foreign Office, 2 abstaining (Lee and Macnamara). The P.M., Bonar Law, Churchill, Addison, Munro,[2] Eric Geddes, Horne, and Shortt, voting for Colonial Office, and Curzon, Chamberlain, Montagu, Fisher, and Milner the Colonial Secretary voting for Foreign Office. I should personally have voted for F.O. had I had a vote, though I should prefer to clear out of both Palestine and Mespot. On Friday afternoon there was no

[1]Diary 15th Dec. 1920.

[2]Robert Munro, 1st Baron Alness 1934 (1868–1955). Politician (Lib.) and lawyer. Secretary of State for Scotland 1916–22. Lord Justice-Clerk 1922–23. Chairman or President of many committees and government bodies appointed to handle Scottish affairs.

Cabinet, which I was thankful for, but I had very heavy and important minutes to draft, and had a great deal of action to take. For example as Montagu had left the Cabinet before the end I had to draft a very important telegram for the India Office to send Cox,[1] the High Commissioner in Mesopotamia, asking him whether a proposal he had made for Faisal's installation as King of Mesopotamia would be acceptable to the people of that country. The Cabinet are much attracted by this proposal, which is Cox's alternative to the proposed withdrawal to Basra, and, according to his estimate, will enable us within a year to cut down our garrison to a division and a brigade, costing perhaps £10 millions a year in lieu of the 2 or 3 divisions otherwise estimated as necessary, which the Cabinet cannot face. Field-Marshal Sir Henry Wilson rang me up while I was drafting this important telegram and told me he had received a private telegram from the G.O.C. (Haldane)[2] in Mesopotamia to the effect that he was prepared to gamble on getting the British force out of Persia at once, in spite of the snow on the passes – hitherto regarded as prohibitive. This would render possible an earlier evacuation of Mesopotamia, if the principle was accepted. I urged him to get the private message made official. H.W. is dead keen on getting out, if he can . . .

Early in the following year, however, Hankey received a letter from Milner declining to carry out the Cabinet's decision that responsibility for the mandated territories should be transferred to the Colonial Office. 'I am quite at the end of my tether', he wrote, 'and so far from taking up any new job I am counting the days till I can shake off the burden which I already carry'.[3] Hankey passed this *cri de coeur* on to the Prime Minister, telling him, that the Cabinet's decision must in consequence be regarded as being 'in abeyance'[4]; but the transfer was made soon after Churchill took over the Colonial Office in February 1921. In the following August the American government claimed the right to be consulted over the allocation of mandates – despite the Senate's total rejection of the Versailles Treaty and so of the League Covenant. On reading the American note Churchill, probably with his tongue in his

[1]Major-General Sir Percy Z. Cox (1864–1937). Joined Indian Political Department 1908. Political Resident, Persian Gulf 1909. Acting British Minister to Persia 1918–20. High Commissioner in Mesopotamia 1920–23.

[2]Later General Sir J. Aylmer L. Haldane (1862–1950). G.O.C., Mesopotamia 1920–22 during the extensive Arab insurrection.

[3]Milner to Hankey 'Strictly Personal' 3rd Jan. 1921, enclosing copy of Milner to Lloyd George of same date.

[4]Hankey to Lloyd George 5th Jan. 1921. Lloyd George papers F/25/1/1.

cheek, accordingly proposed to offer the Americans the mandates for Palestine and Mesopotamia.[1] But, as the British government very well knew, President Harding's administration was most unwilling to accept involvement in Europe or the Middle East; and so it came to pass that, despite all Hankey's misgivings, the mandates in question remained a British responsibility until their termination.

In this somewhat haphazard manner was the fate of the mandated territories, and, incidentally, the future of Faisal, settled. The principles laid down in the Sykes–Picot agreement of May 1916[2] – that the great powers should between them be responsible for 'order, security and legality' in the countries over which they held sway – were now dead.[3] 'English domination of the Middle East', writes a recent historian of that area, presented 'both an opportunity and a responsibility'; but 'the opportunity was missed and the responsibility shirked'.[4] If that judgement be accepted Hankey must bear a share of the blame; for, as we have seen, he had strenuously pressed the view that such commitments should be jettisoned.

Hankey's efforts to 'galvanise the C.I.D. back to life' were recounted earlier. His purpose was probably assisted by Admiralty pressure to initiate a programme of new capital ship construction in 1920, since the proposal led directly to the formation of the 'Naval Shipbuilding Sub-Committee' under Bonar Law's chairmanship early in December.[5] This enquiry produced the first of the numerous post-war clashes between the orthodox sailors, whose gospel it was that the battleship was still 'the unit on which sea power is built up', and the extreme advocates of air power, led by Sir Hugh Trenchard, who declared with equal vehemence that the bomber had rendered the battleship totally obsolete. But the Admiralty's programme also had serious implications in the field of foreign policy, since if Britain restarted capital ship building the U.S. Congress would be powerfully stimulated to complete

[1]Churchill to Lloyd George *ibid.* F/25/2/10. Also C.P. 3076 of 27th June 1921 Cab. 24/125. C.P. 3077 of 27th June 1921 contains interesting correspondence, between Churchill and Hankey on the future development of the Iraq oil fields. Cab. 24/125.

[2]See Vol. I, p. 270, *note* 2.

[3]P. W. Ireland, *Iraq: A Study in Political Development* (Cape, 1957), p. 309 states that Faisal was offered the throne of Iraq as early as 17th December 1920. But Hankey's diary shows that this was only a preliminary approach.

[4]Elie Kedourie, *England and the Middle East*, p. 213.

[5] See Roskill, *Naval Policy*, I, pp. 220–25.

the huge 1916 and 1918 American building programmes; and of course settlement of Britain's war debts to the U.S.A., which the government earnestly desired, would be made far more difficult, if not impossible.

*Diary December 8th 1920*

. . . The meeting of the [Cabinet] Finance Ctee. [on 7th] was a very important one. After nearly two hours' discussion, without any approach to a conclusion the P.M. announced that he would now instruct the Secretary to draft some Resolutions for discussion at the Cabinet next morning with a view to their being read out by Chamberlain in Parliament at the big debate on economy on Thursday [9th].[1] So I had hastily to book a room in town . . . and settle down to cook up something. I invented some high-sounding phrases, and indeed some very drastic proposals for economy in the Navy, Army (Mesopotamia), Air Force and Civil Departments and got Niemeyer of the Treasury[2] and Howorth to 'vet' them. Then I sent advanced drafts to the P.M., Bonar Law, and Chamberlain . . . This morning I conferred with Ll. G. and Bonar Law in regard to them at 10 a.m. and got out a re-draft before the Cabinet. Dr. Addison and Macnamara and some of the others at the Cabinet were as sick as dogs, and made very wry faces when they saw them. I am sorry to say they managed to get them whittled down in important respects, particularly in regard to the expenditure of Local Authorities. Churchill took the military curtailments very well. I had included an inquiry into the lessons of the war as affecting naval strength in the naval part. This was based on a proposal I had received from Archibald Hurd,[3] the naval correspondent of the *Daily Telegraph*, which I ought to have mentioned before in this diary. His idea is that, if we announce an inquiry, the confidence of the Yanks and Japs will be shaken and they will postpone their big building programmes. Walter Long is still laid up, and Lord Beatty and Sir James Craig[4] were invited to the Cabinet in his place. To my astonishment they readily accepted the inquiry, only stipulating that it should be by the C.I.D. Now I am in a quandary. Beatty is pressing for great expedition, as he wants

[1]Parl. Deb., Commons, Vol. 135, Cols. 2473–2582. Debate on a motion by Mr. Lambert to limit expenditure to £808 millions in 1921–22.

[2]Later Sir Otto E. Niemeyer (1883–1971). Treasury official and banker. Vice-Chairman Bank of International Settlements. Director of Bank of England. Controller of Finance, Treasury 1922–27. Member, Financial Committee, League of Nations 1922–37 and Chairman 1927. Carried out financial missions to many countries 1930–41. Chairman of Governors, London School of Economics 1941–57.

[3]See Vol. I, p. 277, *note*.

[4]1st Viscount Craigavon 1927 (1871–1940). Politician (Ulster U.). Parliamentary Secretary, Ministry of Pensions, 1919–20. Parliamentary and Financial Secretary to Admiralty 1920–21. First Prime Minister of Northern Ireland 1921.

it completed before the next budget. The P.M. wants to go slow, because he doesn't want to make provision in the next budget! Subject to amendments in detail, my resolutions were adopted. I am afraid that like other good resolutions they may pave the road to Hell for the Government. The fact is that Lloyd George's pledges about 'a country fit for heroes to dwell in' are not consistent with post-war economy! The Cabinet business is frightfully congested and Ll. G. won't hold meetings to consider anything beyond the whim of the moment. This is a sign that often precedes the collapse of a Government.

The following Sunday 12th December, Hankey's tobogganning with his children was interrupted by a call to return to London to dine with Lloyd George and Haldane at the house of Lord Reading, the Lord Chief Justice. 'Our dinner was very interesting', he wrote, 'and we arranged the general lines of the Naval Inquiry viz:—first consider what enemies we are to prepare to fight; second how; and third with what weapons so far as the Navy is concerned. This was really Lord Haldane's conception of it. Mine was very similar, as I want to make it wide enough to cover the whole political field, so that the Inquiry shall form a foundation for our future defence policy. Haldane was very keen we should drag into it somehow provision for a proper naval staff, but this will be difficult'.[1]

*Diary December 15th*

... On Tuesday [14th] the Naval Inquiry opened with a powerful review by the P.M. of the great risks of our attempting to enter into a shipbuilding competition with U.S.A. We owe them £1000 millions. If we start building they will press for payment ... They will at once 'catch fire' and start to outbid [? outbuild] us; feeling will grow as it did in the case of Germany, until one day the smouldering fire will burst into the flames of war. ... He would prefer a system of alliances – if necessary even with Japan – should they go on building, but we ought first to aim at a naval holiday. Such was the burden of his remarks. Beatty tried to stick to his guns, but these were of course unequal to the P.M's broadside. No-one else very remarkable, but Churchill sturdily stuck to it that our sea-supremacy must be maintained. An interesting and useful start ...

This morning a Cabinet Conference. In the afternoon I [?] had Admiral

[1]Diary 15th Dec. 1920. Haldane's remark about a naval staff shows that he had become very much out of touch. A 'proper naval staff' had in fact been formed – belatedly – in 1918 on very similar lines to those introduced by Haldane at the War Office ten years earlier. It is surprising that Hankey should not have realised this. See Roskill, *Naval Policy*, I, pp. 126–7.

Gaunt[1] (ex-naval attaché) just back from a business trip in U.S.A. with fearful stories of our extreme unpopularity there, mainly due to Sinn Fein propaganda. Afterwards I saw Admiral Leveson[2] for a moment only 'to shake me by the hand' (since the Naval Inquiry began all my old shipmates seem to want that) . . .

*December 20th*

Cabinet at noon to consider the King's speech for prorogation on a draft put up by Philip Kerr – not one of his best efforts. The P.M. rather irritable. I felt instinctively that he was rather cross with me – I think over the Naval Inquiry. He wants to be able to prove that the Capital Ship is doomed – which would be very convenient politically – but I have assured him that he can't. The Admiralty, in a very powerful Memo., have shown that it can't. I forwarded this to him with a covering note stating that their arguments appear incontrovertible. By chance – since I have had no collusion with them – the Admiralty use the same argument as I did, and I believe he suspects me of having conspired with Beatty. What makes me think this is that he remarked the other day to someone – Bonar Law I think – in my presence 'We must watch Hankey very carefully, for this sort of Inquiry has a knack of coming out the way he wants!' He is very suspicious and I nearly always know instinctively when he suspects me. Not that it worries me, for I know I am right. The destroyer can, in favourable conditions, sink the submarine; so the enemy must put up something to beat the destroyer – a light cruiser, perhaps a submersible. Then [?] we must put up something to beat the light cruiser. Then the enemy puts up something stronger, so that, inevitably, you arrive at the capital ship. These are now nearly torpedo proof, and no first class battleship was sunk in the war.[3] . . .

Though one must certainly accept Hankey's word that there was no direct collusion between him and the Admiralty over the Naval Inquiry, and indeed any such action on his part would have undermined his whole position and authority, he did consult his old friend Admiral Richmond[4] about whether the capital ship was obsolete, and gave the

[1]Later Admiral Sir Guy R. A. Gaunt (1870–1953). Naval attaché, Washington 1914–18. Retired 1918 and entered Parliament (Cons.) 1922–26.

[2]Later Admiral Sir Arthur C. Leveson (1868–1929). Commanded 2nd Battle Squadron 1919–20. C-in-C, China 1922–24. Retired 1928.

[3]Presumably Hankey meant by torpedoes. The battleship *Audacious* was sunk by a mine in October 1914 (see J. S. Corbett, *Naval Operations*, I, pp. 239–41) and mines caused a number of losses among old battleships at the Dardanelles (see Vol. I, p. 161). But Hankey's statement none the less gives a false impression, as submarines' and destroyers' torpedoes had a profound effect on strategy and tactics in World War I – notably at Jutland.

[4]See Vol. I, p. 42, *note*.

results to Lloyd George when he submitted the draft terms of reference for an investigation which he hoped to see carried out by a sub-committee of the C.I.D. chaired by Balfour or Haldane.[1] Early in the following year he wrote a long memorandum on whether the submarine had rendered the battleship obsolete, and whether the new Asdic detection device, in which the Admiralty placed great confidence, had mastered the submarine.[2] Two years later he challenged the view expressed by Lord Selborne, who had been Minister of Agriculture and Fisheries in the First Coalition of 1915–16, that the Admiralty was too optimistic in stating that 'by the end of the first three months [of another war] they would have dominated submarine attack'.[3] All in all it is therefore plain that at this stage Hankey's outlook and opinion on the controversial battleship question corresponded to the Admiralty's; and there was some substance in Lloyd George's grumble prior to the Naval Inquiry that the government must be on its guard because 'this sort of inquiry has a knack of coming out the way Hankey wants'. In fact, however, the results were inconclusive. Bonar Law, the chairman, Horne and Geddes signed one report and Walter Long (the First Lord), Churchill and Beatty another. The arguments against the capital ship were rejected in principle but the Admiralty's proposal to build new ones immediately was not approved.[4]

Lloyd George refused to go to Criccieth with his wife and daughter for Christmas 1920 'for a certain reason' – by which Hankey obviously meant that he preferred to spend it in London with Frances Stevenson – so 'spoiling the festival for his private secretaries'.[5] Immediately it was over Hankey got his approval for the composition of the Naval Sub-Committee.[6]

At the end of an extraordinarily busy year Hankey made his usual long diary entry summarising the main problems which had arisen; but

[1]Hankey to Lloyd George 22nd Dec. 1920. Cab. 63/30. Actually Bonar Law was appointed chairman.

[2]Memo. of 18th Jan. 1921. Cab. 63/31.

[3]Memo. of 13th Dec. 1923. Cab. 63/35.

[4]C.I.D. N.S.C. 11 of 2nd March 1921. See Roskill, *Naval Policy*, I, pp. 223–5 for a full account of the Bonar Law Inquiry.

[5]Diary 27th Dec. 1920.

[6]It was composed of Churchill, Long, Horne and Eric Geddes, but Beatty was added on 29th Dec. Long, the First Lord, was however 'very ill with arthritis' (Diary 15th Dec.) and took little part in the inquiry. Beatty stated the Admiralty's case with considerable skill. See Roskill, *Naval Policy*, I, pp. 224–5.

the reader is already familiar with them. As however he made no record in the Cabinet minutes of the discussions which took place after Christmas the relevant extract is reproduced below.

*Diary 31st December 1920*

. . . Our Cabinet meetings have been continued under desperate pressure and we have had great difficulty in the Secretariat to keep abreast of the work. On Thursday morning [30th] we discussed the question of German disarmament, and decided on our general line, viz. to try and induce the French to take a less drastic line towards Germany, whose teeth have been so far drawn as to render them harmless for any aggressive purpose. We are also pressing the French to prevent General Nollet, the French President of the Allied Disarmament Commission at Berlin, not to send drastic and provocative notes to the German Govt. with strong political reactions without first obtaining the authority of the Governments. This led to a very interesting discussion on our general European policy, which, for reasons of secrecy, I thought it better not to record in the official minutes beyond a brief reference. Churchill opened it with a very strong plea for a defensive alliance with France and Belgium. France, he maintained, would only be induced to adopt a more reasonable attitude towards Germany, if her real and justifiable apprehensions were removed. France is dominated by fear of a *Germania rediviva*, with 70 million people animated by the same thirst for revenge as has possessed France herself all these years since 1871. Remove these fears by a definite alliance and France will no longer insist on hectoring Germany and on the absolute letter of the Treaty. By these means we might even succeed in time in bringing about an understanding between the two countries. Chamberlain warmly supported Churchill, and referred to a Memo. on the same lines he wrote a few months ago for the Committee of Imperial Defence. Lord Curzon however took a different line. He alluded, as he had done the previous day in a discussion on Egypt, to the anti-British attitude of the French, to their pin pricks and intreagues [sic] against us in every part of the world, in the Near East, in Washington, Egypt, Persia, Poland and everywhere. The Prime Minister took the same line and pointed out how in Constantinople, Athens and elsewhere it had become almost a fixed habit of the French, after agreeing on a common policy with us, to go behind our backs and allege that we were responsible for all the unpleasant features of that policy. I am glad to say also that he alluded to our traditional policy of aloofness from the affairs of central Europe, only intervening at long intervals when our own safety compelled it, as in the late war and in the Napoleonic wars. A selfish policy, perhaps, but the cheapest and best for our own people, whose interests the Government have to safeguard. It is the policy I have advocated ever since the armistice, and I am glad that the P.M. has at last adopted it. He smothered his opponents in the Cabinet . . .

The discussion on Anglo-French relations which Hankey recorded at the end of the year provides an interesting echo of what Esher had foretold during the last summer of the war. 'If I were the Boche', he then wrote to Hankey, 'I should feel certain of being able to play off England against France, just as Talleyrand played off England against Russia in 1814–15. It is *your* special job to prevent this.'[1] During the first years of peace Hankey certainly tried to carry out his old friend's exhortation; and his lack of success must surely be attributed chiefly to the Gallophobia of Curzon, to Lloyd George's idiosyncratic conduct of diplomacy and foreign policy, and perhaps above all to the relentless vengefulness of the French themselves.

From the point of view of Lloyd George's coalition government 1920 was a year of deteriorating relationships – and not only between him and the Conservatives. For example Hankey recorded how badly he treated Dr. Addison, the Minister of Health, over postponing his Housing Bill, which the Prime Minister considered would be unpopular in the Commons. When Lloyd George proposed that Bonar Law should announce the postponement Addison said it 'would be a slap in the face for him'; but after 'much coaxing, cajoling and hectoring' he accepted the decision. Lloyd George then rubbed salt into the wound by saying 'In old days I should certainly have gone to Asquith ("Arsquith" he pronounced it) in such a case'; but after Addison had left the room Law remarked 'You know George, if ever Asquith had made such a proposal to you, you would have kicked his bottom'.[2] Next day Lloyd George 'bullied Curzon a good deal' about the need to evacuate our forces from Persia, and about 'trade with Russia to which Curzon is an obstacle'. 'He always bullies those Ministers', concluded Hankey, 'who have little popular following'.[3] Such behaviour did not of course tend to facilitate the harmonious conduct of the Cabinet's business. Towards the tirelessly patient Secretary Lloyd George was, as we have seen, consistently inconsiderate; and by the end of the year even Hankey was complaining of fatigue, and showing increasing irritation

[1]Esher to Hankey 29th Aug. 1918. Lloyd George papers F/23/3/11.

[2]Diary 15th Nov. 1920. Addison actually resigned in April 1921, and became Minister without Portfolio.

[3]*ibid.* 16th Nov. 1920.

over his master's unbusinesslike methods.[1] But he did recover fairly quickly after spending Christmas at home in Adeline's care.

To Hankey the year brought further honours and distinctions. In March the Senate of the University of Edinburgh approved the conferment on him of the Honorary Degree of Doctor of Laws. But he was unable to be present for the ceremony until fifteen months later. The Laureation Address read on 18th July 1921 recorded that, after service afloat, he 'took with him into the staid precincts of Downing Street something of the ubiquity, readiness and silent efficiency we associate with the British Navy . . . His adaptability and discretion are vouched for by the fact that he has been Secretary successively to the War Cabinet, the Imperial War Cabinet, the Peace Conference and the Council of Four'.[2] Though Hankey gratefully accepted the honour offered him by Edinburgh he would evidently have appreciated similar action by Cambridge University, since he noted in his diary that Lloyd George had expressed surprise that Balfour, who was then Chancellor, had not nominated him for a degree.[3] In fact he had to wait another twelve years before Cambridge added to the number of honorary degrees he held. Of the six Prime Ministers whom Hankey served, Baldwin was probably the one with whom he was least intimate, and who held him in least regard. It was therefore curious that Cambridge should not have honoured Hankey when his close friend and admirer Balfour was Chancellor of the university but should have done so when Baldwin was elected into that office.[4]

At the Paris Peace Conference the powers had decided that no decorations should be conferred on each other's representatives – an arrangement which Hankey said he cordially approved of, remarking

[1]*ibid.* 28th Dec. 1920.

[2]Copy received from The Secretary, University of Edinburgh 23rd Dec. 1969. Hankey's degree was conferred by Sir Alfred Ewing, the Vice-Chancellor of the university, who had done brilliant work in the Admiralty's famous Room 40 (cryptographic section) under Admiral Sir Reginald Hall during the war. See W. M. James, *The Eyes of the Navy* (Methuen, 1955), p. XX and *passim*; also *Life of Sir Alfred Ewing, the Man of Room 40* by his son (1939).

[3]Diary 13th June 1920.

[4]The Honorary Degree of Doctor of Laws of Cambridge University was conferred in person by Baldwin on 11th June 1932. The Orator's speech, here translated from the Latin, referred to Hankey as 'a man who has made European affairs his special subject; a man, in sum, who is gifted with those qualities which in a ruler our people trust beyond all others'. Information from Miss M. E. Raven, Assistant Keeper of Archives, Cambridge University Jan. 1970.

that 'otherwise I should have received the Grand Cordon of innumerable states'.[1] However while at Lucerne in September Giolitti, the Italian Prime Minister, 'insisted on his having a rise' in his Italian order (Commendatore of the Crown of Italy), for his war services. So he 'capitulated' and accepted the Grand Cross of that Order. In October 1921 he represented to the Prime Minister that his trip to Gallipoli justified the award of the 1914–15 war medal, which the Admiralty had refused him on the grounds that his services were 'of a temporary and special nature'.[2] With some reason he regarded this decision as an injustice, and asked Lloyd George whether he would accept a suggestion put forward by Lord Lee, First Lord of the Admiralty, and recommend to the King that he be granted all the war medals for his services at the Dardanelles and his many trips to the western front.[3] Though Hankey apparently felt slighted by the refusal of the authorities to admit that his contribution to the war had been that of a combatant, it must have been at about this time that he received an honour which in the long view conferred far greater distinction than any strips of ribbon. This was an invitation to become a member of 'The Club', the body of about forty men who had achieved great distinction in almost every walk of life – politics, the sciences, religion, the arts and the fighting services – which had been founded in 1764 by Joshua Reynolds and Samuel Johnson.[4] Hankey's diary shows that he dined for the first time as a member of The Club on 5th March 1921, and he subsequently attended its gatherings so regularly that in 1942 he was elected Treasurer. As The Club never has had a President or Secretary this was the key office, and its conferment on Hankey was a great mark of distinction.

[1]Diary 13th June 1920.

[2]See Vol. I, pp. 188–205.

[3]Though Lawrence Burgis is confident that, after a long campaign with the authorities, Hankey did receive the World War I medals the family is unable to confirm or deny this as, surprisingly, no complete set of his medals has been found.

[4]Professor A. V. Hill, himself a member of the Club, quotes in his memoirs the description of it as having 'never had any serious mission to perform nor any ulterior purpose. It has always been a perfectly useless institution. After the good stories have been told and a piece of business discussed the meeting dissolves without having budged the world an inch from its place . . . The Club claims to have no use and sets up no defence. There is nothing then to do about it except to join in its toast, *Esto perpetua* – may it last for ever!' C. S. Slichter, *Science in a Tavern* (Univ. of Wisconsin, 1938). Quoted A. V. Hill, *The Scientific Dilemma* (O.U.P., 1960).

*Chapter* 8

# The Era of Conferences II. January-October 1921

DURING the early days of 1921 Hankey surveyed world problems, as was his wont, in his diary. Relations with France, which was 'dominated by fear of an eventually resuscitated Germany', were passing through a very difficult phase; but he none the less believed that Britain and France were 'cemented by indissoluble ties', and that in the end 'we shall manage to pull together'. With Italy our relations were 'on the whole good', though her ambitions in Asia Minor remained a cause for anxiety. Germany was 'still an outcast' from the comity of civilised nations, but 'she will surely revive and again be a great power in the world'. Russia he expected ultimately to emerge from the prevailing chaos 'under the overwhelming pressure of economic necessity'; but he pessimistically prophesied that she would then again become 'the cumbrous inefficient mass of corruption' which she had been before 1914. His anxieties were centred chiefly on Greece and Turkey; and the key to restoration of peace between those two nations lay in the hope that King Constantine 'will come to terms with Mustapha [Kemal]', whereby the disputed area round Smyrna would become autonomous under League protection. Hankey blamed the prevailing British troubles in the Middle East, from Egypt to India, on President Wilson's 'Fourteen Points' and his 'impossible doctrine of self-determination'; and he wanted the British entirely to disengage themselves from Persia and greatly to reduce their forces in Palestine and Mesopotamia. Lloyd George, he remarked, believed that by 'adroit diplomacy' and by 'expedients such as setting up Faisal as King of Mesopotamia we can maintain our position'.[1] But Hankey doubted the validity of such

[1]Faisal was expelled from Damascus by the French in July 1920. Early in 1921 at the Churchill conference in Cairo (see below) his nomination as King of Iraq was accepted. After a referendum in Iraq had produced a favourable response he was crowned in August 1921.

arguments – chiefly because 'everything is dominated by finance', and we simply could not afford to continue to carry the heavy overseas responsibilities whilst introducing the promised measures of social reform at home. Voluntary withdrawal from the mandated territories was in his view preferable to accepting the risk of being driven out by nationalist forces.[1]

On 7th January Churchill telephoned to Hankey, who was at home, from Lympne where he was staying with Lloyd George, to tell him 'in cryptic language' that he was to take over the Colonial Office, and to ask for Hankey's help and co-operation in that new responsibility. Churchill was 'so nice and complimentary', wrote Hankey, that he felt obliged to return to London next day, a Saturday, to offer his help and advice before Churchill left for the Riviera.[2] Though the new Colonial Secretary's appointment was not announced until mid-February he actually took over his additional responsibility almost immediately, and proposed to Hankey that he should visit Mesopotamia forthwith. Hankey, however, with 'memories of Antwerp [1914]' in mind, and believing that 'a disaster in Mesopotamia is far from impossible', begged him not to go.[3] In fact Churchill went to Cairo in March, and there tried to find a solution to the problem which was so troubling Hankey – that of pacifying and controlling the three turbulent territories at a time when military retrenchment was regarded as a primary necessity.[4]

Hankey was evidently at this time a good deal worried both by Lloyd George's love affair with Frances Stevenson and by his domineering attitude and rudeness to his colleagues. As to the former, Hankey's puritanism was outraged by the transparent subterfuges adopted by the Prime Minister to stay in London or at Chequers and enjoy the company of his mistress rather than join his family at Criccieth.[5] And his manners, even in Cabinet, were sometimes so bad that even Law was moved to protest. Curzon, for all his arrogant appearance and behaviour, was a sensitive man, and according to Law was 'very hurt' when Lloyd George blamed him for British involvement in Persia, and by the decision to transfer responsibility for the mandated territories from the Foreign Office to the Colonial Office. Chamberlain and Milner apparently shared Law's resentment; but when Law remonstrated with the Prime Minister all he got was 'Well, he [Curzon] has no

[1]Diary 3rd Jan. 1921. [2]Diary 7th Jan. 1921. [3]*ibid.*
[4]Diary 16th March 1921. [5]Diary 7th and 13th Jan. 1921.

following'. To which Law replied, in unmistakably minatory vein, 'Still, he is a very big man, and his colleagues will not stand to have him treated like this'. Hankey concluded, with some reason, that Lloyd George was suffering 'from a touch of swelled head'; though he regarded this as understandable because 'he is much the biggest man among them.' Hankey's talks with Law, Curzon and other Ministers at this time caused him to note that 'the idea which seems to be gradually taking shape in Bonar's mind [is] that the Coalition may not last so very long.' 'This is rather my view,' he added with one of his touches of prophetic insight.[1] An interesting point in the light of the events of 1923, after the Conservatives had regained power, is that Hankey discussed with Law a memorandum Edwin Montagu had written on the anti-dumping Bill, which Sir Robert Horne, who was to take over the Exchequer from Austen Chamberlain in April, had brought before the Cabinet. Hankey remarked that Montagu's paper raised the whole issue of the 'Tariff Reform – Free Trade controversy'. To which Law replied 'This might easily wreck the Government. My view is that if we have a Bill at all, with all the opposition [to Tariff Reform], we may as well have a real Bill. It can only be done, though, if Ll. G. knocks his Liberal colleagues on the head'.[2] That of course Lloyd George was not prepared to do; though after he had left office he undoubtedly did at one time play with the idea of supporting Protection as a means of mitigating unemployment – and, perhaps, of securing his own return to power.[3] Nor did the defeat of the Coalition candidate J. J. Astor by an Independent 'Anti-Waste' candidate in the by-election in the 'safe' seat of Dover in mid-January strengthen Hankey's hopes for the continuation of the Coalition. 'Lloyd George', he wrote, 'said it was a defeat for Moses and the Ten Commandments. He did not seem to mind a little bit. He said it would not worry him at all to be defeated ... His plans were fully matured. He would take a little place in Kent with some fruit trees. He would make a contract with some publisher and settle down and write a book about the war ... He would leave his successors to get in a mess before returning to attack them. He thought the election was a convenient lever wherewith to force his colleagues to adopt his views on economy. I gathered he was nurturing a plan for a "General Post" in the government, in which he would

[1] *ibid.* [2] Diary 8th Jan. 1921.
[3] See K. Middlemas and J. Barnes, *Baldwin* (Weidenfeld and Nicolson, 1969), p. 234. Henceforth cited as *Baldwin*.

get rid of the "duds" (he mentioned Illingworth[1] and Addison) . . . He said significantly, as though giving me a hint, that he wished he could find someone who would tell him how from £100 to £150 millions could be saved on the estimates. I told him I could find half a dozen ways, but they would involve sacrificing reforms with which his name was associated e.g. old age and service pensions, health and unemployment insurance, evacuation of Mesopotamia and Palestine, and scrapping departments such as the Ministry of Transport, Air Ministry and Labour Ministry. He said he did not mind. Times had changed. I suggested his trying Sir Warren Fisher, the Secretary of the Treasury, and a very able man. Ll. G. said Fisher and the Treasury officials were no good. Chamberlain, though good in the House, was hopeless as Chancellor of the Exchequer . . .'.

With the Prime Minister in this difficult state of mind it must have been hard for Hankey to get him to settle down to preparing for the forthcoming Paris Conference, at which Reparations, Disarmament and the Greco-Turkish troubles were again to be discussed with the French.[2] Fortunately the fall of the Leygues government – because it had tried to adhere to the agreement on Reparations accepted by Millerand at Hythe and Boulogne the previous summer – gained Hankey a breathing space.[3] Though Lloyd George hoped Poincaré would return to power in fact the new Premier was Briand. Furthermore, in addition to the Paris Conference, Lloyd George was committed to holding an Imperial Conference in the summer – at which difficult issues such as the renewal of the Anglo-Japanese alliance would have to be considered. As early as January Hankey had all these problems in his mind; but he told Lloyd George that after Paris he absolutely insisted on having three weeks proper holiday.

On Sunday 23rd January he and Lloyd George left for France. Adeline and Robin (now 16 years old) evidently saw them off, for Hankey told his wife that the Prime Minister had said that Robin 'must hurry up and grow up, as I want a new Private Secretary. He would take him now if I allowed it'. In the same letter he recounted how an unnamed Labour M.P. had said 'What the Government want

[1]Albert H. Illingworth, 1st Baron 1921 (1865–1942). Politician (Co. Lib., from 1930 Cons.) and banker. Postmaster-General 1916–21. Member or chairman of many government-appointed bodies e.g. Excess Profits Board.

[2]Hankey to Lloyd George 12th Jan. 1921. Lloyd George papers F/25/1/2.

[3]Diary 26th Feb. 1921.

is a rest, and for us to take their place. But the worst of it is this will not give Hankey a rest. We have our eye on him!'[1] And so it was to prove – in due course.

Conferences began on the Monday, and the rejection by the new French government of the earlier agreements produced a very difficult week for Hankey, since it meant starting all over again on issues he had believed settled. Finally on 28th agreement was reached with Briand whereby German payments totalling £11,300 millions were to be spread over 42 years. The rapid depreciation of the German mark soon made that figure illusory, and in March the Germans offered a total of £1,500 millions – which was of course rejected by the Allies. An odd feature of the Paris figure proposed by the Allies is that it was worked out by a Committee on which D'Abernon and Worthington-Evans were the British representatives. Though the former was a banker by profession the latter could not by any stretch of the imagination be described as a financial or economic expert.[2] Shortly before the agreement was reached Adeline joined her husband, and Hankey experienced the 'strange sensation' of seeing Lloyd George off at the Gare du Nord whilst remaining behind himself. Then he and Adeline set off in a luxurious private saloon provided by Count Sforza for Naples. Hankey took advantage of a stop in Rome to have a long and friendly talk with Giolitti; and of course he sent home his impressions of the Italian government, which were favourable. A copy evidently went to H. A. L. Fisher at the Board of Education, for he replied 'with special admiration for your wonderful capacity for absorbing relevant information in the minimum of time'.[3] Apart from that brief business diversion the Hankeys were left undisturbed for three weeks; and there is no need to enlarge on their blissful enjoyment of Amalfi, Sorrento and other sights on or near the lovely and then entirely unspoilt Bay of Naples. Hankey found time to send Tom Jones a lyrical account of their doings in a setting that 'brings back my old days in the Mediterranean fleet when I was immensely happy'. But his work was evidently not entirely obliterated from his mind, despite 'the atmo-

[1]To Lady Hankey 24th Jan. 1921.

[2]Diary 26th Feb. 1921. See also Nicolson, *Curzon,* p. 216. The Conclusions of the Second Paris Conference are in C.P. 2533 of 3rd Feb. 1921. Cab. 24/119. See also D.B.F.P., 1st Series, XV, Ch. 1.

[3]H. A. L. Fisher to Hankey 24th Feb. 1921. Hankey's report, dated 19th Feb. 1921, is in Cab. 63/31.

sphere of Baedeker, Lytton's "Last Days of Pompeii" and "*dolce far niente*"' in which he was living; for he ended his letter with an outline of his future programme, and even expressed a hope that the Prime Minister might allow him to take an extra week's holiday. Jones, however, replied that forthcoming commitments made such a proposal impossible,[1] and on 19th February they were home again. Jones and Sylvester met them at Victoria Station, and at once whisked Hankey off to Chequers, while Adeline returned to her domestic cares.

While the Hankeys were in Italy the Irish troubles continued to take up much of the Cabinet's time. Though Hankey left this side of his office's work in his deputy's capable hands, Jones always kept his 'chief' *au courant* with the state of opinion as some of the leaders on both sides cautiously felt their way towards abandoning violence and terror and opening negotiations. Sometimes, at crucial moments, Hankey would add the weight of his influence to Jones's. Such was the pressure they jointly exerted on Lloyd George in September not to try and wring further concessions from the Sinn Fein leaders – despite their apparent intransigence.[2] For they both, and indeed some Ministers including Bonar Law, believed that a compromise was possible, and were desperately anxious not to destroy that prospect by demanding more than the Irishmen could reasonably yield. After Hankey's departure in November with Balfour to take part in the Washington conference, of which more later, the Irish negotiations became still more Jones's particular province. But even when his chief was separated from him by the width of the Atlantic Jones kept him informed of the progress towards agreement. And when Hankey heard that, after many anxious moments, the treaty had been signed in the small hours of 6th December he at once wrote to his deputy that 'the news seems too good to be true', and congratulated him 'with all my heart'.[3] Plainly there was no jealousy on Hankey's part when a really big issue was at stake; and although Jones always played the principal part in the Irish negotiations he could hardly have done so without the complete support of his chief. Looking back to-day at their correspondence, and at the letters that passed between both of them and Ministers in 1921, it seems true to say that but for the patience, moderation and humanity of the two civil servants, at a time when most politicians and virtually all soldiers

[1]Hankey to Jones 3rd Feb. and Jones to Hankey 12th Feb. 1921. Jones papers.
[2]*Middlemas*, I, p. 172.
[3]Hankey to Jones 6th Dec. 1921.

were very unyielding,[1] the agreement would not have been achieved.

To go back to February, on arriving at Chequers after his Italian holiday Hankey received a very warm welcome from Lloyd George and his wife, between whom 'an affectionate family scene' took place over the recent success of Ernest Evans, Lloyd George's private secretary in the Cardiganshire by-election.[2] Then, with the inevitable Riddell in the offing, they settled down to prepare for the next round of negotiations on revision of the Treaty of Sèvres, the Greco-Turkish situation and the intractable issue of Reparations. Briand arrived in London on 20th, a Sunday, shortly followed by Sforza, and for the next three weeks Hankey's time was almost completely taken up by the Third London Conference, held at St. James's Palace. This time he acted as Secretary-General, which meant that responsibility for the entire organisation fell on his shoulders. His duties were made more than usually onerous by the fact that the Turks had sent two delegations, one representing the Sultan's government at Constantinople and the other Mustapha Kemal's nationalist government; and although they were 'in reality perfectly friendly' they 'pretended to ignore each other'. To complicate matters still further, as Greece and Turkey were at war Hankey had to avoid a confrontation between their delegates. None the less at the end of the first week he was able to record that 'We seem to be on the eve of securing agreement on a French proposal for a Commission to investigate the rival Greek and Turkish claims to Smyrna and Thrace'. Both parties had, however, felt obliged to refer the proposal to their home authorities, and Hankey was very dubious whether it would be found acceptable in Athens.[3] The conference then moved to Lancaster House and switched to Reparations, and on 28th Dr. Simons, the German delegate, arrived in London. Hankey was determined that there should be no repetition of 'the discomforts and indignities to which the Germans had been subjected at Spa', and went out of his way to welcome Simons and to make him feel he was a collaborator in a joint endeavour rather than a prisoner at the bar. 'I think he was rather touched by my attentiveness', Hankey noted.

[1]As late as 9th Sept. H. A. L. Fisher, President of the Board of Education and a Liberal, described de Valera's latest proposals as 'An insolent, defiant opening, a rude, abrupt and apparently irrevocable rejection of the Government offer, followed by a passage which appears to indicate a readiness to enter into direct negotiations . . .'. Lloyd George papers F/25/2/32.

[2]Diary 26th Feb. 1921.

[3]*ibid.* See also D.B.F.P., 1st Series, XV, Ch. II.

After he had accompanied Simons and the German delegation's secretary to a levée at St. James's Palace – not without misgivings over possible Press reactions – the conference settled down to business. Unhappily Simons 'put forward a perfectly impossible scheme of Reparations which Lloyd George on behalf of the Allies rejected'. Next day the Allies conferred over what should be done. 'The French, of course', wrote Hankey, 'wanted military action'; but Lloyd George stressed that it would be self-defeating, and put up an ingenious proposal to deduct 50% from the purchase price paid in Allied countries for German goods, 'a Treasury receipt being given, in exchange for which the German Government would have to pay in paper marks.' But this only aroused varying degrees of hostility among the French, Italians, Belgians and Japanese – partly because of the steadily depreciating value of the German mark.[1] 'There were some very strong passages', Hankey continued in his diary, 'the net result of which was an agreement that if the Germans did not roll up with a better plan by Monday 7th March the Allies would apply the French sanctions, and each Power would . . . levy Lloyd George's tax'.

Lloyd George justifiably regarded the speech he was to make that day, announcing the failure of the conference, as exceptionally important. Contrary to his usual practice, recorded Hankey, 'he prepared every word of it himself', and wrote most of it out. Then he dictated it to relays of stenographers and interpreters produced by Hankey – though constantly 'interpolating *extempore* passages', which made it difficult to take down exactly what he meant to say. None the less the whole speech was ready for issue to the Press within ten minutes of the conference rising. As *The Times* reproduced it in full, and also gave it the leading article headlined 'Allies to March. The Conference Fails' Hankey's efforts to give the Press good service were evidently not wasted.

On 4th March, while the Reparations issue was still being debated, news came that, as Hankey had expected, the Greek Government had rejected the proposed Commission on Thrace and Smyrna. Lloyd George then engaged in direct negotiations with the Greek and Turkish

[1]By mid-1920 the mark had fallen from parity of 20 to the £1 to 250, where it remained until the summer of 1921 when it again fell heavily. By November 1921 it had fallen to 1,000 to the £ and in the summer of 1922 it collapsed completely. See E. H. Carr, *International Relations since the Peace Treaties* (Macmillan, 1937), pp. 55–6.

delegates, putting up a complicated compromise involving a form of dyarchy for Smyrna. While this was being put to the Greek delegates Hankey suddenly realised that 'the Greek Minister[1] was not correctly interpreting Lloyd George's carefully chosen words'. 'To Ll. G's astonishment I intervened in the Greek language with so large a number of corrections that he left the room until we had between us supplied an agreed version'.[2] But Hankey's linguistic skill was of no avail in bringing the two parties any nearer agreement – the Turks being particularly stubborn in their rejection of any form of shared government for Smyrna. The *impasse* was complete, and that same afternoon Hankey learnt from the Greek secretary what was soon to be proved all too true – 'that the French are making a truce with the Turks in Cilicia, which will release large forces for operations further north against the Greeks . . .'.

That same day, 4th March, Lloyd George met Briand and Simons at Curzon's house, while the respective 'experts' – D'Abernon, Loucheur and Theunis[3] – discussed the technicalities of Reparations. Hankey was at first hopeful of a settlement on the lines of payments being made by Germany 'for five years on the Paris agreement basis, leaving payment for subsequent years to be settled later'. But Loucheur finally turned this down, explaining that 'France must have some scheme which would give her security for an immediate loan'. On Sunday 6th D'Abernon reported that the Germans were willing 'to concede everything essential in the Paris agreement', and Hankey hurried down to Chequers to give Lloyd George the news, closely followed by the three 'experts'. No progress could, however, be made in Briand's absence, so Lloyd George re-transferred the negotiations to London. Hankey's car was involved in what he described as a 'badish smash' at Shepherd's Bush, with the result that he was late to join the conference, which had been renewed at Downing Street and sat far into the night – though with little hope of finding a solution.[4] Next day negotiations with the Germans were broken off, and at the evening Cabinet the application of 'sanctions' was approved. The occupation by Allied troops of Düsseldorf, Duisburg and Ruhrort followed, and a customs

[1]The Greek delegate referred to was Alexander Rizo-Rangabé, Chargé d'Affaires in London at the time. Minister to Egypt and Ethiopia 1932–34.
[2]Diary 5th March 1921.
[3]Georges Theunis. Belgian politician. Prime Minister and Minister of Finance 1921.
[4]Diary 6th March 1921.

cordon was established between the occupied area and the rest of Germany. As Lloyd George had foretold this did not produce any deliveries in cash or kind by way of Reparations: it merely caused the decline of the mark to accelerate.

Having totally failed in one of its purposes the conference returned to St. James's Palace and to the Greco–Turkish *impasse*, and considered a new compromise put forward by Vansittart. That evening, 9th, Hankey delivered a message which was to prove as fatal to Lloyd George as to the Greeks. It is best quoted in his own words.

*Diary 9th March 1921*
. . . At 8.30 p.m. under instructions from Lloyd George I saw M. Kalogeropoulos[1] the Greek Prime Minister at Claridge's Hotel and told him that, if it was of vital importance (*importanza vitale ed primordiale*) to the safety of the Greek army to strike a blow at Mustapha Kemal Mr. Lloyd George as President of the conference could not take the responsibility of restraining them. The old boy, who had been very depressed when I came in, showed every sign of intense relief, declared that he would never have sanctioned an attack without authority, and that the recovery of his freedom was a great relief. He was so keen about it that I took occasion to warn him that Ll. G. was not encouraging him to attack but only removing a ban that had been placed on him. Ll. G. had twice given me instructions to do this, once before and once after the afternoon meeting. . . . He assured me he had told Briand and Sforza he was going to give this warning. . . .

*March 10th*
At 10.45 I attended Ll. G's meeting with Kalogeropoulos, who has now been reinforced by the notorious pro-German Gounaris,[2] who, however, is the real man with whom we have to deal. As Lloyd George put it 'Kalogeropoulos is the Grand Vizier (Tewfik) and Gounaris the Bekir Sami of the Greek delegation'.[3] The conference met at noon to compare notes about the

[1]M. Kalogeropoulos, who had been Finance Minister of Greece, took over as Prime Minister and Foreign Minister shortly before the London Conference.

[2]Demetrios Gounaris (1867–1922). Greek politician. Minister of Finance 1908. Became Prime Minister on dismissal of Venizelos 1915; favoured return of Constantine and again became Prime Minister 1920. Executed 1922 as scapegoat for Greek collapse in Asia Minor.

[3]Ahmed Tewfik Pasha (1843–1936). Turkish diplomat and politician. Ambassador at Berlin 1885–95. Foreign Minister 1895–1909. Became Grand Vizier after Young Turk revolution. Ambassador at London 1909–14. Again Grand Vizier 1919.

Bekir Sami Bey was leader of the Angora (i.e. Kemalist) Turkish delegation. Lloyd George plainly meant that on the Greek side it was Gounaris who, like the Angora Turks, was really calling the tune.

meetings with Turks and Greeks. At 5 p.m. I went to the Foreign Office, where Curzon received the Greeks again – a difficult meeting for me as Secretary, all in French. Then at 6 p.m. to the House of Commons, where the conference was delayed 1½ hours as Ll. G. was making a speech on reparations, Briand, Sforza etc. going in to listen. After a short meeting at 7.30 p.m. we adjourned to enable a document to be prepared for presentation to [the] Greeks. Then Ll. G. asked us all to dine with him at the H. of Commons. Briand in great form. Meanwhile I had summoned General Haddad Pasha, Faisal's man, and at 9.30 p.m. I had to take notes of a long and v. rapid conversation conducted in French without an interpreter between him and Briand. Haddad tried to get Briand to take Faisal or 'Abdulla[1] for Syria, but without any success at all. Then the conference met and went on until nearly 11 p.m. . . .

The last session of the conference took place on 12th March, when both Greeks and Turks were given the Allies' final compromise proposals.[2] Hankey noted that 'the attitude of the Turks [was] harder, due I think to a truce having been concluded with the French, which enables them to reinforce against the Greeks on the Smyrna front'. Three days later the Greek secretary of the conference, Kaptanzoglu, came to see Hankey and hinted 'that the Greeks would shortly attack Mustapha Kemal's forces'. 'I told him', the diary entry continues, 'that they would incur odium, and that they must be very careful to make [it] clear to public opinion that this move had been forced on them as a defensive measure by the Turkish concentration'.[3]

*Diary March 16th 1921*

. . . Curzon much upset at the P.M.'s permission to the Greeks to attack in Smyrna and says that through Philip Kerr he has been telling them to attack. In consequence of his [Curzon's] representations in an interview at 1 p.m. the P.M., in saying goodbye to the Grand Vizier (Tewfik) in my presence at 3 p.m., warned him there was no truce and that we could not prevent Greeks from attacking. He arranged also that Curzon should warn Bekir Sami that, if Kemal attacks us in Mesopotamia we shall consider ourselves free to arm the Greeks at Smyrna.

[1] 'Abdulla, second son of Hussein Sherif of Mecca (King of Hejaz later), and younger brother of Faisal. Played prominent part in Arab revolt 1916–18. Became Emir of Transjordan 1921–46 and King 1946–51.

[2] The 'Proposals of the Allies' are in C.P. 2695 and 2699 of 11th March 1921. Cab. 24/120. The Minutes of the London Conference of 21st Feb. to 14th March 1921 are in Cab. 29/91 and 92.

[3] Diary 15th March 1921.

Two days later Hankey and Lloyd George said goodbye to the Greek delegates. For two Hellenophils it was a sad occasion, since they knew that the Greeks intended to launch their offensive from Smyrna on the following Monday, 21st. Hankey certainly felt grave misgivings about the outcome, and it seems that his master was also far from happy about the action he had so rashly authorised. At any rate Hankey noted that he looked 'very tired and ill'.

On 14th March, just after the London conference had come to such an unsatisfactory ending, the Cabinet decided 'to go ahead with the Russian trade agreement' – despite the strong opposition of Churchill, who on this issue was in alliance with Curzon and the right wing Conservatives.[1] Three days later the Coalition suffered a heavy blow. Hankey was at home when a telephone call from the office brought him the news that Bonar Law had resigned on grounds of health. 'It was not a complete thunderbolt', he wrote in his diary, since that same morning at the House of Commons he had found Lloyd George 'closeted with Sir George Younger,[2] one of the Unionist whips and a great personal friend of Bonar'. On leaving Younger the Prime Minister went to 11 Downing Street to see Law, while Hankey 'gossiped with Younger, Davies and Kerr', from whom he learnt that Law's health was worse than he had supposed. 'Younger said he would retire if Bonar went', continued Hankey, 'as he was only held by personal friendship'; while Kerr remarked that Lloyd George 'would never work in harness with Chamberlain', who was expected to succeed to Law's offices of Lord Privy Seal and leader of the Unionists. Kerr also prophesied – more accurately in this case, since Chamberlain proved deeply loyal to the Coalition – that Lloyd George was 'so tied up in his various pledges to Germany, to France, to the Arabs and in his Irish policy that he ought to clear out for a year or two; that he was in the position Asquith was in in 1916, hanging on without any particular policy or support and would only end, as Asquith ended, by being kicked out ignominiously . . .'.[3]

[1]Diary 14th March 1921. The agreement is in C.P. 2724 of 16th March 1921. Cab. 24/121.

[2]1851–1929, 1st Viscount 1923. Politician (Cons.), businessman and brewer. Chairman George Younger & Sons, Alloa. President, National Union of Conservative Associations of Scotland 1904. Chairman of Unionist Party Organisation 1916–23.

[3]Diary 16th March 1921. See Robert Blake, *The Unknown Prime Minister* (Eyre and

Hankey, Lloyd George, Signor Giolitti (Italian Premier) and Dr Mattoli (interpreter) at the Lucerne Conference August 1920

Lloyd George with (?) Sir Laming Worthington-Evans and Hankey. Probably at the Villa de Albertis during the Genoa Conference 1922

Hankey with Lord Chelmsford (First Lord of the Admiralty) on the formation of the first Labour Government 1924

Hankey at once wrote to Bonar Law 'On behalf of the Cabinet Secretariat to express . . . our deep regret at your resignation, and especially its cause; our strong sense of the privilege it has been to work under you; our gratitude for your inexhaustible patience, sympathy and help at all times; and our fervent wish that you may speedily be restored to full strength and health . . .'.[1] Law replied in his own hand from Cannes, where he had gone to try and recuperate, that 'It was always a great pleasure to me to work not only with you but with your colleagues. I think you realised that the burden had gradually become too heavy for me, and I believe I have just got relief in time, but you know not only how much I admired but how much I liked the P.M., and I am very distressed to think that he is left with a task which is ever getting more difficult and that I can't help him in it'.[2] That letter makes it plain that in March 1921 Law had not envisaged giving his support to a revolt by the Conservative Party against the Coalition – as he was to do eighteen months later.

It is scarcely surprising that Hankey found Lloyd George intensely preoccupied when he buttonholed him a few days later in order to get a decision on the establishment of customs houses on the borders of the newly-occupied zone in Germany – which the French were trying to hasten. Two days later Lloyd George seemed on the verge of collapse. 'Hankey is the only one who can stand it' he remarked to Kerr in Hankey's presence. Then, to the latter, he asked 'How do you do it?'[3] – a matter which had puzzled other Ministers besides Lloyd George, and was to remain a source of amazement to the end of Hankey's career. The answer lay of course in his temperamental tranquillity, in his abstemiousness and physical fitness, and perhaps above all in the love and support he received from his wife.

Hardly had the government adjusted itself to the departure of Bonar Law when renewed trouble flared up in the coalfields. At the end of March the owners resumed control of the mines and the men promptly demanded that their wages should be regulated by a 'national pool' –

Spottiswoode, 1955), p. 423 regarding Law's resignation. This source is henceforth cited as Blake, *Bonar Law*.

[1]Hankey to Law 18th March 1921. Bonar Law papers BL 100/3/24(28). He wrote again in similar vein on 22nd. *ibid.* BL 108/8/11 (46).

[2]Law to Hankey from Hotel Bellevue, Cannes 22nd March 1921.

[3]Diary 18th March 1921.

so that the profitable pits which could pay good wages would in effect subsidise the unprofitable ones. The owners' offer of reduced wages and their settlement on a district basis was rejected, and on 1st April a lockout brought the whole industry to a standstill. Though Jones once again acted as principal secretary to the Cabinet conferences on the dispute, and also played a distinguished part as mediator, he and Hankey fully agreed that Henry Wilson's view that 'Red Revolution' was just around the corner was absurdly alarmist – even after the Railwaymen and Transport Workers had threatened to support the miners.[1] But the Cabinet did take the precaution of organising the maintenance of essential services, moved soldiers and sailors into the coalfields to keep the pumps running and prevent sabotage, and on 8th April decided to call up some reservists. This required a message to Parliament signed by the King, after which the Privy Council could approve the issue of the necessary Proclamation. But the constitutional processes were complicated by the fact that 8th April was a Friday, and under Standing Orders the House rose at 5.30 p.m. on Fridays. To suspend Standing Orders would demand a debate, which the Cabinet found, in Hankey's words 'very inconvenient at that moment'. Accordingly a telephone message was sent to the King at Windsor asking him to come up immediately; and he arrived in 43 minutes – before the message to Parliament was actually ready. Hankey got the accompanying explanatory statement, which was to be made in both Houses, produced just in time – thanks to fast work by Sylvester and Owen. It was actually sent in to Lloyd George sheet by sheet as it was typed, and although he could no doubt have extemporised had there been a delay it was Hankey's organisation that enabled the constitutional difficulties to be surmounted. At the Privy Council that followed Lloyd George's statement in Parliament the King apologised 'for appearing in a frock coat and brown boots, which he had not had time to change'.[2] Evidently George V did not consider that sartorial niceties should be jettisoned – even in an emergency.

The following Friday, 15th April, Hankey described as 'even more dramatic'. Long remembered in Trade Union circles as 'Black Friday' it marked the collapse of the Triple Alliance, and a victory for the

[1] *Middlemas*, I, pp. 132–53, esp. Jones's diary entry for 5th April regarding his and Hankey's talk at the U.S. Club.

[2] Diary 5th May 1921.

government.[1] However the coal stoppage dragged on, with increasing hardship for the miners' families. The first sign of a break occurred early in May when Lloyd George, after making a speech at Maidstone went to stay with the Cazalets at Fairlawne. Frank Hodges, the miners' leader, then asked to see Lloyd George, who told Hankey that Hodges wanted to end the strike, and that he (Lloyd George) would 'do it on the basis of his speech in the House of Commons in August 1919'.[2] On 1st July the miners returned to work – on much better terms than had been offered them in March, including the long-disputed 'National Agreement' on wages.[3] 'The P.M. comes magnificently out of this strike business' was Hankey's final judgement.[4] The reader will recollect that at the time of the railway strike of 1919 the Cabinet formed a Supply and Transport Committee under Sir Eric Geddes to organise the maintenance of essential services during industrial troubles. According to Hankey's assistant St. Quintin Hill, who acted as its secretary, it reached 'its highest state of development' in the coal strike of 1921.[5] In the following November the Home Affairs Committee of the Cabinet decided, somewhat prematurely, to disband the organisation which had been so laboriously built up; but in March 1922 this decision was modified in favour of maintaining a nucleus which 'could be used in emergency' but was not to cost more than £2,000 per annum.[6] Though the Labour Government of 1924 kept the organisation in being, contrary to the fears of J. C. C. Davidson who had been appointed Chief Civil Commissioner in the event of a national emergency, the decision of 1922 to place the nation-wide preparations in cold storage proved short sighted when in 1925 the threat of a coal strike again arose. A costly subsidy had then to be granted to gain the time needed to reactivate the organisation.[7]

While Hankey was deeply involved in the industrial troubles of the summer of 1921 he was worried by an 'absurd accusation' telegraphed by Sir Auckland Geddes, the ambassador in Washington to the effect that he had 'tricked' the Americans during the Paris Peace Conference

[1] *Middlemas*, I, p. 149. But the Editor misdates Black Friday 16th April, which was a Saturday.
[2] Diary 7th May 1921.
[3] See *Baldwin*, pp. 77–80 regarding the precautions instituted to meet the threat of the coal strike of 1921.
[4] Diary 5th May 1921. [5] Note by St. Q. Hill of 23rd June 1922. Cab. 21/232.
[6] H.A.C. 101st meeting 29th Nov. 1921.
[7] See James, *Davidson*, pp. 178–80 and 228–33.

over the mandate for the island of Yap going to the Japanese. We saw earlier how, at the cost of considerable time and trouble, he was able to reply with what he called 'an overwhelming refutation' of the American accusation.[1] Hankey considered Auckland Geddes's behaviour in this matter 'rather hysterical'; for the Ambassador described Charles Evans Hughes, the U.S. Secretary of State, as being in a mentally unstable condition, the symptoms of which Geddes, a physician by training, declared that he was well qualified to diagnose. On reading this unusual despatch Curzon sent it to Lloyd George with a note that he was 'not by any means sure that it is not the British Ambassador who is afflicted with a mild form of mania'.[2] One feels that the Foreign Secretary was probably nearer the mark than the physician-diplomat. There was an amusing aftermath to this affair in Washington a few months later, when Hankey found himself placed at a dinner next to the person who had initiated the whole controversy, but was evidently unaware of the identity of his neighbour.[3] 'I looked him in the face', wrote Hankey to Lloyd George, 'and said "I am Sir Maurice Hankey". Never have I seen a man so embarrassed. He knew that I knew, and quite thirty seconds elapsed before he could speak'. But Hankey was not the man to nurse a grievance or feed the flames of a quarrel, and typically added 'Now we are on excellent terms, and I am to lunch with him alone'.[4]

On 23rd April Lloyd George and Briand met, once again at Sassoon's house at Lympne, to discuss harsher sanctions against Germany, including perhaps occupation of the Ruhr. Hankey was the only secretary present, and had to burn much midnight oil to prevent the record of the conversations falling in arrears. Though Lloyd George was still opposed in principle to draconian measures, he well knew that no French government would survive if it yielded appreciably on the issue of Reparations.[5] A week later the scene shifted to London for another Inter-Allied meeting, which was attended by the Reparations

[1]See p. 82. Geddes's despatch to Curzon of 15th April 1921 is in Lloyd George papers F/13/2/19.

[2]*ibid.*

[3]Hankey names this man as Fletcher, and it presumably was Senator Duncan V. Fletcher (Politician, Dem.). Senator from Florida 1909–15 and 1915–39. Served on many Senate Committees e.g. Commerce, Military affairs, Banking (Chairman) etc.

[4]To Lloyd George 17th Nov. 1921. Lloyd George papers F/62/1/3.

[5]Conclusions of Fourth Lympne Conference are in C.P. 2878 of 26th April 1921. The French plan for the occupation of the Ruhr is in C.P. 2882 of 27th April. Both

Commission.[1] A schedule of payments was drawn up and presented to the Germans, under the threat of occupation of the Ruhr. The German government thereupon resigned, but Wirth[2] reformed his Cabinet and on 11th May – a week after the end of the London Conference – accepted the Allied ultimatum. Hankey found these proceedings the heaviest burden he had borne since the Peace Conference. He left an amusing description of the final scene – which surely shows 'Diplomacy by Conference' at its worst.

*Diary 5th May 1921*

... Last night was the climax. The Supreme Council met from 9.30 until past midnight, having been waiting all day for the result of the deliberations of the Reparations Commission, which had been brought at short notice the night before from Paris in order to persuade them to adopt the Allied scheme of reparations by Germany. At last means were found to induce them to agree, Sir John Bradbury's conscience being the difficulty, and shortly after midnight the Supreme Council got everything fixed up in principle. After that there was a hectic drafting Ctee. – 14 tired and jaded Ministers and officials in the Treasury Boardroom trying to draft complicated financial protocols in two languages. Worthington-Evans in the chair was dropping with fatigue. The Italian and Japanese delegates were not pretending to take any interest. Fromageot, the brilliant and very straight French jurist, was in an armchair, cursing the financiers and saying 'I do not want to go like old Father [i.e. President] Wilson. Let me go to bed.' Malkin, the English jurist's eyes and face were twitching terribly. Loucheur, fresh as a pin, was 'trying it on' all the time, and Sir John Bradbury from time to time shouting abuse at Loucheur and then mumbling apologies. Lord D'Abernon and Worthington-Evans bursting in now and again to keep the peace. Somewhere after 2 a.m. something came out of it, and I had to get it typed.[3] My office staff was there until 5.30 a.m. I had to have all ready for signature at 9.45 so that our guests could get away at 11 o'clock. I was the only person with Lloyd George when he handed the ultimatum to Herr Sthamer, the German

---

in Cab. 24/122. Minutes of the conference are in Cab. 29/92. See also D.B.F.P., 1st Series, Vol. XV, Ch. III.

[1]This was the Fourth London Conference. Minutes in Cab. 29/92 and /93.

[2]Joseph Wirth (1879–1956). German politician (Centre). Minister of Finance 1920. Chancellor in succession to Fehrenbach May 1921–Nov. 1922, when replaced by Cuno. Minister of Interior 1930–31. Left Germany when Nazis obtained power.

[3]C.P. 2908, 2909, 2913 and 2924 of 5th, 5th, 6th and 10th May 1921 are the relevant documents on Reparations etc. produced at this conference. All in Cab. 24/123.

ambassador,[1] an unimpressive person. . . . The pace has been too hot, and we cannot get out these very technical protocols in two languages in such conditions . . .

After May 1921 there is a gap in Hankey's diary until the early days of October 1922, when the fall of the Coalition was plainly imminent; but his letters to his wife, from whom he was often separated during those months, and to Lloyd George, enable us to follow his activities fairly closely. Indeed it may have been his knowledge that these letters would be preserved that caused him to neglect his diary.

In June Hankey continued to keep a watchful eye on the situation developing in Asia Minor, and made certain that Lloyd George was aware of the danger which would arise on the Ismid peninsula opposite Constantinople in the event of a Greek defeat. He set out in some detail the policy he considered should be adopted, including a strong plea to the French to put an end to their selfish and by no means scrupulous action in trying to come to an arrangement with the Kemalist Turks behind the back of the British government; and he foretold with complete accuracy the consequences of a Greek collapse – even to the point of urging that shipping should be prepared 'for a rapid withdrawal' from Constantinople and Smyrna 'in case of necessity'.[2] With the forthcoming Imperial Conference in view he again brought up the question of restoring the Committee of Imperial Defence in its pre-war form, and wrote a long history of its origins, purposes and accomplishments;[3] and he reviewed the work of his own office in the light of the very heavy pressure to which it had been subjected by the long series of Inter-Allied conferences. He pleaded particularly for more consideration over late Cabinet meetings (after 4 p.m.), which inevitably meant his staff having to keep very long hours. Such practices had, he protested, become 3½ times as frequent 'as in the most active period of the War Cabinet'.[4] Almost at the same time he put up his proposals for the Imperial Conference to the Cabinet, including remarks on the personalities and outlook of the Dominions' representatives – Hughes

[1] Dr. Friedrich Sthamer (1856–1931). German lawyer and diplomat. Senator for Hamburg 1904. Chargé d'Affaires for the German Republic in London Feb.–Aug. 1920 and thereafter Ambassador until 1930.

[2] Hankey to Lloyd George 2nd June 1921. Lloyd George papers F/25/1/36. See map p. 278.

[3] Memo. of 1st April 1921. Cab. 21/209.

[4] C.P. 3023 of 13th June 1921. Cab. 24/125.

of Australia, Meighen of Canada, Massey of New Zealand and Smuts – who had arrived in London. Renewal of the Anglo-Japanese alliance, he quickly learnt, would be strongly opposed by Canada, whose delegates were also very dubious regarding Hankey's favourite project for a truly Imperial secretariat.[1] Finally he besought Lloyd George not to hold the conference at St. James's Palace, which was 'very inconvenient for the Secretariat', but at No. 10 – a request with which the Prime Minister complied.[2]

Among the matters to be discussed at the Imperial Conference Hankey obviously considered the construction of a naval base at Singapore, which the Cabinet reviewed on 14th June, of prime importance. 'It appears that our Fleet,' he wrote, 'most of which is now oil driven, cannot be employed in the Pacific without the development of oil fuel and other facilities at Singapore. The total cost of this, spread over some years, will be more than eight millions. The question is therefore a very serious one'.[3] Thus did Hankey come down tactfully but firmly on the side of the Admiralty over the most controversial defence issue of the 1920s.[4] Construction of the Singapore base was approved in principle by the Cabinet on 16th June.[5]

We cannot here follow the Imperial Conference in any detail. It opened on 20th June and continued until 5th August. Lloyd George was elected chairman, and in addition to 34 Plenary Sessions he met the Dominion Prime Ministers eleven times. Their differences of outlook – notably over the Anglo-Japanese alliance, which Australia and New Zealand wished to see renewed, and over the question of a military guarantee to France which had been signed in 1919 but never ratified, soon became apparent. In opposing that principle, and pleading for a withdrawal from European entanglements, Hankey was in accord with Smuts; and he recognised the force of Meighen's claim for the Dominions to participate in the formulation of foreign policy – though he understood how difficult it would prove to put such a proposal into practice. But he was strongly opposed to the Dominion Prime Ministers communicating direct with the British Prime Minister

[1]Hankey to Lloyd George 14th and 15th June 1921. Lloyd George papers F/25/1/40 and /41.

[2]Same to same 16th June 1921. *ibid.* F/25/1/45.

[3]Same to same 14th June 1921. *ibid.* F/25/1/39. Also C.I.D. 143C of 7th June 1921.

[4]See Roskill, *Naval Policy*, I, pp. 290–99 and *passim*.

[5]Cabinet 49(21) and Hankey to Lloyd George of 16th June 1921. Lloyd George papers F/25/1/44.

by cipher telegrams, because it would short circuit the Colonial Office and dislocate the whole administrative machinery of government.[1]

Hankey's papers contain an amusing sideline on the Imperial Conference. Hughes, in his reply to Lloyd George's speech of welcome remarked of the delegates 'We are nearly all of the same race'. On hearing this Edwin Montagu wrote the sentence at the top of a sheet of 10 Downing Street notepaper, and passed it to Hankey with the delegates' racial origins described as follows:—

Balfour, Smartt[2] – Scotch.
Massey, Meighen, Chamberlain – English.
Hughes, P.M. – Welsh.
Churchill – English, American, Red Indian.
Smuts – Dutch.
E.S.M. (himself) – Jewish.
Curzon – Superhuman.

Although at the beginning of the conference Hankey described 'Billy' Hughes as 'altogether quietened and more chastened' – compared with his conduct at the time of the Paris Conference – as the Imperial Conference dragged on ineffectively he began to show all his old restlessness. Towards the end he wrote to Hankey that he was getting 'seriously alarmed at the prospects of this mountain of a conference being delivered of a very small mouse, and a half dead one at that'. He described himself as 'a whole-hearted champion of Empire' but wanted to be able to show his people that Australians were 'partners and not pawns'.[3] Hankey no doubt agreed with much of Hughes's tirade; but he knew that Canada and South Africa would not go nearly as far or as fast as the fiery Australian wanted, and believed it in the best interests of the Empire as a whole to hasten very slowly. His general views on the guarantee to France are well summed up in the last paragraph of a long letter he sent Lloyd George a few days after the opening of the conference. 'Fundamentally, both parties to this controversy agree that the main object of our foreign policy is to secure peace; that it is essential to honour our signature to the various Treaties of Peace; and that this involves working in the closest accord

[1]Hankey to Lloyd George 25th June and 12th July 1921. Cab. 63/31.

[2]Sir Thomas W. Smartt (1859–1929). South African politician (Unionist), actually of Irish origin. Secretary for Agriculture 1921.

[3]Hughes to Hankey from 10 Downing Street. Undated but obviously August 1921. Lloyd George papers F/25/2/5.

with our late Allies. The League of Nations, which includes many nations that were neutral in the late war, will not undertake the execution and enforcement of the Peace Treaties, and consequently, for the present, we must work through the medium of the Supreme Council. It is a matter for future consideration, however, whether, when the outstanding questions have been finally disposed of, we could not exercise, through the medium of the League of Nations or of any body that takes its place, that influence in the maintenance of peace which all desire. By these means we might achieve the same result without accepting obligations that might later on prove inconvenient to fulfil, and from which it might be impossible to extricate ourselves.'[1]

No sooner was the Imperial Conference over than Hankey set off yet again with Lloyd George for Paris, where Curzon had made an unsuccessful attempt to mediate between the Greeks and Turks in June. For the August meeting the main issues were the future of Upper Silesia, a majority of whose people had voted in March for union with Germany rather than Poland.[2] The French refused to accept the decision, and on 12th August the Paris Conference submitted the problem to the League, whose Council finally recommended partition. Though Hankey described the conference as 'comparatively harmonious', he was depressed and angered by the cynical bellicosity he encountered in Paris. 'The League of Nations', he wrote, 'is of no more account than the International Postal Bureau . . . It is never mentioned. It is true it never counted for much in Paris, but the underlying idea was there. Now the League and the idea are dead, and the sabres rattle in their scabbards and people talk of "the next war" and the old game of grab called "Diplomacy" goes on'.[3] On 12th he telegraphed the decision about Silesia to Balfour, who was undergoing a cure. He said that although Lloyd George was very reluctant to interrupt Balfour's holiday he hoped that he would represent the British government at the forthcoming League Council meeting. Hankey briefed Balfour very fully on the subject, ending with the justifiable conclusion that the

[1]Hankey to Lloyd George 25th June 1921. Lloyd George papers F/25/1/48. Also Cab. 63/31.

[2]This was the Third Paris Conference 8th–13th August 1921. Minutes in Cab. 29/93. See also D.B.F.P., 1st Series, Vol. XV, Ch. VI.

[3]To Lady Hankey, from Hotel Crillon, Paris, 10th August 1921. See also Hankey to Lloyd George 15th August 1921 Lloyd George papers F/25/2/4. The Resolutions adopted are in C.P. 3245 of 18th August 1921. Cab. 24/127.

fundamental desire of the French was 'to clip the wings of the Germans', for which purpose they wished to deprive them of the Ruhr in the west and of Silesia in the East.[1] Balfour accepted the task, and at the end of September telegraphed his hopes for a satisfactory solution to Hankey; but French influence proved dominant. Towards the end of October Hankey wrote to Drummond in high indignation about the decision to refer the Silesian issue to four members of the Council, one of whom – the Belgian representative – was certainly prejudiced in favour of the French, while the others were totally unqualified to adjudicate on it. What was needed, he wrote, was 'a perfectly independent and impartial tribunal'. 'I am still sufficiently idealist', he continued, 'to believe in the principle of the League, but this is not much use if the official world has lost confidence'. He gave a copy of this letter to Lloyd George with the addendum 'I had to allow my wrath to cool before I could write civilly'.[2] Though Drummond sent a full and friendly reply, defending the members of the Council who were to hear the case,[3] one feels that Hankey's judgement was much the more realistic, and that the League had taken the first step down the slippery slope leading to the bottomless pit of impotence. At any rate Harold Nicolson later stigmatised its decision as 'unpardonably unfair [to the German majority], and wholly unworthy of the League'.[4]

On 10th July, while the Imperial Conference was still in session, President Harding announced that the United States would issue invitations to the principal powers and to China to participate in a conference on 'the limitation of armament' and on 'reaching a common understanding with respect to principles and policies in the Far East'. This invitation more or less stultified the deliberations in London. Hankey, as we saw earlier, had long viewed the possibility of a naval building race between Britain and the U.S.A. with the utmost misgivings, though he held to the view that a One Power Standard should effectively be maintained by Britain. When Balfour accepted Lloyd George's request to lead the British delegation to Washington Hankey was the obvious choice for the post of Secretary and general adviser. Tom Jones would of course hold the fort in London, with J. R.

[1]B.M. Add. MSS. 49704 pp. 20–27.
[2]Hankey to Drummond 21st Oct. and to Lloyd George 26th Oct. 1921. Lloyd George papers F/25/2/35.
[3]Drummond to Hankey 29th Oct. 1921. *ibid.* F/25/2/39.
[4]*Curzon*, pp. 211–12, *note*.

Chancellor (of whom Hankey held no very high opinion) acting temporarily as secretary of the C.I.D. and of its Standing Sub-Committee. Hankey spent a good deal of the late summer months tidying up odds and ends of the special responsibilities which he could not delegate, such as the Cabinet Committee on the Secret Service, of which Warren Fisher, Eyre Crowe and he were members. Their report, rendered early in November led to the dismissal – or perhaps forced resignation is a better description – of Sir Basil Thomson,[1] head of the Special Branch of the Criminal Investigation Department, on the grounds that he would not subordinate himself to the Chief Commissioner of Police. This decision produced a sharp division in the Cabinet; and, a few days later, an equally sharp exchange of questions and answers, followed by a debate, took place in Parliament.[2] But the Government obtained adequate support for its action. One of those considered as successor to Thomson was Sir Joseph Byrne,[3] head of the hard-pressed Royal Irish Constabulary. Hankey however reported that Lord French, the Viceroy, and Lloyd George both considered Byrne had lost his nerve.[4] He was therefore consoled with a whole series of Colonial Governorships – which must have proved a good deal more congenial than the preservation of law and order in Ireland.

At this time Hankey also had a good deal of correspondence with Stamfordham, Tom Jones and Lloyd George on the burning issue of unemployment.[5] To the Prime Minister he set out his views in full. His main points were an all-round reduction in government expenditure and of the standard of living, the cancellation of war debts, the

[1]See Vol. I, p. 566, *note*.

[2]Austen Chamberlain to Curzon 7th Nov. 1921. Chamberlain papers AC 23/2/4 and 23/2/16. *The Times* of 7th Nov. printed Thomson's protest over his dismissal. In Cabinet Shortt and Macpherson, who backed the Committee's report, were opposed by Long and Bonar Law. See also Parl. Deb., Commons, Vol. 147, Cols. 31, 63, 220 and 1929 (Parliamentary questions) and Cols. 2041–86 (Debate on the Adjournment).

[3]Brigadier-General Sir Joseph A. Byrne (1874–1942). Inspector-General, R.I.C. 1916–20. Governor of Seychelles 1922–27, of Sierra Leone 1927–31 and Governor and C-in-C, Kenya 1931–37.

[4]Chamberlain papers AC 23/2/4, 23/2/16 and 23/2/21.

[5]Stamfordham to Hankey 21st Sept. 1921. RA GV K1740/5. Circulated as C.P. 3329. Hankey to Jones 30th Sept. 1921. *Middlemas,* I, pp. 173–4. Hankey to Lloyd George 5th Oct. 1921. Lloyd George papers F/25/2/27.

starting of relief works, and emigration to the Dominions. But he, like Tom Jones, wished to guard against unemployment benefit being abused and becoming an excuse for idleness; and he reverted again to his favourite project for the diversion of unemployed women into domestic service.

At the end of September Hankey telegraphed to Balfour warning him that he was to be asked to lead the British delegation to Washington, and to the Dominions to invite them to send representatives.[1] Balfour replied that he 'very much hoped the Prime Minister will think better of it', and that Bonar Law was much better suited for the task than he, and was moreover 'one of the unemployed'. But, he added, 'if there is an important reason for my going I am ready to go'.[2] Hankey considered this 'a very sporting gesture' by a man aged 73, who moreover detested sea voyages. But Hankey himself received at least one warm eulogy on his acceptance of Lloyd George's wish that he should accompany Balfour.

*Curzon to Hankey. 1 Carlton House Terrace. 17th October 1921.* Holograph
My dear Hankey,

May I say with what pleasure I heard at the Cabinet (not having then received your letter) that you have consented to go to Washington.

I regard this as the best guarantee for success that has as yet been provided, and no one will be more grateful to you than [the] F.O. for your patriotic self-abnegation.

Yours ever

On 24th October Hankey circulated the provisional organisation of the British Empire Delegation.[3] All was now ready for him to sail for Quebec in the Canadian Pacific liner *Empress of France* on 2nd November, with Lawrence Burgis his private secretary and other members of the delegation. He told Adeline that he 'loathed partings . . . but must just go through with it'.[4] She no doubt agreed fully with the former sentiment, but may well have wondered how many more partings she was to endure. But she never voiced a word of complaint. On her advice Hankey took some whisky to mitigate the dryness of the United States; but as he wrapped the bottles in his tail coat and they got broken the

[1]Lloyd George papers F/25/2/22 and F/25/2/21.
[2]Balfour to Hankey 29th Sept. 1921. Lloyd George papers F/25/2/22.
[3]C.P. 3488 of 24th Oct. 1921. Cab. 24/129.
[4]To Lady Hankey 5th Nov. 1921.

outcome of her thoughtfulness was less agreeable than she intended. Burgis took some champagne – with happier results.[1]

As is to be expected in late autumn the Atlantic passage was less enjoyable than three such indifferent sailors as Balfour, Hankey and Burgis would have wished. But they none the less managed to have useful talks with the Admiralty's representatives. These were led by Lord Lee of Fareham, the First Lord, and Admiral Beatty the First Sea Lord, who had both preceded the others to U.S.A. Admiral Chatfield,[2] the able Assistant Chief of Naval Staff and various junior officers went out with Hankey and Balfour. Before reaching Canadian soil Hankey was able to tell his wife that he had completed the preliminary draft of a naval limitation treaty – which of course took account only of British needs and policy. He had also spent considerable time in 'coaching' Balfour – despite his sea-sickness; and he believed a settlement with the other naval powers 'practicable'.[3]

[1]Interview with Lawrence Burgis 7th April 1967. His champagne was opened to celebrate the signature of the Naval Treaty.

[2]Later Admiral of the Fleet Baron Chatfield (1873–1967). Flag Captain to Admiral Beatty in all the principal North Sea battles of World War I. Fourth Sea Lord 1919. Assistant Chief of Naval Staff 1920–22. Third Sea Lord and Controller of Navy 1925–28. C-in-C, Atlantic Fleet 1929–30 and Mediterranean Fleet 1930–33. First Sea Lord 1933–38. Minister for Co-ordination of Defence 1939–40 and member of War Cabinet under Neville Chamberlain.

[3]To Lady Hankey 5th and 7th Nov. 1921.

*Chapter 9*

# The Washington and Genoa Conferences. November 1921-May 1922

THE *Empress of France* reached Quebec on 8th November and the British delegates went straight on to Washington, where Hankey found that he was accommodated in the 'small, rather noisy, gloomy' Lafayette Hotel, and that offices had been provided for him in the Franklin Square Hotel. The Americans attached a detective to him, but Hankey believed his duty was to spy on his movements on behalf of the State Department rather than ensure his safety. He therefore amused himself by deliberately shaking off the sleuth. The first meeting of the British Empire Delegation took place almost immediately, and Hankey reported with satisfaction that they were 'won to my plan'. But before the mission settled down to serious work they had to be introduced to President Harding and then attend the burial of the American 'Unknown Soldier' in the Arlington National Cemetery; and it was when he came to dress for that ceremony (which he considered very badly organised) that the disaster to the whisky bottle was discovered. Feeling that a British delegate who presented himself before the President of 'dry' America smelling strongly of liquor might produce an unhappy impression Hankey consulted an American colleague, and the advice given to him was 'Wear the tail coat and you'll be the most popular man on this side of the Atlantic!'[1] However he evidently still had misgivings, since he also consulted Balfour's private secretary, who assured him that it would be quite in order for him to appear in a frock coat.[2] The odoriferous tail coat, which might or might not have proved a harbinger of popularity, was accordingly cast aside.

Hankey kept no diary during his time in U.S.A. – probably for

[1]The present Lord Hankey writes that this was one of his father's 'favourite anecdotes'.

[2]To Lady Hankey 13th and 17th Nov. 1921.

reasons of security. But he wrote a series of fifteen very long letters to Lloyd George about the inside story of the conference, and he sometimes enclosed copies of them in the far larger number of letters he wrote to Adeline. This surely suggests that he intended the letters to be regarded as a substitute for his diary. In the official records there is a file of 'Sir Maurice Hankey's correspondence' during the conference which contains interesting material, including holograph drafts of some of his letters to the Prime Minister and drafts of Balfour's despatches.[1] The manuscripts of the former vary very little from the typed versions, but it is typical that Hankey should have drafted those letters in longhand.

The Washington Conference has often been described, and there is no need to include here a detailed account of the long-drawn processes whereby the nine Treaties and twelve Resolutions were finally signed and adopted.[2] What we are interested in is Hankey's part in the successful outcome of the negotiations, and his impressions of the principal participants.

His first letter to Lloyd George, written the day before the opening session, was optimistic, though he gave warning of the 'blackmailing' activities of the American Legion, which was strongly opposed to arms limitation, and of the influence of anti-British factions such as the U.S. Navy League, the Irish lobby and the powerful oil and armaments interests. But he believed that pressure for economy would defeat those opposed to a naval agreement. President Harding struck him as 'a very sincere, likeable sort of man, but not very "quick in the uptake" '. Hughes, the Secretary of State made 'on the whole a very favourable impression . . . He was affable, and talked extremely good sense'. The Vice-President, Calvin Coolidge,[3] he described as 'a sly-looking fellow who does not look you in the face, but I am told he is clever'. Edwin

[1]Cab. 30/31. Copies of all Hankey's letters to Lloyd George from Washington are in Cab. 63/34. The originals are in Lloyd George papers F/63/1 to /15.

[2]See particularly H. and M. Sprout, *Toward a New Order of Sea Power* (Princeton U.P., 1940), Roskill, *Naval Policy,* I, Chapters VII to IX and J. C. Vinson, *The Parchment Peace: The United States and the Washington Conference 1921–22* (Georgia U.P., 1955).

[3]1872–1933. Lawyer and politician (Repub.). President, Massachusetts Senate 1913. Lieutenant-Governor 1915 and Governor 1918. As Vice-President of the U.S.A. 1920 opposed entry to League of Nations. Became thirtieth President on Harding's death 3rd August 1923. Re-elected 1924 but 'did not choose to run for President in 1928'.

Denby,[1] Secretary of the Navy, he found 'a particularly attractive man' – which was a substantial misjudgment; while Admiral Robert E. Coontz[2] the Chief of Naval Operations 'is not a very impressive person and is said to be anti-British'. John Weeks,[3] the Secretary of War, on the other hand 'was immensely friendly and anxious to work with us'. He added that Lord Lee had already confirmed, from conversations with Senators Elihu Root[4] and Henry Cabot Lodge[5] 'that the Anglo-Japanese Alliance is, as we knew, intensely unpopular'; but the Americans were ignorant of 'our intense desire for a Tripartite Agreement [to replace it]'. Where he foresaw trouble was over a Far Eastern settlement, chiefly because of 'the feebleness of the Chinese Delegation'. As to the British Empire Delegation, Sir Robert Borden[6] of Canada was 'much the same as ever, but in a most reasonable frame of mind'; Senator Pearce[7] of Australia was 'not likely to contribute very much wisdom'; while Sir John Salmond,[8] though 'not a very impressive figure, . . . has a curious knack of getting to the essential point of a discussion'.

Hankey anticipated 'intrigue' from both the French and Italian

[1]1870–1929. Lawyer and politician (Repub.). Congressional Representative from Michigan 1905, and twice re-elected. A surprising choice of Harding's for Secretary of the Navy, in which capacity he exerted little influence. Resigned 1924 due to involvement in the notorious Teapot Dome oil lease scandal – though probably not himself corrupt.

[2]1864–1935. Commanded Puget Sound Navy Yard and 13th Naval District 1915–18, and 7th Division, Atlantic Fleet 1919. Chief of Naval Operations 1919–23. C-in-C, U.S. Fleet 1923–25 and commanded 5th Naval District 1925–28.

[3]1860–1926. Politician (Repub.). Senator from Massachusetts 1913–19. Secretary of War under Presidents Harding and Coolidge 1921–25.

[4]1845–1937. Lawyer and politician (Repub.). Secretary of War under President McKinley 1899–1904. Secretary of State under President Theodore Roosevelt 1905–9. Senator from New York 1909–15. Ambassador to Moscow 1917. Member of Committee which established Permanent Court of International Justice 1921. Awarded Nobel Peace Prize 1912.

[5]1850–1924. Politician (Repub.) and writer. Senator from Massachusetts 1893. Played large part in rejection of League of Nations by U.S. Senate 1919.

[6]See Vol. I, p. 120, *note*.

[7]Later Sir George F. Pearce (1870–1952). Australian politician (Lab., from 1916 Nat.) and Trade Union leader. Senator 1907. Acting Prime Minister 1916. Minister for Defence 1908–9, 1910–13, 1914–21 and 1931–34. Minister for Home and Territories 1921–26 and for External Affairs 1934–37.

[8]1862–1924. New Zealand academic lawyer and politician. Professor of Law, Adelaide University 1897–1906 and Victoria University College, Wellington 1907–10. Solicitor-General 1910–20.

delegations, but was confident that 'if we can get on terms of real intimacy and cordiality' with the Americans a limitation agreement, probably based on the draft he had prepared and which Balfour had telegraphed home, would be achieved. Anglo-American relations were, he asserted, 'much better than we thought they were a year or two ago'.[1]

The proposals put forward by Hughes at the opening session on 12th for sweeping reductions in capital ships by scrapping and by cancelling orders were a very well-kept secret, and undoubtedly took everyone by surprise. At a stroke he secured the initiative for the Americans, and rendered obsolete Hankey's carefully prepared scheme, which of course went a long way to meet the Admiralty's views. To his wife he wrote enthusiastically that the American plan was 'really magnificent and stunning. None but a very great nation could have conceived it . . . we have decided to accept it, subject to a few details'. Actually the British reservations were substantial. Immediately after the first session Hankey and Balfour went off to lunch together, and during the meal they considered the reply which the latter was to make at the second session. Balfour scribbled his notes on the back of an envelope and gave it to Burgis after lunch with the remark 'This might help the reporters'. Burgis must have passed the envelope to Hankey, since it ultimately reached Adeline's scrap book. The notes show Balfour's train of thought, and his reaction to Hughes's proposals very clearly; and a large number of his jottings appear in the speech as actually delivered on 15th November:—

'We have admiration and approval' [for Hughes's purposes]
'Spirit and principle' [We accept them in spirit and in principle]
'Give us economy etc. Yes, but something yet *greater*.'
'Idealism turned into facts'
'Britain necessity cf. America' [A reference to the British need for special consideration in the matter of trade protection]
'I am not lamenting' [the sacrifice of British maritime predominance]
'Other questions – 1. Submarines, 2. Cruisers, 3. Replacement'. [British qualifications to Hughes's proposals]

Reading Balfour's speech to-day one cannot but marvel at its smoothness and polish, at the tact with which he hinted at difficulties to come, and at the construction of so exquisite a piece of dialectic from such very slender material. Hankey told Lloyd George that it was 'perfect in

[1]Hankey to Lloyd George 11th Nov. 1921. Lloyd George papers F/63/1/1.

structure', and that Balfour's 'extempore delivery, his pleasant voice and attractive personality made an extraordinarily effective contrast' to the 'raucous voices and unctuous oratory' of the American delegates.[1] The reader will be aware of Hankey's long-standing admiration and affection for Balfour; but it was at Washington in 1921 that it reached its apogee.

As always at an international conference Hankey was soon running not only the British Empire Delegation on his well-tried system and drafting Balfour's despatches to London, but was also tactfully instructing the American Secretary-General John W. Garrett[2] and his staff 'who are very inexperienced' in their duties. Though some of the self-flattery in his letters may reasonably be discounted he gave so many examples of the inefficiency of the American Secretariat that his strictures cannot be totally ignored.

About a week after his arrival he described his routine and the working of the conference to Adeline.

*To Lady Hankey. Hotel Lafayette, Washington. 17th November 1921.*
It is only by breakfasting at 7.30 a.m. that I can get time to write to you . . . My life is very strenuous. [After breakfast] I write letters and telegrams for an hour; see Riddell and Sir Arthur Willert,[3] our Press officer, at 8.45; all the secretaries of the British Empire Delegation at 9.15, and often a number of others. At 9.30 I go to the office . . . and on to Mr. Balfour to give him the latest news before the meeting [of the main conference or one of its committees] at 11 a.m. If there is no official lunch I lunch with Mr. Balfour to meet foreign and British delegates or experts . . . This often involves a note being made afterwards. The B.E.D. meets at 3 p.m., but I often delegate this, and generally [there is] a committee of the Conference at 4 p.m. I have so far written all the Minutes of the conference during the meeting, as the Secretariat-General are inexperienced and I want to help them. When they are more efficient I shall drop this. Then I return to the office and dictate telegrams, despatches and letters until dinner time. I dine with Mr. B. and

[1]Hankey to Lloyd George 17th Nov. 1921. Lloyd George papers F/62/1/3.
[2]1872–1942. Official of U.S. Foreign Service and banker. Held various appointments in U.S. embassies in Europe and South America 1903–19. Conducted negotiations over treatment of prisoners-of-war 1914–18.
[3]1882– . Joined staff of *The Times* 1906. Chief correspondent of *The Times* in U.S.A. 1910–20 (except 1917–18) when serving as Secretary of British War Mission and of Ministry of Information. Head of News Department, Foreign Office 1921. Delegate to many conferences and to meetings of League of Nations 1921–35. Ministry of Information 1939–45.

Mr. Balfour's Note for his great speech, Washington 15 Nov. 1921.

New anniversary - We are discovering
11th v. 12th how hard is Peace

Count myself fortunate. Weary recitative
Sudden blow. Great Event.

Why do I continue debate? Britain
Through no ambitions: necessity
Imaginatively realised? Cf America
communication: Food: Material.

I am not lamenting: Spirit &
Enemies & friends. in Principle

We must consider: We have Admiration & Approval
Not everything: Neither Continental fleets
nor armies
But biggest Battle fleets - & Auxiliaries

Other question - 1 Submarines
2 Cruisers
3 Replacement

Committee points
Leave untouched great lines

Gives us Economy &c Yes but
Something yet greater
Idealism turned into fact

This will make first sitting memorable

Balfour's notes for his speech at the opening session of the Washington Conference, 12th November, 1921

more delegates or experts – unless, as is usual, there is an official or private dinner to attend . . . I hardly ever get to bed before midnight . . .

As was to be expected a few troubles soon arose for Hankey. Such was an injudicious statement by Salmond to the Press about the constitutional position of the Dominions, and 'a very foolish remark in one of the Foreign Office papers' about the alleged inferiority of Asiatic races – which of course gave deep offence to the Indian representatives[1]; but Hankey was always adept at smoothing down ruffled feathers. An interesting point is that as early as 14th November the British realised that limitation of land forces had virtually no place in American plans. Lodge and Root had told Balfour that 'the American people only thought of limitation of armaments in naval terms'; which, at any rate in the light of later events, seems to be an extraordinarily restricted viewpoint.[2] However Hankey noted that Balfour's hint that Britain was prepared to accept total abolition of submarines, given at the second plenary session, was 'received with loud applause from the gallery allotted to members of Congress'. The Admiralty had agreed readily enough to this proposal being put forward; but there never was much reality behind it, since everyone knew that there was no chance at all that the French, or for that matter the Americans, would accept it.

If, as Hankey very well knew, the British proposal about submarines was not likely to be taken seriously he very soon discovered that the American proposal for a ten year naval building holiday was little less disingenuous.

*Hankey to Lloyd George. Private. 18th November 1921*

[Postscript to letter of 17th][3]

. . . Lord Beatty has just been in to tell me of an extraordinary incident which happened at the Naval Technical Sub-Committee. Colonel Roosevelt,[4]

[1]The Chief delegate from India was Right Hon. V. S. Srinivasa-Sastri (1869–1946). Agent for government of India to South Africa 1927–29. Member of Viceroy's Legislative Council 1916–20. Represented India at Imperial Conference and at League Assembly 1921.

[2]Hankey to Lloyd George 14th Nov. 1921. Lloyd George papers F/62/1/2.

[3]Lloyd George papers F/62/1/3.

[4]Theodore Roosevelt Jr. (1887–1944). Son of Theodore Roosevelt, 26th President of U.S.A., and an equally strong 'big Navy' protagonist. Assistant Secretary of the Navy 1921–24. Not to be confused with his relatives Henry L. Roosevelt and Franklin D. Roosevelt, both of whom also served as Assistant Secretary of the Navy (1933–36 and 1913–20 respectively).

the Chairman, is apparently a tremendous babbler. In course of a conversation which the heads of our Naval Delegation had with the heads of the American Naval Delegation, Lord Beatty asked Colonel Roosevelt, in connection with the naval holiday, what America proposed to do with her shipyards, in order that they might be available and efficient at the end of the ten years' holiday. Colonel Roosevelt replied that they would have plenty to do building cruisers and seaplane carriers. Lord Beatty then asked about the armour-plate plant. Colonel Roosevelt replied 'Oh, they will be kept busy reconstructing our old battleships'. Lord Beatty then turned to Admiral Coontz and said 'Are you really going to reconstruct your old battleships?' Admiral Coontz looked very embarrassed and said 'Of course we are not'. Colonel Roosevelt then said, 'Oh yes we are, and we are going to begin with the *Delaware*.' This was a fair give-away . . .

On 23rd Hankey was taken to see Woodrow Wilson, and sent Lloyd George his impressions of that tragic figure.

*Hankey to Lloyd George. Personal and Private. 24th Nov. 1921.*[1]
. . . I think you may be interested that I saw Mr. Woodrow Wilson yesterday for half an hour. I was rather shocked at his appearance, which somehow reminded me of a waxwork. Obviously he is paralysed on one side. . . . He apologised for not getting up, as he had 'a game leg'. I gave him kind remembrances from you, to which he very cordially responded.

His mind was active and his memory fresh. He is extraordinarily bitter against his opponents, and said he was ashamed of his fellow-countrymen for throwing over the League. I reminded him of recent successes of the League, and begged him to take a long view and to believe that he had laid foundations on which some great scheme for world peace would be built; but he reverted almost at once to his bitter scorn for his opponents.

The ex-President was also very bitter against the French, who, he said were 'up to their old games'. Even for Foch he would not have a good word. He regards him as the ultimate author of all our difficulties. I said he was a first-rate General. To that he replied 'That may be, but at the time of the armistice the Germans had broken his spirit and he would not fight on'. This, no doubt, was harking back to Pershing's idea that we ought to have gone on with the war.

He said that at present the British Empire and the United States were drifting towards leadership of the world, which he thought was rather dangerous. For yourself he seemed to preserve very kindly memories. He was so nice to me, and his private secretary had told me that he spoke so often of me, that I ventured to raise the question of Yap . . . He at once violently repudiated the suggestion that any blame could attach to me, but

[1]Lloyd George papers F/62/1/4.

said he feared he had been rather remiss in the matter ... He had quite forgotten the circumstances in which the decisions as to mandates were taken ... though he recalled it when I reminded him.

I left with the feeling that he was a terribly pathetic figure, but with the same liking for the man which I had in Paris. He is not unpopular here now. He has had a number of ovations – in the theatre, outside his house, and out driving ... If you ask me, I think all this is sentiment – devoid of much political significance, though undoubtedly the present Administration have lost popularity ...

I have seen House[1] – another pathetic figure. He has never been able to make it up with Wilson. Indeed, he has never seen him since Paris days ...

Yours ever

On the following day Wilson's secretary wrote to Hankey that 'Mr. Wilson wishes you to know how happy he was to see you again, and he has spoken several times of the pleasant twenty minute chat he had with you. He sends you his warmest regards, in which Mrs. Wilson joins'.[2]

The 24th November being Thanksgiving Day the conference took a holiday; but for Hankey it was totally spoilt. Not only had he caught a cold, about which he was always resentful, but he was intensely perturbed by telegrams from home urging that pressure should be put on the French to accept limitation of land armaments. 'There is absolutely nothing doing in land armaments', he told his wife, 'as the French Chamber has forbidden Briand to discuss it unless America gives the [military] guarantee, which she cannot do. To attack the French on the question would be to irritate them to the point of wrecking the whole scheme of naval limitation ... Balfour is so irritated that he threatened to chuck the whole show. However we spent the whole day drafting a telegram to show the Government their incredible folly ...'[3]

Next day Hankey explained at length to Lloyd George why progress with the naval limitation agreement was not as fast as everyone wished. 'The crux of the whole question', he wrote, 'is the proposed ten years' naval holiday' – which part of the American scheme he considered 'not well thought out'. In effect Hankey was supporting the Admiralty's alternative scheme to a complete holiday in capital ship building, whereby Britain and America would each be allowed to build four

[1]See Vol. I, p. 157, *note*. [2]J. R. Bolling to Hankey 25th Nov. 1921.
[3]To Lady Hankey 27th Nov. 1921.

Nov 24/21



My dear Prime Minister

Apart from an official despatch I ~~have put in~~ on the present position in regard to China and the Pacific, I have put most of my letter writing energy this week into an appreciation of the ~~question~~ position in regard to the naval position which takes the form of a separate letter [margin: and which I have had to re-write four times over].

I think however you may be interested to hear that I saw Mr. Woodrow Wilson yesterday for half an hour. I was rather shocked at his appearance which somehow reminded me of a waxwork. Obviously he is paralysed on one side — I know all the symptoms as a my wife's step sister, ~~who lived with us for a long time was has paralysed~~ is in exactly the same condition. He apologised for not "getting up" as he had "a game leg". ~~How~~ I gave him kind remembrances from you to which he very cordially responded.

His mind was ~~very~~ active and his memory fresh. ~~He was exceedingly cordial to me~~ He is extraordinarily bitter against his opponents, and said he was ashamed of his fellow-countrymen for throwing over the League. ~~When~~ I [margin: reminded him of recent successes of the League and] begged him to take a long view and to believe that he had laid foundations on which some great ~~plan~~ scheme for world peace would ~~rise~~ be built. ~~But~~ He ~~merely~~ reverted ~~to his pa~~ almost at once to his bitter scorn ~~of~~ for his opponents.

The ex-President was also very bitter against the French who, he said, were "up to their old games". Even for Foch

A facsimile of part of the draft of a letter from Hankey to Lloyd George written from Washington on 24th November, 1921

ships of that class between 1922 and 1932, thereby preventing the shipyards and industrial plant which specialised in naval construction falling completely idle.[1] In this letter Hankey exercised his gift for persuasive argument to the fullest extent, since he was completely in accord with Beatty and Chatfield on the rôle of the capital ship 'as the basis of our sea power' – though he had the courage to tell the Prime Minister he 'suspected you are a heretic in this'. But it was all to no avail, as on 10th December the B.E.D. received a telegram from Lloyd George saying 'that the ten year naval holiday . . . should be agreed to'.[2]

It was probably this decision that caused Hankey to tell Adeline that he had 'for a long time felt a little out of sympathy with Ll. G. both on public and private grounds [an obvious if oblique reference to his love affair with Frances Stevenson] and my position with him is not what it was. . . . In peace time his ways are a bit too tortuous for a simple and direct person like me'.[3] Though few who knew him intimately would have accepted Hankey's description of himself as 'simple and direct', there was more than a grain of truth in his assessment of the pitfalls which Lloyd George's methods were digging for the Coalition government. 'Some day', wrote Hankey prophetically, 'he will split the country again on some great controversy and go out of office'; and if and when that happened Hankey's own position would of course be undermined. So he warned Adeline of the need to be 'philosophical' about the troubles he foresaw.[4] He was also strongly opposed to Lloyd George's suggestion that he himself might come out to Washington – so stealing the thunder of success from Balfour, to whom it was properly due; and he tactfully gave the Prime Minister cogent political and social arguments against such an idea.

In contrast to the groundswell of discontent in the B.E.D. over the naval holiday decision, on 29th Hankey told Lloyd George that he was optimistic about achieving agreement on a suitable instrument to replace the Anglo-Japanese alliance. As regards the naval limitation discussions he wholly supported Balfour's proposal that the maximum displacement of aircraft carriers should be 10,000 tons, and also his reservation that Britain 'required a considerable number [of cruisers]

[1]See Roskill, *Naval Policy*, I, pp. 303–6 and 312.
[2]60th meeting of B.E.D. Adm. 1/8630. See Roskill, *Naval Policy*, I, pp. 313–15 for a summary of the whole argument about the naval holiday.
[3]To Lady Hankey 27th Nov. 1921. [4]*ibid.*

above this ratio [i.e. the 5 : 5 : 3 ratio for Britain, U.S.A. and Japan proposed by Hughes] for defending the commerce of the British Empire'.[1] Here we may remark that this issue caused a diplomatic conflagration in 1928 when, after the breakdown of the Geneva naval disarmament conference, the Americans claimed that at Washington the British had agreed to parity with the U.S.A. in cruisers. Hankey at once turned up the relevant papers and telegrams and provided a complete refutation of the suggestion. 'What on earth should we have done', wrote Balfour, 'if you had not developed your admirable machinery for extracting the required needles from the huge bundles of hay which accumulate round any prolonged conference?'[2]

In late November 1921 Hankey's chief anxiety for the limitation treaty stemmed from Japan's claim for 70 % of the British and American capital ship tonnage instead of the 60 % offered by Hughes. But he told Lloyd George he 'could not believe this conference is going to be wrecked on a small difference of 10 per cent in the ratio'.[3] Hankey was puzzled over Hughes's policy of inactivity in this matter; but we now know what Hankey seems not to have guessed – namely that the Americans had broken the Japanese diplomatic cipher, and were fully aware not only of the earlier British proposal to call a conference in London on the Far Eastern questions, but of the fact that the Japanese government had told its delegates in Washington that they were not prepared to risk a breach with Britain and America over the ratio issue. Thus all Hughes had to do was to bide his time in the certainty that the 60 % ratio would be accepted.[4] It seems surprising that Hankey, with his long experience of Intelligence work, and his knowledge of the breaking of the American and German diplomatic ciphers by the

[1]Telegram of 28th Nov. B.M. Add. MSS. 49705 ff. 78–81.

[2]Balfour to Hankey 1st Dec. 1928. *ibid.* f. 85.

[3]Hankey to Lloyd George 29th Nov. 1921. Lloyd George papers F/62/1/6.

[4]See H. O. Yardley, *Secret Service in America* (English Ed., Faber 1931) esp. Ch. XVI. Yardley was head of the State Department's 'Black Chamber' which did brilliant cryptographic work between 1913 and 1929, when it was abolished by Henry Stimson as Secretary of State on the grounds that 'Gentlemen do not read each other's mail'. See L. Farago, *The Broken Seal* (English Ed. Arthur Barker, 1967), esp. Ch. 5. Though full of mistakes (see review by P. Pineau in United States Naval Institute Proceedings, No. 780, Vol. 94, No. 2, Feb. 1968) this book does give a fairly reliable account of Yardley's activities. In 1928 he sold all the secrets of the American cryptographic organisation to the Japanese for $7,000 to pay for his drink and gambling debts (Farago, pp. 57–8) – surely the best value for money ever paid in the Intelligence field.

British during World War I,[1] did not at least suspect that the Americans might have accomplished a similar coup at the time of the Washington Conference. He did, however, warn his wife that the normal mails were insecure, and although he, rather guilelessly, believed 'the administration people' to be 'honourable', he had been told that 'the local intelligence service sticks at nothing'[2] – which could be read as a hint of awareness of the activities of the State Department's 'Black Chamber'.

It may have been at a meeting in Hughes's room early in December that Hankey first appreciated, though dimly, what lay behind the Americans' delaying tactics. On 1st Balfour had a long talk with Baron Kato, the head of the Japanese delegation, who argued forcibly for a 70% ratio in capital ships for his country.[3] Next day Balfour explained the Japanese argument to the B.E.D., and in the afternoon Hankey was present at a meeting between Hughes, Kato and Balfour in the Secretary of State's room.[4] He told Adeline that he now had 'his finger on the whole machine', and was evidently flattered by Hughes's request that he should prepare a memorandum on 'this memorable interview'. These developments, he remarked, made him feel that he was back again at the Paris Peace Conference, acting as Secretary to the Council of Four (or of Three).[5] Hankey's record of the conversation on 2nd produced the following eulogy.

*Charles E. Hughes to Hankey. Secretary of State, Washington. December 5th 1921.*
My dear Sir Maurice,

I return herewith the memorandum you have prepared of the conversation between Mr. Balfour, Baron Kato and myself on Friday afternoon, December 2nd. The memorandum is generally accurate and I must congratulate you on your success in reporting so fairly such a long interview. I have made only a few changes – chiefly in amplification of the report of what I said in answering Baron Kato's statement . . . I think you will at once recognize the propriety of my alterations and additions, but if they do not accord with your recollection do not fail to advise me.

Cordially appreciating the trouble that you have taken to prepare the memorandum, I am

Very sincerely yours

[1]See Vol. I, pp. 246–7 and 81, *note*. [2]To Lady Hankey 27th Nov. 1921.
[3]Appendices I and II to minutes of conference of B.E.D. on 1st Dec. 1921. Cab. 29/28/3.
[4]Memo. of conversation in Cab. 30/31. On 14th Dec. Hankey sent Hughes copies of his notes on all the recent conversations between the heads of delegations.
[5]To Lady Hankey 3rd Dec. 1921.

Two days after the three heads of delegations held their private meeting Hankey told Lloyd George that 'Mr. Hughes has deliberately slowed down the Conference; for, incredible as it may seem, he thinks we are going too fast for these frightened hares of Orientals'.[1] That statement did accurately represent Hughes's policy, even though Hankey probably did not fully appreciate what lay behind Hughes's deliberate procrastination. Hankey himself had put up a draft compromise proposal on the ratio question; but that of course held no appeal for Hughes. In the same letter Hankey once again damped down Lloyd George's enthusiasm to come out himself, at any rate while progress was so slow, and also explained in full detail the trouble between the Japanese and Chinese over the province of Shantung in China, which had fallen under Japanese control as a result of the expulsion of the Germans during the war. In another letter he described how Chinese students had blockaded their country's delegates in their house, lest they should make concessions over Shantung to the Japanese; how he was sent 'with an American official and a crowd of detectives' to break the blockade; and how the Chinese delegates were finally 'smuggled out through a back door'. All of which has a very modern ring about it.[2]

The next few days (5th–8th December) Hankey described as having been spent 'marking time'. For with Balfour away in New York and Hughes unwilling to speed up the naval limitation discussions little progress could be made. But there was of course enough activity in the B.E.D. and in the meetings of the 'experts' to keep Hankey and his staff fully employed. On 9th he told Lloyd George that he would be 'profoundly disappointed if the new quadruple alliance is not announced in public session within the next two or three days'.[3] Next day he wrote to Adeline 'in an exalted state of mind'; for the Four Power Pact (Britain, U.S.A., Japan and France), which was to replace the Anglo-Japanese alliance, had been agreed.[4] Hankey described it 'as a great diplomatic triumph' for Balfour and himself; and it is a fact that both in London at the time of the Imperial Conference and in the preliminary discussions during the voyage out he had pressed the idea of

[1]To Lloyd George 4th Dec. 1921. Lloyd George papers F/62/1/7.
[2]To Robin Hankey 4th Dec. 1921.
[3]Hankey to Lloyd George 9th Dec. 1921. Lloyd George papers F/62/1/8.
[4]To Lady Hankey 10th Dec. 1921. The Four Power Pact was actually signed on 13th Dec.

a multilateral treaty to replace the alliance. An enclosure to his letter to Lloyd George described how, by a combination of tact and firmness, he had managed to dissuade the Italians from pressing to be included in the Four Power Pact. In a long talk with the Marquis Visconti Venosta, the Italian Secretary-General, Hankey managed totally to demolish his country's claims to representation in a treaty which chiefly concerned the powers with big colonial and mercantile interests in the Pacific; and he did so without giving the slightest offence to the Italians. It was in talks like this one that Hankey's unrivalled knowledge of all the conferences held during the war and since proved invaluable; since he knew exactly what were each country's hopes, claims and aspirations.

Only a week after Hankey's spirits had soared with the signature of the Four Power Pact trouble within the B.E.D. caused them to plummet again. He attributed this mainly to the fact that, as Balfour was handling the principal negotiations himself – advised of course by Hankey – the other British delegates and those from the Dominions were not left with enough work to keep them properly occupied. And, remarked Hankey, 'Satan finds some mischief still . . .' The worst case, he said, was Lord Lee who was 'in a thoroughly neurotic state', and was jealous of Balfour conducting the naval limitation discussions, which he considered fell within his own orbit. Then a squall blew up in naval circles. Beatty had returned home late in November to fight the Admiralty's case before the Cabinet Committee on National Expenditure (the Geddes Committee), which was trying to cut naval expenditure very heavily. This left Admiral Chatfield as senior naval adviser in Washington, and on 2nd December he circulated a paper attacking the proposed Ten Year Holiday.[1] But, as we have already seen, the Cabinet overruled naval opinion on this matter. Then on 19th Chatfield sent Balfour a memorandum stressing the right of the naval 'experts' to be consulted on matters which were '*purely technical*' (his italics); and he considered that limitation of capital ships by numbers instead of total tonnage, as in Hughes's proposals, and also agreement on the maximum size of such ships, came within that definition.[2] Chatfield certainly took the rejection of his and the Admiralty's case very badly.[3]

[1]Copy in Adm. 116/2149.
[2]Chatfield to Balfour 19th Dec. 1919. *ibid.* There are several more strongly worded drafts in the same reference.
[3]Roskill, *Naval Policy*, I, pp. 318–20.

Meanwhile Hankey had become involved in these naval grievances through a telegram from Lloyd George to Balfour saying that 'We hope it is not true that our naval experts have been, to quote Hankey "helping the Americans out" by pointing out to them the disadvantages of their own proposal [for the building holiday] from their point of view. This would surely be a gratuitous and wanton task'.[1] Hankey told his wife that this telegram 'quoted or rather misquoted a private letter of mine'; but the expression attributed to him is not in any of his letters to Lloyd George. As it was Churchill who actually drafted the offending telegram it seems likely that it appeared in a letter to him.[2] At any rate the telegram was read by Beatty 'with the utmost amazement', and he at once sent a warm repudiation of the accusation to the Cabinet.[3] Hankey, however, was undefeated. He first showed the suspicious sailors the private letter which contained the offending sentence, and then sent 'a strong disclaimer to the P.M.'[4] But the squall reinforced his feeling that he was becoming unpopular in the Prime Minister's inner circle, and no longer enjoyed his complete confidence. These misgivings may well have been strengthened by the successful negotiation of the Irish Treaty early in December, in which Tom Jones of course played a leading part. Though Jones sent his chief a number of letters describing the negotiations,[5] and showed every sign of loyalty to him, the limelight in Cabinet circles in London inevitably rested chiefly on Jones – while Hankey was toiling away in the outer darkness of Washington.

Hankey had long since abandoned hopes of rejoining his family for Christmas, and the passages for the British delegates booked in the *Olympic* for the last day of the year were cancelled on 21st December. His depression at the prolongation of the separation was aggravated by news that his salary was to be reduced by £500 per annum – a very severe cut for a man with a large young family. He gave Adeline no explanation for these ill tidings, but it must surely have been the Civil

[1] Lloyd George to Balfour. Telegram No. 101 of 9th Dec. 1921. Cab. 30/5.

[2] Roskill, *op. cit.* p. 320.

[3] Dated 10th Dec. 1921. Adm. 116/1776.

[4] To Lady Hankey 17th Dec. 1921.

[5] *Middlemas*, I, pp. 182–4. But Jones's very interesting letter to Hankey of 25th Nov. 1921 telling him of the consequences of the enrolment in Ulster of 'loyalists in military units under the camouflage of police', about which Sir Hamar Greenwood and General Tudor had known nothing, but which had been got hold of and published by Sinn Fein, is not included in that work. See Cab. 63/34.

Service's share of the all-pervading search for economy by the Geddes Committee.[1]

In mid-December the storm over the French demand for a far higher capital ship tonnage than Hughes had proposed broke in full fury, and some very heated debates followed. Hankey noted that the wholly excessive French demands had gravely damaged the public image of their country in U.S.A. 'The shade of Lafayette is very poorly at present' he told Lloyd George.[2] Hankey had suffered so much from French intransigence at Inter-Allied conferences that it was only human of him to show some relish over the strong American reaction to the same phenomenon. However all ended well, for on 18th Briand telegraphed to Hughes that, subject to some awkward reservations about smaller classes of ship, and especially submarines, the French delegates had been told to accept the proposed capital ship quota.

The French reservations led directly to reopening of the question whether submarines could not be entirely abolished – as proposed by the British government. Just before Christmas Balfour argued the case for abolition with such great dialectical skill that Hankey considered it 'unanswerable'.[3] But the French, having given way once, were determined not to repeat such generosity, and on 28th they flatly refused to consider a submarine quota below that accorded to Britain and America. Abolition had of course now receded into the remotest realm of improbability.

On New Year's Day Hankey told Adeline that he hoped to sail on 17th January; but that hope also soon receded – chiefly because of the continued deadlock over the Shantung question. However early in the month he became secretary to the committee of the chief delegates of the five powers, which had been formed to work out the details of the limitation treaty and the specific meaning of the non-fortification clause referring to Pacific territories, which had been agreed in principle as part of the price paid to Japan for accepting the 60% capital ship ration. From 10th January almost to the end of the month a state of deadlock prevailed over the scope and phraseology of this clause. In the end a formula was found which met the British determination not to include Singapore in the non-fortification zone, and also the

[1]To Lady Hankey 21st Dec. 1921.

[2]To Lloyd George. Undated but probably written on 19th Dec. 1921. Lloyd George papers F/62/1/11.

[3]To Lady Hankey 25th Dec. 1921.

Japanese refusal to have it applied to islands such as the Bonin group, which they regarded as part of their homeland. Though Hankey was amused by, and probably relished the lionisation which his work at the centre of the conference produced, he was chafing more and more at the slowness of progress.[1] Tom Jones had sent him an account of the London conference on Reparations and Security held from 18th–22nd December[2] – the first international conference which Hankey had missed for a long time. Then early in January he learnt of Lloyd George's impending departure for Cannes, where he intended to offer the French a security pact – on certain conditions. Hankey saw in this proposal the hand of Churchill and of Sir Edward Grigg,[3] who had recently replaced Philip Kerr, and told his wife that had he been at home he would assuredly have 'blocked' this re-entanglement of Britain in continental affairs.[4] News soon reached Washington that Briand had accepted this offer subject to the inclusion of 'a technical military convention' [i.e. the long-sought guarantee from Britain] – which seemed all of a piece with the hard line taken by his country's delegates to the naval conference. But it was not hard enough for French opinion, and on 13th Briand resigned. Poincaré again became head of the French government, and the likelihood of any amelioration of the Treaty of Versailles, or improvement in Anglo-French relations receded still further. This news increased Hankey's restiveness; and the feeling that he ought to be back in London was aggravated when he heard that the Geddes Committee had proposed the replacement of the three Service Departments by a Ministry of Defence – a proposal which had always been, and was always to remain one of his pet bugbears. The only good news he could send was that the draft of the naval treaty was progressing well – though still held up by Japanese reluctance to compromise over Shantung. In the end the British offer to return to China the naval base at Wei hai wei in the same province, which the Cabinet approved without hesitation, helped the Japanese to

[1]To Lady Hankey 11th Jan. 1922. [2]*Middlemas*, I, pp. 186–7.

[3]1879–1955, 1st Baron Altrincham 1945. A Private Secretary to Lloyd George 1921–22. Governor and C-in-C, Kenya 1925–31. Parliamentary Secretary, Ministry of Information 1939–40. Financial Secretary, War Office 1940. Joint Parliamentary Under-Secretary for War 1940–42. Minister Resident in Middle East 1944–45. (Not to be confused with Sir Percy J. Grigg (1890–1964) who was Principal Private Secretary to Chancellors of the Exchequer 1921–30, Permanent Under-Secretary of State for War 1939–42 and Secretary of State for War 1942–45).

[4]To Lady Hankey 10th Jan. 1922 (misdated 1921).

yield.[1] On 1st February the conference met in plenary session to hear Hughes announce the naval treaty and also the 'Nine Power Treaty' concerning China. Both were signed on 6th.[2]

Meanwhile Hankey's recall had been decided in London. On 19th January Lloyd George telegraphed Balfour saying that the arrangements for the Genoa conference, at which he intended to make his supreme effort for the resettlement of Europe, 'have to be undertaken immediately' as the date of the opening session was only six weeks ahead. The organisation was in the hands of the Italians, but Lloyd George evidently felt considerable doubts regarding the wisdom of leaving the secretarial side entirely to them. 'Much as I dislike to make a request which may inconvenience you', his telegram continued, 'I feel bound to ask whether you can spare Hankey before the end of your conference. Tom Jones is much engaged upon detailed Irish business, and we have no-one with Hankey's organising experience and knowledge of the personnel of foreign secretariats'. Balfour of course felt bound to defer to such a request, and proposed that Hankey should sail on 7th February. In reply Sylvester telegraphed that, as the Italians were 'very inexperienced', Lloyd George felt that Hankey's co-operation with them was essential, and he should therefore sail at the earliest possible opportunity.[3] Doubtless Lloyd George's insistence on Hankey's early return helped to restore his self-confidence, which had recently been rather badly shaken.

On 22nd January news of the death of Lord Bryce, the much-loved and very successful British ambassador 1907–1913, reached Washington. That day Hankey and Balfour had to attend a meeting of the Conference and when the American delegates opened the session with warm tributes to Bryce Hankey realised to his horror that he had not even told Balfour the news, let alone briefed him properly for his

[1]Balfour asked the Cabinet for freedom of action over offering the rendition of Wei hai wei and yielding up to China the British share of the Boxer indemnity in order to help towards an agreement between China and Japan. The Treasury raised no objection to the latter suggestion – despite the current pressure for economy. See P. J. Grigg to Vansittart 22nd Nov. 1921. Lloyd George papers F/15/2/46.

[2]Balfour's final despatches of 4th and 6th Feb. 1922 (Nos. 25 and 27) sum up admirably the last stage of the protracted negotiations over the naval limitation treaty and the agreement over Shantung.

[3]Lloyd George to Balfour, telegram No. 209 of 19th Jan. 1922 *et seq.* Lloyd George papers F/61/2/4, 5 and 8.

reply. And as Balfour hardly ever read a newspaper he was probably completely in the dark about it. Balfour, however, rose splendidly to the occasion and spoke of Bryce with all his usual elegance – to the considerable puzzlement of the secretary. On the way home Hankey asked Balfour how he had been forewarned, and received the reply 'Oh! It was all right! Sarah told me'. Hankey was vastly amused that the coloured cook should have been the agent whereby his own lapse was redeemed.[1]

Hankey actually left New York in the *Scythia* on 26th January. His last two letters to Lloyd George from Washington reflect a little of his uneasiness of mind at that time. His disquiet, and anxiety about the future, were probably aggravated by the publication in January by Ray Stannard Baker of long extracts from the minutes of the Council of Four at the Paris Conference – which all had agreed should be treated as secret.[2] Though he expressed his indignation at 'a scandalous breach of confidence' to Lloyd George, we saw earlier how, when he came to learn the full facts about the premature disclosures, he took a more generous view.[3] One of his last letters to Garrett, the Secretary-General of the Washington Conference, was to press for twenty complete sets of the minutes of the various committees, which were 'a long way in arrear', to be made available for the British and Dominion delegates before their departure.[4] Evidently his experiences in Washington had done nothing to allay his early misgivings about the efficiency of the American secretarial system.

The results of the Washington Conference were greeted with world-wide acclaim – though it has long since been recognised as having created little more than a 'Parchment Peace'.[5] Yet it did prevent the danger of a naval race between Britain and America – at any rate in capital ships; and it did, though only temporarily, dampen the antagonisms between the two democracies, which had become increasingly apparent since 1918. That it handed over strategic command of the western Pacific to the Japanese, though recognised by both British and American naval men at the time, did not become fully apparent until 1941. However if one denies oneself the substantial benefit of

[1]Diary 31st Oct. 1922.

[2]Hankey to Lloyd George 17th and 20th Jan. 1922. Lloyd George papers F/62/1/14 and 15.

[3]See pp. 104–5.

[4]Hankey to Garrett 31st Dec. 1921. Cab. 30/31.

[5]See C. J. Vinson's book of that title (Georgia U.P., 1955).

historical hindsight, and accepts the contemporary assessment of the importance of the treaties at its face value, Balfour's achievement was certainly outstanding, and second only to that of Hughes in bringing the conference to a happy conclusion. And throughout those three trying months Hankey always stood at Balfour's right hand, and often, almost literally held up his arms in periods of difficulty. Taken together they were a remarkable pair, the like of which has not been seen since and is not likely to be seen again. Balfour's charm, his skill in dialectics and his attractive personality were, as Hankey told Lloyd George, of inestimable value. But Hankey's own part was surely considerable, since it was he who got the initially gritty machinery of the conference to run smoothly, who was friendly and tactful to everyone, and who often saw the best road to compromise. It does not go too far to say that without Hankey Balfour's success would certainly have been harder won, and might not have been won at all.

Hankey arrived home from America on 4th February, and was at once involved in clearing the accumulation of business which had piled up during his absence. The Cannes Conference (6th–13th January), at which Tom Jones had deputised for him, had ended in failure and the resignation of M. Briand. With Poincaré holding the offices of Prime Minister and Foreign Minister prospects of an improvement in Anglo-French relations were dim; but Lloyd George was determined to go ahead with his final bid to restore the economic and financial state of Europe by holding a huge conference at Genoa under the aegis of the Italian government, of which Luigi Facta was now the head.[1] Britain and the Dominions and 29 European nations, including the other Allied powers, Russia, Germany, the U.S.A. and 18 states which had been neutral in the war were to be invited; and each (except Luxemburg) was to be allowed to send two delegates. But the auguries soon appeared a good deal less than favourable, since President Harding's administration declined to participate, and European recovery could hardly be effectively initiated without at least the benevolence of the U.S.A. Furthermore Lord D'Abernon had already reported several times from Berlin that Russian emissaries to the Genoa Conference were engaged in discussions with the German government – a warning whose

[1] 1861–1930. Italian politician (Dem.). Succeeded Giolitti as Prime Minister March 1922 after prolonged crisis. Took no effective steps to counter the rise of Fascism, and his government fell 28th October 1922 giving place to that of Mussolini. Senator 1924.

significance does not appear to have been appreciated at the time.[1]

Hankey at once prepared a paper surveying the preparations made up to the date of his return – which were not in fact impressive.[2] Three days later he attended a conference of Ministers (Lloyd George, Chamberlain and Curzon) at which the attitude of the new French government was the main subject. Doubts were expressed whether Poincaré merely repudiated the Resolutions accepted by Briand at Cannes in January or whether he was trying to prevent the Genoa conference taking place.[3] The French ambassador had assured Curzon that the Cannes Resolutions were all that his government disliked; but the British Ministers agreed that preliminary talks with the French to clear the matter up were essential, and an invitation was therefore sent asking for a meeting of the two nations' economic experts.

It must not be thought that, because Genoa loomed large on Hankey's horizon at this time, it was his sole pre-occupation. The reports by the Geddes Committee on National Expenditure had just been issued,[4] and had aroused predictably strong reactions from the Service Departments – and especially the Admiralty; for Geddes had aimed some very hard blows at the department of which he had until recently been the head.[5] The government thereupon appointed a new committee under Churchill to review the Geddes proposals, and Hankey was particularly concerned to convince Churchill that Geddes's suggestion that a Ministry of Defence should replace the three service departments was neither necessary nor practicable. 'It is surely essential both in peace and in war', he wrote to Lloyd George, 'that the Navy, our first line of defence, should be represented in the Cabinet and in Parliament by a separate Minister'.[6] Though the Churchill Committee concluded that a

[1]Diary extracts for 20th Jan. 1922 and later. Copies sent to Curzon and Hankey. D'Abernon papers B.M. Add. MSS. 48924 (Vol. III), folders 5, 6 and 8.

[2]C.P. 3716 of 7th Feb. 1922.

[3]The two 'Cannes Resolutions' were, firstly, Lloyd George's proposal to summon an Economic and Financial conference early in 1922 with the object of restoring trade and re-creating a sense of security in Europe. Secondly the Resolution proposed by the Supreme Council that an International Corporation should be set up with the object of achieving 'the economic reconstruction of Europe'. See Cmd. 1621.

[4]Cmd. 1581, 1582 and 1589 of 14th Dec. 1921, 28th Jan. 1922 and 21st Feb. 1922.

[5]See Roskill, *Naval Policy*, I, pp. 230–3, 267–8 and 318. C.P. 3692 of 4th Feb. 1922 (Cab. 24/132) is the report of the Churchill Committee.

[6]Hankey to Lloyd George from Washington 20th Jan. 1922. Cab. 63/32.

single Ministry 'might well be the ultimate solution to the problem of co-ordinating the activities of the three services', they did not consider the present time appropriate for making such a drastic change. Instead they regarded the C.I.D. as 'a suitable instrument to achieve the desired co-ordination', and proposed that it should be in constant session. This was of course the precise policy which Hankey had long been pressing on Lloyd George, and its insertion in the Churchill Committee's report can confidently be attributed to his efforts.[1]

Other matters which took up much of Hankey's time were the future of the coal industry, the government's proposals to institute unemployment insurance, and the possible amalgamation of the major oil producing and distributing companies – with particular reference to building up reserves of oil at home and at overseas naval bases now that the Navy was almost wholly dependent on the new type of fuel. As regards Imperial and defence policy the future of the Royal Air Force still hung in the balance, the introduction of a new step towards self-government for India was pressing, and the status of Egypt was far from settled. Though Hankey left the industrial negotiations mainly in Tom Jones's hands, as he did when the Irish situation again became menacing in the middle of the year, he could not entirely escape involvement – especially where political questions, such as the acceptance or rejection of the new constitution for Ireland, had military implications.

On 17th February Hankey circulated to the Cabinet a paper stating that decisions were required, firstly as to whether the R.A.F. should continue as a separate service, and secondly, if it did so continue, what responsibilities for Imperial Defence heretofore carried by the Army and Navy should be transferred to the new service. He recapitulated the past history of the long-standing controversy as recorded in a large number of C.P. and C.I.D. memoranda, which showed once again how indispensable was his system of recording discussions and conclusions; but he expressed no opinion of his own.[2] However we know from Hankey's frequent and friendly correspondence with

[1]Roskill, *op. cit.* p. 338. Also Hankey to Jones 20th Jan. 1922. 'I want you to realise that this [i.e. a Ministry of Defence] is a matter on which I feel very strongly indeed . . . I am anxious that the Prime Minister at any rate should know what I think'. Jones papers.

[2]C.P. 3754 of 17th Feb. 1922 which is also C.I.D. 163C. Cab. 24/33 and 21/225. A large number of earlier memoranda in the C. Series deal with this subject e.g. 135, 136, 139, 141, 149, 151 and 153 all of April–July 1921.

Trenchard[1] at this time that, despite his naval background and training, he was no supporter of those naval men who wished to carve up the R.A.F. and revert to the state of affairs which had prevailed before 1918. He did, however, agree with Beatty that the navy should be allowed to control and develop its own aviation branch as an integral part of that service – as indeed Trenchard himself had foretold in 1919 might well be the ultimate solution[2]; and in that belief Hankey surely showed both wisdom and foresight. In March this issue came before the Cabinet as a result of a motion put down for debate in Parliament by Admiral Sir Reginald Hall, the former Director of Naval Intelligence, that the Royal Naval Air Service should be revived.[3] In Cabinet Austen Chamberlain used the brief Hankey had prepared as the basis of the important statement he proposed to make next day in the House, and the Cabinet approved it.[4] Included in that statement was the decision that a Sub-Committee of the C.I.D. should be established to 'enquire into the existing system of Naval and Air co-operation, and to advise as to the way in which the Air Force can give to the Navy the Air Service which the Navy requires'.

A week later Hankey wrote to Lloyd George about the current negotiations between Beatty and Trenchard. Some progress had, he said, been made; but he still thought the sub-committee should be formed. If Balfour could not take the chair he proposed H. A. L. Fisher, President of the Board of Education, as the best alternative. Austen Chamberlain, Lord Lee (First Lord) and F. E. Guest (Secretary of State for Air) had, he wrote, agreed to this suggestion.[5] Unhappily the dispute between the Admiralty and the Air Ministry simmered and seethed throughout the spring and summer until, in July, Hankey felt bound to report that an *impasse* had been reached and that arbitration on the highest level appeared to be the only solution. He proposed that this should be undertaken by Lloyd George, Chamberlain and Balfour 'whose decision should be final'.[6] But the crisis in the Middle

[1]Trenchard papers. [2]Roskill, *op. cit.*, p. 256 and Cmd. 467.

[3]Parl. Deb. Commons, Vol. 151, Cols. 2457–68. Admiral Hall moved an amendment in the debate on the Navy Estimates on 16th March 1922.

[4]Cabinet 18(22) of 15th March 1922. Cab. 23/29.

[5]Hankey to Lloyd George 22nd March 1922. Lloyd George papers F/26/1/21. H. A. L. Fisher did become chairman of the C.I.D. Sub-Committee, but it failed to produce a solution. Cab. 21/225. The relevant C.I.D. memoranda are in the B. Series e.g. 357, 360, 362.

[6]Hankey to Lloyd George 28th July 1922. Lloyd George papers F/26/2/9.

East in the autumn of 1922 submerged that sensible proposal, and the dispute had not been resolved at the time of the fall of the Coalition government. One of the first issues Hankey then took up with Bonar Law was the need to put an end to this interdepartmental strife. Churchill's efforts at mediation between Beatty and Trenchard having proved fruitless Hankey suggested that either a Cabinet Committee should be set up to find a solution or the Prime Minister himself should arbitrate between the two parties. Sir Samuel Hoare, the new Secretary of State for Air, agreed to the former proposal, and he and Hankey both urged that the Prime Minister himself should take the chair.[1] This marked the genesis of the Salisbury Committee and its offshoot the Balfour Sub-Committee of 1923, to which we will revert later.

It was unlucky for Hankey that at such a very busy time he should have been troubled by more cases of leakage of Cabinet documents to the Press. On 24th March the *Daily Sketch* and *Daily Express* both reported accurately the recommendations of the Cabinet Committee appointed to study Unemployment Insurance, though the actual Conclusions of the Cabinet were mis-reported.[2] This serious case came shortly after two less important ones had already caused Hankey to go into action. On 8th he informed all Ministers of the decision that 'in future Cabinet Minutes should not be circulated'; instead the Secretary would send 'reminders' to those Ministers concerned with the execution of any Conclusion. Only one copy of the actual Minutes was to be kept in his office, and another sent to the King. But he quickly found that this system involved him in writing about a score of personal letters to Ministers after each Cabinet;[3] which obviously added greatly to his burden. After the fall of Lloyd George the circulation of Cabinet Minutes was resumed, though their form was much curtailed. Yet the leakages continued, each case was investigated by Hankey, and in some instances the responsibility could be firmly placed.[4]

While Hankey was struggling to progress the very complicated arrangements for the Genoa Conference he accompanied Lloyd George

[1]Hankey to Bonar Law 22nd Nov. 1922. Cab. 21/225.

[2]Cab. 21/457. The proposals before the Cabinet are in C.P. 3865. The actual Conclusion is Cabinet 16(22) Conclusion 3.

[3]Hankey to Churchill 10th March 1922. Cab. 21/222.

[4]For example at about the same time as Bonar Law's notorious letter to *The Times* of 30th Jan. 1923 (see p. 131, *note*) about the American War Debt settlement. A leak on the same subject in Paris was traced to an underpaid official in the French Foreign Office.

to Boulogne for talks with Poincaré on the attitude of the latter towards the 'Cannes Resolutions' and towards disarmament – a subject on which the French Premier was not exactly malleable. Our interest in the talks is limited to the view Hankey expressed on the principles which should govern further disarmament. To Esher he wrote, as a result of the Boulogne meeting, 'My view is that the League of Nations should take up the whole of the work of the Washington Conference on armaments and apply it throughout the world. Thus the principles of the Naval Agreement should be extended to the Powers who did not take part in the discussions on armaments at Washington, and all the nations which are members of the League should be asked to agree to the Poison Gas Resolution [one of the 'Root Resolutions' signed at Washington] and any others of the same type . . . I also made the same suggestion to Eric Drummond'.[1] Later in the 1920s the extreme proponents of the League and the principle of 'Collective Security', such as Lord Robert Cecil and Philip Noel-Baker, regarded Hankey as a major obstacle to their aims and ideals. Yet the letter to Esher quoted above surely shows that *as long as prospects for the success of the League appeared reasonable* Hankey was prepared to support and strengthen it. Only after its failures had become palpable – notably over the Italian aggression against Greece in 1923[2] – did he turn to the alternative of maintaining national armaments at a level necessary to achieve reasonable security in case the League should again fail (as it did do) to deal effectively with plainly aggressive actions.

We have already seen how revision of the Treaty of Sèvres in favour of Turkey had recurred again and again in the deliberations of the British Cabinet; and that the desire to placate Turkey arose in part from the alleged ill effects of the treaty on Moslem opinion in India. This was an issue on which Curzon, who regarded himself, not without reason, as an expert, frequently came into conflict with Edwin Montagu, the Secretary of State for India. On 1st March the Viceroy, Lord Reading, telegraphed home urging that, in deference to Moslem opinion, the Allies should evacuate Constantinople, acknowledge the Sultan's suzerainty over the Holy Places and restore Ottoman Thrace and Smyrna to Turkey.[3] Montagu, who had never been an easy bed-

[1]Hankey to Esher 27th Feb. 1922. Esher papers.

[2]See James Barros, *The Corfu Incident of 1923. Mussolini and the League of Nations.* (Oxford U.P., 1966).

[3]C.P. 3794. Cab. 24/133.

fellow in Asquith's or Lloyd George's ministries, published the Viceroy's proposals – without having consulted any of his colleagues. Hankey at once became involved because Montagu claimed that the Viceroy's telegram had been circulated 'immediately', and also quoted, or rather misquoted, a letter from Curzon marked 'Private' in a speech at Cambridge. These reckless actions caused Chamberlain to protest vigorously, and roused Curzon to a state of almost hysterical fury. The outcome was the resignation of Montagu on 9th March. Though he described himself as 'a victim of Diehard Dislike' Chamberlain told the Viceroy that the sole reason for his resignation was his failure to consult any of his colleagues before taking a step 'which gravely affected the conduct of foreign affairs'.[1] Hankey admitted, however, that the Viceroy's telegram of 1st March which set off the explosion was in the Cabinet Office 'longer than I thought', and acquitted Montagu of deliberately announcing its contents without consulting his colleagues. After a good deal of coming and going, and Derby and Devonshire both refusing the India Office, it was accepted by Lord Peel; but the implications for the Coalition government were anything but happy, and Hankey was obviously distressed by the whole episode. His next task was of course the tricky one of recovering from Montagu his Cabinet papers. On 20th he warned Lloyd George that the outgoing Minister intended 'to take away nearly all his Cabinet papers on leaving the India Office', and that his own proposal of November 1919 that Ministers should be required 'to surrender their papers on leaving office' had never received approval. Lloyd George, however, left the question alone – possibly realising that he himself might well be affected one day if such a ruling were strictly applied.[2]

The explosion provoked by Montagu had hardly subsided before another, and potentially far more serious one appeared likely over Ulster. On 17th March Jones warned Lloyd George of the danger of 'departing from the spirit of the bargain with the South' by 'cloaking a military force [the so-called 'B Special' constabulary] under the guise of a police force', and other steps favoured by Sir Henry Wilson, who had now become a leader of the Orange faction.[3] A few days earlier

[1]Austen Chamberlain papers AC 23/7/1, 29, 65 and 68 contain Chamberlain's correspondence and copies of telegrams and letters about this rumpus. For Montagu's side of the story see S. D. Waley, *Edwin Montagu: A Memoir* (1964), pp. 271–8.

[2]Hankey to Lloyd George 20th March 1922. Lloyd George papers F/26/1/18.

[3]Jones to Lloyd George 17th March 1922 *ibid.* F/26/1/17. In the previous November

Hankey had expressed similar misgivings,[1] and in May a request from the Free State Government for arms with which to attack the rebel I.R.A. plainly threatened renewed British involvement in Irish civil strife – a prospect which Jones and Hankey both viewed with alarm.[2] The summer months were tense and anxious, and Churchill showed renewed bellicosity over Ulster. Then on 22nd June Henry Wilson was assassinated by I.R.A. gunmen outside his house in London.

*To Lady Hankey. Grosvenor Hotel, 22nd June 1922.*
I could not go home to-night owing to the murder of Sir Henry Wilson by the Sinn Feiners . . . I at once went to the P.M. who was very much upset – as I was myself. I have been with him ever since – it is now about 11 p.m. Both the assassins have been caught. I have seen the revolvers with which they did the deed and the documents taken on them. Undoubtedly it was a carefully planned and premeditated assassination. We have had to put back all the precautions for the safety of Ministers, public buildings etc. . . . I was with the P.M. seeing the Home Secretary [Edward Shortt] and other Cabinet Ministers, General Horwood[3] the Chief of Police, the head of the Criminal Investigation Dept. and so forth until dinner and getting various decisions executed. The P.M. generally likes to have me with him on these occasions, so I stayed on to dinner and until bedtime with him and Chamberlain. We are carrying out a number of searches and arrests to-night.

I fear Henry Wilson brought this on himself by his very bitter attitude towards the Irish policy of the Govt., and he was suspected by the extremists of having caused the anti-Sinn Fein pogroms in Belfast. He was probably urged on to all this by his wife who is a rabid fanatic. To Ll. G's telegram of sympathy tonight she replied in her own hand that Henry Wilson's death lies at his door . . . The P.M. took it very well. . . . Personally I believe the assassination, though political, was personal to Henry Wilson, and I don't believe it is part of any general plot. No one can tell what the political effect will be. It might mean a stampede of Unionists against the Coalition, but personally I am convinced it will not, unless followed by other murders. It is a great thing that the assassins were captured, and a great credit to the courage of the police who, though unarmed, captured them . . .

---

Jones had warned Hankey of the dangers inherent in this subterfuge. See p. 253, *note*.

[1]Hankey to Lloyd George 14th March 1922 *ibid.* F/26/1/13. Also Jones to Hankey 28th April 1922. *Middlemas,* I, p. 198.

[2]Jones to Hankey 12th May 1922.

[3]Brigadier-General Sir William T. F. Horwood (1868–1943). D.A.A.G., War Office 1914–15; Provost-Marshal, G.H.Q. British Expeditionary Force 1915–18. Assistant Commissioner, Metropolitan Police 1918–20 and Commissioner 1920–28.

One result of the murder of Wilson was that the government exerted pressure on Michael Collins to deal with the rebels in Dublin who had seized the Four Courts as long ago as 13th April. Jones was away at the time, and Hankey therefore had to handle Irish affairs as well as everything else. Although on 29th June he told Adeline that 'the Dublin business looks ugly' in fact the Provisional Government decided on strong action, and after a bombardment Rory O'Connor and the rebels surrendered on 30th. Despite the sudden death of Arthur Griffith, the President of the Provisional Government, on 12th August and the death in an I.R.A. ambush of his closest associate Michael Collins ten days later, the rebels' attempt to re-involve the British government in the civil war failed, and Ireland ceased to be the major problem it had been ever since Easter 1916. But, perhaps unfairly, the Coalition government emerged with little credit from the prolonged negotiations which had ended in the setting up of the Irish Free State.

We must now return to the middle of March and to the preparations for the Genoa Conference. On 14th Hankey told Lloyd George that the Italians 'were not putting their backs into arranging the conference', and that 'M. Poincaré is doing his best to block Genoa'. He wanted 'the strongest possible pressure' put on the Italians to expedite matters.[1] Lloyd George agreed, and Hankey next reported that he had 'turned on the Foreign Office to drive the Italians'.[2] Then Chicherin, the Russian Foreign Minister[3] sent an 'insolent telegram' demanding that the conference should open on 23rd March, to which Signor Schanzer,[4] his Italian compeer, had replied '*d'une manière assez rude*'.[5] The opening date was now firmly fixed for 10th April, and for the next week Hankey wrote daily to Lloyd George to inform him of the progress made by the preliminary Committee of Experts. Before the end of March he was able to report that it 'was proceeding very satisfactorily', though there

[1]Hankey to Lloyd George 14th March 1922. Lloyd George papers F/26/1/12.
[2]Same to same 15th March 1922. *ibid.* F/26/1/14.
[3]Georgios V. Chicherin (1872–1936). Russian diplomat and politician (initially Social Democrat, then Menshevik, finally Bolshevik). Political refugee 1907–18. Succeeded Trotsky as Commissar for Foreign Affairs March 1918. Replaced by Litvinov 1930.
[4]Carlo Schanzer. Italian politician (Dem.). Foreign Minister 1921.
[5]Hankey to Lloyd George 16th March 1922. Lloyd George papers F/26/1/15. Chicherin's telegram of 15th March is printed in Cmd. 1637.

were obviously serious obstacles to surmount over restarting trade with Russia.[1]

As March drew to a close Hankey attended a series of ministerial meetings at which the instructions to be given to the delegates for the Genoa conference were discussed prior to them being placed before the full Cabinet.[2] No less than four drafts were prepared by Hankey, Chamberlain and Lloyd George separately or together, and a deep cleavage of opinion soon became apparent over the question of recognising the Soviet government.[3] Lloyd George believed that all the great powers wanted to grant recognition – subject 'to some probationary period'; but Churchill and Curzon had always been passionately opposed to such a measure, and the former told Chamberlain that he would resign rather than accord *de jure* recognition to the U.S.S.R.[4] His insistence that he must put down a motion in the House on the terms of reference for the conference made the likelihood of a split in the Cabinet plain. On 28th an important Cabinet was held with Lloyd George in the chair and Hankey and Jones both present to record the proceedings on the Resolution to be submitted to the House on the following Monday (3rd April) and the instructions to the Genoa delegates. As to the latter, the Cabinet agreed to grant wide discretion, subject to limitations regarding recognition of the Soviet government – such as acceptance by the U.S.S.R. of the Cannes Resolutions and appointment only of a Chargé d'Affaires 'for a probationary period'; and the results of the conference were to be finally approved by Parliament.[5] Though Chamberlain stood loyally by Lloyd George during these discussions, the outcome plainly was a substantial success to the dissident Conservative faction in the Coalition.

On 8th April Hankey left London with Lloyd George and his usual galaxy of private secretaries and advisers, including Sir Edward Grigg and Sir Cecil Hurst (legal adviser to the Foreign office). Sir Robert

[1]Hankey to Lloyd George 21st March 1922. *ibid.* F/26/1/42.

[2]At this stage the delegates were to be Lloyd George, Curzon and Horne; but Birkenhead, the Lord Chancellor, was to be 'in the neighbourhood'. Cabinet 21(22) of 28th March 1922.

[3]C.P. 3908 of 29th March 1921. Cab. 24/136.

[4]Chamberlain to Curzon 24th March 1922. Chamberlain papers AC 23/6/21. For Curzon's views see Cmd. 1869, *Correspondence between His Majesty's Government and the Soviet Government respecting the Relations between the two Governments* (1923).

[5]Cabinet 21(22) of 28th March 1922.

Horne (Chancellor of the Exchequer), Sir Philip Lloyd-Greame[1] (Secretary to the Department of Overseas Trade) and Sir Laming Worthington-Evans[2] (Secretary of State for War) went out independently. Curzon, the Foreign Secretary, was not included – probably because his health was not good, he was already at loggerheads with Poincaré, and he did not wish to play second fiddle to Lloyd George at a conference which he considered foredoomed to failure.[3] Poincaré and Barthou joined the British delegates' train while it was passing around the Paris 'ceinture', and Hankey had to take a note of the conversation in a cramped carriage sitting on a footstool.[4] On reaching Genoa Hankey found himself very comfortably installed in the Hotel Miramare. But the conduct of business was made difficult by Lloyd George being installed in the luxurious Villa de Albertis six miles outside the town; while the Russian delegates were still further separated from the headquarters of the conference at the Palazzo Reale, Genoa, by being accommodated at Santa Margherita near Rapallo, which was fifteen miles away and accessible only by an indifferent and very hilly road. Robin Hankey, who came out for the conference, recalls that the reason why the Russian and German delegations were quarantined in this manner was that typhus was rampant in their home countries, and the Italians were extremely nervous about it spreading. The railway stations used by the Russians and Germans were, according to the same source, washed down daily with carbolic. But if the hygienic results were satisfactory the diplomatic consequences were very much the reverse.

The principal figures were of course the chief representatives of the five 'convening powers' – Italy, Britain, France, Belgium and Japan; but around them revolved an immense galaxy of delegates, experts and officials from the other participating states – including of course those from the British Dominions. Hankey was immediately 'up to the neck' in trying to get this enormous and unwieldy gathering organised and

[1]Assumed name of Cunliffe-Lister 1924. 1st Earl of Swinton 1955. (1884– ). Politician (Cons.). Secretary, Overseas Trade Department 1921–22. President, Board of Trade 1922–23, 1924–29 and 1931. Secretary of State for Colonies 1931–35, and for Air 1935–38. Resident Minister in West Africa 1942–44. Minister for Civil Aviation 1944–45. Chancellor of Duchy of Lancaster and Minister of Materials 1951–52. Secretary of State for Commonwealth Relations 1952–55.

[2]See p. 130, *note*.

[3]Nicolson, *Curzon*, pp. 243–5.

[4]To Lady Hankey 9th April 1922.

working efficiently.[1] 'The Italian Secretariat-General', he told Adeline, 'are very good fellows, but really have an impossible task to perform. It is as though we had to organise a conference of 30 nations in (say) Cardiff. The telephones don't function, the operators do not understand English . . . the typewriters have Italian lettering, and they wanted all their Roneos [reproducing machines] themselves'. Luckily he had foreseen such troubles and had brought with him English typewriters and other equipment, and by various dodges he managed to get the opening speeches by the heads of delegations of the convening powers reproduced and telegraphed home – even prior to some of them being actually delivered.[2] By such devices did he always manage to maintain friendly relations with the Press.

The Plenary Sessions were held in the beautiful hall of the Palazzo di San Giorgio (which local wags soon suggested renaming San Lloyd-Giorgio), and at the first of them on 10th April Lloyd George made an eloquent and gracious speech proposing that, as the Italian nation was acting as host to the conference, Signor Facta should be elected President – a motion which was readily accepted. Italian hospitality was indeed lavish, and Hankey was embarrassed to learn that they insisted on paying for his accommodation. His delight at the atmosphere in which the conference opened was, however, soon shaken; for Chicherin the chief Russian delegate, whom he described as 'a foolish, mischievous fellow', introduced 'some very provocative matter' into his first speech. But he was forced to admit that the Russian was 'a clever debater', and at once got the best of a dialectical exchange with Barthou. This early clash between the French and Russians at once made him apprehensive about a breakdown. However Lloyd George calmed the troubled waters temporarily 'with a speech of delightful raillery'.[3] What caused Hankey further misgivings was that it quickly became clear that, whereas the British delegates had been granted reasonable latitude in negotiation, Poincaré had given Barthou the most stringent and rigid brief – leaving him virtually no room for compromise.

Four Commissions – Political, Financial, Economic and Transport – were at once set up. Though Hankey was only directly concerned with the Political Commission he had in addition to organise all the separate

[1] A good contemporary account, though written very much from Lloyd George's point of view, is J. Saxon Mills, *The Genoa Conference* (Hutchinson, 1922).
[2] To Lady Hankey 11th April 1922. [3] *ibid.*

meetings of the British Empire Delegation – as at Washington. He very quickly noticed that 'at every point and in every committee the French hatred of the Bolshevists crops up'; and so marked was it that 'they almost seem to have forgotten their hatred of the Germans'.[1] On the day that the four Commissions settled down to work Hankey sent Chamberlain the first of a series of sixteen long letters about the progress of the conference. These corresponded of course to the letters he had sent Lloyd George from Washington, and were intended to keep the Lord Privy Seal informed on the inside story, and so able to answer questions in the House or make a statement on behalf of the government – should the need arise. He also sent home the full *procès-verbaux*; but Chamberlain understandably found that mass of material indigestible and soon told Worthington-Evans how much he appreciated Hankey's private letters.[2] Certainly they provide an admirable synopsis of the course of events, as well as entertaining descriptions of the personalities involved. The very first of this series told how the French were trying 'to keep the Russians and Germans off the Sub-Committees which are the real working bodies of the four great Commissions', and how Lloyd George, 'ably seconded by M. Facta and M. Schanzer [the Italian delegates]' had frustrated these obstructionist tactics. The Russians, he said, 'do not lack ability, but they seem almost entirely devoid of tact'; but he admitted Chicherin scored a good debating point off Barthou by arguing that Briand having described the large Russian army as 'the bar to peace' at the Washington Conference, if Russia were now prepared to reduce her army there could surely be no obstacle to disarmament. 'I thought his [Chicherin's] eyes were dancing with mischief' wrote the observant Hankey – probably correctly – about this episode.[3]

On April 14th (Good Friday) Hankey was present when Lloyd George had a face-to-face session at his villa with Chicherin, Litvinov and Krassin. 'Naturally', he wrote, 'as one always finds, they were very much like other people'; and he recalled the absurdity of Churchill's metaphor about 'the hairy paw of the baboon'. Barthou, however, refused flatly to sit down to lunch with the Russians, and Hankey himself 'did not much like' doing so. Litvinov he described as 'a

[1]To Lady Hankey 12th April 1922.

[2]Chamberlain to Worthington-Evans 3rd May 1922. Chamberlain papers AC 23/6/22.

[3]Hankey to Chamberlain 12th April 1922.

repulsive looking creature with a fat, puffy face, pug nose, enormous thick sensual lips and rather hanging [? pendulous] cheeks'; but Chicherin he considered 'an intelligent, cultured man', though his voice was 'a squeaky tenor or alto which is sometimes very difficult to follow in a conference'. Lloyd George, however, handled them with great skill, and Hankey found it 'wonderful to watch the play and subtlety of his mind'. One little gem of a story came out over lunch. The reader will recollect that Kamenev was expelled from England in September 1920 for smuggling in and selling looted jewellery and using the proceeds for propaganda purposes.[1] Lloyd George teasingly asked what had become of him, to which Litvinov replied 'In Moscow – still selling diamonds'.[2] In retrospect it is of course plain that Lloyd George by no means held a monopoly of subtlety at Genoa, and that the Russians were in fact engaged in a very clever piece of double-dealing.

Throughout the Friday and Saturday before Easter discussions revolved around the question of the Russian war debt, and whether a formula could be found whereby the debt could be recognised in principle and at the same time allowance made for the devastation suffered by Russia. Chicherin made things harder by putting in a vast claim for the damage done by the White Russian armies and their supporters among the Allies; but in the end a formula was reached which gave some hope of a compromise, and which Chicherin agreed to refer to Moscow.[3] In truth the Russians must merely have been playing for time, since on the very next day, Easter Sunday 16th April, they exploded their bombshell of the bilateral agreement signed at Rapallo with the Germans. Hankey was appalled, and recalled how, ever since the famous Fontainebleau weekend at the time of the Paris peace conference,[4] what he had 'most dreaded had been that Germany and Russia would come together'. Now, he told Adeline, 'it has happened'; but he still hoped that, with patience and perseverance, something of value might be salvaged from the conference.[5] An

[1]See p. 188.

[2]To Lady Hankey 15th April 1922. To Chamberlain 16th April describes this luncheon in rather apologetic terms, as Hankey thought that Lloyd George's act of hospitality 'may be criticised at home'.

[3]Hankey to Chamberlain 16th April 1922. The formula is in I.C.P. 238D Appendix.

[4]See p. 70. [5]To Lady Hankey 18th April (misdated May) 1922.

interesting point is that Hankey at once became aware of the contents of Litvinov's message of 17th to Moscow describing the effect of the Rapallo treaty on the conference. As it was given the Intelligence grading of A1 it is plain that we must have broken the Russian diplomatic cipher.[1]

On 19th Lloyd George had 'a rather stormy conversation' with Wirth, the German Chancellor, and Walther Rathenau,[2] the Foreign Minister, in the gardens of his villa – where a strong wind constantly scattered the papers on which Hankey was trying to keep a record. He described the Germans as 'horribly shifty and equivocal, evading the point and making false insinuations'. Lloyd George was, of course, tactfully trying to persuade them to cancel the Rapallo agreement; but all his wiles and eloquence produced little effect. Then he conceived the idea of calling a large meeting, including the small Allied nations but not the neutrals. This, however, would obviously offend the latter, and Hankey was therefore given the delicate task of persuading the small Allies (Jugo-Slavia, Czecho-Slovakia etc.) not to insist on their rights in order that the neutrals might show equal forbearance. All he got from Lloyd George to help him in this task, which Schanzer had flatly declined to take on, was 'Tell him not to be a bloody fool and sit on his head'. But after a lot of motoring around the scattered headquarters of the various delegations he was successful – except with the Portuguese.[3]

Early in the conference Hankey started to keep a day-by-day diary, a copy of which he sent to Chamberlain in instalments, the first of which (14th–23rd April) dealt chiefly with the discussions with Wirth and Rathenau and the reactions of the French towards their conduct at Rapallo. He said that these were so violent that a complete breakdown was not improbable. He also described the Russian reply to the Allies' memorandum on the settlement of war debts, mentioned earlier. This, he felt, 'could form a basis for discussion'; and with that object in view an expert sub-committee had been set up under the chairmanship of Worthington-Evans.[4] At the end of that week, however, he wrote despondently to Chamberlain 'you will see that we have been ob-

[1]Lloyd George papers F/26/1/30.

[2]1867–1922. German politician and industrialist. Head of office for supply of primary products in World War I. Minister of Reconstruction 1921 and of Foreign Affairs 1922. Earned hatred of Nationalists and anti-Semites by his proposals to socialise industry, and they procured or carried out his assassination.

[3]To Lady Hankey 20th April 1922. [4]Diary 21st April 1922.

structed and delayed by the clumsiness and tactlessness of the Germans and Russians, but above all by the touchiness and obstructiveness of the French' – to whom Lloyd George had twice given 'very serious warnings' regarding the probable consequences of their intransigence. His remarks, continued Hankey, were 'not so much aimed at Barthou, who is a decent fellow, . . . but at Poincaré who deluges Barthou with telegrams and injunctions' – which on one occasion Barthou described as 'his love letters from Poincaré'. Despite all these mountainous troubles Hankey believed 'that the conference will continue', and in earnest of that belief he telegraphed for Adeline to join him.[1] He had been considering this step for some time, but had been deterred by the Italians' insistence on paying for his accommodation, as he was not prepared to allow them to extend their hospitality to his wife. In the end Adeline did come out for about ten days in late April, and brought Robin, now nearly 17 years old, with her.

The third week of the conference began (Monday 24th April) with renewed negotiations with the Germans and discussions on the Russian reply regarding a debt settlement. Hankey told Chamberlain that the conditions which the latter had put forward were 'perfectly impossible'; and that an 'ultimatum' was being drafted telling them 'that we cannot remain here for ever and that they must take our conditions or leave them'.[2] The memorandum would, he wrote, be in two parts, the first of which he described as 'the bunch of carrots', as it set out the benefits the Russians would gain from a settlement, while the second part comprised 'the obstacles which the donkey has to surmount before it reaches them [the carrots]'. But he was obviously anxious and nearing exhaustion over the strain of having 'so many nations here and so many interests to be considered'. Altogether it was 'a most terrible job'; but Lloyd George was, he said, still striving for an agreement 'among the powers as a whole' which would undo, or at least mitigate the consequences of Rapallo. Hankey set out in the most gloomy terms the probable result of failure to reach an agreement. He also described the preliminary discussions with the French, the Czechs and others over a Pact of Non-Aggression; and to his fury Hurst's draft of the pact was leaked to the Press – no doubt deliberately – in Paris. Barthou, he was sure, was 'very much out of sympathy' with Poincaré on many of these questions. But it was of course Poincaré who had the whip

[1] *ibid.* 23rd April 1922.

[2] Hankey to Chamberlain 25th April 1922.

hand; and French opinion was fairly solidly behind him. Hankey ended by assuring Chamberlain that he had 'constantly reminded' the Prime Minister of the need to make a statement in Parliament, but 'things have been in such a state of flux this week' that it had been very difficult to produce what Chamberlain wanted in that respect.[1] At the end of the week he reported clearer indications of Barthou's lack of sympathy with Poincaré, whom 'he sees that he must square or put down'. Barthou meant, he was sure, 'to bring matters to a head', and was returning to Paris with that object in view. But what the outcome of the confrontation with Poincaré would be he 'would not venture to guess'.[2]

The fourth week opened with some hopeful signs – especially regarding the vexed question of Russian war debts. The French and British had at least achieved what Hankey called an '*accord complét*' on the subject – thanks largely to an ingenious draft prepared by Hurst and his French colleague Fromageot. But that of course was only a preliminary step, and Russian acceptance of the idea of acknowledging the war debts but putting them into 'cold storage' for the present was still a major obstacle.[3] It was in fact Poincaré, supported by the Belgians, rather than the Russians who sabotaged this hopeful line of progress; and next day Hankey wrote again to Chamberlain in terms not far short of despair.[4] By 7th May Hankey admitted that 'the conference has reached a stage when it is at the crisis of its fate'. Though his customary optimism had not been entirely shattered, and he was still prepared 'to lay odds of five to three on a settlement with the Russians', he was forced to admit that 'the Franco-Belgian incident has been very unpleasant', and that 'it is by no means unlikely that we shall have a break this week'.[5] At about the same time D'Abernon wrote to Hankey recounting the activities of the Russian delegates Joffé and Radek in Berlin while the former was travelling from Genoa to Moscow. No matter how much the Russo-German rapprochement had been encouraged by French intransigence and British anti-Communism it was by this time plainly a *fait accompli*; and there was no prospect whatever of Lloyd George persuading either party to abandon the Rapallo agreement.[6]

[1]Hankey to Chamberlain 27th April 1922. [2]Same to same 30th April 1922.
[3]Same to same 2nd May 1922.
[4]Same to same 3rd May 1922. Also Grigg to Chamberlain 4th May. Austen Chamberlain papers. [5]Same to same 7th May 1922.
[6]D'Abernon to Hankey 10th May 1922. B.M. Add. MSS. 48924 (Vol. III, folder 5).

They don't seem to be drafting at all. They are conducting a separate Conference on their own

Litvinoff has gone right back on this morning's discussion

A note passed by Hankey to Lloyd George, with a comment by the latter, at the Genoa Conference, April 1922

On 11th May Hankey reported that the Russian reply on war debts 'would be neither a refusal nor an acceptance, but a suggestion to gain time by the establishment of Commissions of Enquiry'. This 'woolly and argumentative' line was in his view 'most difficult to deal with', though it apparently appealed to both the Secretary-General and the American ambassador in Rome,[1] with whom the Prime Minister had recently had conversations. At first this idea did not attract Lloyd George. But, according to Hankey, he came round to the view that 'a Commission or Commissions should be set up by the Genoa Conference to study the questions of Debts, property and credits', and that in the meanwhile 'a provisional pact of Non-Aggression . . . should operate'. This was of course merely a gloss to cover the failure of the conference, which Hankey was now forced to admit.[2] In his next letter he enlarged both on the Russian reply and on Lloyd George's acceptance of the proposal for the Commissions; but he surely was guilty of an exaggeration in saying that the latter would 'snatch a success out of the Genoa Conference'.[3] One feels that Hankey's loyalty to Lloyd George and his admiration for 'the enormous energy which the Prime Minister displayed in order to carry through his [sic] plan' made him ignore, or at least play down the harsh truths of the failure. His final

[1]Richard W. Child (1881–1935). Author and diplomat. U.S. ambassador at Rome 1921–24. Represented U.S.A. at Genoa and Lausanne Conferences 1922.

[2]Hankey to Chamberlain 11th May 1922. [3]Same to same 13th May 1922.

letter from Genoa contained the disappointing news that the Americans would not after all participate in the Commissions, and an account of the drafting of the document setting out the only outcome of a month's deliberations.[1] Truly this 'mountain of a Conference' had – to quote 'Billy' Hughes's remark made in a different context – only 'given birth to a very small mouse'; and the Coalition Government, which had been under heavy fire, especially from the Northcliffe Press, during these wearisome deliberations, had lost further ground in the eyes of the British people – and especially among the increasingly restless Conservative element in the government. Looking back at Hankey's part in this sad story many years later Lloyd-Greame (now Lord Swinton) recalled how he and Massigli, the French Secretary-General, both produced minutes of the Anglo-French discussions. Hankey's version contained all Barthou's indiscretions and Massigli's all those of Lloyd George; so they were instructed to put together joint conclusions and the result was 'a complete anodyne'.[2] As one looks at the resulting documents to-day that description does not seem unfair.[3] But the truth of the matter surely was that the conference was far too large, and the differences of purpose and outlook of the principal powers were so wide that any real degree of success would have been little short of miraculous. In retrospect it is clear that the German–Soviet agreement signed at Rapallo on Easter Sunday 1922, for which the chief responsibility must rest with Rathenau, had very far-reaching consequences; for it marked the first stage on the road leading to the Russo–German pact of August 1939, which made World War II inevitable.[4]

Hankey returned home from Italy exhausted both in mind and in body. Though he had a short holiday with the family in Wales in August he was worried over Adeline's continued ill health, and he knew that the Cabinet Secretariat was being strongly criticised in some sections of the Press. A scurrilous cartoon in *John Bull* depicting 'Hankey Pankey' on a pedestal supervising his 'Stictatorship of the Secretariat' probably caused no more than a smile.[5] But the repeated attacks in the

[1]Hankey to Chamberlain 18th May 1922.

[2]Lord Swinton to the author. Interview 5th April 1968.

[3]Minutes of Genoa Conference in Cab. 29/96. I.C.P. Series 241–249J.

[4]A valuable study of Rathenau's part in the Rapallo agreement is to be found in the article by David Felix entitled *Walter Rathenau* in *History Today*, Vol. XX, No. 9 (Sept. 1970).

[5]*John Bull*, 3rd Dec. 1921. Also 24th June 1922.

*Daily Express*, which told how he had become 'secretary during the war and capitalist after the war',[1] in the *Sunday Express* which described him as a Jew,[2] and still more a hostile editorial in *The Economist*[3] could not be shrugged off so lightly. In the main such attacks were without doubt really directed at Lloyd George's 'Garden Suburb', which the less well-informed newspapers could not, or did not wish to distinguish from the Cabinet Secretariat proper. That criticism aimed at Lloyd George's increasingly large team of advisers should have fallen on Hankey and his overworked staff was extremely unfair. Though there may have been exaggeration in Henry Wilson's diary entry that 'Hankey and his Secretariat was essential, whereas Philip Kerr, Ned Grigg etc. are poisonous',[4] there was also an element of truth in his castigation of the Garden Suburb. None the less the rejection by the House of Commons in June of a motion criticising the Secretariat did not kill the charges or still the criticism.[5] It will be recounted later how the attacks reached a climax in the autumn of 1922, and how Hankey handled what was perhaps the most serious threat ever to arise against the Cabinet Secretariat. For the present it will suffice to remark that his labours at Genoa were ill rewarded, and that during the summer holiday following the failure of the conference his mind must have been anything but easy.

Meanwhile Curzon, from a bed of sickness, had told Chamberlain that he was following 'the Genoa débâcle' closely, and deplored the fact that there was 'no Foreign Office man to guide the P.M.'. He was 'very alarmed' at the prospect of an agreement with the Russians – a view which Churchill, who had visited Curzon that very day, fully supported.[6] The potential rift in the Cabinet had plainly widened during Lloyd George's long absence; but Hankey does not seem to have been fully aware of this dangerous trend until after he reached London on 20th May.

[1]*Daily Express*, 24th and 26th Nov. 1921 and 6th June 1922.
[2]*Sunday Express*, 25th June 1922. [3]*The Economist*, 17th June 1922.
[4]R. R. James, *Memoirs of a Conservative* (Weidenfeld and Nicolson, 1969), p. 138. Henceforth cited as James, *Davidson*.
[5]Parl. Deb., Commons, Vol. 155, Cols. 213–76. Sir Donald Maclean (Lib.) moved to reduce the vote for the Cabinet Secretariat and Asquith, though he paid a warm personal tribute to Hankey, supported it. The motion was rejected by 205–111.
[6]Curzon to Chamberlain and Churchill to Chamberlain 13th May 1922. Chamberlain papers AC 23/6/33 and 23/6/38.

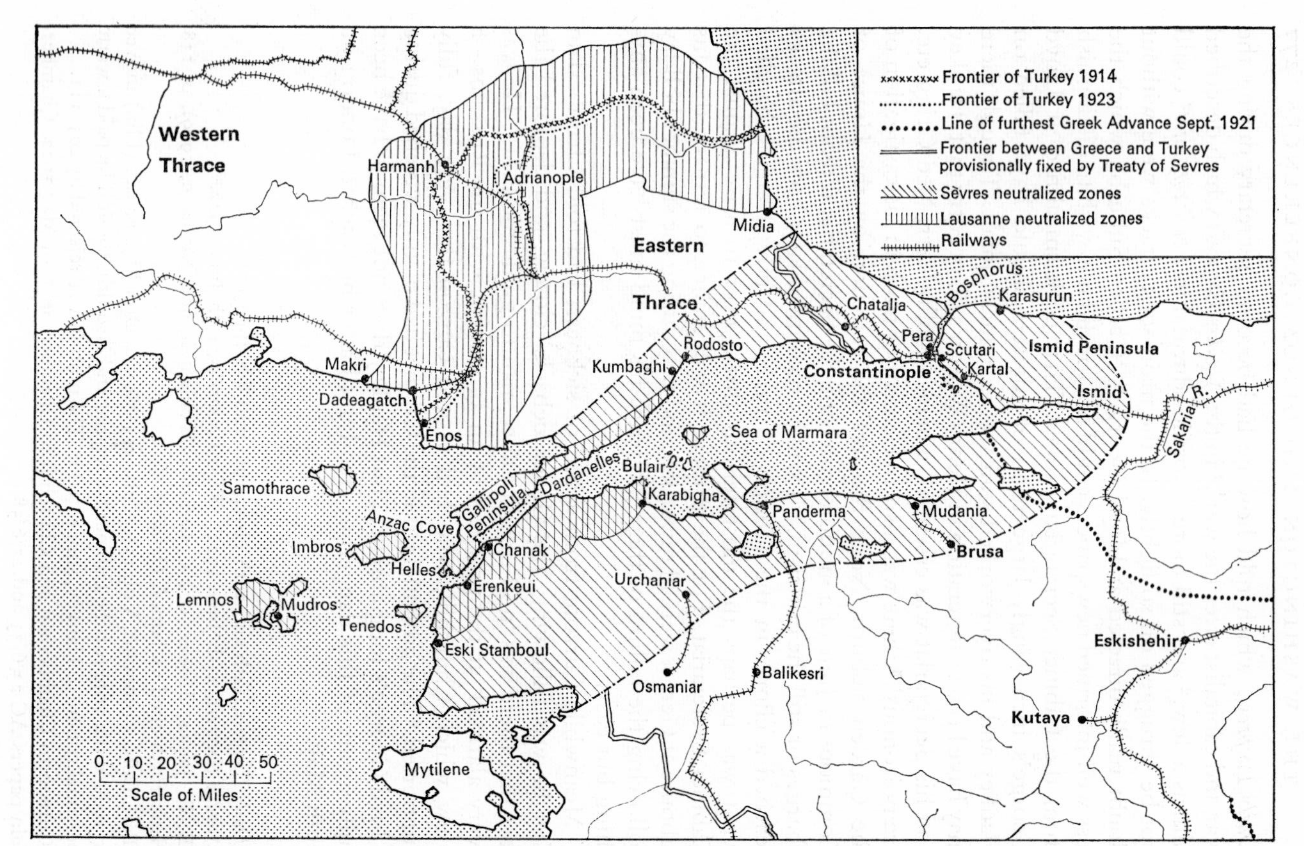


The Dardanelles and Bosphorus and adjacent territories, illustrating the Chanak Crisis of 1922

*Chapter* 10

# The Near East Crisis and the Fall of Lloyd George. June-October 1922

FOR much of June 1922 Hankey's time was taken up in preparing to rebut the offensive launched against the Cabinet Secretariat. Adeline had gone to Frinton with Henry in an endeavour to recover her health completely, and her husband evidently enjoyed the company of the other three children whenever he could get down to Highstead. On 16th he told his wife that he had heard from 'a certain Colonel Grant' that trouble was brewing, and that he had talked the matter over with Lloyd George and Chamberlain after that morning's Cabinet. Chamberlain had remarked, no doubt, correctly, 'that of course the attack was directed against the P.M.', and that they would 'slash at anyone in his entourage'. 'I expect my old friend Beaverbrook is at the bottom of it' surmised Hankey; and the remorseless hostility of the *Daily Express* and *Sunday Express* certainly supported that view. On the other hand the *Manchester Guardian* had published 'a most amusing letter' from Hartington's private secretary to Gladstone's in which the former wrote that 'Harcourt and [Joseph] Chamberlain have both been here this morning, and *at* my chief about yesterday's Cabinet proceedings. They cannot agree about what occurred. There *must* have been some decision, as Bright's resignation shows. My chief has told me to ask you what the devil *was* decided, for he be damned if he knows . . .'.[1] Equally consoling was the fact that Stamfordham had written to Austen Chamberlain 'that the King much prefers the modern Cabinet

[1]To Lady Hankey 16th June 1922. John Bright, Liberal politician, free trade advocate and orator (1811–1889) resigned his office as Chancellor of the Duchy of Lancaster in Gladstone's government on 15th July 1882 in protest against the decision to use force against the Khedive after a massacre of Christians in Egypt. This had resulted in the bombardment of Alexandria on 11th July. Hartington (8th Duke of Devonshire 1891) was Secretary of State for India and Joseph Chamberlain President of the Board of Trade at the time.

system with a secretariat[1] – as indeed [the King] has often told me'.

On 10th June Hankey sent Lloyd George a monumental brief on the Cabinet Office's 'four distinct functions' (the Cabinet Secretariat, the C.I.D., the war histories and the League of Nations), its staff and what it cost, for use in the debate which was to take place in three days' time. He had managed to reduce the estimate from about £65,000 in the previous year to some £53,600, and the Treasury, he reported, did not consider the staff greater 'in numbers or quality' than the work demanded. In an Appendix he pointed out that during the three years 1920–22 secretaries had been provided for 861 Cabinet meetings, 273 of the C.I.D. and its sub-committees, 425 Inter-Allied conferences and 45 Imperial Cabinets.[2] When the debate took place Hankey was distressed that Asquith, who had leant on him so heavily during the war and for whom he still felt a warm affection, had joined in the attack on the secretariat. He believed that, due chiefly to Margot's 'hopeless extravagance', the Asquiths were in financial trouble – despite Lord Cowdray having paid off their debts some years previously.[3] Hankey also 'chaffed' Lord Robert Cecil about his attitude in the debate. Cecil told him that he had expressed the view to Asquith and Maclean, while they were on the opposition front bench, 'that the secretary would never be abolished'; and the two Liberal leaders had 'agreed that probably this was the case'. Cecil also said that at the time of the first Coalition 'the procedure of the Cabinet got so muddled that he [Cecil] wrote (or spoke) to Asquith and offered . . . to put his services at the disposal of Asquith as secretary'. 'Apparently this appealed to Asquith', Hankey continued, 'but Montagu, claiming to have long rendered personal services to Asquith, bleated out a protest at Bob Cecil undertaking it, and Asquith then let the matter drop'.[4] Evidently Cecil and Hankey were on friendly, even intimate terms in 1922.

If Asquith's speech in the Commons on 13th June caused Hankey pain he was heartened by 'the tremendous panegyric' which Balfour,

[1]Stamfordham's letter of 15th June to Chamberlain is in Cab. 21/231. He wrote that 'the King desires me to say how much he appreciates the new methods by which the Sovereign is informed of the proceedings of the Cabinet meetings, which was never the case under the old system'. But he went on to say that the King thought 'the numbers and cost of the personnel of the secretariat are excessive'.

[2]Cab. 63/32. Also in Cab. 21/468. [3]To Lady Hankey 16th June 1922.

[4]To the same 19th June 1922. As no letter containing this suggestion has been found in the Asquith or Cecil papers the probability is that Cecil made it verbally to Asquith.

now an Earl as a result of his labours at Washington, delivered in the Lords a fortnight later 'on the Cabinet Secretariat in general and me in particular'.[1] He also probably derived satisfaction from the head of the French military mission in London asking for information on the working of the British Cabinet system.[2] At the time when he was coping with the Parliamentary assault on the secretariat Hankey also wrote to Lloyd George that he had 'a number of ideas for possible economies in the Cabinet Office', whereby the criticisms of it might be diminished if not stilled; but his problems were aggravated by the many and sudden demands made on the office – such as the recent re-drafting of the Irish constitution, which had necessitated his keeping the staff working into the small hours of the morning. Nor was that 'at all an uncommon instance', as similar demands had frequently arisen during the industrial troubles, the Irish negotiations and the conferences held at home and abroad.[3] The following weekend Hankey spent 'hunting up cases of Cabinet failures due to no Secretary'. He had already unearthed half a score, and intended to search Greville's memoirs and various 19th century political biographies for others.[4]

There followed a visit by Poincaré – without a secretary, so Hankey had to record the conversations between him, Lloyd George and Balfour. As the subject was once again reparations the results were not productive. Hankey was by this time convinced that the French Premier intended to occupy the Ruhr, and that no amount of pressure would deter him from such an ill-advised attempt to exact reparations from Germany. Poincaré, remarked Hankey, was 'a partisan of the old diplomacy through Ambassadors', and had 'declaimed in public against conferences'. But on finding 'that we are stuck on half a dozen questions', he allowed himself to be drawn into conference by Lloyd George; and he had even fished for an invitation to Chequers.

[1]To Lady Hankey 27th June 1922. Balfour's speech of that date in answer to an attack by Lord Middleton on the Cabinet Secretariat is in Parl. Deb., Lords, Vol. 51, Cols. 30–33.

[2]Letter of 26th May to Hankey and reply of 31st May 1922. Cab. 21/468.

[3]Hankey to Lloyd George 15th June 1922. Lloyd George papers F/26/1/52.

[4]To Lady Hankey 18th and 19th June 1922. For the reader who may wish to follow the trail searched by Hankey the latest edition of Greville is *The Greville Diary: Including Passages hitherto withheld from Publication* Ed. Philip W. Wilson (Heinemann, 1927). It is interesting that within a year of Hankey referring to Greville he should have succeeded to the office held by the latter throughout his career – that of Clerk to the Privy Council.

By the end of the month Hankey had his scheme for economies cut and dried; but as they were not actually implemented until after the change of government we will defer considering them for the present. As regards his own future he was philosophical, and recognised that his fate depended on who the next Prime Minister was. Should it be Churchill he felt sure that he would be replaced by Masterton Smith. In that event he might withdraw into private life and help Lloyd George with his memoirs – for which the Prime Minister had been offered £80,000.[1] After Henry Wilson's murder Hankey and Grigg both felt that Lloyd George's 'growing unpopularity' made his resignation likely. 'I can't help feeling', wrote Hankey, 'that it will be difficult for him to carry on with the Unionists very much longer'; but he expected he would 'probably come back in a year or two'.[2] An interesting point is that Hankey, for all his numerous contacts, seems to have been completely unaware of the taint of corruption over the sale of honours at this time, which was to contribute so much to the destruction of Lloyd George. Not one word about Maundy Gregory and his activities as honours broker for Lloyd George appears in his diary or in his letters to his wife.[3] But at the time when the matter came to a head in July he and Adeline were reunited, so no letters passed between them; and there is also a gap in his diary during that period.

The summer months passed very uneasily for Hankey, and still more uneasily for the government as embarrassments such as the Honours scandal came to light, the hostility of a powerful section of the Press mounted, the unrest of the Unionists gathered momentum, and the crisis in the Middle East became increasingly ominous. In August–September 1921 the Greek army had sustained a defeat in Anatolia which utterly destroyed their government's ambitions in Asia Minor.[4] There then ensued a lull, chiefly because both sides were exhausted; but in July 1922 the Greeks unwisely began to strengthen their forces in Thrace – with the obvious intention of occupying Constantinople. The

[1]To Lady Hankey 25th June 1922. [2]To the same 26th June 1922.

[3]See James, *Davidson*, pp. 278–82 for a full account of this unsavoury story. It reached a climax in July 1922 when 'after a sharp debate in the House of Commons' a Royal Commission was set up to investigate the whole matter and recommended measures to prevent abuses. The Honours (Prevention of Abuses) Bill (15 and 16 Geo. 5. c. 72) did not actually become law until 1925.

[4]The battle of Sakarya, 23rd Aug.–12th Sept. 1921. Perhaps the best detailed account is still that in Churchill's *The Aftermath: A Sequel to the World Crisis* (London, 1929), Ch. XVIII.

British government at once made it plain that any attempt to fulfil such an aim would be resisted by force. Preparations were made to carry out that threat, but as the Greek government abandoned its rash intentions they proved unnecessary. All this was of course gall and wormwood to the Phil-Hellenic Hankey; but he saw that the course which the Greeks seemed so bent on pursuing was foolhardy in the extreme. Then in August 1922 the Turks, profiting by the recent transfer of Greek troops to Thrace, resumed the offensive in Anatolia, and routed the Greek army. By the beginning of September it was reaching Smyrna as 'a disorganised and undisciplined rabble',[1] and on 9th the advance guard of the Turks followed it into the city. Four days later a fire started in the Armenian quarter, and soon the city was ablaze from end to end. The British Mediterranean fleet was now involved in a major rescue operation, with a quarter of a million Greeks and Armenians trying to get away. These events led to the second deposition and exile of King Constantine, and the establishment in Athens of a military government favourable to Hankey's old friend Venizelos.

That same month the triumphant Turkish Nationalists had advanced to the boundary of the 'neutral zones' established by the Treaty of Sèvres on the east shore of the Dardanelles at Chanak and on the Ismid peninsula on the Bosphorus. The British government decided that an attempt by the Turks to cross over to the European side of the Straits must be resisted – if need be by the British alone. On 15th September, when Hankey returned from his holiday in Wales, Lloyd George greeted him with 'exceptional warmth' – probably because he knew that a crisis was imminent and, as always on such occasions, wanted to have Hankey at his side.

*Diary 15th September 1922* (Written on 4th October)

The Cabinet met late that afternoon [15th] and decided on a policy which may be summed up as follows:—promotion of a Peace Conference; adoption of measures to enable us if necessary to defy the Turk at the Straits and prevent him from coming into Europe – otherwise we should only be bluffed out of the freedom of the Straits and everything else; concentration of ships, aircraft, guns and troops at Chanak – but no mobilisation yet; appeal to the Dominions to assist, or at least declare themselves for our policy; appeal to Roumania and Serbia to help safeguard the position in the Straits pending the Conference, to which they would be invited if they

[1]Report of Proceedings, C-in-C, Mediterranean of 2nd Oct. 1922. Adm. 1/8640 and 137/1778.

were good boys and shared the responsibilities of safeguarding the key positions on the Straits. As a preliminary Lord Curzon (who had only just returned after a month's illness) was to go to Paris and try to come to terms with Poincaré, but not until we had heard from Roumania, Serbia and the Dominions.

When I had drafted the minutes I went to see first Lloyd George and then Chamberlain and rubbed into them that the Serbians, whose King and Foreign Minister were to be sounded by Hardinge in Paris, would go straight to the Quai d'Orsay and give away the whole show, and the French would be furious if not consulted before Lord Curzon went to Paris next week. Both were unimpressed and thought the French attitude so hopeless and equivocal that, if consulted, they would only dish our policy everywhere. I think they were wrong, because in my experience the trickiness of Latin races is best met by the most perfect candour.

After the Cabinet on 15th Curzon went straight off to Hackwood near Basingstoke, and when Hankey took Lloyd George the minutes of the meeting he 'found him furious at Curzon having gone away in such a crisis'. Hankey himself felt the same way, and sent a special messenger down to Hackwood that evening with the Cabinet Conclusions.[1] Next day, Saturday 16th, the Cabinet met again – with the Foreign Secretary absent – and a statement of policy was issued that afternoon. Hankey had lunched with Lloyd George, and no mention had been made of this so-called 'Manifesto' foreshadowing a possible war with Turkey. He first read it – with astonishment – in the evening paper. He later discovered that Churchill had come round to No. 10 after lunch, and 'that he and Lloyd George had between them settled the matter'. He then expressed the view that complaints about lack of publicity by Lord Riddell, who had been with the Prime Minister the previous evening, might have helped to put the latter 'rather in the mood to respond to Churchill's suggestion'.[2] Sunday 17th Chamberlain spent at Chequers with Lloyd George, Worthington-Evans, Birkenhead and Churchill, and Chamberlain telephoned a protest to Curzon about his absence from London. On Curzon saying that he would be away until the following Tuesday Chamberlain told him 'that he must return first

[1]Diary 4th Oct. 1922.

[2]Hankey to A. Chamberlain 2nd Nov. 1933 reviews these events in detail with reference to Wickham Steed's article in the *Daily Express* of 2nd Nov. 1933. The Cabinet records entirely support Hankey's letter to Chamberlain (AC 40/5/119), as does his recapitulatory diary entry for 4th Oct. 1922.

thing on Monday morning'. When the 'Conference of Ministers'[1] (not the full Cabinet) met again that morning there was what Hankey later described as 'an unedifying row'. Curzon, probably on his own initiative, then went off to Paris to see Poincaré. On his return he gave the Cabinet a lurid account of Poincaré's fury when reproached with abandoning our small force at Chanak – 'a shameful episode for which all French soldiers here are apologising' wrote Hankey.[2] However Curzon and Poincaré did agree on a joint note to be sent to Kemal, which, if accepted, went a long way towards meeting what Hankey called our 'desiderata'.

Unfortunately one item in the policy agreed on 15th immediately went awry; and, to the discomfiture of Hankey, who had for so long worked for closer Imperial co-operation, that was the question of support by the Dominions. The trouble was that they had not been properly consulted before the crisis broke in full severity; and it is surely reasonable to suggest that if Hankey had not been away from the office this blunder would have been avoided. Only New Zealand and Newfoundland offered full support; Hughes of Australia offered a contingent if a conflict broke out; but South Africa wholly demurred and Canada declined any help.

*Diary 16th–22nd September 1922* (Written 4th Oct.)
The next few days were mainly spent in innumerable Conferences and Committees to try and scrape up guns, aircraft, troops etc. for the Dardanelles, and in getting shipping together to carry them. All very well and efficiently done, though the War Office had 'cold feet'. Cavan[3] is new to his job and not very good at stating his case. His D.M.O. – Stuart – is hardly in the

[1]The Conference of Ministers generally consisted of Lloyd George, Chamberlain, Curzon, Birkenhead, Churchill, Peel, Worthington-Evans and Lee. But by no means all of them attended all meetings. At the height of the crisis F. E. Guest (Secretary of State for Air) and the three Chiefs of Staff were also called in.

[2]Diary 4th Oct. 1922. See Nicolson, *Curzon*, p. 273 and *Middlemas*, I, pp. 209–10 for Tom Jones's graphic description of Curzon's 'tempestuous interview' with Poincaré. This arose from the French having sent M. Franklin-Bouillon to Angora in June 1921 without consulting the British. His mission resulted in the conclusion of what amounted to a separate treaty between France and the Kemalist Turks in the following October. It provided for the peaceful evacuation of the Greek population of Cilicia; and the French and Italians both handed over large quantities of arms to the Kemalists. This left the British isolated in support of the Greeks and in defending the 'neutral zones'.

[3]See Vol. I, p. 582, *note*.

saddle.[1] General Chetwode,[2] though sensible, does not like this business. And Col. Bartholomew,[3] who was with me at Washington, appeared very down on his luck. Beatty goes to the other extreme, and made out that, if given proper warning and a free hand, the Navy could do the whole thing. Lloyd George delighted, and annoyed with me because I told him that I knew the Dardanelles and Bosphorus and was certain the Navy couldn't do it without strong military support. Beatty's plan was to round up everything afloat in the straits and the Marmara and to jamb it into the Golden Horn or some other bay. Of course it couldn't be done without precipitating a massacre in Constantinople, and the men on the spot (General Harington,[4] whom I know well; Admiral Brock[5] and Sir Horace Rumbold, whom I stayed with at Warsaw) would not take it on. Trenchard, the genial Air Marshal was splendid, but aeroplanes, most mobile of weapons tactically, are the least mobile strategically, and it took a long time to get them over from Egypt to the Straits.[6]

Hankey also managed somehow to find time to write and circulate a number of memoranda on the Near East crisis, such as one on the importance of the Aegean islands in the event of conflict – no doubt based on the study he had made of those waters when serving in the Mediterranean Fleet early in the century, and on his experiences there in 1915.[7] Another proposed the preparation of a special War Book

[1]Later General Sir John T. Burnett-Stuart (1875–1958). In Sept. 1922 had only just succeeded General Sir William Thwaites as Director of Military Operations and Intelligence. Served as such until 1926. G.O.C. Egypt 1931–34 and G.O.C-in-C, Southern Command 1934–38.

[2]General Sir Philip W. Chetwode, later Field-Marshal and 1st Baron (1869–1950). Commanded 20th Army Corps 1917–18 in final phase of Palestine campaign. Deputy C.I.G.S. 1920–22. Adjutant-General 1922–23. C-in-C, Aldershot Command 1923–27. Chief of General Staff, India 1928–30; C-in-C, India 1930–35.

[3]Later General Sir William H. Bartholomew (1877–1962). Deputy Director, Military Operations and Intelligence 1922. Commandant, Imperial Defence College 1929–31. Director of Military Operations and Intelligence 1931–34. G.O.C-in-C, Northern Command 1937–40. Eastern Regional Commissioner for Civil Defence 1940–45.

[4]Vol. I, p. 493, *note*.

[5]Later Admiral of the Fleet Sir Osmond de B. Brock (1869–1947). Chief of Staff to Beatty as C-in-C, Grand Fleet 1916–19. Deputy Chief of Naval Staff 1919-21. C-in-C, Mediterranean 1922–25 and Portsmouth 1926–29. Hankey had served with Brock in the *Ramillies* 1899-1901. See Vol. I, Ch. II.

[6]This was the subject of a furious row between the Admiralty and Air Ministry. See Roskill, *Naval Policy*, I, pp. 260–1.

[7]C.P. 4243 of 26th Sept. 1922. Cab. 24/139. See Vol. I, pp. 80–85 and 188–205 regarding Hankey's earlier experience at the Aegean and at the Dardanelles.

dealing with that theatre.[1] And he also briefed Lloyd George on answering an attack on the Cabinet Secretariat over the issue of the 'Manifesto' of 16th September made by J. G. Swift MacNeill in a letter to *The Times* – which had obviously got under his skin.[2]

Meanwhile Hankey had become involved with the Admiralty over the precise intention of the Cabinet conclusions of 19th regarding the Navy's task of preventing Kemalist forces from crossing to the European shore. On 22nd Beatty telephoned his desire for further clarification and Hankey, after consulting his notes of the meeting, wrote to the First Sea Lord that he felt satisfied that they would justify an additional conclusion as follows:—

'That the Admiralty should be authorised to notify the Naval Commander-in-Chief in the Mediterranean that measures to prevent the transport of Turkish Nationalist forces to the Marmara Islands or to the shores of the Straits and the Sea of Marmara should not be regarded as provocative action.'

Beatty's secretary, however, replied that the Admiral 'desired a more exact interpretation than this', and as Hankey did not feel justified in going further on his own responsibility he telephoned to J. T. Davies at Chequers to get Lloyd George's personal views. The outcome was that Hankey was able to tell Beatty that 'no Kemalist forces must be allowed to cross the salt-water. The moment a Kemalist gets afloat he must be dealt with'.[3] This was strong stuff, and on 22nd Curzon telephoned from Paris to Sir William Tyrrell saying that he 'considered that these measures would be highly provocative'. However at the Committee (or Conference) of Ministers held that evening with Churchill in the chair the additional conclusion proposed by Hankey and the intentions expressed in his letter to Beatty were approved.[4]

On 20th Hankey wrote to Stamfordham telling him that a Royal Proclamation might be necessary to requisition the shipping needed to carry troops out to the Straits, and Stamfordham replied next day that the Proclamation was in the box which went everywhere with the

[1]C.P. 4246 and 4260 of 30th Sept. and 4th Oct. 1922. Cab. 24/139.

[2]Hankey to Lloyd George 26th Sept. 1922. Lloyd George papers F/26/2/37. See *The Times* of same date.

[3]Hankey to Beatty 22nd Sept. 1922. Lloyd George papers F/26/1/42.

[4]Draft Conclusions of meeting on 22nd Sept. Cab. 23/31. Hankey amended the title from 'Conference of Ministers' to 'Committee of Ministers'. This body's Conclusions were, however, circulated to and approved by the Cabinet.

King.[1] That same day Lord Grey published a letter in *The Times* supporting Curzon's peace-making efforts and describing the Manifesto of 16th as 'a terrible mistake'. The imminent threat of war, coming on top of other causes of mistrust of Lloyd George's personality and policy, was by this time increasing the unrest among Unionist members of Parliament, who felt that their leaders in the government (and especially Chamberlain, Birkenhead and Horne) were completely out of touch with the real feelings of members. But Hankey of course knew little or nothing about the political agitations behind the scenes during these anxious weeks; for his job merely was to put the government's decisions into effect as efficiently as possible. Despite the unusual display of Anglo-French unity in the note agreed between Curzon and Poincaré, which was published on 25th, the Kemalist troops continued to concentrate against the slender British forces guarding the neutral zone at Chanak, advancing right up to the barbed wire guarding the camp, which could obviously be rushed at any time. A repetition of the Smyrna massacres seemed a distinct possibility.

*Diary 23rd–27th September 1922* (Written 4th October)
On 23rd the Cabinet had to agree, though very reluctantly in Lloyd George's case, that one of the bases of the peace conference should be the return of Eastern Thrace to Turkey. Only two or three days later came the news of the Greek revolution, the abdication of King Constantine, with Venizelos hurrying to London full of hope to retrieve the desperate situation of his country.* The moment he read the news of Constantine's abdication Lloyd George bitterly regretted the decision as regards Eastern Thrace. To stand by Greece under Constantine, the traitor to the Allies who had brought his country on to its back by wild adventures in Anatolia, had been unthinkable on the Saturday [23rd]. On Wednesday to back up Venizelos fighting a defensive war to keep the Turk out of Europe seemed a different thing. I dined at Philip Sassoon's house after a late Conference of Ministers on that Wednesday night (27th Sept.). It was an episode characteristic of Lloyd George. After I had left Downing St. to go to my office a messenger caught me up and told me the P.M. wanted me. I found him dressing, Sir Edward Grigg and Sarah, his old Welsh servant, being there – the latter valeting him. 'If you have nothing better to do, drive with me as far as Sassoon's' he said

[1]RA GV M1811/20 and /29. Also Hankey to Lloyd George 20th Sept. 1922. Lloyd George papers F/26/2/29.

*Venizelos was brought to London by Lloyd George who gave a hint to Sir John Stavridi (see p. 199), and the latter went straight to Paris and brought back Venizelos with him.

(it was nearly 9 p.m., I had not dined, and my private secretary and stenographers were still waiting for me). Of course I went. We talked in his car and when we got to Park Lane he said 'You must dine somewhere, there are only Winston and Sassoon, and we might have a talk'. So in I went in my office clothes, and after telephoning to the office to dismiss the staff and book me a bed somewhere, I sat with my friends in evening dress to a sumptuous dinner. We talked late into the night. Winston, hitherto a strong Turkophile had swung round at the threat to his beloved Dardanelles and become violently Turko-phobe and even Phil-Hellene. All the talk was of war. By violating the neutral zone the Turks had released us of the already hated condition re Eastern Thrace in the Paris invitation to a conference. We were not strong enough to keep them from crossing the Bosphorus into Europe. So let them into Europe, we holding meanwhile to Chanak to enable us to keep open the Dardanelles. In Thrace the Turks would come up, not against Constantine's tired, ill-commanded and dispirited army, but against a national resistance, inspired by Venizelos and the revolution, invigorated by having the British Empire at its back, and with its old Generals restored. By the time Mustapha Kemal is beaten and held we shall be strong enough to move up from Chanak to Ismid, where, with a relatively small force we shall cut his communications and compel a humiliating surrender. Such was the burden of the talk. In the end they almost decided to send me to Constantinople to get the people there on the right lines, though I showed no great alacrity to go until I saw how the cat was going to jump. At that moment I was more impressed than they with the intense repugnance that our people feel for war, and the strong feeling against our being tied to Greece and acting against France.

Ever since that night there has been a curious struggle going on in the Cabinet and the Conference of Ministers. Lloyd George and Churchill have enlisted to their cause the powerful aid of Lord Birkenhead, and, though he is much less keen, Sir Robert Horne, as well as Guest, just back from America. They have never fully disclosed their plan – though I heard Birkenhead tell Chamberlain a good deal of it at 1 a.m. on Sunday [1st October] while drinking a whisky and soda in Chamberlain's room after Saturday night's late Cabinet. But all the time they are manoeuvring for position in a way that the Turko-philes, or rather Helleno-phobes, who, for one reason or another, include Chamberlain, Curzon, Lee, probably Worthington-Evans, and Lord Peel[1] – do not understand. What Ll. G., Churchill and Birkenhead dread is

[1]William R. W. Peel, 2nd Viscount 1912, 1st Earl 1929 (1867–1937). Politician (Cons.). Under-Secretary of State for War 1919–21. Chancellor of Duchy of Lancaster and Minister of Transport 1921–22. Secretary of State for India 1922–24 and 1928–29. First Commissioner of Works 1924–28. Lord Privy Seal 1931. Member of Indian Round Table Conference 1930–31.

that Mustapha Kemal will accept the conference, and we shall have to implement the condition of handing over Eastern Thrace to the Turk, thus bringing him back to Europe with all that implies for the future, and losing our credit with the Greeks without gaining that of the Turks – as the French and Italians will of course claim that they forced us to it. . . .

On 28th and 29th September telegrams came in from General Harington which Hankey described as having 'a very alarming character'. The Conference of Ministers was reconvened on Friday 29th with Curzon and the Chiefs of Staff present, and they were told to consider Harington's telegrams and report on their significance. According to Hankey their advice was 'that if the conditions reported by Harington continued the defensive position [at Chanak] would be imperilled and that the moment to avert a disaster had arrived'.[1] He later described these informal meetings of the heads of the fighting services as the 'embryo' of the famous Chiefs of Staff Sub-Committee of the C.I.D.,[2] though that body did not come into being formally until the middle of 1923. Such was the background to the notorious 'ultimatum' sent to Harington on 29th ordering the Turkish commander to withdraw, which Sir Harold Nicolson has described as 'that superb gesture of unwisdom'.[3] Important points are, firstly, that Curzon was present at both Conferences of Ministers held on 29th; secondly that Hankey was present at a meeting late that evening at Curzon's house at which Chamberlain took the chair and 'the whole matter was gone into very carefully'; and, thirdly, that, despite 'a rather encouraging talk' having taken place between Curzon and the Turkish Nationalist representative in London, according to Hankey 'they would not look at Curzon's request for a 24 hours suspension of the ultimatum'. And when next evening, 30th, telegrams came in from Rumbold, the High Commissioner at Constantinople, in similar vein there was what Hankey called 'a furious outcry against Harington' – because his and Rumbold's moderation ran wholly contrary to the views of those whom Hankey justifiably called 'the militants'.[4]

Hankey was meanwhile keeping Balfour, who was at Geneva, fully

[1]To Chamberlain 6th Nov. 1933. AC 40/5/122.

[2]Hankey to Trenchard 5th Feb. 1954. As the Chiefs of Staff met without a secretary during the Chanak crisis no record was kept of their deliberations.

[3]Nicolson, *Curzon*, p. 285. Hankey's 'note' on the ultimatum sent to General Harington and on Venizelos's visit to London on 30th Sept. confirms his diary entries. Cab. 63/32.

[4]Diary 4th Oct. 1922.

informed regarding all these developments, so that he could pass them on to the Dominions, who had complained that they were not getting enough information.[1] Balfour later thanked him very warmly for his 'most interesting and helpful telegrams'.[2] We may quote the description Hankey gave Balfour of that anxious Saturday:—

All Saturday [30th] we waited breathless to know whether the guns had gone off or whether the Turks had withdrawn ... However, the suspense continued. The Conference of Ministers met at 4 p.m. – no news! The Cabinet met again at 10.30 p.m. to consider a telegram which had just come in from Rumbold, who said he had seen a telegram from General Harington to the War Office which had made it quite clear that after all action had not been taken. There was, to put it mildly, a considerable reaction on this news. There was some annoyance in certain quarters [Churchill & Co.] with Harington for not having answered before, and I think everyone felt a little that after his telegrams about the seriousness of the situation [which had of course led to the 'ultimatum'] we had been 'spoofed'. The Cabinet sat until 11 p.m. and until 12 p.m., and it was not until nearly 1 a.m. that we heard that Harington's telegram had arrived in six parts and would take hours to decypher.[3]

On Sunday 1st October the Chiefs of Staff met early and the Cabinet at 10 a.m. It was then learnt with relief that the Turks had withdrawn from the British barbed wire at Chanak, and that the local commander was therefore able to extend his small perimeter. The main Turkish concentration now shifted towards Ismid; but the negotiations which led to the Mudania Conference had begun. On 4th Hankey concluded his long diary entry with the thankful words 'It looks as though the militants are beaten. But they have one chance yet; for Harington's instructions are to be very firm about the neutral zones, and it may be that Mustapha Kemal cannot meet us on that'. 'And', he added prophetically, 'often I ask myself "Can the Coalition survive all this?" '. He thought the Cabinet might hold together; but there would certainly be trouble when Parliament met.

The Cabinet met very late on the evening or 5th October and again the following morning, when it was agreed that Curzon should go to Paris again to place the British government's views before Poincaré. Incidentally there is no truth at all in the assertion by Wickham Steed

[1]Hankey to Grigg 26th Sept. 1922. Lloyd George papers F/26/2/36.

[2]Balfour to Hankey 29th Oct. 1922. Lloyd George papers F/26/2/39.

[3]Hankey to Balfour, quoted Hankey to Chamberlain 6th Nov. 1933.

that Curzon 'resolved to go again to Paris – against the wishes of his colleagues'.[1] Hankey thought that Steed had probably got this idea from Grigg, or possibly, as Chamberlain had suggested, from Curzon himself. The Cabinet minutes for 6th October recorded that 'In these circumstances [i.e. lack of support from France] it was necessary for Great Britain to separate herself from her allies in this and perhaps in other questions, and she would proceed to occupy and hold the Gallipoli Peninsula with such assistance as she could obtain from other quarters. In other respects, she ceased to interest herself or take any responsibility for what might happen in Constantinople or in Thrace. Through the treachery of her allies Great Britain had been rendered powerless to carry out the agreed policy, and the only course consistent with her honour was the one proposed'.[2] An interesting point is that Bonar Law asked Steed that same day to publish a letter in *The Times* ending with the statement that if France would not stand by Britain the latter would withdraw herself 'strictly within the confines of the British Empire' – surely an echo of the discussion in Cabinet – which Law had of course not attended.[3] Steed however refused to publish so drastic a proposal, and Law accepted the alterations proposed by the Editor toning down considerably the last paragraph of his letter.[4] But the letter as published was strongly 'anti-militant', and did provide support for Curzon's efforts to reach an agreement with Poincaré and avoid hostilities with Turkey. Moreover it showed that Law had returned to active politics, and was again a force to be reckoned with.[5]

On 6th October Asquith launched a strong attack on the conduct of diplomacy 'by amateurs in Downing Street' in a speech at Dumfries, and claimed that the accomplishments of 'the old diplomacy' compared very favourably 'with the amateur improvisations of the last few years'. This galvanised Hankey into producing a catalogue of what he regarded as the mistakes made by 'the old diplomacy', going back to the secret Treaty of London of 1915 and the Sykes–Picot agreement of the following year – which the Italians always claimed to have violated Article 9 of the London Treaty; and, he continued, the Treaty of Sèvres with Turkey had in fact been drawn up by professionals. 'So far as Mr. Asquith is concerned', he concluded, 'the moral of it all is that "people

[1]*Daily Express*, 2nd Nov. 1933. [2]Cab. 23/31.
[3]*Daily Express* 2nd Nov. 1933. [4]*The Times*, 7th Oct. 1922.
[5]See *Baldwin*, pp. 114–15 regarding the significance of Law's letter.

in glass houses . . ." '.[1] This strong rebuttal of a former chief for whom he had often expressed a profound affection suggests that there is some substance in the statement 'Jacky' Fisher made in 1916 that Hankey was 'extravagantly loyal to his immediate chief'.[2] Yet, one may reasonably ask, on what other ethical basis could he have operated the machinery of government?

The final breach between Curzon and Lloyd George came about through the speech made by the latter at Manchester on 14th October. Hankey prepared a brief for it, stressing that no member of the Cabinet Secretariat saw the notorious 'Manifesto' of 16th September until they read it in the Press.[3] He gave the same brief to Chamberlain for use in a speech at Birmingham on the day following Lloyd George's. In it he outlined 'the development of our Turkish policy for a peace settlement from the beginning of the war [presumably the Greco–Turkish war]' until the present time. 'The contrast between the two speeches from the same brief', he wrote, 'was extraordinary – the one [Chamberlain] painstaking, accurate and stodgy, the other [Lloyd George] full of sparkle'. As the brief dealt largely with foreign policy Hankey 'begged both the P.M. and Chamberlain before speaking to go through that part of their speeches with Lord Curzon . . .' Chamberlain did so, and Hankey 'warned the P.M. three times of the importance of this', and received a promise that he would follow suit.[4] Unfortunately Lloyd George had an audience with the King on the morning of 13th, and when he returned from the Palace to Downing Street a Conference of Ministers had just ended and he found 'a number of his colleagues still gossiping' in the Cabinet room. So instead of having what Hankey called a 'heart-to-heart' talk with Curzon he 'merely gave a general indication of the line he proposed to take'.[5] Thence arose the Foreign

[1]Hankey to Lloyd George and Chamberlain 10th Oct. 1922. Cab. 63/33.

[2]To C. P. Scott 4th Dec. 1916. Trevor Wilson (Ed.) *The Political Diaries of C. P. Scott* (Collins, 1970), p. 245. Fisher was actually complaining that Hankey had told a lie to the Dardanelles Commission in order to shield Asquith. Hankey's evidence was certainly framed to defend the government; but a scrutiny of the transcript reveals no instance where he can be said to have departed from the truth. See Vol. I, pp. 299–304.

[3]Dated 13th Oct. 1922. Cab. 63/33. [4]Diary 17th Oct. 1922.

[5]*ibid.* Also Hankey to Baldwin 4th Nov. 1927. This letter has a marginal note in Hankey's hand 'As a matter of fact before going to Churt [on Friday 13th] Mr. Lloyd George had given the Cabinet an outline of what he meant to say, and the particulars are on record in the Cabinet Minutes'. (This is correct, see Cab. 23/31.)

Secretary's fury on reading the Manchester speech. But one has to put this final explosion into the context of Lloyd George's outrageous behaviour towards his Foreign Secretary – of which Hankey's diary contains numerous examples. To quote only one of them, he recorded that 'when Curzon complained about the Manifesto of 16th September the P.M. threw in his teeth the fact of his absence [from the Cabinets and Conferences of Ministers on 16th and 17th] – adding his own experiences of the difficulties of getting an answer out of the Foreign Office before 11.30 in the morning[1] . . . "The fact is there is no Foreign Office – except sometimes" he said. Curzon as usual knuckled down before the P.M's rather brutal attack, but several of his colleagues (including Lee) expressed astonishment to me afterwards that he had not resigned'.[2] Hankey's mature conclusion was that 'Personally I never thought Lord Curzon had a leg to stand on over this particular episode as he took an active part throughout'. He considered that the only complaint he might reasonably have concerned the Manifesto of September 16th; but that was his fault for being out of touch at so critical a moment.[3] Be that as it may, Curzon was present at a dinner at Churchill's house on 9th October when Liberal members of the government reviewed the difficulties they were having with some of their Conservative colleagues. When the desirability and ethics of asking for a dissolution of Parliament at a fairly early date and appealing to the electorate came up Curzon remarked 'Well boys, if that's your game I'm with you'.[4] Yet within a week he had changed his mind, and declined to attend another dinner at Churchill's house at which the discussion was to be continued.[5] Nor were many weeks to elapse before Hankey himself suffered from Curzon's two-facedness.

The events leading up to the Mudania Conference are well known,

[1]Here Hankey inserted in parenthesis 'As a matter of fact no-one is there much before that hour'.

[2]Diary 4th Oct. 1922.

[3]To Chamberlain 6th Nov. 1933. Austen Chamberlain papers AC 40/5/122. Towards the end of 1927 Lord Ronaldshay wrote to Baldwin for information about the breach between Curzon and Lloyd George, for use in his *Life of Lord Curzon* (Benn, 3 vols., 1928). On 4th Nov. 1927 Hankey sent Baldwin his views on the subject, taken largely from the diary entries quoted here. Cab. 21/334.

[4]Ronaldshay to Chamberlain 12th Dec. 1927. AC 54/426. This episode is described in bowdlerised form in Ronaldshay, *op. cit.*, Vol. III, p. 312. Churchill gives a somewhat different version in *Great Contemporaries* (Thornton Butterworth, 1939), pp. 281–2.

[5]Ronaldshay, *op. cit.,* Vol. III, pp. 318–19. Also Blake, *Bonar Law*, p. 452.

and although there were many anxious hours, largely caused by the equivocal behaviour of M. Franklin-Bouillon, the French representative, the Convention was signed on 11th. In truth Kemal had gained all that he could hope for; and he probably realised the folly of challenging British power – even if that nation acted alone.[1] Above all the entire Treaty of Sèvres was now as dead as the ill-conceived 'ultimatum' of 16th September. Hankey's diary throws interesting light on how Churchill viewed the end of the crisis.

*Diary 17th October 1922*
. . . I walked across the Park with Churchill one evening towards the end of the crisis and he quite frankly regretted that the Turks had not attacked us at Chanak, as he felt that the surrender to them of Eastern Thrace was humiliating, and that the return of the Turks to Europe meant an infinity of trouble. I don't think the Prime Minister felt very differently. I was constantly with him during the crisis, lunching and dining with him; and even the night before the armistice was signed, when information came in that the Turks were violating the neutral zones, he thought, and perhaps hoped that the [Mudania] Conference would break down. He talked constantly of the possible occupation of the Chataldja lines[2] by the Greeks. . . .
Now we are in the thick of a terrific crisis on the question of whether the Unionist Party is to remain with the Coalition, and Chamberlain, Balfour, Birkenhead and Horne are fighting with their backs to the wall to maintain the Coalition under Lloyd George. Balfour told me this afternoon that Curzon has, he believes, gone over to the enemy,[3] and one of his reasons is that Lloyd George's speech [at Manchester], and especially his references to the French and Turks, has made it impossible for him to carry on at the Turkish peace conference. Luckily that part of the speech was not prompted by me. This, however, is precisely the sort of difficulty which I foresaw. Unfortunately Ll. G. has a low opinion of Curzon, and was very rude to him a week or two ago, which, no doubt, is the root cause of the trouble. It might so easily have been avoided. . . .

Apart from the cleavage in the Cabinet over the militants' 'tough line' policy against Nationalist Turkey, the signs of profound disquiet in the nation over recent events were heavily emphasised by the resounding victory of an Independent Conservative candidate over the Coalitionist in the Newport by-election on 18th October. Plainly with

[1]Roskill, *Naval Policy*, I, pp. 199–200.
[2]The fortified lines in Eastern Thrace guarding the approach to Constantinople from the west.
[3]This was correct. See above.

Bonar Law back in the field of action and Lloyd George's image gravely tarnished a show-down could not be long deferred. It came at the famous and oft-described Carlton Club meeting on 19th, when out of 275 Unionist M.P.s present 185 voted to end the Coalition.[1] Hankey's diary illuminates in some respects the events of these hectic days.

*Diary 21st October 1922*

Within the last four days dramatic events have taken place. The Coalition has broken. Lloyd George has resigned. Bonar Law is forming a Conservative Government [Hankey went on to describe the significance of the Newport by-election]. Moreover before the Newport election came off the split in the Conservative party and the revolt of the 'die-hards' had assumed such formidable dimensions in consequence of the Turkish crisis that Chamberlain, in view of the coming General Election, had had to summon a meeting of Conservative M.Ps to try and assert his leadership. When this meeting was first arranged, early in the week the die-hards 'thought they would be successful'. I lunched with Lloyd George on Tuesday 17th Oct., and Lord Birkenhead, who came in after lunch, said frankly that he was by no means confident of success, though he rehearsed a short but eloquent speech which he intended to make at the Carlton Club, but in fact never did make.[2] On Wednesday however there had been a reaction in favour of Chamberlain and the Coalition. [Hankey then described the outcome of the Carlton Club meeting.]

I heard the result at about 1.15 p.m. and went straight to 10 Downing St. The first person I met was Chamberlain, coming down the passage from the Cabinet room, where he had been telling the P.M. the news. 'I am sorry to hear this' I said. 'Well, anyhow' he remarked 'there is one man who is sorrier than I, and that is Bonar Law' (who had 'gone die-hard' and done the trick). Then I met the P.M. in the lavatory. 'Hankey' he said 'you have written your last Minutes for me. I have asked the King to come to town, and this afternoon I shall resign and you will have another Prime Minister'. Both Chamberlain and Lloyd George were jaunty and cheerful, and showed

[1]The best recent account is in James, *Davidson*, pp. 122–33, which gives the complete list of how members voted. See also *Baldwin*, pp. 120–4 especially regarding the speech he made 'for only eight devastating minutes', and Blake, *Bonar Law*, pp. 447–58. Beaverbrook, *The Decline and Fall of Lloyd George* (Collins, 1963), pp. 189–202 is not wholly reliable.

[2]The invitation to the Carlton Club meeting was addressed 'to all members of the Party in the House of Commons to meet him [Chamberlain] and Unionist members of the Cabinet'. So presumably Birkenhead could have spoken at the meeting, though, being a member of the House of Lords, he could not have voted on the decisive motion proposed by E. G. Pretyman.

no signs of regret at leaving office. There was nothing to be done and I came home early. The P.M. resigned and he and Chamberlain spent the afternoon in meeting their respective party colleagues, issuing manifestos and what not. Meanwhile Bonar Law saw the King and agreed to form a Cabinet if and when the Conservative party should elect him leader.

At about the time when Lloyd George told Hankey about his resignation the latter allegedly penned the following lines of doggerel:—

'And so while the great ones depart to their dinner
The Secret'ry stays, growing thinner and thinner
Racking his brains to record and report
What he thinks that they think that they ought to have thought'.[1]

*Diary 21st October 1922* (cont.)

Next day, Friday October 20th, I called at 10 Downing St. and saw Lloyd George on my way to the office. He was in good fettle, and not a bit cast down by his bad luck. He was ever so – at his best in adversity, but in success rather depressed, as though it were a harbinger of misfortune. He told me that he wanted always to remain close friends with me. He recalled that when he came into office he had never objected to my maintaining good social relations with Asquith, and he assured me that he would never allow anything to pass that would embarrass me in my loyalty to my new chief. He said he would speak to Bonar Law about it. I recalled that every time I had seen Asquith I had reported to him both before and after, and I said I would of course feel bound to do the same with Bonar Law, if he took me on. Then he spoke of his book, and said he would ask Bonar to let Swinton (who is devilling for the book) continue to have access to the War Cabinet records. He said he was not intending to attack Bonar or anyone else in the book. Later I went to the Guildhall *déjeuner* to the Prince of Wales, driving there with Sir James Masterton Smith (Permanent Under-Secretary to the Colonial Office) and Sir John Anderson, Permanent Under-Secretary at the Home Office. Masterton Smith told us a characteristic story of Winston Churchill, who has been stricken down quite suddenly with appendicitis and had been operated [on] two days ago. On coming to from his anaesthetic he immediately cried 'Who has got in for Newport? Give me a newspaper'. The doctor told him he could not have it and must keep quiet. Shortly after, the doctor

[1] I am indebted to Sir John Benn, Hankey's son-in-law for drawing my attention to these lines. Though their attribution and the occasion on which they were produced are both a little uncertain Sir John and Lord Amory (formerly D. Heathcoat Amory. Politician, Cons. 1899– ) are confident that the attribution to Hankey is correct. Sir Arthur Bryant quotes them in *The Turn of the Tide* (Collins, 1957), p. 320 but without giving any source. Bryant's implication that they date to World War II is surely incorrect.

returned and found Winston unconscious again with four or five newspapers lying on the bed. Masterton Smith was to see Winston that afternoon, and the patient had insisted on seeing Lord Birkenhead and others, though less than two days have elapsed since the operation. . . .

While we were awaiting [at the Guildhall luncheon] the arrival of the Prince of Wales and I was standing among a group of Cabinet Ministers – Chamberlain, Worthington-Evans and others, Boscawen[1] edged up to me and behaved in an effusively friendly manner. This annoyed me a good deal, because Boscawen with Baldwin[2] was the 'Judas' of the Cabinet, who betrayed Chamberlain and Lloyd George at the Carlton Club, and his colleagues were distinctly giving him the cold shoulder at the Guildhall. He has been particularly truculent at Cabinet towards Lloyd George, since the latter has been rather down on his luck, and has not behaved well. Lloyd George says he is really a Jew, because he looks like one, and calls him 'Cohen'. Anyhow I managed to edge off a little, and finding myself beside Jack Seely[3] I said 'Well, Jack, you must be smiling' (he had resigned office more than a year ago). His only reply was to look at Boscawen and say 'This is a Judas business'. Then I spied J. H. Thomas, the Labour man, who told me that he had been bred in Newport all his life, and that he had just been there. The election had not been fought on any National or Imperial issue, but on a purely local issue – and he went off into some complicated story of pubs and clubs . . . Anyhow J. H. was confident that Newport was no test whatsoever of British opinion. I also spoke to Lloyd George for a moment and got his permission to place the services of myself and my office at Bonar Law's disposal while he was forming his Cabinet, even before he had formally accepted office. I had a good deal of chaff at the Guildhall owing to recent attacks on the Cabinet Office and several people asked me half chaffingly whether I had resigned and alluded to 'superfluous' officials. . . . On my return to the office I rang up Bonar Law's secretary and told him of the authority I had received from the P.M. He answered rather sulkily I thought, but later on, after seeing Bonar Law, rang me up and thanked me very politely and said Bonar would probably wish to see me on the morrow. Then I dictated a note to Bonar, giving him a list of the really urgent questions

[1]Sir Arthur S. T. Griffith-Boscawen (1865–1946). Politician (Cons.). Parliamentary Secretary, Ministry of Pensions 1916–19 and Board of Agriculture and Fisheries 1919–21. Minister of Agriculture and Fisheries 1921–22 and of Health 1922–23. Chairman, Royal Commission on Transport 1928–31 and of Transport Advisory Council 1936–45.

[2]For Baldwin's side of the story see *Baldwin*, pp. 115–24. The authors argue convincingly that he took no underhand steps, but was merely outraged at the 'moral disintegration' which had taken place under Lloyd George.

[3]See Vol. I, p. 116, *note*.

before the Cabinet on which he could not long defer a decision (Ireland – confirmation of Constitution; Turkish Peace Treaty; mission for funding debt in U.S.A.; observance of armistice day; and report of [Geddes–Churchill] Economy Committee). I also reminded him he must select a man to represent us on the Council of the League of Nations and a Chairman for the Standing [Sub-]Committee of the Committee of Imperial Defence when choosing his Cabinet. It was a carefully worded letter, not assuming that there was to be a Cabinet Secretary, much less that I was to be the man, but showing in a few lines a real desire to help him in his difficulties. Then Lord Balfour, with whom I have been more intimate than ever since Washington, came in and had a long yarn all about the crisis. He was genuinely delighted at his escape from office and at the prospect of a holiday in Scotland. He said that for the first time he was glad to be a Peer, because he escaped all the hateful electioneering. The most interesting thing he told me was of a talk he had had with a doctor he had met at Lord Derby's house in Lancashire. This doctor had attended him many years ago in an illness he had when he was Prime Minister and had asked to sound him now. The doctor had found him in splendid condition to his great surprise, because on the previous occasion Balfour's heart had been so weak that the doctor thought he could never work hard again. The same doctor had also attended Lord Birkenhead and told Balfour very confidentially that he had double myopia from over smoking, and that he was poisoning his brain from excessive indulgence in alcohol. Balfour deplored all this in so brilliant a man, and said he had done all he could to induce him to give up his habits. Birkenhead, he said, had been quite drunk at an evening meeting of Conservative Ministers during the crisis.

Hankey also recorded an amusing incident about Balfour and the Carlton Club meeting. 'He came downstairs [at his home]', he wrote, 'only just in time to go to the meeting. He wanted to know the result of the Newport by-election before he went to the club, and asked Miss Bliss his private secretary to bring him the newspaper. Miss Bliss replied that he did not take one! Miss Balfour took the *Morning Post*, but when she went away she always cancelled it'.[1] Presumably Balfour did not learn about the government defeat at Newport until he reached the Carlton Club.

*Diary 23rd October 1922*

This afternoon I said goodbye to Lloyd George at 10 Downing St. He was in great form – absolutely hilarious. He gave us – his private secretaries, Tom Jones and myself – a most amusing imaginary mimickry of a deputation,

[1]Diary 31st Oct. 1922.

headed by himself, addressing Bonar Law as Prime Minister. Going to a seat on the opposite side of the table to where he has so long sat as Prime Minister he stood up, and in the curious rather halting manner of so many deputations made a little speech introducing a deputation on Welsh education – afterwards changing it to a deputation in favour of assisting Greek refugees from Smyrna. Meanwhile Tom Jones sat in the Prime Minister's chair imitating the very dejected appearance of Bonar Law with his head in his hands. Then the P.M. suddenly changed and pretended to be Bonar Law, imitating his manner exactly.[1] He told me that he was now going to have a quiet time – with occasional cyclones. 'But there will be cyclones for Bonar too, I can tell you that' he added. Then he went off in his Rolls-Royce car to Churt in Surrey with Gwilym Lloyd George.[2] . . . Once I hinted that perhaps after the general election he would after all come back as P.M. 'Oh no, he cried, nothing will induce me to let Bonar off. Birkenhead and I are determined to keep him up to it. Each of us will hold up an arm until sundown'. This means that his fun will come when Bonar is running the show. That morning he had been to see Winston on his bed of sickness. Apparently Winston's pet aversion over all this is Curzon. 'I am going to write some letters next week', he told Ll. G., 'and one of them will let Curzon have it', and Ll. G. twisted his hand round as though he were gouging someone's vitals. I met old Lord Farquhar of Buckingham Palace to-day.[3] He had seen Curzon and said he was very bitter against Lloyd George and there was something behind, which Ll. G. must have said or done to him. Perhaps I knew! I did know, but didn't feel inclined to say – it was Ll. G's brutal behaviour to Curzon at the Cabinet on Sept. 18th. . . . [4] Curzon is very vengeful and never forgives or forgets. This is his revenge.

*October 24th 1922*

Lord Balfour came in to see me this evening to say goodbye before relinquishing the Seals of Office. He said many nice things of my work. He told

[1]*Middlemas*, I, pp. 216–17 gives Tom Jones's version of this charade.

[2]Second son of David, later 1st Earl Lloyd George. 1st Viscount Tenby 1957 (1894–1967). Politician (Lib. then Cons.). Parliamentary Secretary, Board of Trade 1931 and 1939–41. Minister of Fuel and Power 1942–45 and of Food 1951–54. Home Secretary and Minister for Welsh Affairs 1954–57.

[3]Horace B. Farquhar, 1st Earl 1922. (1844–1923). Politician (Cons.) and Courtier. Master of Household to Edward VII. Lord Steward 1915–22. As Treasurer of the Conservative party the chief figure in a somewhat dubious episode concerning the distribution of political contributions to the Lloyd George Coalition as well as to the Conservative party. Dismissed as Treasurer March 1923. See Blake, *Bonar Law*, pp. 496–7.

[4]See p. 294.

me that Bonar Law had offered the Colonial Secretaryship to Lord Ullswater,[1] the late Speaker, who came to consult him about it. Lord U. eventually decided to refuse because he preferred coalition to party, because as Speaker for many years he had been regarded as above party and he thought that it would be a reflection on that attitude to take office in an essentially party Government, and because he liked a country life and was 67 years of age. While Balfour was with me Bonar Law's secretary rang up to say that Bonar was Cabinet making along with Lord Curzon and I think Lord Salisbury. They wanted to know whether there had been a case in the last 40 years when both the Secretary of State for War and the First Lord of the Admiralty had been Peers.[2] Balfour, whom I told, was much amused but greatly interested. I looked it up in Whitaker's Almanack and found the last date when this occurred was 1863–6 when Lord de Grey and Ripon had been S. of S. for War and the First Lord of the Admiralty was the Duke of Somerset. Balfour said it was a very bad precedent as this was the fag end of Palmerston's Govt. just before Gladstone came in and cleansed the Augean stable. He said it had been deliberate that the two offices were never simultaneously held by Peers, as the House of Commons would resent both the great spending departments being headed by Peers. I received the following nice letter to-day from Lord Curzon:— Oct 23 'My dear Hankey, I have suffered as you know terribly from the encroachment of Downing St. but never from yours. You have always been a model of constitutional propriety and personal consideration and I rejoice to think that I shall profit in an even greater degree in the future from your invaluable assistance Yours very sincerely Curzon'.[3] This, of course is a complete refutation of the persistent stories in the Beaverbrook and Rothermere press, that I have interfered in our foreign policy. Yesterday I received a telephone message from Marsh,[4] Churchill's secretary, asking me to burn a Proclamation which had been drafted last February, at the time of the Four Courts business, to be issued if and when the Four Courts were occupied [presumably by British troops]. I turned it up, and found it attached to some manuscript minutes of this episode, in rough draft in the original. I did not feel justified in burning it, but, as it was an Irish (Colonial Office) paper I did feel justified in handing it over to Lionel Curtis, the Colonial Office Secretary of the Cabinet Committee

[1]James W. Lowther, 1st Viscount Ullswater 1921 (1855–1949). Politician (Cons. then Non-Party). Deputy Speaker of House of Commons 1895–1905 and Speaker 1905–21. Member or Chairman of many Royal Commissions and government-appointed bodies both before and after his retirement.

[2]Bonar Law was obviously considering whether Lord Lee could continue as First Lord if Lord Derby went to the War Office. In the end Amery got the Admiralty.

[3]The original of this letter, in holograph, is in the Hankey papers.

[4]See Vol. I, p. 324, *note*.

on Ireland, and I took his receipt for it and attached it to these very secret minutes, which I then sealed up as before.

The last part of the above diary entry suggests that, with the change of government an accomplished fact and Bonar Law's Cabinet-making actually in progress, Churchill was anxious to cover his bellicose tracks at the time of the last Irish crisis. He was defeated at Dundee in the 1922 General Election.

So ended for Hankey a relationship which was to prove unique in his career. For nearly six years he had, in war and in peace, stood at the right hand and acted as the closest and most confidential adviser of a man who, no matter how great his faults, will always be regarded as one of the outstanding figures of twentieth century politics. That Hankey was fully aware of his faults – except possibly the scale on which the sale of honours had been proceeding – will be plain to all who have persevered thus far; and he certainly suffered a great deal from his master's idiosyncratic methods. Yet it is also plain that he admired, even loved Lloyd George – chiefly for his courage in adversity, for his basic sympathy with the poor and under-privileged from among whom he himself had sprung, for his wit and humour, and for his amazing gift of rhetoric. Few if any persons who actually experienced the spell of Lloyd George's speeches, whether in the House or in the constituencies, have forgotten the magnetism he could exert and the authority he could wield. It was not without cause that he was widely, if sometimes pejoratively, referred to as 'The Welsh Wizard'; and Hankey was certainly not immune to the emotional influence of his charm. That Lloyd George was devious in his methods is true; and Hankey often experienced his deviousness at first hand. Yet allowance must be made for the fact that in neither of his governments did he enjoy solid Parliamentary support, and he always had a difficult, fissiparous team to lead. If he treated some of his colleagues, notably Curzon, abominably he retained the loyalty of honourable men like Austen Chamberlain and Balfour to the end. Hankey's affection for him was of a different quality to that which he felt towards Asquith. Whereas in the latter case he was warmed by the benevolent glow of the personality of 'the last of the Romans', in the former he was enkindled, sometimes perhaps dazzled, by the sheer brilliance of intellect and imagination, which almost daily flashed and scintillated before him like an Aurora Borealis. Though Hankey did not of course realise on the day he said goodbye that he would never serve Lloyd George again – indeed it is plain that he expected him to return to office fairly soon – he never lost touch with him; and in later years he was one of Lloyd George's closest advisers in the writing of his brilliant, if sometimes tendentious memoirs. His sadness at the parting in Downing Street on 24th October – despite the buffoonery with which Lloyd George obviously tried to ease the tension of an emotional moment – is plain from their subsequent correspondence and contacts. But Hankey was never the man to repine, and if later he occasionally looked back nostalgically on the Lloyd George era, as on that of Asquith, at the time his mind was full of the future, not the past. And for himself and his staff he knew very well that the future would be difficult, perhaps bleak.

*Chapter 11*

# Under Bonar Law. The fight for the Cabinet Secretariat. October-December 1922

TRAFALGAR Day 1922 was a critical day for Hankey, and its events are best recorded in his own words.

*Diary 21st October 1922*

To-day . . . when I arrived in the office I found that the usual batch of Foreign Office telegrams had not arrived. This looked ominous, as I had read in the newspaper that Lord Curzon had been seeing Bonar Law, and it rather looked as though this was a sign that the insistent and much repeated newspaper stories were true and that they had decided to scrap the Cabinet Secretariat. I had decided, in that event, that I would ask Lloyd George for a peerage among his 'leaving honours' so as to give me some hold on political life and a seat in the House of Lords. However, the first thing to do was to verify the position. I therefore told Burgis, my private secretary, to ring up the distribution department of the Foreign Office, and ask for the telegrams. The reply was even more ominous – it had been done by direct orders from Sir Eyre Crowe, the Permanent Under-Secretary! I was then out for blood and prepared to write a pretty hot letter to Lord Curzon. I decided, however, first to tackle Crowe. As soon as he came to the office I telephoned personally. He was nervous and apologetic, but very friendly, and explained that, as there was practically no Cabinet, Lord Curzon had stopped the whole Cabinet circulation. However, he himself would take the responsibility of seeing that I got my papers as usual – and later in the day they arrived. As there was a prospect of my seeing Bonar Law that day, and as I knew that the only chance of saving the Secretariat was to effect big economies, and had already blocked in the general lines of my plans, I decided at once to see Crowe and explain to him two proposals which affected the Foreign Office. Just as I was leaving for the Foreign Office I had a message that Bonar Law wanted to see me at noon. I had a very friendly talk with Crowe (who looks very ill, in spite of three or four months' leave) and told him that I intended that very day to propose – first that the League of Nations section should be handed over to the Foreign Office, and second that the Cabinet Secretariat should drop out of all International Conferences. I pointed out that I had long favoured both courses, as he knew, and that it was Lloyd George and Balfour who had always insisted on my doing this work.[1] I also recalled that in fact I had never interfered with the advisory functions of his office, and had never had any quarrel with him or the Foreign Office in fulfilling my secretarial functions, but I thought in principle it was only right that for the future he should undertake both functions. He was obviously pleased and grateful, and was very complimentary, saying that we had done the work with a maximum of efficiency and a minimum of friction, though in principle he thought the F.O. should take these duties, even if they did not at first do them so well. He asked for my help in organising conferences, and of course I promised everything. Then we talked of the League of Nations and I told him of Bob Cecil's plan of an Assistant Secretary of State in the Foreign Office to represent us at the Council of the League.[2] He said he went further, and would like a permanent representative at Geneva, who would do all the 'donkey work', just as the Ambassadors' Conference at Paris does the 'donkey work' of the Supreme Council. This corresponds to the original scheme I drafted in Paris, when I was Secretary-General designate of the League,[3] and we agreed it would tend to check the dangerous tendency of the League Secretariat to arrogate to itself too much power. On the other hand, the removal from the League of people of detachment and wide political experience like Lord Balfour and [H. A. L.] Fisher, and its concentration in the hands of Foreign Offices and diplomats will not be good for the League.

Then I left Crowe, after a most cordial talk, and drove to 24 Onslow Gardens to see Bonar Law. Though my fate, and that of the great organisation I have built up were at stake, I did not feel a spark of nervousness, and never felt more cheery in my life. On the doorstep I was joined by Stanley Baldwin, who led the revolt at the Carlton Club, and I thought that the crowd of watching reporters looked surprised at our cordial greeting.

[1]But see pp. 105 and 192–3. Hankey had certainly not been averse to taking the League of Nations side into his organisation.

[2]When on 1st October 1922 the *Observer* carried an interview with Lord Robert Cecil in which he stressed the need for fuller development of the League machinery in Whitehall Hankey sent Lloyd George an angry riposte. He said that a Cabinet Committee for League affairs, such as Lord Robert had proposed, had existed since May 1920; that the League section had 'the whole Cabinet office machinery' behind it; and that many high civil servants attended meetings of the League Council or Assembly. In other words all Lord Robert's *desiderata* were already met. Hankey added that, although he personally favoured the League of Nations section being under the Foreign Office, Balfour did not want it transferred. Lloyd George papers F/26/2/42.

[3]See Vol. I, pp. 482 and 613.

Baldwin and I chatted for some time with Davidson and Fry,[1] the private secretaries, and then a footman came for me. 'I feel as though I were going from a doctor's waiting room to his consulting room to know my fate' I remarked amid a roar of laughter. Bonar received me with great cordiality in an upstairs drawing room, the floor of which was littered, as Bonar's room always is, with papers. His face was very flushed – quite bloated by contrast with his usual rather gaunt appearance – and it was obvious that he had not slept. He looked excited and very worried, and his manner had none of its normal Scottish coolness and canniness. As I shook hands I said 'Congratulations on being about to be . . .'. He shook his head dismally and said it was no cause for congratulations. Then he asked me point blank if I was prepared to serve him as loyally as I had served Lloyd George. I replied that, if he wanted me, I would serve him as loyally as I had served Asquith and Lloyd George and that the latter was quite prepared that I should do so. 'That is the answer I had expected', he said, 'and you can help me at once because your experience in these matters is unique'. Then he asked me to find out how many offices from a constitutional point of view he must fill before he dissolved Parliament on Wednesday, as he could not hope to complete his Ministry by then. I promised to find this out, and then asked him point blank if he intended to have a Cabinet Secretariat or to scrap it. He at once replied that he intended to continue the system of recording Cabinet conclusions, which he thought essential to businesslike procedure. But he thought it essential that the cost should be curtailed. I said that I would work out plans for this, if he would decide the broad lines, and I could suggest the lines to him in three minutes. At this point he sent for Stanley Baldwin, who, I gather, is to be his right-hand man, and who stood in the corner of the room 'belching' – for some time he has had a distressing stomach trouble.[2] I then outlined my proposals – League of Nations to go to the Foreign Office, who would also take all International Conferences. The Committee of Imperial Defence to be the same as before the war (which means 'scrapping' Sir John Chancellor,[3] who is rather a misfit and cannot

[1]Later Sir Geoffrey S. Fry (1888–1960). Private Secretary to Bonar Law 1919–21 and 1922–23, and to Baldwin 1923–29.

[2]Doctors whom I have consulted tell me that this remark suggests that Baldwin suffered from peptic ulcers; but I have found no evidence to support that suggestion.

[3]1870–1952. Assistant Military Secretary, C.I.D. 1904. Secretary, Colonial Defence Committee, 1906. Governor of Mauritius 1911–16 and of Trinidad and Tobago 1916–21. Assistant Secretary, Cabinet Office 1922–23. Governor of Southern Rhodesia 1923–28. High Commissioner and C-in-C, Palestine 1928–31. Chairman of many government committees. Vice-Chairman, British Council 1940–41.

get on with his subordinates). Two of the staff or perhaps three on the Cabinet side to be 'scrapped' and a big reduction to be made in the clerical establishment. I thought I could reduce from £37,000 (including C.I.D.) to £15–16,000, though I would not tie myself to this figure until I had worked it out in detail. Both he and Baldwin were immensely relieved at this suggestion and said it was a great help. I told them that of course they would have a good deal of criticism but I could give them a defence. Then I said I was particularly anxious to keep Tom Jones, but the difficulty was his salary of £1,500 a year. Bonar thought he could carry this, and was very anxious to keep Tom. Then I jokingly asked if I could make two suggestions about his Cabinet, and begged him to bear in mind the importance of appointing someone to a comparatively light office, who could give his time to the Standing Sub-Committee of the Committee of Imperial Defence and someone to represent us at the Council of the League. He welcomed both suggestions, and we proceeded to discuss details and I told him of Crowe's ideas about the League. Next he said he must have a political secretary like Sir Edward Grigg. I told him Grigg was the best available man, but I understood he was standing for Parliament, and I doubted if he would take it on. Eventually he commissioned me very discreetly to sound Grigg. I said the next best man was Lionel Curtis,[1] who is handling Irish affairs at the Colonial office. He thought Curtis might be too opinionated, but I said Ll. G. had improved him in this respect. I then suggested Vansittart[2] of the Foreign Office, but he doubted whether Vansittart was a good enough draftsman, and said he wanted someone who could draft a thing into better language than he would do himself. As I said goodbye I remarked 'You have greatly relieved my mind about Tom Jones'. He replied 'I will save him, if I possibly can' – a less satisfactory answer than his first. Then he asked how Tom Jones would do as political secretary 'for my very short

[1] 1872–1955. Colonial Service Officer and writer on international affairs. Member of Lord Milner's 'Kindergarten' in South Africa after Boer War. Founder of *The Round Table* and an influential member of the group named after it. Founder of The Royal Institute of International Affairs. As a Fellow of All Souls became a close friend of Hankey's, as well as of Tom Jones, Philip Kerr and Geoffrey Dawson; but was never one of the 'appeasers' of Germany in the 1930s. See A. L. Rowse, *All Souls and Appeasement* (Macmillan, 1961).

[2] Robert G. Vansittart, 1st Baron 1941 (1881–1957). Secretary to Curzon as Foreign Secretary 1920–24. Assistant Under-Secretary of State and Principal Private Secretary to Baldwin as Prime Minister 1928–30. Permanent Under-Secretary, Foreign Office 1930–38. Chief Diplomatic Adviser to Foreign Secretary 1938–41. Member of Defence Requirements Sub-Committee (Hankey Chairman 1933). A close ally of Hankey in cause of rearmament in 1930s and outspoken opponent of 'appeasement' of Hitler's Germany.

term of office', – he doubted whether he were a good enough draftsman. I thought Tom would do all right, and it might be a good way out. He said 'Personally I like Tom Jones better than any of them'. Before leaving I mentioned Ll. G.'s wish to maintain his friendship with me and Bonar naturally waived it aside as perfectly legitimate. He added 'I know Ll. G. will attack me ceaselessly, but I don't believe it will make a bit of difference to our personal friendship'. Incidentally he mentioned that at 10.30 on Wednesday evening [presumably 18th October, the day before the Carlton Club meeting] he had been on the point of telegraphing to his constituency to resign his seat, and that his children had been the principal influence in inducing him to take this on.[1] Then I returned to my office. The reporters outside eyed me curiously. . . . At the office I saw most of my colleagues in succession. My worst interviews were with St. Quintin Hill,[2] who is a civil servant and will probably go to the Board of Trade, whence he came, but is most reluctant to leave the office, and Wicks,[3] who is a temporary man with a family, and is left high and dry. I promised to do all I can for him, but it is a bad look-out, as he didn't serve in the war. I told him to go to Carson, who is a friend, and to try and get a private secretaryship, as a stop-gap. Tom Jones is very anxious to stop with me, as is Howorth. Longhurst is all right, but I shall have to do a job to keep Burgis, who is only a temporary man. Bonar Law had promised his help. A very trying business sacking these people. Then I sent Tom Jones to Liddell[4] the Parliamentary draftsman on the constitutional point, and sent Bonar a note before my very late lunch to tell him that constitutionally he need fill no offices . . . It was desirable however to fill the posts of Lord Chancellor and Home Secretary, who had duties to perform in connection with the elections, while administrative difficulties would soon arise if the post of Secretary for Scotland was not filled and (though not essential) there ought to be a Lord President of the Council, as a [Privy] Council meeting would very shortly have to be held. For myself I added that in view of the need of a Turkish peace there should

[1] This somewhat modifies the view tentatively expressed in Blake, *Bonar Law*, p. 456 and James, *Davidson,* p. 126 that Law's sister Mary was the decisive influence on his decision.

[2] Later Sir T. St. Quintin Hill (1889–1963). Civil Servant. An Assistant Secretary, Cabinet Office 1919–23 and 1941–42.

[3] Pembroke Wicks. (1882–1957). Barrister, Civil Servant and Conservative Party official. Private Secretary to Lord Carson 1911–18. An Assistant Secretary, Cabinet Office 1918–22. Private Secretary to Lord Curzon 1923. Political Secretary, Conservative Central Office 1925–31.

[4] Later Sir Frederick F. Liddell (1865–1950). Barrister. First Parliamentary Counsel 1917–28. Counsel to the Speaker, House of Commons 1928–43. An Ecclesiastical Commissioner 1944–48.

at once be a Foreign Secretary; a Colonial Secretary was also needed at an early date for Irish affairs, and I need hardly add how important it was to have a chancellor of the Exchequer. . . .

The very next day Hankey, never a man to let the grass grow under his feet, wrote to Law to give him the results of his 'very discreet inquiries' about a political private secretary for him. Grigg, he said, intended to stand for Parliament, but if he was not elected 'might be induced to come'.[1] Curtis was 'much occupied with Irish affairs in the Colonial Office', but is 'vastly improved by his official experience, and is no longer dogmatic or inelastic'. Warren Fisher, however, wanted Law 'to have a first rate Treasury man' – which would be a reversion to earlier practice. Finally Tom Jones would 'always be at your disposal to the fullest extent you desire'.[2] Hankey then sacked Chancellor, who was 'so unpleasant about it I really could not feel sorry for him'; but he none the less got Masterton Smith to promise 'to try and find him a [Colonial] Governorship', and also to get him a G.C.M.G.[3] Plainly Hankey's loyalty to his staff was not denied even to one of the most difficult characters ever to serve under him.

While the future of the Secretariat hung in the balance the Beaverbrook and Rothermere newspapers stepped up their campaign against it. The *Daily Mail* declared that 'Sir Maurice Hankey's share in the direction of the country has been distinctly unconstitutional'[4]; the *Evening Standard* resurrected Peter Wright, whom Hankey had abruptly dismissed from his Paris office in 1918 as a security risk,[5] to write a long and vindictive article in which he described the Secretariat as 'simply an expansion of Sir Maurice Hankey', who had allegedly 'issued orders to all the Ministers, who became mere subordinates'.[6] Much nearer the mark was the *Observer*'s view that 'the Garden Suburb' was doomed.[7]

High on the list of those whom Hankey took into his complete confidence at this time of crisis stood, of course, his old friend and firm supporter Esher, and a long series of letters passed between

[1]Sir Edward Grigg (see p. 255, *note*) was elected to Parliament as National Liberal member for Oldham in 1922.

[2]Hankey to Bonar Law 23rd Oct. 1922. Bonar Law papers BL 11/21/99.

[3]Hankey was nearly always successful in procuring Honours for his staff, and Chancellor was gazetted G.C.M.G. in 1922. See p. 306 regarding his later career.

[4]28th Oct. 1922. [5]See Vol. I, p. 491, *note*.

[6]*Evening Standard* 30th Oct. 1922.

[7]The *Observer* 22nd Oct. 1922. Copy in Cab. 21/221.

them.[1] On 22nd Hankey wrote 'I think I have saved the ship by chucking ballast overboard'; but that judgement soon proved much too optimistic, since the redoubtable Warren Fisher had hardly begun to bring his big guns into action. As the progress of the dispute is clearly described in Hankey's diary and in the semi-official correspondence which passed between him and Fisher we will follow it in those sources rather than in the Esher correspondence. On 24th, presumably by way of 'chucking ballast overboard', Hankey approached the British Museum about taking over the Historical Section of the C.I.D. Though Frederic Kenyon, the Curator,[2] was 'very favourably disposed' he thought 'the [Imperial] War Museum might be even better'.[3] In fact, however, the Historical Section remained where it was – to the great advantage of the author of this biography, who served in its successor the Cabinet Office Historical Section from 1949–61 while engaged on the history of the maritime side of World War II.

*Diary 25th October 1922*
I have been fighting all day with my back to the wall for my position. I am up against the whole hierarchy of the civil service, who have taken advantage of Lloyd George's fall to try and down me. Luckily their representative was Warren Fisher, a personal friend and a gentleman. I think I have succeeded in retaining all essentials. I have dictated an account of the whole day's proceeding with Bonar Law and Warren Fisher, and hope to insert a copy in this diary.* My object in making this entry is to note an extraordinary statement made to me by Davidson, Bonar Law's parliamentary secretary this morning, while I was waiting for Bonar Law at 24 Onslow Gardens. Davidson told me that Lord Rothermere came yesterday to see Bonar Law. The latter expressed a hope that Lord Rothermere would support him in his

[1]Hankey to Esher 22nd, 25th, 26th, 27th Oct., 8th Nov. (two letters). All in Esher papers. Esher to Hankey 1st, 9th and 21st Nov. All holograph from Roman Camp, Callander.

[2]Later Sir Frederic G. Kenyon (1863–1952). Classicist and bibliophil. Assistant Keeper of Manuscripts, British Museum 1898–1909. Director and Principal Librarian 1909–30. President, British Academy 1917–21 and of many Learned Societies.

[3]Diary 24th Oct. 1922.

*[obviously added later] 'It was left in the Cabinet Office when I retired among my personal records known as *Magnum Opus*'. These files only reached the Public Record Office in November 1970. The document in question is now in Cab. 63/33, but the Hankey papers contain copies of his whole correspondence with Sir Warren Fisher on this matter.

newspapers. Lord Rothermere replied that he would do so on conditions. These were that Lord Rothermere himself should receive an earldom and that his son Esmond Harmsworth, should receive a good office in the Government. Blackmail! The odd thing was that Bonar had thought of offering a very minor post to young Esmond Harmsworth, but this, of course, makes it impossible.[1] Rothermere is the man who has been attacking me.

Next day Bonar Law made a speech at Glasgow in which he assured his audience that, as he had stated in his Election address, the Government 'intend to bring that body [i.e. the Cabinet Secretariat] in its present form to an end'.[2] This differed widely from the assurances Law had given Hankey at their meeting on 21st, and the distress it caused to the latter is therefore easily understood. Furthermore Law's change of front coincided exactly with a letter Hankey sent Fisher describing the economies he had in mind, as already outlined to Law and Baldwin, and emphasising his earnest desire to retain the services of Tom Jones.[3] It is difficult not to feel that, whereas Hankey had laid all his cards face upwards on the table, both Law and Fisher were at this stage engaged in something not far short of double-dealing.

*Diary 27th October 1922*
All yesterday I was worrying at the way Warren Fisher treated me in springing on me his proposal that I should become a Treasury official. He admitted that he had been planning this for years, yet, when I had always put my cards on the table in regard to the office he had kept it back until now. As I shall presently show he did the same thing to-day. In the morning I called together the whole office (Assistant Secretaries), and read to them the passage from Bonar Law's speech in which he said that the Cabinet Secretariat in its present form was to come to an end. I then described the arrangements I was making to obtain employment, and I ended by thanking [them] all for their support. During the morning I found all my colleagues very depressed, and much incensed against Bonar Law. Contrary to his expressed intention Bonar had not read the formula agreed between Warren Fisher and myself. On the contrary he had deliberately omitted the passage to which I attached so much importance, viz. that the Cabinet Secretariat and C.I.D. would be *retrans-*

[1]See James, *Davidson*, pp. 135 and 293 for Davidson's account of this astonishing episode.
[2]*The Times*, 27th Oct. 1922.
[3]Hankey to Fisher 26th Oct. 1922. Fisher replied on 27th 'I share to the full your regard for T.J. as you know. I will gladly see if anything is possible on the lines you suggest . . .'. Jones papers.

*ferred* to the Treasury and Subordinate Departments' vote. He had managed to convey the impression that we were to be absorbed into the body of the Treasury, which was exactly what I wished to avoid. Moreover he had omitted to do what I had begged him to do, and to say something which would make clear that we had in fact not encroached on other Departments, and had done our work efficiently and well. In fact, as Lord Esher said in a telegram, he had conveyed the impression that all the allegations against the office were true. Rawlins, my head clerk, came to me and said that, after all his incessant self-denying work he went about feeling like a criminal. St. Quintin Hill, the quietest and most bovine of men, was speechless with indignation. Longhurst is ill with it. I walked round to Lord Milner's house, thinking he would be a good man to talk things over with, but he had moved. Then I dropped in at the Treasury and saw Warren Fisher for a moment, telling him that I was getting to the point of resignation, which seemed to upset him. But he had a luncheon engagement, so I arranged to see him in the afternoon. I lunched at a Lyons restaurant – I can't face the club – and thought things out. Then I decided that the only possible, honourable course was an inquiry. *The Times* had [published] bitter and false things about us in its leader.[1] I felt I could not honourably or loyally accept the new post until I had removed the stain from the office in regard to my previous administration. I sat down and drafted a letter insisting on [an] inquiry before my appointment. I read this over to Tom Jones, Howorth and Burgis, but, as civil servants dependent on this for their living they asked me to omit reference to 'my colleagues and myself'. Then I saw Warren Fisher, and as usual put all my cards on the table. At first he thought the inquiry a good idea but, as we talked it out, [he] went back on this. Soldiers and sailors are constantly given inquiries, and he understood my desire for this. There was no precedent in the case of the civil service, and there were many precedents to the contrary. Civil servants were supposed to be anonymous, and it was their business to put up with attacks until Ministers defended them in Parliament. Other departments, including the Treasury had been venomously attacked and had just had to stick it. None of this appealed to me at all. Then we discussed possible forms of inquiry. I did not like civil servants. Though ostensibly hostile, if they exonerated me the public would say we were all thieves together. If Beatty and Cavan were added, they would say these were my pals. A select Ctee. of the House of Commons would involve politics and be abominable. A Ministerial Ctee. would not command much confidence. I suggested a judge in the chair, and he agreed this would be

[1]In its first editorial for 27th Oct. *The Times* described the Cabinet Secretariat as 'a Prime Ministerial Department for the conduct of important international affairs apart from, or even in subversion of, well-tried constitutional practices and safeguards'.

best. Still, he did not like to establish the precedent. Eventually he asked if I would be content if Bonar Law undertook during the short forthcoming session in Parliament to make a statement refuting the charges. I rather liked the idea, but having once so nearly walked into a trap, I took jolly good care to be non-committal and said I would think it over. Then an extraordinary thing happened, for he suddenly launched out into a brand new proposal, viz. that in addition to continuing [as] Secretary of the Cabinet and C.I.D. I should also become Clerk of the Privy Council – practically a sinecure. The post will shortly be vacant as Sir Almeric Fitzroy,[1] the present Clerk, has been convicted of bothering women in the Park, and even if he wins his appeal, will probably have to retire. This proposal of course eases everything. The Cabinet [is] constitutionally a Committee of the Privy Council, as the C.I.D. is of the Cabinet. The whole arrangement is symmetrical and logical, and one that I have often thought of. Fisher then astonished me by saying it had been in his mind throughout. Why didn't he say so? Why did he ask me to become a Treasury official, when all the time he had this in his mind? My view is that my draft letter frightened him.[2] It would put the Prime Minister and the treasury in a cleft stick. If they granted an impartial inquiry, I should get such a flaming report that everyone would say – 'Why on earth did you abolish it?' If they refused an inquiry people would say they were afraid of it. Fisher tried to belittle the probable results, but I rehearsed the history of the Cabinet Secretariat, with its development from the War Cabinet into an Imperial War Cabinet and Supreme War Council, to say nothing of Peace Conference developments bringing ever increased prestige. This was not the work of the Treasury – the Central Department of Government to which he is always referring but of the Secretariat. The Treasury had failed utterly. It had shown neither foresight nor imagination nor organising capacity, and had plunged the country into something like administrative chaos until the War Cabinet machine came to the rescue. This he did not dispute, and even strengthened what I said. He must have realised that if I developed this case before an impartial tribunal the Treasury [would] look rather silly. He therefore played his last card, which he had meant to keep back. Why? I suspect the answer is to be found in a hint thrown out by Howorth to one of my assistant secretaries that, if I had to retire, Fisher would himself take my job.[3] If I could be forced out by

[1] 1851–1935. Clerk of the Privy Council 1898–1923. Charged and convicted of 'wilfully interfering with and annoying persons using Hyde Park' 8th Oct. 1922. The conviction and fine of £5 were not upheld on appeal, the magistrates stopping the case and awarding Fitzroy costs against the police. *The Times* 11th Nov. 1922.

[2] This obviously refers to Hankey's draft letter requesting an enquiry.

[3] In his diary entry for 30th October Hankey recalled that on this day Fisher 'let drop . . . that if I went he had no-one in view who was the least bit suited to the

humiliating conditions, well and good. If I could not – then he must give me decent terms. As we both want to be away until to-morrow we adjourned until Monday, and I undertook to consider his proposal that Bonar Law should undertake to whitewash me. I am quite convinced that there is a long dated civil service cabal to get me out. Masterton Smith has always shut up like a knife whenever I have raised the question of the future of the Cabinet Secretariat. Chancellor to-day found him holding forth in an oracular manner about the importance of re-establishing Treasury control, and having a civil servant as principal secretary to the Prime Minister. He also found Baldwin talking sententiously about the importance of Treasury control etc.

It must have been on the day Hankey made the foregoing diary entry, or possibly on 28th, that he told his staff about the latest developments. His announcement 'with a smile' that he was to become Clerk of the Privy Council provoked an acidulous entry in the diary of Tom Jones, who 'relapsed into a painful silence' and 'was speechless and remained so to the end.'[1] Obviously Jones, and probably the other assistant secretaries present, thought that Hankey had advanced his own interests regardless of their prospects and security. Yet the hard fight Hankey waged with Law, Baldwin and Fisher to retain the services of Jones, Howorth and even Burgis (though he told Esher, who always took an almost paternal interest in Burgis's future, that he was very doubtful of success in his case[2]) gives the lie to such an uncharitable suggestion. It is true that Hankey was determined to maintain his position if possible. But he was prepared to resign if the Secretariat was forced into the Treasury's arms; there is every sign that he fought hard to keep on the best of his staff – and especially Jones; and, finally,

---

job'; which contradicts the suggestion here made that Fisher himself intended to take it on. It seems unlikely that so astute a man as Fisher would ever have seriously considered that the Permanent Secretary of the Treasury could also be secretary of the Cabinet and C.I.D.

[1] *Middlemas*, I, p. 219. Hankey was not actually appointed Clerk of the Privy Council until 31st May 1923. Colin Smith had been appointed Deputy Clerk in March 1921 and retained that post until March 1934. He received a special allowance, and did all the routine work for Hankey during most of his time as Clerk. Eric Leadbitter (1891–1971, knighted 1946) took over as Deputy Clerk in March 1934, and remained so until June 1951. Information from Sir Godfrey Agnew, Clerk of the Privy Council, 19th June 1968.

[2] Hankey to Esher 8th Nov. 1922. Esher papers.

he flatly refused Fisher's proposal to continue the Secretariat in its present form *for the duration of his own tenure only*.[1]

*Diary October 29th 1922*

Yesterday morning Bonar Law sent for me to discuss Cabinet business. I said I could not fairly do this unless I knew whether I was able to continue as Secretary to the Cabinet. I had that morning written a letter to Warren Fisher rehearsing all that had happened and saying that nothing would induce me to remain unless the cloud of suspicion regarding my administration of the old Cabinet office was effectually dissipated. As an ex-officer dealing in the C.I.D. with officers of high rank I should prefer the military method of inquiry. If that was impossible some other means must be found. Tactically, if you mean to resign, a document is essential and this was frankly a resigning document for publication if necessary. I gave it to Bonar Law. He read it, asked a few questions, said I was too sensitive, and then promised to meet me everywhere – a statement in Parliament refuting the foul accusations against the Cabinet Office i.e. encroachment on Foreign policy; the statement of Sept. 16th[2]; overstaffing and extravagance; and interference with the press. Bonar also promised that we should revert to the position of a subordinate dept. of Treasury and should not be swallowed by the Treasury, and that I should have my own staff, which I volunteered to reduce to a minimum. I wrote to tell Fisher this.

The first phase of the battle – the defensive phase for me, is over. Frankly I was surprised. While I had all my cards on the table and was parleying with Warren Fisher he opened a long prepared attack with the whole strength of the Civil Service Rifles. My covering forces were surprised and gave way. My principal ally (Lloyd George) had withdrawn from the fray and I felt very isolated. I gave up some positions – but they were awkward salients. The Turkish Peace Conference must be more or less of a fiasco, and in the long run all connected with it will be discredited. The ground can then be recovered, if necessary, under changed conditions. The League of Nations Section was always rather outside our natural scope. We have held our main position – the secretaryship of the Cabinet and the C.I.D., and the independent position we always held until 1920 as a subordinate Dept. of Treasury.

[1]Hankey to Bonar Law 2nd Nov. 1922. This draft memorandum was withdrawn by Hankey after discussion with Sir Warren Fisher that same day. Fisher for his part withdrew his submission of 31st Oct. in which he had proposed the absorption of the Cabinet Secretariat by the Treasury.

[2]That is the 'Manifesto', probably drafted by Lloyd George and Churchill, foreshadowing war with Turkey, which produced such an extremely hostile reaction. Hankey had absolutely nothing to do with its drafting and first read it in the evening paper. See pp. 284 and 293.

The next battle will be on the staff. The Treasury began by trying to swallow us from the head. The mouthful was too big. Now they will try and swallow us from the tail. They will try and put our clerks on the Treasury vote. This I shall refuse. If the vital clerical machine is paid by someone else, it is in the last resort under someone else's control and I will not stand this. When the fight comes I shall transfer the battle to 10 Downing St. and take the offensive against the Treasury in the presence of the Prime Minister. I shall show that the so-called Central Department of the Government has failed as regards the past, present, and future. [Here Hankey repeated his oft-used and vehement attack on the Treasury's failure to prepare for war in 1914.[1]] When I launch this terrific Tank against them it will crumple up their barbed wire and crush them. All I pray is that I may get the opportunity. I now have my forces marshalled for the great counter-offensive. If it fails in the private discussions, I shall resign and make it public. This is a mere summary of a case I have worked out in full detail. I omitted to mention that Bonar Law told me he had already seen Wickham Steed and protested against the references to the Cabinet Office in *The Times* of the previous day [actually 27th October, see p. 312, *note*].

*October 30th 1922*

All has gone according to plan. I wrote Warren Fisher a letter this morning telling him that I could not agree to have my clerks under anyone's orders or on anyone's paysheet but my own, for reasons of discipline and efficiency; and I added that I objected just as much to the Cabinet Office being swallowed from the tail as from the head, but [?] favouring the closest co-operation. He rang me up at once and I went to see him. I was very cool and collected, having absolutely determined to resign if I did not get my way. He argued at great length and I replied, never budging an inch and meeting argument with counter-argument. This time he frankly admitted that he had fully intended to absorb the whole office into the Treasury. In fact, during the meeting, to show how extensive the plot was, one of his colleagues Sir George Barstow, a Controller of the Treasury, burst in and said 'Hallo Hankey, are you one of my colleagues now?' 'Not in the sense you mean', I replied, 'but I hope a colleague all the same'. Fisher looked daggers at him, and he hastily withdrew. I then rather bitterly reproached Fisher for lack of candour in launching this attack on me without warning. He pretended to be very hurt and said that everyone thought out such plans in a general way, and then a moment would come when action became essential. One could not tell people all one's aspirations. Very lame, I thought. After a tremendous wrangle he had to give way, and said I should have my staff on my own vote as a subordinate Dept. of the Treasury, and we parted with mutual com-

[1]See Vol. I, pp. 137–8.

pliments. He said he would put forward a Minute to the effect that in his view the logical plan was the absorption of the Cabinet Office into the Treasury; that owing to my personal position he would not press it . . .; that there was a minor question as to which vote the clerks and typists etc. should be on, in which we also disagreed, but he did not think it necessary to quarrel over it, and would therefore . . . let me have my way. I asked him to send me a copy and to allow me to place myself on record on the questions of principle to the same extent as he did. This he accepted. I left him with the feeling that I had won a great victory and routed the Civil Service Rifles – horse, foot and artillery. Moreover I have done it without bringing up my Tank. Later I saw Bonar Law about Cabinet business. He was deciding which Ministers were to be in the Cabinet. He talked of leaving out the Minister of Education, but I pointed out it would result in a frightful row, and he decided to include him.[1]

Simultaneously with the above entry in his diary Hankey sent Law a memorandum entitled 'Procedure in the Cabinet Office' setting out the practices which had been in force under Lloyd George and asking whether they were to continue.[2] Next day he followed it up with another entitled 'Draft Instructions to the Secretary of the Cabinet'[3]; but that one was apparently never circulated – probably because, as the next diary entry shows, it was overtaken by events.

*Diary 2nd November 1922*

Yesterday morning I attended the first Cabinet meeting of Bonar Law's Govt. Many flattering tributes to myself. I also received Warren Fisher's draft submission to the Treasury Board in regard to the Cabinet Office. I regarded it as an offensive document and inconsistent with our agreement. For tactical reasons I wrote a somewhat acid commentary for the Prime Minister – sending an advance copy to Fisher. As I expected and intended, this flattened out Warren Fisher. I had another very heated discussion with him this evening at 5 p.m. I was adamant and refused to budge an inch, and eventually he gave in – as I thought he would have to – and promised a new draft in accordance with my ideas. I attach the correspondence, which speaks for itself. [Not reproduced, as it adds little to the diary entries.]

*8th November 1922*

On Nov. 6th I had my final row with Fisher. He sent me his second draft submission to the P.M. about the Secretariat. I strongly objected to a passage

[1]Edward F. L. Wood (Baron Irwin 1925, Earl of Halifax 1944) became President of the Board of Education with a seat in Bonar Law's Cabinet.

[2]Hankey to Law 30th Oct. 1922. Cab. 21/223. [3]Dated 31st Oct. 1922. *ibid.*

which was rather tendentious and indicated that the Govt. might one day wish to swallow it into the Treasury. I said if this stood I must forward a companion document protesting against the principle. We then discussed the matter and he agreed to accept a draft I proposed. We then reached agreement, and I hope the matter is closed. Yesterday afternoon the Cabinet met at short notice to consider a renewal of the difficulties at Constantinople, where the Angora Turks have made extravagant demands – withdrawal of [the] Allies, permission to be asked before our ships enter the Straits or Turkish ports, extravagant customs dues, abolition of capitulations etc. Only 9 members present – mostly Peers, the others being away electioneering. The High Commissioner and Generals want to refuse and to declare a state of siege in Constantinople, and Harington wants to abandon Chanak and concentrate all forces in Constantinople. The Govt. telephoned to Paris to ask Poincaré to agree before approving. I stayed in town with Hilda, in case the reply necessitated a late Cabinet, but Poincaré agreed. After the Cabinet I gave Bonar Law solemn warning that if we abandoned Chanak, and [the] Turks occupied the Asiatic shores of the Dardanelles the Allied garrison might be marooned at Constantinople, and might have the utmost difficulty in making their escape down the Straits. It might become impossible to supply them, and there might be a disaster. He made light of it. I can see that their real hope is that, if as usual the French and Italians refuse to assist us in offering force to the Turks, we shall be able to withdraw 'honourably' on the ground that we cannot do the job alone. A nice position when the British Empire cannot stand up to Turkey! . . .

The semi-official letters which passed between Hankey on the one side and Warren Fisher, Bonar Law and Baldwin, now Chancellor of the Exchequer, on the other side add little to the diary entries quoted above. They were all couched in impeccably polite language, and the two protagonists sent each other copies of their submissions. All Hankey's passionate, harsh emotions, and the strident accusations in the diary were of course excluded. Interest in the letters lies, firstly, in the demonstration they provide of how two top civil servants handled an issue over which they were in fundamental disagreement; and, secondly, in the astuteness with which Hankey not only outflanked his formidable antagonist at the Treasury but also the Prime Minister and Chancellor of the Exchequer. The correspondence includes a holograph note by Hankey which in effect heralded his victory. It reads 'As the result of a conversation at 5 p.m. on 2nd November 1922 Sir Warren Fisher agreed to cancel his submission of 31st October and I agreed not to send this [the rebuttal of Fisher's proposals] to the

Prime Minister . . .'. The two letters reproduced below signalise Fisher's surrender and the wise moderation with which Hankey received it.

*Sir Warren Fisher to Hankey. H.M. Treasury. 3rd November 1922.* Holograph.[1]
My dear Hankey,

I have redrawn certain parts of the enclosed [his memorandum of 31st October] on the lines I told you. The draft carries out precisely the idea on which we concluded, and I am sure you will agree that I have left nothing undone in my power to meet you personally, being actuated not merely by my sense of the close and harmonious relationship between us, but also by the feeling that great consideration is due to a man who has devoted himself with such remarkable efficiency to our common service.

Yours sincerely

*Hankey to Fisher. 2 Whitehall Gardens. 6th November 1922.* Holograph.[2]
My dear Warren Fisher,

Many thanks for the revised draft. I have suggested two small modifications, shown in pencil in the margin.

In view of the strong views I hold on the question of principle I propose to put forward the attached short typewritten note to the Prime Minister. I don't think you will object to it. You have affirmed your view on the question and I here affirm mine.

May I take this opportunity to thank you for your personal consideration to me throughout these discussions. If I have had to be obstinate, it was on no personal ground, and solely because I had strong views on the principle.

I ask nothing more than to work with you on the same terms of cordial co-operation, mutual respect and personal friendship as in the past.

Yours sincerely

Hankey's submission to Bonar Law, referred to above, stated the terms on which he and Fisher had come to agreement. Never one to harbour a grudge Hankey ended by saying 'I wish to place on record the great personal consideration which Sir Warren Fisher has shown me in the discussions I have had with him on the subject'. In truth they became firm friends from the day when they buried the axe of the Cabinet Secretariat's future; and in the early 1930s they were close allies in the cause of rearmament. But one cannot but feel that, if Fisher had seen Hankey's diary entries, the whole story of the Secretariat, and indeed of the administration of British government, would have been different.

[1]Cab. 63/33. [2]*ibid.*

The observations made many years later by Sir Horace Wilson[1] about Warren Fisher's aims at this time may not be out of place here. According to Wilson, Fisher's policy was 'to create a universal Civil Service to serve all Ministers with the best men available'. His chief principles were that the Civil Service should 'Keep clear of Honours', that there should be no lobbying or intrigue by them over appointments, and that for two years after retirement they should accept no post in any business with which they had dealings while in the Civil Service. According to Wilson, Fisher himself did, however, interfere in high appointments in the Foreign Office; and if a man was appointed whom he did not consider the best available (Sir Walford Selby was quoted as a case in point[2]) Fisher would move to the attack. Wilson recalled that Fisher 'respected Hankey for his gifts as a highly efficient secretary'; but in 1922 he wanted the post of Secretary of the Cabinet for 'a regular Civil Servant'. The Permanent Secretary of the Treasury should in Fisher's view be 'the most powerful person in Whitehall', and his strong reaction in 1922 was inspired by his hatred of the corruption which had stained Lloyd George's administration, and his dislike of the Garden Suburb and of 'the untidy and inefficient' administrative arrangements of recent years.[3]

On 8th Curzon made in the City what Hankey described as 'an offensive speech in which he referred disparagingly to "the too powerful and too numerous Cabinet Secretariat"'. 'This', he continued in amazement and anger, 'in spite of his letter to me of 23rd October and his promise to say the same in public!'[4] He was not slow in extracting an apology from the Janus-like and fickle Foreign Secretary.

[1]1882– . Civil Servant. Principal Assistant Secretary, Ministry of Labour 1919–21 and Permanent Secretary 1921–30. Chief Industrial Adviser to government 1930–39. Permanent Secretary, Treasury and Head of Civil Service 1939–42. Influential in cause of 'appeasement' towards Germany in 1930s.

[2]1881–1965. Diplomat. Assistant Private Secretary to Lord Grey 1911–15. First Secretary, Cairo 1919–22. Principal Private Secretary to Secretary of State for Foreign Affairs 1924–32. Ambassador at Vienna 1933–37 and at Lisbon 1937–40.

[3]Interview with Sir Horace Wilson 7th July 1967. In discussing Foreign Office appointments Sir Horace doubtless had in mind the famous Treasury Minute of 1919 which placed them at the disposal of the Permanent Secretary of the Treasury – namely Sir Warren Fisher.

[4]This obviously refers to the letter from Curzon quoted in Hankey's diary entry for 24th Oct. 1922. See p. 301.

*Curzon to Hankey. 1 Carlton House Terrace. 9th November 1922.* Holograph

My dear Hankey,

I am very sorry to think that my rather hasty and quite unpremeditated words in the City were thought by you and your staff to reflect upon their ever ready and devoted services.

I think that your criticism is just, and I gladly withdraw the words which were certainly never intended to convey any hostile criticism.

Such, as you know, is the very reverse of my own opinions more than once expressed in public of the work of the secretariat.

You may make any use of this letter inside the office that you please.

Yours ever

Next day, before he had received the above letter, Hankey went to see Curzon and 'took him to task' about his unguarded words. He said that 'too powerful' could only apply to himself, and that he 'did not mind a hint' if such was the case, though he would 'rather have received it in private'. On the score of 'too numerous' he protested strongly, pointing out that the Geddes Committee and Lloyd George himself had both very recently cleared the Secretariat on that charge. He could not, he said, 'maintain the morale of the office', whose staff were constantly being asked to work very long hours on behalf of Ministers – including preparing the speech in question for Curzon himself – if such accusations were made against them. Curzon was 'frightfully upset' by this devastating reproof, and offered to make a public recantation. But Hankey generously excused him from such an embarrassment during an election, so they 'parted on good terms'. Hankey then assembled his staff and read Curzon's letter to them. He did not fail to notice that the offending passage was not printed in *The Times* report of the speech, and guessed, probably correctly, that Curzon himself had it removed. He was amused that, on the very day that he was accused of being too powerful Bonar Law had to ask him to amend the 'shocking bad draft' of instructions to General Harington about Chanak which the Chiefs of Staff had produced for the Cabinet. That evening he visited Law at his house with the Cabinet minutes, and found him very unwell with a cold and a temperature. 'My feeling is', he wrote in his diary, 'as Sir William Robertson said of Marshal Lyautey "That fellow won't last long".[1] I am afraid his health won't stand the strain. He is quite sensible but uninspiring'.[2] Hankey's prediction was to prove as accurate as his summing up of Law's character.

[1]See Vol. I, p. 349. [2]Diary of 10th Nov. 1922.

A few days later Lord Lee, who had just been replaced at the Admiralty by Amery in order to keep down the number of Peers in the Cabinet, answered Hankey's letter of sympathy with some consoling words about the Secretariat. 'I am also greatly relieved', wrote Lee, 'to know that this election talk about the "Cabinet Secretariat" is largely eyewash, and that you are still in business at the old stand. The alternative would be chaos, and I have been working up a savage indictment of the new Govt. for the first opportunity in the House of Lords. Now I hope it may be unnecessary'.[1] Though Hankey, having transferred his services and his loyalty to Law, was not particularly well disposed towards those who had stood by the Coalition at the Carlton Club meeting, words like Lee's were probably balm to his troubled spirit at this difficult time. Even Lord Grey, who was not likely to tolerate the Cabinet Secretariat doing work which in his view came within the province of the Foreign Office, and had made a speech at Manchester voicing his criticisms of latter day practices in that respect, assured Hankey that he 'had the greatest admiration for the value of your devoted services to the country while I was in office'; and he would 'always be ready to acknowledge it'.[2] And Birdwood, Hankey's old comrade of Gallipoli days, wrote from far away Rawalpindi to sympathise with him over 'all the upheavals in the political world', and wondering how Law's announcement about the Cabinet Secretariat would affect him.[3] Such reminders of his past service must have reassured and encouraged Hankey with regard to the future, which had recently seemed ominously cloudy.

It was typical that, no sooner had he got the main issue regarding the Cabinet Secretariat settled, Hankey should return to the charge on the old question of revitalising the C.I.D. On 17th November he wrote to Lord Salisbury,[4] the Chairman of the Standing Defence Sub-Committee which, as long as the Prime Minister could not or would not revive the parent body, he was forced to regard as its *locum tenens*, enclosing an Agenda and suggesting a meeting in the near future. The main issues

[1]Lee to Hankey 13th Nov. 1922. Holograph.

[2]Grey to Hankey 8th Nov. 1922.

[3]Birdwood to Hankey 6th Nov. 1922, from Northern Command, India.

[4]James E. H. Gascoyne-Cecil, 4th Marquis of Salisbury (1861–1947). Politician (Cons.) and landowner. Under-Secretary for Foreign Affairs 1900–3. Lord Privy Seal 1903–5. President, Board of Trade 1905. Lord President of Council 1922–24. Chancellor of Duchy of Lancaster 1922–23. Lord Privy Seal 1924–29. Leader of House of Lords 1925–29.

he wanted to get settled were, firstly, approval of the report of the Committee on Revision of the Laws of War 'because the whole of the defence schemes of ports abroad are held up pending its approval'; secondly a decision regarding the responsibilities of the Army and Air Force for A-A defence and Air Operations; thirdly protection of the south Persian oilfields and the linked question of reserves of oil fuel for the Navy; fourthly the future of the Royal Arsenal at Woolwich, which he described as 'rather a formidable one' as it affected the future of thousands of workmen at a time of high unemployment; and, lastly, the annual report of the Co-ordination Committee on revision of the War Book.[1] In fact even the Standing Sub-Committee of the C.I.D. remained more or less dormant until early in the following year, when it was forced to undertake a major review of the functions and future of the three fighting services.

*Diary 26th November 1922*

... The Labour Party have already, during the first two days of Parliament, 'put the wind up' the new Government on Unemployment. After the Treasury had talked very big about not allowing the new Unemployment Ctee. to spend any money, and the Prime Minister under Stanley Baldwin's inspiration had resisted the entreaties of the Minister of Labour to have a Cabinet meeting on the subject, on Friday [24th] they decided to spend a very large sum, and that evening hastily assembled the Unemployment Committee to discover how to spend it! Bonar Law is himself a very able man, but he has the whole burden on his shoulders. Physically he is unequal to it, and yesterday when I saw him he was flushed and nervous like he was on the day he came into office. He cannot shake off his cold. I really don't know what will happen to them if Bonar's health cracks, as I believe it will soon. Except in Lord Curzon and Lord Cave I have not seen a spark of ability anywhere else. Stanley Baldwin hardly ever speaks. The Duke of Devonshire[2] looks like an apoplectic idol and adds little counsel. The rest – except possibly but doubtfully Amery and Lloyd-Greame – are second rate. Lord Derby told me the other day he doesn't want to remain in office. He assured me that Lord Birkenhead was really a traitor to Lloyd George. His plan had been for the Coalition to hold the election. When Ll. G. came back with but few Liberal Coalitionists he had intended to say politely that of course in the circumstances the Conservatives could not serve under him as Prime Minister,

[1]Hankey to Salisbury 17th Nov. 1922. Cab. 21/469.

[2]Victor C. W. Cavendish, 9th Duke of Devonshire (1868–1938). Politician (Cons.) and landowner. Financial Secretary to Treasury 1903–5. Governor-General of Canada 1916–21. Colonial Secretary 1922–24.

and himself [Birkenhead] usurp his [Lloyd George's] plan. In fact he declared that Birkenhead had last March asked him (Lord Derby) if he would join a Government of which Lord Birkenhead was to be the leader, and he had declined to do anything to upset Lloyd George. I am glad that Boscawen and my old friend Leslie Wilson, both of whom behaved treacherously to Lloyd George and Chamberlain, lost their seats at the election. On the whole, in spite of their good majority, I do not think the prospects of the present Government are very bright.

*30th November 1922*

To-day Bonar Law astonished me by saying that he wants me to undertake the secretarial work for the big conference which is to meet in London next week on reparations – Poincaré, Mussolini, Theunis etc. I urged that the Foreign Office should undertake it, but he said he thought I should have to as the F.O. were already strained in providing a secretariat at Lausanne. I was vastly tickled at this request, after the speeches he and Curzon have made to the effect that never again shall the Cabinet Secretariat take part in International Conferences. Even if I do not act as Secretary it is very humorous that I should have been asked to do so. This evening Stanley Baldwin asked me to come to his room at the House of Commons and over a pipe in the most friendly way pumped me for half an hour about Imperial Defence, and more particularly the situation in the Pacific. I gladly did all I could to help him in the difficult financial situation, but warned him of the risks of cutting down the two battleships.[1]

Hankey had hardly recovered from his astonishment at Law's request, when he was involved in a first-class crisis which threatened to overturn the government. From February onwards Demetrios Gounaris, the Greek politician who had again become Prime Minister in 1920,[2] had conducted a protracted correspondence with Curzon. On 28th November Gounaris and five of his colleagues were, to the horror of the civilised world, executed in Athens as scapegoats for the Greek collapse in Asia Minor. By some still undisclosed means the Gounaris–Curzon letters got into Beaverbrook's hands, and on 3rd December the *Sunday Express* published a letter dated 15th February in which Gounaris warned Curzon that unless Britain supplied arms and money the Greek army would have to withdraw from Asia Minor before it was driven into the sea. This revelation appeared to the leading

[1]This refers to the two battleships, finally named *Nelson* and *Rodney* (35,000 tons, 9 16-inch guns) which Britain was permitted to build under the terms of the Washington Naval Treaty.

[2]See p. 222, *note*.

Conservative ex-Coalitionists, and especially Birkenhead, to provide a golden opportunity to bring about Curzon's downfall. The former Lord Chancellor was sure he had never seen the letter; and Lloyd George, Chamberlain and Worthington-Evans also disclaimed knowledge. If Curzon had not circulated so important a communication to the Cabinet he could reasonably be held responsible for the Greek débâcle. On 7th December Birkenhead, without troubling to consult Hankey or look up the records, read the Gounaris letter in the House of Lords – with obvious evil intent. Hankey merely had to turn up the relevant file to show that not only had the letter been printed and circulated to the Cabinet but Birkenhead had actually initialled it. He and Lloyd George, who now appeared in a most foolish light, were forced to retract and apologise; and what Lord Ronaldshay has aptly called 'a truly remarkable case of collective amnesia'[1] ended in enhancing the standing of Law's government – and his debt to Hankey, who incidentally seems to have warned Lloyd George of his error at the earliest possible moment and received a cordial reply.[2]

Immediately this explosion had subsided Hankey had to turn his attention to the forthcoming conference on Reparations. His diary accurately reports the totally negative outcome.

Before November came to an end Hankey was able to record that, as regards the conduct of Cabinet business and his own position, everything was proceeding as though Law's election promises had never been made. 'I attend all meetings of the Cabinet and keep the Minutes exactly as before', he recorded. 'My relations with Bonar Law are almost the same as my relations were with Lloyd George. In spite of all the talk of "Conferences of Ministers" and "Cabinet Committees" being unconstitutional, force of circumstances has forced the new Government to adopt this method of transacting its business'. However with his reduced staff he could no longer supply secretaries for all the Cabinet Committees (Home Affairs, Ireland, Mesopotamia, Unemployment and the Navy–Air controversy); so he had 'farmed out' some of these to the Ministries most concerned. But the fact that departmental jealousy resulted in two men being produced to carry out what one of his staff, and a far less highly paid man, had previously done aroused his sardonic humour. On 25th he visited Law at his house – and was the recipient of 'an outburst against Boscawen, the chairman

[1] *Life of Lord Curzon*, III, p. 330. See also Blake, *Bonar Law*, pp. 477–80.

[2] Lloyd George to Hankey 14th Dec. 1922.

of the Unemployment Committee', whom Law described as having 'neither the imagination nor the drive for the job'. 'It is untrue', continued Law, '[that] as the Opposition and the Press say, we are deficient in brains, but it is true that we are terribly lacking in Ministers of administrative experience' – a judgement with which Hankey fully agreed.[1]

Meanwhile the first Lausanne Conference, convened to reach a new peace treaty with Turkey, had opened on 20th November. It lasted until 4th February 1923, on which day Curzon refused to conclude a separate treaty and presented Ismet Pasha with an eleventh hour ultimatum. The final result came with the second Lausanne Conference of April–July 1923, when minor concessions were offered to and accepted by the Turks. The treaty was signed on 4th July, and what Harold Nicolson has called Curzon's 'superb direction of foreign policy' breached the Russo-Turkish accord, and restored Anglo-Turkish unity without sacrificing that of France and Italy – no mean diplomatic feat.[2] But as Hankey was only indirectly involved in these prolonged negotiations we must pass over them quickly and return to the events of the closing weeks of 1922.

*Diary 12th December 1922*

We have just finished the Reparations Conference, or rather conversations of the four Prime Ministers – Bonar Law, Poincaré, Theunis, and Mussolini. In spite of the election speeches, according to which I was never again to attend an international conference, I found myself once more in the familiar rôle of secretary to a meeting of Prime Ministers. . . . As I anticipated, the conference has been a complete failure. No matter what was proposed – even when Mussolini hinted that Great Britain should relinquish Allied debts – Poincaré refused it unless security for fulfilment was offered by the occupation of the Ruhr. Of course Bonar Law had to decline this. The French think that the German failure to provide reparations is due to the industrialists, who have fraudulently exported their capital and put pressure on the German Government to water the currency and ruin the country. They believe, or affect to believe, that the way to deal with these gentry is to seize their property in the Ruhr, where they own the coalfields and factories, in which event they will force the German Government to comply with the Allied demands. They repudiate all idea of permanent occupation, but some of us think they protest too vigorously, or at best that circumstances may be too strong for them. In these conditions Bonar Law played for time. He considers a break almost inevitable, but he wants to postpone it for a few

[1]Diary 26th Nov. 1922. [2]Nicolson, *Curzon,* pp. 282–348.

weeks to give the Lausanne Conference a chance. The one chance at Lausanne is a continuance of Allied unity, and the one chance of Allied unity is no break over reparations. He played his hand quite deftly and firmly, and was very lucky to succeed in inducing Poincaré to adjourn until Jan. 2nd. He did this by getting hold of Poincaré alone, and explaining how difficult it would be for him if his first act after coming into power was to announce a break with France. He told Poincaré his Govt. was more favourable to France than any other. How often I have heard Lloyd George use precisely the same language! Anyhow, Poincaré gave him the adjournment, though it may bring about his own fall. Bonar Law is more tricky than I suspected. Before the meeting on Sunday afternoon [10th] he wanted to meet the Belgians (Theunis and Jaspar) alone, and asked them to Downing St., and for some reason he did not want Poincaré to know that they were conspiring. (Vain thought! Foreigners always tell!) I met them all coming downstairs together. Theunis and Jaspar entered the Cabinet room by the usual entrance from the hall. Bonar came in through another door from the private secretary's room. Seeing M. Poincaré in the Cabinet room he turned to the Belgians (whom he had just left at the bottom of the stairs) and greeted them effusively, *shaking them by the hand*. And the *Morning Post* and other papers this morning are contrasting the 'straightness' of Bonar Law with the obliquity of Ll. G.! The latter would not have done this, I feel sure. It makes me suspect that Bonar was behind Warren Fisher all the time.

The new figure at this meeting was Mussolini the Italian Prime Minister, who has come into office on the shoulders of the Fascisti by Cromwellian methods, and has already flouted his Parliament. He raised the one laugh at rather a dour meeting. Poincaré had just been explaining that he had come to London with a mandate from the French Parliament, and Bonar Law had capped it by saying that whatever he agreed to was subject to Parliamentary approval. Mussolini then began, amid a roar of laughter, 'My Parliamentary position is rather different'. He had spoken quite seriously and flushed like a schoolboy when the others laughed. He made one or two half-slighting references to the Italian Parliament. Mussolini has a cruel mouth but is otherwise attractive and far more decided and less balancing than any Italian Prime Minister I have met. He was of course wholly ignorant of reparations and splashed about rather wildly. His experts used to pass in notes from outside and the Marquis della Torretta,[1] the Ambassador, who sat beside him, would push these in front of him at appropriate moments. Mussolini would glare at them with eyes that seemed to get bigger and bigger with lack of comprehension, and would then translate them into French in a way which showed he understood nothing of their contents. His French was

[1] Marchese Pietro della Torretta was appointed Italian ambassador in London 15th Nov. 1922.

very good indeed, and in the main he made a good impression. Bonar Law made the usual mistake of beginners at international conferences of pledging all to secrecy and refusing any information to the Press. Of course the foreigners gave everything away, as they always do, and our Press is furious. I had solemnly warned Bonar that all this would happen, but he refused to listen. Partly to save Bonar embarrassing questions after his silly speeches and partly in order to avoid publicity in my association with the conference, which I knew must fail, I took elaborate precautions to dodge the Press, going in and out through the Treasury. So far my presence has not been announced.

For Hankey, and indeed for Bonar Law, the year ended far better than had at one time seemed likely. Hankey had very skilfully saved the government from the folly of scrapping the Cabinet Secretariat, and had preserved all the essentials of the system he had built up over so many years. As for 'the government of the second eleven' it had survived its first severe tests with flying colours; and despite the slow progress at Lausanne and the prevailing cancer of unemployment at home there seemed no good reason why it should not survive, and even gain strength. For at the end of December Hankey was able to tell Law that Balfour had remarked to Eric Drummond that he 'would be willing to join Bonar Law's government for a year'. To that offer Law replied that 'he would sooner have Balfour than all the rest [of the dissident Conservatives] put together'.[1] But it was not to be; for on his return from Geneva in the autumn of 1922 Balfour confined his activities to the rôle of Elder Statesman until in April 1925 he became Lord President of the Council in Baldwin's second administration.

Meanwhile as was his wont Hankey was keeping in touch with his former chief, towards whom he certainly felt great respect – if not affection such as Asquith had inspired.

*Diary 21st December 1922*[2]

To-day I lunched with Lloyd George. We walked together from Abingdon Street, where he works, to Vincent Square where for the moment he is living and back. I was struck by the extraordinary cordiality and respect with which he was greeted by all classes in these rather poor streets. He displayed no bitterness and warned me against allowing personal bitterness to interfere with one's prospects. The only hint of bitterness was against Lord Curzon

[1]Diary 28th Dec. 1922.

[2]This entry is written on the back of an account of the Lausanne Reparations Conference, and Hankey himself seems to have forgotten its existence.

who, he said, just before the meeting at the Carlton Club had promised to 'play the game'. He did this, according to Lloyd George, in Lord Balfour's presence. Ll. G. did not appear in the least worried at the attacks on his Greek policy . . . He was also not worried about the repudiation by the *New York Times* of the American rights over his book on the war owing to the publication of articles on current topics. He said that he was receiving plenty of fresh offers for the American rights. Ll. G. said that Bonar Law's Ministry had made a very bad impression in Parliament. It was a one man show, and he did not think that Bonar Law unaided could stand the strain of a long parliamentary session. He had special contempt for Baldwin. He himself had no desire to upset Bonar Law. He could bide his time, and when the moment came he would have a real fight on definite issues. Meanwhile, by writing, he was making five times as much money as he ever made as Prime Minister. He intended to show up French policy, contrasting their extravagant expenditure on armaments with their bad financial position. He was very sympathetic about my own difficulties [with Warren Fisher], and commended the line I had taken . . .

During the last days of the year Hankey managed to get a short holiday – after which he was once again drawn into the whirlpool of discussions on Reparations.

*Chapter 12*

# From Bonar Law to Baldwin. January-December 1923

WE have seen how by the end of 1922 Hankey found himself – contrary to his more pessimistic prognostications – working on exactly the same principles as before the fall of Lloyd George. But the drastic reduction of staff which he had accepted in order to preserve the Cabinet Secretariat greatly increased his difficulties when he found that he was still expected to provide the secretaries not only for the Cabinet, the C.I.D. and most of their sub-committees, but also for the International Conferences which Lloyd George's more severe critics had, somewhat ignorantly, proposed to discontinue. Thus there was conspicuous irony, which provoked caustic comments from Hankey, in the fact that on the last day of 1922 he crossed the Channel once again to act as secretary at another Inter-Allied conference on Reparations. The British delegates were Sir John Bradbury and Sir Frederick Leith Ross[1] of the Reparations Commission, Niemeyer of the Treasury and Crowe from the Foreign Office. Bonar Law and Lloyd-Greame represented the Cabinet, and the number of private secretaries and lesser officials were little below the Lloyd George scale. Curzon and Sir William Tyrrell, his chief adviser, joined the party in Paris from the Lausanne Conference. The Marquis of Torretta and Signor Avezzano represented Italy; and Hankey's long-standing acquaintances Theunis and Jaspar once more came from Brussels.

The first deliberations among the British delegates revolved around a new and complicated scheme for the settlement of reparations devised by Bradbury – which, according to Jones, the Cabinet had approved

[1] 1887–1968. Financier and economist. Private secretary to Asquith 1911–13. British representative on Financial Board of Reparations Commission 1920–25. Chief Economic Adviser to government 1932–46. Attended many conferences in between the wars as principal British financial expert.

without really understanding it.[1] When Poincaré and his colleagues came into conclave Hankey found the proceedings 'rather a dour affair', since neither the British nor the French Prime Minister possessed 'the sparkle of Briand and Lloyd George'. Hankey soon found himself taking all his meals with Law – 'just as I used to [do] with Lloyd George'.[2] Though he missed the brilliance of Lloyd George's conversation and repartee he collected some good stories from Law and Lloyd-Greame. When the former enlarged on Birkenhead's 'treachery' to Lloyd George Hankey held up his hands and said he could only echo the favourite phrase of Henry Wilson 'Oh! You frocks!'. To which Lloyd-Greame, not unreasonably, riposted 'Yes. Henry Wilson claimed that soldiers ought to have a monopoly of intrigue'.[3] Curzon was 'very effusive' to Hankey, and 'said he had never missed me so much as at Lausanne, and that without me the Secretariat-General was hopeless'. On hearing this eulogy 'Crowe scowled'.[4] Certainly Hankey was remarkably quick to notice the reaction of any member of his entourage to the remarks or attitude of others present. Perhaps the secret of his influence lay, at any rate in part, in this acute perceptivity.

As regards Bradbury's scheme, Hankey described it as '*mal dressé*'; while Theunis called it 'hopeless in presentation'.[5] 'Lloyd George', added the Belgian, 'would never have presented such a document' – which embarrassed Hankey as he 'felt it was true'. The essence of it was that a large sum in reparations required the restoration of German credit in order that a loan might be raised. Bonds were to be issued which, according to Hankey, Germany 'could redeem on very favourable terms at the outset', but which would become increasingly less favourable if she fell behind with payments. A four year moratorium was to be granted 'to encourage her to restore her finances, raise a loan, redeem early and so pay reparations'. The French would only agree to 'a very partial moratorium accompanied by "*gages productives*" [sureties for production]'; which, remarked Hankey, 'would compel Germany to pay so much that in our view her credit would not be restored and she could not raise a loan. The French scheme would kill the goose that

[1]*Middlemas*, I, p. 224. [2]Diary 7th Jan. 1923.
[3]To Lady Hankey 1st Jan. 1923. [4]To the same 2nd Jan. 1923.
[5]In March 1923 Bradbury threatened to resign from the Reparations Commission, and in the following June he repeated the threat. Bradbury to Baldwin, 16th June 1923. Baldwin papers, Vol. 125, p. 221.

lays the golden eggs'.[1] After three days a complete deadlock was reached. Whatever faults Bradbury's scheme may have suffered from it has a clear affinity with the Dawes and Young Plans of 1924 and 1930, whereby further efforts were made to restore the German economy whilst maintaining the principle that reparations should be paid in some form.

*Diary 7th January 1923*

... On the last day Poincaré tried once or twice to work himself into a rage, but Bonar Law was so good tempered and agreeable in manner that Poincaré couldn't work up anything like a real outburst. The rupture was therefore a mild one, and we parted rather in sorrow than in anger. On the day of our departure some of the French officials were talking about the next conference. There was general regret we could not reach agreement, but nothing of tragedy ... Bonar Law talked to Poincaré and waved to him as the train left. Then he shut the window with a bang, threw himself back in a seat, and said as he glanced back 'Now *you* can be damned!' That was the only sign of irritation he showed, except once when Poincaré, in an outburst early in the conference ... abused Sir John Bradbury ... Bonar was very stiff, and very properly defended Bradbury.

For my own part I was very busy, but mainly with the *procès-verbaux*, which I took single-handed ...[2] I rather avoided intervening in matters of policy, though I did urge Bonar Law, in the event of a break, to refer the whole question to the League of Nations. He was not unfavourably disposed to this suggestion, and may yet adopt it. [Here Hankey analysed the political situation in France, Italy and Belgium now that 'we have definitely broken with them'.] My advice to Bonar was not to withdraw from the Conference of Ambassadors, the Reparations Commission and the Rhine[land] occupation, but simply to watch events. ... The Americans will certainly remonstrate if France goes into the Ruhr ...

One point to note is that the newspapers are quite wrong in suggesting that there was no lobbying or back-chat at this conference [in contrast to Lloyd George's methods of course]. Crowe was sent to try and lobby the Italians into supporting our plan on Wednesday [3rd]. At the President's lunch on Thursday they promised us support, but failed us when the conference met. Lloyd-Greame told me that many nice things were said to Bonar Law and himself about me. 'He is not only Secretary to the Supreme

[1]Diary 7th Jan. 1922. *Punch* published a cartoon at this time using precisely the metaphor in Hankey's last sentence 'The Goose that Couldn't or Wouldn't'. It showed an expostulating Poincaré protesting to a languid Bonar Law over the behaviour of a goose in a *pickelhaube* (German army helmet). See Blake, *Bonar Law,* p. 484. [2]See Cab. 29/97.

Council but also Supreme Secretary' someone (I think Millerand) said ... All this is very good for Bonar Law.

On 11th Poincaré achieved what Hankey had long considered to be his true aim, and the French occupied the Ruhr. The Germans at once embarked on a campaign of passive resistance, reparations deliveries stopped altogether, and the value of the mark plummeted. Obviously the economic recovery of Germany – and with it that of all the western world – was further off than ever. And what was more ominous in the long view was that the militarist and extreme nationalist elements in Germany had received a powerful boost; for the widespread disorder produced in Germany presented Hitler with the opportunity to make his first bid for power – in the abortive Munich 'Beer Hall Putsch' of November 1923.[1]

We saw earlier how, immediately Bonar Law came into power, Hankey placed the settlement of the American debt high on the Cabinet's agenda. Since the middle of 1920 British policy had been that we would demand no more from our creditors than we had to pay to America.[2] But such altruism held little appeal either to President Harding's administration or to the debtor nations of Europe; for the former was as determined to exact full payment from Britain (despite the fact that much of the borrowed money had been passed directly to the other Allied nations) as the latter were determined to exact full payment for all war costs and damage from Germany.[3] Law's Cabinet was therefore under pressure to obtain a settlement of a debt which, by early 1923, amounted to $4,686 millions. It should be mentioned that in June of the previous year Lloyd George had proposed to send a mission to U.S.A. with the same purpose as was placed on the somewhat inexperienced shoulders of Baldwin six months later.[4] We cannot here follow the details of the protracted negotiations conducted with the Americans; but Hankey's diary adds a little to what Jones, Davidson

[1]See Elizabeth Wiskemann, *The Rome-Berlin Axis* (Collins Ed., 1966, pp. 31–2).

[2]See for example Hankey to Lloyd George 19th May 1920 on Churchill's proposal for mutual remission of war debts. The matter had come before the Cabinet the previous day. Lloyd George papers F/24/2/36.

[3]For a full discussion of the War Debts problem see Blake, *Bonar Law*, pp. 490–6, *Baldwin*, pp. 128–48. Lloyd George's *The Truth about Reparations and War Debts* is not reliable in this matter.

[4]*Baldwin*, p. 133 effectively demolishes Lloyd George's later statements about his Cabinet's intentions in 1922.

and others close to the centre of affairs have recorded about the crisis which ensued.

*Diary 3rd February 1923*
The Government had a very near shave from breaking up this week. Baldwin, the Chancellor of the Exchequer, returned from Washington last Saturday [27th Jan.], having been recalled because the Prime Minister could not accept his desire to close with the American terms for funding the Debt. Bonar Law made it perfectly clear that he would resign rather than accept. With two exceptions all the members of the Cabinet were in favour of acceptance.[1] On Tuesday evening [30th] a break up of the Cabinet appeared absolutely inevitable. I saw Bonar Law and obtained his permission to draft the compromise based on the idea of a provisional settlement, justified by the new factors which have arisen since Baldwin left for America. I made a very strong case out of the French action in the Ruhr, which has made the economic future and exchanges very uncertain, so that the moment was extremely bad for committing ourselves to payments extending over 62 years. In the end, however, Bonar Law 'piped down'[2] owing to the extreme difficulties in which his party would be placed if he resigned at this moment. My impression is that Bonar Law would not have been sorry to get out of it. The French action in the Ruhr; the difficulties at the Lausanne Conference, which at that moment appeared almost certain to break down; the visible crumbling of the Entente, which it was Bonar Law's announced policy to maintain, and which had a place in every election address; the danger to our force at Constantinople which Lord Curzon insists from Lausanne in continuing to maintain there against the advice of the soldiers, sailors and diplomats at Constantinople; the danger to our forces at Mosul; the imminent risk of trouble in Egypt and the bleak financial outlook and continued unemployment, have in combination produced a state of affairs which cannot be very attractive to him. . . .

When Hankey remarked that Bonar Law had 'piped down' what he meant was that the Prime Minister had yielded to the strong persuasion of his colleagues, and especially Devonshire, Cave and Baldwin, not to resign. But Hankey's cool feelings towards Baldwin, which undoubtedly derived from his conduct at the Carlton Club meeting, were enhanced by the grave indiscretion he committed when he was interviewed by journalists on arrival at Southampton on 27th January. To a person of

[1]The exceptions were Lord Novar (1860–1934) Secretary of State for Scotland, and, much less emphatically, Lloyd-Greame. See *Baldwin*, p. 146.
[2]Naval slang for 'gave way' or 'shut up', derived from the Bosun's call for the crew of a warship to turn into their hammocks.

Hankey's reticence and long experience in handling the Press it seemed incredible that a Minister entrusted with a very delicate mission should have publicly admitted that he was in favour of accepting the American offer of settlement, and believed it to be the best that could be obtained.[1] The debt negotiations actually dragged on until early July, when the agreement was signed; but argument over the fairness of the terms accepted continued for many years. Hankey's view appears to have been one of moderate satisfaction at getting so tricky a problem out of the way; but he never laid claim to financial or economic expertise.

The American debt settlement of 1922 produced an amusing aftermath about a decade later. On 14th December 1932 Lloyd George crossed swords with Sir Robert Horne in Parliament about the processes whereby the settlement had been reached. He quoted verbatim the Cabinet Minute approving the agreement, and demanded publication of all the papers.[2] This breach of confidence, and of propriety, produced a strong reaction on Hankey's part. He at once consulted the Attorney-General and Lord Chancellor, and then sent Lloyd George through Sylvester a threat of prosecution against the newspaper editors concerned, and against Lloyd George himself if the Minutes were published. Needless to say Lloyd George was far too astute to invite such dire penalties and dropped his demand; but one can easily imagine the cynical smile with which the former Prime Minister received a threat which he must have guessed to have been initiated by his own erstwhile intimate adviser and confidant. And the prolonged battle fought by Hankey himself from 1946 to 1961 to overcome the ban on his own memoirs leads one to conclude that, when it comes to publication of 'indiscretions', it all depends on who is in a position to apply the notorious Official Secrets Act and who wishes to evade its provisions.

To return to 1923, early in March the government was, in Hankey's words 'knocked endways' by a succession of by-election defeats – including that of Griffith-Boscawen, the Minister of Health, in the

[1] *Baldwin*, pp. 143–4. Ten years later Hankey drafted a sharp reply for Baldwin to send to Lloyd George in answer to his proposal that the Cabinet minutes on the Balfour note to U.S.A. of 1st August 1922 regarding cancellation of war debts should be published. Baldwin to Lloyd George (draft in Hankey's hand) 15th Dec. 1932. Baldwin papers Vol. 110.

[2] Cab. 21/372. The Minute quoted by Lloyd George was Cabinet 46(22) Conclusion 2. See also Hankey's memorandum of 15th Dec. 1932. Cab. 63/45.

contest for the previously safe Conservative seat of Mitcham.[1] Cabinet business was disrupted, and Hankey told his wife that 'Bonar Law looks more than ever like a mute at a funeral or an undertaker's assistant'. A lunch alone with Balfour had convinced him that 'this Government will have to come to terms with Chamberlain, Horne, Worthington-Evans, Birkenhead and Balfour if they are to do any good'. A lot depended in his view on Lloyd George. If he came to terms with Asquith then 'his late [Conservative] colleagues' would have 'a decent opportunity to go with Bonar Law'. Otherwise he foretold that the government would get 'rockier and rockier', and finally suffer defeat in Parliament. For his own part he could not 'shed any crocodile's tears over the misfortunes of the government' – despite the fact that he enjoyed 'excellent personal relations with all its members'. But the truth regarding the political manoeuvring of these times was that there was not the slightest chance of the two sections of the Liberal Party composing their differences; and almost two years were to pass before the split in the Conservative ranks was healed.

At this time Balfour showed Hankey his private correspondence with Bonar Law about the request made by the latter that he should continue to represent Britain on the League Council. It included 'some caustic remarks' about the transfer of League business from the Cabinet Secretariat to the Foreign Office; but Hankey told Balfour that he was 'jolly glad to get rid of it'.[2]

Despite the uncertain prospects of the government it did carry out the promise to institute a far-ranging enquiry into 'the co-operation and co-ordination between the Navy, Army and Air Force generally, including the question of establishing some co-ordinating authority, whether by a Ministry of Defence or otherwise'. On 6th March Hankey warned Adeline that he was likely to be extremely busy with 'a big C.I.D. enquiry in the air', and three days later the Cabinet approved the setting up of a sub-committee under Lord Salisbury with the terms of reference quoted above. The other members were Baldwin, Curzon, Derby, Peel, Weir and Hoare. Hankey at once circulated his 'Suggestions as to the conduct of the Enquiry' and put forward firm proposals

[1]Two other government defeats took place almost simultaneously – those of Lieut.-Col. G. F. Stanley, Parliamentary Under-Secretary to Home Office at Willesden on 3rd March and of Major J. W. Hills, Financial Secretary to Treasury, in the Edge Hill Division of Liverpool on 6th.

[2]To Lady Hankey 5th March 1923. See also p. 306.

for the conduct of its first meeting.[1] The Salisbury Committee threw off a sub-committee under Balfour, aided by Peel and Weir, which was to investigate 'the relations of the Navy and Air Force as regards the control of Fleet air work'. In other words it was to decide whether the Navy was to be allowed complete control of the Fleet Air Arm, or whether the status of that branch as a part of the Royal Air Force, instituted in 1918, was to continue.[2] This was of course the issue on which the Admiralty and Air Ministry had been at loggerheads ever since the war, and over which all efforts at mediation had so far proved fruitless. Some two months later Lord Derby, now Secretary of State for War once more,[3] asked Baldwin for a committee to be formed to examine and report on the future strength of the Army; but Hankey stepped in and suggested, very sensibly, that such a proposal must be carried out in co-ordination with the future of the Navy and R.A.F., and that the Salisbury Committee was the obvious body to fulfil such a purpose – a good example of the way he prevented fragmentation of wide-ranging surveys.[4]

Hankey was deeply involved in both enquiries from the beginning, and although his sympathies probably lay with Beatty and the Admiralty on the naval aviation issue he displayed such admirable impartiality that he completely won the confidence of Trenchard and Weir – the two chief advocates of 'unified air'. However, over the suggestion that a Ministry of Defence might replace the three Service Departments he showed no such scruples. For example when Sir Herbert Creedy, the Permanent Secretary of the War Office, wrote to him strongly opposing such a proposal Hankey stored up his arguments for use at an opportune moment.[5] A few days later he dug out and drew Law's attention to a speech Churchill had made in the House of Commons a year earlier, which he described as 'a very valuable contribution to the question of the Navy–Air controversy and to the question of a Ministry of National Defence'. Though Churchill had described such a Ministry as 'an ultimate goal' Hankey judiciously added that 'he clearly explained why

[1] Memo. of 9th March 1923. Cab. 63/35.

[2] See Roskill, *Naval Policy*, I, pp. 372–87 for a full account of the deliberations of both sides.

[3] See Vol. I, p. 251, *note*.

[4] Derby to Baldwin 28th May and Hankey to Baldwin 30th May 1923. Baldwin papers.

[5] Creedy to Hankey 9th March 1923. Cab. 21/351.

the question could not be rushed'.[1] One may reasonably assume that it was with the same object in view that he got Salisbury to invite those old and firm allies of the C.I.D. Haldane and Esher to give evidence to his committee – especially as in a holograph postscript to his letter to Haldane he offered him a preliminary talk over lunch at his club.[2] Having mobilised his forces in this manner – to use the military metaphor which Hankey himself employed over his engagement with Warren Fisher – he could afford to scoff at those sections of the Press which still showed hostility towards him. And when an M.P. asked a Parliamentary Question about the Secretary of the C.I.D. having insufficient work, and alleged 'the objection of the public to creation of "Pooh-Bah" posts of this kind, this gentleman now having three separate posts', the questioner was quietly but firmly put in his place by Baldwin.[3]

We cannot here follow the details of the two enquiries, which were in fact extremely protracted.[4] The Balfour Committee reported to the parent body on 21st July, and came down against the Admiralty on the main issue. This was without doubt primarily due to the efforts of Lord Weir, since both Balfour and Peel were sympathetic towards the Navy's claim.[5] Its recommendations were accepted by the Salisbury Committee – with Derby and Amery dissenting. In the Salisbury Committee's Interim Report of 12th June great stress was laid on increasing the strength of the R.A.F. 'for Home and Imperial Defence'.[6] Actually it was French preponderance in bombers which inspired that

[1]Hankey to Law 13th March 1923. Bonar Law papers BL 111/21/103. Churchill's speech was made on 21st March 1922 during the debate on the Air Estimates. Parl. Deb., Commons, Vol. 152, Cols. 379–93. The remarks to which Hankey drew Law's attention are in Cols. 390–1.

[2]Hankey to Haldane and to Esher 21st March 1923. Haldane and Esher papers respectively.

[3]Question by Commander C. W. Bellairs, 28th March 1923. Parl. Deb., Commons, Vol. 162, Cols. 492–3.

[4]The Salisbury Committee met 19 times and the Balfour Sub-Committee 12 times. For the former 67 memoranda were prepared (N.D. Series) and for the latter 19. In addition both bodies took a great deal of verbal evidence. Roskill, *Naval Policy*, pp. 373 ff.

[5]See W. J. Reader, *Architect of Air Power* (Collins, 1968), pp. 98–109. The Balfour Committee's report is Cmd. 1938.

[6]Cmd. 2029 is the published but incomplete report of the Salisbury Committee. The full report is C.P. 461(23). Cab. 21/469. Also C.I.D. 463B of 15th Nov. 1923.

recommendation – though that fact was omitted from the published version of the Salisbury Committee's report.

In his dealings with the Balfour sub-committee Hankey went to great pains to preserve a strict neutrality between Amery and Beatty on the Admiralty's side and Hoare and Trenchard on the Air Ministry's. That he carried out this balancing act with great dexterity is shown by the letter he sent to Weir towards the end, reminding him of the repeated requests made by Beatty that he should 'wind up the Admiralty case'. 'In this event', said Hankey, 'Air Marshal Trenchard ought also to be allowed to wind up the Air Ministry case'. He therefore urged that, even though the committee's report was completed, both protagonists should be heard again before it was sent in.[1]

When the result of the long deliberations by the Balfour Committee became known in June they were received with very bad grace by the Admiralty. They first tried to upset the recommendations by direct action; and, when that failed, they waged a long and none too scrupulous campaign to achieve the same purpose by indirect means. Hankey continued to try and find a compromise agreement which was acceptable to both parties; and that he accomplished by tactful persuasion and with Haldane's help in the Trenchard–Keyes agreement of April 1924.[2] Unhappily that was not the end of a departmental squabble to which we will revert later.

For the Salisbury Committee Hankey himself wrote a long and detailed memorandum on the 'Existing Methods of Co-ordination in Defence Matters'.[3] It was in six parts, and described not only the machinery which he had done so much to create, but the history of the C.I.D. before and since the war, and the part it played in co-ordinating defence problems with the Dominions. We may usefully quote his peroration:—

'From the above [Parts I–V] it will be seen that the means of co-ordination in operation in the C.I.D. apply not only to the Service Departments but to every Department of State which has any action to take on the outbreak of war. In the larger questions of policy the Treasury, Foreign Office, Colonial Office and India Office are involved only to a slightly less extent than the Service Departments. In matters of detail a great many other Departments are concerned . . . In the widest sense of the term this Committee [of Imperial Defence] may be said to fulfil many of the functions of a Ministry of Defence.

[1]Hankey to Weir 12th June 1923. Weir papers.

[2]Roskill, *op. cit.*, pp. 389–91. [3]N.D. 8 of 3rd April 1923. Cab. 21/469.

Whatever may be said in regard to a Ministry of Defence in the narrower sense of a Ministry for the three Services, it appears essential that our Defence Organisation as a whole should not be less broadly based than at present. The machinery should continue to be sufficiently elastic in character to focus into our Defence Organisation all the resources of the Empire ... Whether, as suggested in some of the memoranda from outside, some further development is required in order to prevent lack of co-ordination between the three Service Departments in the working out of plans ... is a matter for the Sub-Committee [i.e. the Balfour Committee] to consider'.

One feels that the advocates of a Ministry of Defence never stood any real chance of success in 1923 with so formidable, experienced and persuasive an advocate on the other side – especially as Hankey himself wrote the final report of the Salisbury Committee.[1]

Lord Salisbury and his colleagues did, however, recommend one important innovation – namely the institution of the Chiefs of Staff Committee as a sub-committee of the C.I.D. They also recommended placing on the three service heads a collective responsibility for advising the Cabinet on defence policy, additional to their individual responsibilities for their own services. But as Hankey at once became secretary of the new body, which met for the first time on 17th July 1923, and his Military Assistant Secretaries invariably served its numerous subcommittees in the same manner, he at once acquired a powerful influence over it – if only because Chiefs of Staffs came and went, while he went on, seemingly, for ever. He at once started the new series of C.O.S. Minutes and Memoranda which were to become so famous in World War II.[2]

Despite his heavy involvement in the deliberations of the Salisbury and Balfour Committees, and with the birth pangs of the Chiefs of Staff Committee, Hankey managed to prepare at this time a long survey of the history of 'Food Supply in the Great War' for the Agricultural Tribunal of Investigation.[3] This body had been set up to report on the advisability of increasing home food production in order to reduce dependence on imports and so a repetition of the crisis of 1917.

[1]Hankey to Trenchard 5th Feb. 1954.

[2]The first volume of C.O.S. Minutes (July 1923–Jan. 1927) is in Cab. 53/1. That of C.O.S. Memoranda (Nos. 1–50, June 1923–Sept. 1926) is in Cab. 53/12.

[3]C.I.D. 442B of 4th June 1923. In C.I.D. 444B of 9th Aug. 1923 Hankey summarised the preparations made to maintain food supplies in the event of another war. Cab. 4/10.

Hankey enlisted the aid of Ernest Fayle,[1] the author of the official history of 'Seaborne Trade' in this work, and it may have been he who drew Hankey's attention to the findings of the Royal Commission of 1903–4 on 'Supply of Food and Raw Materials in War'.[2] At any rate in the evidence Hankey gave to the Tribunal he quoted the Royal Commission's view that 'in the future, as in the past, we must look mainly for security to the strength of our Navy, and we must rely only in a less degree upon the widespread resources of our mercantile fleet, and its power to carry on our trade and to reach all possible sources of supply . . .'. Hankey reaffirmed that view in 1923, merely adding that 'due co-operation from adequate air forces' as well as naval strength was now essential[3]; and those principles remained a cardinal point in his philosophy of national defence to the end of his days. Nor did the Agricultural Tribunal disagree with his views; yet in 1942 we were again brought to the edge of starvation and defeat by the renewal of the attack on our merchant shipping.[4] Small wonder that when history thus repeated itself in World War II Hankey should have viewed the policy and strategy of the government of the day with strong disapproval.

Before the Salisbury and Balfour Committees had rendered their final reports there took place an event which was to have a profound influence on Hankey's position – namely the resignation of Bonar Law on 20th May. We saw earlier how Hankey had noticed at the beginning of Law's term of office that his health was not good; and he was now found to be suffering from the cancer of the throat which proved fatal five months later. The story of the choice of successor, of Law's refusal to put forward a name, and how it came to pass that the King sent for Baldwin and not Curzon – to the bitter disappointment of the latter – has often been told.[5] Here we need note only two points. The first is that Colonel Ronald Waterhouse,[6] principal private secretary to Bonar

[1]C. Ernest Fayle, author of *History of the Great War: Seaborne Trade* (3 Vols., Murray, 1920–24).

[2]Cd. 2643–5 of 1905 Lord Balfour of Burleigh was Chairman.

[3]'Notes for Hankey's evidence' to this Tribunal, dated 4th June 1923. Cab. 63/35.

[4]See Vol. I, pp. 356–7 and 380–4. The quotation used by Hankey in 1923 is para. 269 of the Commission's Main Report.

[5]See Blake, *Bonar Law*, pp. 516–27; James, *Davidson,* pp. 148–66; Nicolson, *Curzon*, pp. 354–6; *Baldwin*, pp. 160–9 and *Middlemas*, I, pp. 235–7.

[6]Later Sir Ronald Waterhouse (1873–1942). Private secretary to Sir Frederick Sykes as Chief of Air Staff 1918, and to Bonar Law and Austen Chamberlain

Law, whom Davidson has justly described as 'a subtle and somewhat sinister figure',[1] probably made improper use of Davidson's memorandum on the succession when he met Stamfordham at Aldershot on 20th May, by giving the impression that it represented Law's views. The memorandum was 'in fact a cogent argument for choosing Baldwin and rejecting Curzon'[2]; but it did not have Law's authority or approval. The second point is that when Austen Chamberlain criticised Harold Nicolson's account of Curzon's confident expectations on receiving Stamfordham's telegram requesting him to come to London, Nicolson ruefully admitted, on reading the actual text, that 'I must say that Lord Curzon was extremely optimistic in interpreting it as a summons to take office'.[3] There seems little doubt that, of those whom the King consulted, it was Balfour's influence that proved decisive; and he 'recommended emphatically in favour of Baldwin'.[4] We have seen how Hankey wrote long entries in his diary about the fall of Asquith and of Lloyd George; but he left no comparable account of the days following Bonar Law's resignation. Though he was not of course in the inside circle of those who were advising the King (or in Beaverbrook's case intriguing to secure the premiership for Curzon) it is hard to believe that he had no inkling of what was going on. The only clue to his attitude is a diary entry made nearly six months later.

*Diary 11th November 1923*

Once more my diary has been dreadfully neglected . . . I have passed without note Bonar Law's retirement, Baldwin's succession and Bonar Law's death [on 30th October]. Poor Bonar never had the nerve for the job of Prime Minister. The responsibility preyed on his mind and, I feel sure, hastened on his cancer. Baldwin has nerve but scant capacity and I fear will not last long. He is astonishingly maladroit with the Cabinet. For example he sprang his protectionist policy on them only a day or two before he announced it at Plymouth [on 25th October].[5] Half his colleagues were Free Traders by conviction and were horribly shocked. This was straining loyalty too far. It

---

1920–21. Principal private secretary to Bonar Law, Baldwin and Ramsay MacDonald as Prime Ministers 1922–28.

[1]James, *Davidson*, p. 162. [2]*ibid.*, p. 155.

[3]Nicolson to Chamberlain 30th May 1934. Chamberlain papers AC 40/6/34.

[4]James, *Davidson*, p. 157.

[5]This is a considerable exaggeration. Though the Cabinet only discussed the matter on 23rd October, when Hankey took the minutes, Baldwin's colleagues had known the way his mind was moving since at least 15th. See *Baldwin*, pp. 222–30.

was the same with the Imperial Conference, just over. Baldwin and Curzon sent the telegram responding to President Coolidge's hint that he would take part in a Reparations Conference without a word to the Dominion Prime Ministers. I warned him that they were a bit restive, and that he ought at least to ask them to take cognisance of it, more particularly as he had sent it in the name of the [Imperial] Conference. Nevertheless he actually allowed Curzon to send a second telegram to Poincaré before he said a word about it, which evoked a very proper protest . . .

As regards the choice between Baldwin and Curzon there is plenty of internal evidence that Hankey regarded the former as inexperienced and uninspiring; and he had suffered so much from Curzon's arrogance over so many years for us to be sure that he would not have wanted him for Prime Minister. The truth seems to be that Hankey deplored the exclusion from office of the two most brilliant men of the period – Lloyd George and Churchill, and hankered after a new Coalition with Lloyd George again in supreme power. Unhappily British puritanism had been so powerfully stimulated by Lloyd George's dubious methods and irregular life that his acceptance by the electorate was out of the question – at any rate for many years. And most influential Conservatives thoroughly mistrusted the brilliant if erratic Churchill – even after he had crossed the floor of the house and joined their party in 1924. Lloyd George did still have a considerable following among ex-Coalition Conservatives; and it is difficult not to regret that they and the Liberals did not make common cause in mid-1923 when the political situation was highly fluid. Hindsight suggests that the whole history of 'between the wars' might well have been profoundly altered had they done so.

From Hankey's personal point of view the accession to power of Baldwin was a disaster. All observers of the contemporary scene agree that, of all the Prime Ministers whom he served, Baldwin was the one with whom he was least in sympathy. Nor is there any doubt that the lack of sympathy was reciprocated. Lawrence Burgis for example has recalled Baldwin's remark that Hankey 'had no bowels' [of compassion presumably][1]; while Sir Horace Wilson and Lord Bridges both confirmed to the author the lack of rapport between them.[2] Perhaps Burgis's story of how Baldwin would do the *Daily Telegraph* crossword puzzle while travelling up from Chequers on Monday mornings instead

[1]To the author 27th Aug. 1968.

[2]Interviews 7th July 1967 and 15th Aug. 1968 respectively.

of studying the official papers carefully prepared by Hankey for that day's Cabinet best explains the fundamental difference between the two men's outlook and methods. But the accession of Baldwin to power not only marked a signal decline in Hankey's standing and influence – it also marked the simultaneous rise of Tom Jones to the position of close and intimate adviser to the Prime Minister. Though Jones and Hankey continued to work together as a team, and no harsh words seem ever to have passed between them, Hankey would have been less than human had he not felt some hurt at his comparative relegation. To illustrate the extent of his loss of intimacy, whereas the visitors' book at Chequers records that he stayed there four times in 1921 his name does not reappear in it until 1931 – at which time MacDonald was in power.[1]

Jones's diaries and letters reveal very clearly why he was so sympathetic to Baldwin. Not only did Jones exude a pervasive charm, but he could always produce the apt quotation or draft a telling passage for a speech. His friends were innumerable and influential, and his idealism probably made him appear to Baldwin as the perfect representative of the sound and solid British working class, regarding whom the Prime Minister maintained a paternalist, but in fact increasingly obsolete view.[2] A shrewd if hostile observer has remarked that to Baldwin Tom Jones 'incarnated the wisdom of the ages', and administered his 'daily dose of soothing syrup'.[3] But that applied to the period of the 'appeasement' of Germany in the 1930s, when Jones was working busily for friendship with Hitler – while Hankey was struggling to rearm the nation so that it could at least negotiate from strength, and would be prepared for war if it could not be averted. That, however, all lies far ahead of the stage now reached in our story, and we must return to the middle of 1923.

As soon as the Salisbury and Balfour Committees' reports had been approved Hankey made it plain that he intended the Chiefs of Staff 'to get to work at once'. In close consultation with Lord Salisbury, for whom he wrote a paper on 'Co-ordination of the Defence Forces',[4] and with Beatty, Cavan and Trenchard, he circulated the proposed membership of the C.I.D. and 'the individual and collective responsi-

[1]Information from The Curator, Chequers, 8th Feb. 1970.

[2]See *Baldwin*, Chapters I and II.

[3]A. L. Rowse, *All Souls and Appeasement* (Macmillan, 1961), pp. 36 and 37.

[4]C.P. 346(23) of 27th July 1923. Cab. 21/291.

bilities of the three Chiefs of Staff'.[1] It would, however, be a considerable exaggeration to represent that the new body at once proved an outstanding success. The differences between the service departments, and especially between the Admiralty and Air Ministry, were too deep-seated to yield even to Hankey's persuasive tact; and the C.O.S.s were all the time engaged in a struggle to get for their own services the largest possible share of the ever decreasing sums which Parliament was prepared to vote for defence. Nor was Hankey free from complaints by the C.O.S.s themselves about the minutes taken of their meetings. Thus at the end of the year Trenchard represented that their discussions were not being recorded fully enough. Hankey replied in conciliatory vein that 'we of course only want to make the sort of record which the Chiefs of Staff would themselves like to have', and he was prepared to make 'as full a record as you like'. But he anticipated that very soon the Committee would come to discuss 'very secret matters indeed' of which only 'the briefest possible record' could judiciously be made – notably in the case of war plans. Though he would discuss the matter with the triumvirate, he suggested that reports which went to the full C.I.D. might be kept brief, while minutes of the C.O.S.s own discussions 'could be fuller'.[2] The C.O.S. Memoranda and Minutes indicate, however, that as time passed full records were kept in both cases.

As to the usefulness of the new committee, between July 1922 and February 1926 twenty questions were referred to the Chiefs of Staff for 'joint appreciations'[3]; and in many of those cases the result was a vague and unsatisfactory compromise. Though Hankey later defended the Chiefs of Staff of the 1920s and early 1930s against such a charge, Lord Bridges remarked to the author on their tendency 'to fight their own corners', and on their fundamental disagreement with regard to the part that air power would play in war. Although in Bridges's view the Air Staff exaggerated the effects of air bombardment, the other two services were consistently jealous of and hostile towards the Air

[1]*ibid.* The Warrant defining the responsibilities of the C.O.S.s, drafted by Sir Warren Fisher, was circulated at the end of April 1926. C.I.D. 685B (Revise). In the following July Hankey sent Fisher the final proof, which he described as 'a pompous document'. Fisher minuted sarcastically on it 'Almost thou temptest me to ask for one for the civilians [i.e. the top civil servants] likewise'. Cab. 21/291.

[2]Trenchard to Hankey 31st Dec. 1923 and reply by latter of same day. Trenchard papers.

[3]List in Cab. 21/291.

Ministry. He admitted that what he called 'the miserable Ten Year Rule', which Hankey later attacked so severely, made all defence problems vastly more difficult than they need have been; but he considered that the creation of a Ministry of Defence in the late 1920s or early 1930s would have made 'a vast difference'.[1] If Bridges's view be accepted (and this historian feels that it has much force behind it) we cannot acquit Hankey of error in strenuously and repeatedly opposing such a measure – until the first step in that direction, namely the appointment of Sir Thomas Inskip[2] as Minister for Co-ordination of Defence, was virtually forced on him early in 1936. On the other hand it is only fair to record that Lord Bridges, when interviewed towards the end of his life, showed himself to be a markedly hostile witness on Hankey; and, as the reader of our first volume will recall, he had a large hand in the banning of the publication of Hankey's memoirs. Bridges also showed strong disapproval of Hankey having kept a diary while Secretary of the Cabinet.

Hankey had hardly got the Salisbury and Balfour committees reports out of the way, and had by no means yet reconciled himself to Baldwin's seemingly casual ways, when he had to prepare for another Imperial Conference and its subordinate but simultaneous Economic Conference, which the Lloyd George government and the Commonwealth Prime Ministers had agreed upon in principle at the close of the 1921 conference. It now seems plain that the decision to meet again so soon was premature, and that too little time was allowed for the preparatory work. But there were good reasons for the Conservative government to favour a meeting with the representatives of the Dominions; and some of the Cabinet saw in the development of trade within the Empire and Commonwealth, shielded by measures of Preference, a cure for the prevailing disease of unemployment. Here the chief trouble lay in the election pledge given by Bonar Law and inherited by Baldwin that Tariff Reform would not be introduced without a new appeal to the electorate; and Lloyd George was standing on the sidelines of the political field waiting for an opportunity to leap into the fray on the issue of Protection. Nor were the Dominion Prime Ministers unanimous

[1]Interview 15th Aug. 1968.

[2]1876–1947. 1st Viscount Caldecote 1939. Lawyer and politician (Cons.). Solicitor-General 1922–24, 1924–28 and 1931–32. Attorney-General 1928–29 and 1932–36. Minister for Co-ordination of Defence 1936–39. Secretary of State for Dominions 1939 and 1940. Lord Chancellor 1939–40. Lord Chief Justice 1940–46.

on this delicate issue. Whereas S. M. Bruce[1] of Australia came out whole-heartedly for Imperial Preference and received support from W. F. Massey of New Zealand, Mackenzie King[2] of Canada took the opposite view; and Smuts's eyes were chiefly focused on the involvement of Britain in European affairs, which, like Hankey, he viewed with disfavour, and on the peculiar political problems of his own Dominion.

Hankey was, of course, primarily concerned with defence rather than with the economic problems to be discussed. On 20th September he sent Salisbury lengthy 'Draft Notes for a speech on Imperial Defence', and during the next few days he revised and polished those notes into their final form.[3] It is interesting to remark that he stressed the creation of an airship route to the Far East as an important development in Imperial communications. His proposal was that Amery, the First Lord, should then place the Admiralty's views, especially with regard to the Singapore base, before the conference and that Hoare, the Secretary of State for Air, should follow with a statement on his department's policy and purposes. The War Office had declared, somewhat supinely, that they did not 'consider the time ripe' to put forward any proposals on military defence.[4] On the same day that he sent Salisbury the draft notes Hankey forwarded to Bruce a copy of the long memorandum on the history and functions of the C.I.D., originally produced for the Salisbury Committee, for which the Australian Premier had evidently asked.[5]

Baldwin took the chair at the opening session on 1st October, and after his carefully rehearsed speech of welcome he called on Salisbury

[1] 1st Viscount Bruce 1947 (1883–1967). Australian politician (Cons.) and statesman. Represented Australia at League Assemblies 1921–38. President of Council of League of Nations 1936. Prime Minister and Minister for External Affairs 1923–29. Minister, then High Commissioner in London 1932–45. Represented Australia in War Cabinet 1942–45. Chairman, World Food Council 1947–51 and of Finance Corporation for Industry 1947–57.

[2] William L. Mackenzie King (1874–1950). Canadian politician (Lib.). Leader of Opposition 1919–21 and 1930–35. Prime Minister 1921–30 with short break in 1926. Secretary of State for External Affairs 1935–46. Represented Canada at many Imperial Conferences, and at Councils and Assemblies of League of Nations and United Nations Organisation.

[3] Cab. 21/469. Though unsigned these notes bear the clear imprint of Hankey's work.

[4] Dated 25th Sept. 1923. Cab. 63/35.

[5] Hankey to Bruce 20th Sept. 1923. Cab. 31/469.

to present the general aspects of defence problems; and he was followed by Amery and Hoare – exactly on the lines Hankey had proposed.[1] As to the Singapore base, which Hankey had strongly supported from the beginning, he was probably well content with the conclusion that the conference 'took note of the deep interest' of Australia, New Zealand and India in that project, and still more with Massey's announcement of a first contribution of £100,000 towards the cost.[2] Later sessions did not go smoothly. The demand of the Indian representatives for equal citizenship annoyed Hankey and included some telling thrusts at Smuts for his racial policy in South Africa; while Curzon caused a flurry by sending telegrams to Washington and Paris about reparations in the name of the Dominion Prime Ministers.[3] The one absolutely clear outcome of the conference was the insistence of the Dominions on full consultation. No longer were they content to allow Downing Street to speak for them. As to defence, the final conclusions were not without contradictions; since they reaffirmed the need to provide 'adequate defence of the territories and trade of the several countries comprising the British Empire', but expressed 'earnest desire for the further limitation of armaments'.[4] When the conference came to discuss League of Nations' affairs and the recent Italian aggression against Greek Corfu, all delegates deplored the weakness displayed by the League. Smuts, however, described the Ambassadors' Conference, to which the complaints of Greece had been referred, as 'the real villain of the piece'; while Curzon blamed the very unjust decisions reached by that body on France and Italy. He asked for 'a declaration by the British government in agreement with the Dominions' about the League's future, and urged that it should include an expression of 'their intention to give [it] their warmest support'. Hankey recorded that in consequence the Imperial Conference agreed that 'a strong resolution in support of the League' should be placed 'in the forefront' of their conclusions; and so it was, though it did little to strengthen that body.[5]

Hankey's disgruntlement over the differences voiced at the Imperial

[1]*Middlemas*, I, pp. 245–7 contains a graphic description by Tom Jones of the meetings of the conference on 1st, 3rd and 5th Oct.

[2]Cmd. 1987. Roskill, *Naval Policy*, I, pp. 405–8 deals in detail with the naval problems discussed.

[3]See Diary for 11th Nov. 1923. [4]*ibid.*

[5]Hankey's holograph notes, undated but probably 13th Oct. 1923. Baldwin papers, Vol. 110, pp. 76–8.

Conference and the anodyne nature of the resolutions arrived at is made plain by his diary entry.

*Diary 11th November 1923*

. . . Throughout the conference I don't think Baldwin uttered one sentence, unless prompted by the Colonial Office or myself. At the end we got in a dreadful mess because Mackenzie King would not accept a passage on foreign affairs prepared for the [final] report by Curzon, and relating particularly to Egypt and the Near East [this referred to the special British interests in that area, foreshadowing the suggestion of a 'Monroe Doctrine' for Britain made at the time of the Kellogg–Briand pact of 1928]. Curzon would not give way. Mackenzie King could not – for he was asked to put his name to recommendations of the very type which had brought down his predecessor Meighen as the result of his own attacks.[1] No one seemed to care much, and the whole negotiation was left to me. After nearly 24 hours I had reached an *impasse*. Neither side would budge. At last I had to get Mackenzie King to draft a reservation. It was a poisonous document, and would have placed a sword in the hands of Hertzog[2] and the South African secessionists. After showing it to Curzon, in order to frighten him, I took it to Smuts, who said he would go home at once rather than allow it to be entered [in the report]. We then devised a formula and went together both to Mackenzie King and Curzon, inducing both, with some reluctance, to accept rather than break up the Conference. This is the barest summary of a most difficult negotiation.

It was essentially a 'Permanent Official' conference. Our politicians only read out what the officials – mainly Masterton Smith and myself – told them to say. It was a deplorable spectacle compared with Lloyd George & Co. It is the first time I have ever felt that the ability of the Dominions' side was superior to the British side of the table – except for Lord Curzon of course. I still continue as Secretary of the Cabinet, and am on the best of terms with Baldwin and his colleagues. I have however a very low opinion of their ability I regret to say. Curzon is the only first class man, except for Bob Cecil, who is unfortunately a crank. Salisbury, however, has done well in the Defence Committee, where we have had a most fruitful and successful

[1]Arthur Meighen (1874–1960). Canadian politician (Cons.). Solicitor-General 1913. Minister for Mines, then of Interior 1917. Member of Imperial War Cabinet 1918. Prime Minister and Minister for External Affairs 1920–21. Prime Minister again 1926 for few months. Minister without Portfolio 1932–35. Senator 1932.

[2]James B. M. Hertzog (1866–1942). South African politician (Nat.). Fought against British in Boer War. Minister of Justice 1910–12. Prime Minister and Minister for Native Affairs 1924–29. Minister for External Affairs 1929–39. Formed Coalition Government with Smuts 1932, as United Party and carried through policy of racial segregation. Defeated on proposal of neutrality in World War II Sept. 1939.

year. I get on admirably with him. I feel, however, that Baldwin has ruined the Government's prospects with his extraordinarily ill-timed Protectionist stunt. *Quem deus perdere vult, prius dementat.*

An interesting point is that none of Curzon's biographers – Lord Ronaldshay, Harold Nicolson or Leonard Mosley – mentions the clash between Curzon and Mackenzie King at the 1923 Imperial Conference; nor do the official proceedings make clear what happened. Fortunately Mackenzie King himself kept a diary, parts of which have been published; and that entirely confirms the account in Hankey's own diary. The Canadian Prime Minister regarded the Resolutions on foreign policy and defence presented to the conference as 'traps to inveigle the Dominions into matters on which they had no direct interest or responsibility'. 'Why', he demanded, 'should he be asked to approve the fortification of Singapore or endorse British policy in Egypt?' As Hankey had a big hand in the drafting of those Resolutions it must quickly have become plain to him that he was in for a rough passage with Mackenzie King. The latter described how in secret session on 5th November he, standing practically alone, opposed the Resolutions in question, and even threatened that, if they were adopted Canada would not participate in future conferences. He recorded that during the two following days he had talks with Hankey, who did his utmost to close the gap between what Curzon (and no doubt Hankey himself) wanted, and what King was prepared to accept. Finally King 'told Hankey that if Lord Curzon held to the position he did I must add a reservation', and that he would be 'absolutely firm on this'. Hankey then went to Smuts, whose attitude on these questions was somewhat ambivalent; and, after a meeting between the three of them, the offending paragraphs were dropped and a rider added to the effect that all the proceedings of the conference were subject to Parliamentary approval.[1] Though King's biographer calls this outcome 'a triumph' for him, and claims that he 'beat off the attack [of Curzon backed by Bruce and Massey] almost single-handed', the wisdom of hindsight suggests that in the long view it was Curzon and Hankey who were right; since when in 1939–41 new threats arose to western democracy Canada could not escape involvement in either Europe or the Far East.

Though Hankey himself felt little cause for satisfaction over the

[1]R. MacGregor Dawson, *William Lyon Mackenzie King*, Vol. I (Methuen, 1958), pp. 473–8.

outcome of the Imperial Conference of 1923 his efforts to make it a success earned him a warm tribute from one of the Ministers chiefly concerned. The Duke of Devonshire, the Colonial Secretary, wrote that it had been mainly due to Hankey that 'the conference began, continued and ended in an atmosphere of goodwill'.[1]

For an account of the somewhat bizarre processes whereby Baldwin decided to go to the country on the issue of Protection in the autumn of 1923 the reader must be referred to the political biographies and diaries of the period.[2] Tom Jones remarked that 'Hankey and I were given no opportunity of putting out red lights'[3]; but as Jones had become Baldwin's most intimate adviser, and on at least one recent occasion Baldwin had given Hankey a brush-off,[4] it was surely unfair of Jones to attribute any share of the responsibility to his Chief. Hankey's diary makes plain not only the surprise and shock he felt at the way the decision was taken, but that Jones *was* in a position 'to put out red lights'.

The question of policy was settled at a Cabinet on the afternoon of 23rd October. Hankey's minutes end with the clearest of indications regarding what was decided. 'There was only one way, not to cure, but to fight unemployment', they record, 'and that is to protect the home market against foreign manufactures. Without the machinery for this, we are impotent to meet any of the dangers described [i.e. from the competition of foreign, and especially French and German, goods produced by unfair means of competition 'including currency bounties and low wages abroad']. The alternatives, viz: to do nothing, or to temporise by putting the McKenna duties on a few more articles, are of no value'.

Polling Day was fixed for 6th December; and the results left the government in an overall minority of 95 seats. Labour increased its representation from 142 to 191, and became the second strongest party for the first time in history.

*Diary 9th December 1923*
. . . On returning from the Cabinet [presumably of 23rd October] which

[1]Duke of Devonshire to Hankey 13th Nov. 1923.
[2]See *Baldwin*, Ch. X, James, *Davidson*, pp. 182–9 and *Middlemas*, I, pp. 249–62.
[3]*Middlemas*, I, p. 261.
[4]Jones's diary for 23rd Oct. 1923 'but the P.M. gave Hankey a clear indication that he was not wanted' – at a discussion with M.P.s at the House of Commons. *ibid.* p. 250.

reluctantly agreed to allow Baldwin to announce a policy of Tariff Reform to the party meeting at Plymouth I had written the Minutes in manuscript and, after obtaining Baldwin's approval, I sent them to the King. I told no one in the office what had been decided, but I remarked to my private secretary [Burgis] 'Baldwin will be out of office in six weeks'. Yesterday morning I saw him. '*Moriturus te saluto*' he said, and told me he was about to resign. He did not seem particularly dejected. It is an astonishing affair. I found that the Tariff Reform decision had been taken without consulting a single official. When one thinks of the wealth of information on the subject in the Treasury, Board of Trade, Boards of Customs and Inland Revenue, and Labour Department it is incredible that not even a hasty investigation was made before the decision was taken. Lloyd-Greame, the President of the Board of Trade, knew quite well that the figures were against the possibility of Tariff Reform helping unemployment. Neville Chamberlain, the Chancellor of the Exchequer, soon discovered it. He turned on his private secretaries to rake together figures to support the speeches, but found that they all told the wrong way! Fancy a business being conducted on such lines – to take a decision to consult the shareholders before the experts have been asked to examine the proposition and state the figures!

The most extraordinary feature of the election was that almost the whole of all the Prime Minister's speeches was written by Tom Jones, my No. 2, who is a passionate Free-Trader, an intimate and trusted friend of Lloyd George, voted Liberal, and at the 1906 Election was engaged as Professor of Economics at Glasgow University in supplying pabulum for the Free-Trade campaign. Nowadays Tom Jones is a Civil Servant, and is supposed to have no politics. Moreover he is the most loyal creature under the sun, and sweated blood for Baldwin. Still no one could believe that he would be chosen to write the P.M's election speeches in a Tariff Reform campaign. It shocks me inexpressibly that the P.M. should have his speeches written for him, or even read them.[1] But Baldwin, though a nice fellow, is not of the stuff of which British Prime Ministers are made . . .

From all of which one may deduce that, to use his own metaphor about Bonar Law's ministry, Hankey 'shed no crocodile tears' over Baldwin's departure from No. 10.

[1]But Hankey himself provided an enormous amount of material for the speeches of Lloyd George and of other Coalition Ministers e.g. Curzon.

*Chapter 13*

# The First Labour Government. January-October 1924

EVENTS did not actually move as fast as Hankey had anticipated when he wrote up his diary on 9th December, since the King very properly insisted that Baldwin must 'face Parliament and only resign after a defeat in the House of Commons'.[1] Baldwin acquiesced, and the new Parliament accordingly met on 15th January. Four days later Hankey had his first encounter with Ramsay MacDonald. To try and solve the difficulty produced by few of the probable members of the new Government – including MacDonald himself – being Privy Counsellors Hankey got Baldwin's permission to visit him 'and talk things over'. Taking 'careful precautions to elude the vigilance of the Press' he betook himself to Hampstead and found the house 'exactly opposite Belsize Park station'.[2] The resulting interview is best described in the words of his own retrospective diary entry.

*Diary 11th October 1924*
. . . I was taken up to a small room at the very top of the house – almost an attic or garret, with books all round, books and papers all over the tables, and Ramsay in the middle of them looking gaunt and thin and wearing a very ancient and threadbare 'sporty' coat. I took to him at once, and *vice versâ* I think. After discussing the Privy Council arrangements I passed to the Cabinet Secretariat. I said I did not know whether he proposed to have a Cabinet Secretary, but that in any event I recognised it to be a very personal matter, and if he wanted someone else I begged him not to consider my personal feelings . . . He replied very frankly that he had made many personal inquiries about me, and had heard nothing but good of me, and he begged me to remain, and added that he hoped we should become friends as well as associates. After describing in some detail the work of the Cabinet Secretariat I passed (with some trepidation) to the Committee of Imperial Defence.

[1]Harold Nicolson, *King George V* (Constable, 1952), pp. 382–4.
[2]MacDonald's home was at 9 Howitt Road, Hampstead.

Rather to my surprise he displayed a good deal of interest, and, pointing to his bookshelves, he told me that General Smuts had said that he [MacDonald] possessed one of the best military libraries in London. He promised me every support in the C.I.D. He then went on to discuss very frankly his difficulties in finding Labour Ministers suited to take charge of the three Service Departments, and in particular pressed me for details as to how far as Prime Minister he could expect to control their policy. I told him through the medium of the C.I.D. he could do a good deal. After an hour's conversation I had to run the gauntlet of the Press again . . .

Lawrence Burgis recalls that when MacDonald came into power for the first time Hankey greatly feared that he would 'cut the C.I.D's throat'. Such fears no doubt explain the caution, plainly echoed in the foregoing diary entry, with which he broached the subject of the Committee's future. But on returning to his office after his first interview with MacDonald Hankey said to Burgis 'I like that man and am going to do all I can to help him'. Assuming that Burgis's memory is correct – and there is no reason to question it – one must surely conclude that Hankey was taken in by MacDonald's eloquence and personality. At any rate he was to have good cause to modify substantially his initially favourable impression eight months later. Hankey also soon found MacDonald's inexperience a serious handicap. Burgis remembers how he proposed that no memoranda should be put up by departments to the Cabinet without his having first read and approved them. Such extreme centralisation would of course have destroyed Hankey's whole system of running the machinery of government, and according to Burgis, when MacDonald's proposal reached him he 'politely but firmly told him that it was nonsense'.[1] Hankey certainly never lacked the moral courage to remonstrate very strongly – even with Prime Ministers – if they made ridiculous proposals. But he always did so in such a tactful manner that no offence was taken.

On 21st January the Conservatives suffered the expected defeat in Parliament. Hankey was in the House for the crucial debate, which he described as 'very interesting and exciting'. 'It had been intended', he told Adeline, 'to adjourn the House until 12th February, and the Prime Minister moved this. Objection was taken, however, by some of the Liberals, and, as it was past 11.30 [p.m.], under the rules of the House the motion could not be taken, and the matter stood open until to-day'.

[1]Interview with Lawrence Burgis 7th April 1967.

This, he continued, upset the provisional programme he had arranged, whereby Baldwin would resign at 11.15 a.m. on 22nd and a Privy Council was to be held at noon at which MacDonald would be sworn a Privy Counsellor. The King would then immediately have sent for MacDonald, who would have 'kissed hands' as First Lord of the Treasury and completed his Cabinet after lunch. This arrangement would, however, have produced 'a very awkward Parliamentary situation', since the motion for the adjournment of the House stood in Baldwin's name as Prime Minister; and that office was in fact held by MacDonald, who would have had the right to sit on the Treasury Bench as Prime Minister. Since it was 'physically impossible' for the Conservative Ministers to transfer all their seals of office to their successors in time MacDonald would thus have found himself sitting among his opponents. According to Hankey he was 'the first to spot this difficulty'; he spoke to Baldwin and then went to see the Speaker. The outcome was an agreement that the King would ask MacDonald to form a government, but he would not 'kiss hands' until after the adjournment of Parliament. Hankey at once began to search for precedents, and by the morning of 22nd he had found two which 'though not identical served'. This led to his writing at once to Stamfordham informing him that he found it was customary for the Clerk of the Privy Council to 'take the King's pleasure as to whether the Princes of the Blood Royal' should attend a Council at which the seals of office were to be handed over. The Prince of Wales was, he said, the only relevant person in the country at the moment, so Hankey asked whether he should be summoned.[1]

The Baldwin Cabinet met for the last time at 10.30 on the morning of 22nd, by which time Hankey had it 'all cut and dried'. Then the Palace turned 'sticky', and 'wanted to postpone the whole business until after the meeting of Parliament' [on 12th February]; but Hankey considered that this 'obviously created a bad precedent', and finally 'won all parties round to the Speaker's plan'.[2]

Hankey recorded that at the last Cabinet of the outgoing government Baldwin made 'a perfectly delightful speech . . . thanking me for all the help I had given. I was very much moved, as it was quite

[1]Hankey to Stamfordham 22nd Jan. 1924. RA GV K1918/163.

[2]To Lady Hankey 22nd Jan. 1924. Hankey's diary for 11th Oct. 1924 also contains a full account of these events, in almost identical terms to those he wrote to his wife.

unexpected, and I was told to put a Minute in the record'.[1] Then his 'carefully organised meeting of the Privy Council took place', and he was vastly amused when J. H. Thomas came up to him in the ante-room while he was 'gossiping among a group of tall Court officials and said "'Ullo, *Maurice*! 'Ow are you?" '. The Court officials 'looked surprised', but Arthur Henderson, the new Home Secretary, was 'particularly cordial and assured me it was the beginning of a new era'. In the afternoon of this busy day Hankey 'wound up the Cabinet and Defence Committee business of the old Government'. This no doubt included all the work carried out by Davidson who, as Chancellor of the Duchy of Lancaster, had been appointed Chief Civil Commissioner in May 1923 with responsibility for preparing in absolute secrecy for the maintenance of public services in the event of serious industrial trouble. Lancelot Storr,[2] Hankey's former assistant, who was now a close friend and ally of Davidson, recommended 'leaving it to Hankey' to consult Davidson's successor Josiah Wedgwood on the tricky question of the custody of this politically explosive material; but in fact Wedgwood left the whole of it untouched – to the great advantage of the nation when the General Strike was declared in 1926.[3]

To return to the afternoon of 22nd January, at 5.30 Hankey was sent for by the King, who described his interview with MacDonald and kept Hankey for an hour discussing the recent developments. Then he received a message from MacDonald to come and see him at the House, and found him 'surrounded by his new Cabinet'. Hankey was called on 'to address them about the arrangements for to-morrow's [Privy] Council', and 'drilled them in the various formalities'. Lord Thomson,[4] the new Secretary of State for Air, then whispered to Hankey that 'MacDonald was at a loose end as regards dinner'; so he promptly invited the new Prime Minister to dine *tête à tête* at his club, and 'put up champagne to celebrate the occasion'. Contrary to Hankey's expectations, but to his great pleasure, this act of hospitality to the Labour

[1]The Minute reads 'The Prime Minister, on behalf of his colleagues, expressed the thanks of the Cabinet to Sir Maurice Hankey for the ready assistance which he had at all times rendered to members in discharge of his duties as Secretary of the Cabinet'. Cabinet 6(24) Conclusion 2 of 22nd Jan. 1924. Cab. 23/46.

[2]See Vol. I, p. 458, *note*. [3]James, *Davidson*, pp. 178–80 and 228–9.

[4]Christopher B. Thomson, 1st Baron 1924 (1875–1930). Soldier and politician (Lab.). Served on staff of Supreme War Council 1918–19. Secretary of State for Air 1924 and 1929–30. Killed in disaster to airship R.101 on maiden flight to India 5th Oct. 1930.

leader was warmly welcomed by the Committee of the United Service Club.[1]

Simultaneously with Hankey's transfer of his loyalties to his new master a number of tributes reached him from those whom he had been serving. The two reproduced below are particularly eloquent, since the first came from a Minister with whom he had often found himself out of sympathy, and the second from the head of a department in which his naval background could very easily have aroused suspicions regarding his impartiality.

*Curzon to Hankey. 1 Carlton House Terrace. 22nd January 1924.* Holograph

My dear Hankey,

For the first time for nearly 9 years I shall not be sitting with you in Council at No. 10. It will be a great deprivation, so let me say what a pleasure it has been through all these years to profit from your unfailing courtesy, unruffled good temper, sound judgment and immense experience.

You have been a mainstay of Government in these troubled and even perilous times, and I am convinced that you will be able to render services as great – they may be even greater – to Government in the near future.

I am glad of a holiday which you neither get nor take. But the greatest pleasure in coming back if ever I do will be to find myself working with you again.

Yours ever

*Sir Samuel Hoare to Hankey. 18 Cadogan Gardens, S.W.3. 24th January 1924*

Dear Hankey,

We have seen so much of each other during the life of the last Government that I feel I must add a few lines to the hurried goodbye that I said in Downing Street. I am most deeply grateful to you not only for the constant and sympathetic interest that you took in Air questions, but also for the wise and friendly advice that you never failed to give to me. I shall always look back to my work on the Committee of Imperial Defence as the most interesting, and I hope the most useful, that I had in office, and to my relations with you as one of the pleasantest incidents in a somewhat confused and controversial period. I much hope that although our official relations may for the time be ended, we may still see something of each other in ordinary life.

Yours sincerely

[1]To Lady Hankey 22nd Jan. 1924.

*Hankey to Hoare. 2 Whitehall Gardens. 25th January 1924*[1]
My dear Hoare,

Very many thanks for your kind letter. One does not make many new friends at my time of life, so it is with enhanced satisfaction that I can feel that our very cordial official relations have led to the establishment of a personal note. I hope that before long we may again work together officially, and I warmly endorse the hope that we may meet in private life.

Yours very sincerely

It thus came to pass that on the very day MacDonald replaced Baldwin the relative positions of Hankey and Tom Jones as the closest and most intimate adviser of the Prime Minister were reversed. There can surely be no doubt that Hankey welcomed this sudden change of fortune whole-heartedly. A few months later he was able to write to Smuts that his dinner with MacDonald had proved 'the basis of excellent personal relations which have been renewed at Chequers and elsewhere'. MacDonald, he went on, 'affects to regard me as a reactionary, and I retaliate by treating him as a visionary, but this is all more or less banter. I continue as Secretary of the Cabinet as of yore'.[2] According to Hankey only one innovation was introduced in Cabinet when Labour took office. 'The old convention', he wrote many years later, 'was "No Smoking before lunch". It was observed until 1924 when MacDonald renewed it at the outset of his first meeting. But J. H. Thomas came in later and, knowing nothing of the rule, continued to smoke. Soon others lit their pipes, and the rule vanished – to the intense discomfort of non-smokers!'[3] If Hankey was delighted to find himself once more in the favoured position he had enjoyed under Asquith and Lloyd George, Tom Jones was, not surprisingly, somewhat sore over the fact that he was apparently 'to have nothing to do with the new Prime Minister'. But it was unfair of him to write that Hankey 'has not lifted a finger to help'[4]; for Hankey had always fought to retain Jones in the Secretariat – even when Warren Fisher had brought his heaviest broadsides to bear. And Jones's reappointment as Principal Assistant Secretary soon after MacDonald came into power certainly owed a great deal to Hankey. In sum, though Hankey cannot

[1]Templewood papers. Tem. V. 1.
[2]Hankey to Smuts 1st April 1924. Smuts Archive.
[3]Aide-Mémoire by Hankey on Cabinet Procedure, written for Sir Norman Brook, then Secretary of the Cabinet 10th Nov. 1949.
[4]*Middlemas*, I, pp. 267–8.

have relished the special relationship which Jones achieved with Baldwin, he never gave vent to such feelings; but when Jones found himself relegated to his proper status of deputy to Hankey he seems to have shown less forbearance than his Chief. His resentment was, however, probably mollified when in February new troubles arose in Ireland over the appointment of a Boundary Commission to establish the frontier between the Free State and Ulster, and he once more found himself called upon to play a leading part in the delicate negotiations between President Cosgrave and Sir James Craig.[1]

Hankey's delight at having so easily won MacDonald's support for the C.I.D. (though it was soon to be severely shaken) was no doubt heightened by the appointment of his old friend and supporter Haldane to act as Chairman in the Prime Minister's absence. The intimate correspondence between them, which had never altogether lapsed during Haldane's years in the political wilderness, was now renewed with very evident pleasure on both sides. Haldane at this time wrote 'It is a great advance having a Cabinet Secretary with an agenda and minutes, and Hankey does the job to perfection. MacDonald is a better chairman than Asquith was, which may be due to the new system'.[2] And when their new association proved brief Haldane wrote 'a kind and sympathetic letter', to which Hankey replied 'I cannot express how much I have appreciated working under you during the last few months', and assuring Haldane that 'real progress' had been made.[3]

In fact the 'progress' consisted chiefly of the immediate circulation by Hankey of a number of papers dealing with the future work of the C.I.D. and what he regarded as the most important current problems in Imperial Defence. Probably because he was dealing with Ministers who were not familiar with the C.I.D's organisation he produced a full

[1]The editorial notes in *Middlemas*, I, pp. 271–87 are very confusing. The Boundary Commission was set up under Article XII of the Anglo-Irish Treaty which provided that, in the event of Northern Ireland opting out of the Free State (as it at once did) a commission should be set up to determine the boundary 'in accordance with the wishes of the inhabitants, so far as may be compatible with economic and geographic conditions'. The neutral chairman appointed was the South African Judge Mr. Justice Feetham, and after long delays, caused chiefly by Ulster's refusal to nominate a member, the Commission met on 6th Nov. 1924 – two days after the fall of the Labour government. Its deliberations were concluded on 3rd Dec. 1925, and only minor adjustments of the boundaries were recommended. See *Report of the Irish Boundary Commission* (Irish Univ. Press, 1970).

[2]Dudley Sommer, *Haldane of Cloan*, p. 404.

[3]Hankey to Haldane 10th Nov. 1924. Haldane papers.

statement of its Standing Sub-Committees, their history and their functions. It may help the reader to have a summary of the organisation as it was early in 1924. The Standing Sub-Committees were the Chiefs of Staff's Committee, the Overseas Defence and Home Defence Committees, which together formed the Joint Defence Committee and had sub-committees on Man Power and Censorship; the Committee for Co-ordination of Departmental Action (or War Book Committee); the Imperial Communications Committee; the Committee on National Service in a Future War; and, finally, the Committee on the Official Histories. In addition an Advisory Committee on Trading and Blockade, the Principal Supply Offices Committee and one to handle Insurance of Shipping were being formed.[1] As to current problems, these included the defence of Egypt and the Suez Canal, regarding which Hankey summarised all the past history, and the building up of oil reserves for the Navy.[2] But he can hardly have been surprised that the new Cabinet chose rather to turn their attention to the question of building new cruisers, for which the Admiralty was pressing, and to the future of the Singapore base. On 24th February they set up a committee under J. R. Clynes,[3] the Lord Privy Seal, to review both issues.[4] Admiral Beatty, the First Sea Lord, made such a masterly statement of naval policy and needs that J. H. Thomas, the Colonial Secretary, was moved to remark that 'from a strategical point of view he considered nothing more need be said' about Singapore. But other considerations than strategy prevailed, and on 17th March the Cabinet approved a statement MacDonald was to make next day that the government 'could not ask Parliament to go on with this scheme', since their policy was to support 'international co-operation through a strengthened and enlarged League of Nations'.[5] The views of the Dominions were obtained, but whereas Canada and the Irish Free State offered no opinion, Australia, New Zealand and Newfoundland all wished to go ahead with the base. From South Africa, however, Smuts telegraphed that he 'welcomed the abandonment of the scheme, which would be out of keeping with the spirit of the Washington agreement' – a curious statement, observing that Singapore had been deliberately excluded from the non-fortification clause in the Four Power Pact signed at Washington. Hankey later

[1]Memo. by Hankey of 30th Jan. 1924. Cab. 63/36.
[2]C.I.D. 478B and 479B of 31st Jan. and 2nd Feb. 1924.
[3]See Vol. I, p. 571, *note*. [4]C.P. 15(24) of 20th Feb. 1924.
[5]Minutes in R.S.(24) Series Cab. 27/236.

told Smuts, rather ruefully, that his telegram 'was of the utmost assistance' to the government.[1] In the House MacDonald said that he thought he 'might claim that we have a large measure of sympathy in the Dominions with our international policy'[2]; which, bearing in mind the emphatic disapproval of the government's policy with regard to Singapore expressed by three of the Dominions, provides an early example of MacDonald's capacity for equivocation.

Sir Harry Batterbee,[3] a close associate of Hankey's over the many years during which he served in the Colonial (later Dominions) Office, recalls an interesting example of Hankey's methods of working to achieve his purposes, and how he tried to stop the cancellation of the Singapore base in 1924. Batterbee visited Singapore that year in order to study the problem of the base from the point of view of the Dominions, and soon after his return he discussed the matter, and the government's intentions, with Hankey. He at once took Batterbee round to No. 10 to see MacDonald. Batterbee urged the Prime Minister to regard the construction of the base as 'an expression of gratitude towards Australia and New Zealand for their help in the war', and stressed that those two Dominions would regard its cancellation as something not far short of betrayal. MacDonald, who at first showed signs of boredom over the subject, was plainly impressed by Batterbee's argument; but he could not carry his Cabinet with him on such an issue.[4]

A few days after MacDonald announced the government's decision regarding the Singapore base Hankey took him severely to task about a remark in his speech of 18th March in the House to the effect that the C.I.D. was not an adequate 'organ of co-ordination'. After quoting the Prime Minister's exact words[5] he said that 'there may or may not be weaknesses in our present system of co-ordination, but I submit that Singapore is about the worst case that can be taken to illustrate them', since 'no question has been more exhaustively studied in the last twenty years'; and he went on to recapitulate the history of the project. The decision to build the base might, he continued tactfully, 'have been

[1]Hankey to Smuts 1st April 1924. Smuts Archive 138.

[2]Parl. Deb., Commons, Vol. 171, Col. 321. [3]See Vol. I, p. 572, *note*.

[4]Interview of Sir Harry Batterbee 10th April 1970.

[5]Parl. Deb., Commons, Vol. 171, Col. 322. The words which caused Hankey offence were 'So far as Singapore is concerned I say that we have created a Defence Committee with the Prime Minister as Chairman. That is an excellent idea, and an excellent machine if it could work. But it cannot work! It shows certain weaknesses ...'.

wise or unwise'; but it was 'impossible to contend that it was not in full accordance with the policy of successive governments'. The decision of the present government to cancel the project had been taken 'because you had adopted an entirely different foreign policy' – not because 'of any lack of co-ordination in principle or in detail among Departments or different portions of the Empire'. In consequence of MacDonald's somewhat heedless remark that the machinery of which he was the head 'cannot work' Hankey felt it 'difficult to leave matters where they are'. An enquiry appeared unavoidable 'if only in justice to those who have been trying, as they thought with success, to make it work'. He himself would welcome such an enquiry – despite the fact that the ground had been exhaustively covered by a body appointed by the previous government – presumably meaning the Salisbury Committee. 'Apparently', he added with some acerbity, 'you will not accept their report'; but he hoped that MacDonald would at least make himself 'acquainted with the facts', and offered his own services for that purpose. 'I believe', he concluded, 'that I could remove many, if not all, of your misgivings'. This was strong stuff for any civil servant to address to a Prime Minister; but Hankey had obviously been touched on the raw. All he got by way of reply was a somewhat incoherent holograph note from MacDonald 'I really have gone into this matter. The weakness is the P.M. himself and this is what I had in mind. Also the Admiralty (not as a matter of machinery but of spirit). But I shall have a talk with you one day soon. Meanwhile leave it where it is'.[1] Doubtless this brought little comfort to Hankey; nor does the promise of a talk on the subject appear to have been fulfilled.

Though the decision regarding Singapore caused dismay, even anger, in the Admiralty, and Hankey certainly sympathised with Beatty and was opposed to Smuts on this issue, the Navy fared unexpectedly well over the cruiser building programme. This was certainly not because MacDonald and his colleagues agreed with those who argued the case on strategic, Imperial or economic grounds, but simply because they were seeking fairly quick-acting measures to relieve unemployment. The true reason was made abundantly plain when C. G. Ammon, Parliamentary Secretary of the Admiralty, announced the decision to build five large cruisers in the House on 21st February;[2] and although

[1]Hankey to MacDonald 22nd March 1924 and minute by latter of 23rd. Cab. 21/469.

[2]Parl. Deb. Commons, Vol. 169, Cols. 1971 ff.

there were renewed hesitations in Cabinet during the succeeding months, chiefly because MacDonald was hoping to call a world disarmament conference, the Admiralty got their way.[1] Though there is no possible doubt regarding where Hankey's sympathies lay on these issues, which had in fact been under almost continuous discussion since 1919, it is difficult to measure how much influence he actually exerted – because he always used the method of indirect approach to achieve his ends.

In May the draft Treaty of Mutual Assistance, which had been presented to the League Assembly in the previous September after three years of deliberation, came before the C.I.D. and the Cabinet. The clauses that caused most misgivings in London were those that laid an obligation on members of the League to come to the aid of each other in the event of aggression against one of them. The Admiralty feared, with some reason, that this might involve the British fleet in conflicts which were of no concern to the nation. Hankey put forward his objections in tactful but firm terms. They rested, firstly, on the difficulty of determining who was the aggressor, and of notifying the League's Secretary-General accordingly within the period of four days specified; secondly that the decision regarding who was the aggressor had to be by unanimous vote of the Council; and thirdly on the slowness with which such forces as might be available to the League could be brought into action. His general standpoint is made clear by his statement that 'the real force of the League is moral rather than material'; and that 'material force . . . should be contemplated only in the last resort'.[2] As the C.I.D. was also opposed to this novel concept, of which Lord Cecil was the chief protagonist, it is not surprising that on 30th May the Cabinet approved a letter to the Secretary-General stating that 'The British Government is definitely opposed in principle to the proposed Treaties'.[3] Final rejection came in July.

An interesting example of Hankey's methods, which arose at about the same time as the cruiser controversy, may be mentioned here. We

[1]See Roskill, *Naval Policy*, I, pp. 419–25.

[2]'Preliminary Suggestions as to the British reply' dated 20th March 1924. Cab. 63/36.

[3]C.P. 309(24) and Conclusions of C.I.D. in C.P. 311(24). The Cabinet Minutes are Cabinet 35(24) Conclusion 3 of 30th May 1924. Cab. 23/48. In referring to 'treaties' in the plural the Cabinet was referring to the Treaty of Mutual Guarantee of 1923 as well as the Treaty of Mutual Assistance of 1923–24. Both were largely Lord Cecil's work.

saw earlier how the Channel Tunnel was always one of his bugbears, ever since it had first been adumbrated in 1906. In June 1924 the proposal was revived by MacDonald, and, after receiving a strong all-party deputation on the subject, he ordered the C.I.D. to carry out a fresh investigation. Hankey at once compiled a long paper recapitulating the whole history of the project.[1] Then he 'summoned' the former Prime Ministers who had been in power at the time when the Cabinet or C.I.D. had deliberated the matter (Balfour, Asquith, Lloyd George and Baldwin) to attend the Committee 'in solemn conclave'[2]; and he obtained an adverse report from the Chiefs of Staff as well. Small wonder that, to quote his own words, the Channel Tunnel was 'flooded out' in 1924 – despite the powerful lobby of businessmen who favoured it.[3]

If the Channel Tunnel was ancient history to Hankey so was the oft-recurring trouble over 'leakages' of Cabinet secrets; and the Labour Government seems to have been particularly prone to indiscretions – probably because most Ministers were inexperienced in handling the Press. Thus in mid-1924 the *Daily Mail* carried articles on the Cabinet's plans for dealing with Communist propaganda and the extension of strikes, and even with the C.I.D's deliberations on the Channel Tunnel.[4] When Labour returned to power again in 1929 the same phenomenon recurred, and Hankey decided that it would be best to treat the matter in humorous vein. He therefore prepared and circulated 'by direction of the Prime Minister' a collection of quotations from the classics – including Polybius, Thomas à Kempis, Francis Bacon and Hobbes – illustrating both the need for discretion and the consequences of the lack of it.[5] A copy was sent to the King, who minuted 'Very amusing, but will it have any effect?'; while Warren Fisher wrote to Hankey 'You're a perfect joy! I believe the element of ridicule may keep their

[1]C.I.D. 122A of 3rd June 1924. Memoranda 122A–129A of June–July 1924 all deal with the Channel Tunnel, and on 7th July MacDonald made a long statement on the subject in answer to a Parliamentary Question (Parl. Deb., Commons, Vol. 175, Cols. 1782–5). Hankey was present when on 26th June MacDonald received the deputation referred to here.

[2]Hankey to Asquith 19th June 1924 is the invitation to him. Asquith papers, Box 82, Item 141.

[3]Hankey to Smuts 17th July 1924. Smuts Archive 140. Hankey's 'observations' on the subject and his draft for MacDonald's statement in Parliament are in Cab. 63/36.

[4]Cab. 21/443 and 21/391. [5]Memo. of c. 12th Dec. 1931.

tongues quiet . . .'.[1] And when MacDonald himself read the memorandum in Cabinet Hankey noted that it 'provoked much hilarity'. Certainly he was far more likely to improve discretion by reminding Ministers that Carlyle had written 'Men are very porous, weighty secrets oozing out of them like quicksilver through clay jars',[2] or that à Kempis had recorded 'Oftentimes I could wish that I had held my peace when I have spoken; and that I had not been in company',[3] than by reprimanding them like naughty schoolboys. But in his dealings with the great Hankey always showed a degree of psychological perception which, in his day, was very advanced.

As was to be expected the Labour government of 1924 created a number of new Cabinet Committees, with the object of tackling problems in which its members were particularly concerned. The chief ones were the Unemployment Policy Committee under Snowden (Chancellor of Exchequer), the Industrial Disputes Committee under Clynes (Lord Privy Seal), the Committee on Indian Affairs under Lord Olivier[4] (Secretary of State for India) and the Poor Law Reform Committee under John Wheatley[5] (Minister of Health).[6] But in the long view perhaps the most important new body, and certainly the most long lived, was the Principal Supply Officers' Sub-Committee of the C.I.D. This extension of the earlier Sub-Committee on the Production of Warlike Stores was created in mid-January, and consisted of the Principal Supply Officers of the three fighting services and a representative of the Board of Trade, with the C.I.D. providing the secretary.[7] Indeed all Hankey's apprehensions about MacDonald's attitude towards the C.I.D. quickly proved without foundation; for at the first meeting he attended he said that it was 'a pleasure as well as a duty to meet the Heads of the three Service Departments and their Chiefs of Staff'. He went on to announce that as he himself could not always be present he had selected Haldane, who 'as the Committee well

[1]Clive Wigram to Hankey 11th Dec. 1931 and Fisher to Hankey 10th Dec. 1931.
[2]From *Frederick the Great*. [3]*Of the Imitation of Christ*.
[4]1859–1943. 1st Baron 1924. Colonial Service Officer and politician (Lab.). Secretary, Fabian Society 1886–90. Colonial Secretary, Jamaica 1899–1904. Governor of same 1907–13. Permanent Secretary, Board of Agriculture and Fisheries 1913–17. Secretary of State for India 1924. Author of many books on colonial government and socialist theory.
[5]1869–1930. Politician (I.L.P.). Minister of Health with responsibility for housing 1924. Became identified with advanced and revolutionary socialist views.
[6]Cab. 21/394. [7]179th C.I.D. of 14th Jan. 1924, Item 1. Cab. 2/5.

knew possessed unique experience' to act as Chairman. 'The old traditions of the Committee', MacDonald concluded, 'must be maintained', and its functions 'should be continued on the same lines as in the past'.[1] This must all have been music in Hankey's ears.

Providing the secretaries for the aforementioned new bodies was of course all in the day's work for Hankey. But early in April he ran into trouble over a complaint by Sir Patrick Hastings,[2] the Attorney-General, that the Law Officers were being insufficiently consulted about government measures before they were presented to Parliament. Hankey at once arranged a meeting with Hastings and Sir Henry Slesser, the Solicitor-General,[3] and as a result he circulated the draft of a Treasury Minute which Warren Fisher was to sign stressing the need for full departmental co-ordination on proposals before they came before the Cabinet. This was typical of Hankey, who evidently realised that Hastings's complaint had wider significance than the Attorney-General realised; and only a Treasury Minute could bring the matter to the attention of all government departments with adequate force behind it.[4] In exactly three weeks his proposal had passed through all stages and been issued. Judged by any standard this was fast work.

Perhaps the best view of the Labour government as seen by Hankey after a few months' experience is contained in a long letter he sent Smuts on 1st April.[5] He reported that they had so far received 'a great deal of good will from the British people' who, in Henderson's words, had shown 'a sporting feeling' that they 'should be given a chance'. Looked at from the inside he was able to say that they had proved 'a very business-like government' – indeed the best in that respect that he had ever served. 'They read their papers and get up their subjects', he continued; and they never allowed arrears to pile up as Lloyd George used often to do. He attributed the efficient and speedy conduct of affairs largely to MacDonald himself; but he made a very strong reservation about his carrying the Foreign Office as well as the Premier-

[1] 180th C.I.D. of 4th Feb. 1924. Cab. 2/4.

[2] 1880–1956. Barrister and politician (Lab.). Attorney-General 1924, returning to private practice after fall of Labour government as a result of disillusion over MacDonald's handling of the Campbell case (see pp. 375–80).

[3] 1883– . Barrister and politician (Lab.). Solicitor-General 1924.

[4] Cab. 21/294. The matter was discussed in Cabinet on 7th April. Cabinet 25(24) Conclusion 6. The Prime Minister approved the draft Treasury Minute on 11th and the Cabinet on 15th. It was issued as Treasury Minute F. 6064 on 28th April.

[5] Smuts Archive 138.

ship. He wrote that after Curzon's departure there was at first 'one big sigh of relief in the Foreign Office'; but it had soon become plain that 'no man or super-man' could do the two jobs properly. And he found the consequential 'signs of overwork in our Prime Minister distressing'. As to the other members of the government, though none was outstanding 'they are quite a competent lot and their team work is excellent'; and he had been pleasantly surprised to find them 'better informed' than he had expected. This he attributed to their service on the wide range of committees established earlier at Labour Party headquarters. Of course their Parliamentary position was precarious, and he had watched with amusement how they got their majority 'one day from one Party and the other day from the other'; but so far all had been well. Turning to Imperial Defence Hankey gently took Smuts to task for his opposition to the Singapore base; and he foresaw trouble 'if Japan knows that both we and the U.S.A. are powerless to exert our strength in the Far East'. Japan, he remarked prophetically, 'did not care a hang for public opinion in Europe', and 'the League of Nations is no good in her case'. As regards Europe he was sure MacDonald was 'going to work up to a big Disarmament Conference', and was engaged in trying to 'create a good atmosphere'. But Hankey had 'no use for "atmospheres" '. He had seen Lloyd George, Bonar Law and Baldwin all try to do precisely this with Poincaré; and in each case it had come to nothing. These experiences, Hankey told Smuts, explained his support of MacDonald's scepticism towards the Treaty of Mutual Assistance, mentioned earlier, for which Cecil had been working, and also his dislike of any military guarantee to France. The outlook for negotiations with Egypt was, he continued, 'not very hopeful', though MacDonald himself was optimistic. Finally Philip Snowden's first budget had reassured the City and business circles; and, although the recrudescence of strikes was disturbing, the economic outlook appeared favourable, with the number of unemployed substantially decreased. Meanwhile Lloyd George was 'biding his time', and Hankey felt that he 'hoped to get his chance when everyone else has more or less failed'. At the time of writing neither Conservatives nor Liberals wanted another election; and that helped the government. But he did not believe 'that they can hang on until the summer recess', though Curzon thought they might last until the end of the year.

Like his three predecessors MacDonald soon found that the recovery of Europe was indissolubly linked with the problem of reparations payments by Germany; but he at least had the advantage that the government of the 'hard line' French Premier Poincaré had fallen from power on 11th May and had been replaced by a left-wing coalition under Edouard Herriot.[1] The moment seemed auspicious, and in July MacDonald called a conference in London. The first stage was to consist of conversations between the former Allied powers, and especially the British and French; but after agreement had been reached between them the Germans were to be invited to take part.[2] As Adeline had taken the family to St. David's, where they had rented the Archdeaconry for a holiday, her husband was forced to put up at his club during the conference.[3]

*Diary 11th October 1924*
. . . I had not expected to be asked to take part in it [the conference], but Miles Lampson[4] of the Foreign Office, who had worked very closely with me at the Washington Conference and by now had become head of the Central European Department, insisted that I must be Secretary-General. So the Foreign Office (popularly supposed to be jealous of me, though in fact always friendly and intimate) themselves asked me to do this job! I responded by asking for Spring-Rice[5] or young Wigram[6] of the Paris

[1] 1872–1957. French politician (Rad. Soc.). Minister of Public Works and Transport 1916, and of Education and Fine Arts 1926–28. Premier and Minister for Foreign Affairs 1924–25, again Premier 1926 (for a few days) and 1932 (for six months). Minister for Public Instruction under Poincaré 1926–28 and Minister of State in various governments 1934–35. President of Chamber 1936–40. Arrested by Vichy government and sent to Germany 1944. Re-elected to Chamber on release 1946. President of National Assembly 1947.

[2] For the preliminaries to the London Conference see Cabinet 41, 43, 44(24) of 15th, 22nd and 30th July 1924. All in Cab. 23/48.

[3] Lady Hankey recalls the Archdeaconry as 'a lovely place because the front looked out on to a long path ending in the cathedral'. To the author 25th March 1970.

[4] Sir Miles Lampson, 1st Baron Killearn 1943 (1880–1964). Diplomat and Pro-Consul. Minister to China 1926–33. High Commissioner for Egypt and Sudan 1933–36, then Ambassador to Egypt until 1946. Special Commissioner in South-East Asia 1946–48. An intimate friend of Hankey in the 1950s and an ally of his against concessions to Egyptian nationalism.

[5] Thomas A. Spring-Rice, 3rd Baron Monteagle 1926. (1883–1934.) Diplomat. Served in British delegation to Paris Peace Conference, 1919. First Secretary, British Embassy, Paris 1920, and Brussels 1921.

[6] Ralph F. Wigram (1890–1936). Diplomat. 1st Secretary, Paris 1924–33. An intimate friend of Lord Vansittart and, with him, a strong opponent of 'appeasement' in 1930s. See Ian Colvin, *Vansittart in Office* (Gollancz, 1965), p. 120 regarding Wigram's tragic death.

Embassy as my assistant . . . It all worked splendidly and I received many thanks. In the end, however, through no fault of mine, I became what I had not intended to become – the principal adviser and counsellor to Ramsay MacDonald[1] . . . When Parliament rose his colleagues left town and I was almost the only friend he had left. For the last ten days of the conference we were almost inseparable. MacDonald worked in almost as irregular a way as Lloyd George – often seeing people early in the morning and late at night[2] . . ., I, having nothing else to do, living at the Club, feeding with him and fully in his confidence naturally became his assistant and abetter. This was all the more so because he and Snowden, the Chancellor of the Exchequer, . . . do not hit it off and could not work together. Often I would go on missions to Marx[3] or Herriot or Theunis after midnight, and several times MacDonald rang me up at 7.15 a.m. to know the results of my negotiations. Thus . . . the more delicate diplomatic negotiations on points of high policy and on irreconcilable differences of opinion passed more and more into my hands. [Here Hankey enlarged on MacDonald's unsystematic methods, and his initial refusal to allow a secretary to be present at and record the discussions – 'like Lloyd George in the early days of the Council of Four'.] I made many protests, verbally and in writing . . . He would not listen, but consented to have a record of all discussions attended by the Germans. Later on he asked me to try and get some notes out of Camerlynck the interpreter, but this was of course impossible. It is interesting to recall that Lloyd George in the same way tried to get notes from Mantoux, the interpreter of the Council of Four. As a matter of fact this sloppy procedure did give rise to a serious *contretemps*. [Here Hankey described how, because notices of meetings were not issued, Herriot did not turn up on one occasion. When telephoned for he at once suspected that the other delegates had been plotting behind his back, and had 'a most terrible outburst of rage and even tears' – which Hankey by chance witnessed. That evening he had to restore peace with Herriot, who 'became very confidential', and also with Theunis who was 'in high dudgeon' and alleging that the French had been negotiating with the Germans behind the backs of the Belgians. Hankey found Herriot 'deficient in political courage and very emotional'. 'He more than once cried in the presence of MacDonald and Crowe' he recorded.]

[1]Hankey must surely have meant that he intended not to usurp the Foreign Office's prerogatives at the conference; for he had worked hard to achieve the position of 'principal adviser and counsellor' since the day MacDonald achieved power.

[2]This conflicts oddly with the praise of MacDonald's business-like methods Hankey expressed in the letter to Smuts quoted above (p. 366).

[3]Wilhelm Marx (1863–1946). German politician (Catholic). Chancellor 1923–25. Opposed Hindenburg for Presidency 1925. Then Minister for Justice. Again Chancellor 1926–28.

Hankey's separation from his wife and family while they were at St. David's in August 1924 produced the historical benefit of a long series of letters which give us a more intimate insight into the proceedings at the London Reparations Conference than is contained in the official records.[1] As early as 2nd he wrote optimistically that progress was good, that the Allied powers had been able 'to tumble into agreement ("*tomber d'accord*") on most issues', and that the Germans had been invited to come over. MacDonald, he said, was 'leaning on me a good deal', and had given him 'his entire confidence'. However the 'serious crisis' over the Irish Boundary Commission was 'diverting a good deal of his own and the Cabinet's attention from the discussions on reparations'. Then, as so often happened, difficulties arose through Herriot feeling obliged to refer any agreement to the French Parliament; and the Germans would not be ready to join in the negotiations as early as he had hoped.[2] Over the Bank holiday weekend Hankey was kept very busy with Cabinet meetings on the Irish crisis, which was eased somewhat by Henderson and Thomas going over there to try and bring the two parties together, and by the need to prepare for the arrival of the German delegates. Typically he set out to create a favourable atmosphere by making a friend of the German delegation's secretary – 'a nice fellow who seems to have been brought up in England'.[3] On 5th the German delegates arrived, Hankey met them and at once had a long talk with von Schubert, the head of their Foreign Ministry.[4] The first Plenary Session took place that afternoon,[5] and it at once became plain that the crucial issue was whether the French would agree to an early evacuation of the Ruhr. As the eastern frontier of France, and that country's desire to hold the left bank of the Rhine, played such a large part in every post-war conference it is interesting to find Hankey suggesting to the Foreign Office, shortly

[1]The minutes of the conference are in I.C.P. Series. Cab. 29/103 and 104.

[2]To Lady Hankey 1st, 2nd and 3rd August 1924.

[3]To the same 4th Aug. 1924. The German secretary in question was probably Herr M. Kiep, who attended the Plenary Session on 5th August. He was joined by Doctor E. Wiehl later, and the two of them then worked as joint secretaries.

[4]Carl T. C. von Schubert (1882–1947). German diplomat. Counsellor in London before World War I and then in charge of British Section at the Wilhelmstrasse. Under-Secretary of State for Foreign Affairs 1925–30. Ambassador to Italy 1930–32.

[5]Cabinet 47(24) Conclusion 3. Cab. 23/48.

before the London Reparations Conference opened, that the League of Nations should become the sovereign authority for the river.[1] Unfortunately Lampson, to whom he sent his proposal, does not appear to have followed it up.

On the day that the German delegates arrived Hankey lunched with MacDonald and 'took him to task about his unconcealed hatred of Lloyd George whom he always belittles'. He stressed that the present conference 'was simplicity itself compared with the Paris [Peace] Conference', that Lloyd George 'had never allowed anyone to run him [MacDonald] down ... when he was the underdog', but had described him as 'a very considerable fellow fighting a lonely battle very pluckily'. Hankey attributed MacDonald's attitude 'to jealousy of a much bigger man than he'. But MacDonald gave Hankey one interesting piece of information – that on 2nd August 1914 Asquith had invited him to join the government, and that Morley, who was about to resign on the issue of joining in the war, had urged him to accept. MacDonald refused – 'apparently because he thought the famous White Paper [on the negotiations leading to war] had been "doctored" ';[2] but he did not contradict Hankey's view that after the violation of Belgium's neutrality Britain could not honourably stand aside. None the less he blamed the conflict chiefly on France and Russia.[3]

On 7th Hankey reiterated to his wife that an agreement depended entirely on France 'evacuating the Ruhr within a reasonable time', and found an analogy between that issue and the prolonged negotiations over Shantung at the Washington Conference – 'something outside the conference but on which the whole thing turns'. At least the French had condescended to meet the Germans in formal visits lasting five minutes – which marked some progress and eased the 'distinctly sulphurous' initial atmosphere. Hankey himself was all the time acting as *amicus curiae* (friend of the court); but 'the unconcealed differences' between the financially orthodox Snowden and the Prime Minister worried him greatly. Whereas the former wanted to press the French and Belgians 'far enough to induce the British and American bankers to

[1]Hankey to D'Abernon 23rd May 1924 enclosing a copy of his letter to Lampson. B.M. Add. MSS. 48927, Vol. VI, p. 7.

[2]Presumably Cd. 7445, *Correspondence respecting the European Crisis*. Continued in Cd. 7467 and 7596 of August and September 1914.

[3]To Lady Hankey 5th Aug. 1924.

provide the loan which is essential for the Dawes Report,[1] the latter held that if a political agreement was reached 'the Bankers will have to come into line'. Thus arose the odd situation that 'Snowden and the Germans were on one side, and MacDonald and the French on the other'; with the French and Belgian delegates complaining bitterly to Hankey about the obdurate Chancellor's attitude. Nor were things made easier by an injudicious remark by MacDonald that 'only Satan can separate us [from the French]' being leaked to the French Press, which promptly published an article on Snowden headed 'Satan is here'. In addition to these troubles Sir John Bradbury was 'perpetually threatening to resign from the Reparations Commission' if the French were allowed to have their way.[2]

As the negotiations dragged on Hankey became increasingly irritated at the slow progress, and depressed by the separation from his family. On 9th he sent Adeline 'more indiscretions' – notably about the arrangement for a meeting between Stresemann[3] and Herriot 'without the Press discovering it'. This he accomplished by organising a dinner at the American embassy, which proved a success, followed for Hankey by a long and friendly talk with Stresemann, who 'poured forth many of his troubles'. However that same day all the French delegates returned to Paris 'to consult their Cabinet' – especially over the delicate subject of the timing of the Ruhr evacuation, which Herriot and Clémentel[4] were prepared to accept but to which General

[1]The report of the Committee under the American diplomat, lawyer and banker General Charles G. Dawes (1865–1951) which met in Paris in January and reported on 9th April 1924. German stability was to be restored on a gold basis by the new 'Rentenmark', and she was to pay amounts rising from £50 millions for four years to £125 millions. The evacuation of the Ruhr and a loan of 800 million gold marks (£40 millions) were integral conditions of the Dawes Plan. See G. M. Gathorne-Hardy, *A Short History of International Affairs 1920–1938* (Oxford U.P., 1938), pp. 47–8 and C. L. Mowat, *Britain between the Wars* (Methuen, 1955), pp. 179–83.

[2]To Lady Hankey 7th Aug. 1924, ending 'Keep this indiscreet letter carefully and do not leave it about or talk about it'. Obviously Hankey regarded these letters as a substitute for the diary which he neglected at this time.

[3]Gustav Stresemann (1878–1929). German politician (Nat.-Lib.). As Chancellor 1923 ended passive resistance in Ruhr. As Minister for Foreign Affairs 1924–29 accepted Dawes Plan, arranged evacuation of Ruhr 1924 and entry of Germany into League of Nations 1926. Signatory, with A. Chamberlain and Briand, of Locarno Treaty 1926 and Kellogg Pact 1928. A staunch advocate of reconciliation with France.

[4]Etienne Clémentel (1864–1936). French politician. Minister of Commerce 1916–20 and held many other ministerial offices 1905–24. Senator 1920.

Nollet, the Minister of War, was strongly opposed. Hankey learnt of this schism in the French delegation through 'a violent and prolonged altercation on the subject at 10 Downing Street', which caused MacDonald 'to get rid of them from their room upstairs', whereupon they continued the argument in the Cabinet room until midnight, and then carried it on 'even into the street'.[1]

Sunday 10th produced a lull and Hankey 'risked a day in the country' with his brother Clement and his family. But late in the evening the discussions were renewed, and MacDonald sent Hankey off to fetch Marx, the German Chancellor, from the Ritz Hotel to join in a prolonged session which lasted far into the night. Now it was the Germans who proved difficult because, although 'Herriot has power to make great concessions . . . they say that these are not sufficient for their [the Germans'] Parliament'. MacDonald, he wrote, had shown 'very great resource all through the conference . . . Whether he remains in office or not I shall always look back with pleasure to my association with him . . . Unlike some of his predecessors [presumably Law and Baldwin] he has all those rare qualities in combination which make him a great statesman'. Evidently Hankey had not yet penetrated beneath the attractive veneer of mellifluous eloquence and urbanity sufficiently to detect the fundamental meretriciousness which flawed MacDonald's character. In course of one of their many intimate talks he had 'astonished' Hankey by declaring himself 'a great admirer of Jacky Fisher', and had said that 'if Jacky had lived he would have offered him office'. As Fisher would have been 83 years old in 1924 it is hard to take MacDonald's remark seriously.

But Franco-German intransigence was not the only cause of the delays which so irritated Hankey. Snowden's tactlessness constantly produced friction, and even provoked from Camerlynck the interpreter, 'a very mild man', a threat to use his position to expose the Chancellor's maladroit methods. 'It is a pity', wrote Hankey, 'Snowden is so tactless. I think he could say what he wants to say without rubbing people so much the wrong way. It makes it harder for the Germans to make concessions . . .'. However, when the Belgian delegates Hymans and Theunis complained about Snowden he described him as 'a very honourable, straight fellow who says what is in his mind'.[2] Thus, as always, did Hankey try to smooth ruffled feathers and soften clashes of personality in order to achieve the object in hand.

[1]To Lady Hankey 9th Aug. 1924. [2]To Lady Hankey 12th Aug. 1924.

The triangular discussions between the French, Germans and Belgians dragged on, and when on 13th Hankey was with MacDonald at an evening performance of Bernard Shaw's *Saint Joan* he was called out to deal with a crisis by getting the Prime Minister to see the German delegates. He collected them all at No. 10 and the talks went on into the small hours. 'This [14th] is the critical day', Hankey told Adeline. 'I would eat my hat to have Ll. G. in charge for 24 hours. He could fix it all right. Ramsay MacDonald . . . tries to do too much himself, and has in consequence been a little out-manoeuvred'. The French had rallied the Italians, Belgians and even the Americans to their claim to stay in the Ruhr another year. 'Ll. G. never would have allowed this', he asserted – with some justice. Despite Hankey's misgivings agreement was reached on 16th on the basis of acceptance of the Dawes Plan and evacuation of the Ruhr within a year – a considerable personal success for MacDonald which paved the way to the Locarno Conference of the following year.[1] A week later Hankey joined his family at St. David's for the holiday he had been awaiting so impatiently.

The successful outcome of the London conference brought him the usual shower of congratulatory letters from the British Empire delegates and participating officials, including a very warm letter from Haldane and one from Clive Wigram, assistant secretary to the King,[2] in which he expressed the Monarch's appreciation of 'the prompt and efficient manner in which the record of all these conferences has been kept'.[3] In his reply to the Lord Chancellor Hankey wrote 'make no mistake, it was Ramsay MacDonald's conference'; and he added that, had Haldane not joined the Labour Government 'I believe we would have had something like disaster on the defence side'.[4] His retrospective summing up in his diary read 'What with the mutual suspicion of the French and Germans; the friction between MacDonald and Snowden; MacDonald's irregular methods; the difficulty of maintaining constant contact between the British delegates and the B.E.D.; conferences two or three times a day with my good friend Sir Arthur Willert,[5] the admirable official in charge of the Press at the Foreign

[1]See Gathorne-Hardy and C. L. Mowat, *op. cit.*

[2]1873–1960, 1st Baron Wigram 1935. Assistant Private Secretary and Equerry to the King 1910–31. Private Secretary and Extra Equerry 1931–35. Keeper of Privy Purse 1935–36.

[3]Wigram to Hankey from Bolton Abbey 18th Aug. 1924.

[4]Hankey to Haldane 20th Aug. 1920. Haldane papers. [5]See p. 242, *note*.

Office – it was a strenuous and difficult time'.[1] But he certainly relished finding himself once more at the hub of international politics.

The summer of 1924 also marked the opening of the British Empire Exhibition at Wembley. Its purpose was of course to stimulate trade, and, less overtly, to emphasise the unity of the Empire. Though it was scarcely a financial success, and the guarantors were called on to meet part of the deficiency, it did perhaps help to encourage the feeling that, after the disastrous experiences of the Ruhr occupation, better times were on the way. The Hankeys attended the garden party given by the King for distinguished overseas visitors at Hampton Court on 27th June, and also visited the exhibition with the Cabinet a month later.

At the end of July the first moves took place in a train of events which was in the end to bring about the downfall of the government and shatter Hankey's confidence in MacDonald as Prime Minister. Though he never said so in his diary or in his letters to his wife his general attitude strongly suggests that the admiration, even affection, which he had felt towards MacDonald at the beginning of his Premiership never recovered from the shock he suffered over his handling of the notorious 'Campbell Case'. As a good deal has already been published about it there is no need to recapitulate the story in detail here.[2] Suffice it to say that on 30th July the Director of Public Prosecutions drew the attention of Sir Patrick Hastings, the Attorney-General, to an open letter in a little-known Communist paper *The Workers' Weekly* addressed to the men of the fighting services urging them not only to adopt 'passive resistance' in the event of war but to refuse to 'turn your guns on your fellow workers' in the event of industrial strife. Simultaneously questions were asked of the Home Secretary in Parliament regarding what he intended to do about the letter.[3] Next day detectives visited the office of *The Workers' Weekly*, of which J. R. Campbell was acting temporarily as editor, and a warrant was issued for his arrest. Campbell, who had a good war record, then visited James Maxton,[4] the Clydeside

[1]Diary 11th Oct. 1924.

[2]Though the source references are not always correct a valuable account entitled *The Campbell Case and the First Labour Government* by Professor F. H. Newark was published in The Northern Ireland Legal Quarterly, Vol. 20, No. 1 (March 1969). I am indebted to Professor Newark for supplying me with an offprint and for interesting letters about the Campbell case.

[3]Parl. Deb., Commons, Vol. 176, Cols. 2059 and 2085.

[4]1885–1946. Politician (Ind. Lab.). Chairman, Independent Labour Party 1926–31 and 1934–39.

Independent Labour Party member, at the House with the result that Hastings and his colleague the Solicitor-General realised that a prosecution was most unlikely to succeed. MacDonald was much disturbed by these developments, and saw Hastings and the Assistant Director of Public Prosecutions. The decision was then taken that the prosecution of Campbell should be withdrawn by Travers Humphreys, the Treasury Counsel, when the case came before the magistrate on 13th August. Humphreys, however, at once appreciated that none of the instructions given to him provided adequate legal grounds for withdrawing the prosecution; but he none the less offered no evidence in court, and Campbell was accordingly discharged. *The Workers' Weekly* was, expectedly, lyrical about the outcome; and when Parliament reassembled on 30th September the Attorney-General was severely heckled – especially about Humphreys's statement in court that '*it has been represented that the object and intention* of the article was not to seduce men in the fighting forces from their duties and allegiance . . . (italics supplied)'. Members of the opposition were not slow to follow up the question thundered in *The Times* of 15th – 'BY WHOSE REPRESENTATION?' When MacDonald himself was asked whether he had given any directions on the matter his answer contained several blatant untruths. Indeed when Hankey learnt that MacDonald had said that he had not been consulted about the withdrawal of the prosecution, had first learnt about it from the Press, and had never recommended any such action he exclaimed 'That's a bloody lie'.[1] As Hankey was not given to the use of such expletives it is obvious that he was outraged. The question inevitably arises 'Who prepared the answer to the Parliamentary Question for MacDonald?' The normal practice in such a case would be for it to be done at 10 Downing Street by one or other of the private secretaries; and the Principal Private Secretary at the time was that same Colonel Ronald Waterhouse whose conduct at the time of the negotiations regarding the succession to Bonar Law had, to put it mildly, not been above criticism.[2] Waterhouse must surely at least have seen the answer drafted for the Prime Minister's use – though when on his feet in the House MacDonald may of course not have used it, but have gone off on a tangent on his own. One point which can be stated with confidence is that, although Hankey often provided all the Prime Ministers whom he served with drafts or notes for their speeches, and he had quite recently helped MacDonald with those he made at the

[1] *Middlemas*, I, p. 296. [2] See pp. 341–2.

Reparations Conference, neither he nor Tom Jones had any hand in preparing the answer given by the Prime Minister. The outcome is clearly expressed in the unsigned draft of a Cabinet minute in Hankey's hand. Though not dated it was probably written on 5th October. 'Cabinet decided', it reads, 'to treat both resolution [i.e. the Conservative vote of censure] and the amendment [i.e. the Liberal amendment to appoint a Select Committee] as votes of no confidence, as the wording of the amendment is intolerable. It proposes to put the honour of the Government in the hands of a partisan Committee composed of seven opponents and three supporters. Impossible to say what will happen Wednesday night [8th]'.[1] The debate took place on 8th, and one cannot but agree with Philip Snowden's description of MacDonald's performance on that occasion as 'incoherent, evasive and prevaricating'.[2]

The truth of the matter is that the Cabinet discussed the Campbell case on 6th August, with MacDonald present and Jones recording the discussion. The Cabinet then decided, firstly, that 'no public prosecution of a political character should be undertaken without the prior sanction of the Cabinet'; and, secondly, approved the proposal put forward by Hastings that the prosecution of Campbell should be dropped.[3] On 2nd October Hankey added a holograph note to the foregoing minute reading 'On September 22nd 1924 the Prime Minister, in the presence of a number of his Cabinet colleagues, asked me to show him the Cabinet Conclusion in regard to the prosecution of the *Workers' Weekly* . . . On reading the Minute the Prime Minister at once challenged its accuracy, more particularly in regard to Conclusion (b) [i.e. the dropping of the prosecution]'. On 3rd November Hankey added another holograph note reading 'The Prime Minister . . . asked me to-day to be sure that if ever the Cabinet Minute of 6th August 1924 was called for, I should also bring to notice the enclosed transcript of notes made at the meeting by Mr. T. Jones . . .'.[4]

In fact the notes taken by Jones at the meeting on 6th August were not one of his best efforts as regards either clarity or accuracy;[5] but they do indicate the general trend of the discussion, and fully support

[1]MacDonald papers 1/197.

[2]*Autobiography*, Vol. II (Ivor Nicholson & Watson, 1934), p. 695.

[3]Cabinet 48(24) Concl. 5. [4]In Cab. 23/48. See also Cab. 21/294.

[5]Professor Newark, *op. cit.* pp. 36–8 points out several mistakes. Jones's notes as printed in *Middlemas*, I, pp. 287–90 contain several errors additional to those made by Jones himself.

the Conclusion recorded. Furthermore Hankey was able to show that the Minutes of the meeting were circulated in draft in the normal manner, and that no requests for corrections were received. Though he could not prove conclusively that MacDonald saw them during a day which was extremely busy Hankey was able to state that 'I do not think there is the smallest doubt that I did show you the Minute'; and he added a note that Jones recalled that 'I definitely informed him that the Prime Minister approved this particular minute'.[1] Such, in brief outline, is the chain of events which led to the defeat of the first Labour government by 364 to 198 votes on the motion debated on 8th October. If Hankey had been any less meticulous in his procedure for recording and circulating Cabinet Minutes he would have found himself in a very tight corner when MacDonald declared that he had never seen the Conclusion of 6th August and questioned its accuracy.

As soon as Hankey heard that MacDonald intended to bring up in Cabinet on 5th October the question of 'Custody of Cabinet Minutes' he went into action in defence of the secretariat and of the system he administered. He sent the Prime Minister the memorandum on the subject which he had circulated immediately after the very first meeting of his Cabinet, in which the instructions on which he acted were summarised.[2] He went on to stress 'the very elaborate precautions' taken in his office to comply with those instructions, and pointed out that Ministers were themselves responsible for communicating the contents of Cabinet minutes within their departments. Thus once the draft minutes had left his hands he had 'no further responsibility for them'. Some of the present Cabinet (including Haldane the Lord Chancellor and Wedgwood, Chancellor of the Duchy of Lancaster) regularly returned their copies to his office; but in every government there were others 'who made a point of retaining permanently all copies of Cabinet minutes, and taking them away with them when they go out of office'. 'I could mention', he continued, 'one or two ex-Ministers who to my knowledge have complete files of the Cabinet minutes for their period of office'. Obviously he had Lloyd George and Churchill principally in mind. He then outlined the varying practices followed by different departments in handling the minutes internally. The chief difficulty was, and always had been, that the need for secrecy clashed with the

[1]Hankey to MacDonald 2nd Oct. 1924. Cab. 23/48.

[2]Appendix I to C.P. 30(24).

'sound administration' of the government's policy. 'If your officials do not know the policy', he wrote, 'they will not be good administrators', and would 'often fail to give advice consistent with the broader policy'. He went on to analyse the 14 cases of leakage which had occurred since 1919, only two of which had been 'definitely traced'.[1] Leakages of C.I.D. proceedings were, he said, 'extraordinarily rare'; and that alone provided 'strong evidence in favour of exonerating the staff of this office'. As to the sources of leakage, he quoted several cases of carelessness with documents. One which had been circulated to the Chancellor of the Exchequer of the time had been picked up in a tube station, and a Foreign Office telegram had been found on the Horse-guards' Parade. Hankey was sure that carelessness in conversation was 'by far the commonest source of leakage' – especially 'in the lobbies of the House of Commons'. Treachery he considered 'extremely rare although not absolutely unknown'. He concluded by claiming that, as regards the *Workers' Weekly* case there had been no leakage 'which cannot be accounted for', since 'any intelligent journalist' would have deduced that, when the Cabinet met at the House of Commons on the evening of 6th August 'such an important question must have been raised' – especially as it was probably known that the Attorney-General had been summoned to attend. All in all therefore Hankey closed any loophole MacDonald may have hoped to find through establishing that a leakage of the Cabinet proceedings of that day had occurred. The way the Prime Minister's mind was working when he read the paper is shown by the notes he made on it. They read 'No copying': 'Abstract of Discussion': and 'Sidelined paras'.[2]

The epilogue to this tangled affair took place shortly after the Conservatives had returned to power. On 8th December Hankey added a third holograph note to the two already mentioned (of 2nd October and 3rd November). In it he stated that the controversial minute of 6th August was discussed by Baldwin's Cabinet on 3rd December, and Hankey had then carried out MacDonald's instruction to produce Jones's notes as well as the minute. Though Joynson-

[1]These were a leakage on motor legislation, which an official had deliberately given to the Press in the belief that he was intended to do so, and a leakage traced to the Admiralty on the naval aviation dispute and the Balfour Committee's recommendations – almost certainly the *Daily Mail* article of 30th July 1923. See Roskill, *Naval Policy*, I, pp. 379–80.

[2]Memo. of 4th Oct. 1924. MacDonald papers 1/195.

Hicks,[1] the Home Secretary, appears to have wanted to use the minute as a stick with which to belabour the late government the Cabinet decided that it was 'highly undesirable and would furnish a most unfortunate precedent' to make it public 'in any form' – a decision which no doubt accorded fully with Hankey's views, and with the principles which always guided him in his work. The Conservative Cabinet did, however, cancel the first part of the minute, which had stated that no prosecution 'of a political character should be undertaken without the prior sanction of the Cabinet'.[2] They evidently desired to leave the responsibility for such action where it had always belonged – namely with the Law Officers of the Crown.

MacDonald's challenge to the accuracy of the minute of 6th August was not the only time Hankey had trouble with him over the recording of Cabinet Conclusions. On the afternoon of 22nd September – the very day when he wrote his note recording the Prime Minister's dissent – another Cabinet took place with MacDonald in the chair and Haldane, Snowden, Clynes, Olivier, Chelmsford, Trevelyan, Hartshorn, Sidney Webb, Buxton and Wedgwood present. Next day Hankey circulated the draft minutes because he had been unable 'to get access to' the Prime Minister. MacDonald scrawled across the first page 'This was not a meeting of the Cabinet at all and no record shd. be made'. Hankey, loyal as ever despite the trials to which he was being subjected, thereupon circulated a note that the meeting was 'to be treated as a purely informal conversation' of which no record was to be kept. The minutes were to be returned to him for destruction.[3] Apart from the reasonable deduction that MacDonald was feeling uncomfortable at the time over developments about the Campbell case, the cancelled minutes give us two clues regarding the reasons for his action. During a discussion on the proposed Anglo-Soviet Treaty the possibility of an arrangement being made with the Liberal Party to secure its acceptance was mentioned. MacDonald wrote in the margin 'This was a joke'; to which one may reasonably ask why it should have been so regarded by the secretary? Secondly a discussion took place on Arbitration, Security

[1]William Joynson-Hicks, 1st Viscount Brentford 1929 (1865–1932). Solicitor and politician (Cons.). Postmaster-General and Paymaster-General 1923. Financial Secretary to Treasury 1923. Minister of Health 1923–24. As Home Secretary 1924–29 a frequent butt for David Low's cartoons as the pompous and moralistic 'Jix'.

[2]Cabinet 65(24) of 3rd Dec. 1924. Cab. 23/49.

[3]Cabinet 51(24) of 22nd Sept. 1924. Cab. 23/48. Hankey recovered all copies except Lord Haldane's.

and Limitation of Armament, and against a reservation regarding the use of the British Fleet against a nation which had refused arbitration MacDonald wrote a peremptory 'No' and deleted the minute. Yet we know that his Cabinet was deeply divided over the 'Geneva Protocol', and that Chelmsford, the First Lord, had entered a strong caveat regarding the perils he saw in the acceptance of it.[1] Indeed it seems unlikely that, had the Labour Government remained in office, the Protocol would have been signed. On the other hand it is a fact that Hankey was strongly opposed to the Protocol, and supported the Admiralty's line; so MacDonald may have wished to avoid recording views contrary to those held by Henderson and Parmoor,[2] his representatives at Geneva.

Looking back to-day at the confused events described above it is obvious that MacDonald's cardinal error lay in acting as his own Foreign Secretary. One has only to glance at the Cabinet minutes of the period to realise that with so many important and highly complicated issues under discussion – the Irish boundary agreement, negotiations with the Egyptian nationalists, the possibility of an Anglo-Soviet treaty, the Geneva Protocol and the admission of Germany to the League, Reparations, relations with the U.S.A. and so on – it was beyond the powers of any one man to master all of them. Indeed it was on the day before the fateful Cabinet of 6th August that Snowden the Chancellor 'announced that the Anglo-Soviet Conference, after sitting through last night, had broken down on the question of compensation for nationalised property'[3]; and that unwelcome news may have contributed to MacDonald's amnesia about the discussion on the Campbell case. But even if there is substance in that suggestion it does not excuse MacDonald's evasiveness and prevarication two months later.

[1]The 'Protocol for the Pacific Settlement of International Disputes' was drafted by a sub-committee appointed by the Third Assembly of the League of Nations (1st Sept.–2nd Oct. 1924) under President Beneš of Czecho-Slovakia. See Roskill, *Naval Policy*, I, pp. 430–1.

[2]Charles A. Cripps, 1st Baron Parmoor 1914 (1852–1941). Lawyer and politician (Cons., then Lab.). Lord President of Council 1924 and 1929–31. British representative on League of Nations Council and British Empire Delegate to Assembly. Leader of House of Lords 1929–31.

[3]Cabinet 27(24) Conclusion 3 of 5th Aug. 1924 in Cab. 23/48. In fact left wing pressure on Arthur Ponsonby, Under-Secretary at the Foreign Office, to resume negotiations with Rakovsky, the Soviet Trade Commissar, resulted in negotiations being resumed on 6th and an agreement was reached – subject to Parliamentary ratification – that evening. See *Baldwin* pp. 271–2.

For Hankey the exposure of the chief whom he had so taken to at first encounter, and who had certainly done well at the London Reparations conference, must have been a bitter blow. Moreover he well knew that the return of the Tories would bring back Baldwin, and so restore Jones to his former privileged position. To Jones's credit he came out strongly against a dissolution. Hankey was away from the office on the day of the government's defeat, and Jones wrote to him as follows:—

*Jones to Hankey. Cabinet Office. 8th October 1924.* Holograph[1]

Dear Chief,

What a pity you are not about to look after us all! Don't you think in as much as (1) we have a minority govt. and (2) no-one (except some Labour men) wants an election, that the King should refuse a dissolution until he has exhausted all alternatives i.e. seen Baldwin and Asquith. I am sure this view is held by responsible persons, and if you were about you could convey it to H.M. If the King simply takes a P.M's advice and does not react at all, what is the good of a King? – so it was put to me by an M.P. yesterday.

I suppose you can't come down? But to-morrow we shall know, and probably you could hardly be here in time to affect matters.

Yours ever

But it was not to be. On 9th the King signed a note which Stamfordham sent on to MacDonald that same day. It read 'In granting the Prime Minister's request to dissolve Parliament, I could not help regretting the necessity for doing so' – because in the King's opinion the country 'strongly deprecates another election within a year'.[2] Then began perhaps the most extraordinary election campaign since Britain became a Parliamentary democracy.

So much has been published in recent years about the notorious 'Zinoviev letter' that it is unnecessary to do more here than sketch its story in barest outline.[3] That it was a not very skilled forgery, produced by White Russian émigrés in Berlin, may be taken as proven; as is the fact that it was 'planted' on the Foreign Office with the connivance of the Conservative Central Office and of the British Intelligence services.

[1]Rather oddly this letter is in the Esher papers (Eshr. 12/10). Presumably Hankey showed it to Esher and forgot to recover it from him.

[2]MacDonald papers 1/197. See also Nicolson, *George V*, pp. 399–401 and *Baldwin*, pp. 273–4.

[3]See especially L. Chester, S. Fay and H. Young, *The Zinoviev Letter* (Heinemann, 1967). Though this book is by no means free from errors, mostly of a minor nature, the authors have followed up every clue with great persistence and have uncovered a good deal of new information.

How far Sir Eyre Crowe, the Permanent Secretary of the Foreign Office, and J. D. Gregory the Head of the Northern Department were willing dupes cannot be said; but the manner in which they handled the letter does lend some support to such a suggestion. On the other hand, even though the letter was a forgery, its contents were not out of line with much of the inflammatory propaganda issued by the Third Communist International (or Comintern), of which Grigory Zinoviev had been President since 1919[1]; and this no doubt contributed to the readiness with which the letter was accepted as genuine by politicians such as Baldwin and Austen Chamberlain, whose integrity is beyond dispute.

A copy of the letter (the original has never been found) reached the Foreign Office on 10th October, and the Northern Department received it four days later. MacDonald was at the time stumping the country on a prolonged and very exhausting tour of political speech-making. The letter came into his hands late on 15th together with a great many other official papers sent from Whitehall. He ordered its authenticity to be carefully checked, and a protest to the Russian Chargé d'Affaires Christian Rakovsky to be drafted. Gregory had originally minuted 'I very much doubt the wisdom of publication' – because the authenticity of the document was bound to be challenged at once. But Crowe was of contrary view; he had convinced himself that the letter was genuine, and although it was Gregory who actually signed the protest 'in the absence of the Secretary of State', on 24th Crowe himself took the decision not only to despatch the protest but to release it and the Zinoviev letter to the Press. And he did so without informing MacDonald or giving him any opportunity to see whether the Foreign Office had taken account of the cautionary note he had sounded and

[1]An interesting account of the Comintern's purposes and methods in working for world revolution is to be found in a long letter dated 9th November 1935 by Walter Newbold of Durham, who had been a member of the British Communist party until August 1924 when he resigned in disgust. 'In the old days', wrote Newbold, 'the couriers of the Comintern and the Red International of Trade Unions and the instructors came in at Blythe and the Tyne–Weir ports off ships from Hamburg and the Baltic . . . The Soviets and the Comintern work very subtly and on a long date and a world plan'. He went on to describe the Soviet view of another world war, ending with the declaration that by 1941–42 such a conflict would be regarded as 'desirable and will be provoked'. Baldwin papers, Vol. 47, pp. 151–5. The pamphlets circulated to the men of the Home Fleet at the time of the so-called 'Invergordon mutiny' of September 1931 fully support Newbold's views.

the amendments he had made to the draft of the protest. The letter and protest were published in the *Daily Mail*, which had actually already received a copy of the former from other sources, next day. Though there is little doubt that a number of persons in the underworld of secret intelligence had for some time been working hard and without the slightest scruples to secure publication of the letter in order to destroy the Anglo-Soviet treaty and discredit the Labour Party,[1] circumstantial evidence strongly suggests that Gregory himself was implicated in the plot and played a crucial part in its success. A point which those who have investigated this extremely complex story have missed is that Gregory was a Roman Catholic, and so likely to be strongly anti-Communist. Hankey first met him in Athens on his return from Gallipoli in 1915, and came in contact with him several times later in the War.[2] His diary entry describing him as 'a curious continental sort of man in the Foreign Office' suggests that, with his customary shrewdness in judgement of character, he was mistrustful of Gregory. In 1928 the lawsuit between Messrs. Ironmonger, foreign bankers, and Mrs. A. M. Bradley Dyne, who had worked as Gregory's private secretary in the Foreign Office some ten years earlier, revealed that he and other officials had speculated in various foreign currencies.[3] Gregory himself had speculated very heavily, and after an Inquiry conducted by Sir Warren Fisher he was dismissed from the Foreign Service.[4] Two other officials, Owen O'Malley and Lieutenant-Commander H. F. B. Maxse, were also found to have 'acted in a manner inconsistent with their obligations as Civil Servants'. O'Malley was 'permitted to resign' but was reinstated about a year later. During the

[1]Such as the notorious British agent Sidney Reilly, Donald im Thurn, a London business man who had connections with the Secret Service, his friend in the city Guy Kindersley, the head of the Secret Service Admiral Sir Hugh Sinclair, and his close associate the former Director of Naval Intelligence Admiral Sir Reginald Hall, a Conservative M.P. in 1924.

[2]See Vol. I, pp. 204, 401 and 451. Trevor Wilson in *The Political Diaries of C. P. Scott 1911–1928* (Collins, 1970), pp. 477–8 records an interview Scott had with Ramsay MacDonald on 4th March 1925 during which MacDonald said that 'if there was a villain of the piece [in the Foreign Office] it was Gregory'. Also 'there were too many Roman Catholics high up in the Foreign Office. Gregory was one of them . . .'.

[3]Messrs. Ironmonger sued Mrs. Dyne for £39,178.1.3. incurred by losses in these speculations and obtained judgement against her.

[4]See *The Times* of 27th, 28th and 31st Jan. and 1st and 2nd Feb. 1928 for the law reports on the Ironmonger v. Dyne case.

lawsuit other officials were mentioned as having indulged in similar speculations, including Hankey's close friend of later years Sir Miles Lampson, then Minister in China. He telegraphed offering his resignation, which Sir Austen Chamberlain refused to accept.[1]

To return to October 1924 polling took place only four days after publication of the Zinoviev letter, and the results quickly showed that the plotters had succeeded – probably beyond their wildest dreams. Though the Labour vote actually increased by over a million compared with the December 1923 election their party lost 40 seats; but it was the Liberals who were overtaken by disaster, with a greatly reduced poll and the loss of 119 seats. The Conservatives with 419 seats won a huge majority over all the other parties. Among the first actions taken by the new government were the refusal to ratify the Anglo-Soviet treaty and the continuation of the inquiry by a Cabinet committee, initiated by the Labour government shortly before it left office, into the authenticity of the Zinoviev letter. Austen Chamberlain, the new Foreign Secretary, now took the chair at the inquiry,[2] and on 15th December he informed the House that four independent sources had established that the letter was genuine.[3] Hankey was as convinced as any of the politicians concerned that this was so,[4] and the Soviet's announcement in March 1928 that they had uncovered the source of the forgery did not shake his or their conviction. There can be no question that he, like Baldwin and his colleagues, acted in perfectly good faith – which certainly cannot be said of those who had operated in the twilight world of covert intelligence and political intrigue. Nor was it known until much later that in April 1928 the Conservative Central Office paid £5,000 down and guaranteed an annuity for ten years and then payment of the balance of £10,000 to one of the principals in the plot.[5] But by that time Hankey had become aware, as

[1]Telegram of 8th April and Chamberlain's reply of 19th May 1928. Austen Chamberlain papers AC 55/300 and 301.

[2]The other members were Lord Cave, the Lord Chancellor (see Vol. I, p. 502, *note*), Lord Curzon and Lord Robert Cecil.

[3]Parl. Deb., Commons, Vol. 179, Cols. 673–4.

[4]See Hankey's holograph Addendum to the Cabinet Minutes of 17th March 1927, Cabinet 17(27), giving Sir Douglas Hogg's report on the authenticity of the Zinoviev letter and Austen Chamberlain's review of the 'impression made on foreign Governments by the British note of protest to Russia [of 24th Oct. 1924]'. Cab. 23/90B.

[5]See C. L. Mowat, *Great Britain since 1914* (Sources of History with Hodder and Stoughton, 1971) Ch. 8.

will be told later, that the Conservative Party included some individuals who had few scruples regarding where money came from for their own or the party's purposes.

Early in October, after the school and university terms had begun, Hankey and Adeline set off for Venice where they spent an idyllic fortnight. On the very day that the 'Red Letter' election took place Hankey sent his children a long description of the sights they had seen, and the trips they had made around the lovely islands of the Venetian lagoon. Adeline had, he wrote 'saturated herself in guide books and histories'; and the two of them were 'doing the sights most conscientiously'. It seems that, probably under Adeline's influence, the strong prejudice he had felt as a young man in favour of classical Greece and against Renaissance Italy had evaporated.[1] Robin, now 19 years old and at New College, Oxford, was treated to a thoughtful account of political developments in Fascist Italy – some aspects of which evidently impressed his father favourably.[2] By the end of October they were back in England again – Adeline to resume her domestic chores and her husband to face the inevitable difficulties produced by a change of government.

[1]See Vol. I, p. 46.
[2]To Robin Hankey, 19th Oct. 1924 from Grand Hotel, Venice.

*Chapter 14*

# Back to Baldwin. November 1924-December 1925

WE now come to the least well documented period of Hankey's whole career – the four and a half years of Baldwin's second administration; and one may hazard a guess that, except for the years preceding and following the disaster of 1956 in the Middle East, this was also the most unhappy period of his life. Not only was Hankey temperamentally out of sympathy with his new Chief, but, although he never uttered a word of complaint about it, he would have been less than human had he not been pained by the knowledge that Tom Jones had once again supplanted him as the Prime Minister's principal and intimate adviser. Gone were the days when a stream of notes emanated from Whitehall Gardens beginning 'My dear Prime Minister' and ending 'Yours ever', such as Hankey had constantly addressed to Asquith and Lloyd George. Indeed such communications as passed between him and Baldwin, and they were not very many, were couched in the most formal terms, and generally received only a formal reply – if any. Nor did the change in the relative status of the Secretary and Deputy Secretary of the Cabinet escape the notice of the Press, which must have rubbed salt into Hankey's wounds of the spirit. In 1926 a well-informed political commentator, possibly Lord Riddell, published a long article entitled 'Politics Unmasked'.[1] After describing Hankey's rapid rise under Asquith and Lloyd George, and paying tribute to his services, the correspondent went on to say 'For some reasons, however, Colonel Hankey's influence has declined. The chief reason I now propose to give. It involves a delineation of his character'. 'Cross-Bencher' went

[1]Under the pseudonym 'Cross-Bencher', which was used in the *Sunday Express* and other papers in the 1920s. Unfortunately the cutting in Lady Hankey's scrap book is undated and has no indication of its provenance. Nor has prolonged search in newspaper files of the period identified it.

on to describe Hankey as 'a man but he is also a machine'; and his gifts were alleged to be of greater service in war than in peace. 'But', the correspondent continued, 'now life is not lived at such a pace and fewer documents are needed [sic]. It is Mr. Tom Jones who with his subtle mind and powers of persuasion has gained the ears of Ministers, and Colonel Hankey has been relegated to his true place, that of efficient secretaryship.' 'Cross-Bencher' declared that Hankey had 'many consolations' in the rewards he had received and 'wears a smile on his face and there is no sadness in his hazel eyes'.[1] Though the last sentence was probably true it is difficult not to feel that there must have been some sadness, as well as anxiety for his country's future, in Hankey's heart.

We saw earlier how whenever a Minister or service man of distinction received promotion or an honour, or left office for no matter what reason, Hankey wrote a letter of congratulations or of sympathy, which was always acknowledged in the friendliest terms. The gulf between him and Baldwin is perhaps best illustrated by the fact that not one such letter passed between them, either at the time of Baldwin's various promotions and his receipt of honours, or on the occasion of his electoral defeats in 1923 and 1929.[2] Even his final retirement in 1937 was allowed to pass without a line of farewell from Hankey. Furthermore Baldwin restarted in modified form the 'King's Letters' describing proceedings in Parliament, though not in Cabinet, which Lloyd George had dropped, largely on Hankey's initiative, in December 1916.[3] Though they are often succinct and witty descriptions of debates, and Jones may well have had a hand in their composition, their style is certainly not Hankey's.[4] And Hankey, who had long been accustomed to compose the agenda for Cabinet meetings himself, merely submitting it to the Prime Minister for approval, now often received instructions

[1]*ibid.*

[2]The Baldwin papers (Vols. 140–3) contain many congratulatory letters – on his Privy Counsellorship (July 1920), on his appointment as President of the Board of Trade (April 1921), and Chancellor of the Exchequer (Oct. 1922) etc. Hankey's former assistant, now Sir Clement Jones, wrote to Baldwin on 7th April 1921 comparing the life of a Minister with that of a secretary at Whitehall Gardens. But in all these huge collections not one congratulatory letter from Hankey has been found.

[3]See Vol. I, pp. 340–1.

[4]Baldwin papers Vols. 60–3.

from Geoffrey Fry or one of the other Private Secretaries at No. 10 regarding what items were to be discussed.[1]

But the lack of intimate letters to and from the Prime Minister is not the only handicap which besets Hankey's biographer at this time. His diary was badly neglected for much of the period, and because he was separated less frequently from his wife far fewer letters passed between them – so depriving us of yet another valuable source. However the fact that during the period described by Baldwin's biographers as 'The Appeasement of England'[2] Hankey was able to enjoy a more stable home life than ever before at least brought benefits to his family; and from letters to his children which have survived we gain an interesting glimpse of him in the exacting rôle of father to adolescent sons. To give one example Christopher, his second son, went to Rugby School (of which Hankey became a Governor at this time) for his first term in September 1924, and his father 'rushed up to Euston' to see him off. Unfortunately he only arrived in time to see the train steaming out of the station. 'I only saw the wave of a hand' he wrote to Christopher that evening; and added 'Or was it the shaking of a fist?' A paragraph of paternalistic but sensible advice followed. 'I suppose at present you are feeling rather strange and unsettled, and may be a little homesick', he wrote. 'The great thing is to take everything calmly as it comes and not [to] worry. Don't feel upset if you don't do well in your work at first. You may be sure that I shall not worry as long as I know you are trying. I do not attach much importance to book-learning. A steady, level character is much more important'.[3] One feels that the last sentences were probably included because Hankey knew that Christopher had developed more slowly than Robin or Henry. Though the underlying seriousness of Hankey's attitude towards his children was never in doubt, Ursula recalls that her father was also 'a great teaser'; and his letters of the 1920s certainly confirm that description.

At this time Hankey constantly joined his children in singing rounds, catches, madrigals and part songs – some of which he composed himself. He would either extemporise the accompaniment on the piano, or if, as was more usual, the singing was unaccompanied, he would

[1] See for example letters of 15th and 30th May 1928 from 10 Downing Street to Hankey. Baldwin papers Vol. 65, pp. 50–2.

[2] *Baldwin*, Ch. 12.

[3] To Christopher Hankey 28th Sept. 1924 from Highstead.

conduct his little choir. It is a tribute to his taste, and to the way he could communicate his own enthusiasm for song, that the family's repertoire has been preserved to this day, and has been produced on several occasions for this biographer's enjoyment; and to-day Hankey's grandchildren are as familiar with his favourite songs as his own children became in the 1920s.

To return from the family to the service side of Hankey's life, it was natural that in the changed circumstances in which he now found himself, he should have concentrated his efforts on the C.I.D. side of his office's work rather than the Cabinet side. Curzon, though deeply offended at being asked to leave the Foreign Office, trimmed his sails to the new wind and accepted the Lord Presidency of the Council and chairmanship of the C.I.D. Hankey never budged from his view that the Prime Minister should be the titular, and if possible the active chairman of the Committee,[1] and in February he therefore arranged for Baldwin to meet the heads of the Service Departments and the Chiefs of Staff at a C.I.D. meeting.[2] Though Hankey was well aware of Curzon's qualities 'at making a lucid exposition of a tangled situation' he was also very much aware of the unpopularity he had incurred in the Foreign Office – chiefly by his arrogant and inconsiderate behaviour to his subordinates. Though Curzon 'begged Baldwin not to impose this burden [the C.I.D.] on me', the Prime Minister could find no other way of consoling him for his replacement as Foreign Secretary by Austen Chamberlain. In fact Hankey soon 'got to like and appreciate him [Curzon] as a chief', and found him (unlike Baldwin) 'extraordinarily prompt in dealing with business'.[3] Thus their brief partnership proved more fruitful and less burdensome than Hankey had feared. Early in 1923 he had written for the Bonar Law Cabinet a long paper entitled 'Strategical Preparation for War', and tried to get a small sub-committee of the C.I.D. formed to consider it.[4] Though he had no success on that occasion the advent of Curzon provided a new

[1]See for example his lecture 'The Origin and Development of the C.I.D.' delivered at the London School of Economics 11th March 1927, with Balfour in the chair. It was published in *The Army Quarterly* for July 1927. Also a lecture on 'Higher Control in War' dated 28th Oct. 1927, probably delivered at the Imperial Defence College. Copies of lectures given by Hankey while in office are preserved in Cab. 21/736. Lectures given after his retirement are preserved in his own papers.
[2]180th C.I.D. on 4th Feb. 1924. Cab. 21/469.
[3]Hankey to Curzon 8th Nov. 1924. *ibid.*
[4]Memo. of 29th Jan. 1923. Cab. 63/35.

opportunity, and in November 1924 Hankey sent him a full synopsis of the C.I.D's work since the last government came into office, and asked for chairmen to be nominated for its various sub-committees.[1] Furthermore his long and happy association with Haldane was not entirely severed, because Baldwin, with the cordial agreement of Curzon, Birkenhead and Cave, invited him to continue to serve on the C.I.D. and act as chairman of its sub-committee on Emergency Legislation. This was a subject to which Hankey, who was all too well aware of the likelihood of industrial strife, attached great importance. 'I do hope you will accept' he added in a postscript to the invitation.[2] Despite MacDonald's overt misgivings about a member of his recent Cabinet serving on the C.I.D. under his successor Haldane agreed to do so.[3] In addition Haldane's mind was returning to the field of 'civil research' – economic as well as scientific – to which he had first been drawn in 1918, and in which he had endeavoured, unsuccessfully, to interest MacDonald in 1924.[4] A year later, thanks to Balfour's intervention, the Committee of Civil Research was actually formed; and its organisation was based, as Haldane had originally proposed, on that of the C.I.D. Though Tom Jones acted as secretary of the C.C.R. until his retirement Hankey always took great interest in the many, far-reaching projects considered by its numerous sub-committees, and kept in close touch with Balfour on its work.[5] In February 1926 Balfour sent Hankey a memorandum urging that economy should not wholly stultify 'research in fields essential to the modernisation and prosperity of industry'. He wrote that he addressed himself to Hankey 'partly because you are Secretary to the Cabinet and the proper channel through whom matters affecting many departments can most easily be distributed, and partly because you are Secretary of the Defence Committee, which is not unconcerned with some of the issues on which I shall touch'.[6] Hankey showed this impressive missive to Baldwin, and after discussing the matter with the Treasury he replied reassuringly.[7] But Balfour was evidently still uneasy, since a few days later he wrote

[1]Diary 22nd March 1925.

[2]Hankey to Haldane 13th Nov. 1924. Haldane papers.

[3]Dudley Sommer, *Haldane of Cloan* (Allen and Unwin, 1960), pp. 411–12.

[4]R. B. Haldane, *An Autobiography* (Hodder and Stoughton, 1929), p. 331.

[5]See Roy M. MacLeod and E. Kay Andrews, *The Committee of Civil Research: Scientific Advice for Economic Development 1925–30*, Minerva, Vol. VII, No. 4 (1969).

[6]Balfour to Hankey 12th Feb. 1926. B.M. Add. MSS. 49704, pp. 50–67.

[7]Hankey to Balfour 15th Feb. 1926. *ibid.*

again stressing that 'Industrial Research ought not to be regarded as a desirable luxury like good motor roads', but in the opposite sense – namely "Can we afford *not* to spend the sums on research which the general economic policy of the government and our national position among world producers seem to require?" '[1] Again Hankey assured his old friend and ally that the Prime Minister entirely agreed, and so he felt sure did the Chancellor of the Exchequer. And as Balfour had proposed in the House of Lords that the new body should be modelled on the C.I.D. he forwarded a full statement on that body's organisation and functions[2] – with which the reader will already be familiar. A short time later he sent Haldane a similarly optimistic report, and received in reply:—'What you tell me of the P.M. is very reassuring. The business of the Committees [i.e. the C.C.R.] is under his supervision, and you and he can shape it. It is important that it should be the P.M. who takes the active ministerial part, whenever he can make time to do so. And this one cares about his work in this as in other reforms' – a surprising tribute to a political opponent and to a Prime Minister often criticised for sloth.[3]

It will be convenient here to carry on the story of the C.C.R. to the end. In 1930 it was transformed into the Economic Advisory Council,[4] and that body was in turn the forerunner of the Cabinet's Scientific Advisory Committee of 1940, of which Hankey, then Minister without Portfolio, became chairman. He must then have felt that his appointment forged the final link in the chain of ideas propagated some twenty years earlier by two of his closest friends, Haldane and Balfour.[5]

At his return to office in 1924 Baldwin succeeded in healing the breach in the Conservative party which had been opened by the Carlton Club meeting. Austen Chamberlain and Birkenhead, shortly followed by Balfour, now returned to the fold. The surprise appointment in the new Cabinet was of course that of Churchill as Chancellor of the Exchequer. But, taken as a whole, Baldwin's new team was far stronger than that which he had inherited from Bonar Law; and in the autumn of 1924 the auguries for the future of the new government appeared

[1]Balfour to Hankey 19th Feb. 1926. *ibid.* pp. 88–91.

[2]Hankey to Balfour 22nd Feb. 1926. *ibid.* pp. 92–3. Also in Cab. 63/37.

[3]Haldane to Hankey. Holograph. 5th March 1926.

[4]By Treasury Minute of 27th June 1930. Cab. 21/482.

[5]On the prolonged birth pangs of the Scientific Advisory Committee, and the pposition to it expressed by some scientists in 1938–40, see Cab. 21/711.

very favourable.[1] Hankey lost no time at all in getting Baldwin to confirm that the conduct of Cabinet business was to continue as before[2] – despite the misgivings about the recording of discussions which still existed in some quarters. A year later he told the Prime Minister that a valuable precedent for this practice had been discovered through John Fortescue's research in George III's papers. Therefore, he wrote, 'if the question should ever be raised again we should be in a much stronger position to meet the criticisms of the constitutional pundits'.[3] In fact the keeping of Cabinet minutes was not seriously challenged after the debate of 1922; and the system introduced by Hankey in 1916 has endured to this day.

At about the time that Hankey stabilised the situation regarding Cabinet procedure he sent Baldwin, at the request of the latter, 'some notes in regard to the personnel of the C.I.D.' He proposed that 'for your present period of office' membership should remain the same as the Salisbury Committee of 1923 had recommended[4]; and he was opposed to any large increase of numbers such as had taken place before the outbreak of World War I. Lord Salisbury himself was, because of his long experience, the only addition he now suggested; and he tactfully threw cold water on Baldwin's own proposal that Lord Peel should join the committee. As to the urgent matter of considering the Geneva Protocol, which had been left unsettled by the MacDonald government, he thought that Lord Cecil, who 'has by far the widest knowledge of this question' should be invited to attend on an *ad hoc* basis. Hankey then added the glancing blow that, except for Sir Cecil Hurst, Lord Cecil 'is the only person, I think, in the government or government service who has a good word to say for the protocol'.[5]

It will be convenient here to carry on the story of the Geneva

[1]*Baldwin*, pp. 278 ff.

[2]Hankey to Baldwin 6th Nov. 1924. Also C.P. 508(24) of 27th Nov. 1924. Cab. 21/294.

[3]Same to same 13th Nov. 1925. Cab. 21/294. Fortescue to Hankey 11th Nov. 1925 describes the precedent he had discovered regarding the keeping of records of Privy Councils in the 18th century. Cab. 63/38.

[4]See pp. 336–41. The Salisbury Committee recommended that the members should be the Chairman (Deputy to the Prime Minister), the Secretaries of State for Foreign Affairs, War, Air and India, the first Lord of the Admiralty, Chancellor of the Exchequer, Permanent Secretary of the Treasury and the three Chiefs of Staff.

[5]Hankey to Baldwin 26th Nov. 1924. Cab. 21/469.

Protocol to its final demise. Actually Cecil was not invited to attend the meetings of the C.I.D. sub-committee appointed on 16th December to consider whether the Protocol was 'susceptible of being amended', and what principles should govern any alternative which the committee might recommend. But early that month he sent Hankey the draft of a paper he was thinking of circulating, and also asked the busy secretary for answers to a number of difficult questions on the history of the League Covenant, and especially Article 16 – the much disputed 'sanctions' clause, which Hankey had always cordially disliked. Cecil declared that the Foreign Office tended 'to play fast and loose with our obligations under the Covenant', which he considered 'disastrous'; and, somewhat sweepingly, he declared that 'all the Continental nations' regarded Article 16 'as their sheet anchor'.[1] Hankey as usual had all the history at his finger tips, and replied next day not only answering Cecil's questions but bringing him back to reality by stressing that 'Had we ever been able to foresee that America would not join [the League], I do not believe the Covenant would ever have included any sanctions or commitments.' The more closely these were examined, wrote Hankey, 'the more impracticable they appear'; and every effort by the League 'to cross the T's and dot the I's of Article 16 appears to lead them further into the morass'. His own fear was, and always had been, that 'these repeated efforts to achieve the impossible' would discredit 'the priceless work' the League was doing 'for the peaceful settlement of disputes'.[2] The chief British advocate of the Protocol can have been left in no doubt that he was faced by a formidable adversary. And when the C.I.D. nominated Hankey as chairman of the sub-committee appointed to report on it, the fate of the document was in no very great doubt.[3] It began its sessions on 24th December and reported a month later.[4] Curzon called the report 'a

[1] Cecil to Hankey 8th Dec. 1924. Cab. 21/289.

[2] Hankey to Cecil 9th Dec. 1924. *ibid.*

[3] 192nd C.I.D. meeting of 16th Dec. 1924. Cab. 2/4. The other members of the Hankey sub-committee were Sir Eyre Crowe, Sir Arthur Hirtzel and Sir Henry Lambert, Permanent Under-Secretaries of the Foreign, Colonial and India offices respectively. Cecil's memorandum defending the Protocol is C.I.D. 547B of 11th Dec. 1924.

[4] C.I.D. 559B of 23rd Jan. 1925. Amery proposed to Baldwin (18th March 1925, Baldwin papers Vol. 132, pp. 24 and 25) that this paper should be sent to the Dominions. But as Curzon's forthright and critical memorandum (C.P. 105(25)) and other papers were essential to full understanding of the story Chamberlain

powerful but measured condemnation of the Protocol in its more salient features' – which was certainly no overstatement[1]; while Balfour, whose views Hankey had sought, referred to it contemptuously as 'this intolerable theme'.[2] As to the Dominions, though Australia at first thought it would be 'most unwise to reject' the Protocol, S. M. Bruce, the Prime Minister of the Commonwealth, later told Amery he was opposed to the principle of compulsory arbitration[3]; New Zealand considered 'the whole proposal mischievous'; South Africa, after some hesitation, the Irish Free State and India proposed rejection; while Canada, after sitting on the fence for three months, came to much the same decision. In such circumstances the idea which had been mooted of holding an Imperial Conference in London 'to concert a united policy' was dropped.[4] Apart from Hankey's dislike of sanctions and his belief that it was impossible to define aggression or identify an aggressor, mentioned earlier, the basic reasons for his opposition to the Protocol are made clear in a memorandum he wrote in January 1925. In it he repeated his long-standing opposition to giving a military guarantee to France and Belgium, and the Protocol, he wrote, 'tends to favour such a development'. There never had been the slightest doubt, he declared, that if the countries in question were threatened – presumably by Germany – we would go to their aid. But a guarantee 'might involve us in quarrels' which did not threaten French security, and would also encourage the intransigence of France, of which he had such long and bitter experience ever since 1919. The only merit of the Protocol was 'that it provides for French security'.[5] For Britain it might well involve 'great military commitments and armaments'. He disliked 'vague, unlimited commitments' over which we could not exercise full control, and emphasised the opposition of the Dominions to the Protocol. He therefore declined to sign the report of the sub-committee which had considered it.[6] He did not, however, share

was opposed to sending the C.I.D's report. Instead the correspondence with the Dominions and India on the Geneva Protocol was published. Cmd. 2458 and 2492 of 1925.

[1]C.P. 105(25) of 19th Feb. 1925.

[2]Hankey to Balfour 19th Jan. and reply by latter of 9th Feb. 1925. Cab. 21/289.

[3]Bruce to Amery 6th May 1925. Baldwin papers Vol. 115, p. 76.

[4]Telegram Colonial Secretary to all Dominions of 19th Jan. 1925. Cab. 21/289.

[5]See C.I.D. 540B. Cab. 4/12.

[6]Memo, of 23rd Jan. 1925. Cab. 63/37. Many papers on the Hankey sub-committee on the Geneva Protocol are in Cab. 24/172.

Curzon's outright opposition to a Security Pact between Britain, France, Belgium and Germany, and greatly preferred that alternative, for which Sir Eyre Crowe had prepared a draft, to the Protocol.[1]

*Diary 22nd March 1925*

Almost his [Curzon's] last official act was to oppose the Four Power Pact . . . [which] had been proposed on 2nd March. On 3rd I went in succession to the Prime Minister, Lord Curzon, [and] Lord Balfour to point out the objections to this arrangement. I pointed out that the average Englishman was prepared to fight for his country, and that . . ., in order to keep his home secure from aircraft attack, he might be persuaded to fight with [alongside] Belgium and France. But that in my opinion he would never consent to guarantee the German frontier against France, because this could never be really a British interest. Baldwin had to go off that evening to his aged mother's bedside, but Curzon and Balfour (who is a member of the C.I.D. though not of the government) were much moved by my arguments, and went off to Austen Chamberlain, who was to preside next day at the Cabinet in Baldwin's absence. The result was that Curzon was asked to put the point at the Cabinet. Owing to this intervention Chamberlain had to go to Paris and Geneva to meet Herriot with instructions severely limiting his initiative and powers in the matter of the Four Power Pact. Next day, March 5th, Curzon presided over a Committee meeting of the Privy Council . . . and afterwards he and I had some talk. Almost his last words to me – in fact they were his last words – were satisfaction at having, as he thought, killed the idea of a Four Power Pact of guarantee (though of course he had no objection to a pact of non-aggression). A fortnight later he died, and within seven hours of his death the Cabinet had decided to authorise Austen Chamberlain to announce a policy of aiming at the Four Power Pact of Guarantee. I took the draft Minutes to Chamberlain that afternoon . . . and took the opportunity to point out that the question had not been considered from the point of view of commitments. While I recognised that his policy was a peace policy and not a war policy, nevertheless it did involve commitments. Some day the cheque might be presented, and we should have to honour it. Had he considered the desirability of having the question of the commitments involved in his policy considered by the [service] staffs and the C.I.D. ? His reply was what I expected. He thought that by this quadruple pact he might secure a permanent peace, and get rid of the war spirit which is so rife in Europe. If he failed he thought that Europe would inevitably drift in time into another war. He did not wish to wreck his policy on the technicalities of military considerations. Military men were bound to look at the

[1]Hankey to Curzon 23rd Dec. 1924 and to Chamberlain 24th Jan. 1925. Cab. 21/289

question from rather a narrow point of view – and so forth. I then suggested that at least he and the Prime Minister should see the Chiefs of Staff of the three services, and explain the policy to them and enlist their good will. He liked this idea and put it to the P.M. I then saw Baldwin, whom I caught as he was leaving for Chequers, and put the whole thing to him. Baldwin also favoured the idea of seeing the Chiefs of Staff. Baldwin also told me that he was going to ask Balfour (who is on his way to Palestine)[1] to take Lord Curzon's job as President of the Council. He himself intends to take the C.I.D. I am unhappy about this Four Power Pact. It is not so bad as the Geneva Protocol, but it will be unpopular. If I were behind Lloyd George to brief him what hay we would make of it! But I have done as much as I ought, and shall now leave them to work it out. Amery accepts it, only because he is certain the French won't take it – a bad reason.

Such was Hankey's initial reaction to the treaty which ultimately became known as the Locarno Pact. On 12th March Chamberlain announced at Geneva that the British government had rejected the Protocol, and gave as reasons the objections stated at length in the Hankey Committee's report. But he went on to outline the alternative proposal – namely for 'special arrangements to meet special needs . . . these arrangements to be purely defensive in character, framed in the spirit of the Covenant and working in close harmony with the League and under its guidance'.[2] Lord Cecil was, very naturally, distressed by the government's decision to reject the Protocol – of which he had been the foster parent during the discussions in the fifth League Assembly (1st Sept.–2nd Oct. 1924). He wrote to Baldwin more in sorrow than in anger, and suggested a Tripartite (British–French–German) pact as a first step to the establishment of enduring peace in Europe.[3] This, of course, was very much what Chamberlain had in mind. At this stage Cecil and Hankey, though fundamentally divided in their concepts of the best policy for the achievement of peace, were still on friendly terms; and the letters that passed between them, though neither attempted to gloss their differences, were perfectly cordial.[4]

[1]At the end of March 1925 Balfour paid his only visit to Palestine, accompanied by Dr. and Mrs. Weizmann, to attend the opening of the Hebrew University on Mount Scopus outside Jerusalem. He received a great welcome from the Jewish population. See Blanche Dugdale, *Arthur James Balfour* (Hutchinson, 1936), Vol. II, pp. 364–70.

[2]Roskill, *Naval Policy*, I, p. 436.

[3]Cecil to Baldwin 22nd March 1925. Baldwin papers Vol. 115, pp. 68–71.

[4]See for example Cecil to Hankey 8th Dec. 1924 and reply by latter of 9th. Cab. 21/289.

But as Cecil became more and more extreme in his views and outlook, and finally embarrassed the government grievously by the timing and manner of his resignation in 1927, their relations steadily worsened. Hankey then came to regard Cecil as a hopelessly impracticable idealist, even 'a crank'; while Cecil stigmatised Hankey as a 'militarist' – which he certainly was not.

Among historians and biographers of the post-World War I generation, and especially those with a left-wing bias, it has become customary to regard the Geneva Protocol as the most promising instrument for the improvement of international relations and the preservation of peace produced during the 1920s, and to represent its rejection as a disaster.[1] But such views benefit too much from the historically dubious but oft-exploited benefit of hindsight. Viewed in the context of the time the Protocol did contain serious dangers – especially with regard to the responsibilities it could have placed on the British Navy. Faced by the indifference, and in some cases the hostility of the Dominions, not to mention the fact that American opinion was very lukewarm,[2] it is surely inconceivable that any British government would have accepted it. Though MacDonald later attacked the Baldwin administration for rejecting it,[3] we have already seen how, when in office, he himself had been extremely cautious in the instructions given to his representatives at the League Assembly when the Protocol was to be considered.

Certainly Hankey bore a share of the responsibility for its rejection, and he never attempted to play it down. Nor did he at any later period regret his action or express any doubts regarding its wisdom. His antagonism derived of course from his dislike of the 'sanctions' article enshrined in the League Covenant, and from his belief that the automatic application of sanctions against an 'aggressor' imposed an unlimited obligation over a very wide field. 'I do not know quite what "aggressive war" is' he told Balfour during their correspondence on the

[1]See for example Philip Noel-Baker, *The Geneva Protocol* (P. S. King & Son, 1925) and *Disarmament* (Hogarth Press, 1926) esp. Ch. XVII.

[2]C.P. 48(25) of 27th Jan. 1925 is a memorandum by Chamberlain on the American attitude. He had ascertained that the American administration considered it contained 'many sources of trouble', and they anticipated that it 'will die a natural death'.

[3]At a meeting of the Socialist Party and of representatives of socialist organisations in foreign countries held on 9th April 1926. Chamberlain papers AC 53/355.

subject.[1] Nor did anyone else. Hankey very well knew that 'sanctions' was merely a new word for the ancient strategy of blockade; and that blockade, though slow-acting, could prove an extremely potent instrument of war. But for a blockade to achieve its purpose the nation or nations applying it had not only to possess the forces necessary to make it effective (as indeed was recognised in International Law), but had to be prepared *to use those forces*. And such measures constituted of course an act of war – even if war was not declared. Hankey well knew that the British blockades of Napoleonic France and of Imperial Germany had in the end proved extremely effective, even decisive; and that they were made so by the steady application of sea power. How, he asked prophetically, could Britain apply sanctions against Japan in the event of an aggression by her against China – without grave risk of finding herself at war with Japan over an issue which was not of vital concern to Britain? Such a possibility caused him grave, and entirely understandable concern. And, if it comes to reaping the benefits of hindsight, has experience of sanctions applied either by the League of Nations or the United Nations produced any evidence to vitiate Hankey's arguments of 1925? The action taken in the cases of Japan and Manchuria 1931–32, Italy and Abyssinia 1935–36, and Britain and Rhodesia in the 1960s surely support his view; for in none of those cases were sanctions effective – because no nation supporting them was prepared to follow the policy to its logical and inevitable conclusion – namely the use of force – even if it meant war.

The death of Curzon only a week after the rejection of the Geneva Protocol removed one of those whom Hankey called 'the great war figures' from the stage. He considered him 'a good man in the second class', 'a very proud man and very particular about matters of precedence'. Thus Curzon was annoyed that Chamberlain as Deputy Leader of the House of Commons took precedence over himself in Baldwin's Cabinet; and he constantly 'badgered' Hankey to get this changed.[2] Naturally stories about Curzon's idiosyncracies, many of which he himself actually propagated, were revived, and probably embellished, after his death. Hankey recorded one which he received at second hand. When Curzon lay dying he wrote a memorandum in his own hand thanking his doctors and nurses, and asked that it might be published. As the end drew near he 'ordered all the four doctors away from his bedside', adding 'Besides they are drinking up my best

[1]Hankey to Balfour 16th Feb. 1925. Cab. 21/289. [2]Diary 22nd March 1925.

brandy'![1] No matter what his faults may have been, and Hankey often suffered acutely from his irregular hours and exacting habits, he will always remain one of the outstanding figures of the era.[2] In May 1927 Hankey was evidently asked to contribute to a memoir on Curzon, and sent Tom Jones his impressions. 'Frankly, when I searched my heart', he wrote, 'I can't form a very high opinion of Curzon, and my memories of him are not always pleasant. "No man is a hero to his valet!" I have been "intellectual valet" to many – Asquith, Balfour, Lloyd George remain heroes. Curzon does not! That is the difficulty! . . . '.[3] None the less Hankey did produce – after making four drafts – a long memoir of Curzon, and when he sent it to Vansittart for remarks the latter replied 'You have trod with delicacy and discretion and yet with a clear intimation of the truth'. In Vansittart's opinion Curzon was 'An A.1 Class 2 man' – which corresponded closely to Hankey's view.[4]

We have already seen how Hankey worked very hard to bring the Dominions fully into the organisation of the C.I.D. In October 1924 Australia took an important step in the direction he desired, when Richard Casey[5] arrived in London as the special emissary of Mr. Bruce, Prime Minister of the Commonwealth. Casey carried introductions to the British Prime Minister, to the Foreign and Colonial Secretaries[6] – and to Hankey. But his arrival was greeted with what Casey

[1] *ibid.*

[2] A recent assessment of Curzon by Sir Oswald Mosley published in *The Times* 15th Oct. 1968 was headed 'Lord Curzon: a great public servant shabbily treated'. But as the author is Curzon's son-in-law his view can hardly be accepted as objective.

[3] Hankey to Jones 10th May 1927.

[4] Hankey's memoir dated 19th May 1927, and Vansittart's reply undated. Cab. 63/39.

[5] 1st Baron Casey 1960 (1890– ). Australian soldier, politician (Lib.) and diplomat. Liaison officer with British Foreign Office 1924–27 and 1927–31. Assistant Federal Treasurer 1933–35 and Federal Treasurer 1935–39. Minister for Development 1937 and for Supply and Development 1939–40. Minister to U.S.A. 1940–42. Minister of State Resident in Middle East, and member of U.K. War Cabinet 1942–43. Governor of Bengal 1944–46. Minister of Works and Housing 1949–51, of National Development 1950–51, of Scientific Research and Organisation 1950–60 and for External Affairs 1951–60. Governor-General of Australia 1965–70.

[6] Responsibility for 'the autonomous communities within the Empire' passed from the Colonial Secretary to the Secretary of State for Dominion Affairs on 1st July 1925. Leo Amery, the Colonial Secretary, was then appointed Dominions Secretary additionally, and the two offices were generally held by the same Minister until 1938.

has euphemistically called 'very moderate enthusiasm' by Sir Joseph Cook,[1] the Australian High Commissioner in London, because his instructions were to communicate direct with Bruce. A sharp interchange of telegrams between Cook and Bruce followed; but the latter insisted on maintaining his arrangement. When Casey called on Hankey the latter said 'This is splendid. It's what I've hoped for for years. If you are not fixed up with an office I'll give you two rooms in this building'. Thereafter Hankey gave Casey his 'firm and warm support'; and although he did not see all C.I.D. papers, Casey came to regard him as 'my father and mother, who made my task possible of achievement'.[2] So began another of the life-long friendships which brought Hankey so much happiness, and contributed so greatly to his own achievements. But Casey admits that, as Hankey and Adeline 'lived on carrots and salads and very little else' (referring to the period of their vegetarianism[3]), his weekends at Highstead were 'rather a torture' – though his host and hostess 'seemed to thrive' on the diet they had adopted.

In his endeavours to strengthen the ties between the Mother Country and the self-governing Dominions Hankey had two powerful allies in Baldwin's government – Austen Chamberlain and Leo Amery; and by this time he seems to have entirely overcome the mistrust he had felt towards Amery when he first joined the Cabinet Secretariat.[4] It may well have been Casey's arrival that spurred Chamberlain to tell Baldwin he would do all he could 'for any accredited representative of a Dominion', and considered 'the proper place for this liaison officer is

[1] 1860–1947. Australian politician (Lib. then Coalit.). Held many Ministerial appointments 1894–1910. Commonwealth Prime Minister and Minister for Home Affairs 1913–14. Minister for Navy 1917–20. A representative of Australia at Paris Peace Conference 1919 and Genoa Conference 1922. Commonwealth Treasurer 1920–21. High Commissioner for Australia in U.K. 1921–27.

[2] Lord Casey to the author, 6th Feb. 1968. Casey remarks that two distributions for C.I.D. papers were unofficially introduced – 'K' for 'King' and 'C and C' for Cabinet and Casey.

[3] In fact the Hankeys did not adopt the 'Nature Cure' until 1931, following Adeline's five months of serious illness. Casey must therefore have been referring to visits to Highstead after that date. The result of the new diet was the complete restoration of Adeline's health, which had been very poor ever since 1918 when she nearly died of influenza (see Vol. I, pp. 629–31). When deep in her eighties she still possessed remarkable physical and mental vigour.

[4] See Vol. I, pp. 344, 349 and 352–3.

in the Cabinet Office, where *all* information centres';[1] while Amery constantly bombarded the Prime Minister with proposals for closer economic, financial and military co-ordination with the Dominions.[2]

The cancellation of the Singapore base by the first Labour government made it certain that their successors would have to give high priority to the question whether that decision should stand; and that of course meant that the Admiralty, the C.I.D., and Hankey himself had to do all over again the work which had taken up so much time and effort between 1919 and 1924. Very naturally Churchill as Chancellor, and an extreme advocate of economy, quickly appeared on the stage in the rôle of opponent. In November 1924 he held informal discussions with the First Lord (Bridgeman) and First Sea Lord (Beatty), and was infuriated to learn that they had the intercepts of the Japanese Ambassador's report on his own talks with Chamberlain about the Singapore base. Evidently Churchill as Chancellor was no less aware of the great value of intelligence derived from cryptographic sources than Churchill as First Lord had been![3]

Within a month of assuming office the Baldwin Cabinet approved in principle that the Singapore base project should go ahead, though the rate of progress was left open for discussion in the C.I.D.[4] A new sub-committee, initially under Curzon's chairmanship, was set up early in 1925 to review the whole question, and during that year it produced two reports.[5] The committee remained in being throughout Baldwin's second administration, with Balfour as chairman in succession to Curzon and then, from late 1925 to the end, Baldwin himself in the chair. A third report was issued in July 1926,[6] and Hankey acted as secretary throughout the whole of the committee's existence. He therefore had to handle not only the violent controversy which arose between

[1]Memo. of 20th Dec. 1924. Baldwin papers Vol. 93.

[2]For example Amery to Baldwin 6th June 1925 and 30th Sept. 1926 – in which he proposed a Joint Secretariat for the 1926 Imperial Conference. Amery was of course an advocate of Empire Preference, and indeed a strong protectionist – causes which Baldwin handled very gingerly after the electoral débâcle of 1923.

[3]Churchill to Chamberlain 21st Nov. 1924. Chamberlain papers AC 21/9/24.

[4]C.I.D. 236C of 5th Dec. 1924 recorded the Cabinet decision of 26th Nov. C.I.D. 238C of 31st Dec. 1924 refers to the rate of progress.

[5]The first meeting of the sub-committee took place on 16th Jan. 1925. Its two reports of that year are in C.I.D. 243C of 27th Feb. and 253C of 23rd Oct. 1925. A special series with the self-evident title S.P. (25)1–22 was started for the memoranda submitted to the committee.

[6]C.I.D. 275C of 20th July 1926.

the Admiralty and War Office on the one side and the Air Ministry on the other side over whether the defences of the base should consist mainly of heavy guns or of shore-based bombers, but the constant pressure of the Chancellor for economy, and the very full discussion on the project which took place at the 1926 Imperial Conference. We cannot here go into the details of the controversial aspects of the question, which this biographer has in fact dealt with fully elsewhere;[1] but it should be remarked that Hankey managed to maintain friendly relations with both Beatty and Trenchard, the First Sea Lord and Chief of the Air Staff, throughout their arguments over the defences, and often managed to lower the temperature of a heated debate. Indeed in mid-1926 he conceived a very sensible compromise arrangement, involving the installation of some fixed defences and the employment of some shore-based aircraft, which, one feels, should have been acceptable to two less opinionated men.[2] The Chancellor proved even more difficult to handle, and in the end the Admiralty was forced to accept a 'truncated scheme' which would only cost some two-thirds of the £12 millions estimated for the full scheme.[3]

Simultaneously with the renewal of the controversy over the Singapore base Hankey was involved in the Admiralty's fight to obtain approval for a modest but steady building programme to replace the ageing war-built ships. This produced a fierce battle between the Admiralty and the Chancellor, who took the initiative on 26th November 1924 by suggesting that the C.I.D. should resurvey 'the situation as a whole and the dangers to which the British Empire is exposed', should consider the desirability of renewing the 'Ten Year Rule' established in August 1919, and should also review the Admiralty's proposals for naval construction. At about the same time Churchill launched a violent attack on that department in letters to Baldwin and Chamberlain.[4] To the former he wrote that Admiralty policy in the Far East was 'provocative'. 'Why should there be a war with Japan?' he asked rhetorically, adding that he did not believe 'there is the slightest chance of it in our life time' – one of his less happy predictions. He sent a copy

[1]Roskill, *Naval Policy*, I, esp. Chs. XII and XVI.

[2]Hankey to Trenchard 23rd June 1926 and replies by latter of 24th and 26th. Trenchard papers.

[3]Roskill, *op. cit.* pp. 463–4.

[4]Churchill to Baldwin and Chamberlain 15th Dec. 1924. Chamberlain papers AC 51/66 and /67.

of this letter to Chamberlain with a note saying 'What I seek is a declaration to the Cabinet by you ruling out war with Japan from among the reasonable possibilities to be taken into account in the next 10, 15 and 20 years'. This was tantamount to asking the Foreign Office to trim its sails to the cold wind blowing from the Treasury. The result of Churchill's onslaught was that on 5th February 1925 the Cabinet set up a Naval Programme Committee under Birkenhead; and then the fight over the Navy Estimates was joined in earnest.[1] Hankey's sympathies undoubtedly lay with the Admiralty over this issue, and on 9th February he circulated a memorandum setting out the desperate straits to which Britain's heavy industries, which he described as 'the basis of Imperial Defence', had been reduced for want of orders for armaments.[2] This paper brought him into conflict with his deputy Tom Jones, who wrote direct to Baldwin, apparently without his Chief's knowledge, attacking the construction of warships as a measure for ameliorating unemployment, and indeed the whole thesis that the time had come to modernise and re-equip the fighting services. 'In so far as [defence expenditure] is indispensable . . . to safeguard the citizens in the discharge of their daily duties – a policy of insurance – it is justified', wrote Jones. 'But every sixpence beyond this is sheer waste. It is a special kind of economic loss. It robs the country of goods and services which all engaged on "armaments" might otherwise have produced . . . Further the devotion of brain to armaments seems to lead to multiplication of appliances at increasing cost, and to more and more rapid obsolescence . . .'[3] One may see in this attack by Jones the genesis of his support for the appeasement of Germany in the 1930s. And Hankey's marginal notes on his letter such as 'Doles! which rot the morale of the people and promote the interests of the shirker' and 'Employment on armaments [is] a better form of insurance against unemployment than the dole', show how wide was the gulf between them.[4] However, despite Jones's intervention the outcome of the long and acrimonious debate over the 1925–26 Navy Estimates was a victory for Bridgeman and Beatty over Churchill – because the First

[1]Roskill, *op. cit.* pp. 445–53.
[2]Memo. of 9th Feb. 1925. Cab. 63/37.
[3]Jones to Baldwin 28th Feb. 1925. Baldwin papers Vol. 6, pp. 40–50. This letter is not printed in Middlemas, *Whitehall Diary*.
[4]Cab. 63/37.

Lord was fully prepared to resign rather than accept the Chancellor's cuts.[1] But, as will be told later, Churchill had by no means exhausted his armoury of weapons with which to attack the Service estimates.

One of the new C.I.D. sub-committees formed at this time in consequence of the threat (initially from France) of air bombardment of our cities was the Air Raid Precautions (A.R.P.) sub-committee. Sir John Anderson[2] was chairman, Hankey became a member of it (as opposed to secretary) early in 1924, and its first report (of 37 printed pages) clearly bears the imprint of his style.[3] Here we may introduce, as counter-balance to Jones's lack of sympathy with Hankey, the impression the latter made on a civil servant who attended the A.R.P. committee. 'I first met Maurice Hankey', writes Ronald Wells,[4] 'in the twenties, when as a youngish Assistant Principal in the Home Office I went to an A.R.P. meeting in Whitehall Gardens in place of my Assistant Secretary . . . Naturally I was rather overwhelmed until Hankey [apparently on this occasion acting as chairman] turned to me and said "And what does our colleague from the Home Office think?". From that moment, as you will imagine, I became his devoted admirer and disciple'.[5]

Almost simultaneously with the rendering of the first report by the A.R.P. Committee Hankey put pressure on the Sub-Committee on the Co-ordination of Departmental Action – colloquially known as the War Book Committee – to bring its work up to date. It met, still with Sir Eyre Crowe as chairman, in mid-December 1924, and took note of the fact that a year had elapsed since its last report.[6] Hankey now got himself instructed to draft a statement on the progress achieved in 1924 – which meant he could call on every department to report what

[1] Roskill, *op. cit.* pp. 445–53 and *Baldwin*, Ch. 13, aptly titled 'Defence: the Price of Churchill'.

[2] 1st Viscount Waverley 1952 (1882–1958). Civil servant and politician (Nat. Cons.). Secretary, Ministry of Shipping 1917–19. Chairman, Board of Inland Revenue 1919–22. Permanent Under-Secretary, Home Office 1922–32. Governor of Bengal 1932–37. Lord Privy Seal 1938–39. Home Secretary and Minister of Home Security 1939–40. Lord President of Council 1940–43. Chancellor of Exchequer 1943–45.

[3] The first report of the sub-committee is C.I.D. 135A of 8th July 1925.

[4] 1894– . Civil servant, Home Office 1919–54. Member of War Book Committee 1935–39 and of Security Executive 1940–45.

[5] Letter to the author 20th April 1970.

[6] C.I.D. W6 of 18th Dec. 1923. Approved at 179th C.I.D. meeting in Jan. 1924.

they had done, and were doing on the subject.[1] Though the War Book always remained a great speciality of his, derived from his experiences of 1912–14, this provides a nice example of the way he would use a C.I.D. sub-committee to get what he wanted from all government departments – some of which he knew very well to be sluggardly over producing their own sections of the War Book. Ronald Wells, the civil servant already quoted, later became the full time Home Office member of the War Book Committee, and has described it as 'one of the most beautiful pieces of engineering I have ever seen – everything tied up and working together'.[2]

Another new committee at whose birth Hankey assisted at this time, and which was ultimately to prove important, was the Anti-Aircraft Defence Sub-Committee, later known as the Tizard Committee after its chairman of the 1930s.[3] On 8th April 1925 Hankey wrote to Professor F. A. Lindemann[4] of Oxford University saying that the Prime Minister had set up a sub-committee of the C.I.D. with Haldane as chairman 'to investigate scientific aspects of A.A. defence'. It was to meet for the first time at Whitehall Gardens on 29th, and he asked the Professor to serve on it. Lindemann accepted the invitation, which was almost certainly issued on Churchill's initiative, and at first everything went smoothly. Early in 1926 the sub-committee's first report was ready for consideration by the full C.I.D., and with Baldwin's approval Hankey invited Haldane to attend the meeting at which it was to be discussed.[5] But thereafter the impetus applied by Haldane and Hankey was lost, and in November 1928 Baldwin decided that the committee

[1]The Admiralty's copy is in Adm. 1/8682–128/25. Doubtless every department received copies.

[2]Letter to the author 20th April 1970.

[3]Sir Henry T. Tizard (1885–1959). Scientist, administrator and educationist. Permanent Secretary, Department of Scientific and Industrial Research 1927–29. Rector, Imperial College of Science and Technology 1929–42. President, Magdalen College, Oxford 1942–46. Chairman, Aeronautical Research Committee 1933–43. Additional member of Air Council 1941–43. Chairman, Advisory Council on Scientific Policy and Defence Research Policy Committee 1946–52. President, British Association 1948.

[4]1st Viscount Cherwell 1956 (1886–1957). Scientist. Professor of Experimental Philosophy, Oxford 1919 and 1953–56. Personal Assistant to Churchill as Prime Minister 1940. Paymaster-General 1942–45 and 1951–53.

[5]Hankey to Haldane 20th Jan. 1926. Haldane papers. The sub-committee's report was C.I.D. 651B.

should be 'suspended'.[1] It was not revived until 1933, and then led to perhaps the most notorious scientific feud of modern times.[2]

In the field of Imperial Defence the two most troubled areas in the middle 1920s were Egypt and China. The murder of Sir Lee Stack,[3] the Sirdar, in Cairo on 22nd November 1924 produced a strong reaction in Britain against the long-drawn attempt to come to terms with the Egyptian nationalists; and at about the same time Chamberlain found himself increasingly at odds with Lord Allenby the High Commissioner, who had so resented the appointment of Arthur Henderson as Minister Plenipotentiary on his staff at Cairo that he wished to resign. After Chamberlain's attempt to reach a *modus vivendi* with Allenby had failed he informed the Cabinet that he proposed to accept his resignation.[4] The manner in which Hankey recorded the discussion provides an interesting example of his method of handling a very secret and delicate issue. The Cabinet minute (one copy only) is in his own hand; he sent it to Chamberlain and Baldwin for their remarks, and the former made a number of holograph amendments.[5] When Baldwin had initialled it he sent the gist of the minute to Stamfordham for the information of the King, who apparently accepted without demur that Allenby's attitude had been 'unfortunate'.[6] However Lord Lloyd,[7] Allenby's successor, proved no more amenable to direction from Whitehall, and before long Chamberlain was again to find himself at loggerheads with the High Commissioner in Egypt. These troubles did not, of course, help progress towards the British government's policy of negotiating a new treaty by which Egypt's sovereignty and independence would be

[1] Hankey to Lindemann 8th and 16th Nov. 1925 and 1st Nov. 1928. Cherwell papers.

[2] See Ronald Clark, *Tizard* (Methuen, 1956) and Lord Birkenhead, *The Prof. in Two Worlds* (Collins, 1961) for the two sides of the Tizard–Lindemann controversy of the 1930s.

[3] Soldier and administrator (1868–1924). Civil Secretary, Sudan Government 1913–16. Acting Governor of Sudan and Sirdar of Egyptian Army 1917–19. Governor-General of same and Sirdar 1919–24.

[4] Chamberlain to Baldwin 29th Nov. and 22nd Dec. 1924. Baldwin papers Vol. 114, pp. 242–6.

[5] Addendum to Cabinet (3)325 of 21st Jan. 1925. Hankey misdated it 1924. Cab. 23/49.

[6] Stamfordham to Hankey. Very Secret. 27th Jan. 1925. *ibid.*

[7] George A. Lloyd, 1st Baron Lloyd 1925 (1879–1941). Traveller, politician (Cons.) and Pro-Consul. Governor of Bombay 1918–23. High Commissioner for Egypt and Sudan 1925–29.

recognised, but special privileges would be granted to Britain in view of her vital interest in the Suez Canal. Amery on the other hand wanted to strengthen the British position by acquiring the balance of the Suez Canal Company's shares as part of a financial settlement with France.[1] Over the Egyptian imbroglio Hankey, who was acutely conscious of the vulnerability of Britain's maritime communications with India and her possessions in the Far East, was overtly imperialistic; and George Lloyd later became one of his intimate friends and confidants.

In the Far East the setting up of a Nationalist Chinese government under Sun Yat Sen at Canton in 1923, and the military offensive organised by his disciple Chiang Kai Shek three years later, led to widespread and often violent anti-British strikes and boycotts in Hong Kong and the Treaty Ports. The British government, beset by grave economic and financial problems at home, about which Sir Warren Fisher, Permanent Secretary of the Treasury, and Churchill were constantly circulating Cassandra-like warnings,[2] had no desire whatever to accept military commitments in that remote area; but commercial interests were strong and vociferous, and it gradually became plain that some measures would have to be taken. In June Hankey sent Baldwin a letter from Sir William Tyrrell[3] of the Foreign Office about the despatch of troops to North China, suggesting that the C.I.D. should refer the matter to the Chiefs of Staff Committee.[4] At about the same time Beatty put up a somewhat arrogant thesis that 'China has always been a naval responsibility [sic] and the views of the Admiralty upon recent developments must therefore receive attention.'[5] He proposed that Japan should be allowed 'to restore tranquillity in China' – despite the fact that the United States would 'resent this bitterly'. Hankey was inclined to go along with Beatty on this issue.

[1]Amery to Baldwin 29th June 1923. Baldwin papers Vol. 114, pp. 7–9.
[2]For example Churchill to Baldwin 15th Dec. 1924. Baldwin papers Vol. 2, pp. 26–35 and Fisher to Baldwin 22nd Jan. 1925. *ibid.* Vol. 5.
[3]See Vol. I, p. 521, *note*.
[4]Tyrrell to Hankey 19th June 1925 and Hankey to Baldwin of same date. Baldwin papers Vol. 110, pp. 107–10.
[5]Undated memo. c. July 1925. Beatty papers.

*Hankey to Beatty. 2 Whitehall Gardens 10th July 1925.* Holograph[1]

PERSONAL

Dear Lord Beatty,

I have been carefully considering your notes on policy and I am rather attracted by the general idea, which would require very careful handling in execution.

If some policy of the kind is not adopted I am afraid of the following situation arising. We shall have a real 'bust-up' in China. Japan will have to rescue the Legations and pull the chestnuts out of the fire for us all. Once at Pekin Japan will say *'j'y suis, j'y reste'*. We and America will make a hullaballoo, and produce that very situation of antagonism to Japan which we all want to avoid. In fact Japan would then get alongside China against us.

If we adopt your policy we escape this. We say to Japan 'Good luck to you. Do your best. We shall not oppose you, as long as you let our commercial people alone. You will want them and their money to develop China. So leave it at that'.

To America we say: 'You and we are not prepared to take this country in hand. Better leave it to Japan. She may get the lion's share, but the general improvement of China under her guidance will also benefit our trade as compared with the present chaos'.

I wonder if you could not, as a personal suggestion, develop your ideas when the China Report comes before the C.I.D.

Yours ever

As the situation steadily worsened, and Foreign Office reports became increasingly alarmist,[2] the issues were referred to the C.I.D. In March 1926 that body recorded that a blockade of Canton was the only practicable measure, but that 'offensive action on a large scale was not possible for the British Empire acting alone'. The government's policy was at first not to be drawn into intervention.[3] None the less Chamberlain asked for more warships to be sent out, and early in 1927, by which time Hankow had fallen to the Nationalist forces and the threat to Shanghai, with its large foreign trading community, was serious, the Admiralty prepared plans to send out a force of Royal Marines.[4] Amery, supported by Davidson and Churchill, was actively interventionist; and even Balfour thought that blockade, though 'an act of war', might produce the desired result.[5] The final outcome was

[1]Beatty papers.

[2]Foreign Office Memo. of 18th Sept. 1926. Baldwin papers Vol. 111.

[3]C.I.D. 677B of March 1926.

[4]Baldwin papers Vol. 111.

Amery to Baldwin 18th Sept. 1926; Davidson to Baldwin 10th Jan. 1927 ('Please

the intervention which the government had hoped to avoid. It assumed considerable proportions, and provided a pretext for the far more aggressive action by Japan at Shanghai in 1932. Typically Churchill, heretofore the great opponent of the Admiralty's plans to build up naval strength in the Far East, sent Baldwin fulsome congratulations on the despatch of troops early in 1927. 'Short of being actually conquered', he wrote, 'there is no evil worse than submitting to wrong and violence for fear of war'.[1] A C.I.D. Sub-Committee was appointed to consider ways and means of putting 'economic pressure' on China, and Lord Cecil, who had of course gained much experience of such matters as Minister of Blockade in World War I, agreed to serve as Chairman. When the draft report reached Hankey he urged on Cecil that, if we went to war with China, we should not 'connive at some trade [being carried on] with that country', as the Sub-Committee had proposed. A blockade, as he well knew, could not possibly be effective if applied half-heartedly. Hankey's long memory recalled that the pre-war committee on Trading with the Enemy had accepted similar arguments regarding neutral countries' trade with Germany.[2] 'I was always strongly against this paragraph', he wrote, 'and was certain it would not be realisable in practice. So it turned out'. Cecil agreed, and the report was amended accordingly.[3]

To return home and retrace our steps to 1925, it was in the spring of that year that the government took the decision to return to the Gold Standard. Hankey never laid any claims to expertise in economic matters, and accepted without demur the views of the Treasury officials, such as Sir Otto Niemeyer, and the bankers. But the claim that Churchill acted entirely under very severe pressure from such quarters, and finally yielded against his own better judgement[4] is at the very least rendered questionable by a letter he had sent Baldwin in the previous

burn'); Balfour to Baldwin 10th Jan. 1927. Baldwin papers Vol. 115, pp. 122–3 and 185–7.

[1]Churchill to Baldwin from Eze, Alpes Maritimes, 22nd Jan. 1927. *ibid.* pp. 205–8.

[2]This was the C.I.D. Sub-Committee under Lord Desart. It reported on 16th Feb. 1911. C.I.D. 124B. See also *Supreme Command*, I, pp. 90–1.

[3]Hankey to Cecil 1st Feb. 1927, with minute by latter in holograph. Cab. 21/299.

[4]See for example *The Times* of 17th March 1969 'Churchill's resistance was broken . . . he lived to count it the worst mistake of his life'.

December. 'It will be easy to attain the gold standard', he then wrote, 'and indeed almost impossible to avoid taking the decision'.[1]

In the early summer of 1925 the coal industry, which had suffered a catastrophic drop in exports, faced yet another crisis. For the story of the protracted negotiations between the government, the Miners' Federation (backed by the Trades Union Congress) and the Mining Association (the coal owners' organisation) the reader may be referred to the latest biography of Baldwin, where it is told in full detail, and to Tom Jones's diary[2]; for, as in 1919–21, it was Jones rather than Hankey who acted as chief conciliator in the endeavour to reach a compromise. Hankey's principal concern was to ensure the efficiency of the Supply and Transport Committee's preparations to keep essential services running in the event of a General Strike; and he appears to have organised that work on the same general lines as the famous War Book. Nor did he share Cunliffe-Lister's[3] opinion that in July the preparations were not yet far enough advanced to meet a national emergency – a view which may have influenced the decision of the government to grant a subsidy for nine months to enable wages to be paid at the current rates and an average level of profit for the mine owners to be maintained. This substantial victory for the T.U.C., achieved on 31st July, the day which was to pass into Trades Union mythology as 'Red Friday', caused serious misgivings among a substantial section of the Conservative party.[4] Shortly after the Cabinet had reached its decision on the subsidy Hankey sent a long letter on the subject to Stamfordham for the information of the King. It shows that his own point of view was by no means unsympathetic to the miners.

[1]Churchill to Baldwin 15th Dec. 1924. Baldwin papers Vol. 2, pp. 26–35. The main theme of this long letter was an attack on the probable rise of £10 millions in the supply estimates.

[2]*Baldwin*, pp. 394–94. *Middlemas*, I, pp. 323–9. Many documents of great interest for the detailed study of the negotiations are to be found in the Baldwin papers, Vol. 13.

[3]Cunliffe-Lister offered to resign from the government at this time, because as a coal owner with responsibility for the Mines Department he felt he could not properly continue at the Board of Trade. Baldwin begged him to defer action, and early in 1927 Cunliffe-Lister told him that his 'intimate interest with the coal industry had been terminated'. Baldwin papers Vol. 18, pp. 83–6.

[4]In the Conservative Press 31st July 1925 was referred to as 'Blackmail Friday'.

*Hankey to Stamfordham. 2 Whitehall Gardens. 31st July 1925*[1]

. . . It seems that, while Unionist Members . . . are opposed in principle to a subsidy, there is a strong feeling that the miners have a certain amount of right on their side. The miners asked for [an] inquiry on certain points as long ago as last February. I am not clear as to why there was no inquiry, but in fact it has not taken place.[2] Although a good many of the miners' points will be found to have no substance, there are others in which this may not be the case. In any event, it was felt that the case before public opinion could not be fully made until the facts had been brought out by an inquiry. If the result of the inquiry is to show that the miners are in the wrong, then one of two things will happen: either the miners will have to make some concession, or alternatively, if they insist on striking, their case before public opinion will have deteriorated. To put it bluntly, it was felt that public opinion would not be convinced that the miners were completely in the wrong, and that in these circumstances it would not be justifiable to plunge the country into so dire a struggle as that which is now threatened. [Here Hankey stated that the cost of the subsidy was estimated at £10 millions, compared with at least £70 millions for a 3 months' strike; 'to which must be added the appalling dislocation of trade and industry'. Actually the nine month subsidy cost £23 millions.] It was on a balance of these considerations that the Cabinet took their decision.

Yours sincerely,

Thus, by the appointment on 5th September of the Royal Commission on the Coal Industry under the chairmanship of Sir Herbert Samuel (after Lord Grey had declined Baldwin's invitation to serve), was a breathing space of some nine months gained – at a price.[3] As soon as that was accomplished Hankey turned his mind to the question of dis-

[1]RA GV B2015/19. Part of this letter is quoted in *Baldwin*, pp. 387–8, but it is wrongly referenced.

[2]In fact an 'Inquiry into the Coal Mining Dispute 1925' was instituted on 25th July under H. P. (later Lord) Macmillan, W. Sherwood and Sir Josiah (later Lord) Stamp. It reported on 28th July, Cmd. 2478. Stamp introduced an Addendum blaming the export slump chiefly on the return to the Gold Standard. The reason why the Inquiry was not instituted earlier was that Baldwin believed profoundly in the principle that the dispute should be settled by direct negotiation between the two parties, the government only intervening if such negotiations proved totally abortive. Hankey must have known this, and one can only assume that he felt it no part of his duty to explain the Prime Minister's principles to the King.

[3]The Royal Commission reported on 6th March 1926. Cmd. 2600. It recommended the nationalisation of coal royalties, but not of the mines themselves.

armament, and also became involved in the government's preparations for a conference whose purpose would be to reach accord with France, Belgium and Germany on a Treaty of Mutual Assistance – in substitution for the defunct Geneva Protocol. As regards disarmament, on 4th August (an appropriate date!) he produced a historical survey of the rise and fall of nations entitled 'An Introduction to the Study of Disarmament'.[1] Hankey sent it to Trenchard, the Chief of the Air Staff, for remarks, telling him that he had not made it 'an official paper', and to Lord Cecil. From our point of view its chief interest lies in its demonstration of the breadth of Hankey's reading, and of the way his mind was working in the middle 1920s. Certainly it was 'determinist' in character, and the quotations which he introduced from J. H. Breasted the elder's *Ancient Times: A History of the Early World,* Lord Bryce's *Holy Roman Empire*, Gibbon's *Decline and Fall of the Roman Empire*, St. Augustine's *De Civitate Dei* and Balfour's Sidgwick Memorial Lecture of 1908 were too obviously chosen to illustrate his thesis that if disarmament was carried too far and too fast a decrease in 'national virility' would result, unemployment would be created, and trade would suffer; also that the ideals for which the League of Nations stood were already out of date. Cecil in his reply quoted historical examples which controverted Hankey's case, and argued that war was 'necessarily evil in itself' – a proposition which Hankey refused to accept. His long letter which closed the correspondence sets out his philosophy so clearly that we may quote some extracts from it. He denied that his original paper had been written 'in opposition to peace', as Cecil had suggested. Rather had he tried to show that 'whatever you do war will come sooner or later, and if you carry disarmament too far, and crush the military spirit, your civilisation will go under . . . I think that the League of Nations has done something and will do more to postpone and avert wars. But there are lots of cases which the League may not be able to cope with'. He could not agree with Cecil 'that public spirit is a substitute for military spirit'; and the military spirit he considered 'necessary even for the League, if it is to carry out the Covenant. It is certainly necessary for the British Empire'. In conclusion he reiterated his view that 'decline of civilisations was connected with decline of the military spirit', and ended with a renewed plea for caution over disarmament. As the letter was signed 'Yours

[1] Hankey to Chamberlain from Highstead 21st August 1925. Chamberlain papers AC 24/7/16. Also in Cab. 63/37.

ever' it is evident that, at this time, no hard feelings existed on Hankey's side.[1]

The fact that about a fortnight after Hankey circulated his ruminations on peace, disarmament and the military spirit he wrote to Chamberlain on the same theme suggests that he was chiefly concerned with the Foreign Secretary's forthcoming meeting with Briand and Stresemann; for the German Foreign Minister had already made a tentative and informal approach for a security pact with France. At any rate Hankey told Chamberlain that he did not share the optimism expressed by the latter 'about the military spirit in this country'. 'Some of the propaganda of the extremists of the League of Nations', he continued, 'is pernicious, particularly at the Universities'; and Lord Riddell had told him that in some parts of the country the history text books used in primary schools 'teach nothing but internationalism and are contemptuous of patriotism as we understand it'. None the less he was 'broadly convinced that the nation is sound at present'.[2] Incidentally Churchill expressed rather similar views at about the same time. 'Proceeding on the present lines [of granting "uncovenanted benefit" to the unemployed]', he wrote, 'we are rotting the youth of the country and rupturing the mainspring of its energies'.[3] He wanted no relief to be granted to men under 25 without their doing a full day's work.

Hankey took no part in the negotiations which opened at Locarno on 5th October, but after the agreement had been signed he wrote very warmly to Chamberlain about his achievement. As we saw earlier Hankey vastly preferred a treaty of 'Mutual Assistance' or a 'Security Pact' to the principle of compulsory arbitration or to any form of mandatory sanctions against an 'aggressor'. It is likely therefore that his welcome to the Locarno Treaty was tinged by a sense of relief.

*Hankey to Chamberlain. 2 Whitehall Gardens. 19th October 1925.* Holograph[4]

Dear Mr. Chamberlain,

Without burdening you with as long a letter as would be necessary to express my feelings in full, I feel that I must at least send a line or two to express my enthusiastic congratulations on your achievement at Locarno.

I have been something more than a spectator of all the efforts made since

[1]Hankey to Cecil 18th Aug. 1925. Cab. 63/39.

[2]Hankey to Austen Chamberlain. Holograph, from Highstead 21st Aug. 1925. Chamberlain papers AC 24/7/16.

[3]Churchill to Steel-Maitland 19th Sept. 1925. Baldwin papers, Vol. 7, pp. 378–80.

[4]Chamberlain Papers. AC 37/169.

the war to bring about a durable peace, and I know that very soon after you took office you drew your course on the chart and that you have pursued it unerringly to your destination, which you have reached in an incredibly short space of time.

It is a marvellous achievement for which the credit rests almost entirely with you personally. It is certainly the greatest achievement of any Rugbeian, past or present, and, as a Rugbeian, I feel very proud of you.

Yours very sincerely

About a month later Hankey sent Mrs. Chamberlain, at her husband's request an extract from the minutes of a Privy Council, probably of the time of Henry V, which he had 'dug up'. The Foreign Secretary had, he wrote, given no reason why he wanted his wife to have the minute, but Hankey said he suspected it arose 'from some Locarno incident', and felt sure she 'must have enjoyed Austen's triumph'.[1] The Locarno Conference reassembled briefly in London on 1st December for the formal signing of the treaty. It aroused widespread joy and the most hopeful expectations for the future – especially with regard to the rapprochement between France and Germany. Chamberlain himself received the Garter and the Nobel Peace Prize.

In mid-November, by way of heralding the new era, the C.I.D formed a special Disarmament Sub-Committee with Lord Cecil as chairman.[2] Its Terms of Reference were 'to draw up instructions for the guidance of the British representatives at the forthcoming preliminary committee [that is the Preparatory Commission] of the Council at Geneva'. Hankey certainly never displayed any very great interest in this sub-committee's deliberations, and on Disarmament his favourite quotation was '*chi va sano, va piano, chi va piano va lontano*'.[3] None the less in April 1926 the C.I.D. approved that the Cecil sub-committee's

[1]Hankey to Mrs. Chamberlain 23rd October 1925. Holograph. Chamberlain papers AC 6/3/62. The extract in question read 'And these words and many other gentle words he [the Duke of Bedford] said so benignly and goodly, that tears sprang as well out of his eyes, as out of the eyes of all my said lords that were present'.

[2]205th C.I.D. meeting of 17th Nov. 1925. Cab. 21/305. A special series of R.L.A. (*R*eduction and *L*imitation of *A*rmaments) papers was started.

[3]'He who goes wisely goes slow; he who goes slow goes far'. A maxim of Francesco Guicciardini's (1483–1540), the foremost historian of the Italian renaissance. Hankey ended his study on disarmament (see p. 413) with these words, and often made use of them on other occasions. But he actually misquotes Guicciardini, who wrote '*Chi va piano, va sano, e chi va sano va lontano*' (he who goes slowly goes wisely, and he who goes wisely goes far) – which conveys a significantly different meaning.

reports on the Reduction and Limitation of Armaments and the Private Manufacture of Armaments should go to the Cabinet – subject to a good many amendments; and the Cabinet approved the reports as amended.[1]

The year 1925 ended with the application by the Cabinet of the 'Ten Year Rule' to the current expansion scheme for the Royal Air Force, which had been announced in June 1923.[2] In other words the Air Estimates had to be framed on the principle that the expansion for Home Defence would not be completed before the end of 1935. Nor, as we will see later, was this by any means the end of the pressure to extend the expected period of peace and defer the replacement of obsolescent equipment for all the fighting services. Constant and heavy pressure from Churchill and the Treasury[3] had become allied to the 'Locarno spirit' and to the propaganda of the disarmament lobby headed by Cecil. Hankey obviously realised that it would be futile to try and swim against such powerful currents, so held his peace – for a time. But the letters and papers he wrote in this period show that even at this early stage, he felt we were going too far and too fast in the direction of unilateral disarmament. Then, early in the New Year, Baldwin made one of his many statements which, though intended to encourage civilised man's hatred of war, actually did more to aggravate his very natural fear of it. 'Who in Europe', the Prime Minister asked of an academic audience, 'does not know that one more war in the West and the civilization of the ages will fall with as great a crash as that of Rome?'[4] There was irony in Baldwin and Hankey both using the history of the decline and fall of the same Empire at about the same time – for almost antithetical purposes.

[1]C.I.D. 682B of 28th April and 684B of 29th April 1926. Approved by Cabinet 19(26) Conclusion 7. Cab. 16/71.
[2]Cabinet 57(25) of 3rd Dec. 1925.
[3]See for example letter to all Ministers of 16th Oct. 1925 stressing the need to find economies equivalent to the coal subsidy. Baldwin papers, Vol. 3.
[4]Address at annual meeting of the Classical Association, 8th Jan. 1926.

*Chapter* 15

# The Essentials of Defence. January 1926-May 1929

FROM the beginning of 1926 until the fall of Baldwin's second administration in May 1929 Hankey was mainly concerned with preserving the essentials of Imperial, and especially naval defence, in face of relentless pressure from Churchill and the Treasury and strenuous propaganda for disarmament by the advocates of 'collective security' led by Lord Robert Cecil and the 'Peace Lobby'. Churchill's defeat by Bridgeman and Beatty over the 1925–26 Navy Estimates in no way weakened the Chancellor's onslaught on the service departments, and in August 1925 a committee was set up by the Treasury under the Chairmanship of Lord Colwyn[1] to propose drastic economies in all the service estimates. The Admiralty unwisely seized the opportunity to reopen the question of control of the Fleet Air Arm, which had been settled by the Trenchard–Keyes agreement of 1924 – thereby bringing down on their heads one of the heaviest fusillades ever fired at a government department.[2] But the Colwyn Committee's strictures were so severe that even Tom Jones was a little shocked, and advised Baldwin to 'go slow on some of these proposals'.[3] Hankey preserved strict neutrality in the dispute over naval aviation, though subjected to a prolonged bombardment by Bullock, the Permanent Secretary of the Air Ministry,[4] whose violent partisanship and prolixity on paper

[1] 1859–1946. 1st Baron 1917. Business man. Chairman or member of many government committees including the Fighting Services Economy Committee of 1925 referred to here. See Roskill, *Naval Policy*, I, pp. 454–6.

[2] *op. cit.* pp. 473–84. On 15th Jan. 1926 Bridgeman, the First Lord, wrote to Baldwin protesting vigorously over 'the offensive tone of the Colwyn Report', and expressing the indignation he felt on behalf of the naval and civil staff of his department. Baldwin papers Vol. 2.

[3] Jones to Baldwin 26th Feb. 1926. *ibid.*

[4] Later Sir Christopher L. Bullock (1891– ). Civil Servant. Principal Private Secretary to Churchill as Secretary of State for Air 1919, and to Sir Samuel Hoare

certainly did not help to moderate the inter-departmental strife.[1] Hankey plainly considered that the Admiralty had been tactless, if no worse, in reopening a question which he himself had helped Haldane to settle by arbitration some 18 months earlier.[2] When in February 1926 Baldwin himself had to settle whether the Admiralty's claim for complete control over the Fleet Air Arm should be conceded or the Colwyn Committee's recommendation that the Air Ministry's share in its control should be strengthened Hankey came down strongly against the Admiralty. He told Baldwin, quite correctly, that the Admiralty's real purpose was 'to swamp the Air element and to stake out a claim to take over the whole Fleet Air Arm'. The two principles which he considered fundamental were, firstly, the 'permeation of the Navy' by the essential expertise on air warfare; and, secondly, to prevent the elimination of the Air Force interest so that the latest knowledge and experience of that service were available to the fleet.[3] And that was exactly the compromise accepted.

But although Hankey could not dissociate himself from these unsavoury squabbles, and he was well aware of the passions they aroused in both naval and R.A.F. circles, he seems to have regarded them as less momentous to Imperial Defence than the construction of the Singapore base, the preservation of the naval building programme and the need to restrain the enthusiasts for unilateral disarmament. A letter from Cecil to Baldwin protesting against what he called the 'purely obstructive attitude' of 'the three Fighting Officers' (that is the Chiefs of Staff) in the Inter-Departmental Committee on Disarmament showed clearly enough which way the wind was blowing from the disarmament quarter.[4] At about the same time Hankey had to brief MacDonald on the constitutional position and authority of the C.I.D., which some members of the Labour Party and the Trades Union Congress regarded with grave suspicion. Hankey evidently realised that this was a potentially explosive issue, since he showed MacDonald's letter and

---

and Lord Thomson in same office 1923–36. Assistant Secretary, Air Ministry 1929–30 and Permanent Secretary 1931–36. Resigned after enquiry into his approach to Sir Eric Geddes regarding a post on the Board of Imperial Airways. See Cmd. 5254.

[1]The Bullock–Hankey correspondence of Feb. 1926 is in Cab. 21/290.

[2]See Roskill, *Naval Policy*, I, pp. 392–6 regarding Haldane's arbitration and the Trenchard–Keyes agreement of July 1924.

[3]Hankey to Baldwin 19th Feb. 1926. Cab. 63/38.

[4]Cecil to Baldwin 6th Jan. 1926. Baldwin papers Vol. 129, pp. 8–9.

his draft reply to the Prime Minister[1]; and although his carefully worded explanation that the C.I.D. was purely 'a consultative or advisory body' satisfied the Labour leader, who admitted that 'there seems to be a big bee in some people's bonnet about the C.I.D.'[2] suspicions in left-wing circles that it wielded undue influence were by no means allayed. At any rate Hankey was put to the trouble of composing a lengthy rebuttal of the T.U.C.'s views – though he did describe them as 'temperate and restrained'.[3]

Next he was troubled by a recurrence of what may be called Ministry of Defence fever, and the question of amalgamation of the supply services. As soon as he noticed that these matters were to be raised in the debate on the Air Estimates of 1926 he wrote to Baldwin reminding him that the creation of a Ministry of Defence had been thoroughly investigated and turned down by the Salisbury Committee of 1923; while the amalgamation of supply services had been fully examined by the Mond–Weir Committee of 1922. He also sent Baldwin the draft of a letter to the heads of the Service Departments calling for reports on progress made in the latter respect.[4] Then he enlisted the support of the Chiefs of Staff, the Permanent Secretaries of their departments and Sir Warren Fisher of the Treasury on the Ministry of Defence issue; and in answer to suggestions put forward by Churchill he wrote 'I am glad to see in your last paragraph that any new organisation must be brought into harmonious relations with the C.I.D. For modern war we have to organise the whole resources of the nation. At the C.I.D. this has been done to a considerable extent, and the process is going on without any special expenditure'.[5] This was an astute line to take with the Chancellor, who was at that very moment attacking the defence estimates, which he wanted to restrict to a maximum of £110 millions for all three services together.[6] Having thus 'loaded the gun' for the forthcoming debate Hankey primed the fuze by sending Balfour and Salisbury his draft for the Prime Minister's speech, and

[1]MacDonald to Hankey 15th Feb. 1926 and reply by latter of 16th Cab. 21/469. MacDonald's inquiry was instigated by Professor A. B. Keith, who apparently caused the C.I.D's powers and functions to be raised in the Labour Party's Memo. 336B of Feb. 1926.

[2]MacDonald to Hankey 17th Feb. 1926. *ibid.*

[3]Hankey to MacDonald 25th Feb. 1926. *ibid.* Also Cab. 63/38.

[4]Hankey to Baldwin 1st March 1926. Baldwin papers Vol. I, pp. 202–3.

[5]Hankey to Churchill 19th March 1926. Cab. 21/469.

[6]Churchill to Baldwin 19th March 1926. Baldwin papers.

getting it circulated as a C.I.D. Paper.[1] The Liberal Party's Resolution of 1926 on the centralised organisation of defence stood little chance of acceptance in face of Hankey's carefully planned campaign against it. Two years later the same issue was raised again, and was debated in Parliament.[2] Hankey then described the proposal to Balfour as 'a mischievous idea'; but he added that, in spite of all he had done and was still doing, he feared that popular support for a Ministry of Defence was 'gradually growing'.[3] In that respect he was at least to be proved correct.

Here we may digress from defence issues to recount one of the more bizarre episodes in which Hankey was involved. On 16th March 1926 Sir John Power, a Conservative M.P.,[4] called at Whitehall Gardens 'urgently recommended' to Hankey by Lionel Curtis of All Souls' College, Oxford.[5] Power recounted an extraordinary story, the gist of which Hankey recorded in his own hand, marked 'Very Secret' and left with his papers in a sealed envelope. Power described how in the previous year he had been approached about joining a mission to some of the ruling Princes of India 'for the purpose of discussing agricultural development'. Having only recently returned from Canada he was reluctant to accept, and only did so after he had been told that Birkenhead, the Secretary of State for India, 'attached some importance to this mission'. It was led by Sir Warden Chilcott,[6] a Conservative

[1]C.I.D. 696B. Cab. 4/14.

[2]On 27th March 1928. Parl. Deb., Commons, Vol. 215, Cols. 1013–1070. The debate was on the Consolidated Fund Bill. General Sir Robert Hutchison (See Vol. I, p. 548, *note*) spoke in favour of a Ministry of Defence and was answered by Baldwin to the effect that the prevailing system as run by Hankey was efficient and adequate. Lloyd George wanted the principle of the small War Cabinet applied in peacetime. The debate was continued on 28th (Cols. 1111–1140) and the proposal to create a Ministry of Defence received a good deal of support from private members.

[3]Hankey to Balfour. 16th May 1928. B.M. Add. MSS. 49705, pp. 22–8.

[4]1870–1950. Businessman, politician (Cons.) and benefactor of many causes concerned with improvement of international relations. Founder, Institute of Historical Research. Hon. Treasurer, Royal Institute of International Affairs 1921–43. Member, Executive Committee, League of Nations Union 1929–36. Associated with founding of British Council 1934.

[5]See p. 307, *note*.

[6]1871–1942. Politician (Cons.). Served in R.N. Air Service in World War I. Owned a large estate near Warsash on Southampton Water with a private 18-hole golf course. Also an old castle in Corsica where he hunted wild boar with a mounted hunt and

M.P. and a colourful, not to say extravagant character, whose manner of living suggested that he was endowed with vast wealth. His yacht 'reconstructed to resemble a Trafalgar frigate'[1] was one of the more exotic sights of Cowes Week in the 1920s, and on board it he lavishly entertained his friends – who included Birkenhead and Austen Chamberlain. Power was told that Chilcott would pay the expenses of the mission, but soon discovered that the cost was in fact 'defrayed by some of the Indian Princes, for whom the Jam Sahib of Nawanagar acted as Treasurer'. He also quickly found out that 'the agricultural object of the mission was mere camouflage', and nothing in that line was even attempted. Meanwhile Chilcott held conferences with the Princes, and 'told his colleagues little about those interviews'. Power became 'more and more disillusioned about the mission . . . and the atmosphere of mystery which pervaded the whole business' – which appeared to be chiefly designed 'to enhance the importance and prestige of Chilcott'. Eventually it came to Power's knowledge that certain of the Princes had combined to form a substantial joint fund. The Jam Sahib was again Treasurer, and it was to be used under Chilcott's direction 'to promote the cause of the Princes in London'. A still larger scheme was contemplated for founding 'a great establishment in London on the lines of a High Commissioner's office, under Chilcott, to look after the affairs of the Princes'. What 'made the matter particularly unsavoury', wrote Hankey, 'was that Chilcott was given to bragging about his influence with Lord B[irkenhead], and seems to have boasted that he managed Lord B.'s financial affairs'. Power had not the slightest reason 'to believe that Lord B. had ever consciously taken a penny of the Princes' money'; but he was convinced that the Princes had gained 'the impression that by making use of Chilcott as an agent they were obtaining some influence over the Secretary of State'. Power's 'disquiet' became 'so great that he decided to get clear of the business'. So he sent a cheque to the Jam Sahib to cover his share 'of this unsatisfactory expedition', returned home and consulted his friend Curtis.

Hankey thought the matter over, and came to the conclusion that the evidence was not strong enough for him to mention it to the Prime

---

50 boar hounds. His huntsmen wore pink and carried pikes. (*The Times* 12th March 1942.) James, *Davidson*, p. 104 contains a scathing reference to Chilcott as 'a sycophant' and deplores Chamberlain's friendship with him.

[1] *The Times* 12th March 1942.

Minister. With Power's full concurrence he therefore decided to keep it to himself – unless confirmation came to him from other sources. There the matter rested until the last day of May, when Curtis invited Hankey to lunch in his private room at the Institute of International Affairs to meet Sir Stanley Reed,[1] formerly editor of the *Times of India*. Reed's story 'did not differ materially' from Power's, but went back a year or two earlier to the time when Chilcott had first gone to India 'under the auspices of Lord Birkenhead and Mr. Austen Chamberlain to interest the Indian Princes in combatting socialism'. Eight of the Princes had then formed a fund of £100,000 with the Jam Sahib as Treasurer, 'to enable Chilcott to exercise his personal influence on the affairs of the Princes in London'. Reed gave Hankey 'a detailed account of how one young Prince consulted Chilcott on some difficulty in regard to the ownership of a railway in his state'. Chilcott had engaged 'a well-known counsel to undertake the affair', and told the Prince he 'must pay a retaining fee of £20,000 – which was paid to Chilcott'. The Prince then 'smelt a rat' and consulted Reed, who advised him 'to demand his money back, less expenses, and drafted the Prince's letter for him'. In this case the money was returned, but Reed also spoke of the larger scheme mentioned by Power, 'for which £750,000 was to be found'.

Reed declared that 'the whole business was common knowledge among the Indian Princes', who 'universally believed that Lord B. was in Chilcott's pocket for financial reasons, and that consequently Chilcott could do what he liked with Lord B.' Reed, like Power, did not 'suspect Lord B. of wittingly taking the Princes' money, but he blamed him for laxity, and showed considerable personal animus against him'. What incensed Reed was 'the thought that the Indian Princes believed that they could exercise corrupt influence over the Secretary of State through Chilcott'; and he declared that 'certain recent decisions taken in London' were 'universally, though probably incorrectly, ascribed by the Princes to such influence'. Reed felt that before he left London 'someone ought to know this story', and he had therefore given it to Geoffrey Dawson, the editor of *The Times*, as well as to Curtis.

Hankey next 'tested the position a little' by asking Reed 'what action, if any I could or should take'. He said that he felt little justification in

[1] 1872–1969. Journalist and politician (Cons.). Joined staff of *Times of India* 1897. Special correspondent during Royal tours of India. Editor of *Times of India* 1907–23. Founder of *Indian Year Book*. M.P. 1938–50.

telling the Prime Minister, overburdened as he was with the coal crisis. Baldwin would be bound to send for Birkenhead, and the latter would then complain, with good reason, that Hankey should have gone to him in the first instance. If he went to Baldwin all the latter could do would be either to order an enquiry or leave the matter alone; and Hankey felt that either course would produce 'very great difficulties, and very likely he would fail to get to the bottom of it'. The same objections applied to his consulting 'some neutral person like Lord Balfour or Sir Austen Chamberlain' – a remark which suggests that Hankey was unaware of Chamberlain's friendship with Chilcott. But, he continued, such action had 'the added disadvantage that it brought an additional person into the secret'. On the whole he preferred to go to Birkenhead direct, as being 'more open and more honest'. He did not 'for one moment suspect B. of any corruption', but 'it would be only fair to put him on his guard' by bringing to his attention 'the risk he was running'. Such action would, he felt sure, 'put an end to Chilcott's activities'. Reed, however, 'became rather alarmed' at this proposa l,and said that his belief was that, 'bad as the business had been in the past, the Princes had lost confidence in Chilcott and the whole affair was probably at an end'. He asked Hankey 'to suspend action for a day or two' until he had received the further information which he expected; and to that request Hankey acceded, though he made it clear that 'these confidences were an embarrassment' to him. 'It is difficult for an official in my position', he concluded, 'to hear these stories affecting Cabinet Ministers and M.Ps, and reacting on our good name in India, and to do nothing.'

There matters rested until 13th July, when Reed called again on Hankey and told him that 'the subject was beginning to be talked about rather widely in London'. Apparently an officer of the Indian Political Service who was at home had raised it in conversation with Reed, who added that Chilcott had, to his knowledge, 'written to one of the Indian Princes quoting the decision in the Bhopal Succession case as a proof of his influence'.[1] He pointed out 'how undesirable it was that

[1]Bhopal was the principal Muslim state of Central India (population about 730,000). In 1926 the Government of India decided that the Begum's surviving son should be recognised as her heir, to the exclusion of the sons of her elder deceased sons. The Begum abdicated voluntarily on 17th May 1926, and the succession therefore took place in accordance with the Government's decision. The new ruler was also assured that 'he will be succeeded by an heir of his body'. Full particulars of a

Chilcott should claim, or that India should believe he had a hand in it'. Furthermore Birkenhead had given a luncheon to the Maharajah of Alwar at which 'the only person to be invited, outside regular official circles, was Chilcott'; and the latter had also been present at the Maharajah's 'return entertainment'. Plainly Birkenhead was laying himself open to serious misunderstanding, if no worse.

Reed said that Chilcott had asked for £25,000 'for the expenses of the Parliamentary Committee [to India], and that £12,500 had been granted'. As the cost could not have exceeded £500 a head, and there were only five or six members, 'this had made a disagreeable impression on the Princes'. Reed 'insisted very strongly that before long we should hear of this matter from other quarters'; but that does not seem to have happened, and Hankey's memorandum appears to be the only record of some very murky transactions.[1] One is left wondering how much the Indian Princes contributed to Chilcott's 'Trafalgar frigate' and to his Corsican pike-bearing huntsmen.

As Hankey remarked in his ruminations on the *affaire Chilcott*, Baldwin and his Cabinet were very much absorbed in the coal dispute in the spring of 1926. The report of the Royal Commission, chaired by Sir Herbert Samuel, was published on 11th March, and protracted negotiations between the representatives of the coal owners and the miners followed. At the end of April, a state of complete deadlock was reached, and the 'Emergency Regulations 1926', on which Hankey had for some time been working, were introduced by Royal Proclamation. The 1st May produced the fateful decision of the Trades Union Congress to call a General Strike as from midnight on 3rd–4th. The government then brought into effect the long-prepared measures worked out by the Supply and Transport Committee – very much on the lines of Hankey's famous War Book. On 2nd, a Sunday, the Cabinet met three times to put the final touches to the organisation. Hankey was of course working almost round the clock, and after the last Cabinet had ended at 1.30 a.m. on the Monday morning he stayed at his desk signing letters and documents. Tom Jones, he told Adeline, 'is quite worn out'. He himself, knowing that everything possible had been

---

complicated story, which was a pre-occupation of the Government of India and the India Office between 1924 and 1926, will be found in *Memoranda on the Indian States* (New Delhi, 1940). I am indebted to the Librarian, India Office Library, for furnishing me with particulars.

[1]Dated 31st May and 13th July 1926.

done, took the situation very calmly. 'It is going to be interesting seeing if we can beat these fellows', he wrote. 'I think we can, but it involves a big effort'.[1] Next day the Illegal Strike Bill was prepared in great secrecy, and on 8th Hankey sent a first draft of it to Stamfordham.

*Hankey to Stamfordham. 2 Whitehall Gardens 8th May 1926.* Holograph[2]

VERY SECRET

Dear Lord Stamfordham,

The Cabinet decided this evening to introduce a Bill on Tuesday 'to declare and amend the Law with respect to illegal strikes'. Among other things the Bill aims at making it illegal 'to apply any Trades Union Funds to a strike which is intended to coerce or intimidate the Government or the community etc'.

The Bill has to be circulated on Monday, and between that event and its passage into law the Trades Unions may be able to get large sums of money from the banks. The Communists also may be able to get hold of some money that has been sent to them from Moscow.

The [Privy] Council to-morrow is required for the purpose of approving a regulation under the Emergency Proclamation, which will enable the Government to prevent this being done, pending the passage of the new Bill into law.

This, as far as I understand it, is the object of the Council. I have summoned the Lord President, Lord Chancellor and Attorney-General, and the latter will be able to give the King a better explanation.

I am circulating no Cabinet Minute for a day or two, as the whole matter is extremely secret.

Yours sincerely,

P.S. I enclose a first draft of the Bill, which is *especially secret.*

Jones was strongly opposed to hasty legislation in the overcharged atmosphere of those hectic days, and has recorded how, after he had pressed his views on all and sundry, he saw Hankey, who 'in his unemotional way said that he rather felt that the thing was being hurried'.[3] Perhaps it was fortunate for the country that, while Churchill was breathing fire and slaughter at the *Morning Post*'s offices, and treating the strike as an operation of war, someone at the heart of government was unemotional.[4] In fact Hankey watched the working out of the government's preparations with calm detachment, and was glad that the Illegal Strike Bill was dropped. Nor was he surprised when on

[1] To Lady Hankey 3rd May 1926. [2] RA GV B2052/17. [3] *Middlemas*, II, p. 46.

[4] James, *Davidson*, pp. 235–46 contains a graphic account of Churchill's activities at the *Morning Post* offices in producing the *British Gazette.*

12th the T.U.C. decided to throw over the miners and called off the General Strike.[1] Then followed the long-drawn attempt at mediation between the coal owners and miners, in which Churchill, showing great moderation, was nearly successful. But it was in fact cold, hunger and a steady drift back to work that brought the miners' long agony to an end in November. While Jones's time and efforts were almost wholly devoted to the coal dispute Hankey returned to the field of defence, and especially to the Singapore base and the forthcoming Imperial Conference.

At the end of March the Admiralty proposed that development of the base at Singapore should be brought up at the Imperial Conference[2]; but Hankey was already mediating in the dispute between the Admiralty and Air Ministry over the defences of the base, and he took no action until late in July, when he reminded Chamberlain that the Cabinet had directed that policy with regard to the base should be reviewed every year.[3] He wrote that he was therefore circulating the report of the C.I.D.'s Singapore sub-committee, and the Foreign Office's memorandum on the principles governing British foreign policy.[4] This latter had formed the basis of the Chiefs of Staff's 'Review of Imperial Defence', in which they drew attention 'once more to the urgent necessity for providing for the development of a naval base in the Johore Strait and for its defence . . .'.[5] This paper was approved by the Cabinet on 30th July 'as a general statement of Imperial policy'; and Hankey at once followed it up with a short history of the development of the C.I.D. and the Chiefs of Staff's Sub-Committee.[6] Having got these important statements of principle off his hands, and also given rein to the Air Staff's claim to provide the main defences of the base, Hankey turned to the problem of providing the secretariat for the Imperial Conference, and to the details of organisation. He undoubtedly welcomed Amery's proposal for a joint secretariat, with a representative from each Dominion and from India[7]; but he knew only too well the difficulties such a proposal would encounter – especially from

[1]On the General Strike see *Baldwin*, Ch. 15; *Middlemas*, II, pp. 44–53; James, *Davidson*, Ch. 8.

[2]Cab. 21/335.

[3]Hankey to Chamberlain 21st July 1926. Chamberlain papers AC 53/345.

[4]C.I.D. 700B. [5]C.I.D. 701B of 22nd June 1926.

[6]C.I.D. 713B of 3rd Aug. 1926.

[7]Amery to Baldwin 30th Sept. 1926. Baldwin papers. Vol. 93.

Canada and South Africa.[1] As no definition of Dominion status had been reached at the 1923 conference it was vital that agreement should be reached this time. The Permanent Secretaries of the departments concerned therefore held prolonged preliminary discussions with Hankey and Hurst (legal adviser to the Foreign Office) in order to decide the form in which it should be put forward. The genesis of the very important Committee on Co-ordination of Imperial Relations is to be found in these discussions. Sir Harry Batterbee, then Assistant Secretary in the Dominions Office, recalls that 'all the organisation of the conference was Hankey's', and that it was he who conceived the idea that the Co-ordination Committee should sit at a round table.[2]

To smooth the transaction of this difficult business, on 11th October Hankey sent Smuts a friendly reminder of their close association at previous conferences.[3] Next day he wrote to Balfour to tell him that if constitutional questions were referred to a special committee, as Baldwin thought likely, he would be asked to take the chair. This, he said, would be 'a fairly formidable task, but less formidable to you than to most people'; and he enclosed the notes he had prepared for Baldwin's opening speech.[4] Balfour accepted the task, and told Hankey he thought his 'draft speech for Tuesday's opening excellent in all respects'.[5] Further correspondence followed, in which Hankey reported his discovery of 'a perfectly delightful passage' about the C.I.D. in a speech Balfour had made as long ago as 1904, and which he had now incorporated in Baldwin's speech.[6] He also proposed that when Imperial relations were discussed 'some use ought to be made of the Committee of Civil Research', which, as we saw earlier, was a favourite child of Balfour's. The reason, wrote Hankey, was that the C.I.D. and the C.C.R. between them 'cover almost every form of government activity', and each of them 'provides exactly the machinery for continuous

[1]See Mackenzie King to Baldwin 20th April and reply by latter of 18th May 1926. *ibid.*

[2]To the author 10th April 1970. However Hankey's idea may not have been original, as a round table was deliberately used for the prolonged Anglo-Dutch negotiations at Breda in 1667, which finally ended the Second Dutch War. Hankey's historical reading was so wide that he very probably knew this. See P. G. Rogers, *The Dutch in the Medway* (O.U.P., 1970), p. 63.

[3]Smuts Archive, folio 153.

[4]Hankey to Balfour 12th Oct. 1926. B.M. Add. MSS. 490704, pp. 110–11.

[5]Balfour to Hankey 14th Oct. 1926. *ibid.* p. 114.

[6]Hankey to Balfour 15th Oct. 1926. *ibid.* pp. 115–16.

contact between the Dominions and ourselves in a form which they ought to be able to accept'.[1] To drive home this point he circulated a 'Scheme of Inter-Imperial liaison' with a diagram which showed the Cabinet's Foreign Policy Committee, the C.I.D. and the C.C.R. as 'organs of consultation and liaison' during the intervals between Imperial conferences.[2]

The conference opened on 19th October, the day that Hankey gave Balfour the last of his series of suggestions, and lasted until 23rd November. After the first few days Hankey was able to tell his old friend Esher that 'I think we shall get round the constitutional corner all right. Mackenzie King, with a decent majority at his back and a stronger personal position, is really very helpful. The Irish are behaving decently, and everyone is saying "Poor old Hertzog, decent old body, we must find some way of saving his face" '. 'The attitude of the Dominions used to be very critical', he went on, 'and I always dread these conferences. This year I have the impression that they sympathise very much in our difficulties, admire our pluck, and especially our attitude towards American debts . . .'.[3] On 29th Hankey sent Baldwin a full account of that day's meeting of Balfour's Committee at which his own and General Hertzog's draft statements on the status of the Dominions had been discussed, and Birkenhead had produced a new version incorporating some elements of both drafts.[4] He also sent a copy to Chamberlain, explaining that trouble had arisen because Hertzog objected to any mention of 'Empire', and that word did appear in Balfour's draft. 'Commonwealth' was therefore substituted; and although Chamberlain replied that he considered 'British Commonwealth of Nations is not a term of art',[5] and Coates of New Zealand considered the new draft 'a poisonous document', and declared he could not go home with a statement which contained no reference to the British Empire,[6] in the end the new definition was accepted, and the delegates all left for their home countries more or less satisfied with the famous 'Balfour formula'. Hankey received the draft from Balfour's

[1]Hankey to Balfour 19th Oct. 1926. *ibid.*

[2]Dated 11th Nov. 1926. Cab. 63/38.

[3]Hankey to Esher. Holograph postscript to Personal and Confidential letter of 23rd Oct. 1926. Esher papers.

[4]Hankey to Baldwin 29th Oct. 1926. Cab. 21/295.

[5]Chamberlain papers AC 53/348, 352 and 353.

[6]Hankey to Balfour 1st Nov. 1926. B.M. Add. MSS. 49704, pp. 141–5. Also in Cab. 21/295.

own hands, and played a big part in gaining its acceptance.[1] But, he remarked philosophically to Balfour, 'There is always some Dominion that gives trouble at an Imperial Conference, but it is hardly ever the same one twice running'. Before the war it had on one occasion been Australia – 'now one of the most loyal'. In 1921 it was Smuts 'who in 1923 was most helpful'. This time it had been Hertzog; but he wondered 'what his position will be in 1929'.[2]

Lord Casey, who was of course deeply involved in the Imperial Conference of 1926,[3] has told the author that it was at that gathering that the principle that 'no critical comment of the policy of the Dominions should be voiced by the British representatives' was first applied. It was apparently 'adumbrated and accepted' when the Dominions Office was formed in the previous year. Casey always regarded this principle as 'a negation of leadership', and held that it was bound to result in failure to share effectively in 'the corporate responsibilities of the Empire'. He had many talks on the subject with Sir Edward Harding[4] of the Dominions Office and with Hankey. Harding, however, would have nothing to do with Casey's ideas, because he feared they would make the Imperial or Commonwealth Conferences a battle ground. Plain speaking and critical comment by Dominion representatives had of course often been evident at earlier meetings – notably by 'Billy' Hughes of Australia and Mackenzie King of Canada; and one feels that it was too cautious of the Mother Country to deny itself what should be a parent's right, and even her duty. Thus Casey's argument, to which he repeatedly reverted on later occasions, had a great deal of force behind it.[5] As Hankey was a close friend of Harding, and collaborated with him constantly on Commonwealth affairs, it seems certain that the two of them were in agreement on the principle which Casey regarded as so misguided. Moreover compromise was the very essence of Hankey's system, as it was of Balfour's. If therefore plainer speaking would have avoided the gross inequality between Britain's

[1]See Blanche Dugdale, *Arthur James Balfour* (Hutchinson, 1936), Vol. II, pp. 374–83.

[2]Hankey to Balfour 1st Nov. 1926. B.M. Add. MSS. 49704. [3]See pp. 400–401.

[4]1880–1954. Civil Servant in Colonial (later Dominions) Office. Deputy Secretary, Imperial Conferences 1923 and 1926. Assistant Under-Secretary of State, Dominions Office 1925–30 and Permanent Under-Secretary 1930–40. British High Commissioner for High Commission territories and for Union of S. Africa 1940–4.

[5]Interview with Lord Casey 23rd June 1970. Also letter to the author of 5th August 1970. Lord Casey enlarges on this problem in his book *The Future of the Commonwealth* (Muller, 1963), pp. 54–5.

and the Commonwealth countries' expenditure on defence in between the wars,[1] and so led to better preparation to withstand the blackmail of the dictators in the 1930s, Hankey cannot escape a share of the responsibility.

The end of the 1926 conference brought Hankey a shower of letters of congratulation. Sir Edward Harding wrote that he could not go back to the Dominions Office 'without saying how grateful I am both to you personally and to all the staff here [at 2 Whitehall Gardens] for very great kindness during the last few weeks'. It was, he said, 'always a pleasure to work for, and with you'; but this time 'it looks as if the conference might really have achieved something of lasting value'. Harding was 'quite confident' that no one but Hankey could have carried through so successfully 'the very formidable task'.[2] Amery wrote 'to thank and congratulate you on your own personal share in a big achievement. We have co-operated now for a good many years, but never more fruitfully than in the last six weeks'.[3] And Esher wrote hyperbolically 'The combine A. J. B. and M. H. is a marvel! That is what I call a real State Paper. A crowning glory for A. J. B. But, of course, one expects that sort of thing from you. I hope the P.M. – sloppy and idle – is grateful'.[4] Hankey modestly replied that 'it was more A. J. B. than me. I did much lobbying but little drafting', and gave most of the praise for the drafting to Harding. He added that he was applying for a C.M.G. for Esher's protégé Lawrence Burgis[5]; and a few weeks later Burgis wrote very warmly thanking Hankey for his trouble and interest – which 'really give me more pleasure than the

[1]The Admiralty pointed out at the 1926 conference that whereas the British people contributed 25/7d per head annually for defence, the corresponding figures for Australia, Canada and South Africa were 17/2d, 0/8d and 0/2d respectively. These figures were circulated at the conference and reproduced in Cmd. 2769. See Roskill, *Naval Policy*, I, pp. 465–6.

[2]Harding to Hankey. Holograph. 25th Nov. 1926.

[3]Amery to Hankey 29th Nov. 1926. cf. Hankey's early unfavourable impression of Amery. Vol. I, pp. 352–3.

[4]Esher to Hankey. Holograph 23rd Nov. 1926. The State Paper referred to was Cmd. 2768, *Summary of Proceedings of the Imperial Conference 1926*.

[5]Hankey to Esher. Holograph. 24th Nov. 1926. Esher papers. In *The Times* of 22nd March 1930 Amery claimed a share of the credit for the 'Balfour formula'. Harding of the Dominions Office queried this claim to Hankey, who replied on 29th with a full account of how it was produced. There was, he concluded, 'not much to cavil at in Amery's account', and he himself 'would not like to deny Amery's claim to have suggested the idea'. Cab. 63/38.

honour itself'. 'It is nearly six years', continued Burgis, 'since you made me your private secretary, and, thanks to you, they have been supremely happy ones . . . You may have other private secretaries, and more efficient ones than myself, but never one more devoted to you personally.'[1] As a postscript to the story of Hankey's success it may be mentioned here that early in the following year he wrote to tell Balfour that a relation of Adeline's in South Africa had reported that 'Hertzog the malcontent has come back satisfied and even grateful'. 'Your "Diplomacy by Conference" has triumphed again' he concluded.[2] Eighteen months later he reported to Balfour that 'the Prime Ministers of Australia, New Zealand and South Africa have agreed to allow their High Commissioners to take part in the work of the C.I.D.' No reply had yet been received from Mackenzie King – which Hankey interpreted, correctly, as 'a bad sign'.[3] In fact the Canadian Prime Minister was not idle in this matter, though his mind was working on different lines from Hankey's. In May 1927 he asked Burgon Bickersteth,[4] then Warden of Hart House in the University of Toronto, to leave that post and come to Ottawa as his personal assistant, with a view to his becoming ultimately secretary of his Cabinet on the Hankey principle. King greatly admired the British system, though he did not really grasp the difference between the Private Secretaries at No. 10 and the secretariat at Whitehall Gardens. That same summer Bickersteth was in London, and Hankey and Jones 'did all they could' to help him in studying the work of the Cabinet and C.I.D. secretariat.[5] The outcome was a long memorandum from Bickersteth for Mackenzie King on the British machinery, and the way in which it might be adapted to suit Canadian needs; and Hankey vetted the draft before it was despatched. Though Bickersteth turned down King's proposal

[1]Burgis to Hankey. Holograph. 18th Dec. 1926.

[2]Hankey had used 'Diplomacy by Conference' as the title of the lecture he gave at the Institute of International Affairs in Nov. 1920 (see pp. 194–5). As Balfour was in the chair on that occasion and in 1926 Hankey referred to '*your* Diplomacy by Conference' it seems possible that it was Balfour who suggested the title. Hankey used it again as the title of the book on the subject which he published in 1946.

[3]Hankey to Balfour 14th Jan. 1927. B.M. Add. MSS. 49704, p. 183.

[4]John Burgon Bickersteth (1884– ). Educationist. Warden of Hart House, University of Toronto 1921–47. Adviser on Education to G.O.C-in-C, Canadian First Army 1940–42. Director of Army Education, War Office, 1942–44.

[5]See *Middlemas*, II, pp. 106–7 *et seq.* regarding Bickersteth's contacts with Hankey and Jones.

of 1927, and a Canadian Cabinet Secretariat was not actually introduced until 1940, it was then based on the memorandum written thirteen years earlier. However the first negotiations had an interesting by-product. Bickersteth remained a close friend and admirer of Hankey, and he adopted the practice of writing an annual report for him on Canadian affairs. These Hankey circulated to the C.I.D., the Prime Minister and the Palace – according to which was most concerned. Thus did Hankey, by his gift for friendship and personal contact, supply in some degree a link in the Commonwealth chain which the Canadian Prime Minister was not prepared to place on a formal footing.[1]

The Imperial Conference's redefinition of Dominion status inevitably altered the position of the Monarch in relation to the Dominions, and Stamfordham soon took the matter up with Hankey, because he considered that he had 'probably formed the best idea of what will be the result of the changes agreed upon'.[2] In fact in the following year the channel for official communications between the Mother Country and the Dominions was changed from the Governor-General to the Prime Minister or Minister for External Affairs – as indeed Mackenzie King had proposed to Balfour's Committee of 1926. Misunderstandings did of course arise occasionally – as when in 1928 Hertzog spoke in the South African parliament stressing that it was open to any member of the Commonwealth not to come to the assistance of any other member in the event of war, and claimed that the recent conference had accepted this principle.[3] Hankey at once took the matter up with Harding, because he was not sure that Hertzog's statement was true. But Harding was obviously reluctant to reopen such a delicate issue, and replied that Hertzog's statement was substantially correct. The anxiety expressed by the Admiralty about the effect that South African neutrality in a war in which Britain was involved could have on the security of the sea route via the Cape of Good Hope was therefore unallayed[4]; and the principles established in 1926 remained unchanged until the Statute of Westminster of 1931 put the final seal on the complete independence of the Dominions. Yet, despite the fact that ambiguities did exist in the 1926 Balfour Resolution, and despite the reluctance of Canada, South Africa and the Irish Free State to participate actively in

[1]Bickersteth to the author. Undated letter received 19th May 1970.
[2]Stamfordham to Hankey 29th Nov. 1926. Copy in B.M. Add. MSS. 49704, p. 161.
[3]Cab. 21/295. [4]Cab. 21/311.

the planning of Imperial Defence, it did mark an important milestone on the boulder-strewn road leading to full co-operation by the Dominions.

Though Hankey did not send Smuts his impressions of the Imperial Conference until a year later we may usefully quote them here. 'I was of course "up to the neck" in the Imperial Relations settlement', he wrote, 'and was used as the intermediary in the final settlement, which, I was glad to see at the time, won your approval, though I agree in your criticism that it really changed nothing. But what it did change was men's hearts, and that was important . . .'.[1] History was to justify the far-reaching claim in Hankey's last sentence; for the seeds sown at the 1926 conference were to yield an abundant harvest during Britain's ordeal of 1939–42; and for that accomplishment the free world will always remain in the debt of Balfour and Hankey.

While Hankey was busying himself with the constitutional and defence problems raised at the Imperial Conference all was not quiet on the disarmament front. In March Cecil complained to Baldwin that he was 'continually having to accept responsibility for League policy to which I am opposed', and that his troubles with Chamberlain were about as bad as those from which Curzon had suffered at Lloyd George's hands.[2] But the Foreign Secretary was unsympathetic; he described Cecil as 'more of a pacifist than I am', and resented being presented at the end of a long day's work with 'the threat of immediate resignation by Bob'.[3] Though Balfour remarked that the heart of the matter lay in 'Bob Cecil having a resigning mind', on this occasion a placatory letter from Baldwin caused him to defer his departure from the government – for a time. While Cecil was fuming about the lack of support for his policy in the Cabinet he was also acting as chairman of the C.I.D. sub-committee appointed 'to draw up instructions for the guidance of the British representatives at the forthcoming preliminary committee of the [League] Council at Geneva'.[4] In April 1926 the Cecil committee produced reports on the Reduction and Limitation of Armaments and on the Private Manufacture of Arms, which the C.I.D. approved subject to a good many amendments and passed to the Cabinet.[5] Hankey's note

[1]Hankey to Smuts. Holograph. From Highstead 25th Nov. 1927. Smuts archive.
[2]Cecil to Baldwin 17th March 1926. Baldwin papers, Vol. 115, pp. 138–51.
[3]Chamberlain to Baldwin 18th March 1926. *ibid.*
[4]205th C.I.D. on 17th Nov. 1925. Cab. 2/4.
[5]The reports are C.I.D. 682 and 684 of 28th and 29th April 1926. Cab. 16/71.

on these reports suggests a marked lack of enthusiasm for the subjects in question. But he seems to have been content to allow discussions to continue, and many reports and draft Disarmament Conventions to be produced, without making any comments.[1] However, when Cecil proposed to bring up the subject of Disarmament at the Imperial Conference Hankey demurred – on the grounds that the Dominions were 'rather afraid of coming to the C.I.D.'; which reads a little oddly, since he was at the same time doing his best to get the Dominions more fully involved in that body's work.[2] When Cecil produced his draft treaty on the Limitation of Armaments early in 1927 Hankey replied in strongly critical though friendly terms. Apart from the fact that the details, 'which will prove a matter of the greatest difficulty internationally' had not been fully worked out, he considered Cecil's draft 'much too rigid'. And he quoted the recent despatch of a division of troops to Shanghai, though we were not at war with China, as an example of the need for flexibility. Furthermore he took exception to the fact that under Cecil's proposed rules we would have been obliged to report to the League our actual and proposed expenditure on the Singapore base – a procedure which would very probably have 'blocked [the project] in its infancy'. 'When we review the increasing chaos in the Far East could we regard this with equanimity?' he asked. Emergencies might, he pointed out, arise at any time and anywhere, and 'to go to the League for permission to spend money might precipitate the very crisis we wished to avoid'. Finally he stressed that 'it is when the shadows [of war] first begin to appear that military precautions must begin too . . . It is not on the eve of war that you can create a great base like Singapore. You have to do it gradually, and safeguard yourself beforehand'. Hankey declined to criticise the draft treaty 'line by line until these criticisms [of principle] are met', and signed himself 'Yours ever'.[3] His policy seems to have been to allow matters to take their course, confident that nothing would come of the Cecil committee's proposals as long as Baldwin's government remained in office. The last of the dozens of memoranda in the R.L.A. (Reduction and Limitation of Armaments) series is dated 27th April 1929 – just

They were approved by Cabinet 19(26) Conclusion 7 subject to the C.I.D.'s amendments.

[1]See Cab. 16/71, 72, 73 and 74.

[2]Hankey to Cecil 19th Oct. 1926. Cab. 21/305.

[3]Hankey to Cecil 8th Feb. 1927. *ibid.*

a month before the electorate declined to renew Baldwin's mandate.

When Hankey quoted the China crisis to Cecil as an example of a sudden emergency the Nationalist threat to Shanghai was in the forefront of the Cabinet's deliberations. In January 1927 Balfour reviewed ways and means of putting pressure on the Chinese Nationalist government without risking the extremes of 'unconditional surrender' or adopting the attitude of 'dying in the last ditch' in defence of our interests. Two things that the Chinese had not got and could not obtain from their Russian supporters were, he said, sea power and money. We could apply a blockade, and although it would ruin our own trade that looked like happening anyhow.[1] The mention of blockade, and the fact that Balfour sent Hankey a copy of his letter, indicates that they were collaborating closely on this, as on many other issues. Hankey replied at once that he was 'immensely tickled by the way you had foreseen the military situation without having seen the military appreciation', and circulated Balfour's letter to the Cabinet. 'Sooner or later', he far-sightedly remarked, 'we shall have to come to terms in the matter of the settlements [i.e. the Treaty Ports]; and, typically, he produced a historical analogy between the Treaty Ports and the 'German steel yard established in 1250 where Cannon Street station now stands'. He was, however, 'very keen on making sure Shanghai is properly equipped with reserve weapons, barbed wire, hospital appliances and all the things which a loose international body like the Shanghai Municipality probably overlooks'. He had asked the Chiefs of Staff to propose that Lord Cecil's committee, referred to earlier, should consider blockade, and was himself going to discuss the matter with Cecil.[2] Balfour found this epistle 'both amusing and interesting'.[3] Next day Hankey wrote again that 'I feel sure the Cabinet will decide to hold Shanghai, if the Japs play up'. The naval C-in-C, Admiral Tyrwhitt[4] and the Chiefs of Staff favoured doing so, and considered a division of soldiers would be needed.[5] That same day Hankey wrote to all three Chiefs of Staff to warn them that, in the last resort, evacuation of

[1]Balfour to Baldwin 11th Jan. 1927. B.M. Add. MSS. 49704, pp. 166–74.

[2]Hankey to Balfour 13th Jan. 1927. *ibid*. pp. 176–80. The Chiefs of Staff's appreciation is C.O.S. 59.

[3]Balfour to Hankey 14th Jan. 1927. *ibid*. p. 181.

[4]Later Admiral of the Fleet Sir Reginald Y. Tyrwhitt (1870–1951). Commanded Harwich Force with distinction and was engaged in all major North Sea battles of World War I except Jutland. C-in-C, China 1927–29 and The Nore 1930–33.

[5]Hankey to Balfour 15th Jan. 1927. B.M. Add. MSS. 49704, pp. 187–8.

Shanghai might be necessary, and the preparations should therefore be put in hand. He himself thought such action would be 'disastrous' even if it were possible – which he doubted.[1] Meanwhile Stamfordham had represented to Chamberlain that although the Monarch had not demurred over the action of the men on the spot in evacuating the concession at Hankow, he was 'much perturbed' at the thought of the same thing happening at Shanghai. The Foreign Secretary replied reassuringly that Hankey had all the necessary measures in hand, that evacuation was only being prepared as a last resort, and that prospects of joint action with the French, Americans and Japanese were now better.[2] The King was evidently reassured, though he continued to watch the situation anxiously. In Parliament and in the by-elections which took place in 1927 the Labour party strongly opposed the despatch of troops, so provoking Baldwin to write to Conservative candidates that 'It is the bounden duty of the Government to protect the lives and interests of British subjects in any part of the world', and accusing their opponents of communicating with the Chinese Nationalists and spreading false propaganda at home and abroad.[3]

Throughout the early months of 1927 the situation at Shanghai remained tense and anxious, and in fact neither the Americans nor the Japanese took part in the defence of the International Settlement, as Chamberlain had hoped. At the end of March Hankey produced for the Chiefs of Staff Committee what he called his 'China report', and circulated this comprehensive study of a very complicated situation to the C.I.D. and the Cabinet.[4] To Adeline he confided that it had 'a *succès fou*'.[5] Meanwhile the question of establishing a blockade was still being considered, though Hankey very sensibly remarked that, as the Hankow government had 'blockaded itself', no action by Britain was necessary.[6] By April Lord Irwin,[7] the Viceroy of India, was able to

[1]Hankey to Trenchard 15th Jan. 1927. Also to C.I.G.S. and D.C.N.S. Trenchard papers.

[2]Stamfordham to Chamberlain 14th Jan., and reply by latter of 15th Jan. 1927. Chamberlain papers AC 186 and 188.

[3]Baldwin papers Vol. 49.

[4]C.O.S. 69. It became C.I.D. 784B of 29th March 1927. Cab. 4/16. Also C.P. 110(27).

[5]To Lady Hankey 30th March 1927.

[6]A.T.B. (*A*dvisory Committee on *T*rade and *B*lockade) 50 of 7th March 1927. Cab. 21/299.

[7]Edward F. L. Wood, 1st Baron Irwin 1925, 1st Earl of Halifax (new creation)

congratulate Baldwin on having 'prevented Shanghai from being a second Smyrna'[1]; and it is a fact that firmness at home, good organisation by Hankey and the service departments, and the moderation of the men on the spot resolved a situation which at one time looked very nasty indeed. But the defensive measures cost some £3–4 millions, which the Chancellor soon tried to recoup from the fighting services by other means.[2]

The China crisis of 1927 brought about a considerable increase of activity by the C.I.D., which met seven times between February and May, with Baldwin himself in the chair on every occasion.[3] It also contributed to the formation of the Joint Planning Sub-Committee of the Chiefs of Staff Committee, which met for the first time on 18th April with the crisis as the sole item on its agenda. It consisted of the Directors of Plans of the three service departments, and was to become a key body in British defence organisation right through World War II.

Another defence problem in which Hankey and Balfour collaborated at this time was a scheme put forward by the former to plant 'deep afforested belts' instead of building fortifications along the eastern frontier of France. He derived the idea from his study of the campaign of Genghis Khan,[4] sent copies of the resultant paper to the Foreign Office, Balfour, Milne, Trenchard and the chairman of the Forestry Commission; and proposed to place it on the agenda of the Cecil committee.[5] Though Balfour thought there was a good deal to be said

(1881–1959). Politician (Cons.), educationist, diplomat and High Churchman. Under-Secretary for Colonies 1921–22. President, Board of Education 1922–24 and 1932–35. Minister of Agriculture 1924–25. Viceroy of India 1926–31. Secretary of State for War 1935. Lord Privy Seal 1935–37. Lord President of Council 1937–38. Secretary of State for Foreign Affairs in succession to A. Eden (resigned) 1938–40. Ambassador at Washington 1941–46.

[1]Irwin to Baldwin 11th April 1927. Baldwin papers, Vol. 102. Irwin was of course referring to the holocaust of the Greeks and the burning of Smyrna in September 1922. See p. 283.

[2]Letter of 20th June 1927 from Cabinet Committee on Expenditure to all departments. Baldwin papers, Vol. 4.

[3]221st to 227th meetings. Cab. 2/5.

[4]1162–1227. Mongol conqueror. After devastating much of central Asia in 1219–21 the 'Mongol horde' swept into Europe and reached the eastern shore of the Adriatic. Though the brilliance of his military leadership is not in doubt, it is the killing of huge numbers of people and the destruction of their cities for which his campaigns are chiefly remembered.

[5]Memo. of 18th Oct. 1927. Cab. 21/300. Also in Cab. 63/29, dated 28th Oct.

for the idea,[1] the service departments were unenthusiastic, and Hankey let it drop. At least it shows how widely his mind ranged, and how he was always ready to put forward new ideas – in marked contrast to the conservatism of the fighting services.

While the Cabinet was deliberating the despatch of troops to the Far East, and the Admiralty was scraping together reinforcements for the China fleet, other influences were at work, paradoxically, to press ahead with disarmament and to call a new conference on naval limitation. In February Cecil sent Baldwin an Admiralty memorandum proposing that instead of persevering with discussions 'of an interminable character' in the Preparatory Commission at Geneva we should call a 'Washington type conference' in London to consider extending the life of existing warships, reducing the size and armament of future ships, and also cutting down the numbers to be maintained by the principal naval powers.[2] The Admiralty was of course under heavy pressure for economy at the time. They believed that a policy such as Cecil proposed could best be achieved by reducing the displacement and guns of capital ships, and that large numbers of small cruisers would provide the best protection for British trade. Furthermore they had been impressed by the benefits gained by the U.S.A. through the initiative the Americans had secured at Washington in 1921, and wished to emulate them in that respect. However such purposes were frustrated when on 10th February President Coolidge proposed that a new naval conference should be called at Geneva.[3] Meanwhile Cecil was becoming increasingly annoyed by what he described as the Admiralty's 'malevolent neutrality' towards the work of the Preparatory Commission; and even Salisbury complained that they were 'as stiff as a poker' towards its deliberations.[4] Cecil was probably glad to be appointed a delegate to the conference which opened at Geneva in June, though he was very much out of sympathy with Bridgeman, the First Lord, who was also a delegate. Hankey took no part in the organisation of the conference, towards which he was very lukewarm; but at the end of June he sent Baldwin a copy of the letter he had written to Balfour on the subject of the

[1] Balfour to Hankey 20th Oct. 1927. See also K. Young, *Arthur James Balfour* (Bell, 1963), pp. 445–6.

[2] Cecil to Baldwin 4th Feb. 1927. Baldwin papers Vol. 130, pp. 4–9.

[3] Roskill, *Naval Policy*, I, p. 498 ff.

[4] Cecil to Chamberlain 12th April and Salisbury to Chamberlain 15th April 1927. Chamberlain papers AC 54/78 and 58/440.

*impasse* which was by this time becoming evident at Geneva. As he had anticipated, the Americans had demanded parity in cruisers, and the big Navy lobby in U.S.A. had put down 'a heavy press barrage designed to stampede us into granting parity at once'. He saw no reason why we should make a declaration on such lines, and preferred to let the British Empire Delegation 'carry through their own plan of operation' – which was in fact to insist on Britain's special needs for large numbers of small cruisers. 'I have been at many conferences with the Americans', wrote Hankey. 'Time after time we have been told that, if we made this or that concession, we should secure the goodwill of America. We gave up the Anglo-Japanese alliance. We agreed to pay our debts . . . I have never seen any permanent result follow from a policy of concession. I believe we are less popular and more abused in America than ever before, because they think us weak . . . I would refuse either to be blackmailed or browbeaten, and stand absolutely to our preconceived plan of action'. Churchill endorsed Hankey's covering note to this forthright statement 'I agree'.[1]

It was probably because there was no Hankey to organise the conference that misunderstandings soon developed between Geneva and London. On 1st July he told Baldwin that although Bridgeman had evidently made a statement about parity, and American intransigence appeared to have been mollified, we had no knowledge regarding what had been said.[2] A few days later Cecil protested about Beatty's 'extreme sensitiveness as to the use of the word "parity" '.[3] Although on 12th July an Anglo-Japanese compromise solution on 'auxiliary surface craft' (i.e. cruisers and destroyers) appeared possible, and Cecil was optimistic, such hopes soon faded. On 17th Cecil asserted to Chamberlain that we had agreed at the Washington conference to parity in cruisers, and could not now claim that we did not really mean it.[4] But Hankey had long since proved that British cruiser needs were specifically and designedly excluded from the Washington Treaty, and that Balfour had never given any promise of parity in that class.[5] With

[1]Hankey to Baldwin 29th June 1927 enclosing Hankey to Balfour of same date. Baldwin papers, Vol. 130, pp. 58–64. Latter also in B.M. Add. MSS. 49704, pp. 200–3.

[2]Hankey to Baldwin 1st July 1927. Baldwin papers, Vol. 130, pp. 63–4.

[3]To Chamberlain 5th July 1927. Chamberlain papers, AC 54/88.

[4]Cecil to Chamberlain 17th July 1927. Chamberlain papers, AC 54/89.

[5]Hankey to Balfour 5th Aug. 1927 repeated his earlier emphatic denials of this statement. 'Do nail this lie' he wrote. B.M. Add. MSS. 49704. On 21st July 1927

Cecil's health causing concern, and Baldwin about to leave for a long-planned visit to Canada, on 19th the Cabinet decided to recall the delegates for discussion. Hankey at once prepared and circulated a full statement on the events leading to this decision,[1] and the Cabinet agreed that the delegates should return to Geneva and negotiate 'on lines of the Anglo-Japanese proposals, subject to such modification of detail as the Admiralty might suggest'.[2] Baldwin then departed leaving Chamberlain in charge. It must have been at about this time that Hankey drew up a balance sheet showing 'What we gain' and 'What we lose' from coming to terms with the Americans. The 'great loss' would in his opinion be the admission *by treaty* of the right of the U.S.A. to build up to parity with Britain by 1931. The refusal to agree to this had hitherto been regarded as 'a vital principle'.[3]

The next development was the reading in Parliament of a statement by Balfour (described later by Bridgeman as 'a casuistical essay'[4]) explaining that although we accepted parity with the Americans in the short term, no long-term precedent would thereby be created. According to Cecil, Hankey 'was sure the Americans would not accept the Balfour document, and rather rejoiced at it'.[5] At about the same time Sir Esmé Howard,[6] the ambassador at Washington, reported to Chamberlain that there was little prospect of agreement because 'The Admirals here are in the saddle and intend to stay there' – which was no exaggeration.[7] Cecil certainly felt that the same was true on this side of the Atlantic, and was again threatening to resign. So were a number of other Ministers – though for the opposite reason to Cecil's.[8]

---

he circulated a memorandum to the Cabinet stating that 'The whole subject [of parity in cruisers] was avoided' at Washington, and Balfour had never agreed to it. Cab. 63/39.

[1]Cab. 24/188. [2]Cabinet 43(27) Conclusion 1.

[3]Undated Memo. Cab. 63/39. [4]Bridgeman diary June–Aug. 1927.

[5]To Chamberlain 24th July 1927. Chamberlain papers.

[6]1st Baron Howard of Penrith 1930 (1863–1939). Consular Service Officer and Diplomat. After serving in Consular posts in Crete and Hungary, Minister to Switzerland 1911–13 and to Sweden 1913–19. Ambassador to Spain 1919–24 and to U.S.A. 1924–30

[7]Howard to Chamberlain 21st July 1927. Chamberlain papers, AC 54/276.

[8]Hankey to Baldwin 28th July 1927 is 'taken out' of the Baldwin papers – presumably because it described the difference of opinion among Ministers. Fortunately in nearly all such cases the private correspondence of Ministers, in this case Austen Chamberlain's letters to his sister Ida, provide the missing clues. Opposed to Cecil were Churchill, Birkenhead and Bridgeman.

On 28th July the British delegates returned to Geneva, and the final Plenary Session, at which failure to reach any agreement was admitted, took place on 4th August.[1] Three days later Cecil wrote to Chamberlain announcing his intention to resign – which provoked a protest from the Foreign Secretary over Cecil 'becoming an advocate of the large cruiser and the big gun'. Chamberlain strongly defended the line adopted by the Cabinet and his colleagues, all of whom wanted an agreement – though not on the American terms, which Cecil had supported.[2]

In April Adeline went to Paris, where Robin was studying in preparation for taking the examination for the Diplomatic Service and Ursula, now 18, was continuing her chosen vocation of music. Hankey could not get away from London, so went to stay with his sister Hilda – as he had so often done during periods of great pressure during the war. As soon as the Geneva débâcle was over the King approved his going on leave,[3] and to compensate himself for the loss of a French holiday he took Christopher and Henry (now 16 and 13 respectively) to Norway for ten days. His letters home show how relaxed he became as soon as he had shaken the dust of Whitehall off his feet, and how greatly he enjoyed the company of his two adolescent sons.

On his return home Hankey was immediately involved in the crisis provoked by Cecil's resignation which, if published in the terms he originally proposed, would have been very damaging to the govern ment and, in American eyes, to the British nation. Moreover as it included statements made, or alleged to have been made, in Cabinet publication could not be approved unless the King agreed to release Cecil from his Privy Counsellor's oath. Quite apart from ethical considerations Hankey considered Cecil's letter 'a poisonous document'.[4] He told Baldwin that 'the whole statement is completely misleading', and searched the records as far back as Lord Randolph Churchill's resignation of 1886 to produce a large volume of evidence to support his

[1]Cab. 63/45 has a valuable account by Hankey of the 1927 Geneva Conference and the subsequent Anglo-French compromise – written of course from the British point of view.

[2]Cecil to Chamberlain 7th Aug. 1927 and reply by letter of 14th. Chamberlain papers AC 54/92 and /94.

[3]Telegram of 5th Aug. 1927 from Sir Clive Wigram.

[4]Hankey to Balfour 26th Aug. 1927. Cab. 21/297.

view that publication of Cecil's letter was 'unthinkable'.[1] Hankey suggested to Baldwin that he should consult Balfour, with the result that on 26th August he went to Whittinghame armed with Cecil's letter of resignation (second version), his correspondence with Chamberlain, and a statement of his own views regarding the line the government should take. All this he handed to Balfour on arrival early next morning.[2] On 28th, a Sunday, he was back in London, and dined with Baldwin at the Bath Club to report the result of his expedition. That same day Cecil produced a third version of his letter, which Baldwin gave to Hankey 'to check for facts'.[3] Hankey saw Cecil next day, and the latter took away his letter 'in order that he might incorporate in it the agreed amendments' and produce a fourth version. Meanwhile, Baldwin who was about to leave for Aix-les-Bains for his annual holiday, had given 'general approval' to the reply drafted by Chamberlain and Hankey, which would be published simultaneously with Cecil's letter of resignation. Then, at the last moment, Cecil altered his letter yet again, so Baldwin's reply was withdrawn. Austen Chamberlain wrote to his brother Neville telling how Baldwin 'left it to Hankey and me to settle what Cecil might publish, and what his reply might be . . . I can only say that Hankey was a brick as always, but I do not think it is fair of the Prime Minister to leave a matter of this personal character to be dealt with by others'.[4]

The dénouement is best described by quoting Hankey's final letter to Baldwin.

*Hankey to Baldwin. 2 Whitehall Gardens. 30th August 1927*[5]
VERY CONFIDENTIAL
Dear Prime Minister,

After you left on Monday morning [29th], I had an interview of two hours with Lord Cecil. On some points we found it very difficult to agree. He was relying on his memory, I on the official documents plus my memory. I would not budge an inch, and eventually we reached an agreement as to the final version of the minute he had submitted to you on the previous evening. I had secured the omission or alteration of the offending passages, and Sir Austen Chamberlain confirmed my action.

[1] Hankey to Baldwin, undated but c. 27th Aug. 1927. *ibid.* Actually by this time Cecil had produced a second edition of his letter.
[2] Hankey to Balfour 26th Aug. 1927. Cab. 21/297.
[3] Holograph note by Hankey of 30th Aug. 1927. *ibid.*
[4] Letter of 29th Aug. 1927. Chamberlain papers AC 35/1/39. [5] Cab. 21/297.

I lunched with Sir Austen Chamberlain, and we agreed the reply which you had approved in its general lines in the final shape. It really was a peach of a reply, and I verily believe would have smashed Cecil's whole case to smithereens. Although for reasons I shall give in a moment it had to be superseded later, it will be invaluable if Cecil dares raise the matter in the House of Lords. In the afternoon Cecil's new minute (which was the fourth draft of his reasons for resignation) arrived. Waterhouse had obtained by telegram permission from The King to publish both Cecil's paper and your reply. Everything was being typed, and the incident appeared [to be] in its last phases. At that moment (about 4.15), Cecil came to my office to say he had changed his mind, and would like to adopt the suggestion you had made to him (and which I had repeated at one moment when an *impasse* seemed to have been reached at our morning interview), to cut out the whole of the controversial description of Geneva, including what passed at the Cabinet, and confine himself to the more general matter at the beginning and end of his minute. He gave as his reason that some of his friends thought it would re-awaken controversy in America (an argument which we had all used to him but which had fallen on deaf ears). Having in mind the crushing nature of your reply (which of course he had not seen, although I had told him a reply was coming), my first instinct was to tell him he was too late. Having regard, however, to the fact that you had made this suggestion to him, I resisted this instinct, stopped all the machinery that was in operation, and referred the matter to Sir Austen Chamberlain. The latter agreed that it was best in the public interest to adopt the new proposal. It involved the excision of all the really effective passages of the draft letter. We revised your reply, and you will have seen both documents, which were published in this morning's papers, and I am sure Waterhouse will have sent them to you.[1]

I have drawn up a full account of the whole of these transactions as the basis for Waterhouse's letter to Stamfordham. I am sending a copy to Lord Balfour and another to Lord Cave, and I am keeping all relevant material carefully in case of a debate in the autumn.

I hope you and Mrs. Baldwin will have a very nice rest. On no account think it necessary to answer this letter.

Yours very sincerely,

On the same day Hankey wrote to Balfour enclosing a copy of the memorandum he had 'jotted down in intervals in town', describing 'the whole of the events', and telling how Balfour's advice 'was in the end, after many vicissitudes, followed'.[2] Hankey's efforts to resolve

[1]See *The Times*, 30th Aug. 1927.

[2]Hankey to Balfour 30th Aug. 1927. B.M. Add. MSS. 49704, pp. 213–14. Hankey's memorandum of the same date gives a full account of Cecil's resignation. Cab. 63/39.

the crisis provoked by Cecil brought him one of the very few letters he received from Baldwin which shows real warmth. Perhaps the Prime Minister's gratitude owed something to the settlement being achieved without his holiday being interrupted.

*Baldwin to Hankey. Regina Hotel Bernascon, Aix-les-Bains. 3rd Sept. 1927.* Holograph

My dear Hankey,

Your delightful letter gave me great pleasure, increased, if possible, my respect for you, and certainly made me more than ever grateful, I left you a most tiresome task and nobly have you accomplished it.

Now I hope you will have a restful time, as so far I am having.

Most sincerely yours

But that was not quite the end of the story of what Baldwin described as Cecil's 'somewhat unnecessary and emotional exit from the Government'.[1] On 16th November Cecil made the statement in the House of Lords which Hankey had foretold,[2] and in it he reverted largely to the first draft of his resignation letter – 'to which', in Hankey's words, 'at the time strong exception was taken'. This speech resulted in the production of a lengthy riposte – presumably by Hankey, though the copy in the Cabinet records is unsigned.[3] But Baldwin was not the man to rekindle flames of enmity which were dying down, and evidently preferred to leave Cecil's speech unchallenged.

In the autumn of 1927, soon after the Cecil crisis blew up, and possibly as a consequence of it, the question whether it was justifiable, or wise, for Hankey to continue his triple functions was raised – apparently by Esher to the Palace. Hankey wrote at great length to Esher on the subject. In the first place he declared that, as compared with the war years, he was not now overworked. Indeed in that respect he considered himself no worse off than the Permanent Secretary of any of the great Departments of State. If a change was to be made his initial inclination was that he should relinquish the Clerkship of the Privy Council. But he argued that the routine work of the Privy Council Office was in fact done by his 'very capable assistant' [Colin Smith]; and that in an emergency, such as arose over the General Strike, there were great advantages in the secretary of the Cabinet also holding the Clerkship. The only matter that troubled him was that it was sometimes 'terribly inconvenient to dress up for a Council immediately before

[1]Baldwin to King George V. Baldwin papers, Vol. 62.

[2]Parl. Deb., Lords, Vol. 69, Cols. 84–100. [3]Cab. 21/297.

some important meeting of the Cabinet or C.I.D.'! The combination of the secretaryship of the Cabinet with that of the C.I.D. had, he considered, 'enormous advantages' – especially because it ensured that defence problems in general and the defence aspect of any major political issue were kept permanently before the Cabinet, or were brought immediately to its attention. Furthermore the secretary's direct access to the Prime Minister ensured that the latter was kept fully informed about all aspects of any problem. None the less he thought that, at some future date, the Secretary of the C.I.D. might become Deputy Secretary of the Cabinet. He refuted the argument that if he was absent from London the conduct of business suffered, by pointing out that Tom Jones had frequently filled his place to everyone's satisfaction. After discussing, and rejecting, various other possible solutions Hankey made it plain that he wanted his position to continue unchanged.[1] Esher sent this letter on to Stamfordham, who replied that the King thought Hankey 'makes out a very good case for leaving things as they are'. His own comment was 'that Hankey is almost a phenomenon', and if he died to-morrow he doubted whether 'any Prime Minister would attempt to continue a position which almost requires something like the Athanasian Creed to explain it'. He thought that at some future date the Clerkship would be made a separate appointment, and that 'if anything were to happen to Hankey it is possible that a Civil Servant would become Secretary of the Cabinet, and a Naval or Military Officer Secretary of the Defence Committee'.[2] The outcome of this correspondence was that no change was made; but it is interesting to remark that when Hankey finally retired in 1938 the reorganisation corresponded exactly to what Stamfordham had foretold eleven years earlier.

In the autumn of 1927 Hankey was struck down by a sharp attack of influenza, from which he made a surprisingly slow recovery. And while he was still convalescent he had to handle two awkward problems. The first concerned the chairmanship of the Chiefs of Staff's Committee if the Prime Minister was absent. Beatty had fulfilled that duty since the beginning; but he had retired from the office of First Sea Lord in July. His successor Admiral Sir Charles Madden[3] considered that he, being

[1]Hankey to Esher. Private and personal. 29th Sept. 1927. Esher papers.
[2]Stamfordham to Esher 3rd Oct. 1927. *ibid.*
[3]1862–1935. Fourth Sea Lord 1910–11. Commanded 3rd and 2nd Cruiser Squadrons, Home Fleet 1912–14. Chief of Staff to Jellicoe as C-in-C, Grand Fleet 1914–16.

the senior in rank of the three Chiefs of Staff, was heir apparent to the Chairmanship. But the Prime Minister had decided that it should circulate between the service chiefs, and that Trenchard, by virtue of his seniority as a member of the committee, should become chairman. In August Hankey wrote to all three Chiefs of Staff telling them of Baldwin's decision.[1] But Madden took it very badly, and protested vigorously over the fact that 'contrary to the custom of the Fighting Services I am, while sitting on a Committee of members of the Fighting Services, to waive my seniority and take my seat under the presidency of an officer who is junior to me'.[2] An interview with Baldwin having failed to make the Prime Minister change his mind, Madden accepted his subordinate position under protest. So ended a squall in which Hankey, despite his naval associations, sided with Trenchard.[3] It is a tribute to Hankey's tact and persuasiveness that his relations with the strong-willed Chief of the Air Staff remained generally cordial. Indeed only a few weeks after the fracas produced by Madden he persuaded Trenchard not to reopen the thorny issue of employing aircraft in place of heavy guns for the defence of the Singapore base, regarding which a 'concordat' had been reached in July 1926 after prolonged argument and much correspondence and committee work.[4] When in the following month Hankey was still convalescent Trenchard wrote to him affectionately, assuring him that nothing was 'going badly wrong without your guidance', and urging him 'to take it easy and get well and let me know if I can do anything to help you at all'.[5]

We may conveniently mention here a few more examples of Hankey's beneficial influence on Air Staff thinking during the period covered by this chapter. Towards the end of April 1928 Trenchard sent him an advance copy of a paper on 'The War Object of an Air Force', which he wanted the Chiefs of Staff Committee to consider with a view to the

---

Second-in-Command to Beatty as C-in-C, Grand Fleet 1917–19. C-in-C, Atlantic Fleet 1919–22. First Sea Lord 1927–30. Admiral of the Fleet 1924.

[1]Hankey to Trenchard and Milne. 26th Aug. 1927. Copy in C.O.S. 58th Meeting of 21st Oct. 1927.

[2]Madden to Hankey. *ibid.*

[3]Hankey to Trenchard 24th Oct. 1927. Trenchard papers.

[4]Hankey to Trenchard 21st Nov. 1927. *ibid.* The 'concordat', whereby only three 15-in. guns were installed instead of the eight originally proposed by the Admiralty and War Office was approved by the Prime Minister at the 35th C.O.S. meeting on 26th July 1926.

[5]Trenchard to Hankey 17th Nov. 1927. Trenchard papers.

principles it outlined being enshrined in the R.A.F. War Manual. Hankey replied in two capacities – as Secretary of the C.O.S. Committee and as a private individual. In the former capacity he recommended Trenchard to circulate the paper privately to his colleagues with a view to informal discussion in committee. Obviously he was anxious lest Trenchard's claims and ideas should arouse the hostility of the Navy and Army. In his private capacity he wrote at length, and in critical vein – especially about whether Trenchard's bombing doctrine, which he considered might 'cross the border line of humanity', and about the implication that air power by itself could win a war.[1] He added a postscript in his own hand 'Please don't be cross with this note. It is exclusively my own and I have consulted no-one in writing it'. Trenchard replied that he was 'not a bit annoyed' by Hankey's criticisms, and admitted that his draft had gone too far in the claims made. 'I will try to correct the impression that I expect to win the war without the Army and Navy' he wrote.[2] Later in that same month Wing-Commander Sir Norman Leslie,[3] presumably with Hankey's approval, sent Trenchard a suggested 'formula' regarding 'The War Object of an Air Force' which might, he considered, be acceptable to his colleagues. It admitted that bombing of enemy towns might well be forced on us, and moderated the Air Staff's claim by making it plain that an Air Force could only '*contribute* towards the breaking down of the enemy's means of resistance'.[4] But despite Hankey's efforts the doctrine that the only defence against air attack was counter-bombing, and that it would prove decisive in war, remained Air Staff gospel until well after the outbreak of World War II. In July 1928, when the Service chiefs were at loggerheads over the claim of the Air Ministry that aircraft could to a great extent fulfil the rôle of coastal guns, Hankey wrote that he was doing his best to counter the view of the Admiralty and War Office 'that the Air Force is out to grab everything'.

One of the few occasions when Hankey crossed swords seriously with Trenchard was over a paper written by the latter shortly before his

[1]Hankey to Trenchard 28th April 1928 No. 2. Trenchard papers. The paper under discussion was C.O.S. 147 of 2nd May 1928. Cab. 53/14.

[2]Trenchard to Hankey 2nd May 1928 *ibid.*

[3]See Vol. I, Appendix B. Sir Norman R. A. D. Leslie, Bart. (1889–1937) was Assistant Secretary (Air) to the C.I.D. at this time. He must not be confused with Sir Norman Leslie, Hankey's ally in the campaign for the adoption of convoy in 1917. See Vol. I, pp. 382–4.

[4]Leslie to Trenchard 24th May 1928. Trenchard papers.

retirement in December 1929, which the C.A.S. described as his 'Swan Song'. In it he set out without qualification the Air Staff's claims that aircraft should replace military and naval forces on the North-West frontier of India, in the Red Sea, the Sudan, and in British possessions in East and West Africa; also that bombers should to a great extent replace coast defence guns all over the world.[1] Though World War II was to confirm Trenchard's thesis regarding the dominant influence of air power, his paper did contain exaggerations; and its one-sidedness was bound to arouse the hostility of the Admiralty and War Office – especially when Lord Thomson, Secretary of State for Air in the second Labour government, circulated it to the Cabinet. Hankey fully shared the dislike of the other two Chiefs of Staff for this forthright statement on a contentious issue; and it seems true to say that it caused a deterioration in the good relations in the C.O.S. Committee for which he had worked so hard.[2] At any rate in October 1931 Hankey reported to the Prime Minister that co-ordination between the three fighting services had not been satisfactory since the circulation of Trenchard's paper which had, he wrote, irritated the Admiralty and War Office and had 'fanned the missionary zeal of the Air Ministry'. Not only was the C.O.S. Committee no longer working well but the C.I.D. itself was in consequence handicapped. What was now needed, wrote Hankey, was 'a very firm hand at the top', and he urged MacDonald to see the three Service Ministers together with the object of resolving the 'key questions' on which their departments were at loggerheads.[3] At the end of 1935 Trenchard stirred up these muddy waters again in a letter to *The Times*, and Hankey wrote to him 'more in sorrow than in anger' that it had taken him three years 'to get over the damage you did to the C.O.S. Committee by your Swan Song', and protesting that he had now done the same again.[4] But the truth was that by that time the C.I.D. system itself was under heavy fire, and Hankey was fighting against the increasing pressure in favour of a Minister, if not a Ministry of Defence.

Hankey seems never to have been on such intimate and friendly

[1]C.P. 332(29) of November 1929. Cab. 24/207.

[2]See Boyle, *Trenchard*, pp. 579–80 and B. H. Liddell Hart, *Memoirs*, Vol. I (Cassell, 1965), pp. 150–1 regarding Trenchard's 'Swan Song'.

[3]Hankey to MacDonald 28th Oct. 1931. Cab. 63/44.

[4]Hankey to Trenchard 16th Dec. 1935. Holograph from Highstead. Trenchard papers.

terms with General Milne, the C.I.G.S. of this period,[1] as he was with Beatty and Trenchard. For example when in April 1928 Hankey circulated his proposed organisation for the Supreme Control in war, based of course on his experiences of 1914–18, Milne replied stiffly that 'the tendering of technical advice as to the conduct of war is indubitably the duty of the heads of the three services' (by which Milne must have meant the service, as opposed to the political heads); and that they were therefore 'entitled to offer advice to the C.I.D. as to the military aspects of control in war'.[2] Hankey had of course seen quite enough of the consequences of senior officers 'tendering technical advice' in war to mistrust such processes thoroughly. But in the present instance he evidently considered it politic to allow Milne to have his say; so he circulated his paper to the Chiefs of Staff for discussion prior to placing it on the C.I.D.'s agenda.

Though Hankey never succeeded in reconciling the older service departments to the Air Ministry's views – and even its existence – it is fair to claim that, but for his efforts, the jealousies and the internecine strife which bedevilled all the discussions in the Chiefs of Staff's Committee in between the wars would have become worse; and a stage might even have been reached, as was the case with the German armed forces, where inter-service co-operation was totally frustrated – with fatal results.

The period March 1927 to September 1928 was a very busy one for the Chiefs of Staff Committee, and so for Hankey.[3] Apart from the large amount of work produced by the disarmament discussions at Geneva and the abortive naval conference, they had to handle the China Crisis and the debate on the Singapore base; and they were also preparing their second Annual Review of Imperial Defence Policy. As one goes through the volumes of C.O.S. papers of the late 1920s one cannot but marvel at the number of reports and memoranda – on the Chiefs of Staff side alone – which passed through Hankey's hands. Though he delegated a lot to his able Military Assistant Secretaries he must at least have read all those papers; and many of them bear the clear imprint of his style of writing. For considerable periods reports

[1]1866–1948. 1st Baron Milne 1933. Commanded British Salonika Force 1916, and in command at Constantinople until 1920. G.O.C-in-C, Eastern Command 1923–26. C.I.G.S. 1926–33. Field-Marshal 1928.

[2]Milne to Hankey 26th April 1928. Copy in Trenchard papers.

[3]Minutes of meetings 44–75. Cab. 53/2.

came in daily, and sometimes two per day; and most of them covered at least six pages of foolscap typescript, often with several Appendices. To give only one example, the Second Annual Review fills fourteen pages and is signed by Hankey.[1] It begins with a statement of the 'Political and Strategical Assumptions for Defence Preparations', and goes on to survey recent troubles in China and Afghanistan, relations with Russia and Egypt, and the Singapore base. Turning to Home Defence, the Review considered Air Raid Precautions, the control of Anti-aircraft services, the protection of vulnerable points and the possibility of invasion. It follows with Military Commitments on the continent of Europe, in the Mediterranean theatre, in India and in the Far East. And it ends with 'Other questions before the C.I.D.', which included the current disarmament negotiations, the private manufacture of arms, chemical warfare and the work of the Advisory Committee on Trading and Blockade. Altogether it was a masterly summary of the problems involved in defending a world-wide Empire; and no Minister who read it carefully would be left in any doubt regarding their scope and significance. Though long experience and his prodigious memory did of course make the production of a survey such as this easier for Hankey than for anyone else, the fact remains that he continued to produce documents of this nature month by month and year by year. And they were, of course, only one side of his triple responsibilities.

In the summer of 1928 the Overseas Defence Sub-Committee produced under Hankey's guidance an important paper entitled 'Some General Principles of Imperial Defence'. Hankey's long memory recalled that this subject had first been dealt with as long ago as 1896! The representatives of Australia, New Zealand and Canada in London, but not those of South Africa, attended the O.D.C.'s discussions, and after the first draft report had been criticised by the Dominions and the British Service departments, and a large number of amendments made, it was circulated. It stressed strongly that 'the policy underlying the principles of Imperial Defence remains purely defensive'; the maintenance of sea supremacy was named as a cardinal purpose; each service's responsibilities were defined, and reasonable account was taken of the influence of air power. Finally, in what were undoubtedly Hankey's own words, it described the organisation and functions of the C.I.D. and its principal sub-committees.[2] If this paper added little to the

[1]C.O.S. 118 of 28th Oct. 1927. Cab. 53/14.
[2]O.D.C. 537M of 3rd Aug. 1928. Cab. 21/315.

knowledge of those who had attended the recent Imperial Conference it did set out the broad aims of the C.I.D. very clearly.

The second problem Hankey had to deal with while still unwell was the thorny and intricate question whether Britain should try to improve her relations with the U.S.A. by voluntarily surrendering her long-standing claim to 'Belligerent Rights' – the right to 'visit and search' neutral merchant ships for contraband during a war, to detain ships found to be carrying contraband goods, and to seize such ships and their cargoes in prize after proceedings before a nationally constituted Prize Court. The reader of our first volume will recall that the exercise of Belligerent Rights produced many protests from neutrals, and especially from the Americans, during the 1914–18 war; and that at the 1919 Paris Peace Conference Lloyd George stood out firmly and successfully against President Wilson's wish to incorporate 'Freedom of the Seas' in the League Covenant and so in the Peace Treaty.[1] In the autumn of 1927 the whole issue was re-opened in the Cabinet. This arose partly because our Arbitration Treaties with a number of countries, including the Root–Bryce treaty of 1908 between Britain and the U.S.A., had either expired recently or fell due for renewal in the near future[2]; and some Ministers and civil servants held that re-negotiation or extension of the American treaty would be made easier if we could go some way towards meeting their views on Freedom of the Seas. Another element in bringing about a review of this tricky question was a letter from Lord Cushendun,[3] who had succeeded Cecil as Minister responsible for League affairs, to Chamberlain asking whether the moment was not opportune 'to abandon, or modify our traditional doctrine of blockade in time of war'.[4] The Foreign Secretary's initial reaction had been favourable to Cushendun's proposal[5]; but Hankey's was very much the reverse. On the last day of October he sent Chamberlain a historical review of the subject, and told him that

[1]See Vol. I, pp. 105–6, 149, 310 and 336–7.

[2]The Root–Bryce Treaty had already expired and a new treaty was put forward by Kellogg in January 1927. The British arbitration treaty with France expired in October 1928, and those with Italy and Spain in February 1929.

[3]Ronald J. McNeill, 1st Baron Cushendun 1927 (1861–1934). Politician (Cons.). Parliamentary Under-Secretary for Foreign Affairs 1922–24 and 1925. Financial Secretary to Treasury 1925–27. Chancellor of Duchy of Lancaster with responsibility for League of Nations 1927–29.

[4]Cushendun to Chamberlain 4th Nov. 1927. Chamberlain papers AC 54/387.

[5]See Chamberlain's memo. of 26th Oct. 1927. Cab. 63/39.

he was convinced it would be 'a profound mistake', repeating the errors we had made by accepting the Declaration of Paris of 1856 and that of London of 1908.[1] Despite the fact that he was still far from well he quickly followed this up with a survey of 'Blockade and the Laws of War'.[2] Though he and Chamberlain were initially in opposing camps, when the Foreign Secretary sent him his own views on blockade he assured Hankey that he was 'one of those whose absence makes itself felt'.[3] Hankey, though grateful for the sympathy, replied that he hoped that if Chamberlain was determined to initiate an enquiry he would be 'as non-committal as possible'. As one would expect Hankey soon brought Balfour into the controversy, telling him that he suspected Colonel House – 'a fanatic on the subject of Freedom of the Seas' – of being the '*fons et origo*' of the new attempt to whittle away Britain's Belligerent Rights.[4] On 19th November he opened his heart to Tom Jones, telling him that he had 'decided years ago that if ever "Freedom of the Seas" went through' he would resign, because 'Imperial Defence would then be a sham'. Jones promptly showed this letter to Baldwin remarking that it seemed to him 'a very wrong conception of a civil servant's function to threaten resignation on policy'; which was not exactly a display of loyalty by Hankey's deputy.[5] In the following month Hankey wrote a number of letters to Esher, telling him that Lloyd George was still opposed to any sacrifice of Belligerent Rights, describing the views of Chamberlain, Bridgeman and other Ministers, and commenting on the opinions expressed in the Press.[6] The following letter is the last of the series to Esher:—

*Hankey to Esher. 2 Whitehall Gardens. 21st December 1927.* Last two lines and postscript Holograph

SECRET

My dear Esher,

Many thanks for yours of the 19th.

I am afraid it is really out of the question for me not to appear in some degree as a protagonist in the question we discussed. I first heard of this matter in an exchange of confidences with A. C. I was very alarmed, and at

[1]Hankey to Chamberlain 31st Oct. 1927. Cab. 21/307. Also C.P. 258(27). Cab. 24/189.

[2]C.P. 286(27) of 14th Nov. 1927. Cab. 24/189.

[3]Chamberlain to Hankey 10th Nov. 1927. Chamberlain papers, AC 54/238.

[4]Hankey to Balfour 11th Nov. 1927. B.M. Add. MSS. 49704.

*Middlemas*, II, pp. 116–17.

Hankey to Esher 13th and 17th Dec. 1927. Esher papers.

once wrote hastily and sent him a memorandum as to the dangers of raising the question. In this I made no secret of my bias. While I was away with the influenza he brought the whole matter before the Cabinet and circulated my memorandum among others. You see then that I am irrevocably committed. On our Sub-Committee I have been put – not as Secretary but as an expert assessor, whatever that means. I shall in appearance preserve as neutral a view as I can, but I know so much more about the question than anyone else that this will only be a façade and I am sure my predilections will always be cropping up.

There have been about three occasions since I came here when I have had to adopt this rôle, and it is the more effective when I do because of my known impartiality in the great mass of questions.

H.M. is fairly boiling on this question.

All good wishes for Xmas.

Yours ever

P.S. If things go well I shall say nothing. But if they go badly I shall be compelled to drop a depth charge, which is fully loaded. But I will reserve fire to the last moment and be discreet.

The Belligerent Rights Sub-Committee of the C.I.D., referred to in the above letter, was formed in November with Salisbury as Chairman – a duty which Balfour had declined to undertake.[1] Hankey asked that he and Bridgeman might both be made members; but that proposal must have appeared to Baldwin too much like packing the committee. Though he agreed to Bridgeman serving on it, Hankey, Hurst and Madden were only nominated 'expert assessors'.[2] Even so Chamberlain was soon protesting that all the assessors were opposed to his ideas, and wanted one added 'who takes the Foreign Office view'.[3] He proposed to replace Hurst with Tyrrell; but Hankey had got in first, and had already given Chamberlain's nominee all the adverse arguments.[4] He also produced the help of his old friend Sir Herbert Richmond, who produced arguments from naval history in favour of Belligerent Rights going back to the War of 1812.[5]

[1]The other members were Austen Chamberlain, Balfour, Bridgeman, Cunliffe-Lister, Peel, Cushendun and Hogg. Commander C. P. Hermon-Hodge acted as secretary, with H. F. Batterbee of the Dominions Office as his assistant. Batterbee was, as mentioned earlier (see p. 361) a close friend and admirer of Hankey.

[2]Hankey to Bridgeman 2nd Dec. 1927. Cab. 21/307.

[3]Chamberlain to Hankey 6th Jan. 1928. *ibid.*

[4]Hankey to Tyrrell 16th Dec. 1927. *ibid.* Cab. 63/40 contains copies of all the papers accumulated by Hankey during this controversy.

[5]Richmond to Hankey 30th Jan. 1928. *ibid.*

The Sub-Committee met for the first time on 11th January 1928, and Hankey at once started a new series (B.R. papers) to cover all its deliberations. He included in them a number of war time memoranda which supported his view, and a long survey of his own.[1] On Chamberlain's side stood Cushendun, Steel-Maitland (of whom Hankey never had any high opinion[2]), Sir Esmé Howard, the ambassador in Washington, and M. L. Gwyer, the Procurator-General.[3] One feels that such a miscellaneous team stood little chance against the well-ordered and solid ranks in which stood the King, Balfour, Esher, Bridgeman, Hurst, Madden and Bullock (Permanent Secretary of the Air Ministry) – all of whom had been well briefed and coached by Hankey. Early in December he protested vigorously to Salisbury about Chamberlain's 'extraordinarily irregular procedure' in 'unfolding plans on a vital matter' in Cabinet as though he was ignorant of the existence of the sub-committee appointed to consider policy on Belligerent Rights. This, wrote Hankey, had the result that 'the controversy was suddenly and unexpectedly transferred to the Cabinet' – most of whom had not seen the relevant papers.[4] Next he wrote to Balfour complaining that the Foreign Secretary had 'suddenly indicated a preference for Freedom of the Seas'. 'I confess', he added, 'to having felt once or twice a shade of doubt as to whether his judgement is as good as it was'.[5] At about the same time he asked the Salisbury committee to record his opposition to the submission of Belligerent Rights to compulsory arbitration.[6]

How much Hankey's assiduous campaign contributed to the Foreign Secretary's change of front cannot be said; but early in 1928 he was able to tell Balfour and the King that Chamberlain now stood firmly against the abandonment of Belligerent Rights, and that Cushendun

[1] B.R. 21 of 19th March 1928. *ibid.*

[2] See Vol. I, pp. 342–5.

[3] Later Sir Maurice L. Gwyer (1878–1952). Lawyer. Fellow of All Souls' College 1902–16. Lecturer in International Law, Oxford University 1912–15. Legal Adviser to Ministry of Shipping 1917–19. Solicitor and Legal Adviser to Ministry of Health 1919–26. Procurator-General and Solicitor to Treasury 1926–33. First Parliamentary Counsel to Treasury 1934–37. Chief Justice of India 1937–43. Vice-Chancellor, Delhi University 1938–50.

[4] Hankey to Salisbury 10th Dec. 1928. Cab. 63/40.

[5] Hankey to Balfour 18th Dec. 1928. B.M. Add. MSS. 49704.

[6] Memo. of 13th Dec. 1928. Cab. 63/41.

was the only Cabinet Minister in favour of doing so.[1] From the Palace he received a flattering acknowledgment.

*Stamfordham to Hankey. Buckingham Palace. 15th January 1928.* Holograph

My dear Hankey,

The King has sent me your 'Most Secret' letter of 12th inst. to thank you for it with the following note: 'Thank Hankey for his letter. If he is satisfied with F.O. over this question then I am'.

Now, *what* greater faith could any Sovereign have in any subject?!!

Personally I hope the F.O. will *not* indulge in any *over* 'waiving' of 'some small part of the Belligerent Rights as exercised by us during the great war' [a quotation from Hankey's letter].

I shall be surprised if we get *anything* out of our trans-Atlantic cousins. You may count upon absolute secrecy from us.

Yours ever

The Belligerent Rights Committee continued its deliberations throughout 1928, and became involved not only in the question of Arbitration Treaties and whether they should be linked with the disputed rights, but in a highly academic argument initiated by Philip Kerr. He wished to draw a distinction between 'private wars', which would be outlawed, and 'public or League of Nations wars', which would be legal. Hankey sharply told his associate of former times that it was 'infinitely desirable to leave the question of Belligerent Rights alone'.[2]

In February P. J. Grigg[3] sent to Hankey at Churchill's request a survey on Anglo-American relations, with particular reference to naval policy, which the Chancellor had written. Churchill considered that 'to repose final faith in any international instrument is vain', and that 'we in this island must have a good navy, whatever other powers may do'. But in a war with Russia or the U.S.A. 'a convention protecting seaborne commerce from attack would be of priceless help to a small over-crowded island and scattered Empire'. Nor should we 'too readily accept the suggestion that all naval competition with the United States is hopeless'. The British would, he considered, be more ready than the Americans to 'make far greater sacrifice for sea-power over a long period'; and the addition of '20 or even 30 millions a year [to the Navy Estimates], which we could easily afford if we had to' would soon

[1]Hankey to Balfour 12th Jan. 1928. B.M. Add. MSS. 49704.

[2]Hankey to Kerr 14th Dec. 1928. B.M. Add. MSS. 49704.

[3]See p. 255, *note*.

give us a fleet 'which the United States could not surpass without encountering the gravest internal problems'. Furthermore 'the mere suspension of our debt payments would subtract £35 millions from their revenue and add it to our own'. These were curious arguments for a Chancellor who had so recently attacked the Navy Estimates with gusto to put forward. He ended his survey with the following conclusions: 'First, that we should accept, and indeed advocate the immunity of peaceful commerce at sea for all nations. Secondly, that we should reject all proposals for a treaty of mathematical parity with the United States. Thirdly, that apart from any agreement that may be possible about the age and size of battleships, we should preserve entire liberty in numbers and design; and, lastly that we should do our utmost to keep a Navy which as a whole is stronger and better than that of the United States'.[1] Hankey replied two days later that he 'welcomed all the conclusions' in Churchill's paper except the first, which he rebutted in terms and on grounds with which the reader will by now be familiar. As they had both agreed that no one else should see these papers it appears that they never went any further; but Hankey must have had the Chancellor's advocacy of Freedom of the Seas in mind when he gave the King a forthright account of the attitude of Cabinet Ministers – including Chamberlain and Churchill – to that issue.

A short time later Churchill evidently developed these arguments more fully in Cabinet; for Hankey told Chamberlain that he had made 'the most notable contribution to the discussion' on reduction of armaments. He was, Hankey reported, 'opposed to any agreement [with the U.S.A.] whether now or in the future in regard to cruisers' – at any rate those of the smaller type. He was also opposed 'to disclosing any particular programme such as the Admiralty's 70 cruiser programme'. The policy he recommended was one of 'no agreement and low programmes and expenditure', and of temporizing. 'My own impression', concluded Hankey 'is that the Cabinet was a good deal moved by Mr. Churchill's intervention'. There were, he considered, advantages in keeping our hands free as regards small cruisers, and in showing 'a real desire to support France on the military side'. In brief while Churchill favoured going our own way in naval construction Hankey supported the ill-fated Anglo-French compromise which was then

[1]Enclosure to Grigg to Hankey, Personal and Private of 10th Feb. 1928.

coming to the boil. The disillusion of them both with the U.S.A. is readily apparent.[1]

It will be convenient here to carry on the story of the Belligerent Rights Sub-Committee to the end of the Baldwin government. Early in 1929 Vansittart, who had recently replaced Waterhouse, whom Hankey had never liked or trusted, as Principal Private Secretary to the Prime Minister, sent Hankey his views. He wrote that we should '*have* to negotiate [with the Americans] or say "No" about Belligerent Rights'; and, he asked, 'was anyone prepared to do that?' Vansittart wanted therefore 'to make a virtue of necessity' and open negotiations.[2] But Hankey was fully prepared to give the flat negative which Vansittart deprecated.

In February 1929 Hankey told Richmond that Chamberlain had now 'swung round' against a conference with the Americans. 'Thank God', he added, 'they are all for high Belligerent Rights now, except Cushendun'.[3] On 13th he asked the Committee that his opposition to submitting such rights to compulsory arbitration should be recorded in their conclusions.[4] The Committee, having met 16 times and considered nearly 100 memoranda produced two reports. The majority report recommended against holding a conference to decide on the 'agreed law' over Belligerent Rights; while the minority report accepted Hankey's view that there should be no submission of the question until after a conference had established the agreed law.[5] As he remarked the two reports were in effect 'mutually destructive'. What he wanted done was to tell the Americans 'the whole truth', explaining what we wanted and why.

In March Balfour sent Hankey his proposed reply to an enquiry from Sir Robert Borden, the former Canadian Prime Minister who was now representing his country at the League of Nations, about the British government's views on compulsory arbitration and whether Belligerent Rights should be excluded from that concept. Balfour was strongly opposed to 'any system of rigid and compulsory arbitration', and Hankey described his draft as 'an admirable exposition' of the

[1]Hankey to Chamberlain 7th June 1928. Cab. 63/40.
[2]Vansittart to Hankey 30th Jan. 1929. Cab. 21/310.
[3]Hankey to Richmond 8th Feb. 1929. *ibid.*
[4]Memo. of 13th Feb. 1929. Cab. 63/41.
[5]B.R. 62 and 82, which became C.I.D. 943B and 944B of 13th Feb. and 6th March 1929.

defects of the principle of compulsion.[1] Obviously they were of one mind on this, as on many other issues.

Hankey's diary entry dealing with his campaign against the emasculation of Belligerent Rights was written long after it was over, and tells us nothing that is not contained in the letters and memoranda already mentioned. But the end is worth quoting.

*Diary 18th October 1929* [Probably misdated as it precedes entry for 7th Oct.] . . . The final report of the C.I.D. Sub-Committee, which I drafted, and which was a very long one reached the conclusion that we ought to maintain Belligerent Rights as high as possible; that we should avoid any international discussion if possible; but that if we could not avoid it we should try and come to terms with the Americans. The report did not come before the C.I.D. or the Cabinet for discussion during the life of the Unionist Government, and the whole subject was postponed until after the election. Then Baldwin's government was defeated; MacDonald came into office and at once began his conversations with General Dawes with a view to a naval disarmament agreement. I sent him, to Lossiemouth, where he was to see Dawes, both reports of the B.R. Ctee. and he acknowledged them. On June 22nd and 23rd there was an exchange of telegrams with Howard, our ambassador in Washington in which it was made clear that neither Dawes nor President Hoover wanted to take up the question, after which we all assumed that it was to be dropped until after the [London 1930] naval agreement had been reached . . .

We will return to the sequel later. Whatever view one may take of the rights and wrongs of the case over Belligerent Rights and compulsory arbitration there can be no doubt that Hankey fought an extremely skilful, and ultimately successful battle against any relaxation of the British claims. Sir Harry Batterbee recalls an amusing example of his methods. When one of the memoranda proposing the reduction or abandonment of Belligerent Rights was circulated Hankey got him to take it to Balfour, who was staying with his brother near Woking. Balfour looked at the signatures, and said to Batterbee 'Do you think them all wrong?' They then discussed the issues involved, and when they had finished Balfour sat down and drafted 'a perfect memorandum totally controverting the views expressed'.[2] It was probably this memorandum on which Balfour based the cogently argued statement

[1]Balfour to Hankey 20th March and reply by latter of 21st March 1929. B.M. Add. MSS. 49705.

[2]Interview with Sir Harry Batterbee 10th April 1970.

he made at the Sub-Committee's 4th meeting on 27th July 1928. He then suggested that 'the Committee was wandering about in a gloomy penumbra, where even the ghosts lacked definition'; and he reminded them of Lord Melbourne's statement that 'when you know nothing it is better to leave it alone'. He stressed that it 'should be entirely left for the Americans to open up the question' [of Belligerent Rights], and ended by urging the Committee 'to make no direct advances on this question'.[1] This evidence must greatly have delighted at least one of the Committee's 'expert assessors'.

While Hankey was actually corresponding with Balfour on Belligerent Rights his old friend's 80th birthday was celebrated. It produced a letter which shows how profound were the affection and admiration Hankey felt towards Balfour; and how wide of the mark was Baldwin's judgement that Hankey 'had no bowels'. Nor can it be doubted that, in so far as Balfour was capable of experiencing any deep emotion, he reciprocated Hankey's feelings.

*Hankey to Balfour. 2 Whitehall Gardens. 24th July 1928.* Holograph[2]

Dear Lord Balfour,

As one who, during the most eventful period of his life, has benefited amazingly from the privilege of your friendship and unstinted help, I feel I must send you just a line to express my very warm congratulations on your 80th birthday. You will be overwhelmed with letters so I will not burden you with all I should like to say. I was not allowed to subscribe to the motor car [a gift from Balfour's political colleagues] as I am not a member of either House, but I cannot let the occasion pass without some tribute, however trivial.

You once told me you had never read Kipling's story 'The Village that Voted the Earth was Flat'. It is a priceless story, so I send the volume containing it – the marker is put in at the first page of the story.[3]

Wishing you many happy years to enjoy your great and unique position,

I am, yours affectionately

One of Hankey's last 'business' letters to Balfour dealt, significantly, with the subject of illegal German rearmament. Hankey reported that

[1] 4th Meeting of B.R. Sub-Committee. Cab. 16/79.

[2] B.M. Add. MSS. 49705, pp. 36 ff. It may be remarked that after 1928 Hankey regularly ended his letters to Balfour 'Yours ever'. The nearest Balfour came at first to reciprocating the intimacy was to begin letters 'My dear Maurice Hankey'; but in January 1929, the year before his death, 'My dear Maurice' at last appears.

[3] In *A Diversity of Creatures*. Hankey probably sent Balfour the Macmillan 1917 edition.

a 'Professor Morgan'[1] had written 'a very alarmist letter' to *The Times*, with the result that the matter was discussed in the C.I.D. on 16th December.[2] He reported that 'on the whole Milne [C.I.G.S.] thinks there is not much danger. There seems to be no doubt, however, that the Germans are doing everything they can (as we should do in their case[3]) to prepare for a rapid expansion of their forces. Milne thinks that they have no hidden reserves of heavy guns, and that in the absence of heavy guns and tanks there is nothing to be alarmed at'.[4] This was altogether too complacent a view; for in fact the Germans had, ever since 1919, done everything they could to evade the disarmament provisions of the Versailles Treaty – as Morgan, who had served on the Control Commission, very well knew.

On 1st June of the following year, the day after the General Election which had proved fatal to Baldwin, Hankey wrote to him about whether Parliament should meet and the government await an adverse vote before resigning, as had been done after the 1923 Election; and, if Baldwin decided to reconstruct his government, whether all Ministers should place their resignations in his hands. He had discussed the matter with Balfour who, though very weak, accepted the precedents of 1915 and 1918 cited by Hankey. He placed his resignation in Baldwin's hands, and authorised Hankey to tell him so.[5] Nine months later, on 19th March 1930, Balfour passed away peacefully – to Hankey's profound sorrow.

Here we must retrace our steps to 1927. Consideration of the Trade Disputes Bill, whereby the government hoped to make a repetition of the General Strike impossible and eliminate abuses in the Trade Unions, took up a great deal of Hankey's time early in the year. Though

[1]Brigadier-General John H. Morgan (1876–1955). Lawyer. Emeritus Professor of International Law, London University. Counsel to many bodies in India and the Commonwealth. Deputy Adjutant-General in Inter-Allied Control Commission, Germany 1919–23. Adviser to U.S. War Crimes Commission, Nuremberg 1947–49.

[2]Presumably Hankey was referring to Morgan's long letter in *The Times* of 15th Nov. 1928. But it seems surprising that he was apparently unaware of the article on the same theme he had published in the *Quarterly Review* of Oct. 1924. See Roskill, *Naval Policy*, I, p. 98.

[3]This is a very surprising statement by Hankey. He surely cannot have meant that any British government would disregard treaty obligations as flagrantly as the Germans were doing.

[4]Hankey to Balfour 18th Dec. 1928. B.M. Add. MSS. 49705, p. 93.

Hankey to Baldwin 1st June 1929. Baldwin papers Vol. 36, pp. 199-202.

it was finally bulldozed through by the Conservative majority, and remained on the Statute Book until 1946, Hankey described his attitude to it as one of 'indifference' – because he was sure that it could never be enforced.[1] What he called the 'racket' in Cabinet during the discussions prior to the introduction of this controversial measure troubled him less than the leakages regarding its contents which appeared in many newspapers in March.[2] Nor does the source of the leakages ever appear to have been traced. The government's attitude towards Soviet Russia was of course intimately connected with the desire of its right wing elements to curb the power of the Trade Unions; but they were more successful in bringing about a breach with the Soviets than in legislating against another General Strike. As far back as December 1926 J. D. Gregory of the Foreign Office, the sinister figure whom we encountered at the time of the Zinoviev letter forgery, was pressing for diplomatic relations to be broken off.[3] But Gregory was soon to be dismissed as a result of the Bradley–Dyne case mentioned earlier.[4] Incidentally the revelation that officials had indulged in large-scale speculations in foreign currencies shocked Hankey profoundly, and it was perhaps to underline the need for officials to keep wholly clear of such transactions that he told Robin that he himself had always been 'hyper-scrupulous' in money matters.[5] He was also troubled over his friend Sir Miles Lampson being involved, and considered that he 'had rather a narrow squeak, and would probably have been done in but for the admiration in which he is held by the Government'.[6] In March 1927 Hankey wrote in his own hand two long Confidential Annexes to the minutes of the Cabinets at which Chamberlain gave 'highly secret information' regarding the activities of the Third International in this country, and its links with the British Communist party.[7] The Attorney-General, Sir Douglas Hogg, reported that in his opinion the information received was genuine. Although the government decided that it should not be published for

[1]To Lady Hankey 3rd May 1927. See *Baldwin*, pp. 446–53 and *Middlemas*, II, pp. 96–102 regarding the preliminary discussions in Cabinet and the debate on this measure.

[2]Cab. 21/391 and 21/443. Leakages appeared in many newspapers on 24th March.

[3]Memo. of 10th Dec. 1926. Baldwin papers Vol. 113, pp. 47–56.

[4]See pp. 383–4. [5]To Robin Hankey 6th Feb. 1928.

[6]To the same 4th March 1928. See also p. 385.

[7]Confidential Annexes to Cabinet 17(27) of 17th March and 14(27) 1A of 18th March 1927. Cab. 23/90B.

the present, and that relations with the U.S.S.R. were not to be disrupted, the raid on the offices of Arcos Ltd. and the Russian Trade Delegation soon followed on 12th May; and diplomatic, though not trade relations were broken off.[1]

Towards the end of 1927 Hankey wrote a long letter to Smuts reviewing the political situation at home, which he described as 'rather quiet', the personalities of the leaders of the three parties and their prospects, and the international situation. He considered Baldwin's government 'on the whole sound if rather stodgy', and expected them to get back at the next election 'unless they make a bad mistake or have some stroke of bad luck'. He regarded MacDonald as the only possible leader for Labour, but considered him 'not quite first class' and 'never really fit' because he overtaxed his strength. The failure of the Geneva conference he described as 'deplorable'; but success on American terms would have been too dearly bought. As to disarmament, he reminded Smuts that a small but steady naval building programme 'kept the shipyards alive, and is more economical and less sensational than a sudden burst of building'. He applauded Austen Chamberlain's regular attendance at League Council meetings, and expected the League to 'succeed in keeping the peace'. What made him anxious was that 'public opinion in Europe lags far behind this country' on disarmament. 'I don't much mind being a pacifist', he wrote, 'provided all the world is pacifist. But if we are the only pacifists we shall one day suffer a greater disillusionment than we ever did in 1914'. Russia he considered no longer to be a serious menace; but France was 'as militant as ever and suffers from an inferiority complex *vis à vis* Germany'. In that country the League was widely regarded 'merely as a convenient instrument to keep the peace until they recover their strength'; and he feared that the militarist elements 'will get on top'. In Italy, he reported, 'force is rampant', and he had no sympathy at all with the Fascist régime. Judged by any standard this was a remarkably statesmanlike survey; and at the end of it Hankey recorded with pride and pleasure that Robin had been accepted for the Diplomatic Service.[2]

At the time when Hankey wrote to Smuts the Admiralty was fighting hard to obtain approval for the small and steady building programme referred to by him, in face of strenuous opposition from Churchill, who wanted no cruisers at all to be included in the 1927–28 or 1928–29

[1] See *Baldwin*, pp. 457–8.

[2] Hankey to Smuts. Personal. Holograph from Highstead. 25th Nov. 1927.

programmes.[1] Hankey unquestionably sympathised with the Admiralty on this issue, and probably welcomed the decision of March 1928 that the Naval Programme (or Birkenhead) Committee was to become a sub-committee of the C.I.D.[2] At any rate it resulted in an acceptable compromise, midway between the Admiralty's original proposal and the Chancellor's total negative. But the forces working against expenditure on armaments were very powerful – and very vociferous. As far back as November 1926 Arthur Ponsonby[3] asked Baldwin to receive a deputation to present his 'Peace Letter', and by the end of the following year it had been signed by nearly 129,000 persons.[4] Though Baldwin pointed out to Ponsonby that a totally disarmed Britain would have very adverse effects on the League, his reasonable and reasoned reply did not in any way dampen the ardour of the propagandists against armaments. And in July 1928 Churchill put a trump card in their hands by getting the C.I.D. to accept that the Ten Year Rule of 1919 should be made permanent and self-perpetuating.[5] In the following November the decision was taken that the rule should no longer be reviewed annually, though it would be open to any department to bring it up at any time.[6] And a few weeks after MacDonald returned to power in June 1929 he declared the self-perpetuating rule to be 'a change for the better'.[7]

The reader of our first volume will recall that prior to 1914 the C.I.D. had made no study of the measures necessary to mobilise the nation's industries for total war, and to change from a peacetime to a wartime economy. Nor had intelligence been collected regarding the industrial capacity of our possible enemies, and their needs regarding imports of raw materials.[8] Hankey had always believed that what he called a 'seapower and blockade' strategy, applied in conjunction with peripheral operations, would bring about the collapse of the Central European powers. He was convinced that, although the process would be slow, it would be far less costly in men and in resources than the frontal attacks and war of attrition in the west to which the War Office

[1]Churchill to Baldwin 19th Oct. 1927 and 29th Jan. 1928. Baldwin papers Vol. 2.
[2]234th C.I.D. of 29th March 1928. Cab. 2/5.
[3]1st Baron Ponsonby 1930 (1871–1946). Politician (Lib. then Lab.) and lifelong pacifist. Under-Secretary, Foreign Office 1924 and Dominions Office 1929. Chancellor of Duchy of Lancaster 1931.
[4]Baldwin papers Vol. 134, p. 5. [5]236th C.I.D. of 5th July 1928. Cab. 2/5.
[6]238th C.I.D. of 8th Nov. 1928. *ibid.* [7]243rd C.I.D. of 27th June 1929. *ibid.*
[8]See Vol. I, pp. 105–6 and 138–41.

and General Staff were totally committed. He was not the man to forget such lessons, and ever since 1919, when he began work on the new edition of the famous War Book, he had applied his mind to meeting those needs in the event of another war. Though the political atmosphere of the 1920s was not helpful to his purposes he found ready support in the Chiefs of Staff Committee, which accepted his proposal that a special sub-committee of the C.I.D. should be formed to study such problems. Another strong supporter was Sir Philip Cunliffe-Lister (later Lord Swinton),[1] who had been Secretary of the Overseas Trade Department under Lloyd George, and served in Baldwin's first two administrations as President of the Board of Trade. It was largely thanks to Cunliffe-Lister's efforts that strong Treasury objections to the formation of this committee were overborne. Hankey had been working on this idea since 1924, but it was not until some five years later that it actually bore fruit. His ultimate object was to build up the skeleton organisation for what would on the outbreak of war, become a fully fledged Ministry of Economic Warfare. The chairman of the new committee was Sir Edward Crowe,[2] who had succeeded Cunliffe-Lister at the Department of Overseas Trade; but the hostility of the Treasury towards it became apparent at the very first meeting, when a clash took place between that department's representative and the Chiefs of Staff. Incidentally the hostility which Lord Bridges showed towards Hankey and his whole organisation after he had succeeded him as Secretary of the Cabinet in 1938 probably dates to this time; for Bridges was then serving in the Treasury, of which he later became Permanent Secretary.[3]

Hankey's work in this field brought him into close touch with Desmond Morton,[4] and it is plain that Morton, like nearly all civil servants, service men and politicians who knew Hankey well, soon

[1]See p. 268, *note*.

[2]1877–1960. Consular Service officer, mainly in Far East. Seconded to Department of Overseas Trade as Director of Foreign Division 1924–28. Comptroller-General of same Department 1928–37. Not to be confused with his relative Sir Eyre Crowe, Permanent Secretary of Foreign Office 1920–25 (see Vol. I, p. 500, *note*).

[3]This hostility towards Hankey was made very apparent in two long interviews Lord Bridges gave to the author in 1968.

[4]Later Major Sir Desmond Morton (1891–1971). Soldier, intelligence officer and expert on war industries. A.D.C. to Field-Marshal Haig 1917. Principal Assistant Secretary, Ministry of Economic Warfare 1939. Personal Assistant to Churchill as Prime Minister 1940–45. Ministry of Civil Aviation 1950–53.

developed a profound admiration for his tact and persuasiveness, and for the skill with which he would manipulate both individuals and the departmental machinery to achieve any purpose on which he had set his heart.[1] He always knew exactly the right people to consult or inform; nor did he hesitate to go to Ministers, or even the Prime Minister, if he considered it expedient to short-circuit the 'normal channels'. Furthermore his contacts and friendships in all departments were so widespread and influential that he, and he alone could act in such a manner without arousing jealousy or antagonism. Incidentally Morton became a friend and confidant of Churchill's; he participated in his struggle for rearmament in the 1930s, and in his plans and efforts during the critical months of 1940 when France was disintegrating in utter disaster.[2]

While employed on secret intelligence work Morton had developed many contacts in British commercial and industrial circles; and he used the knowledge and experience gained from such contacts to provide the raw material needed by Hankey. In 1927 he produced a series of reports entitled 'Preparations for Industrial Mobilisation Abroad', which aroused great interest among the officials and service men concerned with defence. Hankey was in the forefront of those who appreciated their importance. Two years later, with Hankey's strong support, an Industrial Intelligence Centre was formed to carry this work a stage further. Its terms of reference were 'To discover and report the plans for manufacture of armaments and war stores in foreign countries'. Morton was the obvious person to become head of the new organisation, and in fulfilling his task he maintained his close association with Hankey and the C.I.D. Germany was the first country on which the new centre reported; but it gradually extended its activities to cover all the major powers.[3]

We saw earlier how Hankey was never in any degree deceived by the realities of the Nazi movement and the significance of Hitler's accession to power early in 1933.[4] Soon after that took place he pro-

[1]Even Lord Bridges admitted to the author that 'Nobody was cleverer than Hankey at getting his own way'. Interview 15th Aug. 1968.

[2]See Churchill, *The Second World War*, Vol. I, pp. 62–3 and Vol. II, pp. 180, 182, etc.

[3]See W. N. Medlicott, *The Economic Blockade*, Vol. I (H.M.S.O., 1952), pp. 12–16 regarding the formation of the I.I.C. Vol. II of the same work (H.M.S.O., 1959) refers, p. 51, to 'the crusading zeal of the I.I.C. under Major Morton's leadership'.

[4]See Vol. I, p. 18.

duced a report in which he used the information provided by Morton's organisation to draw a striking picture of the gulf between authoritarian Germany's industrial war potential and Britain's deficiencies. He pointed out that in 1918 we had thousands of factories, and hundreds of thousands of skilled or semi-skilled men and women, engaged on the production of every conceivable sort of equipment and stores needed by the fighting services. But the drastic economies of the 1920s had resulted in the widespread closure and dismantling of plant, and the dispersal of the skilled staff which had operated it – too often to join the ever-lengthening queues of unemployed. To restore this capacity and retrain the operatives would, Hankey stressed, not only require a long time but demanded a radical departure from normal peacetime procedures and practices.[1] If an emergency arose an Act of Parliament could quickly conscript men for the fighting services; but they would be useless if the equipment they needed, and the capacity to produce it, were non-existent. All this information was made available by Hankey to the Defence Requirements Sub-Committee of the C.I.D. of 1933, of which he was chairman and to which further reference will be made later. It is also likely that it influenced Hankey's decision to give evidence himself before the Royal Commission on the Private Manufacture of Armaments of 1936 – which shocked his erstwhile deputy Tom Jones, then one of the leading 'appeasers' of Germany.[2] Unhappily the long and short of the outcome of all these efforts was that, with the exception of the creation of the shadow aircraft factories in the mid-1930s, which owed a great deal to Swinton, Secretary of State for Air from June 1935 until Neville Chamberlain dismissed him in May 1938 in order to relieve himself of so strong an advocate for rearmament,[3] little was done to prepare the country to negotiate with the dictators from strength. And when war came the deficiencies to which Hankey had repeatedly drawn attention became glaringly apparent. Armour plate for the new warships had to be ordered from the Skoda works in Czecho-Slovakia, because the British plant had been dismantled for lack of orders; and Europe was scoured for the anti-

[1]Hankey's report on the parlous condition of British firms which had been largely dependent on orders for armaments, dated 2nd March 1933, is in the MacDonald papers, Box 1/6 (Brown). It was addressed to the Chancellor of the Exchequer, Neville Chamberlain, but he sent a copy to MacDonald, the Prime Minister.

[2]See Jones, *A Diary with Letters 1931–1950* (Oxford U.P., 1954), p. 262. 'So unlike Hankey to have done this.'

[3]Interview with Lord Swinton 5th April 1968.

aircraft weapons which British industry was incapable of producing.[1] It was of course knowledge of these deficiencies that caused the Chiefs of Staff of the 1930s to view with alarm the tendency in some quarters to provoke a simultaneous conflict with two or even three of the dictatorships – a subject to which we will revert in our final volume.

In March 1928 Hankey was greatly worried by Lloyd George raising the old issue of creating a Ministry of Defence, though he wanted the C.I.D. to be retained. Hankey first had a long argument with his former chief on this issue, and having failed to move him he briefed Baldwin for his reply. Lloyd George's idea of abolishing the Service Ministers was, he wrote, based on the assumption that 'we are in for a long period of peace', and 'nowhere in the world does he see any risk'. Thus Lloyd George wanted to cut £40 millions off the Defence estimates, and believed that America and Japan 'would imitate such a gesture'. 'But', asked Hankey prophetically, 'what happens if Japan takes an aggressive line in China . . . and snaps her fingers at our protests, knowing our Navy is ineffective?'[2] Once again he was successful in getting the proposal shelved.

The breakdown of the Geneva naval conferences of 1927 led directly to the notorious 'Anglo-French Compromise' of the following year – which produced an explosion in U.S.A. and brought Anglo-American relations to their nadir. Briefly stated the compromise included the withdrawal of British opposition to the limitation of 6-inch cruisers of displacement under 10,000 tons, cancelled her willingness to see *all* submarines abolished, and accepted the French claim for parity with the largest naval power in two important classes of warship – 8-inch gun cruisers and large submarines. In return Britain agreed to abandon her long-standing opposition to the French policy of conscription for military service. Hankey evidently considered the compromise acceptable; for he wrote to Chamberlain that 'if we treated France reasonably over her Army Reserves, she would come round to our view on cruisers'.[3] And so it might have proved had not premature disclosures

[1]In 1939 the author of this biography was involved on behalf of the Admiralty in the purchase of 500 20 mm. guns from the Oerlikon factory at Zürich, for which £3 millions in gold were to be paid. Only about 150 had been delivered when the fall of France cut us off from the source of supply. Other A.A. weapons tried were the 40 mm. Bofors (Sweden), the 20 mm. Madsen (Danish) and 20 mm. Hispano-Suiza (Spanish-Swiss).

[2]Memo. of 26th March 1928. Cab. 63/40.

[3]Hankey to Chamberlain 7th June 1928. Chamberlain papers Ac 55/215.

produced a furore in the Press on both sides of the Atlantic, and provided all the anti-British elements in the U.S.A. with a field day. The convulsion did not die down until the government published the correspondence relating to the compromise,[1] but in the autumn, Houghton, the American Ambassador in London,[2] was able to report home that 'we now see a molehill where we formerly saw a mountain'.[3] On the British side there certainly was a good deal of clumsiness in the handling of an issue which was bound to arouse American antagonism; and the division in Baldwin's cabinet over naval policy and disarmament was starkly revealed. A curious feature is that the compromise was not handled according to Hankey's normal practice – namely consideration in the first instance by the Chiefs of Staff Committee, which would report to the C.I.D., which would then place a full summary of the problem, with recommendations on the policy to be adopted, before the Cabinet. Instead the proposal was handled entirely by the Cabinet Committee on Reduction and Limitation of Armaments, which had been established in October 1927 under Lord Salisbury.[4] The Foreign Office received copies of all the letters sent to the Admiralty by Vice-Admiral W. H. Kelly, their representative at Geneva, regarding his preliminary and unofficial discussions on the compromise proposals with the French Captain Deleuze (whom the French government later disavowed)[5]; and at least one note of warning was sounded in the Foreign Office.[6] But the Admiralty and Austen Chamberlain appear to have been determined to rush the proposal through, and no full study of the implications was ever made. The recommendation to accept the compromise was made by Salisbury's committee on 24th July and approved next day by the Cabinet.[7] The very unusual manner in which this controversial issue was handled, and the departure from Hankey's well-tried and highly efficient system, probably contributed to the muddle that resulted, and to the fact that Chamberlain and Bridgeman tied themselves in knots when the matter was debated in Parliament.[8]

[1]Cmd. 3211.

[2]Alanson B. Houghton (1863–1941). American businessman and diplomat. Ambassador in London 1925–29.

[3]To State Department 12th Sept. 1928. U.S. National Archives R.G. 80, Box 171.

[4]Cab. 27/361–363. [5]Roskill, *Naval Policy*, I, pp. 546–7.

[6]Minute by Victor Wellesley of 20th June 1928. F.O. 13377.

[7]C.P. 253(28) of 24th July and Cabinet 31(28) of 25th July 1928.

[8]For a valuable study of these events see David Carlton, *The Anglo-French Compromise on Arms Limitation, 1928*. Journal of British Studies, Vol. VIII, No. 2

On 27th August, while the reverberations produced by the Anglo-French compromise were echoing around the Chancelleries of Europe and the U.S.A. the International Treaty for the Renunciation of War, commonly known as the Kellogg–Briand Pact, was signed in Paris. In fact this document was more an expression of pious aspirations than an effective measure for the prevention of war. Hankey gave his opinion on it in a letter to Balfour. 'Looked at from a realistic point of view', he wrote, 'the whole thing is a great fraud . . . It is to a great extent an American electioneering move'; for the Presidential elections were due to take place in the autumn. He went on to say that, as we had already accepted an obligation not to resort to war, we were merely renouncing what 'we have already undertaken not to resort to'. And all 'special interests', such as the Monroe Doctrine for the U.S.A. and the British position in Egypt and the Persian Gulf, were already covered by treaties.[1] Though neither Hankey nor the British service departments raised any overt objections to the pact they were not deceived by the euphoria it aroused all over the world.

The Hankeys' silver wedding fell on 15th September 1928, and they felt an understandable desire to return to Pontresina, where they had spent their honeymoon. In the end they settled for Wengen, and there they spent a blissful but very energetic three weeks in September and October. Hankey showed that his energy was unabated by racing the mountain railway train, with Adeline on board it, down 3,000 feet from Scheidegg and achieving a dead heat! But the problems arising out of the Anglo-French compromise pursued him to the mountains, largely because the American reply to the British note on the subject arrived on 1st October. Hankey ruminated on it during his long walks, and on 2nd he sent Tom Jones his views, which were harsh towards the American counter-proposals. He thought the best step would be 'to pursue the Anglo-French proposals at the Preparatory Commission', hoping that other nations would accept them, and leaving America out; but he felt sure that this line would not succeed, because Italy

---

(May, 1969). I am also much indebted to Herr Wolf-Heinrich Bickel, whose book *Die Anglo-Amerikanischen Beziehungen 1927–1930, im Licht Der Flottenfrage* (Zürich, 1970), pp. 79–88 contains a full and authoritative account. Also for several interesting letters on the subject from Herr Bickel, who supports the conclusions I have reached regarding the unusual handling of this proposal in London.

[1]Hankey to Balfour 16th May and 11th July 1928. B.M. Add. MSS. 49705, pp. 22–8 and 29–32.

'would be nearly sure to refuse to come in'.[1] Jones took a softer line towards the American proposals, and stressed the difficulty that the government were in through being unable to publish the whole correspondence on the compromise on the eve of the American Presidential elections – which had resulted in a lot of very ill-informed criticism appearing in the Press. Their correspondence continued until the end of Hankey's holiday, and he held to his view that Jones's appeasement policy towards America had been tried for ten years and had failed. He wrote that we should therefore 'drop the attitude of sycophancy towards U.S.A.', and 'go our own way over cruisers', but 'in as friendly a manner as possible'.[2] After spending three nights in Paris Hankey was back in London on 13th October. Soon afterwards the correspondence about the compromise was published, and Howard reported from Washington that this had done much to clear the air.[3] None the less in the following month the Foreign Office considered it 'probably safe to say that at no time since 1920 have Anglo-American relations been in so unsatisfactory a state'.[4] It was not a happy beginning to Herbert Hoover's term as President.

Towards the end of November the attention of the Press was diverted from the government's troubles to the serious illness of the King, and the whole world watched the bulletins issued from the Palace with a degree of anxiety which probably surprised that modest Monarch. On 4th December a Privy Council took place to consider the appointment of Counsellors of State to act for the King; and Hankey left a moving account of the scene in the audience chamber adjacent to the King's bedroom. When asked if he was ready for the Council to begin the King replied ' "Yes certainly" in tones as loud as his ordinary voice'. And when Lord Dawson,[5] one of his physicians, took him for signature the Order-in-Council appointing the six commissioners he was able 'to make his signature in all respects in the usual form'.[6] Obviously all Hankey's long-standing affection for George V was stirred by his brave conduct on this occasion.

After the King's recovery the fact that no Regency Bill existed, even

[1]Hankey to Jones 2nd Oct. 1928. *Middlemas*, II, pp. 144–5.
[2]Jones to Hankey 9th Oct. and Hankey to Jones 11th Oct. 1928. *ibid.* pp. 146–9.
[3]Howard to Vansittart 26th Oct. 1928. Baldwin papers Vol. 109.
[4]Memo. of 12th Nov. 1928. *ibid.* [5]See Vol. I, p. 591, *note*.
[6]H. Nicolson, *King George V*, p. 431 has Lord Stamfordham's account of this Privy Council, which corresponds closely to Hankey's.

in draft form, caused Hankey a large amount of work. In 1935 an Inter-Departmental Committee was set up with him as chairman to draft the necessary legislation, taking account of the change in the relationship of the Monarch to the Dominions produced by the Statute of Westminster of 1931. By the following year he and the Law Officers had managed to get a Bill into shape. But it had not been passed at the time of the final illness of George V; and his death on 10th January 1936 actually rendered it unnecessary as the succession was secured.[1] Incidentally it was at the stage now reached in our narrative that the informal arrangement whereby Hankey kept the King personally informed on defence problems, originally approved by Asquith[2] but continued by Lloyd George, was placed on a formal footing by the Lord Chamberlain granting Hankey 'the privilege of entrée' to the Palace.[3] This was a most unusual, and almost certainly a unique privilege to be granted to a Civil Servant; and it speaks volumes for the discretion and tact which Hankey always displayed in his relations with George V and with members of his Household – who might well have resented his intrusion into their own sphere.

At the time when George V's illness of 1928 was causing Hankey great anxiety he was also worried about Balfour's declining strength.[4] It was, however, his equally old friend and supporter Haldane who died first, and on 20th August Hankey sent a long letter of tribute and sympathy to his sister. He described Haldane's death as 'a very real loss to the whole nation'. What Hankey particularly admired was his 'matchless adaptability to new ideas', combined with 'the wisdom of experience'[5] – qualities which can reasonably be attributed to Hankey himself. The closeness of his relations with Haldane is perhaps best demonstrated by the fact that in 1925 he wrote, most unusually and in

[1]Hankey's memo. of 30th June 1934 gives the whole history of the Regency Bill since George V's illness of 1928. Cab. 63/49. Baldwin papers, Vol. 9 contain papers on the Committee of 1935 and Hankey's proposal of 9th March 1935 to Baldwin that the draft Bill should be discussed with the Dominion Prime Ministers when they were in London for the King's Jubilee celebrations. Premier 1/209 has papers dealing with the final Regency Act of 1937, but it is wrongly listed in the P.R.O. Index. Premier 1/208 and 1/209 have obviously been exchanged. The Act received Royal Assent on 19th March 1937.

[2]See Vol. I, p. 117.

[3]Lord Cromer (1877–1953), Lord Chamberlain 1922–38, to Hankey 10th April 1928.

[4]To Lady Hankey 26th Nov. 1928. In fact Balfour lived until 19th March 1930.

[5] Hankey to Miss Haldane 20th Aug. 1928. Haldane papers.

strict anonymity, the article for the *Encyclopædia Britannica* on Haldane's connection with the C.I.D. He showed the draft to Asquith (now Lord Oxford and Asquith) who described it as 'both full and accurate', and to Warren Fisher who found it 'quite excellent, alike in form, substance and perspective'.[1] Though it was too long for the Encyclopædia to print in full, the published summary may be regarded as Hankey's final tribute to the man who in 1912 was chiefly responsible for opening the way to his career in public service.[2]

It must have been in this same year that 'a furious row' took place between Birkenhead and Hankey – probably because the secretary had suggested that Austen Chamberlain should take the chair at a Cabinet when Baldwin was abroad.[3] Though Hankey was by no means alone in suffering from the arrogance and insobriety of Birkenhead, and was caused much trouble by his writing articles for the Press,[4] when he left the India Office and the Cabinet for good in October 1928 Hankey sent him a letter of sympathy. Birkenhead replied that his 'generous letter' gave him 'real pleasure'; and because it was a case of *laudari a viro laudato* [to be praised by a man who is himself praised] it would 'be given a high place in my list of collected papers'.[5]

The last six months of Baldwin's second administration were not a happy period for the Conservative party. The failure at Geneva and the row with America over the Anglo-French compromise produced a feeling that all was not well with the conduct of foreign policy; the antics of Joynson Hicks at the Home Office, notably over the Arcos raid, had produced widespread derision; and Churchill's urgings for 'a big measure' for 1928–29 which would restore the electorate's confidence, and which he visualised in his proposals for rating relief,[6] pro-

[1]The draft is dated 23rd Nov. 1925 and the relevant correspondence is in Cab. 63/28.

[2]See Vol. I, pp. 111–12.

[3]See William Camp, *The Glittering Prizes* (MacGibbon and Kee, 1960), p. 198.

[4]In January 1923 it was established that Ministers should not write for the Press while in office. Cabinet 3(23) Conclusion 7. But in 1925 Birkenhead wrote a number of articles – because he was chronically short of money. Baldwin was anxious not to lose his services, and the outcome was that large sums were paid to him by the Conservative Central Office. 'In this manner', writes Robert Rhodes James, 'the political services of Lord Birkenhead, and his silence in the Press, were secured for another two years'. *Davidson*, pp. 276–7. Baldwin papers, Vol. 56 have much correspondence on this subject.

[5]Birkenhead to Hankey, from Christ Church, Oxford 17th Oct. 1928. Holograph.

[6]Churchill to Baldwin 6th June 1927. Baldwin papers, Vol. 5.

duced disappointing results[1]; unemployment was high, and the Trade Disputes Bill, though ineffective, had provided the Labour party with excellent propaganda. Finally such reorganisation of the Cabinet as Baldwin had carried out had not inspired confidence. Amery had seen the writing on the wall as early as the spring of 1927. He wanted Churchill put in charge of defence in replacement of Balfour, and proposed himself for the Exchequer.[2] But Amery was of course a convinced Protectionist, and that was a policy Baldwin would not touch after his experience in the 1923 election. The future of Churchill was, as often, a major problem – because his brilliance was so marred by what many Conservatives regarded as his erratic temperament. Baldwin evidently considered appointing him to the India Office and Neville Chamberlain to the Treasury; but the former suggestion aroused serious apprehensions in the breast of Lord Irwin, the Viceroy.[3]

In May 1928, when Ursula was presented at Court, her father described her, with obvious pride, as 'about the most attractive of the débutantes'.[4] As he also remarked to Robin on 'the prodigious number of dances she has on hand' he cannot have been greatly surprised when she announced her engagement to John Benn early in the following year. As he had already met John, and found him 'an awfully good fellow',[5] their betrothal plainly gave him great happiness. They were married at St. Margaret's, Westminster on 23rd July 1929, and Ursula recalls that her father 'really enjoyed planning a very large ceremony with three Prime Ministers or ex-Prime Ministers [Baldwin, MacDonald and Lloyd George] present'. 'It was all planned with naval precision', continues Ursula; and the timing was so exactly worked out that after it was all over she and her husband 'could hardly believe we were married'. Meanwhile Robin, though only a Third Secretary in the Diplomatic Service had been transferred from Berlin to a post in Paris normally filled by a First Secretary. The change was made on the initiative of Sir William Tyrrell, the ambassador in Paris, and with Austen Chamberlain's approval; but Hankey hastened to tell Robin that he himself had nothing to do with it. However he considered the new appointment 'a great compliment', and gave Robin introductions to some of his closest friends and associates of wartime and post-war

[1] James, *Davidson*, p. 298.
[2] Amery to Baldwin 10th April 1927. Baldwin papers, Vol. 29.
[3] Irwin to Baldwin 28th March 1929. Baldwin papers, Vol. 103.
[4] To Robin Hankey 22nd May 1928. [5] To Lady Hankey 5th Dec. 1928.

years in Paris. In the following year Robin's engagement to Frances Stuart-Menteth was announced, and with the two oldest children married the inevitable dispersal of the closely-knit Hankey family had obviously begun; and Highstead must have become a quieter place – until the arrival of grandchildren restored its former gaiety.

In the spring of 1929, when the Dissolution of Parliament was in prospect, Hankey had to advise on 'the precise legal position' regarding Prorogation and Dissolution. He searched the records with all his usual care, and produced what he considered to be the answer – only to be challenged by Sir Claud Schuster, Permanent Secretary to the Lord Chancellor.[1] But to his satisfaction it turned out that he was right and Schuster wrong.[2] Parliament was actually dissolved on 10th May, and eight days later Baldwin made the speech at Drury Lane theatre in which he claimed that 'performances not promises' justified the continuation of his mandate. But recent by-elections had shown all too clearly, and without the aid of 'pollsters', that the trend of public opinion was running strongly against the government. Polling took place on 30th and the 1924 Conservative majority of 223 over all other parties was changed to a minority of nearly 100. Labour with 288 seats was once again the largest party. And, although Hankey had believed that Lloyd George's strenuous campaign, and the proposals in his 'Orange Book',[3] were having considerable effect, the Liberals only increased their representation from 40 to 59. On 4th June Baldwin, having decided not to face the new Parliament as he had done in 1924, resigned, and next day the King sent for MacDonald who agreed to form an administration.[4]

[1] 1st Baron Schuster 1944 (1869–1956). Lawyer and Civil Servant. Clerk of the Crown in Chancery and Permanent Secretary to the Lord Chancellor 1915–44.
[2] Hankey to Baldwin 25th March 1929. Baldwin papers, Vol. 36, pp. 93–108.
[3] This was the report of the Liberal Industry Enquiry entitled *Britain's Industrial Future* published in February 1928 and usually referred to as the 'Yellow Book' to distinguish it from the report entitled *The Land and the Nation* which was known as the 'Green Book'. The pamphlet *We Can Conquer Unemployment* was a summary of these reports and of the contemporary 'Brown Book'. I am grateful to Mr. A. J. P. Taylor of the Beaverbrook Library for clarification of this matter.
[4] H. Nicolson, King George V, pp. 434–5.

*Chapter* 16

# The Second Labour Government. June-December 1929

In the Birthday Honours for 1929 Hankey received a G.C.M.G., which surely suggests that Baldwin was more appreciative of his services than had been outwardly apparent. The announcement of the honour brought him a flood of congratulations from his political and service friends and associates, including a telegram from Lord Riddell who considered that 'a Peerage would not have been sufficient reward for all you have done'. And this time there were no acidulous comments in the Press. But when on 5th June MacDonald 'kissed hands' on becoming Prime Minister again Hankey must have viewed the future with some misgivings. Although he probably felt no qualms about the continuation of his own appointment and the preservation of the Cabinet Secretariat and the C.I.D., as had been the case in 1924, his earlier experiences cannot have imbued him with great confidence either in the capacity of his new chief or in the likelihood of the team he had chosen working together harmoniously. For he knew that a basic antipathy existed between MacDonald and both Philip Snowden, his Chancellor of the Exchequer, and Arthur Henderson his Foreign Secretary[1]; and when the principal personalities in the Cabinet were so little in accord the Secretary's lot was not likely to prove enviable.

To place his own position and the system to which he and his staff would work on a firm footing Hankey at once produced his proposed 'Instructions to the Secretary on Cabinet procedure'. In it he again used Fortescue's discovery that Cabinet minutes had been kept during

[1]Emanuel Shinwell's memoirs published in the *Sunday Express* 15th March 1970 emphasise MacDonald's mistrust of Snowden, and David Carlton's *MacDonald versus Henderson* (Macmillan, 1970) deals fully with the Prime Minister's relations with his Foreign Secretary in the second Labour government. Sir Oswald Mosley's *My Life* (Nelson, 1970) makes no attempt to conceal the contempt felt by the author as Chancellor of the Duchy of Lancaster for his colleagues, and especially for MacDonald, Hugh Dalton, J. H. Thomas, Herbert Morrison and Philip Snowden.

the reigns of George III and George IV as an argument in favour of continuing the practice[1]; and in addition to reciting precedents from fairly remote history he emphasised once more the confusion which had prevailed before the institution of the Cabinet Secretariat in 1916. Finally he outlined the duties of the C.I.D. and other Standing Sub-Committees of the Cabinet, including the Committee of Civil Research.[2] Towards the end of July MacDonald, in answering a hostile Parliamentary Question about the Secretary of the Cabinet, reaffirmed that the appointment would be continued. But when asked in a Supplementary Question whether it was the case 'that the Secretary . . . still attends Cabinet meetings and makes out the minutes' the Prime Minister declared that the suggestion was 'absolutely without foundation'.[3] The fact that he was possibly referring to informal 'Conferences of Ministers' does not adequately explain the evasiveness, not to say untruth, of MacDonald's answer. In fact as early as 10th June the Cabinet, with MacDonald in the chair, had approved the circulation to all Ministers of Hankey's Instructions to the Secretary; and the conclusions of that meeting merely stated that in drafting the minutes the Secretary was 'to avoid any reference to opinions expressed by any individual, and to limit the Minutes as narrowly as possible to the actual decisions agreed to'. The 'utmost secrecy' was to be 'observed in regard to the proceedings of the Cabinet by all concerned', and great stress was laid on the need to preserve the security of all Cabinet documents. But the whole conclusion made it absolutely plain that the recording of Cabinet minutes was to continue.[4] The form and style of Cabinet minutes does, however, alter appreciably after the meeting of 10th June. Up to that time Hankey had customarily recorded discussions which had revealed differences of opinion in phrases such as 'The Secretary of State for Foreign Affairs recalled that . . .' or 'The Chancellor of the Exchequer emphasised that . . .'. But after that meeting he recorded disagreements in a much more impersonal manner, such as 'After discussion the Cabinet agreed that . . .'. Though Ministers who

[1]See *The Times*, 3rd, 4th and 5th Nov. 1925, turn-over articles by Fortescue on the discovery of George III and IV's papers at Windsor in 1912.

[2]C.P. 153(29). Cab. 24/104. Also Hankey to MacDonald 14th June 1929 (26 pages) on the C.I.D. and all its sub-committees. It is endorsed by MacDonald 'Discuss on my return'. Cab. 21/470.

[3]Parl. Deb., Commons, Vol. 230, Col. 5, 1292–3. The suggestion that the Secretary no longer attended Cabinet meetings appeared in the *Morning Post* of 18th July 1929.

[4]Cabinet 22(29) of 10th June 1929, Conclusion 1. Cab. 23/61.

had circulated papers were still named as introducing or amplifying the subject in question, the principle of anonymity in discussion was at first observed fairly strictly. But in the middle of 1932, when Hankey was abroad at the Lausanne Conference and Howorth[1] or Hodsoll[2] was acting in his place, the minutes reverted in some degree to their pre-1929 form, and the views of individual Ministers were often recorded. This phenomenon is especially noticeable when Baldwin, then Lord President of the Council, was in the chair. When Hankey took over again he at first reverted to the strict interpretation of the instructions of 1929; but after Baldwin succeeded MacDonald as Prime Minister in June 1935 he too relaxed the principle of anonymity, and thereafter it is quite common for the views of individual Ministers to be quoted.[3] The variations of practice between 1929 and 1935 suggest that Baldwin was much more willing than MacDonald to recognise and accept that the attempt to represent that Cabinet decisions were invariably unanimous was a ridiculous fiction, and that there were advantages in preserving a record of the views put forward by Ministers either as individuals or on behalf of their departments.

To return to June 1929, in marked contrast to MacDonald's equivocal and evasive statements about the functions of the Cabinet Secretary Stamfordham wrote to Hankey at about the same time referring to the remarks made by the King when Margaret Bondfield,[4] the first woman to be sworn a Privy Counsellor, was received, and when some of the new Labour government had 'kissed hands'. 'What an admirable custom', wrote Stamfordham, 'to record any particulars connected with [Privy] Council meetings'.[5] In that same month Stamfordham cele-

[1]Later Sir Rupert B. Howorth (1880–1964). Barrister and Civil Servant. Joined Treasury 1915 and Cabinet Office 1920. Deputy Secretary of Cabinet in succession to Tom Jones 1930–42. Secretary to British delegations to Ottawa Conference 1932 and London Economic Conference 1933. Clerk of Privy Council in succession to Hankey 1938–42. Secretary of Commissions to Lord Chancellor 1945–48.

[2]Later Wing-Commander Sir E. John Hodsoll (1894–1971). Served in R.N.A.S. in World War I, transferring to R.A.F. 1918. Assistant Secretary, C.I.D. 1929–35. Assistant Under-Secretary, Home Office, in charge of Air Raid Precautions 1935–37. Inspector-General of Civil Defence 1938–48, and Director General, Civil Defence Training 1948–54. Chief Civil Defence Adviser to N.A.T.O. 1954–61.

[3]Minutes in Cab. 23/61 *et seq.*

[4]1873–1953. Politician (Lab.) and trade unionist. Chairman, General Council of T.U.C. 1923. Parliamentary Secretary, Ministry of Labour 1924. Minister of Labour 1929–31.

[5]Stamfordham to Hankey 12th June 1929. RA GV K2223/103. The King had

brated his 80th birthday, and in answer to Hankey's congratulations he wrote that 'Both our personal and business relations have always been a joy to me. I am most grateful for your invaluable help and always feel I can claim you as a friend and certainly value you as such'.[1] If the King's Private Secretary was guilty of some exaggeration in suggesting that his relations with Hankey had never been marred by disagreements, the occasion which prompted the eulogy makes it forgivable. Actually they had quite recently had a tiff over the 'summoning of Princes of the Blood Royal' to Privy Councils, and in answer to Stamfordham's protest Hankey had apologised for his failure to follow precedent, and assured him that 'Precedent is everything to us in the Privy Council Office and we should undoubtedly have taken His Majesty's pleasure as to the summoning of the Princes of the Blood Royal'.[2]

As soon as the formalities of swearing in and receiving seals of office had been completed Hankey had to cope with a number of difficult and complicated issues. We saw earlier how in Austen Chamberlain's time as Foreign Secretary the high-handed attitude of George Lloyd as High Commissioner in Egypt had caused reverberations in Whitehall. When Henderson took over the Foreign Office the trouble quickly came to a head. In mid-June 1929 Chamberlain, though now out of office, expressed the doubts he had entertained about extending Lloyd's appointment in a letter to Sir Ronald Lindsay, the Permanent Under-Secretary of the Foreign Office.[3] Lindsay replied that 'it was no use pretending his [i.e. Lloyd's] mind went on liberal lines', and that he had not concealed his desire to have the High Commissioner replaced.[4] Shortly afterwards Henderson sent Chamberlain Lloyd's unyielding reply to the former Foreign Secretary's despatch setting out the lines

---

recently suffered a relapse, and apologised for bringing the new Privy Counsellors to Windsor, instead of receiving them, as he had intended, at Buckingham Palace.

[1]Stamfordham to Hankey. Holograph, from Windsor Castle 21st June 1929.

[2]Stamfordham to Hankey 10th June 1929 and reply by latter of 11th. RA GV K2223/93 and 97.

[3]1877–1945. Diplomat. Assistant Under-Secretary, Foreign Office, in charge of Near Eastern affairs 1921–24. Ambassador to Turkey 1925–26 and at Berlin 1926–28. Permanent Under-Secretary, Foreign Office, 1928–30. Ambassador at Washington 1930–39.

[4]Chamberlain to Lindsay 17th June 1929 and reply by latter of same date. AC 55/314 and 315.

on which negotiations for a treaty with Egypt should be handled.[1] In his 'present obscurity' Chamberlain declined to comment; but Henderson obviously realised that Lloyd's recall would not arouse any strong protest from his predecessor. This greatly strengthened his hand both in reaching a decision and in handling the matter when it was debated in the Commons.[2] Hankey's view was that only a new treaty could resolve the *impasse* in Anglo-Egyptian relations, which had prevailed ever since 1919. At the end of July he therefore summarised the events of the previous month, and arranged for the C.I.D. to refer the draft treaty to the Chiefs of Staff 'for examination'.[3] Only on 26th of that month did the C.O.S.s see the treaty officially, and in their report they very naturally concentrated chiefly on the defence of the Canal Zone – a matter over which Hankey felt great concern. On 24th Henderson informed the Cabinet of Lloyd's resignation. Six days later Hankey lunched with him to hear his version of the quarrel, 'but was careful to avoid any comment'.[4] Although Hankey appreciated Lloyd's realistic understanding of British interests in the Middle East, his high-handed attitude towards his chief was the antithesis to his own method of handling Ministers; and Hankey must surely have realised that to a great extent Lloyd brought his troubles down on his own head.[5]

Hankey's profound interest in Egyptian problems continued, of course, long after Lloyd's recall; for he had always realised that a satisfactory solution would greatly strengthen British Imperial defence. In the 1930s he therefore gave Sir Miles Lampson, then High Commissioner and his close friend, all possible support in the negotiations which culminated in the treaty of 1936. That agreement secured for Britain the position she maintained in Egypt throughout World War

[1]Henderson to Chamberlain 24th June 1929. AC 38/3/87.

[2]Parl. Deb., Commons, Vol. 230, Cols. 1637–46 contain Henderson's statement of 26th July 1929 in reply to Baldwin. The debate on the Egyptian treaty negotiations took place on 23rd Dec., and the government secured satisfactory support for its handling of the matter. *ibid.*, Vol. 233, Cols. 1953–2076. See also Cmd. 3050 (1928) *Negotiations for a Treaty of Alliance with Egypt*.

[3]C.I.D. 954B, 957B and 1011B are concerned with the discussions of the Anglo-Egyptian treaty.

[4]Memo. of 30th July 1929. Cab. 63/41.

[5]It is only fair to record that Lord Vansittart in *The Mist Procession* (Hutchinson, 1958), p. 372 remarks that 'a set in the Foreign Office [presumably led by Lindsay, see above] had long incited Austen against George Lloyd . . . The professionals never wanted an outsider there [in Egypt]'. He also recounts how he prevented Henderson dismissing Lloyd out of hand while on his way home for consultations.

II; and part of the credit for the successful outcome to the long years of patient negotiation must be accorded to Hankey for his efforts in the C.I.D.

In May 1929 Hankey asked the Cabinet to review the question of sending C.I.D. papers to the Dominions. As matters stood Newfoundland and the Irish Free State got none of them. By Baldwin's instructions Casey saw them all but was only allowed to send a proportion to the Australian Prime Minister. As regards Canada, New Zealand and South Africa the decision depended on whether their High Commissioners in London had been present or represented when the subject of the paper was discussed.[1] The Labour government followed their predecessors' principles in this respect, though Hankey had to exercise particular care over inviting Dominion representation at C.I.D. meetings and recommending what papers should be sent to them – because there were many issues, notably the Singapore base, over which some Dominions were at odds with the Mother Country. In the following month, by way of instructing the new Ministers, he produced a long paper on the history and organisation of the C.I.D., and explaining the functions of all its Standing and *ad hoc* sub-committees.[2] But as the reader is familiar with those subjects they will not be repeated here.

While the fracas produced by George Lloyd was reverberating around Whitehall the completion of the Young Report[3] set in train the events which were to result in Hankey's deep involvement in the Hague Conferences of 1929 and 1930. Early in July he wrote to Robin that all his plans were dependent on the Reparations and Naval Conferences, both of which seemed 'to be hanging fire a bit'. 'I trust I shall not be caught for any international conferences', he went on, 'as I have quite forgotten the tricks of the trade'. Moreover he thought that 'in these days the F.O. would take it on themselves'. His hope was quickly shown to be vain; and events were to prove that he had lost none of his

[1]Memo. of 7th May 1929. Cab. 63/41. [2]Memo. of 14th June 1929. *ibid.*

[3]Owen D. Young (1874–1962) was the leading American representative on the committee of experts appointed in January 1929 to achieve a definitive settlement of the Reparations question in supersession of the Dawes Plan of 1924. This was closely linked with the problem of the evacuation of the Rhineland, which the League Assembly had discussed in September 1928. Premier 1/83 contains interesting papers of June–July 1929 on the report of the Experts' Conference, and Young's eulogy of the British representatives on it – Sir Josiah Stamp, Lord Revelstoke and Sir Charles Addis.

The Imperial Conference 1926. Hankey in back row seventh from left

'Pop' at ease in the loggia at Highstead, *c.*1929

Sir Warden Chilcott with Lady (Austen) Chamberlain and her daughter Diane at Deauville August 1932

Sir Warden Chilcott's auxiliary brigantine 'Dolphin'. Probably at Cowes, *c.* 1926

great gift for organising such conferences. 'Things are not so easy as they were with the new crowd [of Ministers]' he told Robin; and they 'have methods of their own of doing business', which might well 'get them in a muddle'. But although everyone agreed MacDonald 'is not too easy to work with', he personally 'got on very well with him'.[1]

By the beginning of August plans had clarified, and Hankey wrote to Tom Jones that 'in spite of violent protests' on his part the Cabinet had insisted on his attending the Reparations Conference, which, he foretold accurately, would prove 'a most unpleasant one'. Indeed he expected that 'sooner or later we shall have a bust-up at The Hague'. He put his deputy, who was away from the office, fully into the picture about current Cabinet business, and gave him some wise tips about handling MacDonald. If a crisis arose at the conference he had arranged 'to get the Prime Minister over'; but he had 'one or two cards' up his sleeve 'before we reach that point'.[2] On Saturday 3rd August he crossed to Holland with only the vaguest instructions 'to help the Dutch get ready for the conference'. Certainly it had never entered his head that he would be appointed Secretary-General; nor had he any ambitions to fill a post which, under the agreement he had made with Warren Fisher in 1923, belonged properly to the Foreign Office. Moreover Hankey entertained grave misgivings about the composition of the British delegation, which he described to Robin as 'like nothing on earth'. Snowden and Henderson, he wrote, were 'not only rivals politically' and 'personally uncongenial to one another', but they had 'poor ideas of team work'. Worst of all they were 'diametrically opposed on the policy we should adopt at The Hague'. Whereas Snowden 'thought we should stand firm for an equitable financial settlement', even to the point of breakdown, Henderson 'held with the Foreign Office that [Sir Josiah] Stamp[3] had given the case away, that the situation was well-nigh irretrievable, and that the price of acceptance of the Young Report was worth paying in order to get a settlement in the Rhineland'.

[1]To Robin Hankey from Highstead 3rd July 1929.

[2]Hankey to Jones, 1st Aug. 1929. *Middlemas*, II, pp. 196–7.

[3]1880–1941. 1st Baron Stamp 1938. Banker, statistician and business executive. Joined Inland Revenue Department 1896. Member of Royal Commission on Income Tax 1919 and of Coal Industry Inquiry 1925. British representative on Reparations Commission's Dawes and Young Committees of 1924 and 1929. Director, Nobel Industries 1919–26 and of I.C.I. 1927–28. Chairman L.M.S. Railway. Director of Bank of England 1928. Member of Economic Advisory Council 1930. A prolific writer and lecturer on financial, economic and educational subjects.

The officials, Hankey continued, were 'ranged behind their respective chiefs, and were barely on speaking terms – the Treasury behind Snowden and the Foreign Office behind Henderson'.[1] Furthermore the departmental representatives were separated physically by a distance of three miles, the former being accommodated at Scheveningen and the latter at The Hague. Rarely can a conference have been convened for which the auguries were less favourable.

On reaching The Hague Hankey found a state of considerable confusion, with the delegates from twelve nations arriving, accommodation scarce, and transport and communications inadequate. Though he felt it wrong that he should be appointed Secretary-General, because he could not claim to be impartial on the issues to be discussed, he yielded when at the first meeting he was 'elected with acclamation'. M. Chéron, the French Minister of Finance,[2] remarked that '*Un conférence ou Sir Maurice Hankey est le Sécrétaire-Général ne peut pas échouer*' – a compliment which helped to allay Hankey's misgivings.[3]

*To Lady Hankey. Grand Hotel, Scheveningen. 7th August 1929*

So far I have been too busy to write a serious letter. First I had to get the conference going, and now I am Secretary-General and am getting it organised. The difficulties of both tasks are considerable, and require patience and a sense of humour. Nearly all my difficulties have been with the French, who, though forcing me into the thankless position of Secretary-General, give me very little help . . .

I came to the conclusion that the only way to get the conference going by Tuesday [6th] was to have an informal meeting of the Heads of Delegations of the Inviting Powers on Monday . . . Oh the effort of accomplishing that meeting! All day different delegations were arriving at hotels far apart – some [at] The Hague, some at Scheveningen. No-one ever knew what hotels they were going to. The meeting could not be just arranged by telephone. Each senior delegation had to be seen, and explanations given as to what was to be discussed, what proposals would be made etc. In fact I spent Monday [5th] in trying to persuade the statesmen of Europe to meet at an hour which upset their dinner arrangements . . . In the end the impossible

[1]To Robin Hankey, 5th Sept. 1929.

[2]Henri Chéron (1867–1936). French lawyer and politician. Senator 1913. Minister of Labour 1913, of Agriculture 1922, of Commerce (briefly) 1928, of Finance 1928–30 and of Justice 1930–31 and 1934. A strong supporter of Poincaré and of the peasants' interests.

[3]'A conference at which Sir Maurice Hankey is Secretary-General cannot fail'. To Robin Hankey, 5th Sept. 1929.

was achieved. Poor lame Snowden and his faithful watchdog Mrs. S. were persuaded that, in spite of the fatigues of his journey, he must hobble to Briand's room at The Hague [Hotel des Indes]. Dr. Stresemann was convinced that there really were over-riding reasons for meeting at the French [delegates'] hotel – and so on. The meeting took place, and subject to slight modifications my plans were adopted. ... I get my morning bathe every day ...

Hankey's management of the conference was, as usual, smoothed by his excellent relations with the British diplomats such as Sir Odo Russell,[1] the Minister at The Hague, whom he had first encountered as private secretary to Grey, and Eric Phipps,[2] who came specially from Vienna to represent the Foreign Office and had been 'personally friendly and congenial' to Hankey ever since the Paris Peace Conference. With the heads of the foreign delegations Hankey quickly re-established the cordial relations he had built up at previous conferences; while the junior members and their secretariats seem to have fallen very quickly under the spell of the Secretary-General's tact and his unobtrusive but all-pervading efficiency. As happened at the Genoa Conference Hankey's chief difficulties were produced by tiresome trivialities, such as shortage of properly trained typists and of Roneo machines.[3] 'I spend one half of the time receiving the intimate confidences of half the Prime Ministers of Europe', he wrote to Robin, 'and the other half in these ridiculous affairs of typists'.[4]

One of Hankey's first actions was to assemble the whole British delegation, and he 'got Snowden to tell them all about the policy he intended to pursue and to appeal to them all, throughout the conference and in all their talk to preserve a united front and never to suggest that in any circumstances would we desist from our 100% claim'. He described this as 'a most valuable and fruitful step'. But the unity of purpose he aimed at was soon vitiated by the discovery that 'Snowden and Henderson hardly ever saw one another'. Indeed the Foreign Secretary and his deputy soon came to complain to Hankey that, whenever they wanted to discuss matters with the Chancellor,

[1]1870–1951. Diplomat. Private Secretary to Sir E. Grey 1905–8. Counsellor at Vienna 1909–15. Diplomatic Secretary to Secretary of State for Foreign Affairs 1915–19. Minister at Berne 1919–22 and to the Holy See 1922–28.

[2]Sir Eric C. E. Phipps (1875–1945). Diplomat. British Secretary to Paris Peace Conference 1919. Counsellor at Brussels 1920–22. Minister Plenipotentiary at Paris 1922–28 and at Vienna 1928–33. Ambassador at Berlin 1933–37 and at Paris 1937–39.

[3]See pp. 268–9. [4]To Robin Hankey, 7th August 1929.

Mrs. Snowden remained present and 'joined in the talk'. They flatly declined to discuss Cabinet policy in her presence, and besought Hankey 'to do something about it'. His solution was to persuade the badly crippled Chancellor to hobble from his own apartment to the delegates' conference room for the daily 'Cabinet meetings', while someone took Mrs. Snowden for a drive or a shopping expedition. His next troubles came from MacDonald, who acted as though 'we were making a mess of it and was always sending embarrassing messages'. 'Temperamentally', he remarked, the Prime Minister and the Chancellor were 'poles asunder'. Whereas the former believed in 'astute and tactful diplomacy', the tactics of the latter were 'simply to stick his toes in and starve the other side out'. Snowden's habit of 'dropping bricks every time he opened his mouth' caused Hankey to build him up as 'a bogeyman' in the foreign delegates' eyes – which he found easy, even though it 'jeopardised a settlement'. But he 'set himself to support Snowden for all I was worth . . . in the sure conviction that we could win through'; and he was confident that, in the long view, a firm policy would pay. This however meant that he had to send a stream of explanatory letters to MacDonald 'to try and keep his nose straight'.[1]

At the first plenary meeting Snowden, true to form, dropped what Hankey, varying his metaphor, called a 'bombshell' into the conference. This was the total rejection by the British government of the Owen Committee's proposals for the re-allocation between the Allied nations of sums paid by way of Reparations.[2] Hankey wrote that 'Snowden's speech was a magnificent performance, reminding me of Ll. G. – very firm but not offensive. I really felt proud of him. Henderson has also done well, so far'.[3] Snowden's later description of how Britain was to be fobbed off with 'ordinary shares of a perhaps not very sound concern, whereas the unconditional payments might be regarded as

[1]To Robin Hankey 5th Sept. 1929.

[2]The Young Plan removed responsibility for transfer of the sums from the recipients, as agreed by the Dawes Plan, to Germany. But to achieve a long-term settlement payments were divided into two classes called 'Unconditional Annuities', which amounted to the mortgage interest derived from the German State Railways, and 'Conditional Annuities' the transfer of which into foreign currencies Germany could postpone for up to two years. The Owen Committee also completely upset the proportions to be paid to the Allied nations agreed at the Spa Conference. About five-sixths of the Unconditional Annuities were to go to France.

[3]To Robin Hankey 7th Aug. 1929.

first-class debentures' was apt.[1] His grievance on behalf of the British taxpayer was aggravated by the fact that Britain alone had started repayment of her war debt to U.S.A., and had done so before receiving anything by way of repayment of the sums due to her by the Allied nations.

*To Lady Hankey. Grand Hotel, Scheveningen. Undated but probably 9th August 1929*
... The conference at the moment is at a bit of a deadlock, which came a few days earlier than I expected. This is due to Snowden having fired his big gun and followed it up with a second round. He made it clear in his first speech that he would not accept the Experts' [i.e. the Owen Committee's] Report without modifications. Then, on all hands we heard that foreigners thought we were bluffing. So yesterday he fired a second charge. The foreigners are rather puzzled. But Briand is playing the game I expected. On the political side he is displaying an extraordinarily conciliatory spirit, offering to abandon the Rhineland etc. – but always subject to one condition, namely that there is a settlement of Reparations. In other words he means to get into a position to represent that the British government in general, and Snowden in particular, are blocking the peace of Europe for a matter of £2½ millions a year! Our people don't at all look like budging an inch, and we are rapidly driving up to a deadlock ...

*To the same. First Chamber of the States General. 10th August 1929*
... I am much in demand in connection with the difficulties arising out of Snowden's speeches. To-day I thought he went too far. Chéron, rather a decent old Frenchman, made a speech combatting Snowden's figures. His reply was, practically, to the effect that all Chéron's figures were false, and the deductions he had drawn from them wrong! No arguments and no figures but merely a reiteration that they must submit to his terms. That fairly blew the lid off! Jaspar, the Belgian Prime Minister,[2] came to me afterwards in a great state of annoyance and exasperation, and told me they really didn't know how to deal with Snowden. He wouldn't discuss, and he had even refused to come to a private meeting of the six [inviting] powers. I replied I was certain this was incorrect. 'No', he answered, 'he told Hilferding

[1]Quoted G. M. Gathorne-Hardy, *A Short History of International Affairs*, p. 257. See also Philip Snowden, *An Autobiography* (Nicholson and Watson, 2 Vols. 1934) Ch. LXIII. The loss to Britain against which Snowden fought so strenuously was about £2 millions per annum for 37 years.

[2]Henri Jaspar (1870–1939). Belgian politician. Minister for Economic Affairs 1918 and Foreign Affairs 1920–24. Prime Minister of national coalition government 1926–31. Finance Minister 1932–34 and again Minister for Foreign Affairs 1934.

(a German)[1] that'. So I went and asked Snowden, who said it was quite untrue. I then dashed after Jaspar and told him, and started to arrange a 'hush, hush' meeting for Sunday [11th] ... Of course the reason for Snowden's stiffness is that he wants to remove the current illusion that he is bluffing ...

Yesterday also I had a difficult day. They were all so upset by Snowden's speech on Thursday [8th] that some of them wanted to put off to-day's meeting of the Financial Commission. As Secretary-General I protested violently, saying that postponement would produce the worst possible public impression and ... perhaps wreck the conference ... [Hankey then went on to describe how he persuaded the French, Belgian and Italian delegates to hold the meeting]. But really we are at a deadlock, unless it is removed by the 'hush hush' meeting on Sunday [11th]. At present it seems to depend on me to find a way out ...

During the week-end of 10th–11th a mistake in London resulted in what Hankey called 'a slightly defeatist message' from MacDonald being telephoned to the British delegation *en clair*. This of course strengthened the hands of those who believed Snowden was bluffing. So MacDonald was at once asked to send 'an open message of support' for Snowden, which he did. But the leakage of other messages to the Press suggested that the lines between Holland and England were being tapped. Hankey and Jones therefore 'resorted to one of Lloyd George's expedients'. The former had with him a junior Foreign Office official who spoke Welsh, and he told Jones to install another Welsh speaker in the Cabinet Office in London. An Inspector of the Welsh Education Board was sent to Lossiemouth, where MacDonald was staying, for the same purpose; a 'glossary of invented words for all key words', for which there was no equivalent in Welsh, was produced, and a code was devised for proper names. Hankey even went to the length of having all Welsh or Welsh-speaking tourists then in Holland investigated. The long and short of these precautions was that 'we got safe communication', which 'proved of the most decisive importance ... in the final stages of the conference'.[2]

What Hankey called his 'worst moment' in the conference occurred at the 'hush hush' meeting he had organised for Sunday 11th, when

[1]Rudolf Hilferding (1877–1941). Austrian-born German journalist and politician (Soc. Dem.) Director of *Freiheit* 1918. Minister of Finance 1923, 1928 and 1929. Fled first to Prague on Hitler's seizure of power 1933, and then to Paris 1938. Arrested by Gestapo in Paris and committed suicide.

[2]To Robin Hankey 5th Sept. 1929.

Snowden described a remark of Chéron's as 'grotesque and ridiculous'. Hankey's sharp eye noticed that the interpreter hesitated, and then substituted 'some milder expression'; and on investigation he discovered that, translated literally, Snowden's words would have been 'a perfectly appalling insult'. 'For some hours', he told MacDonald, 'the situation was dangerous'.[1] A more intimate account of the incident is to be found in the long letter Hankey wrote to Robin soon after the end of the conference.

*Hankey to Robin Hankey. 8 The Esplanade, Seaford. 5th September 1929*

. . . The French flatly declined to take any further part until an apology was offered. Snowden said that there was nothing to apologise for. I was of course appealed to as go-between. With Snowden I had to treat the matter as a screaming joke; with the French and Belgians as a most serious affair. For five hours I was journeying between the French at the Hotel des Indes in The Hague and Snowden at the Grand Hotel, Scheveningen, three miles apart. The decisive moment occurred when Jaspar, the Belgian P.M., asked me to accompany him to the Hotel des Indes. While he saw Briand I was left in a large salon opening from the stairs [and] crowded with French journalists. Someone said to me 'How can you preserve a smiling face in such circumstances?!' I could not say that I regarded it all as the biggest joke ever, so I said I had been through the war alongside the French, and after that nothing could disturb me much. Then I was ushered into a room where were assembled Briand, Loucheur, Chéron and Jaspar, looking very solemn. I began to explain that it was evidently a matter of difference of language, talking in English with Loucheur translating. '*Parlez en français*' said Briand. So I started in French somewhat on these lines. '*Vous savez bien que je ne parle français que très mal. Et si vous dites qu'un Sécrétaire-Général qui ne peut pas parler français bien est grotesque et ridicule, je le traiterai comme une plaisanterie*'.[2] Loucheur burst out laughing, Briand's eyes twinkled. And Jaspar looked incredulous. But it did the trick. Thereafter it was merely a matter of drafting a communiqué – not easy, but manageable. Next day old Chéron came to me with tears in his eyes, and delivered a most affecting speech as to how no-one else in the world could have brought about a settlement. I told Snowden. He spoke up gracefully in public conference. Chéron made a charming reply. The reconciliation was complete and the atmosphere better than at any previous moment. But after the incident I woke in the early hours of the morning with this horrible thought. 'What about

[1] Hankey to MacDonald 11th Aug. 1929. Part published in *Middlemas*, I, pp. 197–8.

[2] 'You know very well that I only speak French indifferently. And if you said that a Secretary-General who could not speak French well was grotesque and ridiculous I would treat it as a joke.'

the 500 journalists who were waiting? Loucheur, quite unscrupulous, will have gone out and told them Sir Maurice Hankey had described himself as '*Un Sécrétaire-Général grotesque et ridicule*'. And Robin, when he picks up his *Echo de Paris* this morning will see it in headlines. I never slept another wink! But Loucheur, who has always been a good friend to me personally, played the game. I could find no trace of it when the French press arrived.

Then there were other incidents of the same kind. Once at the end of the conference, when Snowden had flared up about unbusinesslike procedure, one of the Germans, Dr. Curtius,[1] lost his temper and said Snowden had no right to adopt the rôle of *Schulmeister*. 'You want one' said Snowden! And everyone laughed; but I had to cut it out of the *procès-verbal* . . .

One may doubt whether, before or after the Hague Conference of 1929, that extraordinary compound of experience, tact, urbanity, linguistic skill and psychological insight which were embodied in Maurice Hankey's intellectual conformation were shown to better advantage.

Although on 13th Hankey reported that Snowden and Henderson were 'rather optimistic', and hoped that the heads of delegations and the Secretary-General might be able to leave in the near future,[2] five days later he wrote that 'the atmosphere is highly charged' and that 'we look rather near a break'.[3] He was however cheered to receive the following letter.

*MacDonald to Hankey. 10 Downing Street. Undated but probably 15th August 1929.*[4] Holograph

My dear Hankey,

Your letters are splendidly useful – like yourself at The Hague. I knew you would save the situation if anyone could. The substance of our claims is backed by everybody and also our standing by them and fighting them through. I believe we can get fair dealing without either breaking up or even adjourning the Conference. Snowden is the man of the moment and I rejoice. The poor old country wants it badly and if he pulls it off, it will be a tremendous lift to our prestige. I did tremble at one period, not because he was firm but because he seemed to be treating the Conference like the House of Commons. Still success will be a justification which will overshadow

[1]Julius Curtius (1877–1948). German politician (Soc. Dem.). Minister for Economic Affairs 1926–29. Foreign Minister 1929–31. A close friend and ally of Stresemann. Defended Young Plan when Dr. Schacht attacked it. President of Reichsbank 1934–37.

[2]To Lady Hankey 13th Aug. 1929. [3]To the same 18th Aug. 1929.

[4]Hankey mentions receiving this undated letter in his letter of 16th Aug. to Lady Hankey.

every incident which may not contribute to it. Your letters give me a clear idea of how things go and what is making them go. I do wish, however, you could snatch some rest. Couldn't I send you to the House of Lords or some other Isle of Avalon? Thank you so much.

Yours most gratefully

What Hankey called 'the supreme crisis' began on 22nd August. The British delegates' instructions were that the Cabinet was to be consulted before matters were pushed to the point of breakdown. Hankey's view was that if Snowden and Henderson returned to London the impression would be given that we were weakening. If on the other hand MacDonald came to The Hague Snowden's prestige would suffer. Hankey therefore urged that the Cabinet 'should trust the men on the spot', and on 24th that decision was confirmed in London. 'One up for me' remarked Hankey to Adeline.[1] Next day, a Sunday, Hankey had 'a heart-to-heart talk' with Snowden, and told him he was sure he could get 75% of the Chancellor's demand; but the latter 'would not look at less than 80 to 85%'. The furthest the other nations would go was 60%, which Snowden and Hankey both considered 'derisory'. Hankey thereupon 'played his last card but one', and sent Tom Jones 'a private message hinting that the P.M. must send a personal appeal'. MacDonald responded on 27th,[2] and that evening Snowden reopened negotiations. 'We turned the corner last night' wrote Hankey to Adeline on 28th, and at 1.30 a.m. that morning an agreement was signed.[3] 'Everyone has congratulated me as if I did it' he added in haste as he issued the Press communiqué and thankfully wound up a task which had taxed all his physical and mental reserves to the limit. If the sum at stake at The Hague seems trivial, especially in the light of the world economic crisis which was looming on the horizon, one has to remember that a breakdown would have set back Anglo-French relations very badly. The chief beneficiary of the agreement was of course Germany, which obtained the evacuation of the Rhineland, the removal of foreign control and a reduction of Reparations. These gains should have strengthened the Weimar Republic; and the conference certainly

[1]To Lady Hankey 25th Aug. 1929. [2]*Middlemas*, II, pp. 202–3.

[3]The agreement actually conceded 83% of the British claim. *Punch* of 4th Sept. 1929 published a cartoon showing John Bull welcoming Snowden in cricketing garb back to the pavilion with a score of 83 to his credit. It is titled 'The Yorkshire Stonewaller'. On the results of the conference see also F.O. Memo. of 31st May 1932. Cab. 21/355.

marked another stage on the boulder-strewn road towards the full re-admission of Germany into the comity of nations. The fact that all such gains were to be swallowed up and lost in the disaster of the great depression does not materially diminish the credit due to Hankey. In retrospect Snowden himself wrote that 'The work of the conference at this stage [i.e. 22nd–23rd August] would have broken down altogether if it had not been for the energy and skill of Sir Maurice Hankey, the Secretary-General, who I believe, never went to bed for two nights'.[1]

One result of the prolonged negotiations at The Hague was that the Hankeys' summer holiday was once again disrupted. While it was in progress he urged Adeline not to await his return, but to take the younger members of the family away on her own. After it had ended he had no desire to go abroad again, so they settled for a short holiday at Seaford early in September. One of his first 'relaxations' was to write Robin the remarkable eighteen-page letter giving the inside story of the conference, parts of which we have already quoted. His official report to the Cabinet was completed before he left Holland.

Meanwhile MacDonald's plan to visit U.S.A., chiefly for preliminary talks on naval limitation, had matured. He toyed at first with the idea of taking Hankey with him; but on 17th September Hankey told Robin that he could not go because he was wanted at home to prepare for the renewal of the Hague conference, and because he was regarded in America as 'a pundit in defence matters' and the talks were to be conducted 'nominally at any rate on the political plane'. So Tom Jones was to go, and 'devil' MacDonald's speeches. This of course meant that Hankey would have to take complete charge of the office.[2]

Actually it was the prospect of another naval conference rather than the continuation of the Hague meeting that chiefly occupied Hankey's attention during the closing months of 1929. In the previous June the Foreign Office had produced a historical survey of Anglo-American relations and the effect on them of naval limitation, for use by MacDonald in the preliminary talks he was to hold with General Dawes,[3] who was coming to London for the purpose.[4] The question at once arose whether 'a single Empire quota' should be taken as the basis of British naval strength, or whether the Dominions should have separate quotas. Hankey supported the Admiralty, which strongly favoured the

[1]Viscount Snowden, *An Autobiography*, p. 825.
[2]To Robin Hankey 17th Sept. 1929. [3]See p. 372, *note*.
[4]By R. L. Craigie, dated 10th June 1929. Premier 1/73.

single quota.[1] The abolition of submarines, which the British had unsuccessfully proposed at Washington in 1921, was also raised once more. Rather surprisingly the King came out strongly in favour of abolition[2]; and, despite the discouraging history of previous British efforts to achieve that object which Hankey produced, Stamfordham wrote to him that 'The King hopes that his present Government will not be content with the *non possumus* attitude of France, and will endeavour in co-operation with America to overcome the opposition of our friends across the Channel'.[3] The Dominions were of course kept informed of all these preliminaries by the usual 'Circular telegrams', and when South Africa replied that 'the question of the prohibition of submarines for purely defensive purposes is one which should be discussed more fully' MacDonald exploded. 'This sort of thing is intolerable' he wrote on the telegram; 'Purely defensive purposes! Is the draftsman an ass?'[4] Hankey never budged from the view he had expressed at Washington – that abolition simply was not practical politics. Perhaps it was just as well that the principle of 'no critical comment' of Dominion policy, referred to earlier, prevailed on this occasion, and that MacDonald's expletives were not communicated to Pretoria.

The preliminary exchanges did little more than re-emphasise the gulf between American insistence on big cruisers with 8-inch guns and British insistence on large numbers of smaller ships. They also exposed the impossibility of producing the much-discussed 'yard stick', whereby the Americans hoped to establish the relative value of ships of different displacement, age and gunpower. None the less on 20th September the British government informed its ambassadors in Paris, Rome and Tokyo that invitations would be issued to a five-power naval conference.[5] Eight days later MacDonald left for America. Meanwhile Hankey had become increasingly disturbed about the possibility of the old question of Belligerent Rights being raised either in the MacDonald–Hoover talks, or as part of a bargain at the forthcoming conference.

*Diary 18th October 1929* (Continued from p. 458)
I didn't think it worth while to prime MacDonald on the subject [of Belligerent Rights], as I had been told it would not be raised at Washington; but I did prime Tom Jones a little, and gave him two very informing [?]

[1]Admiralty to Vansittart, 3rd Aug. 1925. *ibid.*
[2]Stamfordham to MacDonald, 10th July 1929. Premier 1/71.
[3]Stamfordham to C. P. Duff, 15th July 1929. *ibid.*
[4]On telegram of 19th Aug. 1929 from South Africa. Premier 1/73. [5]*ibid.*

reports of the B.R. Committee to take with him. We were all very astonished, and I was very shocked, when we learned that the whole subject had been raised at MacDonald's Sunday [6th October] conversations at Hoover's lumber camp [on the Rapidan river, Virginia].[1] It looked like a plant. First MacDonald is told in June that the question is off. Then he comes to Washington [and] gets a tremendous ovation. When drunk with success he is brought to the lumber camp, and without any experts to consult with – for there was an understanding that he should take no experts to Washington – the question is sprung on him in a most acute and contentious form. Here is the story from our end. Monday 7th October. Cabinet meeting with Snowden in the chair, which lasted all day.[2] About 4.30 p.m. I received a telegram which I was too busy to read until the Cabinet rose at about 5 p.m. The gist was that Hoover had produced a draft communiqué regarding the conversation, to be issued on Wednesday evening [9th October], which *inter alia* was to include a statement that the Americans agreed that our bases in the West Indies were not a threat to them; we were to announce that we would not increase them materially, while they were to undertake to have no bases in the eastern hemisphere. In addition, and even more important, they were to announce conversations to be begun on Belligerent Rights . . . and, most important of all, Hoover was in the communiqué to express the hope that foodstuffs would . . . be excluded from the scope of blockade, food ships being treated like hospital ships. Supplementary telegrams from Vansittart made it clear that they hoped we would agree. I showed Snowden the telegram, and though I had never discussed the subject with him, found that he was intensely irritated at this suggestion. Before I left the office late that evening . . . I had a message from Admiral Madden asking for a meeting of the Chiefs of Staff Committee early to-morrow, which I arranged. I also arranged to attend a meeting at the F.O. to-morrow at 11 a.m. I spent the evening drafting the following telegrams:— (1) from the Chiefs of Staff to the P.M.: (2) from Snowden to the P.M., which I hoped to persuade him to send: (3) from myself to the P.M. – the three covering most of the ground.

The next diary entry records that the Chiefs of Staff, with Hankey of course acting as Secretary, asked MacDonald to reject the proposal about the West Indian bases, because the British garrisons had been reduced to a nucleus and we might, irrespective of the Americans, want to increase them again. They also deprecated the

[1]See Raymond G. O'Connor, *Perilous Equilibrium. The United States and the London Naval Conference 1930* (Kansas U.P. 1962), pp. 48–51. Henceforth cited as *O'Connor*. It is here made clear (p. 48) that 'the explosive question of "freedom of the seas" was raised by Hoover' – not by MacDonald.

[2]Cabinet 37(29) in Cab. 23/62.

raising of the issue of Belligerent Rights, and urged that the question of ships carrying foodstuffs should not be discussed. The meeting at the Foreign Office produced a telegram pointing out that the question of foodstuffs was 'in contradiction to our obligations under the Covenant'. Then Hankey saw Snowden, and got his approval to send both telegrams – subject to amendments to meet his views – 'which', Hankey remarked, 'were as strong as my own'. The gist of the final telegram was that these subjects had never been discussed in Cabinet, and that at the moment it was impossible to call 'an efficient Cabinet meeting' because so many Ministers, including Henderson and the heads of the Service departments, were away. Hankey's personal telegram warned MacDonald that in all his twenty-one years experience of the C.I.D. these were 'the most controversial subjects of all'; that a storm would arise if the proposal about food ships were published, and that MacDonald would in consequence lose 'the national support he was receiving'. 'A pretty hot telegram' was Hankey's reasonable description. He showed Snowden's telegram to Lord Passfield and J. H. Thomas, respectively Colonial and Dominions Secretary and Lord Privy Seal, and Thomas declared 'the Government would not last 10 minutes if the amendment included the food proposal'. Hankey then 'went home happier'.[1]

On 9th October Hankey learnt that Henderson 'fully endorsed the action we had taken', and a message from Washington announced that Hoover had 'consented, though reluctantly, to drop the foodstuffs proposal'. MacDonald for his part declared that he had never agreed to it. Hankey then drafted another telegram for Snowden to send stressing that if the matter were mentioned in a communiqué it 'would be interpreted as tacit acquiescence' by the two statesmen participating in the conversations. Then Snowden spoke to Tom Jones on the trans-Atlantic telephone 'much in this vein' though he had 'to use careful language for fear of interception'.[2]

When the communiqué actually appeared on 10th everyone in Whitehall Gardens was astonished to find no mention of the West Indian bases or of Belligerent Rights. Snowden was, according to Hankey, 'astonished at his own success in getting the objectionable paragraphs deleted'.[3] On 16th Hankey followed up this success by sending MacDonald a long letter urging that the question of Belligerent Rights should not be taken up at all. Hankey remarked, not without

[1]Diary 8th Oct. 1929. [2]*ibid.* 9th Oct. 1929. [3]*ibid.* 10th Oct. 1929.

some self-satisfaction, that despite the opposition of Tyrrell, Craigie, Vansittart and Esmé Howard 'it looks as if I might win'. In the letter to MacDonald he had told how, ever since 1915, Colonel House had been the instigator of American proposals for Freedom of the Seas, and he guessed that his hand was to be detected in Hoover's proposal. After Tom Jones had returned home Hankey learnt that his guess had been correct, and that at a lunch with MacDonald, House had admitted that, although his influence had decreased, he had 'got at Hoover through his entourage'. Hankey passed this news on to MacDonald, probably with some relish, while waiting for the King to receive the Privy Council on 5th November. The Prime Minister was 'furious', and declared that House 'always wanted to claim credit for every idea', but that in the present instance the initiative had been solely Hoover's. On 10th Dawson, editor of *The Times*, sent a reporter to Hankey to find out his views, and 'for the first time to a newspaperman' he gave them.[1] The result was an 'admirable leader'.[2]

Hankey was delighted that newspapers 'of every complexion' gave Hoover's proposal a bad Press, and that Lloyd George administered 'a nasty jolt' to MacDonald by interrupting the general plaudits which the House of Commons was according to his account of his visit to America to press him hard about whether he had given anything away'.[3] He also prepared another 'monumental memorandum' on Belligerent Rights for the new C.I.D. sub-committee set up by the Cabinet on 6th November to consider the matter yet again, and to review the policy of the previous government.[4] On 14th the King sent for Hankey and was 'very violent about Hoover's proposal, which he criticised with great ability'. When Hankey entered the Cabinet room that day MacDonald said 'Here is Sir Maurice Hankey. As long as he

[1]*ibid.* 15th Nov. 1929.

[2]Unquestionably the first leader of 12th Nov. 1929, which strongly deprecated the discussion of Belligerent Rights at the forthcoming naval conference.

[3]Hankey was probably here referring to Lloyd George's speech in the debate on the Adjournment on 5th Nov. 1929. He asked about 'the commitments, if there are any, which he [MacDonald] made', and urged that 'we ought to proceed very cautiously with regard to abandoning any of our rights'. Parl. Deb., Commons, Vol. 231, Cols. 890–1. The Cabinet minutes for 1st Nov. contain the statement that MacDonald 'who was warmly greeted by his colleagues, made a very full statement in regard to his visit to the U.S.A. and Canada, and his conversations with President Hoover and Mr. Mackenzie King'. Cabinet 44(29) in Cab. 23/62.

[4]B.R.L. 1 of 9th Nov. 1929. Cab. 21/328.

remains in office there are two institutions which are quite safe. One is the Monarchy. The other our Maritime Belligerent Rights'; which pleased Hankey as it showed that his 'strong views on the latter question' had not antagonised the Prime Minister. In fact he seems at this time to have been on excellent terms with all the Labour Ministers – despite the disagreements existing among themselves. Early in November he learnt from Batterbee that Lord Passfield had included his name in the short list of 'possibles' for the Governor-Generalship of New Zealand; but MacDonald had crossed it out saying that 'he could not possibly spare me'.[1] 'As a matter of fact', he recorded, 'he has asked me to be Secretary-General and Organiser-in-Chief of the forthcoming Naval Conference, so I am clearly not in his bad grace'.

Hankey did, however, have some strong words to say to Craigie[2] when he learnt from Jones that it was he who had allowed MacDonald 'nearly to acquiesce in Hoover's proposal'. And he confessed to his diary that when Craigie defended his actions he had, most unusually, 'rather lost my temper and told him that in my opinion he had got nearer to wrecking the British Empire than anyone in recent times'. 'Still', he typically concluded, 'I shall have to work with him at the Naval Conference, and so I thought it best to bury the hatchet'.[3]

In conclusion, though some readers may feel that Hankey's opposition to any tampering with Belligerent Rights had by 1929 become something of an obsession, it none the less remains true that Britain entered World War II unencumbered by agreements such as those which

[1]Diary 15th Nov. 1929. Hankey also recorded that the King told him that the names submitted to him had included Charles Bathurst, 1st Baron Bledisloe (1867–1958); Air Vice-Marshal Sir Philip Game (1876–1961), Governor of New South Wales 1930–35, Commissioner of Metropolitan Police 1935–45; and Commander J. M. Kenworthy M.P. (1886–1953), 10th Baron Strabolgi 1934 – a somewhat catholic selection. Bledisloe was actually appointed, and served as Governor-General of New Zealand 1930–35. When the King mentioned Bledisloe Hankey told him that when Lloyd George, who had recommended him for a Peerage, was told the title he proposed to take, he had 'roared with laughter' and exclaimed 'Lord Bloody Slow! How appropriate!' The King, he wrote, 'was delighted with the story'. Monarch and secretary seem to have shared a somewhat juvenile sense of humour.

[2]Later Sir Robert L. Craigie (1883–1959). Diplomat. Counsellor, Foreign Office 1928. Under-Secretary of State 1934–37. Ambassador to Japan 1937–41. U.K. representative on United Nations War Crimes Commission 1945–48.

[3]Diary 15th Nov. 1929.

had so weakened the blockade of Germany in 1914–15. In the second conflict a blockade was immediately declared, and although the susceptibilities of neutral nations, and especially the U.S.A. and Italy, caused us to apply the right of 'visit and search' with caution, and on occasions to relax its full stringency, the absence of the embarrassments of World War I was an advantage. And of course as soon as America entered the war they applied the strategy of blockade with full and unrestricted vigour. All thoughts about Freedom of the Seas were then totally dissipated.

It must not be thought that, because the first Hague Conference and the controversy over Belligerent Rights took up so much of Hankey's time during the first six months of the second Labour Government he was not involved in other difficult negotiations. MacDonald himself and the majority of his colleagues wished to restore the decision of 1924 cancelling the Singapore base – a decision to which they considered themselves 'deeply committed'.[1] The position at the time when Labour returned to power was that the big floating dock had been constructed and towed out; the 'truncated scheme' for repair and storage facilities had been approved; the contract for the main shore works, including the graving dock, had been signed in September 1928 and should be completed in seven years from that date; the first stage in the installation of fixed gun defences (including three 15-inch guns) had been approved but no expenditure was to be incurred in the 1929–30 financial year; a flying-boat squadron had arrived, and the airfield and associated buildings to accommodate one naval or R.A.F. squadron were well advanced.[2] On 25th July MacDonald told the C.I.D. that 'the large and overruling problem' was that 'the conditions of the international situation governing Imperial strategy, and perhaps of Imperial strategy itself, which prevailed when the Singapore base was projected have undoubtedly changed' – though he gave no clue as to how or why this was so. Instead he asked 'What modifications in the conclusions come to in those days are now required?' Hankey's interjection in the discussion pointing out that the Dominions had already received the Chiefs of Staff's Committee's report on the defence of Singapore, and his inclusion in the minutes of a strongly worded

[1]Memo. of 8th July 1929. Premier 1/67.

[2]C.I.D. 346C of 4th June 1930 is a comprehensive history of the development of the base prepared by the Overseas Defence Committee for the 1930 Imperial Conference.

telegram from Mr. Bruce of Australia stating that his country 'attached the greatest possible importance to [the] Singapore Base' show clearly enough where his own sympathies lay.[1] Reading between the lines of all the many documents on the subject which were produced in his office at this time one is left with the strong impression that he was working determinedly, though with all his usual tact and diplomacy, to temper the cold wind which was beginning to blow in the direction of an increasingly alarmed Admiralty. However the discussion of 25th July ended with the admission that the financial gain from stopping all work on the base would be 'comparatively small', and that the contract for the graving dock was not to be disturbed. The Cabinet subsequently endorsed those conclusions; but towards the end of the year the whole issue was thrown into the melting pot again by the acceptance of all the Powers concerned of the invitations to the Naval Conference referred to earlier. The government then considered that 'to continue the entire Singapore scheme in complete disregard of the possibilities of the conference would be indefensible'. In October they therefore decided that the work already contracted for 'should be slowed down as much as possible', that 'all work that could be suspended should be suspended', and that 'no new work should be embarked on'.[2] This was a bitter pill for the Admiralty and for Hankey to swallow; and it was made even less palatable by the decision of 28th May 1930 that, in view of the agreements made at the Naval Conference (to which further reference will be made later), 'the present "slowed down" programme should be allowed to continue, and that arrangements should be made to obtain at the forthcoming Imperial Conference a definite and permanent settlement of the question of the Singapore base'.[3] In other words the whole scheme was once again imperilled.

Hankey did not accept this decision tamely: but he must have realised that he was up against heavy odds – especially as C. P. Duff, MacDonald's Private Secretary,[4] took exception to the historical survey of the Singapore base story which he had prepared.[5] That 10 Downing Street and Whitehall Gardens were in opposing camps is shown by a

[1]244th C.I.D. of 25th July 1929. [2]C.I D. 346C. [3]*ibid*

[4]Later Sir C. Patrick Duff (1889– ). Civil Servant. Private Secretary to successive Presidents of Board of Trade 1919–23 and to Baldwin and MacDonald as Prime Ministers 1923–33. Secretary, Ministry of Public Buildings and Works 1933–41. High Commissioner for U.K. in New Zealand 1945–49.

[5]C.I.D. 346C.

note from Duff to Hankey saying that MacDonald felt the paper in question 'as it stood gave a rather pro-Singapore impression', and the Prime Minister had suggested that 'a more colourless *résumé* of the situation might meet the purpose better'.[1] Duff also wrote to MacDonald that 'the large space given to recommendations of the C.I.D. . . . definitely load the dice against the Labour Party decision in 1924 and even against the decision to slow down in 1929'[2] – which no doubt accurately reflected Hankey's intentions. He, however, replied to Duff that the paper in question had already been circulated to the C.I.D., and on 27th June MacDonald accepted that it should stand.[3] The issue remained in that unsatisfactory and unsettled state to be swallowed up in the crisis of 1931 and the fall of the Labour government. Observing that, as Hankey pointed out in several C.I.D. papers, £3¾ millions towards a total cost of some £8 millions had been promised by the Dominions and Crown Colonies, and by mid-1930 over £1½ millions had actually been paid over by them, the charge that the government of 1929–31 committed a breach of faith and of contract towards the countries most concerned is hard to refute. It is difficult to see what more Hankey could have done than place the facts squarely before the C.I.D. and Cabinet. Moreover his efforts to preserve and progress the Singapore base as an essential element in Imperial Defence were probably handicapped by the fact that, ever since the retirement of Beatty as First Sea Lord in 1927, most of the naval members of the Board of Admiralty had been singularly undistinguished; and the replacement of the energetic and determined Bridgeman as First Lord by A. V. Alexander two years later was little short of a disaster for the navy. A stronger Board of Admiralty might well have given Hankey and the Chiefs of Staff Committee greater support on issues such as the Singapore base. Be that as it may, the decisions taken in 1929 left Britain with an uncompleted and ill-defended base in the Far East when it was needed twelve years later.

While the future of the Singapore base thus hung in the balance once again the League Preparatory Commission renewed its attempts to gain acceptance of the 'Model Treaty to strengthen the means of Preventing War'. This document had been approved by the League Assembly in September 1928; but, after referring it to Lord Salisbury's committee,

[1]Duff to Hankey 23rd June 1930. Premier 1/152.

[2]Duff to MacDonald 20th June 1930. *ibid.*

[3]Hankey to Duff 25th June 1930, and note by MacDonald of 27th. *ibid.*

Baldwin's cabinet had declined to accept it.[1] In September of the following year the British delegation proposed that the treaty, which had heretofore been intended as a model which any two or more states could adopt, should be converted into a General Treaty. MacDonald referred this proposal and others connected with disarmament to a committee chaired by Henderson.

Hankey now represented that the Service Departments were being 'steam rollered by Lord Cecil', and that the matter should be handled 'in the normal manner' by placing it first before the Chiefs of Staff Committee.[2] However Colonel Ismay, his Military Assistant Secretary,[3] who was deputising for him, assured him that as Henderson would put forward 'arguments that appeal to him [Hankey] at the C.I.D.' his protest to MacDonald was superfluous.[4] In fact the Chiefs of Staff did report on the Model Treaty in May 1930, and their objections to it came before the C.I.D.[5] Discussions continued during the next year, with the C.O.S.s still voicing their objections both to the draft treaty itself and to the tactics employed by Cecil to secure its adoption[6]. In May 1931 the issue came before the Cabinet.[7] But, like so many other long-gestating and intricate problems, it was submerged in the economic crisis of the following summer. Our interest in the matter lies only in the fact that Hankey regarded the draft treaty as open to serious objections – particularly with regard to military action by Britain, such as had recently been taken at Shanghai, being made subject to League approval, and the possibility that it might be stigmatised as 'aggression'. This danger was certainly very real; nor does study of the draft treaty provide any solid ground for considering that it would in fact

[1]C.P. 253(28).

[2]Hankey to MacDonald 10th Jan. 1930. Draft letter which was not actually sent. Cab. 21/348.

[3]Later General Sir Hastings L. Ismay, 1st Baron 1947 (1887–1965). Assistant Secretary, C.I.D. 1926–30, Deputy Secretary 1936–38 and Secretary in succession to Hankey 1938. Deputy Secretary (Military) to War Cabinet 1940–45 and Chief Staff Officer to Churchill and Attlee as Minister of Defence 1940–46. C.O.S. to Viceroy of India 1947. Secretary of State for Commonwealth Relations 1951–52. Secretary-General, N.A.T.O. 1952–57. Chairman, North Atlantic Council 1956–57.

[4]Ismay to Hankey 3rd April 1930. Cab. 21/348.

[5]C.O.S. 246 which became C.I.D. 1000B. Cab. 4/19.

[6]See for example Admiral Field (First Sea Lord) to Hankey 12th March 1931 objecting to proposals 'introduced by Lord Cecil at Geneva without authority from home'. Cab. 21/348.

[7]C.P. 114(31), considered on 6th May 1931. Cabinet 27(31).

have proved an effective instrument for the prevention of war.[1] Hankey's views on the usefulness and the limitations of the League in accomplishing that purpose are clearly shown by a letter sent to MacDonald at this time. 'I am a profound believer in the League's capacity for conciliation and gaining time for averting war', he wrote; 'I am an equally profound disbeliever in its capacity to advise action . . . Nevertheless sanctions have a certain value. They are like a big stick believed to be in the cupboard; so long as the boys do not realise that it is made of paper it is a deterrent. But if you bring the stick out into the light of day I fear its true character will be exposed'.[2]

It is not surprising that, with Labour in power once more, the old issue of creating a Ministry of Defence should have been raised yet again in Parliament.[3] Hankey at once sent MacDonald the very full brief on the subject which he had prepared for Baldwin's use on the similar occasion in March 1928.[4] Once again he was successful in fending off what he regarded as a threat to the Service Departments and the C.I.D. But when in March 1931 the Economy Committee under Sir George May[5] was set up to propose far-ranging measures to bring the Budget into balance and stop the run on the pound Hankey found himself called on to give evidence on whether a Ministry of Defence would produce an appreciable reduction of expenditure. He obviously realised that, in the climate of the times, the danger of such a measure being forced through was greater than ever before. He therefore produced a historical survey of the whole subject, with strongly-worded arguments against the creation of such a Ministry in time of war as well as in peacetime, and whether it was substituted for the Service Departments or 'superimposed on the existing organisation'. Nor did he consider that 'a Ministry of Defence is the way to achieve economy', because 'economy runs with efficiency', and efficiency was in his view

[1]The text of the Model Treaty as finally approved by the League Assembly is in C.I.D. 993B. Cab. 4/19.

[2]Hankey to MacDonald 10th April 1930. MacDonald papers.

[3]In the debate on Co-ordination of Defence Services, 4th Dec. 1929. Parl. Deb., Commons, Vol. 232, Cols. 2399–2460. During the same session MacDonald had already answered several Parliamentary Questions on the proposal for a Ministry of Defence with firm negatives. *ibid.* Cols. 36 and 485–6.

[4]Hankey to MacDonald 4th Dec. 1929. Cab. 21/351.

[5]1871–1946. 1st Baron May of Weybridge 1935. Businessman. Secretary of Prudential Assurance Company 1915–31. Chairman, Import Duties Advisory Committee 1932.

bound to suffer.[1] He sent a copy of this paper to Sir Warren Fisher of the Treasury, who described it as 'a *locus classicus*' and told Hankey his evidence had 'left a profound impression on the [May] Committee'.[2] Though Hankey was prepared to 'deliver a strong attack on the May Committee report if it suggests there is no proper control of Defence Policy without proving it to the hilt',[3] on the same day that Fisher commented so favourably on his evidence he was able to tell MacDonald that the May Committee 'will report definitely against a Ministry of Defence'.[4] And so it proved.[5] Though that was by no means the end of Hankey's fight to preserve the C.I.D. system, in March 1932 Baldwin, in answering a Parliamentary Question, confirmed the recommendation of the May Committee.[6]

But long before the crisis of 1931 had overwhelmed the second Labour government Hankey became deeply involved in the second Hague and London Naval Conferences of the previous year, and in the Imperial Conference of the same extraordinarily busy period. We must therefore now retrace our steps to the beginning of 1930.

[1]Memo. of 2nd July 1931. Cab. 21/351. Hankey's notes for his evidence to the May Committee are in Cab. 63/44.
[2]Fisher to Hankey replying to his letter of 7th July 1931. Cab. 21/384.
[3]To Waterfield (Treasury). *ibid.*
[4]Hankey to MacDonald 7th July 1931. *ibid.*
[5]The May Committee reported on 24th July 1931, and it was published on 31st. Cmd. 3920.
[6]Parl. Deb. Commons, Vol. 262, Cols. 1105–6.

*Chapter 17*

# A Year of Conferences. 1930

On the last day of 1929 Hankey, accompanied as usual by Lawrence Burgis and a number of the office staff from Whitehall Gardens, crossed again to Holland in order to finalise acceptance of the Young Plan and other questions connected with Reparations and the evacuation of the Rhineland which had been left unsettled when the First Hague Conference adjourned at the end of the previous August. The British delegation was again led by Philip Snowden, who was supported by William Graham, the President of the Board of Trade.[1] Leith-Ross was once more head of the British expert advisers, and Sir Eric Phipps, now Minister at Vienna, represented the diplomatic interest. Hankey had asked the Foreign Office to provide him with an assistant who was fluent in French and German, and Sir Ronald Lindsay, the Permanent Under-Secretary, tactfully seconded Robin from the Paris embassy to fill the bill. This was the only occasion when he served under his father in an official capacity.

Hankey did not take this further separation from Adeline lightly. He complained, with some reason, that international conferences always seemed to be arranged during the summer months, so disrupting their holidays together; and this time he found it harder to bear because he left behind the photograph of his wife which had so often kept him company on his foreign trips, and which served as a vicarious substitute for her physical presence.[2] At least he was able to report that the administrative arrangements and the accommodation and transport provided by the Dutch government were far better than at the previous conference. But whereas he had then only dealt with the representatives

[1] 1887–1932. Politician (Lab.) and economist. Prominent in financial and Scottish legislation. Member, Royal Commission on Oxford and Cambridge Universities 1920–21 and of many other government-appointed or Scottish committees. Financial Secretary to Treasury 1924. President of Board of Trade 1929–31.
[2] To Lady Hankey 1st Jan. 1930.

of the former Allied Powers and of Germany, this time all the ex-enemy countries except Turkey had to be brought in; and the presence of Austrian, Hungarian and Bulgarian delegations produced 'dreadful complications'. 'It is incredible', he told Adeline, 'how much tact is required all the time'; and he himself narrowly escaped giving offence to the Dutch by referring in his draft for the opening speech by M. Jaspar, the Belgian Prime Minister who was President of the conference, to The Hague as 'the capital city' – which apparently 'would have caused a riot in Amsterdam' – and to the Queen and Prince Consort as 'Their Majesties' when the latter was not a 'Majesty'.[1] Despite such troubles over protocol with their hosts, which were probably an echo of the 17th-century jealousies between the Seven Provinces, by 4th January Hankey was able to report that the conference was 'successfully launched'. But he expected the usual quarrels to take place in the committees dealing with specific subjects, such as Finance and Political issues, into which he had, in accordance with his invariable practice, divided the conference.[2] Whenever the 'Inviting Powers' met in secret session Hankey alone was allowed to be present to keep the record. This meant that he 'had to do all the interpreting' as well as keeping the *procès-verbaux*. He was soon able to report that Robin was 'quite invaluable and most popular'; and in between the sessions they managed to get away together either for walks among the sand dunes of Scheveningen or on sight-seeing expeditions to Delft and Leyden. Obviously father and son both enjoyed each other's company. Among the more amusing incidents at The Hague recalled by Robin is his father catching a photographer called Solomons walking into a secret session of the conference dressed up as a delegate; and next day his catching the same man on a ladder photographing a meeting through a window. Doubtless the activities of such gentlemen accounts for Hankey's enduring dislike of the Press.

One interesting change which Hankey was quick to remark was that Philip Snowden, whose obstinacy had produced so many difficulties at the previous conference, was now 'probably the most popular figure'. And 'old Chéron', the French Finance Minister, and his wife

[1] To the same 2nd Jan. 1930.

[2] The Hague Conference papers are in Cab. 29/107–16. Hankey's various series were prefaced H for Plenary Sessions, H(D) for meetings of the six 'Inviting Powers', H(F) for Finance, H(GR) for Reparations, H(P) for Political and B.D.(R) for meetings of the British delegates.

delighted Hankey as 'the perfect example of a French married couple', 'still most devoted – like us' he told Adeline.[1] What he found far more burdensome than the actual sessions of the conference was 'the continual round of incredibly dull entertainment'. The climax to this ordeal came with an 'interminable affair' one evening at the Palace, when the guests had first to endure an hour's wait huddled in groups according to nationality, and were then presented in turn to the Queen, the Queen Mother and the Prince Consort and his 'young princess'.[2] Hankey managed 'to make them all laugh'; but there then followed three hours of what Robin described as 'Court Music'. When at last the party broke up Philippe Berthelot, Secretary-General of the French Foreign Ministry, remarked acidulously that '*Les meilleures plaisanteries sont les plus courtes*'.[3] Though Hankey endured the Palace entertainment to the end his usual technique was to put in an appearance at 'the endless succession of dinners and balls' wearing 'a blaze of decorations', salute his host and then 'slip out by the back door' to return to his hotel or office and complete the record of the day's discussions.[4]

After ten days Hankey was becoming increasingly impatient over the slow progress made, and was worried about what would happen if he was not back in London by 21st January, when the Naval Conference was to begin. He told Adeline that he was 'looking forward to that event "with inspissated gloom" as Asquith would have said'.[5] 'I don't see daylight there', he continued, 'and I don't feel at all in the mood for the turmoil of another difficult conference so soon after the strenuous days here'. Though he 'would not mind getting out' of responsibility for a conference which he 'hardly hoped to succeed' the fact that the King had already summoned him to discuss the matter on 20th, taken with MacDonald's reliance on his organising ability, would obviously make it very difficult to secure his release.[6]

As to progress at The Hague, on 14th Hankey drafted a letter from Snowden to MacDonald describing the difficulties encountered, the

[1]To Lady Hankey 7th and 14th Jan. 1930.

[2]These were respectively Queen Adelheid Emma Wilhelmina Theresia (1858–1934) the widow of King William III (1817–1890), Queen Wilhelmina (1880–1962), abdicated 1948 after a reign of 50 years, and Princess Juliana (b. 1909) who married Prince Bernhard zu Lippe-Biesterfeld and succeeded her mother 1948.

[3]'The best jokes are the shortest ones.' [4]To Lady Hankey 12th Jan. 1930.

[5]Though Asquith may well have used this aphorism it was in fact originated by Dr. Johnson. See Boswell's *Life*, 16th Oct. 1769.

[6]To Lady Hankey 11th and 14th Jan. 1930.

French attitude and the doubts felt regarding whether the Germans would honour their obligations. MacDonald's reply was to the effect that Snowden should be told he could rely on full support from the Cabinet whatever course he decided to take.[1] On the same day that Snowden expressed his misgivings Hankey told his wife that 'last night we took all the main decisions to fix up matters [i.e. acceptance of the Young Plan] with Germany', that the details had been remitted to the Committee of Experts, and that the Drafting Committee had started work on the text of the actual agreement. Then Dr. Hjalmar Schacht, the President of the Reichsbank,[2] 'dropped a bomb into the conference' by suggesting that the draft agreement on the organisation of the Bank of International Settlements conflicted with the German Bank Law of August 1924.[3] The result, Hankey reported, was that 'the Committee of Bankers are on strike', and the arrangements with Austria, Hungary and Bulgaria were 'at a standstill'. Obviously Hankey's presence at the opening of the naval conference was becoming increasingly doubtful; but he told Adeline that he was prepared if necessary to go straight to the office on reaching London and, instead of returning home, throw himself immediately into his new task. None the less he was determined to see through to the end the Hague conference, which he regarded as 'the end of a great historical episode' – namely the Paris Peace Conference.[4] In a sense this was true; but it could also be argued that the Hague Conferences put a term to the clauses of the Versailles Treaty which had established Reparations and the occupation of the Rhineland, so making plain that such measures had totally failed.

As always when Hankey was at an international conference and the Prime Minister in London he kept his 'Chief' informed of progress by letter, and on 17th he told MacDonald that although the final stage had been reached at The Hague, 'on the non-German Reparation side things have been sticking badly'. Jaspar, he wrote, 'depends on me a

[1]Snowden to MacDonald 14th Jan. 1930 and note by latter of 15th. Premier 1/83.
[2]1877–1970. German banker. As President of Reichsbank 1924–29 played a large part in negotiation of Dawes and Young Plans. Again President 1933–39. Minister of National Economy under Hitler 1934–37, then Minister without Portfolio to 1943. Arrested 1944 and interned in concentration camp. Tried as a Major War Criminal at Nuremberg 1946 and acquitted. Tried and sentenced by de-Nazification court 1947, but sentence quashed. President of Schacht & Co., bankers 1953–63.
[3]Cab. 29/110.
[4]To Lady Hankey 14th Jan. 1930.

good deal'; 'I am the only Secretary who has been present at all the meetings of the Inviting Delegates . . . I have the whole machine under my hand; [and] the foreign Secretaries will take orders from me, as I am certain they would not do from anyone else'. If he could not get home on 20th he proposed that Vansittart should act for him at the opening meeting of the naval conference; and he was sending home Burgis and other key men of his staff to give the necessary help.[1] To Adeline he confided that the signature of the agreement at The Hague would be an event of great importance, and that he was determined to be one of the two representatives 'who alone sign the final Act'.[2] And so he was.[3]

The 'Stenographic Notes' of the final Plenary Session, of the Conference, held at 4 p.m. on 30th January, record M. Jaspar as saying, after paying a tribute to his colleagues, 'I centralise the expression of our thanks on one person, our incomparable Secretary-General (Loud Applause). We all know Sir Maurice Hankey, we know how for years he has spent his days and nights in carrying out the most delicate and the most important duties as well for his Government as, I may say, for the whole world. But we have never seen him work with such cheerfulness, with such fixity of purpose, and with that unforgettable modesty which is perhaps the quality that adorns him most – than during the month of August [1929] and these last few days. We have had as Secretary-General a man of outstanding personality, and I wish to express my affectionate admiration to him (Renewed Applause)'.[4]

The agreement signed on that day approved the carrying out of the Young Plan, and on 12th March the necessary measure passed the German Reichstag. It was ratified by Germany on 26th and by Britain, France and Italy soon afterwards. The British occupation force had been withdrawn from the Rhineland in December 1929, and on 17th

[1]Hankey to MacDonald 17th Jan. 1930. Premier 1/83.

[2]To Lady Hankey 18th Jan. 1930.

[3]The Protocol of 31st August 1929 was, on the proposal of M. Jaspar, signed only by himself and Hankey. At the 7th and last Plenary Session on 30th Jan. 1930 Snowden and Hankey signed for Britain. Cab. 29/107.

[4]Cab. 29/108. In addition to this tribute on 3rd February 1930 Jaspar sent Hankey a long letter expressing his gratitude. Part of it reads (author's translation) 'I am happy to have this further opportunity to express to you my very lively gratitude for the speed and perfection with which all these documents have been prepared . . . It is useless for me to repeat my opinion of yourself; on that score I can only recur to the homage I paid to you publicly at The Hague on 30th January'.

May 1930, when the Reparations Commission declared that the Young Plan would come into force from that day, the French government began the reluctant withdrawal of troops from the third and final zone. It was completed by the end of June – the time limit agreed at The Hague.[1]

Unhappily for those who had striven so hard to set Germany on her feet again, and to undo the effects of the draconian clauses of the Versailles Treaty and of subsequent French attempts at enforcement by military measures, the evacuation of the Rhineland produced an upsurge of xenophobia in Germany. President Hindenburg at once issued a Manifesto (countersigned by Dr. Brüning's cabinet[2]), putting forward totally new demands – for the restoration to Germany of the Saar valley, and for the repeal of the demilitarisation of the Rhineland. It ended with the words 'Let us all unite in the cry "*Deutschland, Deutschland über alles*" '.[3] Sir Horace Rumbold wrote in great concern from the Berlin embassy that this formulation of new demands immediately a concession had been granted was entirely typical of German methods; while Orme Sargent[4] of the Foreign Office wrote that the 'undemilitarisation' of the Rhineland 'cut at the very roots of Locarno'.[5] These events foreshadowed the results of the German General Election of September 1930 when the National Socialists polled 6½ million votes, second only to the Social Democrats' 8½ millions, and increased their representation in the Reichstag from 12 to 107 seats. We may here remark that two of Hankey's closest friends in the Diplomatic Service – Rumbold at Berlin, with whom he had worked so closely at the time of the Warsaw mission of July 1920,[6] and Phipps in Vienna – viewed these developments with alarm; and as Hankey kept in close touch with them both – by correspondence and by personal meetings – he was never in any doubt about the realities of the Nazi movement.

[1]D.B.F.P., 2nd Series, Vol. I, No. 301, note 1.

[2]The Müller government which signed the Hague agreements fell on 27th March 1930 and was replaced by a more right wing coalition under Dr. Heinrich Brüning (1885–1969, Chancellor 1930–32).

[3]The Manifesto is reproduced in D.B.F.P., 2nd Series, Vol. I. Enclosure to No. 308.

[4]Later Sir Orme Sargent (1884–1962). Diplomat. Served with British delegation to Conference of Ambassadors 1919. Head of Central Department, Foreign Office 1926, then Assistant Under-Secretary in charge of western European affairs. A strong opponent of the Munich agreement of 1938. Permanent Under-Secretary, Foreign Office 1946–49.

[5]D.B.F.P., 2nd Series, Vol. I Nos. 308 and 327. [6]See pp. 180–7.

Furthermore he saw all the Secret Intelligence reports which showed that undercover rearmament was being carried out on a wide scale in Germany, and that energetic steps were being taken by the militarists to encourage what Rumbold sarcastically called '"Wehrgeist", the precious heritage of Frederician Prussia'.[1] The anxiety which Hankey expressed on paper after a talk with Vansittart in November arose not so much from the increase in the Nazi vote as from the fact that virtually all German political parties were now committed to revision of the Treaty of Versailles.[2]

Hankey's forecast that he would have to go straight from the conference table at The Hague to the opening session of the naval conference, held on 21st January in the Royal Gallery of the House of Lords, proved accurate. But that gathering 'of many of the world's most illustrious statesmen' was in fact the outcome of long months of patient preliminary negotiation – the object of which was to undo the harm done by the breakdown of the Geneva Conference of 1927 and the furore produced by the Anglo-French Compromise of the following year, or at least avoid a repetition of those mishandled exchanges. The preliminary negotiations were conducted at several different levels and in various settings. We cannot here follow them in detail,[3] but some outline must be given of the two aspects in which Hankey was principally concerned – namely the discussions between the Admiralty and the Cabinet on the redefinition of British naval needs, and the Anglo-American negotiations designed to reduce, if not eliminate, the strident antagonisms aroused in 1927–28.

As to the former, it has already been remarked that from Beatty's retirement in 1927 until Admiral Chatfield became First Sea Lord in 1933 the Board of Admiralty became collectively one of the weakest ever to sit in the splendid Board Room which has witnessed so much of Britain's maritime history. Beatty's selection of Admiral Sir Charles Madden as his successor was influenced by his desire to heal the schism which had developed in the navy between his own and Admiral Jellicoe's supporters over the unsatisfactory outcome of the battle of Jutland in 1916; for Madden had been Jellicoe's Chief of Staff at that time. But Beatty also intended that Roger Keyes, an officer of his own

[1]D.B.F.P., 2nd Series, Vol. I, p. 569.

[2]Memo. of 21st Nov. 1930. Cab. 63/43.

[3]*O'Connor* contains an excellent short account of the preliminary political negotiations, though based only on American sources and published British works. The official British records were not open to students at the time this study was written.

school and the hero of the Zeebrugge raid of 1918, should succeed Madden after about two years. Unhappily Keyes's command of the Mediterranean fleet (1925–28) was not a success, and culminated in the thoroughly discreditable publicity produced by the quarrels of certain of his senior officers generally known as the '*Royal Oak* affair'. It thus came to pass that when Alexander became First Lord he declined to accept Keyes as his chief naval adviser because he considered him 'insufficiently amenable to political requirements'. Madden's term of office was therefore first extended, and in July 1930 Admiral Sir Frederick Field was appointed to succeed him.[1] Field was a colourless personality, and at Geneva in 1927 his physical and mental stamina had already been shown to be doubtful. Thus came into being the Board of Admiralty on whose shoulders must be placed the chief responsibility for the Invergordon mutiny of September 1931, which was to have such far-reaching consequences and to which further reference will be made later. Here we may remark that it seems most unlikely that the Bridgeman–Beatty régime, which had successfully defeated Churchill's onslaught on the Navy Estimates of 1925–26,[2] would have accepted the reduction in trade defence warships forced on their successors in 1929 in order to improve the prospects for the London conference. Hankey viewed the consequential weakening of the navy, and the drastic reduction of the industrial capacity on which it depended, with alarm; but he was powerless to do more than frustrate the emasculation of Belligerent Rights, to which reference was made earlier.

The principal proposals which the British Naval Staff agreed should be placed before the conference were, firstly, the reduction of capital ship tonnage and armament from the Washington Treaty figures of 35,000 tons and 16-inch guns to 25,000 tons and 12-inch guns; secondly the reduction of the cruiser total for the Royal Navy from the 70 insisted on in 1927 to 50; thirdly the reduction of the displacement of aircraft carriers from 27,000 to 25,000 tons; fourthly the limitation of displacement and armament of destroyers, which had been left unrestricted at Washington; and lastly the total abolition of submarines.[3] It was the reduction of cruiser strength which caused the gravest con-

[1]See Roskill, *Naval Policy*, I, pp. 45–8 regarding the succession to Beatty and pp. 559–60 regarding the *Royal Oak* affair.
[2]*ibid.* pp. 445–48.
[3]Draft Memorandum on proposals to be submitted to the naval conference of 27th Dec. 1929. Adm. 116/2717.

cern to the Navy, and Madden somewhat feebly asked the First Lord to tell the Prime Minister that 'our cruiser requirements are 70 . . . based on war experience and security. In view, however, of the apparently quiet conditions we have agreed to limit the number of cruisers to 50 for the period of the agreement viz. 7 years'.[1] His Deputy Chief of Naval Staff, Admiral W. W. Fisher,[2] felt more strongly on this issue, and wrote that in accepting the 50 figure the Board was 'assuming the most grave responsibility, and one which could only be justified on political and economic grounds for a strictly limited period'.[3] In fact by that time MacDonald and Alexander had irrevocably committed Britain to the total of 50 cruisers. On 8th January MacDonald announced that 'Britain, with the full consent of the Admiralty up to now, is prepared to make proposals which will mean considerable reductions in naval programmes *without in any degree impairing the security of the Empire*'. The italicised sentence certainly did not accord with the advice tendered by the Admiralty; but two days later Alexander stated that 'The Admiralty is prepared to reduce the number of cruisers from 70 to 50'.[4] The government also stopped work on two cruisers of the 1929–30 programme and delayed the construction of other ships. In the Upper House Lord Stanhope asked awkward questions about how the figure of 50 cruisers had been arrived at, whether the Admiralty had been relieved of its constitutional responsibilities for the defence of commerce, and what were the Government's intentions regarding the Singapore base. Lord Beatty was also soon on his feet to declaim against the cut in cruiser strength; but the debate revealed no very ardent opposition to the government's policy.[5]

The preliminary negotiations between Britain and the United States may be dated to the election of Herbert Hoover as President in the autumn of 1928, and his appointment of Henry L. Stimson[6] as Secretary

[1]Madden to Alexander 28th Nov. 1929. Adm. 116/2689.

[2]1875–1937. Director, Anti-Submarine Division 1917–18. Chief of Staff, Mediterranean Fleet 1919–22 and Atlantic Fleet 1922–24. Rear-Admiral, 1st Battle Squadron 1924–25. Fourth Sea Lord 1927–28. Deputy Chief of Naval Staff 1928–30. Second-in-Command, Mediterranean Fleet 1930–32. Commander-in-Chief of same 1932–36, and Commander-in-Chief, Portsmouth 1936–37.

[3]Minute of 4th Jan. 1930. Adm. 116/2689.

[4]*Daily Telegraph* 8th and 10th Jan. 1930 respectively.

[5]Parl. Deb., Lords, Vol. 75, Cols. 1467–74.

[6]1867–1950. American lawyer and politician (Rep.). Secretary of War under President Taft 1911–13. Governor-General Philippine Islands, 1927–29. Secretary of State 1929–33. Chairman, American delegation to London Naval Conference

of State. But the General Board of the U.S. Navy Department, 'the big Navy lobby' and the usual strident anti-British elements made any diminution of American insistence on 'parity' with Britain in the classes of warship left unrestricted by the Washington Treaty, and any reduction in the demand for 23 big cruisers with 8-inch guns delicate issues for the administration. In February 1929 the Cruiser Bill, providing for the construction of fifteen big ships of that class and one aircraft carrier became law. But with the inauguration of President Hoover in March and the return of Labour to power in England in June the atmosphere changed on both sides of the Atlantic, and the arrival of General Charles G. Dawes (with the rank of ambassador) to open conversations with MacDonald in August was widely welcomed. Among politicians Churchill, who had so strenuously opposed the naval building programmes while Chancellor of the Exchequer, was almost alone in publicly declaiming against the granting of 'parity' to the U.S.A. Though the idea of introducing the notorious 'yardstick' for equating the value of ships of different size, armament and age, first propounded by Hugh Gibson in April 1929,[1] proved totally impractical, and MacDonald's first suggestions regarding the two countries' cruiser strength obviously did not provide parity,[2] some progress towards a compromise was made, and on 28th September MacDonald sailed for America. Though his talks with Hoover produced no concrete results – Hankey having successfully eliminated all mention of Freedom of the Seas – their joint communiqué stating that 'in a new and reinforced sense' not only was 'war between the two governments unthinkable', but that 'distrusts and suspicions must cease to influence our national policies' was well received[3]; and the visit was a great psychological success. On 7th October the British government issued

1930 and General Disarmament Conference 1932. Secretary of War under Presidents Roosevelt and Truman 1940–45.

[1] *O'Connor*, pp. 25–28.

[2] This was as follows, for ships built or projected:—

| | *Britain* | *U.S.A.* |
|---|---|---|
| 8 inch | 18 – 176,800 tons | 23 – 230,000 tons |
| 7.5 inch | 4 – 29,400 tons | NIL |
| 6 inch | 40 – 179,270 tons | 10 – 70,500 tons |
| Totals | 62 – 385,470 tons | 33 – 300,500 tons |

[3] *Daily Telegraph* 10th Oct. 1929.

invitations to France, Italy, Japan and the U.S.A. to meet in London in the following January.

The auguries were not good. A wide gulf existed between the British and American computations of their current needs; Japan was determined that the 5:5:3 Washington Treaty ratio for capital ships should not, as the Americans desired, be applied to smaller vessels; while Italy insisted on parity with France, which the latter refused to consider. Such was, in brief outline, the situation when Hankey returned to London on 20th January. Fortunately he had put in hand the basic preparations for the conference before leaving for The Hague,[1] and had arranged for two of his Assistant Secretaries, Wing-Commander E. J. Hodsoll[2] and Commander L. E. H. Maund,[3] to act as British Secretaries. He was concerned at the decision to hold the conference, after the inaugural session, in St. James's Palace, where there was no central heating. 'Foreign delegates', he wrote, 'are apt to be rather sensitive to the lower temperatures in which business is usually conducted in this country'. But when the decision was confirmed he took the precaution of having electric heaters installed.[4] Towards the end of 1929 he also organised the new series of documents in which the deliberations of the conference were to be recorded, and their distribution. The main L.N.C. series was to go to all delegations, L.N.C.(E) only to British Commonwealth delegates, and L.N.C.(B) only to the British; later he added the (D) series to record the discussions held by Heads of Delegations and the (F) series to cover talks with the French. The (D) series conversations took place at 10 Downing Street, in MacDonald's room at the House of Commons or at Chequers as might be most convenient. To give only one example of the scale of the secretarial work no less than 28 meetings were recorded in the (D)

[1]Hankey to A. Flint, Admiralty, and to other departments 11th Dec. 1929. Adm. 116/2717.

[2]See p. 477, *note*.

[3]Later Rear-Admiral Loben E. H. Maund (1892–1957). Naval Assistant Secretary, Cabinet Office 1928–31. Commanded Combined Operations Development Centre 1939 and H.M.S. *Ark Royal* 1941. Director of Combined Operations, Middle East and India 1942–43. Rear-Admiral Landing Ships and Craft 1944–45. One of the few British officers to stress the vital importance of the specialised techniques of amphibious warfare prior to World War II.

[4]L.N.C.(1) of 25th Nov. 1929. Cab. 29/107. Copies of most of the London Conference papers are also to be found in the Admiralty's records, often with interesting minutes attached. See Adm. 116/2717 in this case, and Adm. 116/2741–2745 for later meetings.

Procession for the installation of the Knights Grand Cross of the Order of the Bath, Westminster Abbey, May 1928. Hankey on extreme right

The Imperial Conference 1930. Hankey in back row directly behind Ramsay MacDonald

King George V opening the London Naval Conference in the Royal Gallery, House of Lords, 21st January 1930
*Left to right*: Lord Lewisham, M. Briand, – ? –, M. Tardieu, Hankey, MacDonald, King George, Arthur Henderson, W. Wedgwood Benn

The London Naval Conference 1930. British Empire and Commonwealth delegates
*Back row*) Philippe Roy (Canada), J. E. Fenton (Australia), C. te Water (South Africa), T. M. Wilford (New Zealand), T. A. Smiddy (Irish Free State), Sir A. Chatterjee (India), Hankey (Secretary-General)
*Seated*) A. V. Alexander (First Lord of the Admiralty), Arthur Henderson (Foreign Secretary), Ramsay MacDonald (Prime Minister of Britain), W. Wedgwood Benn (Secretary of State for India), J. L. Ralston (Canada)

series during the conference. In addition to the formally kept proceedings mentioned above Hankey also had to record, and sometimes actually arranged, informal talks between the principal delegates. These he recorded in his normal manner but added the cautionary statement that they did 'not bear any official character as a Conference Document and should not be quoted'. Delegates were 'invited to treat them with the strictest confidence'.[1]

Meetings between the British and Commonwealth delegates began early in December 1929 with MacDonald in the chair, and a Departmental Organisation Committee was then formed under Hankey's chairmanship (recorded in the N.C.(O) series). The object of these meetings was of course to thrash out a common British policy; and that was not made easier by the fact that Australia and New Zealand, ever conscious of their dependence on sea communications, were as mistrustful of the proposed reduction of British cruiser strength as they had disliked the Labour Government's attitude towards the Singapore base. At one time there was even talk of Australia demanding, and building, a separate quota of cruisers; but in the end that came to nothing. Hankey appealed – not very successfully – to delegates to limit the length of their speeches, and at the end of the month the draft 'Proposals to be submitted by His Majesty's Government' to the conference were agreed.[2]

At the first Plenary Meeting, after the King's speech of welcome, Stimson proposed and André Tardieu, the French Premier, seconded a motion that MacDonald should be appointed chairman. The fact that this had been arranged beforehand without consulting the Italians or Japanese, and so would cause offence to those countries' delegates was overlooked. Furthermore the same two countries had ignored the British request that naval officers, though they could serve on the Committee of Experts and act as 'Advisers' to their delegations, should not be accorded the status of delegates.[3] This request was based on the widespread view that the breakdown at Geneva in 1927 had been

[1]All the London Conference papers are in Cab. 29/117–135. The last number contains Hankey's notes on unofficial meetings. See for example that of 24th Jan. 1930 with note by Hankey. Copy also in Adm. 116/2744.

[2]Dated 27th Dec. 1929. It consisted of 35 pages of printed foolscap. Cab. 27/117. It also became C.P. 5(30).

[3]Admiral Giuseppi Sirianni, Minister for the Navy, and Admiral Alfredo Acton, a Senator, were among the Italian delegates; and Admiral Takeshi Takarabe, the Minister of Marine, was a Japanese delegate.

chiefly attributable to the Admirals – which now appears a considerable over-simplification.

The second Plenary Session took place at St. James's Palace on 23rd January,[1] and it was then that Dino Grandi,[2] the Italian Foreign Minister and senior delegate, formally proposed that Hankey should be Secretary-General. Reijiro Wakatsuki, the senior Japanese delegate and a member of the House of Peers, seconded the motion, which was carried unanimously. Various delegates (but not Stimson) then made statements defining the attitude and needs of their countries. That by Tardieu was extremely long-winded and evidently irritated Hankey; while Grandi's at once placed the fundamental cleavage between France and Italy in the foreground of the conference's deliberations. MacDonald then attempted to summarise the issues which faced the delegates. Referring to Italy's insistence on parity with France, he said that 'to build up a navy merely upon need is an exceedingly foolish undertaking', and that the essential consideration was 'how far there is a threat of the deprivation of those needs'. That of course took the conference right back to the old question of the link between disarmament and the search for security, which had plagued the League's Preparatory Commission ever since its inception. MacDonald also put to the conference what were in fact Hankey's proposals regarding procedure. Apart from the Plenary Sessions, which would be called as necessary to review the recommendations of the various subsidiary bodies, a 'Working Committee' was to be formed from members of the various delegations; and it would throw off sub-committees to handle particular subjects.[3] At the end of January a 'First Committee' was formed, initially under MacDonald and later under Alexander's chairmanship, to consider questions on the agenda[4]; and it appointed a 'Committee of Experts' to handle technical matters and a 'Committee of Jurists' to draft legal documents such as those governing the use of submarines in war. The Committee of Experts held 19 meetings between early February and mid-April.[5]

[1]Cab. 29/119.

[2]1895– . Italian politician. (Fascist.) Took part in 'March on Rome' 1922 and became member of Fascist Grand Council. Foreign Minister 1929–32. Ambassador at London 1932–39. Minister of Justice and President of Fascist Chamber 1939–43. July 1943 voted an order for approach to Britain and for restoration of the King's power. Condemned to death by the neo-Fascist rump at Verona 1944. Retired from politics after liberation of Italy.

[3]L.N.C. 2nd Meeting. Cab. 29/119. [4]Cab. 29/123. [5]Cab. 29/124–125.

Though no one who took part in the conference ever questioned the efficiency of Hankey's secretarial arrangements, his system did amass a veritable mountain of paper. Furthermore the actual negotiations did not begin until, after the second Plenary Session, Hankey organised a series of formal and informal talks between the various delegations with the object of settling the agenda. It was finally divided into 'General Questions' and 'Special Questions', which between them covered the whole field of naval limitation both on matters of principle (e.g. limitation by 'global tonnage' or by 'categories') and on matters of detail (e.g. listing the ships which were not limited by the Washington Treaty, and their armaments).

The third Plenary Session took place on 30th January,[1] and each nation's delegates then made speeches reaffirming their already well-known preferences and their particular problems. The reluctance of delegates to offer concessions or suggest compromises re-emphasised the handicap of holding such meetings in the full glare of publicity. Meanwhile the American delegation was formulating a plan to be presented to the other nations, and on 5th February their proposals – except those concerning capital ships – were communicated to the British and Japanese.[2] The Americans categorically rejected the Japanese demand for a 10:10:7 ratio in cruisers. On 7th the British proposals, referred to earlier, were released somewhat hastily as a result of Stimson issuing a statement about cruiser ratios at very short notice. His excuse was that the documents had already got into the hands of a journalist; but to the British it appeared that 'the Americans had stolen a march on us and we had to look after our own public opinion'. Hankey gave Tom Jones the story of 'what had happened behind the scenes', and how the chief result of Stimson's precipitancy had been to infuriate Tardieu because the French delegates had not been given a copy of the American statement, which appeared to them, quite wrongly, to have been 'rigged up' between the Americans and the British.[3]

Despite this flurry British and American conversations began on 11th, and continued even after a financial crisis had caused the fall of the French government on 17th and necessitated the conference adjourning. The outcome was a preliminary accord by which the

[1]L.N.C. 3rd Meeting. Cab. 29/119. [2]*O'Connor*, pp. 69–72.
[3]See Jones's diary for 7th Feb. 1930. *Middlemas*, II, p. 243. *O'Connor*, p. 72 glosses the effects of Stimson's action on the British and French delegates.

Americans dropped their demand for a new battleship and accepted a total of only 18 8-inch gun cruisers in return for the reduction of the British total in that class from 70 to 50 ships. Destroyer and submarine tonnages were left open pending knowledge of French and Japanese demands. After six months of negotiations and one month of conference Britain and America had virtually eliminated their differences. But a very great deal still remained unsettled; and negotiations between the U.S.A. and Japan were 'complex, difficult and exasperating'.[1] Not until MacDonald and Stimson had threatened to sign a two-power treaty was a compromise accepted by the Japanese. It gave them 70% in 8-inch cruisers, 60% in 6-inch cruisers, 70% in destroyers and parity in submarines. On 9th April a three-power treaty became a reality, and the conference then concentrated on trying to solve the problems common to all five powers.

At the fourth Plenary Session on 11th February each delegation gave its views on the submarine problem. Alexander pressed hard for total abolition, and Stimson supported him. The French totally opposed such a far-reaching measure; the Italian delegates accepted abolition in principle, and in any case both they and the Japanese were prepared to sign an agreement restricting the use of such vessels in war.[2] The issue was passed to the First Committee, which was requested to report on the resolutions put forward by France and the U.S.A. These latter were referred to the Committees of Experts and Jurists; but the First Committee failed to reach agreement on abolition, and the conference ended with the issue unresolved. The submarine question thus remained exactly where the Washington Conference had left it eight years earlier – except that a new Declaration restricting the use of submarines clarified and strengthened the somewhat vague 'Root Resolutions' of 1922. Limitation of the size and armament of destroyers produced less difficulty, as did the tonnage of 'special vessels', which came within no regular category of warship, allowed to each nation. Rules for the disposal of ships which were to be struck off the active fleets, and for the age at which ships became replaceable under the treaty, were also accepted fairly easily.

But the large tonnage of cruisers and smaller warships claimed by France staggered the British delegation. The First Sea Lord described them as 'impossible to contemplate' and 'a demand for expansion

[1] *O'Connor*, p. 77.
[2] L.N.C. 4th Meeting. Cab. 29/119.

rather than reduction'[1]; and when MacDonald saw the French schedule he asked 'How could such a figure be brought to a Disarmament Conference Committee?' Acceptance of it would, he declared, 'mean that this was a Military not a Disarmament Conference'.[2] Briand then restated the French position, which was of course profoundly influenced by the long-standing absence of any military guarantee by Britain and the U.S.A.; and he complained, with good reason, that no statement of the tonnage asked for by Italy had ever been placed before the conference. By the end of March MacDonald was brought face to face with the virtual certainty that a Five Power Treaty could not be achieved.[3] Discussions about a 'Mediterranean Locarno', or a consultative pact covering that area, came to nothing in face of American unwillingness to participate and French insistence that it would add nothing to the provisions incorporated in the League Covenant. A personal appeal by MacDonald to Grandi to 'take his courage in both hands' and 'make some further contribution' towards agreement with France proved equally fruitless.[4] On 10th April negotiations to bring France and Italy together were conclusively abandoned. 'The Five Power Treaty', writes O'Connor, 'was a victim of Italian pride, French fears, British caution and American isolation'.[5]

The drafting of a Three Power Treaty was now placed in the hands of a committee chaired by Dwight Morrow,[6] which laboured incessantly from 13th to 21st April. During that period the 5th Plenary Session took place to approve reports by the First Committee and the Committee of Experts which, according to MacDonald, furnished the 'raw material' for the treaty.[7] The 6th and final Plenary Session took place on 22nd. MacDonald then made claims some of which, in the perspective of history, seem hard to justify. 'The Conference', he said, 'has done great work . . .'; 'We have secured a Three Power Agreement on building programmes – no mean or unimportant achievement . . .'; 'We have proved how . . . the menace of arms can be removed by

[1]L.N.C.(E) 18. Cab. 29/134. [2]L.N.C.(D) 15. Cab. 29/121 of 12th March 1930.
[3]L.N.C.(D) 16. of 24th March 1930. *ibid.*
[4]Unofficial conversation MacDonald–Grandi on 24th March. Cab. 29/135.
[5]*op. cit.* p. 103.
[6]1873–1931. American lawyer and diplomat. Adviser to Allied Maritime Transport Council 1918. Chairman, President Coolidge's Aircraft Board 1925. Ambassador to Mexico 1927. Delegate to Pan-American Conference 1928 and London Naval Conference 1930.
[7]L.N.C. 5th of 14th April 1930. Cab. 29/119.

treaties . . .'.[1] More to the point was the glowing tribute he paid to Hankey, who had of course, been under tremendous strain ever since 21st January. 'You do not know Sir Maurice Hankey' MacDonald told the assembled delegates. 'You meet him at International Conferences. I meet him every day. All the virtues and the resource and the indispensableness [sic] which Sir Maurice shows you when you meet him at international conferences occasionally, he shows to me every hour of the day. There is no man with whom I have come into personal relationship who has impressed me more with his extraordinary capacity to yield public service than my friend Sir Maurice Hankey . . .'.[2] He then adjourned the conference, but that same day he followed up his public praise of the Secretary-General with a personal tribute.

*MacDonald to Hankey. 10 Downing Street. 22nd April 1930.* Holograph
My dear Hankey,

I said a few imperfect things about you to-day, but I must put down on paper an expression of my admiration and gratitude for your work. I do not know what we should have done without you. You were the master engineer. I shall never forget your services, given not only with wonderful ability but with whole-hearted devotion.

Believe me to be

Yours very sincerely

Eight days later the arrival of the Hankeys' first grandchild, a daughter born to Ursula and John Benn, brought them as much happiness as the reasonably successful conclusion of the naval conference brought them relief.

MacDonald also wrote at length to the King repeating in the main the claims he made at the final session. He described the attitude of the French and Italians as 'deplorable' and demanding 'much patience and delicate handling to prevent an angry and an open rupture'. He protested strongly against French attempts to place Britain in a position of having to act 'mechanically and without freedom of judgement should trouble arise in Europe'. But none the less he claimed that 'the results of the Conference will be of great benefit if they are allowed to mature, and one of these will be our improved relations with the

[1]L.N.C. 6th of 22nd April. *ibid.* The terms of the London Treaty were summarised in Cmd. 3547 of 15th April 1930. The treaty is printed in full in *O'Connor*.
[2]Cab. 29/119.

United States'. The King graciously replied congratulating his Prime Minister on the results achieved by his 'untiring labours, patience and tact'.[1]

We may conclude this brief summary of the first London Naval Conference with some remarks on the effects it had on the Royal Navy. Ever since 1919, when the inevitable post-war cuts were imposed, morale in that service had been uneven. The 'Geddes Axe', whereby scores of officers were discharged with pitifully small bounties, left a bitter taste; pressure for economies all along the line was powerful, especially in Churchill's time as Chancellor; the introduction of a reduced scale of pay in 1925 had the result that ratings doing identical jobs were receiving different emoluments – which was not conducive to contentment; cuts in fuel and ammunition allowances reduced sea time and training exercises; and in one case, that of Roger Keyes's term as C-in-C, Mediterranean, the conduct of the high command certainly left something to be desired. For the men of a fighting service to be contented they need not only the conviction that they are employed on and dedicated to a worthwhile task – such as may reconcile them to long separations from wives and families even in peace time – but knowledge that their equipment is reasonably modern and capable of fulfilling the demands which will fall on it in war. The fact that throughout the 1920s many of the British navy's ships and much of their equipment deteriorated for lack of modernisation was not conducive to high morale. The Bridgeman–Beatty régime fought hard, and with some success, against these trends. Their successors were more amenable to the pressure exerted by the politicians, and the London Treaty was widely regarded in the fleet as yet another example of the wide gulf that divided the Board Room in Whitehall from the officers and men serving afloat. A bitter harvest was to be reaped 27 months later from that failure in communication.

In the sphere of international politics it is true that the London conference damped down Anglo-American rivalry, and a degree of stability in the relative naval strength of the three principal powers was achieved for a period of five years. No one could of course foresee that the same period was to produce the rise to power of Hitler in Germany – though danger signals were certainly flying in 1930, as had been recognised in some British circles. But, as O'Connor has remarked,

[1]MacDonald to the King, holograph, 12th April 1930 and reply by the King of 13th. RA GV G2258/18 and /19.

The London Conference 'put the control of weapons in the wrong sequence on the road to security'. The choice lay between a world order based on the moral force of the Kellogg–Briand Pact or on the military clauses of the League Covenant. 'The equilibrium of naval power created at London', the same historian concludes, 'was not only deceptive, but it was created on an illusory foundation'.

As to Hankey's part, we have often remarked on his affection for and concern with the well-being of the British naval service; and the sincerity of those sentiments cannot be disputed. But in 1930, a year throughout which he was working at tremendous pressure, he does seem to have concentrated all his powers of organisation and of persuasion on reaching an agreement – at almost any price. His papers and diary contain no sign whatever of awareness both of the immediate and of the longer term consequences of the agglomeration of compromises reached in order to achieve a treaty. We have already noted the weakness of the contemporary Board of Admiralty; but Hankey seems never to have used his close relations with that body and with the Chiefs of Staff Committee to give any warning of the dangers which strewed the road along which MacDonald and his colleagues were striding with a fixity of purpose which blinded them to other problems and considerations. When the conference was over the Board of Admiralty merely took note of the First Lord's statement that the government appreciated 'the valuable assistance' rendered by his department during the conference[1]; and the Naval Staff stated that, while they did not 'recede from the position that 70 cruisers represent the minimum for our full defence requirements . . . under international conditions to-day, however, a number of 50 cruisers has been accepted for a strictly limited period . . .'.[2] MacDonald directed that this memorandum was to be circulated to the Dominions.

Soon after the end of the conference the effects on British commitments in Europe and the Far East were reviewed by the Admiralty. Their conclusion was that the treaty 'will result in an increase in the relative strengths of the U.S.A. and Japan as compared with us. French and Italian programmes also foreshadow considerable increases. Great Britain is reducing her strength as compared with the others'.[3] Here in a nutshell were stated the developments which were to result in Hankey, as Chairman of the Defence Requirements Sub-Committee

[1]Board Minute 2702. Adm. 167/81. [2]Memo. of 1st Dec. 1931. Adm. 167/84.
[3]Adm. 1/8741.

of 1933, having to strive hard to undo most of what had been accomplished three years earlier. It is only fair to add that the treaty also came under heavy fire in naval circles in America, particularly during the hearings before the Senate Committees on Foreign Relations and on Naval Affairs.[1] Of all the delegations to the conference only the Italians received the unqualified approval of their national Press, and of the great majority of their countrymen. In the British Parliament the attack on the treaty was led in the House of Lords by Carson and Bridgeman, both former First Lords, supported by Admirals Jellicoe and Beatty, both former First Sea Lords; in the Commons by Churchill.[2] But on 24th July the Commons approved the treaty. Despite bitter opposition in Japan, and a rough passage for Hoover's administration, ratifications were deposited in London on 27th October 1930. Early in the following year Henderson and Alexander visited Rome and Paris to try and bring Italy and France together. Though their report claimed that 'complete agreement' had been achieved, in fact those countries only accepted Part III of the London Treaty – and subject to substantial qualifications.[3] And the announcement by the German government of the building of three 'pocket battleships' in 1931–34 rang alarm bells in all the capitals of western Europe. Clearly the dreaded 'naval building race' had not been called off – as MacDonald had claimed.

Early in May 1930 Vansittart circulated a paper which Hankey had printed for the C.I.D. It foretold very accurately the probable trend of events in Europe, including the new claims for which Germany was likely to press.[4] A few months later Hankey discussed these matters with Vansittart, and it seems that their close accord on the threat presented by Nazi Germany dates to this time. Hankey's 'note' on this conversation shows that his chief concern was the continuation of the self-perpetuating Ten Year Rule of July 1928, which he regarded as 'living in a fool's paradise'. 'Germany', he went on, 'could rearm comparatively quickly. Her army was small, but almost certainly efficient . . . Her manufacturing industry was ample to produce material [a statement almost certainly derived from the reports of the Industrial Intelligence Centre]. Once she was armed no-one could say that

[1] *O'Connor*, pp. 109–14.

[2] Parl. Deb., Lords, Vol. 77, Cols. 436–51 and Commons, Vol. 238, Cols. 2098–2110.

[3] D.B.F.P., 2nd Series, Vol. I, No. 299. Also published as Cmd. 3812.

[4] C.I.D. 991B of 1st May 1930. Cab. 4/19. See also D.B.F.P., 2nd Series, Vol. I, p. 501, *note*.

stability existed any longer in Europe . . .'. Vansittart evidently agreed with Hankey's anxieties. He said that the Foreign Office had not 'as an office' endorsed 'the ten-year assumption this year',[1] and he would press ahead with revising and bringing up to date the paper of the previous year in which he had warned that 'the old Adam' of militarism was again raising its ugly head in Germany. Hankey agreed to hold his hand until the new paper was ready, and would then tackle the Prime Minister about the Ten Year Rule. If Vansittart's paper was delayed he would 'take independent action'.[2] Thus began Hankey's campaign to get the 'miserable Ten Year Rule' cancelled.

Only a week after the signature of the London Treaty Hankey had to turn his hand to preparing the Chiefs of Staff Committee's Fifth Annual Review, which had to be circulated well in advance of the Imperial Conference fixed to take place in October. A large amount of material had been sent to Whitehall Gardens by the departments concerned, including the Foreign and Colonial Offices,[3] and the resultant document summarised the effect which the London Treaty would have on all aspects of defence. The picture drawn was certainly not alarmist, though a strong undercurrent of anxiety about such issues as the Singapore base and the continuation of the Ten Year Rule can be detected in it.[4]

While the London conference was actually sitting Hankey was troubled by the resurrection of another of his most notorious bugbears – namely the proposal for a Channel Tunnel, which had been dormant since 1924. After another prolonged enquiry the Home Defence Sub-Committee produced a report in May. Then the Chiefs of Staff went into action – no doubt briefed by Hankey, who produced a paper of his own on the subject for the C.I.D.[5] On 1st June Hankey wrote to Robin that he had killed a scheme which he disliked almost as much as Freedom of the Seas 'with the knife of common sense', having employed the weapon of 'lack of economic attractiveness' rather than the military arguments. MacDonald, he said, had come round to his view because 'French intransigence at the Naval Conference' had made

[1]It was however reaffirmed at the 249th meeting of the C.I.D. on 4th June 1930. Cab. 2/5.

[2]'Note of a conversation with Sir Robert Vansittart, November 21st 1930'. Cab. 21/372.

[3]C.I.D. 1008B of 29th July 1930. Cab. 4/20. [4]C.I.D. 1009B. *ibid.*

[5]C.I.D. 176A is the Chiefs of Staff's report. Hankey's paper is C.I.D. 174A.

him determined not 'to be tied to the leg' of that nation.[1] The announcement to Parliament was made on 5th, and the full arguments were published later as a Command Paper.[2]

Meanwhile Hankey and Adeline had set off to Vienna for their long-promised stay at the embassy as guests of Sir Eric and Lady Phipps. The lovely and still unspoilt city enchanted Hankey, and it was typical that his visit should have been divided between arduous sight-seeing and discussions on international politics.[3] The latter included the threat of an 'Anschluss' between Germany and Austria, which had figured in Vansittart's survey of probable developments. Hankey and Eric Phipps always saw eye to eye on the realities of the Nazi movement, and some of the material used by Vansittart unquestionably originated in the Vienna embassy.

From Vienna the Hankeys went on to St. Anton-am-Arlberg for a week in his beloved mountains, which he climbed as energetically as on his first visit to the Alps nearly 30 years earlier. When they arrived home on 19th Hankey learnt that Tom Jones had just accepted the Secretaryship of the Pilgrim Trust, and had resigned as his Deputy.[4] Rupert Howorth was his natural successor at Whitehall Gardens, and was at once appointed as such. No letters of appreciation seem to have passed between Jones and Hankey to mark the end of nearly 14 years of close association. But they had never been really intimate friends, and for some years they had clearly been moving apart on political and defence issues.[5]

As each month of 1930 passed with the economic situation deteriorating and unemployment rising Hankey turned his mind to the internal state of the nation, and in September he put his views on paper. His chief anxiety evidently lay in the spread of what he called 'national demoralisation' – to which he considered that unemployment contributed greatly. He had no quick-acting or simple panacea to offer, but supported the idea of holding a 'Conference of Parties' to decide the broad principles of the policy to be adopted; and he evidently hoped that would lead to the formation of a National Government. He attacked the long-standing emphasis on 'maintaining the standard of living', and

[1]To Robin Hankey 1st June 1930.

[2]Parl. Deb., Commons, Vol. 239, Cols. 2386–7. Also Cmd. 3591.

[3]To Robin Hankey from St. Anton-am-Arlberg 14th June 1930.

[4]*Middlemas*, II, p. 266.

[5]In contrast see Howorth's warm letter of 12th Aug. 1930 to Jones. *ibid.* p. 272.

urged that the nation should be told 'quite plainly how serious is the [industrial] competition with which we are faced'. All new expenditure on social services, except where it contributed to reducing unemployment, should be stopped 'for a term', and the abuses in the National Insurance scheme, which he believed to be widespread, investigated and checked. By a 'sustained propaganda' campaign he wanted to convince the people that they had 'to pull in their belts' and 'reduce expenditure on luxuries . . . until we have recovered our economic position'. What he called 'reconditioning the people' should be furthered by inaugurating, after the matter had been investigated by the Economy Advisory Council, a 'national health campaign'. Finally he wanted to see British agriculture pulled out of the depression which afflicted it – presumably by clapping duties on imported food; domestic employment he hoped to see 'placed on a sounder footing' (which he had often stressed before), and lastly the question of 'filling the ranks of the army' should be tackled.[1] But none of these proposals was at all likely to appeal to a Labour government.

Preparations for the 1930 Imperial Conference had actually begun as long ago as 24th February, when MacDonald formed a Cabinet Policy Committee under his own chairmanship, and with Hankey as secretary. At the first meeting the committee agreed that the Dominions should be warned that economic questions, not excluding 'the effects of preference, cartels etc.' would be discussed. In other words the government was veering towards some measure of protection for British industry.[2] Then there was an interval while the Naval Conference was in session, and the Policy Committee did not meet again until 7th May, when Foreign Policy and Defence were discussed. It was agreed that, as in 1926, the chairman of the C.I.D. and of the C.O.S. Sub-Committee should make agreed statements to the conference, but that the C.O.S.'s Annual Review was not to be sent to the Dominions prior to the conference. The Singapore base question was to be held up until the Cabinet had made a final decision on its future. Meetings of the Policy Committee then continued fairly regularly until 3rd October, and decisions were taken about the despatch of papers to the Dominions on such subjects as naval policy and disarmament.[3]

Meanwhile a Foreign Policy and Defence Sub-Committee of the C.I.D. had been formed, and met for the first time on 21st March.

[1]Memo. of 19th Sept. 1930. Cab. 63/43. [2]Cab. 32/70.
[3]The Policy Committee held in all 13 meetings. Cab. 32/70.

Hankey was chairman of this body, which agreed initially on the manner in which the important issues referred to it should be handled. It did not meet again until 22nd September, and although it rendered an Interim Report to the Cabinet Policy Committee, and the 18 papers in the I.C.(FD) series are a mine of information on every aspect of defence, it never made a final report.[1] The reason probably was that the subjects dealt with all reached the Cabinet elsehow – most of them through the deliberations of the C.I.D. itself. For example in July the Foreign Office produced an admirable survey of British commitments in the light of the current foreign policy of the government, and Hankey sent MacDonald an advance copy saying that he proposed to use it to provide material for discussion by the Imperial Conference.[2] It was considered by the C.I.D. at the end of September and approved.[3] Then, at Hankey's instigation, the Chiefs of Staff drew the Prime Minister's attention to the need to treat Imperial Defence 'in a complete, integrated manner', and not to expect Britain alone 'to shoulder the bulk of responsibility . . . in a major war'. They drafted Resolutions urging 'collective responsibility' for defence which they wanted to submit to the conference.[4] The influence of Air Power on Imperial Defence was also reviewed, and here Hankey went a good way towards meeting the views which Trenchard had pressed on him earlier and was still urging.[5] On the maritime side Hankey consulted his old friend Richmond, whose interest in naval affairs had not diminished with his approaching retirement from the navy, though he was in very bad odour with the Admiralty for publishing in *The Times* a series of articles advocating a drastic reduction in the size and armament of capital ships.[6] Towards the end of July Hankey produced and circulated a comprehensive survey of Imperial Defence Policy.[7] The opposing field of disarmament was not, of course, being neglected at this

[1]Cab. 32/77.
[2]F.O. Memo. of 1st July and Hankey to MacDonald 16th Sept. 1930. Cab. 21/368.
[3]C.I.D. 1009B and 250th meeting of C.I.D. on 29th Sept. 1930. Cab. 2/5.
[4]C.O.S. Memo. of 3rd Oct. 1930. Cab. 21/368.
[5]C.I.D. 1005B of 17th July 1930. Cab. 4/20.
[6]Hankey to Richmond 16th July 1930. N.M.M. (R.I.C.7/5) and Richmond to Hankey 28th Oct. 1930. See also A. J. Marder, *Portrait of an Admiral* (Cape, 1952), pp. 29–31. Richmond did not actually retire until 1st April 1931. The articles in *The Times* entitled 'Smaller Navies' were published on 21st and 22nd Nov. 1929 shortly before the London Naval Conference.
[7]C.I.D. 1008B of 29th July 1930.

time, and in September the C.I.D. also reviewed the Draft Disarmament Convention, in which various forms of limitation of armaments, including by budgetary expenditure, were put forward. The C.I.D. referred this matter to a sub-committee under Henderson.[1] In the same month Hankey circulated another paper stressing that rearmament could relieve unemployment as well as insure the country against the dangers which he saw gathering in Europe and the Far East. France, he pointed out in another paper on the same subject written nine months later, had the highest expenditure on armaments of any European country and the lowest unemployment.[2] But in the prevailing climate of political and public opinion such arguments fell on deaf ears.

The Imperial Conference opened at 10 Downing Street on 1st October, with MacDonald in the chair and all the Dominions except the Irish Free State represented by their Prime Ministers.[3] Hankey and Batterbee served as secretaries. In all 28 meetings took place, and Hankey was present at all of them. His usual procedure was followed – for example by referring naval, military and air policy to a Committee of Experts drawn from the fighting services, and economic questions to another body of specialists.[4] At the 12th meeting on 31st October the draft of the Statute of Westminster Bill, which was to carry the evolution of Empire into Commonwealth a stage further, was discussed for the first time; and at the 17th meeting the conference agreed to accept the reluctant decision of the British government that the Singapore base should not be wholly cancelled, though expenditure was to be postponed as far as possible during the next five years.[5] Snowden took the chair at the Singapore Base Committee, and although Scullin of Australia[6] and Forbes of New Zealand[7] protested against the

[1]250th C.I.D. Item 3. Cab. 2/5.

[2]Memos. of 19th Sept. 1930 and 19th June 1931. Cab. 63/43 and /44 respectively.

[3]These were R. B. Bennett (Canada): J. H. Scullin (Australia): G. W. Forbes (New Zealand): J. B. M. Hertzog (Union of South Africa) and Sir R. Squires (Newfoundland). Mr. P. Gilligan, Minister for External Affairs represented the Irish Free State, and Mr. W. Wedgwood Benn, Secretary of State for India, represented India and Burma.

[4]1st and 10th Meetings of Imperial Conference 1930. Cab. 32/79.

[5]12th and 17th Meetings held on 31st Oct and 4th Nov. 1930. Cab. 32/79.

[6]James H. Scullin. (1876–1953). Australian politician (Lab.). Leader of Parliamentary Labour Party 1928–35. Prime Minister and Minister of Industry 1929–31.

[7]George W. Forbes (1869–1947). New Zealand politician (Lib., then Reform). Minister of Lands and Agriculture 1928–30, and of Finance and Customs 1930–31. Prime Minister (Coalition) and Minister of External Affairs 1930–35. Also under-

government's decision the dour Chancellor gave them no chance for argument, but virtually presented them with a *fait accompli*. It is not surprising that this body met only once.[1]

At the main conference the later meetings produced a flurry over the British attitude towards the introduction of some measure of Imperial Preference. Here again Snowden was the chief stumbling block, and after lengthy discussions had proved futile R. B. Bennett, the Prime Minister of Canada,[2] boldly proposed that a 10% increase of duties should be levied on all goods imported from outside the Empire. Though this proposal stood no chance of acceptance by the British government it did provide the opportunity for the Conservatives to turn it to political advantage.[3] Hankey was very sympathetic towards any measure of closer co-operation and integration within the economic field as well as that of defence; and Baldwin's acceptance of the substance of Bennett's proposal may be said to mark the first step towards the Ottawa Conference of 1932.

In the autumn of 1930 the old questions of maritime Belligerent Rights and of the desirability of including some relaxation of British claims in that respect in a new Arbitration Treaty with the U.S.A. was resurrected while the Imperial Conference was in session, and Henderson seems to have been attracted by the idea. At any rate Hankey wrote to him giving the whole previous history and setting out what he regarded as the dangers of such a policy – using the same arguments as in 1927–28. He told the Foreign Secretary that he had 'seen more than one Government rather badly split' by these issues, and would not be surprised if the same happened to the Imperial Conference. Nor did he believe that the Americans were seriously interested in the subject – as Stimson had not raised it at the recent naval conference. He therefore tactfully pressed the Foreign Secretary not to embroil the govern-

took offices of Railways, Attorney-General and Native Affairs for various periods while Prime Minister.

[1] On 16th Oct. 1930. Cab. 32/91. The Committee's report is E(30)36 of 27th Oct 1930. *ibid.*

[2] 1st Viscount Bennett 1941 (1870–1947). Canadian lawyer and politician (Cons.). Minister of Justice and Attorney-General 1921. Minister of Finance 1926 and 1930. Prime Minister and Minister of External Affairs 1930–35. Chairman, Ottawa Imperial Economic Conference 1932. Led Canadian delegation to World Economic Conference 1933 and represented Canada at League Assembly 1934.

[3] *Baldwin*, pp. 576–7.

ment in an issue which was bound to cause serious troubles. The records do not show whether it was Hankey's intervention that caused Henderson to hold his hand; but the Imperial Conference did keep off the subject.[1]

Meanwhile a Committee on Arbitration and Disarmament chaired by Mr. Maurice Dupré of Canada was meeting at the Foreign Office, and gave birth to a series of resounding platitudes such as 'The Committee desired to record its conviction that the future peace of the world depends upon the early adoption of some general scheme of disarmament by international agreement'.[2] The Committee of Experts of the Fighting Services, at which Sir George Milne the C.I.G.S. took the chair, held only three meetings, and the British representatives received little except cold comfort from the Dominions. New Zealand promised to continue to maintain two light cruisers, but none of the others offered significant help. The most important recommendation, which almost certainly originated from Hankey, was that those Dominions which had not yet set up a body corresponding to the British Principal Supply Officers' Committee should do so.[3] The Committee on Inter-Imperial Relations under Lord Sankey, which drafted the Statute of Westminster, held 13 meetings and Hankey's close friend and associate Batterbee acted as secretary.[4]

Hankey was plainly ill satisfied with the decisions (or lack of decisions) produced by the 1930 Imperial Conference. On 4th November he wrote to MacDonald that 'the procedure adopted for defence questions . . . was not altogether satisfactory', and enclosed a letter he had received from A. V. Alexander on the subject.[5] But in truth it was too late in the day, and the British government's line was too hard set, to effect any improvement. At least he got MacDonald's tardy permission to send the Dominions the Chiefs of Staff's Annual Review.[6] His paper entitled 'The Association of the Dominions with the C.I.D.', prepared for a meeting of that body on 28th November with the Dominion Prime Ministers present, had a less happy fate. In deference to Mr. Bennett of Canada it was never circulated, and the subject was

[1]Hankey to Henderson 21st Oct. 1930. Cab. 63/43.
[2]E(30)40 of 30th Nov. 1930. Cab. 32/86. [3]Cab. 32/87.
[4]The Statute of Westminster (22 Geo. 5 Ch. 4) became law on 11th Dec. 1931. But it was never ratified by Australia because the adjective 'British' was excluded from the title of the Commonwealth.
[5]Cab. 21/470. [6]Hankey to MacDonald 19th Nov. 1930. *ibid.*

deleted from the agenda.[1] Once again we come up against what Lord Casey called 'the principle of no critical comment' by the Mother Country.

Looking back to-day at this fairly lengthy conference the whole proceedings seem rather futile, and the fundamental disagreements were in fact merely papered over. No measures of common policy were agreed, and the Chiefs of Staff's hopes regarding 'collective responsibility' for Imperial Defence were totally ignored. The Dominions were determined only to secure the statutory recognition of their complete independence, and did so. But in foreign, economic and defence policy the conference did no more than bring out the differences between the nations involved. Small wonder that, as Hankey told Smuts, he 'always rather dreaded' Imperial Conferences; and that held in 1930 must have been the most depressing of the whole series which he organised and recorded. Probably his best reward was a warm letter from Lord Sankey, who had taken the chair at the committee on Inter-Imperial Relations. After thanking Hankey for all his hard work the Lord Chancellor remarked that 'at any rate there is one thing upon which we can congratulate ourselves – the Conference has come to an end but the Empire has not'.[2]

After the end of the conference Hankey circulated a pessimistic paper on the experiences gained. The heavy pressure under which his office had worked earlier in the year had, he said, prevented the preparations being made in good time, and the result was a rushed job in September. Then the decision to allow the delegates to the Indian Round Table conferences to arrive before the end of the Imperial Conference proved 'almost disastrous'; and the fact that Parliament had met two or three weeks earlier than usual aggravated his troubles. The conference itself was, he considered 'over-papered' by memoranda being produced 'on every conceivable subject'. The burden on MacDonald himself was, he protested with good cause, excessive; and there were too many of the social functions which Hankey had always disliked. The hour of 10 a.m. was too early for the conference to meet, and resulted in excessive pressure on himself and his staff, and in delegates skimping their own briefing. He was also critical of the decision not to discuss Foreign Policy or Defence in Plenary Sessions or at meetings of the Heads of Delegations. Finally he protested

[1]The draft is in *ibid.*, dated 20th Nov. 1930.

[2]Lord Sankey to Hankey 12th Nov. 1930.

vigorously at having been physically separated from the Prime Minister – for the first and only time in all his long experience of conferences. If the secretary could not be placed beside his Chief – as had been the practice at most of the conferences he had attended – he should at least sit immediately behind him.[1] One feels that there was substance in all the points on which Hankey was critical of the 1930 Imperial Conference.

By way of a change from his constant involvement in the recurrent problems of defence and disarmament, in the autumn of 1930 Hankey had to handle the very delicate subject of MacDonald's tentative approach for a political alliance with Lloyd George. Hankey had always kept in touch with his erstwhile 'Chief', and was in fact helping him with his World War I memoirs. There is no doubt that he would have welcomed very warmly the return to office of perhaps the most brilliant politician of the time; but he knew full well how difficult it would prove to heal the split in the Liberal party, as well as get the majority of Labour M.P.s to accept a person who was almost bound soon to dominate their own leaders. After a good deal of correspondence MacDonald and Lloyd George met on 19th September, the former accompanied by Snowden and the latter by Philip Kerr, now Lord Lothian, and not by one of the leading Liberal M.P.s as MacDonald had expected. Lloyd George's proposals to alleviate unemployment were then discussed, and, according to Hankey's notes, were found in most cases to be defective. MacDonald had also held talks with Sir Herbert Samuel, who thought the present government should 'be kept in office for two years longer, and that this might be arranged on terms'. The Cabinet much disliked the idea of holding a General Election in the near future, but the price of Liberal co-operation was the introduction of electoral reform – either by means of Proportional Representation (which the Labour Party Executive strongly disliked) or by introducing the Alternative Vote, or by some combination of the two.[2] MacDonald and Lloyd George met again on the day after the Cabinet discussed the matter. Hankey 'thought it more discreet not to take notes' at that Cabinet, so he wrote a summary of the discussion afterwards in his own hand and sent it to MacDonald for comment. Apparently none were made, since Hankey sealed his unamended notes

[1]Memo. of 17th Nov. 1930. Cab. 63/43.

[2]Holograph notes (5 pages) by Hankey of discussion in Cabinet on 25th Sept. 1930. Cab. 23/90B.

in an envelope inscribed 'Only to be opened by you [MacDonald] or on your instructions'.[1] From the national point of view the pity of it was that nothing came of the discussions, and Lloyd George remained in the political wilderness, where he was soon to be joined by Churchill.

In the autumn of 1930 Hankey's greatly-valued Military Assistant Secretary Colonel Ismay left Whitehall Gardens, and Hankey wrote him a letter which reveals very clearly why he gained such devoted service from his staff.

*Hankey to Ismay. Highstead, 27th November 1930.* Holograph[2]
My dear Ismay,
. . . It was very nice of you to write me such a delightful letter. I value it much more than letters from my various chiefs. The man on one's staff sees more of one's weaker side, and is really in a better position to judge than one's chief. Moreover, every man in a position of responsibility is necessarily carried to a great extent by his staff. They do the work. He takes the credit! That is inevitable to some extent, however careful the Chief may be to let it be known where the responsibility really lies. And, after all, if things go wrong it is the Chief who is hanged – and quite rightly!

Except me, no-one knows better than you yourself how far I have relied upon *you*. Also, no-one knows better than I how reliable you have proved. I ask myself whether I have done all I can to express my gratitude? After the fiasco of my attempt to get an honour through India, and their insulting response of an offer of an O.B.E., I decided to abandon that channel. I have now put in a strong claim for a C.B. I don't think there is a chance of getting it, but the mere recommendation direct to the Prime Minister will be of some value, and the members of the Departmental Committee, who sift the list, are all useful people.[3] All this will help later on, perhaps in getting you a job at the I.D.C., in which I hope Bartholomew will help, if it suits your book.

I am just finishing off my biennial disappearance on to the sick list, and am recovering from a very slight dose of influenza. To-morrow I return, as some of the Dominions' P.M.s are coming to a meeting of the C.I.D.

My wife and I both wish we had seen more of you and Mrs. Ismay during the last few years. My activities spread over so wide a field that I cannot see nearly as much as I want of people I should like to see. . . .

[1]Hankey to MacDonald 25th Sept. 1930. Covering note to above.

[2]Ismay Papers, IV/Han./1 University of London, King's College, Centre for Military Archives.

[3]In the New Year Honours for 1931 Ismay's name appeared twice – for a C.B. and a C.S.I., so the India Office evidently relented without telling Hankey. Ismay was told that he could not accept both so accepted the C.B. The result was that he never received an Indian Order. Lawrence Burgis to the author 3rd Aug. 1971.

Whether it was because Hankey was sickening for another bout of what he always described as ''flue', or the frustrations of the London Naval and Imperial conferences, or the sheer mental and physical exhaustion produced by an extraordinarily taxing year we cannot tell. But a note in his papers in Burgis's hand stating that during 1930 he attended 300 meetings of the Cabinet and its numerous committees (not to mention 80 official dinners and lunches excluding those held during the Hague conference), suggests that he was finding the pace too hot. What is certain is that towards the end of the year he was seriously considering retirement. He had it in mind to devote his energies entirely to writing the account of World War I which he had for some time been considering, and for which he knew he possessed unique material in his diary and his letters to his wife. At any rate on 2nd December he put out a feeler in a long letter to Lloyd George, pointing out that Balfour, Asquith, Bonar Law, Smuts, Lothian and other distinguished people had all at some time and in some manner expressed the view that he should 'give up my official career and devote the remainder of my life to writing a history of the War period'. So far he had 'unhesitatingly rejected' all such proposals, but he had recently come round to the view that recently published memoirs and diaries 'sometimes present a very incorrect and biassed picture of events'. He therefore felt that a corrective was needed, and if he undertook to produce it he would aim 'at giving an unbiassed story of the exercise of the supreme control of our war effort from the period of defensive preparation . . . until the armistice, or possibly even the conclusion of peace'. Though he realised that objections would probably be raised in some quarters, he wrote that 'I rather incline to the view that it is my duty to attempt this difficult task', for which 'the facts are undoubtedly at my disposal, especially if I am allowed discreet use of official records'. And he emphasised the invaluable help that his diary and the 'summaries of particular episodes of the war' which were in his possession would afford. His only misgivings lay in 'the doubt I feel as to whether I possess the skill to write this tremendous epic', and he certainly would not undertake it without 'the good will of those principally concerned' – including Lloyd George himself.[1]

Rather oddly no reply from Lloyd George has survived; nor is there any clue in Hankey's papers regarding his reaction, though 27 years later, when he was trying to get Harold Macmillan to lift the ban on

[1]Hankey to Lloyd George, 2nd Dec. 1930. Lloyd George papers G/8/18/15.

publication of *The Supreme Command 1914–1918* he did write that Lloyd George in his own *War Memoirs* had 'relied on my Diary, notably in briefs for speeches'.[1] The implication obviously was that Lloyd George fully approved his having kept the diary, and had never raised any objection to Hankey himself publishing at any rate the more discreet parts of it. Possibly he and Lloyd George discussed the suggestion in 1930; and the latter may well have felt that a book such as Hankey had in mind would have cut right across the memoirs on which he himself was working. At any rate Hankey did not pursue the matter, and within a few years he was acting as both official and unofficial editor of Lloyd George's work – and in the latter capacity often trying to get him to soften some of his harsher remarks about the British Generals and Admirals, and about his erstwhile political colleagues in the wartime Coalition – especially Winston Churchill.[2] It is interesting to remark that when Henry Wilson's diaries were published in 1927, and were found to contain criticisms of Lloyd George he was deeply offended and wrote to Hankey to protest. The latter assured the former Prime Minister that Wilson 'knew perfectly well that you were the man who won the war, and never concealed it'; a reassurance Lloyd George described as 'a joy and a solace'.[3] Yet in 1936 when Hankey told Lloyd George 'I do still . . . deprecate the violence of your attacks on Haig' he failed to persuade him to moderate his language.[4] On the other hand when Churchill in his final volume on World War I attacked Lloyd George 'for sending the Greeks to Smyrna during the Peace Conference' Hankey told Balfour that he had 'warned him [Churchill] that he may get across Lloyd George'.[5] And when in the third volume of his *War Memoirs* Lloyd George in turn directed his fire at Churchill Hankey wrote to him 'Although Churchill is my friend I am not pleading for him on that ground. At the present time [1934] he is rather down on his luck and this passage will hit him dreadfully. It will always be quoted against him if he is ever in, or aspires to get into office

[1]Hankey to Macmillan, 1st May 1957.

[2]Lloyd George papers, box G/212. Captain B. H. Liddell Hart was also acting as adviser to Lloyd George over his war memoirs, and he and Hankey had an extensive correspondence on the former Prime Minister's handling of controversial subjects. See Liddell Hart, *Memoirs*, Vol. I (Cassell, 1965), pp. 360–70.

[3]Hankey to Lloyd George of 9th Oct. and reply by latter of 11th Oct. 1927. *ibid.* G/8/18/3.

[4]Hankey to Lloyd George 16th July 1936. Lloyd George papers, box G/212.

[5]Hankey to Balfour 27th Nov. 1928. Bm. Add. MSS. 49705 folio 112.

again'.[1] In that case he was successful in getting Lloyd George to blunt his historical barbs, since although he protested most vigorously against the 'stream of criticism polluted with much poisonous antagonism' directed against himself in books published by Generals and Admirals, he agreed 'to tone down the acerbities of truth' regarding 'Personalities', and was sending Hankey 'a refurbished Winston – acting on your suggestions'.[2] It seems certain that Churchill never knew about the debt which he thus incurred to Hankey in 1934, or he might have mollified the criticisms he expressed some eight years later, and arranged to dispense with his services in a less hurtful manner. Hankey's defence of Churchill in 1934 is made more ironical by the fact that when at the end of 1926 he had been asked to criticise and edit the final volume of *The World Crisis* he defended Lloyd George against the charges made by Churchill of swallowing too readily the proposal for the Nivelle offensive of April 1917, and of not trying to stop the Third Battle of Ypres later in that year.[3] Rather did he stress how Lloyd George 'snatched advantage out of disaster' – an expression he recalled and used again to MacDonald in the crisis of 1931.[4] All of which shows not only how very subjective are the memoirs of politicians, but how difficult it was for a man in Hankey's position to preserve a steady friendship with someone as subject to the swings and sways of emotion as Winston Churchill.

[1]Hankey to Lloyd George 16th March and 16th April 1934. Lloyd George papers, box G/212.

[2]Lloyd George to Hankey. Wednesday [probably 19th April] 1934. Holograph from Churt.

[3]See Vol. I, pp. 376–8, 400 and 444.

[4]Hankey to Churchill 8th Dec. 1926. Cab. 63/38. In his 15 pages of criticism Hankey told Churchill he had included 'too many of your own Memoranda and Minutes'. He also urged that the final chapter entitled *The Aftermath* should be made into a separate book. That suggestion Churchill accepted, and the final volume with that title was published in 1929.

*Chapter* 18

# Crisis. 1931

WHILE the effects of the great slump, which had begun in 1929, spread steadily across the world, with the number of unemployed in the industrialised countries rising all the time and acute distress prevailing among the primary producers, the politicians of the democracies were expending most of their time and effort on questions relating to disarmament. In consequence that subject became Hankey's chief preoccupation during the first eight months of 1931.

We have seen how in the previous year the Foreign Office, when tactfully prodded by Hankey about the Ten Year Rule, showed slight signs of unease about its continuation.[1] Early in 1931 Hankey produced a prescient and ominous survey of military developments in Germany and urged to the Prime Minister that the Rule should be re-examined. All he got was an acknowledgment from Patrick Fry saying that MacDonald 'cannot disagree with your conclusions', but there was 'scarcely any likelihood of any action being taken pending the General Disarmament Conference'.[2] In March the Admiralty raised the issue in the Chiefs of Staff's Committee, and Hankey then pointed out that they 'were fully justified in suggesting that the Ten Year Rule should be re-examined'.[3] None the less when he brought the issue before the C.I.D., with a very full history of how the rule had come into being in 1919 and the modifications it had subsequently undergone, that body recommended that it should continue unchanged for at least another

[1]See pp. 107, 112, 416 and 463 for the earlier history of this rule.

[2]Memo. by Hankey of 9th Jan. and letter from Fry of 28th Jan. 1931. Cab. 63/44.

[3]C.O.S. 98th Meeting, 9th March 1931. Vice-Admiral F. C. Dreyer, the Deputy Chief of Naval Staff, who was representing the First Sea Lord, raised the matter. Cab. 53/3.

year.[1] And on 15th July the Cabinet accepted that recommendation.[2]

At about the same time Hankey began work on the Chief of Staff Committee's Annual Review. But in fact none was issued for 1931 because the C.I.D. considered that 'the present moment was inopportune'. It could more logically have been argued that the very fact that disarmament was so much in the forefront of the political stage made the preparation of the Annual Review particularly opportune. The C.I.D. did however agree to the Chiefs of Staff submitting a comprehensive review later in the year 'if the course of events should render this desirable'[3]; and Hankey evidently felt compelled to leave the matter there – for a time.

On 15th July 1931 the Cabinet considered a Foreign Office paper and a note by Hankey on the Ten Year Rule. They decided 'That the situation should again be thoroughly examined in the light of developments in 1932 on which the continuance or otherwise of the present policy must necessarily depend'. In other words procrastination was still the order of the day. In February 1932 Hankey informed the Chiefs of Staff Committee in diplomatic language that 'as the present Cabinet as a whole is not very fully informed about the situation of Imperial Defence', he thought it would be a good idea for them to submit their Annual Report 'rather earlier than usual'.[4] By that time Japanese activities in Manchuria, which coincided, happily for them, with American and European preoccupation with disarmament and the economic crisis, had of course turned a spotlight on our inability to defend our interests in the Far East, and on the League of Nations' impotence. Pressure to progress the Singapore base and, still more, to get the Ten Year Rule rescinded then increased.[5] On 22nd March 1932 the C.I.D. referred to the Cabinet the recommendation 'that the assumption governing the Estimates of the Defence Services that from any given date there will be no major war for 10 years should be cancelled',[6] that defensive requirements in the Far East should be given first priority, and that the government should not await the results of

[1]C.I.D. 1055B. Though dated 23rd June 1931, presumably the date when it was circulated, it was considered by the C.I.D. on 19th March, 252nd Meeting, Item 1. Cab. 2/5.

[2]Cabinet 38(31), Conclusion 13.

[3]C.I.D. 1053B of 16th June and 253rd Meeting of C.I.D. on 29th June 1931. Cab. 2/5.

[4]C.O.S. 101st Meeting on 4th Feb. 1932. Cab. 53/4.

[5]C.I.D. 1082B of 23rd Feb. 1932. [6]255th Meeting. Cab. 2/5.

the [General] Disarmament Conference before taking such steps. 'Recent events in the Far East are ominous', concluded the C.I.D., and 'We cannot ignore the "Writing on the Wall" '.[1]

The Cabinet considered the C.I.D.'s recommendations, supporting the Chiefs of Staff's report, and a note on the financial implications by the Treasury, on 23rd March. The Conclusions state that 'No dissent was expressed from the acceptance by the C.I.D. of the recommendation of the Chiefs of Staff Sub-Committee in favour of the cancellation of the assumption . . .'.[2] Unhappily expressing 'no dissent' from a recommendation was by no means the same thing as positive approval of it; and we may conveniently here continue the story to the end. On 16th January 1933 (the month when Hitler achieved supreme power) Hankey wrote to MacDonald 'I think I ought to remind you . . . that the question of the assumption governing the Estimates of the Defence Services that . . . there will be no major war for ten years is in an unsatisfactory state'. The Chiefs of Staff had, he pointed out, again recommended cancellation in their Annual Review for 1932; but 'At present no-one quite knows whether the rule stands or not . . .'.[3] None the less in a letter to Neville Chamberlain, the Chancellor of the Exchequer, written ten weeks later on the subject of the deplorable state of the armaments industry it is surprising to find Hankey saying that 'the ten years assumption had been abolished'. 'The international situation is so grave', he went on, 'that I for one find it impossible to believe that the greatly needed rehabilitation of our Services can be much longer delayed . . .'.[4]

That the rule had not in fact been cancelled in March 1933 is confirmed by the minutes of a Cabinet held eight months later. On 15th November they had before them the Annual Review of Imperial Defence Policy for that year, and this time they *approved* the proposals of the C.I.D. with regard to the Chiefs of Staff's recommendations.[5] However MacDonald then said that 'the proposals of the official committee [i.e. the Defence Requirements Committee, of which Hankey was chairman] which would set forth our major deficiencies . . . would, according to the plan he had in mind, then be considered by a Ministerial Committee. The Cabinet would be quite uncommitted until these pro-

[1] *ibid.* Conclusion I(c). [2] Cabinet 19(32). Cab. 23/70.
[3] Hankey to MacDonald 16th Jan. 1933. Cab. 63/46.
[4] Hankey to N. Chamberlain 2nd March 1933. Cab. 63/46.
[5] C.P. 264(33), 261st meeting of C.I.D. Cab. 23/77.

posals had come before them'.[1] In other words with the setting up of the D.R.C. and the Ministerial Committee the Ten Year Rule at last effectively lapsed. And by the time it lapsed Germany had walked out of the Disarmament Conference and abandoned the League of Nations. Thus was initiated one of the most important and greatly needed steps to face realities in Europe as well as in the Far East; and the voluminous files of the C.O.S. Committee and the C.I.D. leave no room for doubt that it was largely instigated by Hankey.

To return to 1931, on 4th February the Cabinet set up an important committee under Henderson, to recommend on the policy to be adopted regarding disarmament, with particular reference to the forthcoming Geneva conference. The other members were Snowden and the three Service Ministers (A. V. Alexander, T. Shaw and Lord Thomson), and Hankey served as its secretary throughout its life.[2] This committee was empowered to consult the other political parties if it desired to do so, but was *obliged* to consult the Dominions and India. Thus when early in August it produced a series of Draft Resolutions to be placed before the conference (which were in fact little more than pious platitudes) they were telegraphed to the Dominions.[3] Hardly surprisingly New Zealand received them very coolly.

Two days after this committee was formed MacDonald approached Lloyd George with the object of framing an 'all-party' proposal for the Disarmament Conference.[4] He suggested that a C.I.D. Sub-Committee should explore the ground – which was in fact merely continuing a practice established by the previous government.[5] A month later he invited Baldwin and Lloyd George each to nominate three members of their party to serve on the committee. The offer was accepted, and the committee came into being under MacDonald's chairmanship.[6] British policy on disarmament was not, however, finalised until the

[1]Cabinet 62(33) of 15th Nov. 1933. *ibid.*

[2]Memoranda of this committee are in the D.C. (P) Series, Minutes in D.P.C.(31) Series. Cab. 21/347.

[3]F.O. Circular Telegram B.98 of 10th August 1931. Copy in Cab. 21/346.

[4]MacDonald to Lloyd George 6th Feb. 1931. Cab. 21/344.

[5]Cab. 21/346 and 347.

[6]MacDonald to Baldwin 5th March and reply by latter of 12th March 1931. Baldwin nominated Austen Chamberlain, Hoare and Eden to serve. Baldwin papers Vol. 129, pp. 46–7. Lloyd George nominated himself, Samuel and Lothian, and to balance numbers MacDonald then offered Baldwin a fourth place. He nominated Hailsham.

middle of 1932, when a Command Paper on the subject was published.[1]

The 'Three-Party Sub-Committee' met for the first time on 18th March 1931, and at Hankey's initiative the Chiefs of Staff were invited to attend the second meeting.[2] Obviously he was determined that the heads of the services should at least have a hearing. On 9th May he gave MacDonald an interesting brief on 'the one definite conclusion' which had emerged from the discussions in the Three-Party Committee. The unanimous view was that 'France holds the key to disarmament'; that she was 'greatly over-insured' in armaments; and that the conference would achieve little 'unless the French are prepared to make concessions'. To put France in the pillory would in his view be 'perfectly useless' – as had been demonstrated again and again since 1919; and moreover everything pointed 'to the desirability of a friendly France'. The most promising line was therefore to try and persuade the French voluntarily to accept 'that they and their group really are over-insured'.[3] At about the same time Hankey and Vansittart agreed on the futility of 'holding France up to the world as the incarnation of the Old Adam if she will not concede all we want'.[4] Before the end of May Hankey told MacDonald that he had 'been putting a good deal of work into the papers of the Three-Party Committee on Disarmament', and he suggested that after the Whitsun recess that body should turn to consideration of the actual Draft Disarmament Convention. He proposed that this document, to which the League Preparatory Commission had devoted five years' work, should be taken 'article by article', and that the Committee should decide on acceptance or modification, and in cases where other countries had made reservations, whether they should be supported or opposed. MacDonald agreed to this proposal,[5] and on 28th Hankey accordingly sent him a new draft agenda for the Committee. MacDonald endorsed it 'This is very well done'.[6] A month later Hankey sent the Prime Minister 'a brief for the Debate on Disarmament', which he had 'framed in accordance with what I conceive

[1]Cabinet 41(32) Conclusion 4 of 30th June 1932. Also Cmd. 4122.

[2]Held on 7th May 1931. Cab. 21/344. C.P. 96, 100 and 108(31) are the Memos. submitted respectively by the C.I.G.S., First Sea Lord and C.A.S.

[3]Hankey to MacDonald 9th May 1931. Cab. 21/344.

[4]Hankey to Vansittart 12th May 1931. Cab. 21/344. Vansittart's original 'Old Adam' paper, as Hankey called it, is C.P. 125(31).

[5]Hankey to MacDonald 19th May 1931, with endorsement by latter. Cab. 21/344.

[6]Same to same 28th May 1931. *ibid.*

to be the policy of the Government'; but he took the opportunity again to warn against the ill effects which would result 'if we press the French too hard'. He added a postscript saying that he had just heard from Sylvester that 'L.G. is delighted with the draft' brief.[1] Obviously Hankey had completely won MacDonald's confidence by his handling of the government's approach to the long-promised General Disarmament Conference.

At this time the tide of public opinion, in America as well as in Britain, was flowing very strongly in favour of disarmament, and if need be unilateral disarmament, as the best if not the only hope for world peace. And such currents were greatly strengthened by the sustained propaganda campaign waged by bodies such as Lord Cecil's Central Disarmament Bureau and the League of Nations Union.[2] In July a Resolution was proposed and carried at a mass meeting of such bodies at the Albert Hall. It read 'That the Societies represented at this meeting pledge themselves to do their utmost to ensure that the Disarmament Conference shall succeed in bringing about a genuine reduction in the Fighting Forces of the World'. MacDonald and Lloyd George readily agreed to attend the meeting. Baldwin at first declined – it was on a Saturday afternoon and he wanted to go to Lords' for the Eton and Harrow cricket match; but he finally yielded to Cecil's strong pressure.[3] Hankey may well have felt that any attempt by himself to swim against such powerful currents would be utterly futile, and would probably destroy his own position as trusted adviser to and confidant of Ministers of all parties. Yet it is hard to believe that he felt any real faith in the cause for which he was now required to work. At least he saw to it that the Chiefs of Staffs received a hearing – as in the C.I.D. Sub-Committee already referred to. To give only one example, in February Field-Marshal Milne, the C.I.G.S., submitted a well-argued and prophetic paper on Italian aims and intentions, concluding with the statement that her policy was 'playing with fire and so long as it persists must render Italy a focus of European unrest and a potential danger to European peace.'[4] Hankey brought this before the C.I.D., and MacDonald said that 'the Staffs of the Service Depart-

[1]Hankey to MacDonald 26th June 1931. Cab. 21/345 and Cab. 63/44.
[2]Baldwin papers Vol. 129 has much interesting material on the activities of the 'Disarmament Lobby', and the cleverness of its leaders in involving politicians of all parties in their activities 1931–34.
[3]*ibid.* Vol. 133. [4]C.I.D. 1034B of 6th Feb. 1931.

ments could rest assured that interesting documents of this kind were considered most carefully . . .'.[1] – a piece of equivocation which probably deceived no-one.

Hankey himself sometimes passed advice privately to a service department at this time which certainly did not accord with government policy. For instance in February Christopher Bullock, the Permanent Secretary of the Air Ministry, wrote to him protesting strongly against the whole concept of advocating a 'percentage reduction' in armaments, as had been proposed by the Cabinet Sub-Committee. Hankey replied that 'there is a good deal of politics in all this', and suggested that the real aim was 'to gain electoral advantage'. In effect he briefed Bullock on how to circumvent the Cabinet Committee's recommendation, wisely adding at the end 'This is really Personal and Confidential'. Bullock was duly grateful, and the outcome was 'a strongish paper on air disarmament by the Secretary of State, and one on the international air situation by the Chief of the Air Staff'.[2] Sir Basil Liddell Hart, who knew Hankey well, and to whom the latter certainly confided some of his innermost thoughts, has written that in 1931 Hankey's real apprehension was that the Disarmament Conference would merely aggravate national rivalries.[3] The memoranda and letters which he wrote certainly lend support to such a view.

In June issues which were already complicated enough were made still more so by the French suggestion that armaments should be divided into Offensive and Defensive categories, and that only the former should be limited.[4] This proposal was passed to the Chiefs of Staff; and, rather oddly, it produced from Snowden a strong recommendation that, because the total abolition 'of Air Forces as national weapons' was 'perhaps too much to expect', the Disarmament Conference 'should be moved to agree to the total abolition of all *sea-borne* aircraft'.[5] While the Admiralty very naturally viewed this idea with strong disfavour, it was received with relish in the Air Ministry, which had always cordially disliked the Fleet Air Arm and was fully prepared to use almost any weapon to emasculate, or if possible abolish

[1] 252nd C.I.D. of 19th March 1931. Cab. 2/5.
[2] Bullock to Hankey 18th Feb. and reply by latter of 20th Feb. 1931. Also Bullock to Hankey 27th Feb. and 31st March 1931. Cab. 21/347.
[3] B. H. Liddell Hart, *Memoirs*, Vol. I (Cassell, 1965), p. 185.
[4] The French proposal is C.P. 236(31) of 15th July 1931.
[5] Snowden to Henderson 22nd June 1931. Cab. 21/345.

it. By mid-July however Hankey told the C.O.S.s that the government had abandoned the attempt to divide weapons on the lines of the French proposal, so they need not report on it. Then the Conservative members of the Three-Party Committee insisted on reviving the issue, so Hankey had to call for a report from the C.O.S.s after all.[1]

While the Cabinet was thus involved in the Disarmament debate the financial crisis was deepening all the time. In July an Economic Conference was called in London to try and resolve the acute trouble which had arisen in Germany. As so often before Hankey was appointed Secretary-General; but the conference broke down because, as was the case with Disarmament, the French government held all the trump cards and endeavoured to impose unacceptable political conditions as the price of affording financial help to countries like Austria which were in difficulties over their balance of payments and urgently needed credits. Then, at the end of July, the May Committee on National Economy, which had been appointed in March, reported. The effects were cataclysmic; and as Parliament had adjourned no public debate of the issues was possible. On 11th August MacDonald returned to London, and during the succeeding days the Cabinet's Economy Committee met several times and agreed to open talks with the leaders of the opposition parties, the Labour Party Executive and the Trades Union Congress.[2] On 19th the full Cabinet met 'in circumstances of exceptional gravity and urgency to consider the recent serious developments in the financial situation', and the memorandum giving the Economy Committee's proposals for balancing the budget was circulated. The reduction of 20% in Unemployment Assurance, proposed by the May Committee to save nearly £15 millions, was decisively rejected.[3] Discussions with the other parties and with the T.U.C. followed, and on 21st Snowden told his colleagues that 'it appeared that the members of the General Council had no real appreciation of the seriousness of the situation'. The Cabinet agreed, after much discussion, to adopt MacDonald's proposal that the government 'should proceed with the programme and include in it sufficient economies to restore public confidence'. Parliament was to be recalled.[4] Next day MacDonald

[1]Cab. 21/346. [2]Premier 1/96.

[3]Cabinet 41(31) of 19th Aug. 1931. In Cab. 23/67. The memorandum in question is C.P. 203(31).

[4]Cabinet 43(31) of 21st Aug. 1931. *ibid.*

reported that the situation had deteriorated further, and that more support must be obtained for the pound from New York and Paris. He 'assured the Cabinet in the most emphatic terms that there was no ground whatever for the suggestion that the present crisis was in any respect due to a conspiracy on the part of the Banks, all of which were most anxious to render assistance to the Government'.[1]

Meanwhile Hankey had, for once, given priority to his own and his family's interests – though not without considerable misgivings. When early in August he had learnt that the King was going to Balmoral and MacDonald to Lossiemouth he felt justified in carrying out his plan to go to La Grave in Dauphiné with Adeline, Christopher and Henry. He was, he wrote later, 'exhausted after a long and harassing period . . . without any respite of more than two or three days'; and Monarch and Prime Minister both urged him to go. On 22nd two telegrams reached Hankey from London – one recalling him and the other cancelling it. Then Robin wired from the Foreign Office to say that he had consulted Burgis and they felt instinctively that he should return at once. He reached London next day. But before we quote Hankey's account of the political crisis which he then found in full spate we may quote his views on how and why the crisis arose. It is not surprising that in this respect he went along wholly with Sir George May and those of his colleagues who signed the Majority Report of the Economy Committee.[2] But to a generation which, nearly half a century later, has suffered from the constant erosion of the benefits of its thrift through rampant inflation such views will probably seem more solidly based than they did to the critics of deflationary fiscal policy in the 1930s.

Shortly after Hankey's return home he received from the Palace the 'strong commendation' of the King for the excellent work done by Howorth in producing the Cabinet Conclusions during the prevailing crisis. Hankey, ready as always to give credit to his staff whenever it

[1]Cabinet 44(31) of 22nd Aug. 1931. *ibid.*

[2]Sir Mark Jenkinson (Industrialist and Chartered Accountant, 1878–1935) made a Reservation regarding two paragraphs of the Report, where blame was laid on politicians of all parties for pledging themselves to 'vast and expensive schemes' even before they were returned to Westminster. Charles Latham (later 1st Baron Latham. Accountant and politician (Lab.), 1888– ) and Arthur Pugh (Trade Unionist 1870-1955) signed a Minority Report wholly dissenting from the conclusions and recommendations of the majority of their colleagues. Cmd. 3920.

was due, at once replied to the Private Secretary that 'Mr. Howorth is quite overwhelmed with the King's notice of his work'.[1]

*Diary September 6th 1931*

We are living just now through the most serious crisis since the war and the future outlook is black. After the war we failed to adopt the measures of economy necessary to a nation that had dissipated a large part of its wealth in smoke and explosions. The beginning of it all was Ll. G.'s election speech in 1919 about 'a home for heroes to live in' – as I have more than once noted in this journal. Thereafter it has been a 'rake's progress' for which each successive Government has its share of responsibility. As I once told Ll. G., many years ago, when he was Prime Minister, and as I have told his successors, the only real cure is to preach to the people that they must pull in their belts and economise, and that the standard of living must be lowered so as to enable us – a nation dependent on oversea trade – to compete effectively with our rivals. Nevertheless, the exigencies of party politics have compelled each party leader to declare repeatedly, and right up to the present time, that the standard of living must be maintained. While our fighting strength has been reduced by repeated 'cuts' – relatively to foreign nations – there has been an orgy of extravagance on social reform. Old age pensions have both increased and extended; widows' pensions have been adopted and absorb the whole of the money accruing from the diminution of war pensions; wages have risen – especially in the non-competitive industries like railways, and are much higher than they are abroad; the cost of education has been prodigiously increased; unemployment has increased to about 2¾ million; but the doles have been increased by the Labour Government and the precautions against fraud reduced, so that there are wide-spread abuses, only partially checked by the recent Act of Parliament.[2] Our policy in India, Egypt and China has been weak and reacts on our prestige in all Eastern countries. The result has been a great fall in our prestige throughout the world. Broadly speaking, foreigners, and especially the French, who have a great following in Central Europe, and the Italians, who are still Fascists, have lost confidence in us. They don't believe in our policy on disarmament – especially the reduction of the fleet and the insufficiency of our air force to defend London; they disagree with our policy in India, China, Egypt, and our general pacifism and idealism. Some understand, and in theory approve it. But many

[1]Wigram to Hankey 25th Aug. 1931 and reply by latter of same date. RA GV K2330(2)/4 and /8.

[2]Hankey must have been referring either to the Unemployment Insurance Act, 1931 (21 Geo. 5, Ch. 8), which received Royal Assent on 3rd March 1931, or to the Anomalies Bill, which was introduced in Parliament on 18th June 1931. See R. Skidelski, *Politicians and the Slump* (Pelican Ed. 1970), pp. 353–5.

– as I know from conversations at the Hague Conferences and the London Naval Conference – think that it is really due less to idealism than to our realisation of our exhaustion and economic weakness. Above all there is almost universal criticism of our policy of doles, and our insistence on maintaining a much higher standard of living than our economic circumstances justify. Our wage regulations, relatively short hours of work, inelasticity of labour and general subservience to the Trade Unions are more especially mistrusted. In short, we are regarded as being definitely on the down grade, and that view is held especially strongly in financial circles. Personally I agree with all these criticisms.

Hankey went on to quote, approvingly, André Siegfried's recently published book *La Crise Britannique au 20me Siècle*,[1] and to recount how the crisis could be said to have begun with the proposal for an Austro-German Customs Union. The French saw in this move the first step towards the 'Anschluss' between Germany and Austria which was forbidden by the Peace Treaties. They therefore refused to offer any credits to Austria until the Customs Union proposal was dropped. Hankey wrote that 'outwardly' the British government preserved 'rather a cautious attitude', but 'the real opinion of the government was that finance should not be mixed up with politics'. He gave no indication, however, of how the two could be kept separate. When the Bank of England 'gave an accommodation to Austria without political conditions' he remarked to Snowden's Private Secretary that the Bank would lose its money; for his trip to Vienna in the previous year had left him with 'a very bad impression of the financial and economic stability of the country'. According to Hankey the French were 'a good deal annoyed' by the British attitude towards the Austro-German Customs Union.

The German economic collapse and the Hoover moratorium of 20th June, remitting Allied debts for a year, followed. Though the London Conference 'extended the moratorium to Germany and reparations' it brought only 'a temporary alleviation'; and the German failure to repay short-term credits granted by Britain and their inability to pay 'Bills for imports as they matured in London', together with financial troubles in many other countries, reacted on the British financial position in the same way. Hankey called it 'an incredible coincidence of troubles'; but in fact the steady worsening of the economic situation had been apparent for several months. At that moment the May

[1]Librairie Armand Colin, 1931.

Committee's report disclosed an anticipated budget deficit of 'over 100 millions – mainly due to unemployment insurance', remarked Hankey. 'That', he concluded, 'lifted the lid off'; and he went on to describe how gold 'began to flow out at an alarming rate'.

At a Cabinet held late in the evening of Sunday 23rd August the proposal that Unemployment Insurance benefit should be reduced by 10% was discussed at length. An unsigned and undated note, almost certainly by Howorth, shows that, although no vote was apparently taken, eleven Ministers were prepared to accept such a measure and eight or nine were against doing so.[1] In view of the fact that, as the minutes of the meeting record, adoption of the 10% cut 'would involve the resignation of certain Ministers', MacDonald said that he would at once inform the King of the situation which had arisen and 'advise him to hold a conference with Mr. Baldwin, Sir Herbert Samuel and himself on the following morning'. The Cabinet approved this proposal, and also authorised MacDonald to tell the King that all Cabinet Ministers 'had placed their resignations in the Prime Minister's hands'. MacDonald left for Buckingham Palace at 10.10 p.m. and returned half an hour later to report 'that it was impossible for them to continue in office as a united Cabinet'.[2]

As soon as Hankey reached London at 5 p.m. on Monday 24th he went round to Downing Street without even changing out of his travelling clothes.

*Diary 6th September 1931*

[On reaching Downing Street] I found him [MacDonald] in the Cabinet room with Baldwin and Herbert Samuel – MacDonald looking very tired and haggard – discussing the formation of the new National Government, and they put to me various constitutional problems, on which I asked to retire to consult the Privy Council Office and Parliamentary Counsel. All that evening I was very busy. But gradually I pieced the story together. The drain on London had been proceeding catastrophically. The Bank of England had come to the Government – Montagu Norman,[3] the Governor was worn

[1]The majority was headed by MacDonald, Snowden and Herbert Morrison, and the minority by Arthur Henderson and Graham. The latter also included Adamson, Lansbury, Alexander, Addison, Johnston, Greenwood and possibly Clynes against whose name there is a question mark. Premier 1/96.

[2]Cabinet 46(31) of 23rd Aug. 1931. Cab. 23/67.

[3]Montagu C. N. Norman, 1st Baron Norman 1944 (1871–1950). Banker. Governor of Bank of England 1920–44.

out and had had to go for a holiday and had insisted on going to his cottage on the coast of Maine, U.S.A. The Government wanted (a) a loan to enable them to help the Bank to deal with the situation (b) to restore confidence abroad and stop the rot. The American bankers, who were most anxious to help, said that, in order to reassure public opinion abroad it was necessary to balance the budget; to accomplish this to the extent of at least half by economies; and that there must be a reduction of at least 10% in the insurance payments. Short of this they did not believe that the loan could be assured. The Labour Government had worked at economies for a week, and had arrived at a plan. But about 10 of them would not swallow the 10% cut. So the Prime Minister had no alternative but to resign. Luckily the King had come back from Balmoral 'off his own bat'. . . . Baldwin had been recalled from Aix-les-Bains. Ll. George being ill, Herbert Samuel had taken his place. A consultation had taken place at Buckingham Palace that day, and Mr. MacDonald had undertaken to form a National Government.

In fact at a Cabinet held at noon on 24th August, with Howorth still acting as secretary, MacDonald reported that 'as the result of failing to reach agreement the financial position had greatly deteriorated . . . No useful purpose would be served by consideration of any question other than saving the country from financial collapse. The proposal was that His Majesty would invite certain individuals, as individuals, to take upon their shoulders the burden of carrying on the government, and Mr. Baldwin and Sir Herbert Samuel had stated that they were prepared to act accordingly'. MacDonald proposed therefore to tender the resignation of the government, and felt that 'no other course was open to him than to assist in the formation of a National Government on a comprehensive basis for the purposes of meeting the present emergency'.[1] Thus was the die cast a few hours before Hankey reached London and resumed duty as secretary of the Cabinet.

*Diary 6th September 1931* (cont.)

That evening [Monday 24th August] I was sent for again to Downing St. at 7.30 p.m. and asked to draft a Manifesto by the new Government. MacDonald gave me general instructions and Baldwin and Samuel each gave me a written contribution. It was to be ready for their consideration at 8.30. It was an awkward thing to draft. It was impossible to say, as they wanted to say, that the *intention* of the new Cabinet was 'so and so'. For the new Cabinet was not formed, much less sworn, and technically the old Ministers were in office until the new ones were sworn. However I did it and

[1]Cabinet 47(31) of 24th Aug. 1931. Cab. 23/67.

got it 'vetted' by Graham-Harrison[1] (parliamentary counsel, whom I dragged away from his dinner) before submitting it. They modified, but approved my draft, which was issued that night.

The draft, written in Hankey's hand, has survived in his papers. 'The specific object for which the new government is being formed', it states, 'is to deal with the national emergency that now exists. It will not be a Coalition Government in the usual accepted sense of the term, but a Government of co-operation for this one purpose. When that purpose is achieved the political parties will resume their respective positions'. At about the same time MacDonald approved making the announcement that Parliament would be recalled on 8th September 'when proposals will be submitted to the House of Commons for a large reduction of expenditure and for the provision *on an equitable basis* of the further funds required to balance the budget'. This draft is on Downing Street notepaper and is undated. The italicised words, inserted in red ink, appear to be in MacDonald's hand.

*Diary 6th September 1931* (cont.)

When I saw the King, to coach him before the swearing-in Council he said 'Thank God you are back'. Indeed everyone from the King and the Prime Minister downwards seemed very glad to see me. I could not help recalling that on the last day of Parliament Mr. Baldwin had walked across the yard outside [the House of Commons] and had said 'I will do everything I can to help the Government in making economies, but I will not enter a Coalition Government.' But circumstances had compelled him to enter a National Government, which is to all intents and purposes a Coalition!

Ever since then I have been desperately busy; first as Clerk of the Council in carrying out the many formalities incidental to the formation and inauguration of a new Government; second, as secretary to the Cabinet, in keeping the Minutes of the new Cabinet, which has been formulating its economy and taxation policy. It is a Cabinet of Ten with a lot of outside Ministers, and has to be run like the War Cabinet, but I am allowed to send the Minutes to most of the outsiders. It is an awkward machine with its three parties, all rather jealous of their own position. As the only neutral person all sorts of odd difficulties arise for me. On the first day [Tuesday 25th August] when they gave me the list I found that nothing had been arranged about precedence. This is no formality, because if the Prime Minister or other leading Ministers happen to be away at an International Conference or elsewhere, the senior

[1]Later Sir William M. Graham-Harrison (1871–1949). Barrister. Second Parliamentary Counsel to Treasury 1917–28 and First Counsel 1928–33. Chancellor of Dioceses of Durham 1934–40, of Truro 1935–40 and of Portsmouth 1938–40.

Drafted for Mr. MacDonald, Mr. Baldwin + Sir H. Samuel late on the evening of Monday Aug. 24. 1931 and published in the papers next morning

The Prime Minister, since kissing hands [M.P.H.] on appointment by His Majesty this afternoon, has been in consultation with Mr Baldwin, Sir Herbert Samuel and Mr. Snowden as to the names ~~to be~~ ~~to be~~ to be submitted to the King for inclusion [as Ministers] in the new ~~G~~ Government [Government]. Considerable progress has been made. The ~~reason~~ [sole object] for [which] ~~the constitution of~~ the new Government is being formed is to deal with the [existing] national emergency [that now exists]. ~~now~~ It will not be a Coalition Government in the [usual] accepted sense of the term, but a Government of cooperation for this one purpose. When that purpose is achieved the political parties will resume their respective positions

Hankey's draft 'Manifesto' on the formation of the National Government, 24th August, 1931

man presides. They left me to submit a draft and I put – P.M., Baldwin, Snowden, Samuel, Reading, Sankey. The P.M. insisted on Sankey, the Lord Chancellor coming fourth. Samuel was uncomfortable about being in front of Reading – but I told him that he had represented Ll. G. at Buckingham Palace and must take his responsibility. He agreed and it was fixed up. Several troubles have arisen. N. Chamberlain objected to Reading being added to the Finance Committee, which consisted of Snowden, Samuel and himself, on the ground of the balance of parties being upset, and I had to get the P.M. to smooth it out. He [presumably Neville Chamberlain] also objected to Cecil being selected to lead us at Geneva.

Still, the first week has been surmounted quite successfully and the policy is ready for the meeting of Parliament on Tuesday [8th September]. But, meanwhile, the drain on London has not ceased and on Friday three millions went out. I have also been busy on a number of other matters – co-ordinating and collecting 'briefs' for the P.M.'s speeches and a thousand details. This will be a critical week.

Hankey was determined that all the necessary ammunition should be at MacDonald's disposal before the critical debates took place. On 3rd September he therefore wrote to the Prime Minister that he had been 'very actively at work informally and unobtrusively' with this object in view, and had secured the co-operation of civil servants such as Warren Fisher at the Treasury and of politicians such as Cunliffe-Lister, now President of the Board of Trade, with regard to 'all the financial aspects'. Then, to widen the scope of the brief he had in mind, he had informally warned Vansittart, Batterbee, Horace Wilson and others to be 'prepared to furnish information about what the effects on the Dominions, colonies and foreign countries would have been if the pound sterling had "gone west" [i.e. off the gold standard] last week'. He suggested that the informal action he had taken should be strengthened by issuing formal instructions to the departments to prepare what was needed; and MacDonald endorsed his letter 'Most grateful. Make these suggestions into official instructions'. Hankey ended with a warning that he had 'heard everywhere that the late [i.e. Labour] Under-Secretaries have got into their heads that there never was a serious crisis and that the whole thing was a bankers' ramp'. He was therefore working to show 'beyond dispute, first, that the crisis was imminent, and second, how serious its effects would have been'.[1] The events of the following fortnight were to show Hankey's far-sightedness in a somewhat ironical light; but one has to remember that

[1]Hankey to MacDonald 3rd Sept. 1931. Cab. 21/350.

Approved

10, Downing Street.
Whitehall.

In order to correct without delay the
excess of national expenditure over revenue
it is anticipated that
H. M. Govt have decided to
Sep 8th
will be summon Parlt on
when proposals will be submitted to the
House of C for a large reduction of expenditure
on an equitable basis
and for the provision of the further
funds required to balance the Budget
which will be raised in a way to ensure
that the sacrifice necessary shall be
distributed equitably amongst the
various sections of the people

A note with amendments in MacDonald's hand on measures to meet the financial crisis of September 1931

the fight to keep the pound on gold was not lost when he called up all forces to prevent devaluation.

*Diary September 13th 1931*

The critical week has passed. The policy of the National Government of co-operation, hatched out during the previous weeks with so much effort, has been launched. The crisis has passed from the Cabinet to Parliament. Policy was discussed on Tuesday [8th]; procedure on Wednesday [9th]; finance on Thursday [10th], when Mr. Snowden, introducing his vast scheme of taxation received an astonishing ovation from Conservatives and Liberals; economy on Friday [11th], when the Prime Minister introduced the Economy Bill, providing for £70 millions of economies, to be operated by Orders-in-Council.[1] The Government have had much the better of the debates and majorities of at least 60. But the results are not wholly satisfactory. Gold is still running out of the Bank of England at a rate of about £2 millions a day. There are serious critics of the whole policy of maintaining the value of sterling. Lord d'Abernon, whom I was commissioned to induce to broadcast on the effect of the German period of inflation in 1922–3 (when he was Ambassador in Berlin), and with whom I lunched at 12 Arlington St. on Tuesday, was, I found, a violent opponent of the policy – though unwilling to attack it during the crisis. He evidently favoured an inflationary policy, but admitted the dangers of local inflation. What he wanted was a world inflation, especially in America. He spoke bitterly of Sprague,[2] the American economic adviser of the Bank of England . . . Keynes also has published a critical article in the *Evening Standard*, and considers the forecasts of going off the gold standard made by Government speakers as grossly exaggerated. A Cabinet Committee will meet to-morrow to consider the problem of the restoration of our trade balance. It is difficult to see how this is to be accomplished without tariffs, to which Snowden and Samuel are bitterly opposed, and which are barred by the 'Gentleman's Agreement' on which the Government is based. It is difficult to see how a solution is to be found without a general election . . .

During the debates of the past week the opposition (Henderson, Graham & Co.) have sought to disassociate themselves from the greater part of the economies, in order to curry favour with the electorate. This is extremely disingenuous on their part, as they themselves agreed provisionally to £56 millions of economies, most of which are identical with those included in the economy White Paper. The Prime Minister had to show this up in debate on Friday [11th], and J. H. Thomas hammered it home with overwhelming power in winding up Friday's debate and discomfited the opposition to an extent such as I have never before witnessed in Parliament. Unfortunately he had to base himself on the Cabinet Minutes of the late Government and this produced great indignation. Both the Prime Minister and I had seen him separately and urged him to be discreet. He accomplished this (a) by sticking to points which Henderson had been the first to refer to; e.g. the

[1]See Parl. Deb., Commons, Vol. 256, respectively Cols. 13–22 for 8th Sept.; Cols. 139–196 for 9th; Cols. 297–412 for 10th (Committee of Ways and Means); and Cols. 419–490 for 11th (debate on the National Economy Bill).

[2]Oliver M. W. Sprague (1873–1953). American academic economist. Professor of Banking and Finance, Harvard University 1913–41 and, under leave of absence, economic adviser to Bank of England.

£56 millions figure . . . and (b) by mentioning only matters which had been communicated by decision of the late Cabinet to the other party leaders. Still, he sailed near the wind in his very remarkable speech, and I am nervous for the whole secrecy of Cabinet Minutes.[1]

The Prime Minister has been very seedy. When under severe nervous strain he is apt to vomit in the morning, and this leaves him terribly weak. I fear he is feeling the break with the rest of the Labour party very badly. but he enjoys leading a Cabinet composed largely of Conservatives, and says their faults are as bad as those of the Labour men – which is true. Snowden, who is [as] hard as nails in spite of his physical infirmities, is quite unaffected by his separation from Labour colleagues many of whom he despises and dislikes. . . .

On 9th September the statement by Arthur Henderson in the House that on 22nd August the leaders of the three political parties had wanted to add £25–30 millions to the proposals for economies[2] forced Hankey to undertake a hectic search through the Cabinet records, including those kept by Howorth while he himself had been in France, to see if there was any substance in Henderson's claim. Hankey finally reported to MacDonald that he could 'find no reference to those figures. If they were mentioned (which I doubt as Mr. Howorth never mentioned them to me) they were not recorded . . .'.[3] In other words he was not able to provide evidence controverting Henderson's statement, and was therefore not prepared to allow MacDonald to commit himself to a flat contradiction of his erstwhile colleague – a good example of the thoroughness and fairness with which Hankey handled tricky political issues.

It was perfectly natural that at this time Hankey should review the effects which the cuts in salary and increase in taxes would have on himself and his family. His salary was apparently £3,000 per annum,[4] but he estimated his total loss of income at about £700, and feared that it would prove 'difficult to make both ends meet'. In fact however Adeline's good management and her husband's very abstemious habits seem to have combined to avert the 'economies all round' which he anticipated would be necessary.[5]

The week following the foregoing diary entry produced the traumatic

[1]See Parl. Deb., Commons, Vol. 256, Cols. 481–90, especially the opposition interventions on whether Thomas was quoting from Cabinet minutes (Col. 484 ff.).
[2]Parl Deb., Commons, Vol. 256, Cols. 139–196.
[3]Hankey to MacDonald 9th Sept. 1931. Cab. 21/350.
[4]*News Chronicle* of 18th Aug. 1931. [5]Diary Sept. 13th 1931.

occurrence generally referred to as the Invergordon Mutiny.[1] The Atlantic Fleet, whose Commander-in-Chief Admiral Sir Michael Hodges,[2] had just been taken seriously ill, left its home ports on 8th September to concentrate in the Moray Firth for a period of intensive exercises. Meanwhile Austen Chamberlain had taken over the Admiralty from A. V. Alexander – though without any great enthusiasm as he had hoped to return to the Foreign Office under the National Government. The other members of the Board, with the exceptions of Lord Stanhope (Parliamentary Secretary)[3] and Rear-Admiral R. R. C. Backhouse[4] the Third Sea Lord (whose responsibilities actually lay in the field of material and not personnel) were, at the best, undistinguished. Furthermore Admiral Field, the colourless First Sea Lord, was away from the office ill. The Labour Government had accepted the May Committee's general recommendation regarding cuts in service men's pay before it left office; but the Admiralty could not immediately issue a clear statement regarding the government's intentions because the May Committee itself had proffered two alternatives – namely a 10% overall cut or the reduction of the pay of men entered under the 1919 rates to the substantially lower rates introduced in 1925. Not until after the change of government was it decided that the second alternative was to be adopted. This proposal had for a long time been pressed by the Treasury, but had always been strongly resisted by the Admiralty

[1]See David Divine, *Mutiny at Invergordon* (MacDonald, 1970). The author is the first writer to be allowed access to the long-withheld Admiralty records of these events. Unfortunately the book bears very evident signs of hasty writing and production. The author has not consulted some highly relevant personal papers, nor such sources as the Royal Archives. Dates, officers' ranks and titles, and sometimes even names are incorrectly given. Thus although the book is valuable until a more complete account is available it must be treated with caution.

[2]1874–1951. Chief of Staff to Admiral Sir Charles Madden 1918–20. Naval Secretary to First Lord 1923–25. Second-in-Command, Mediterranean Fleet 1925–27. Second Sea Lord 1927–30. C-in-C, Atlantic Fleet 1930–31.

[3]7th Earl Stanhope (1880–1967). Landowner and politician (Cons.). Parliamentary Secretary, War office 1918. Civil Lord of Admiralty 1924–29. Parliamentary and Financial Secretary to Admiralty 1931. Under-Secretary of State for War 1931–34 and for Foreign Affairs 1934–36. First Commissioner of Works 1936–37. President Board of Education 1937–38. First Lord of Admiralty 1938–39. Lord President of Council 1939–40. Leader of House of Lords 1938–40.

[4]Later Admiral of the Fleet Sir Roger Backhouse (1878–1939). Commanded 3rd Battle Squadron, Atlantic Fleet 1926–27. Third Sea Lord and Controller of Navy 1928–32. As Vice-Admiral commanded First Battle Squadron, Mediterranean Fleet 1932–34. C-in-C, Home Fleet 1935–38. First Sea Lord 1938–39.

as 'a breach of faith' to the long-service men involved. Furthermore when the decision had been taken there followed such an extraordinary succession of administrative blunders that the contents of Snowden's budget speech of 10th September became known to the Atlantic Fleet through the Press and the B.B.C. before any warning had arrived from Whitehall, let alone directions on how the government's measures should be explained to the men. During the week-end of 12th–13th meetings took place in the canteen at Invergordon, but the naval authorities did not regard them seriously. Nor is there any evidence that, at this stage, Communist party influences were at work to stir up trouble. On Monday 14th however a mass meeting at the canteen took on a far more menacing shape, and showed beyond doubt that the pay cuts had produced such a degree of unrest that an explosion was likely.

Though it was the older men, who had been on the 1919 rates of pay, who were worst affected – and their loss could amount to as much as 25 % – the younger men on the 1925 rates soon made common cause with them. On Tuesday 15th the majority of the crews of the big ships refused to sail for exercises. Next day support for what was in fact a sit-down strike rather than a full-scale mutiny had plainly become more widespread; and although no serious violence had yet been perpetrated, Rear-Admiral Wilfred Tomkinson,[1] the acting Commander of the fleet, now reported, somewhat belatedly, that it was possible that the situation would 'get entirely out of control'. In fact he and his officers had lost control of the fleet since the previous Monday evening.[2] On 16th Chamberlain gave the Cabinet an account of what had happened during the previous forty-eight hours; but his colleagues, while admitting 'that grievances of a specially onerous kind might exist in the fleet, were deeply concerned with the effect' that concessions in that respect would have 'on the whole scheme of Government economies'. The very cautiously expressed minutes in which Hankey recorded the discussion state that 'doubts were felt as to whether it was expedient

[1] 1877– . Chief of Staff to Admiral Keyes as C-in-C, Mediterranean Fleet 1927–28. Assistant Chief of Naval Staff 1929–31. Vice-Admiral in command of Battle Cruiser Squadron 1931–32.

[2] Mr. Divine is wrong to suggest that the mutiny was confined almost wholly to the men who had enjoyed the 1919 rates of pay. Commander H. Pursey, the future Labour M.P., who was serving in the *Hood* at the time, has assured the author that men on the 1925 rates were just as fully involved, though some of the 'ringleaders' were found among the older men.

... to withdraw the ships to the home ports as desired by the Sea Lords'; but the proposal 'was eventually agreed to on the understanding that it was made clear that this was done in obedience to an order from the Admiralty'.[1] Hankey's diary, quoted below, reveals with stark clarity the extent to which this was an equivocal and face-saving formula. That same afternoon the Admiralty accordingly ordered all ships to return to their home ports in order that cases of hardship should be investigated. Some anxious hours followed, but late that evening all ships did sail. Next day these events were debated in the House of Commons on a Motion for the Adjournment, and at the end of his speech Chamberlain declared, in answer to an appeal by J. M. Kenworthy that there should be 'no penalisation', 'The past is past. It is in the interest of everyone in the Navy or out of it to forget it ... there will be no looking back to what has happened on this occasion, but we shall go forward together in the service of the country'.[2] From the point of view of those responsible for the restoration of discipline and the rebuilding of morale in the fleet this was an unfortunate promise, since it was absolutely inevitable that there should be a very great deal of 'looking back', and if proper enquiries were forbidden it was very unlikely that justice would be done, let alone be seen to be done.

*Diary 20th and 26th September 1931*

... It has been a difficult and depressing week. The mutiny in the Atlantic Fleet against the cuts in naval pay created a peculiarly distressing situation and immensely stimulated the flight from the pound ... On Monday [21st] information was received from secret sources that the men of the fleet intended to repeat at the home ports their action at Invergordon last week, and to walk out of the ships as a protest against the cuts.[3] No means being available to enforce discipline at such short notice the Cabinet anticipated them by the expedient of reducing the cuts – not only in the Navy but also in the Army, Air Force, among teachers and police to a maximum of 10%. This did the trick and there has been no trouble. All naval officers from the

[1]Cabinet 56(31) of 16th Sept. 1931, Conclusion 3. Cab. 23/68.

[2]Parl. Deb., Commons, Vol. 256, Col. 1120.

[3]See also Hankey's draft 'Most Secret' notes on Chamberlain's statement made to the Cabinet on 21st Sept. 1931. The First Lord then described the situation in the home ports as 'extremely serious'. Although the outbreak at Invergordon had been 'purely naval and the Communists had been rather taken by surprise', now 'the Communists were active in the ports and had sent some of their best agents there'. Cab. 23/90B.

Board of Admiralty downwards believed it [the mutiny] was a spontaneous protest against an intolerable grievance, which ought to be remedied. Not a word has leaked out as to the true cause of the reduction in the cuts, and the seamen don't know that the Government was aware of their intentions. But it is no use blinking the fact that the Cabinet yielded to force and that it was mutiny. It bodes ill for the future and for the discipline of the fleet. Both Baldwin and J. H. Thomas have told me that they cannot leave the question where it is, and they consider some inquiry indispensable.

On 25th September Chamberlain sent the King his apologia for these events. He declared that 'a moderate cut' in pay would have been accepted by the men, but that 'the severity of the cuts . . . burst upon them like a thunderclap'. He defended the Board of Admiralty against the charge, unstated but implicit in all these exchanges, of having mishandled the whole affair by pleading in extenuation 'the rapidity with which events moved' and 'the very difficult conditions in which the Board had to act'. Though there certainly was some truth in his statement that the origin of the outbreak was to be found in 'decent men driven to distraction about their homes', to say that 'this was no mutiny as the word is generally understood' was a gross *suppressio veri*.[1] This unconvincing defence evidently did not satisfy the Monarch. When he met Bridgeman, the former First Lord, some months later he told him that he considered that the Sea Lords should all have resigned.[2] In fact only one of them, Admiral C. T. M. Fuller,[3] the Second Sea Lord, who was responsible for personnel, was relieved of his post. But the complete lack of any inquiry by an impartial judicial body did result in injustices among officers and men. Admiral Tomkinson, who had taken over command of the Fleet at very short notice, was replaced before he had served his full term afloat, the Captains of the ships which had been worst affected were relieved of their commands, and a large number of ratings were discharged 'Services No Longer Required' – a polite euphemism designed to cover up the fact that they were believed to have been seriously involved in stirring up or organising the mutiny. They were not given any opportunity to defend themselves, let alone call witnesses on their own behalf, but were abruptly dismissed – often

[1] RA GV K2330(3)/14. [2] Bridgeman, Political Notes (MSS.), Vol. II, p. 253.
[3] 1874–1942. Chief of Staff, Atlantic Fleet 1920–22. Assistant Chief of Naval Staff 1922–23. Third Sea Lord and Controller of Navy 1923–25. Commanded Battle Cruiser Squadron, Atlantic Fleet 1925–27. C-in-C, America and West Indies Station 1928–30. Second Sea Lord and Chief of Naval Personnel 1930–32.

to join the ever-lengthening queue of unemployed. Though it is certainly the case that the Boards of Admiralty which succeeded to the ill-starred Board of 1931 had a very difficult and delicate task to perform, and it is hard to quarrel with the view that restoration of the morale of the Navy had to be their paramount task, one does wish that the officers who were adjudged to have failed, and the men who were deemed to have been prime movers in bringing about the events of September 1931, had been given the ordinary Common Law right to defend their own actions. As regards the men it should be recorded that one of these unfortunates, Able Seaman Copeman, fought later in the International Brigade during the Spanish Civil War and then performed most gallant service in the London Civil Defence service during the city's ordeal by bombing in 1940–41.[1]

On 21st September MacDonald announced in the House that the reductions in pay to be imposed on teachers and police as well as on the fighting services were to be limited to 'not more than 10 per cent'. But that still left the position of service men on the 1919 rates of pay in a state of ambiguity. On the last day of the month the Cabinet was forced to consider their problems again, and admitted that it was 'politically impossible' to interpret the Prime Minister's statement otherwise than meaning that no man, whether on the 1919 or 1925 rate of pay, should be left worse off than 10%.[2] Truly the intricacies introduced under Treasury pressure in 1925 came home to roost with a vengeance six years later.

*Diary 20th September 1931*

I write in the train on my way to a Sunday Cabinet. All the decisions were taken on Friday night [18th] and confirmed yesterday for us to fall off the gold standard to-morrow. The Cabinet is little more than a formality to confirm decisions already taken. All the week the drain of credits and gold on London has been increasing. On Wednesday it was £5 million, on Thursday £10 million, on Friday nearly £18 million. The end of the £80 million credit is in sight. On Monday [14th] the Bank of England told us that at the then rate of withdrawals they could hold out for three or four weeks. By Thursday [17th] the estimate had fallen to two weeks, but they still wanted to continue the fight, and induced the Government to appeal to the U.S.A. and

[1] Sir John Hodsoll, who was Inspector-General of Civil Defence in World War II, to the author 20th March 1964. I am indebted to Mr. Richard Ollard, who met Copeman while on the teaching staff at the R.N. College, Greenwich, for information about his career after he was discharged from the Navy.

[2] Cabinet 67(31) of 30th Sept. 1931, Conclusion 1. Cab. 23/68.

French Governments for further aid – though the Treasury were convinced it could not be given, which has proved correct. On Friday night, after several nights in town working late, I got home at about 5 p.m. and, on arrival, received a telephone message that the P.M., who had left for Chequers earlier, was on his way back as Sir Ernest Harvey,[1] Deputy Governor of the Bank of England, and Mr. Peacock[2] were to see him at 9.45 p.m. I went back to the station but just missed the train. It was too foggy to motor, so I caught the 9.30, which needless to say, was 20 minutes late! I found the Bankers with the P.M., Warren Fisher and Leith Ross. They had decided to give up the fight and were discussing ways and means for going off the gold standard – a Bill on Monday to be passed through all its stages (necessitating summoning the House of Lords); taking of powers to proclaim a Bank Holiday in the event of a run on the Banks, powers to stop export of credit; propaganda etc. Rather a dismal affair. On Saturday morning [19th] I was very busy on the Bank Holiday proclamations – a most complicated business. If the powers were wanted at all, they would be needed at the shortest notice. But, for fear of creating a panic, it was necessary to keep quiet that we were taking these powers. If the King had been in London it would have been easy to have the necessary instruments ready and to summon a Privy Council meeting at short notice to pass them. But the King was [at] Balmoral. The lawyers would not let us have a Proclamation with the date left blank. So, as we could not tell on which day a panic might arise, if it does arise, we had to get the King to sign five separate Proclamations proclaiming a Bank Holiday, i.e. one for each day from Monday to Friday. Privy Counsellors had to be collected from places within reach of Balmoral, and elaborate arrangements made for secrecy. The Council is fixed for 4 p.m. this afternoon. Clive Wigram, who has succeeded Stamfordham as private secretary, was very cool, and I fixed the whole thing up by telephone. I also looked into our food supply, which appears satisfactory and the national strike organisation, as we cannot foretell what will happen. I had a long talk with the P.M. in the morning, and we lunched together at the U.S. Club. He showed good courage after the prolonged strain. I told him that in the war, whenever we met disaster, we tried to get some good out of it:—The Supreme War Council out of Caporetto; the unified command out of March 21st 1918 etc., and I urged that we must do the same now. A depreciation of the £ should enable us to improve our export trade; to manufacture our own petrol from coal; to get agriculture on its legs; and,

[1] 1867–1955. (Not Hervey as written by Hankey). Comptroller, Bank of England 1925–28. Deputy Governor 1929–36.

[2] Later Sir Edward R. Peacock (1871–1962). Canadian-born banker. A director of Bank of England 1921–24 and 1928–46. A managing director of Baring Bros., and director of C.P.R. and Hudson's Bay Company.

with proper handling, to get our extravagant standard of living down. His mind worked like lightning on these ideas and we were both cheered and stimulated by our talk, though all this will take time and in the meantime we shall have every kind of trouble.

It has been a difficult and depressing week. . . . The political situation also has been very difficult, even in the Cabinet. Having balanced the budget the next step is to try and restore the balance of trade. Tariffs appear to be the only solution, but a general election would be essential for this. Anyhow, if the National Govt. was to continue, a general election to secure a better majority in Parliament than 50 was held widely to be essential. The original idea at the formation of the National Government had been that, as soon as sterling was secured, the general election should be held; the National Government remaining in office during the election, but each party being entirely free to preach its own nostrums. During the present week it became clear that this course was fraught with danger. The bankers advised that public opinion abroad would view with misgiving a general election in such circumstances. But if the National Government could go to the country with a national policy for restoring the trade balance, they thought opinion abroad would be reassured and that the prospects of a further loan would be improved. The question arose, therefore, in an acute and urgent form as to whether an agreed policy could be found to enable the re-establishment of the balance of trade. The Prime Minister's efforts to accomplish this were met by insuperable obstacles. The Conservatives could not contemplate a general election in which tariff reform was not in the forefront. The Liberals could not yield an inch on free trade, and represented their position to be as patriotic and convinced as that of the Conservatives. Thomas, of course, has long favoured a tariff. The P.M., I have no doubt, would support it, and Lord Sankey would follow him. Snowden, I think, would agree to a prohibitive duty on certain luxury goods – a prohibition of import being contrary to the Anglo-German Commercial Treaty of 1924, the benefits of which are secured to some other countries by most-favoured-nation treaties – but not to tariffs for any other purpose. I think Samuel, like Snowden, might have been persuaded to this if they were satisfied that it was necessary to secure the balance of trade. On this question negotiations, which were transferred from the Cabinet to the P.M., Baldwin and Samuel, had reached an impasse on Friday [18th]. The dilemma was acute. Without a general election the National Government was likely to decline steadily in popularity and before long to become ineffective owing to the absence of any sufficient common denominator of agreement. Confidence in it would fail and the £ sterling must collapse. An election without a national policy was equally disastrous, and sufficient credits were not likely to be obtained to tide over the period of the election. Yet in the state of parties, a national policy was unattainable. At this precise moment the Bank of England fell off the gold standard. The whole question of a general election disappears in the overwhelming need for national unity. It is probable that, if the £ falls in value, the argument for a tariff will disappear, as the devaluation will itself provide protection if we do not allow wages and doles to rise in proportion. All these matters I discussed with the P.M. at lunch at the U.S. Club on Saturday; also other matters such as the criticism of our whole field of policy in France and in parts of the continent under French influence.

On Saturday afternoon [19th] I was present at conferences between the P.M., Baldwin, Samuel, the Deputy Governor of the Bank (Sir Ernest Harvey), Mr. Peacock and Treasury officials. I got home late and found a telephone message awaiting me that a Cabinet must be summoned [for] Sunday at 4.30 p.m. My office was closed, my private secretary out of touch, and I found myself compelled to telephone to each member of the Cabinet, who were widely dispersed – Baldwin in Dorsetshire, Cunliffe-Lister in Oxfordshire etc. – a most tiresome job and I was dead tired already. Baldwin was furious with Samuel, who had asked for the Cabinet, especially as he had had to travel up to town and back from Cranborne that day.

I spent the morning sun-bathing, interrupted by a long harangue on the telephone by Winston Churchill (who has Charlie Chaplin as his guest at Chartwell[1]) on the situation. I could not enlighten him that we were going off the gold standard to-morrow, and had to listen to a torrent of suggestions to deal with a situation that had already passed out of history. I write this in the train at 9.30 p.m. on my way home from the Cabinet, after completing the Minutes. I left the P.M. closeted with Arthur Henderson, the leader of the opposition, showing him the Bill taking us off the gold standard.[2]

On 26th Hankey recorded that the £ sterling had dropped to about 15/- or 16/-, but 'the people have kept steady and there has been no case for using the Bank Holiday Proclamations'. Then he became involved in complicated and acrimonious exchanges between London and Delhi over whether the Indian rupee should be maintained at about 1/6 and linked to the £ sterling or 'cut adrift'. In the latter event London

[1]Hankey actually wrote 'Churt' where Lloyd George was of course then living. But he must have meant Chartwell, where the visitors' book confirms that Charlie Chaplin stayed for the week-end of 19th–21st Sept. 1931. Information from the Curator, Chartwell, Nov. 1970.

[2]The Cabinet minutes entirely confirm Hankey's diary entry. The only interesting point is that the minutes record that MacDonald explained why 'it had been necessary for him to take action expeditiously and with the utmost secrecy' on 19th, and so had not been able to summon the full Cabinet. The Conclusion states that 'The Cabinet recognized the circumstances in which the Prime Minister had to act on their behalf'. Cabinet 60(31) of 20th Sept. 1931. Cab. 23/68.

felt sure it would fall to its silver bullion value of about -/4d, with catastrophic results for India. Delhi on the other hand was equally sure that the British policy would result 'in all their currency reserves being drawn to London in an impossible effort to support the rupee'. Sir George Schuster,[1] the Finance Member, threatened to resign over this issue, and the Viceroy himself 'gave a barely concealed hint that he and the whole Government [of India] would do the same'. The Cabinet, however, 'stuck to its guns', and 'a strong personal appeal' by MacDonald and Baldwin to Lord Willingdon[2] and Schuster produced the desired result.

*Diary 26th September 1931*

... The Press is full of the idea of a general election. The majority of the Cabinet favour the idea. Sam Hoare (S. of S. for India) told me on Thursday morning that the pressure from the Conservative rank and file for an election is so overwhelming that the members of the Cabinet 'would be left high and dry' if it does not come off. They want the P.M. to go to an election as leader of a National Party, but they insist on a tariff reform policy. I suggested that, if the National Party were successful at the polls, the Conservatives would come back with the bulk of their members. After a year or two there would be nothing to prevent them from 'carting' Ramsay MacDonald as they carted Ll. George in 1922. What guarantee could they give against that happening? His reply was 'Well! We just won't do that'. But, of course, the trouble is the usual one that behind Conservative Ministers, most of whom play the game, is the Carlton Club! Hoare ended by appealing to me to say a word to MacDonald. I grunted. That afternoon Baldwin opened up on the same subject. He considered a general election to be absolutely essential. The National Cabinet had no mandate and an insufficient majority. It could not carry on much longer, and the sooner an election was held the better. 'Your position' I remarked 'is the same as when you took over the post of P.M. from Bonar Law. I remember that you were always restless because you had not your own majority'. He agreed. Like Hoare, he wanted the National Government to go to the country with an agreed programme that must

[1] 1881– . Banker and financial expert. Financial Secretary, Sudan Government 1922–27. Economic and financial adviser to Colonial Office 1927–28. Finance Member, Executive Council of Viceroy of India 1928–34. Member of many government committees especially on finance, colonial development, industrial and economic policy etc.

[2] Freeman Freeman-Thomas, 1st Marquess of Willingdon 1936 (1866–1941). Politician (Lib.) and Pro-Consul. Governor of Bombay 1913–19 and of Madras 1919–24. Governor-General of Canada 1926–31. Succeeded Lord Irwin (later Earl of Halifax) as Viceroy of India April 1931 and held that office until 1936.

include tariff reform. 'If the Conservative majority is very large' he added 'our fellows may make some difficulty about the Prime Ministership; but I think it can be arranged'.... A few minutes later I saw J. H. Thomas and told him how matters stood. He also is overwhelmingly in favour of a general election, and told me that the P.M. is also – which I know is not correct. J. H. wants as a programme a simple mandate for five years to straighten out our financial and economic position, with a free hand to do the best for the country, nothing barred, not even tariffs. Of course he is an out and out tariff reformer. He said that Snowden would not object, as he is deliberately sitting back on the question, having already announced his intention to retire. Lord Sankey would follow the P.M. (Sankey, by the way, gave me as his private view that by March Lloyd George would be P.M.) Thomas spoke of the sacrifices he had made and assured me that in the last six months he had lost £150,000 – an almost incredible statement! Next day [Friday 25th] the P.M. spent a few hours in town on his way from a short spell at Sandwich to Chequers, and took a Cabinet. Just before the meeting I told him of the attitude of the Conservatives and (without mentioning names) of my [talk] with Sam Hoare. He remarked 'In fact, they will keep me in, as long as I lead the Conservative party!' After the Cabinet he saw Baldwin and Samuel each separately. Samuel is the difficulty. He has circulated an extremely powerful Memo, against an election, and criticising Tariff Reform – though I thought he did just leave the door ajar on the subject, in case it was found that the balance of trade could not be adjusted without resort to tariffs in some form. The trouble is that all the Conservative members of the Cabinet cordially detest Samuel, both in his opposition to tariffs and in his personality.

An interesting minor development this week has occurred at Geneva. The Japanese have been indulging in some rather high-handed proceedings against the Chinese in Manchuria, whom they represent (probably correctly) as having been more than usually intractable. The Chinese appealed to the League, which is meeting in the Assembly. The Japs have very politely but firmly told the League to go to the devil. The League had asked the British, French, Italians, Germans and Spaniards to make representations at Tokyo. The British at once sent instructions. Up to now the others have not. Spain was included because the Spanish Foreign Minister was in the Chair at the Council. He sent his instruction by mistake to Pekin instead of Tokyo!!! This caused much bewilderment!...[1] Why do we do these silly things? That is one of the reasons why we are so mistrusted. We will poke our nose into everyone's business at the League.

[1]The Japanese were evidently not above exploiting Lord Cecil's unpopularity in some quarters by 'hinting' that the British were courting the hostility of Japan through following his initiative. Hankey recorded this, but then scrupulously added that 'the Japs were wrong' in attributing the League's representations to Cecil.

It must have been at a Cabinet held on 30th September or 1st October that, according to a later entry in Hankey's diary,[1] he drafted and handed to MacDonald a suggested 'formula' which the three political parties might all accept as a solution 'to the difficult question of tariffs'. It read as follows:—

'*National Government seeks a Mandate*:

To take all means to re-establish the national economy. Nothing is barred; tariffs to be considered on their merits according to developments.

*Conservatives* to be free to say "We believe tariffs are essential, but we will keep an open mind".

*Liberals* to be free to say "We believe Free Trade will stand, but we will keep an open mind".

*Labour* According as they are Tariff Reformers or Free Traders'.

MacDonald 'read half' the draft 'and then stopped abruptly and put a pencil through the lower half'. Yet, as Hankey remarked, it was 'substantially the ultimate settlement'.

*Diary October 3rd 1931*

The political crisis continued all the week.[2] . . . On Wednesday afternoon I had some business with him [MacDonald] and found him closeted with Baldwin. He was lying down with a bad headache. When we had finished the business, he and Baldwin kept on gossiping about old times for half an hour or so, and wouldn't let me go. [Here Hankey repeated a story MacDonald told him about how, on the eve of the outbreak of war in 1914, Sir John French learnt from Lord Riddell, with whom MacDonald was dining, that he was to command the B.E.F. MacDonald also described how 'influenced to some extent by Morley', he had refused to join the government.] At the end of our talk Ramsay MacDonald suddenly jumped up from his sofa and said 'My head-ache has quite gone', and went to his desk to tackle his papers. I then saw why he had kept me gossiping. He had been so oppressed by the weight of the political crisis that he simply had to talk of something else. The trouble is that he insists on staying in the House every night until

[1]For 7th Oct. 1931.

[2]Hankey here recorded that he had dictated an account of the crisis 'in case the P.M. wanted it', and had attached a copy to his diary. It is entitled 'Notes of events during week ending Saturday October 3rd' and is now in the loose-leaf section of the diary. Another copy is in the 'Magnum Opus' file Cab. 63/44. It does not, however, add anything significant to the entries quoted here. There is also a valuable diary compiled by C. P. Duff and covering the period 11th–24th August 1931 in Premier 1/96.

it rises: sleeps very badly; starts work again before 8 a.m., and never lets up. All this week, with this frightful crisis on hand, he has spent his mornings presiding at a Committee of the Indian Round Table Conference,[1] besides dashing off to his constituency at Seaham, where he has been repudiated, on Friday [? 18th September] – the most fateful day of the crisis, as it turned out. . . .

An amusing incident occurred in this connection at the Cabinet on Wednesday [30th September]. They were discussing the dates of future meetings. Samuel was to go to Churt to see Lloyd George that afternoon, so they could not have a Cabinet that evening. Reading also wanted to see Ll. G. before the Cabinet met, but could not go until Thursday afternoon. 'Please remember' said MacDonald 'that on Friday I go to "See-im"' (that was how it sounded). 'What! *You* going to see Lloyd George!' several voices cried. 'I am going to Sea*ham*' said MacDonald. Loud and general laughter interrupted what had become a tense moment – for the Conservatives had been protesting against the further delay in the long, protracted crisis, which is getting on the nerves of their party. . . . In a word it [the crisis] has been a long wrangle in the search for a formula on tariffs, on which the Conservatives and Liberals can unite in going to the country as a National Government. On Friday [2nd October] they seemed very near at one time. Baldwin was in the chair at first. Later on, after a short adjournment, Snowden came in from the House, where he had been making a speech on the Finance Bill, rather pleased with himself, as he had been trouncing his opponents. Baldwin asked him to take the chair, as he was more detached in the controversy. Snowden asked Samuel and Chamberlain to explain their respective points of view. When they had finished he said he could see no difference between them. 'It is Tweedledum and Tweedledee. We shall look absolute Ninnies if we break on so narrow an issue'. But they could not agree, and at the end they instructed me to report to the P.M. on his return from Seaham early on Saturday morning. I was a bit fogged myself at the moment, with all the rapid fire of argument, though I had taken copious notes. So, after the Cabinet had risen, I asked Snowden to give me his version of the point of difference. He replied 'I assure you that I am quite incapable at this moment of explaining what the difference is!' So I went to

[1]Hankey is here referring to the second session of the India Round Table Conference. The first session had opened on 12th Nov. 1930 and was prorogued by MacDonald on 19th Jan. 1931. The second session began in the following September, and was chiefly concerned with trying to reconcile the rival claims of Moslems and Hindus under an all-India Federal constitution. The famous White Paper of March 1933 was the ultimate product of the prolonged deliberations initiated by the 'Irwin Declaration' of October 1929 naming Dominion Status as the goal for India.

Samuel's room and got him to dictate his version of the difference. Then I went to Neville Chamberlain's room and got him to do the same. Next I went to 10 Downing St. and spoke on the telephone to the Prime Minister at Seaham. He asked me, if I spoke to any members of the Cabinet, to let them know that he was 'fed up' with the whole business and inclined to run out. Then to the Cabinet Office, where Clive Wigram, the King's Private Secretary was waiting to see me, and was perturbed to learn of the virtual break. He told me that Samuel had seen the King that morning, and had been very unyielding and had made the King very cross by his attitude. He had told someone – Harding,[1] I think, perhaps also the King – that he had in mind a new coalition – Ramsay MacDonald, the Liberals and the Labour Party under Henderson. Shortly after I found it necessary to telephone to Samuel (about 6.40 p.m.) to ask him about how his formula on tariffs fitted into another formula drawn up by a Cabinet Committee. I took the opportunity to tell him that MacDonald was 'fed to the teeth' and in the mood to drop out. 'Oh. He needn't think of it!' said Samuel. 'There are other combinations that might be tried. You can tell the P.M. that I am at his disposal to-morrow if he wants me!' So, putting Wigram's news to Samuel's I saw the whole thing. When Samuel came to the Cabinet that afternoon, after difficult interviews with his Liberal colleagues outside the Cabinet, he had this new combination in mind, and had no idea of getting a settlement, or at any rate of any further concession. The Conservatives, I knew, who dislike Samuel, had been determined to make no further concessions beyond the considerable ones already made. So, as I had sensed at the time, there never was a chance of a deal, in spite of their seeming so near. I reported all this in writing – rather flippantly, I fear – to the P.M. I also drew up a very full Cabinet Minute for the P.M., and sent a copy to Samuel to check. I am to show it to Baldwin [on] Monday [5th], before circulating – there are occasions when it is wise to be slow in circulating, just as there are times when one cannot be too quick. In a crisis like this Minutes are a delicate business! I got to dinner about 10.30 p.m. The previous night the Cabinet had sat until 11.30 p.m.! . . .

On Saturday morning [3rd] I went to 10 Downing St. at 7.40 a.m. in order to make sure of catching the P.M. before he saw J. H. Thomas at breakfast at 8 a.m. I was most anxious that he should see my purely objective official account of yesterday's proceedings, before he heard Thomas's version, which would be partisan and highly coloured, Thomas being in favour of a break with the official Liberals. I found the P.M. reading my

[1]Though Hankey wrote 'Harding', and he may have been referring to Sir Edward Harding of the Dominions Office (see p. 429, *note*), in this context it seems more probable that he meant Sir Alexander Hardinge (1894–1960), later 2nd Baron Hardinge, who was Equerry and Assistant Private Secretary to the King 1920–36.

Minutes, which I had left at No. 10 myself the night before. I told him that the Conservatives wanted power to deal with limitation of imports by tariffs – and made no secret of their determination to use the power. The Liberals were ready, if investigation showed the necessity, to resort to tariffs in particular cases, but made no secret of it that they still stood for free trade and would only agree to tariffs in the last resort and if it was a proved necessity. To the layman that might seem a narrow distinction, comparable to the 'homo-ousian' of the Arian controversy,[1] or the 'filioque' which separated the Roman and Orthodox churches. But in the constituencies, it would be difficult to prevent Liberals, who were keen free-traders, and Conservatives, who were keen tariff reformers, to refrain from putting up rival candidates on any formula that had yet been proferred. There was not a broad enough basis of agreement. If the National Government got a majority, I feared that this difference of point of view would be constantly splitting the Cabinet and the majority in Parliament, and would soon weaken the Government. Ramsay was cross at Samuel's hint of another combination, and cross with the Conservatives for not being more elastic. 'Samuel will co-operate, if I will bring in some other fellow', he said, 'and the Conservative attitude is just the same'. (The Conservatives want Simon[2] and the tariff reform Liberals instead of Samuel). Then Thomas came in with his son, who was at Rugby with Christopher, a nice-looking boy. It was Thomas's 57th birthday. As I expected, he was all out to get rid of Samuel & Co., but thinks Reading will stay. An hour or two later I again saw the P.M. on his return from seeing the King. But he had no news, beyond an account of the King's rather heated interview with Samuel. He went off to Chequers, but was to see Baldwin surreptitiously en route at Trent [Park],[3] Philip Sassoon's place which he has lent to Baldwin for the week-end. I had to wait in town until MacDonald had reached Chequers and telephoned that there would be no Cabinet Monday morning. The result was I missed a perfectly lovely autumn day. But I slept 10 hours and we went off this morning [Sunday 4th Oct.] to Tide Mills (between Newhaven and Seaford). . . .

[1]This refers to the controversy over the identity of substance of the three persons of the Holy Trinity. The Council of Nicaea, convened by Constantine in A.D. 325, ruled against the Alexandrian presbyter Arius that the Son was 'homo-ousios', i.e. 'of the same substance', with the Father.

[2]John A. S. Simon, 1st Viscount Simon 1940 (1873–1954). Lawyer and politician (Lib. until 1931, then Lib. Nat.). Solicitor-General 1913. Attorney-General 1913–15. Home Secretary 1915–16. Chairman, Indian Statutory Commission 1927–30. Foreign Secretary 1931–35. Again Home Secretary 1935–37. Chancellor of Exchequer 1937–40. Lord Chancellor 1940–45.

[3]In Hertfordshire. Not to be confused with Sassoon's house near Lympne where the conferences of 1920–21 took place. See pp. 166–8, 173–4, 187 and 228.

The night's rest on 3rd–4th October, followed by the sea bathe and 'a good tramp on the downs' above Lewes made Hankey feel like 'a giant refreshed', and on the Monday he was back in the office to find the political crisis still in full spate.

*Diary 5th October 1931*

The Prime Minister spent his morning at the Indian Round Table Conference and his afternoon seeing Baldwin and Samuel, trying to get an agreed formula, but without success. Cabinet meeting at 6 p.m. Most dramatic! Everyone thought the National Cabinet was going to break up; that Samuel, and perhaps Reading, would resign and that Simon, Runciman and the dissident group of tariff reform Liberals would replace them. The P.M. put the alternatives:—a break-up; to continue in office without an election; to go to the country on a general programme to stabilise sterling, leaving the question of tariffs for each party to deal with in its own way. The news from the City was so bad, and from Central Europe so disquieting that a break-up was generally deemed impossible. To continue in office without an election was equally unacceptable to all except the Liberals. It was known everywhere, at home and abroad, that the Cabinet for a week had been trying to agree on an election programme, and it was felt that everyone would know that the decision to continue in office was due to a failure to agree. In these circumstances the Cabinet would not inspire the confidence . . . to enable it to take the national and international measures necessary to re-establish the balance of trade and stabilise the currency. When the Prime Minister declared for a general election, all fell into line, even the Liberals, notwithstanding that Lloyd George, whom the P.M. had visited at Churt that morning, was known to be obdurate on the point. There were two interesting episodes; first an extraordinary outburst by Jim Thomas, when the P.M. suggested remaining in office without an election. He had only suggested it in order to show the Liberals how impossible it was; but Thomas took it seriously and hinted at the influence on the P.M. of people who had no political experience. He was, I think, referring to Jowitt,[1] the Attorney-General; for, before the Cabinet, he had deplored to me that the P.M. was dining with the Jowitts whom he supposed to be a bad influence. As a matter of fact Jowitt had told me earlier that he was convinced that the P.M. must go on, so Thomas was wrong for once. Anyhow, he nearly spoilt the P.M's tactics. The other incident was the reading by Samuel of a typewritten statement on behalf of the Liberal Ministers. This was quite a useful statement of willingness to

[1]William A. Jowitt, 1st Earl 1951 (1885–1957). Lawyer and politician (Lib. until 1929 then Lab.). Attorney-General 1929–32. Solicitor-General 1940–42. Paymaster-General 1942. Minister without Portfolio 1942–44 and for National Insurance 1944–45. Lord Chancellor 1945–51.

co-operate, if the P.M. decided on an election, but then he began to read from a manuscript note of a much more controversial character. Whereupon Reading interrupted him with 'No! No! Don't read *that*!!' And Samuel hastily put it in his pocket. So all ended in perfect harmony. It was nearly midnight, but I had to go back to the office and work on the revise of my draft of the King's speech, which had to be printed and sent to the King first thing to-morrow, and to write a letter to Schuster, the Clerk of the Crown Office, telling him to have the election writs ready for issue on Wednesday night [7th]. . . .

Next day, 6th, Hankey was in the office early in order to complete the previous day's Cabinet minutes. Then he went round to No. 10 and found MacDonald, Baldwin and Samuel putting the final touches to the government's Manifesto to the electors and 'fixing up a lot of election business'. In the afternoon the final Cabinet of the caretaker National government took place, after which Hankey had to arrange for two meetings of the Privy Council on 7th – one to approve the Order-in-Council proroguing Parliament and the other the Proclamation dissolving it.[1] Both passed off without incident, the King 'was in great form and was particularly nice to me' wrote Hankey.[2] 'So the crisis is over', he concluded, and then added 'The Prime Minister has been splendid . . . and has proved himself a worthy leader of the nation. In the early part [of the crisis] he gave the impression of being worn out and hardly equal physically to the terrific burden put upon him. But he has an extraordinarily elastic constitution, and in spite of late hours, sleepless nights and incessant toil for 16 hours a day, he recuperated and won through in what seemed to most of us to be an impossible task'. As Hankey was one of those best placed to observe MacDonald closely during the crisis of 1931 his final tribute must surely carry weight.

On 2nd October the King kept Hankey behind after a Privy Council and 'gossiped about election news'. When he said to the Clerk 'Of course you are going to vote' Hankey explained that, ever since the war, he had 'rather made a point of not voting' in elections in order to emphasise his detachment from party politics. 'But', said the Monarch, 'this time it is different. I want the National Government to get every vote possible'. When he confirmed to Hankey that this was 'a command', the latter said 'Very well, Sire. Your Majesty can claim to have canvassed one vote for the National Government'. And when Hankey

[1]Diary 6th Oct. 1931. [2]*ibid.* 7th Oct. 1931.

deplored the controversy which had continued throughout the election campaign regarding 'what had happened in the Cabinet', to his surprise the King said 'he didn't mind much so long as they didn't drag him in'.[1]

Two days later Hankey was at No. 10 while the election results were coming in, and 'every hour showed the eclipse of Labour to be greater'. Geoffrey Dawson, editor of *The Times* was there, and on hearing that MacDonald had arrived in town and was lunching with Lord De la Warr,[2] Hankey, Dawson and Ralph Glyn[3] went round to Buckingham Mews to find him. The 'tiny house', wrote Hankey, was 'an odd place to find the P.M. of the National Government at the very moment of his unprecedented success'.[4] MacDonald was obviously in splendid form and gave an amusing account of how he had got the better of a hostile audience of Durham coal miners during the election campaign. But Hankey very soon got him down to serious business.

*Diary 28th Oct. 1931*

. . . In our short conversation [at 3 Buckingham Mews, Lord De La Warr's house] I said I hoped that there was no truth in the rumour that the P.M. intended to delegate the leadership of the House of Commons to Mr. Baldwin, and reminded him how unpopular Mr. Lloyd George had been in the House of Commons for doing this. He said he would not do so. I also strongly advised him to have a large Cabinet again. After the huge number of Conservatives had been elected, he could hardly hope to keep his three Labour colleagues in a Cabinet of 10, but could do so in a Cabinet of 20. He agreed, and said he had come to the conclusion that this country could not be governed permanently with a Cabinet of 10. At the end I got him alone and suggested that he could solve some of his difficulties by appointing Baldwin as Chancellor of the Exchequer. He was not such an extreme Tariff

[1]Diary 26th Oct. 1931.

[2]Hankey here wrote 'Delaware', but there is no such title. Obviously he meant Herbrand E. D. B. Sackville, 9th Earl De La Warr (pronounced 'De la Ware') (1900– ). Landowner and politician (Cons.). Parliamentary Secretary, Ministry of Agriculture 1930–31 and 1931–35. Parliamentary Under-Secretary for Colonies 1936–37. Lord Privy Seal 1937–38. President, Board of Education 1938–40. First Commissioner of Works 1940. Postmaster-General 1951–55.

[3]Major Ralph G. C. Glyn. (Not Glynn as written by Hankey.) (1885–1960). 1st Baron Glyn 1953. Politician (Cons.) and businessman. Parliamentary Private Secretary to Ramsay MacDonald as Prime Minister and as Lord President of Council 1931–35.

[4]The National Government won 554 seats, of which no less than 473 went to Conservatives. Labour slumped from the 288 in the previous Parliament to 52.

Reformer as Neville Chamberlain, yet it would satisfy the Conservatives. Moreover it would give a £5,000 a year job to Baldwin, who is a poor man and the Treasury like him.[1] He replied that Baldwin had not a very good reputation as Chancellor, and that Runciman was his man.

*October 30th*

When I took the Cabinet Minutes to the P.M. this evening I took the opportunity to refer again to the question of the new Chancellor of the Exchequer. I said I hardly liked to speak of a personal friend in this way, but I felt bound to say that I had misgivings as to whether Runciman would fill the bill. . . . I recalled Kitchener's verdict that Runciman was always very impressive in Cabinet, but failed to deliver the goods. I added that Ll. G. (who, of course, did not like Runciman) often quoted this. I added that in my experience R. was not a very easy man in a Cabinet. He has, like McKenna, Donald Maclean[2] or Samuel (to a less extent), that hard uncompromising radical mind that bases itself on principle, and is not easily moved. I agreed however that he was firm, had a gift of exposition in Parliament, and [was] competent. The P.M. said he could not let the Conservatives have both the Exchequer and the Board of Trade, and that he must not leave Runciman out. He agreed that Simon would not do for Chancellor. He thanked me for speaking so frankly. I have sent him a long Memo. on the task of the National Government, in which I air my views as to the root cause of the crisis – our want of 'guts' since the war, which has led other nations to lose confidence in us.[3]

A week later Hankey's intervention in MacDonald's Cabinet-making bore fruit in the announcement that Neville Chamberlain would shift from the Ministry of Health to the Treasury, and Runciman take over the Board of Trade. And it is hard not to feel that, even if the expression of his personal preferences for Ministers may not have been constitutionally correct action by a civil servant, his unwillingness to see

[1]Although in June 1919 Baldwin valued his estate at £580,000 and gave 20% of that sum anonymously to reduce the national debt (see *Baldwin*, pp. 72–3), the shares in his family firm, which had stood at 50/- at the height of the postwar boom, had slumped to 3/6 by 1927, and the firm was paying no dividends. (*op. cit.* p. 260.) Thus Hankey's description of him as 'a poor man' in the early 1930s was well justified.

[2]Sir Donald Maclean (1864–1932). Politician (Lib.). As Chairman, Liberal Parliamentary Party 1919–22 inherited the somewhat tattered cloak of Asquithian Liberalism.

[3]Memo. dated 28th Oct. 1931 entitled 'Notes on the task of the National Government'. Hankey sent it only to MacDonald, and discussed it with him at Chequers during the weekend of 21st–22nd Nov. Cab. 63/44.

Runciman, not to mention Simon, as Chancellor of the Exchequer was fully justified.

The formation of the National Government in the early days of November 1931 provides a convenient point at which to end this volume. Hankey had then passed his 53rd birthday, and no visible sign of any decline in his astonishing stamina and vitality had yet become apparent. He himself attributed his fitness to what he described as the 'very low diet' which he had adopted about 1929. This comprised 'a Continental breakfast (coffee and whole-meal bread and butter); a few nuts and some fruit for lunch; nothing with my tea; and a light dinner of fish or eggs or Welsh rarebit, usually very late in the evening ... and a lemon and hot water without sugar at bed time'. In addition he did 'Müller's exercises for a quarter of an hour every morning, took a cold bath all the year round, and had breakfast out in the loggia [at Highstead]' whenever possible. He always wore 'very light clothes' and 'ate lettuce and grated raw carrots at least once a day'. 'Rather a spartan régime', he admitted, certainly without exaggeration, 'but a pleasant one' – except, as we saw earlier, to his less hardy friends.[1]

Intellectually he was still at the peak of his powers, and even Tom Jones, who was by no means always a friendly critic, was constrained to describe him as 'an amazing person' a few months after the National Government took office.[2] Yet the biographer, who has inevitably lived very close to his subject over a long period, can hardly fail to observe that a change did take place in his subject's character and outlook during the 13 years covered by this volume. Something of warmth and spontaneity in his feelings and reactions, not to mention the compassion he felt for suffering – notably that of the soldiers of World War I – is no longer so evident. Even his letters to Adeline, though no less regular than before, are more perfunctory, and often end on a note of exhaustion or even of exasperation such as 'No time for more now' or 'It is past midnight and I have not yet finished the record of the day's discussions'. Furthermore the endless drafting of minutes, memoranda and *procès-verbaux*, in which the avoidance of any suggestion of disagreement or recrimination were a dominant requirement, had vitiated the gift for producing the vivid phrase and the flashes of insight about

[1] Diary 3rd Oct. 1931.
[2] *A Diary with Letters 1931–1950* (Oxford U.P., 1954), p. 33. Diary entry for 5th March 1932

people and places which are so evident in his early letters. Plainly this loss was all part of the price he had to pay for being what he was. Yet its effects do appear to have resulted in a hardening of character and a loss of sentiment and sensibility. For example, although one can readily understand Hankey's militant attitude towards the General Strike of 1926, which was shared by millions of his countrymen, he never seems to have appreciated what to-day appears to be the astonishing patience of the vast army of unemployed of the period, or to have understood how very hard the economies introduced in 1931 hit those who were least able to withstand the shock.

The fall of Lloyd George undoubtedly marked a climacteric in Hankey's career. Not only were his relations with that mercurial character of a nature which was never repeated, but he was on equally intimate terms with nearly all the statesmen of Europe during the Lloyd George era. Clemenceau, for example, remarked in his memoirs on Hankey's 'superior qualities of order, of loyalty and of impeccable discipline'; while Frances Stevenson, the future second Lady Lloyd George, wrote of the same period that Hankey's 'serenity in trouble had to be seen to be believed, and his loyalty to Ll. G. was unfailing'. She considered, with good reason, that 'his spiritual resources and the happiness of his home must have upheld him in times of need'.[1]

Hankey's association with Bonar Law was too brief for either to have made a deep impression on the other; and if Baldwin really felt that, as Lawrence Burgis recalls, 'Hankey had no bowels' he certainly suppressed such thoughts successfully whenever it suited him to dump into Hankey's lap a particularly awkward issue – such as Lord Cecil's resignation – which he certainly ought to have handled himself. It can hardly be mere coincidence that all the letters from Baldwin which show warmth were either written while he was on a holiday which he obviously did not want to have disrupted, or when Hankey was at a European conference in which Baldwin himself might well have taken an active part.

Ramsay MacDonald's relations with Hankey provide something of a puzzle. That Hankey cordially disapproved MacDonald's dishonesty about the Campbell case of 1924 is beyond dispute, as is the fact that he was not taken in by MacDonald's capacity for equivocation and self-deception on not a few other issues. Yet Hankey served him with the utmost loyalty right to the end; and MacDonald for his part unques-

[1]To the author 3rd June 1970.

tionably relied greatly on Hankey. Possibly this reliance derived from the fact that neither in 1924 nor in 1929 did MacDonald enjoy the support of a solid Parliamentary majority, and from 1931 to 1935 he was completely dependent on Conservative support. In such uneasy circumstances he may well have felt that Hankey's great experience of public and international affairs was an invaluable asset, and also found in him the sheet anchor which his political supporters were either too few or too mutually unsympathetic to provide. Certainly MacDonald wrote a large number of appreciative letters to Hankey; but there is in them such a marked degree of fulsomeness and of flattery that one is inclined to doubt their sincerity.

As regards Hankey's relations with other Ministers of all parties it is almost impossible to find in their letters to him, or in their memoirs and autobiographies, a single discordant note except from Lord Cecil – until one comes to Churchill after 1937. With those exceptions all applaud Hankey both for his work and as a person.

In the Cabinet and C.I.D. sub-committees with which Hankey was chiefly concerned either as secretary or as chairman he was universally admired for his ability to reconcile violently conflicting points of view or opinions. This was particularly the case between Trenchard and Beatty in the Chiefs of Staff's Committee. Indeed study of that body's minutes and memoranda leaves no possible room for doubt that it was Hankey who dominated its deliberations, who produced many of the ideas which had to be considered, and who advised the service chiefs on how their own special problems should be handled.

More surprising than Hankey's great influence in the C.I.D. and the C.O.S. Sub-Committee is the fact that he established such excellent relations with the senior civil servants in every government department – with Warren Fisher at the Treasury (after their battle of 1923), Vansittart at the Foreign Office, Harding and Batterbee at the Dominions Office, Bullock at the Air Ministry and so on. For the senior men in any established organisation – be it a government department, a fighting service or an academic institution – are always inclined to cast distrustful, not to say jealous eyes at the outsider who has broken through the walls of their ivory towers. And the more able the outsider the more likely is he to arouse such antagonism. Yet, although no member of the establishment could possibly deny that Hankey's ability was outstanding, he almost always won their confidence, and even their affection in the end – even though in some cases it took a long time. His exemplary tact, so often remarked on, no doubt contributed to this, but so did his inexhaustible patience. He became indeed an artist not only in the handling of men but in the manipulation of the machinery of government of a vast empire – and even on occasions that of most of the nations of the world. The only exception to the record of Hankey's success with senior civil servants is Sir Edward (later Lord) Bridges, who came from the Treasury to take over one side of Hankey's work in 1938, and seems to have disliked his system as much as his personality. Though we may here remark that Bridges's membership of Churchill's 'secret circle' of World War II probably prejudiced him against his predecessor as Secretary of the Cabinet we must defer detailed consideration of the strange story of their mutual antipathy until our final volume.

Turning to the more intimate view of Hankey available to those who worked inside the closely guarded doors of 2 Whitehall Gardens, we are fortunate in having the first-hand recollections of several of his erstwhile assistants. Thus the late Sir John Hodsoll described him as 'a very great public servant . . . a good person to work for, as he let you get on with your job but was always accessible. And every now and again he would sit down in one of his armchairs, put you in the other and talk about the general situation or some current problem of special importance'.[1] Air Chief-Marshal Sir William Elliot, another of Hankey's Air Force assistants, writes that 'Foch somewhere in his book "On War" describes a harassed German General on the eve of, I think, the battle of Sadowa.[2] He is surrounded by his Staff Officers proferring advice. Eventually he can stand it no longer and exclaims, "To hell with strategy! *What is the problem*?" That is what I learnt from Hankey – the importance of discovering and recognising the problem' – a form of instruction in which the Service Staff Colleges were, in Sir William's opinion, very deficient.[3] The views of Lord Casey have already been quoted; and until General Ismay fell under the very powerful and hypnotic influence of Winston Churchill he too showed himself to be a warm admirer of Hankey. And so it continues down the list of those who knew him at first hand. Though some were readier than others to recognise Hankey's less admirable traits of character – such as his enjoyment of power and his reluctance to relinquish the

[1]To the author 22nd April 1970.
[2]Ferdinand Foch, *Des Principes de la Guerre* (1903).
[3]To the author, 9th Jan. 1969.

power which his knowledge and experience had gained him – there is not one who does not acknowledge the greatness of his qualities. Furthermore he was one of the very few men in high places who by the early 1930s had recognised that the rise of the dictatorships in Europe and the Far East presented a deadly threat to the democracies; that to attempt to negotiate with such rulers from weakness was foredoomed; and that the only hope of controlling their aggressive intentions lay in re-creating such armed strength as would enable our diplomats and statesmen to face them on something like equal terms. Though much that Hankey strove to accomplish was left far too late, and avoidable diplomatic defeats were thereby incurred, the fact that Britain did not succumb in the cataclysms of 1940–42 at the very least owes something to his clear-sightedness and perseverance.

# Index

Compiled by The Rev. S. B-R. Poole

Where a note reference is given in brackets, this signifies that there is a short biographical note on the person concerned.

Abdullah, Emir (later King) of Transjordan, 223 (and *note* 1)
Abraham, Captain E., 48 *note* 4, 103, 147, 162
Acton, Admiral Alfredo, 513 *note* 3
Adams, Professor George, 22
Adamson, W., 546 *note* 1
Addis, Sir Charles, 480 *note* 3
Addison, Dr. Christopher (later 1st Viscount), Minister of Reconstruction, then of Health, 36, 134, 202, 205, 210, 216, 546 *note* 1
Admiralty, reaction to scuttling of German ships at Scapa, 94-5; conflict with Air Ministry over control of naval aviation, 107; threat of naval building race, 112-13; proposal to build capital ships referred to Bonar Law Committee, 204-8; sponsors Singapore base, 231; delegation to Washington Conference, 237; their attitude there, 244 *et seq.*; their views overruled, 248; opposition to Geddes Report, 259; renewed controversy with Air Ministry, 260-2; attitude to Near Eastern Crisis, 286-7; continuing dispute with Air Ministry, 325; temporarily settled by Salisbury and Balfour Committees and Trenchard-Keyes agreement, 336-9, 344-346; continued interest in Singapore base, 347, 360-2; cruiser building programme, 362-3; opposition to Geneva Protocol, 381; renewed support for Singapore base, 402 and renewed friction with Air Ministry, 403; naval reconstruction programme carried, 403-5; claim that China was a naval responsibility, 408-10; reaction to Colwyn Committee and control of Fleet Air Arm, 417-18; policy at Geneva Conference, 438-41; further strife with Air Ministry, 445-9; attitude to Belligerent Rights, 452 *et seq.*; Churchill's attitude towards, 455-6, 462, and decision of Birkenhead Committee, 463; support for Anglo-French Compromise, 468; differences of outlook with U.S.A., 490 *et seq.*; dissatisfaction over progress on Singapore Base, 496-8; weakness of Board of, 508-9; preparations for and policy at London Naval Conference (1930), 509-12, 513-17, 519-20; review of naval commitments, 520-2; prejudice against Richmond, 525; efforts to revise Ten Year Rule, 534 *et seq.*; effect of May Report and Invergordon Mutiny, 554-8, *see* also Belligerent Rights, Freedom of the Seas and Ten Year Rule.
Adriatic question (Italo-Yugoslav dispute), 30-1, 57 *note* 1, 78, 80-2, 89, 91, 96, 100, 135, 138, 142,

Adriatic question [*contd.*]
143-4, 146-8, 162, *see* also Fiume.
Air Ministry and Royal Air Force, abortive proposals to discontinue Air Ministry, 32, 46-7, 107; idea of controlling Mesopotamia by aircraft, 169; controversy over future role (particularly with Admiralty), 260-2; attitude to Near Eastern crisis, 286; continued crisis with Admiralty, 325 and its temporary solution in Trenchard-Keyes agreement, 336-9; continued friction with Admiralty, 344-5, 402-3, 415-417, 446-9; work of Swinton for, 466; contribution to Singapore base, 496; influence of Air Power reviewed at Foreign Policy and Defence Sub-Committee of C.I.D., 525
Air Raid Precautions Sub-Committee, 405
Albert I, King of the Belgians, 176 (and *note* 1)
Aldington, Richard, 117
Aldrovandi, Count Luigi, 81, 83
Alexander, King of the Hellenes, death of, 199
Alexander, Rt. Hon. A. V. (later 1st Earl Alexander of Hillsborough) First Lord of Admiralty, 498, 509, 510, 514, 516, 520, 521, 528, 538, 546 *note* 1, 554
Allen, Sir James, 175 *note* 2
Allenby, Field-Marshal 1st Viscount, given peerage, 31; High Commissioner in Egypt, 115, 117, 407; his wartime campaign, 128
Alwar, Maharajah of, 424
Amery, Rt. Hon. Leopold C. M. S., employed in Cabinet Secretariat, 34, 38, 127; First Lord of Admiralty, 301 *note* 2, 322, 323, 338, 339, 347, 348; Secretary of State for Colonies, 397 and for Dominions, 401 *note* 6, 408, 409, 426, 430, 473
Ammon, C. G. (later 1st Baron), 362
Anderson, Rt. Hon. Sir John (later 1st Viscount Waverley), 196, 297, 405 (and *note* 2)
Anglo-French Compromise (1928), 456, 467-9, 472, 508
Anglo-Japanese Alliance (1902), 112, 216, 231, 240, 248; replaced by Four Power Pact 1921, 251, 439
Annunzio, Gabriele d', 162 *note* 1
Asquith, Rt. Hon. H. H. (later 1st Earl of Oxford and Asquith), H's unsuccessful attempt to include in Peace Conference Delegation, 21, 22, 23, 25, 42; defeat at General Election and H's letter of sympathy 40-1; his tribute to H, 109; supports motion against Cabinet Secretariat, 277 *note* 6, 280; attacks modern diplomatic methods, 292; approves H's article on Haldane, 472. Mentioned, 70, 194, 210, 224, 264, 293 *note* 2, 297, 303, 306, 336, 342, 359, 364, 371, 387, 400, 471, 504, 532
Asquith, Margot, 280
Astor, J. J. (later 1st Baron Astor of Hever), 103 and *note* 4, 215
Astor, Nancy, Viscountess, 114, 123, 146
Astor, Waldorf, 2nd Viscount, 114, 123, 146
Auchincloss, Gordon (Colonel House's Secretary), 41
Australia, claims and attitudes at Peace Conference, 30, 36, 37, 38, 45, 46, 51, 52, 54, 55, 77-8; attitude to Reparations, 175; attends Imperial Conference of 1921, 230-2, and Washington Conference, 240; offers help over Chanak crisis, 285; attends Imperial Conference of 1923 and displays deep interest in Singapore Base, 347-50; concerned at decision to halt work at Singapore, 360-1; attitude to Geneva Protocol, 395; Casey mission, 400-401; participates in Imperial Conference of 1926, 429 and has representatives at C.I.D. meetings, 431 and O.D.C. discussions, 450;

again strongly supports Singapore base, 497; attitude at London Naval Conference of 1930, 513 and at Imperial Conference of 1930, 526-7

Avezzano, Signor, 330

Backhouse, Rear-Admiral (later Admiral of the Fleet) Sir Roger R. C., 554 (and *note* 4)

Baker, Ray Stannard, 104, 257

Baldwin, Rt. Hon. Stanley (later 1st Earl),

(1) *Political Career*

(a) *Early Days* – Financial Secretary of Treasury, 105; at Carlton Club Meeting, 298, 305-6, 334; Chancellor of Exchequer, 307, 311, 314, 318, 323, 324; Lloyd George's view of, 329; settles American Debt, 333-5; Member of Salisbury Committee, 336-7, 338

(b) *Prime Minister* (1923-4), becomes Prime Minister, 341-3; views on Tariff Reform, 346; presides over Imperial Conference, 347, 349; defeat at election, 351-2; end of ministry, 353-6

(c) *Prime Minister* (1924-9), 387 *passim* 416; 417 *passim* 474

(d) *Joins National Government* (1931), 546 *et seq.*, 560 *et seq.*, 567 *et seq.*, 570-1

(2) *Relations with H*, 211, 334, 342, 343-4, 351, 352, 355-6, 358, 387-9, 390, 444, 475, 573

(3) *Mentioned*, 56 *note* 1, 328, 358, 359, 364, 367, 373, 379, 382, 385, 475, 477, 480, 499, 500, 501, 527, 540

Balfour, Rt. Hon. A. J. (later 1st Earl) – as Foreign Secretary prepares for Peace Conference, 21, 30, 36, 38, 39, 41, 48; in Paris, 49 *note* 1, 52, 55, 57, 58, 61, 63, 64, 68, 81, 89, 91, 92, 95, 104; declines peerage, 129; contribution to Cabinet reconstruction, 132; opposed to Channel Tunnel, 134; leaves Foreign Office, 142, but retains senior position (Lord President of Council) in Cabinet, 156, 157, 188, 189, 208; approves of H's attitude to League of Nations, 192; appointed to lead British Delegation to Washington, 218, 236-7; at Imperial Conference of 1921, 232; attitude to Silesian Plebiscite, 233-4; at Washington Conference, 238, 239, 241-4, 246, 248-9, 250-3, 254, 256-7, 258; created Earl, 280-1; kept informed by H of Chanak Crisis, 290-1; attitude during last days of Coalition, 295, 299, 329; resigns 300-1; not in Bonar Law's Ministry, 328, but remains in C.I.D. where initiates Committee of Civil Research, 391-2, 427; attitude to Geneva Protocol, 395 and to Four Power Pact, 396; again Lord President of Council, 397; chairs sub-committee on Singapore Base, 402; attitude to Shanghai crisis, 409 and to proposed Ministry of Defence, 419-20; produces formula for recognising Dominion status at Imperial Conference of 1926, 427-9, 430, 432; opinion on Cecil, 433, 442, 443; attitude to renewed crisis in China, 435; reaction to H's ideas on defence of eastern frontier of France, 437-8; views on naval parity with U.S.A., 440; attitude to Belligerent Rights, 452, 453, 457, 459; resignation and death of, 460.

Close relations with H, 52, 129, 211, 258, 280-1, 291, 391, 392, 442, 452, 459, 460, 471

Mentioned, 127 *note* 1, 138, 139, 166, 171, 302, 336, 364, 398, 413, 423, 431, 469, 471, 473, 532, 533

Balfour Sub-Committee of Salisbury Committee (1923) to investigate relations of Navy and Air Force as regards control of Fleet air work, 262, 337, 338-9, 340, 344, 346, 379 *note* 1

Barnes, Rt. Hon. George N., 127 *note* 1, 195
Barstow, Sir George, 316
Bartholomew, Colonel (later General Sir) William H., 286 (and *note* 3), 531
Barthou, Louis, 137 (and *note* 2), 268, 269, 270, 273, 274, 276
Batterbee, Sir Harry, 361, 427, 453 *note* 1, 458, 495, 526, 528, 550, 574
Bauer, Gustav, German Chancellor, 95 (and *note* 3), 150 *note* 1
Beale, Sir John F., 26 (and *note* 1)
Beatty, Admiral Sir David (later Admiral of the Fleet 1st Earl), awarded peerage, 31; as First Sea Lord supports H over future of C.I.D., 155; accepts Naval Inquiry by C.I.D., 205-6, 207, 208; at Washington Conference, 237, 244-5 (where overruled by Lloyd George, 248); resists Geddes Report, 252-3; quarrel with Air Ministry, 261-2; plans for Chanak Crisis, 286-7; renewed strife with Air Ministry, 337, 339; supports Chief of Staffs Sub-Committee of C.I.D., 344; evidence to Clynes Commission, 360; concern over Singapore Base, 362, 402; relations with Trenchard, 403; struggle over 1925-6 Navy Estimates, 404, 417, 509; ideas on situation in China, 408-9; interpretation of naval parity with U.S.A., 439; retirement and plans for his successors, 508-9; protests against cut in cruiser strength, 510; attacks Three Power Treaty after London Naval Conference, 521. Mentioned, 312, 449, 519, 574
Beaverbrook, 1st Baron, 279, 324, 342
Beckett, Hon. Mrs. Rupert, 188 (and *note* 2)
Bekir Sami, 222, 223
Belligerent Rights, H's determination to preserve, 135, 451-9, 491-6, 509, *see* also Freedom of Seas
Beneš, Dr. Eduard, 75, 183
Benn, Sir John (H's son-in-law), 297 *note* 1, 473, 518
Bennett, R. B. (later 1st Viscount), Canadian Prime Minister, 526 *note* 3, 527 (and *note* 2)
Bernhard, Prince of the Netherlands, 504 *note* 2
Berthelot, Philippe, 137 (and *note* 3), 147, 150, 160, 161, 162, 182, 200, 201, 504
Bhopal Succession Case, 423
Bickersteth, John Burgon, 431 (and *note* 4), 432
Birdwood, General Sir William (later Field-Marshal 1st Baron), 322
Birkenhead, Rt. Hon. 1st Earl of, Lord Chancellor, 124, 127 *note* 1, 130, 172, 267 *note* 2; actions during Chanak Crisis and last days of Lloyd George's Ministry, 284, 285 *note* 1, 288, 289, 296, 299, 300, 323-4; unsuccessful attempt to blame Curzon for Greek débacle, 325; relations with Bonar Law, 331, 336; rejoins Government (as Secretary for India), 392; part played in Chilcott affair, 420-4; at Imperial Conference of 1926, 428; retirement and H's letter to, 472. Mentioned, 391
Birkenhead Committee of investigation into naval shipbuilding programmes (1925), 404, 463
Black, Dr., 91
Blackett, B. P. (later Sir Basil), 167 (and *note* 1)
Bledisloe, 1st Viscount, 495 *note* 1
Bliss, Miss (Balfour's private secretary), 299
Bonar Law, Rt. Hon. Andrew, views on Kaiser's trial, 20; activities as Cabinet Minister (Chancellor of Exchequer), 21, 29, 31, 34-5, 36, 39, 42, (Lord Privy Seal), 60, 78, 103, 115, 120, 123, 125, 127 and *note* 1, 131 *note* 4, 134, 138, 139, 152, 164, 170, 172, 174, 189, 190, 194, 196, 197, 198, 199, 200, 202, 207, 210, 214-15; resignation because of

ill-health, 224-5; returns to political life, 292; becomes Prime Minister, 296-302; controversy over Cabinet Secretariat, 304-19, 322, 324; H's relations with, 325-6; conduct at Reparations Conferences in London, 326-8, and Paris, 330-2; sends Baldwin to U.S.A. to settle Debt and threatens to resign, 333-4; weakness of his Government, 335, 336; involved in Navy-Air Strife, 337; resignation and death, 341-2; H's view on 323, 336, 342, 573. Mentioned, 236, 262, 346, 352, 367, 373, 376, 390, 392, 532, 562

Bonar Law Committee: Sub-Committee of C.I.D. on Naval Shipbuilding (1920), 204-5, 206-8

Bondfield, Rt. Hon. Margaret, 477 (and *note* 4)

Borden, Sir Robert, Prime Minister of Canada, at Paris Peace Conference, 20, 29-30, 31, 36, 38, 39, 46, 49, 55, 92; Canadian Representative at Washington Conference, 240, and at League of Nations, 457

Boscawen, *see* Griffith-Boscawen

Botha, General Louis, 35-6, 38, 53, 61, 107, 121, 177

Botha, Mrs., 35

Boulogne; Conference on Reparations at (1920), 171, 174-5, 198; Anglo-French meeting at (1922), 262-3

Brace, William, 190 (and *note* 3), 191

Bradbury, Sir John (later 1st Baron), 164 (and *note* 2), 167, 229, 330, 331-2, 372

Bratianu, J., Prime Minister of Roumania, 56

Breasted, J. H., 413

Briand, Aristide, 137, 145, 216, 219, 221, 222, 223, 228, 246, 255, 258, 259, 270, 331, 414, 483, 485, 487, 517, *see* also Kellogg-Briand Pact

Bridgeman, Rt. Hon. William S. (later 1st Viscount), First Lord of Admiralty, 402, 404, 417 (and *note* 1), 438, 440, 452, 498, 509, 519, 521

Bridges, Sir Edward E. (later 1st Baron), 343, 345-6, 464, 575

Bright, John, 279 (and *note* 1)

British Empire Delegation (B.E.D.), at Paris, 21, 29-30, 36, 43-4, 45, 46, 48, 49, 51-2, 53-5, 63, 94, 96, 100; before Boulogne and Spa Conferences, 175; at First League Assembly, 195-6; at Washington, 240, 242, 248, 250, 252; at Genoa, 268, 270; at London Reparations Conference, 374; at London Naval Conference, 513

Brock, Admiral (later Admiral of Fleet Sir) Osmond de B., 286 (and *note* 5)

Brockdorff-Rantzau, Count Ulrich, 88 (and *note* 2)

Bruce, S. M. (later 1st Viscount), Prime Minister of Australia, 347 (and *note* 1), 350, 395, 497

Brüning, Dr. Heinrich, German Chancellor, 507 *note* 2

Bryce, 1st Viscount, 40, 256-7, 413

Budienny, Marshal, 185

Bullock, C. L. (later Sir Christopher), 417 (and *note* 4), 541, 574

Burgis, Lawrence, H's private secretary, 19-20, 212 *note* 3, 236, 241, 304, 308, 312, 314, 343, 352, 354, 430-1, 502, 506, 532, 543, 573

Burnett-Stuart, General Sir John T., 285, 286 (and *note* 1)

Buxton, Noel Edward (later 1st Baron Noel-Buxton), 380

Byrne, Brigadier-General Sir Joseph A., 235 (and *note* 3)

Caccia, Anthony M. F., 29 (and *note* 1)

Caccia, Major H. A., 48 *note* 4, 147

Cadman-Berthelot Agreement (1920), 163 *note* 4

Cambon, Paul, 152

Camerlynck, Monsieur, 100, 369, 373

Campbell, J. R. (The Campbell Case), 366 *note* 2, 375-8, 573

Canada, participates in Paris Peace Conference, 29-30, 36, 38, 45, 46, 52, 55; suggests alteration of title of B.E.D. to suit Dominions, 195;

Canada [*contd.*]
at Imperial Conference of 1921, where opposes renewal of Anglo-Japanese alliance and claims a say in foreign policy, 231; at Washington Conference, 240; refuses help over Chanak Crisis, 285; attitude at Imperial Conference of 1923, 347, 349-50; disinterested in Singapore Base, 360; opposed to Geneva Protocol, 395; at Imperial Conference of 1926, 427, 428, 429; interest in setting up own Cabinet Secretariat, 431-2; attends O.D.C. discussions, 450; attitude to Belligerent Rights, 457; at Imperial Conference of 1930, where strongly supports Imperial Preference and produces a disarmament formula, 528

Cannes Conference (1922) and Resolutions, 258, 259 (and *note* 3), 263, 267

Carlton Club Meeting (1922), 296, 299, 305, 322, 329, 334, 562

Carnegie, Andrew, 109 (and *note* 1)

Carson, Baron, 308, 521

Casey, Richard (later 1st Baron), 400 (and *note* 5), 401, 429, 480, 529, 575

Cavan, Field-Marshal 10th Earl of, 285, 312, 344

Cave, 1st Viscount, Lord Chancellor, 323, 334, 391, 443

Cazalet-Keir, Mrs. Thelma, 188 (and *note* 3), 227

Cecil, Lord Robert (later 1st Viscount), Assistant Secretary for Foreign Affairs, 32; British Representative on Commission on League of Nations, 57 *note* 2, 60-1; receives H's ideas on League, 75 and his letter declining to be candidate for post of Secretary-General, 79-80; criticised by H for rigidity of League Constitution, 135; his views on Supreme Council, 194-5; Balfour critical of, 196; suspicious of H, 263; attitude to Cabinet Secretariat, 280; stresses need for close Foreign Office link with League, 305; H's opinion of, 349; his work on Treaty of Mutual Assistance, 363, 367; support for Geneva Protocol 393-4 and distress at its rejection, 397-8; his work for disarmament, 438-40; resignation from Government (Chancellor of Duchy of Lancaster with special responsibility for League affairs) and its aftermath, 441-4, 451; his attitude to Service Departments criticised by H, 499; hostility of Neville Chamberlain towards, 550; his unpopularity exploited by Japanese, 563 *note* 1. Mentioned, 573

Cecil Committee on Reduction and limitation of Armaments, 415-16, 433-4

Chamberlain, Rt. Hon. Austen, position and activities in Coalition Government, 21, 33, 35, 36, 96, 113, 127 *note* 1, 154, 157; at First Lympne Conference, 167, 168; attitude to Russian trade agreement, 173, to unemployment, 191, to mandated territories, 202, and to national economy, 205; supports defensive alliance with France, 209; resents Lloyd George's treatment of Curzon, 214; leaves Exchequer (to become Lord Privy Seal), 215-16, 224; at Imperial Conference of 1921, 232; attitude to Navy-Air controversy, 261, and to Montagu's resignation, 264; supports recognition of U.S.S.R., 267; receives H's reports on Genoa Conference, 270, 272, 273, 274; actions during Chanak Crisis, and last days of Coalition Ministry, 284, 285 *note* 1, 288, 290, 292, 293, 295; summons Carlton Club Meeting, 296-7, 298; continuing loyalty to Lloyd George, 302; becomes Foreign Secretary, 390, 392; supports Four Power Pact, but rejects Geneva Protocol, 396-7; anxious to strengthen ties with Dominions, 401; attitude to Japan, 402, 403, 404; his Egyptian policy, 407; firm attitude to China, 409; negotiates Locarno Pact, 414-15; involvement in Chilcott affair, 421, 422, 423; briefed by H for Imperial Conference of 1926, 426, 428; conflict with Cecil over disarmament, 433; action over Shanghai, 436; final conflict with Cecil (who resigns), 439-41, 442, 443; attitude to Belligerent Rights, 451-2, 453-4, 456, 457; his regular attendance at League of Nations meetings applauded by H, 462; sponsors Anglo-French Compromise, 467-8; critical of Lloyd's régime in Egypt, 478-9; joins National Government as First Lord of Admiralty and has to deal with Invergordon Mutiny, 554, 555, 556, 557. Mentioned, 259, 265, 277, 279, 324, 325, 336, 342, 383, 385, 399, 472, 473, 538 *note* 6

Chamberlain, Rt. Hon. Neville, Chancellor of Exchequer in Baldwin's First Ministry, 352, Minister of Health, 473; Chancellor of Exchequer in National Government, 537, 550, 565, 566, 571. Mentioned, 442, 466

Chanak Crisis (1922), 283-96, 318, 324-7

Chancellor, Sir John R., 157 *note* 2, 238, 306 (and *note* 3), 309, 314

Channel Tunnel, H's opposition to, 133-5, 139, 364, 522

Chaplin, Charlie, 561

Chapman, Professor (later Sir) Sydney J., 107 (and *note* 2), 111, 113

Chatfield, Admiral (later Admiral of Fleet 1st Baron), 237 (and *note* 2), 252, 508

Chelmsford, 1st Viscount, First Lord of Admiralty, 380, 381

Chéron, Henri, French Minister of Finance, at Hague Conferences, 482 (and *note* 2), 485, 487, 503

Chetwode, General Sir Philip (later Field-Marshal 1st Baron), 286 (and *note* 2)

Chiang Kai Shek, 408

Chicherin, Youri, Russian Foreign Minister, 266 (and *note* 3), 269, 270-1

Chilcott, Sir Warden (Chilcott Affair), 420-3, 420 (and *note* 6)

Child, Richard W., U.S. Representative at Geneva Conference, 275 (and *note* 2)

China, Shantung and Kiaochow discussed at Paris Peace Conference, 83, 84; delegation at Washington Conference, 240, where Shantung again discussed, 251, 254, 371; Wei hai wei restored to, 255-6; activities of Nationalists in and threat to Hankow and Shanghai, 407, 408-10, 434, 435-7, 449-50; weakness of British policy towards, 544; Japanese aggression against, 399, 563

Churchill, Lord Randolph, 441

Churchill, Rt. Hon. Winston S., succeeds Milner as War Minister, 32, and assumes responsibility for Air Ministry, 46-7; presses for full intervention against Russia at Council of Ten, 62; his role at War Office commented upon by H, 107; proposes rewards for War Generals, 108; views on Cabinet re-organisation, 110; again presses for measures against Russia, 115; views on Cabinet Secretariat, 128, 130; policy towards Ireland, 154; suggested by H as Chairman of Standing Committee of C.I.D., 157; at First Lympne Conference, 166; suggests Mesopotamia be controlled by aircraft, 169; opposed to trade agreement with Russia, 172-3, 224; proposes new line of defence in Mesopotamia, 201, and supports ideas that mandates be a Colonial Office responsibility, 202; takes over Colonial Office, 203, 214; position over Naval Inquiry,

Churchill, Rt. Hon. Winston S. [*contd.*] 208; advocate of defensive alliance with France, 209; at Imperial Conference of 1921, 232; criticises B.E.D. at Washington Conference, 253; unsuccessful attempts to mediate between Beatty and Trenchard, 262; bellicosity over Russia, 277; position over Chanak Crisis and end of Coalition, 284, 285 *note* 1, 287, 289, 291, 294, 295, 297-8, 300, 302; views on Ministry of Defence, 337-8; his exclusion from Government deplored by H, 343; Chancellor of Exchequer, 392; advocates economy and makes onslaught on 1925-6 Navy Estimates, 402, 403-5, 509; behind invitation to Lindemann to serve on C.I.D. subcommittee, 406; attitude to China crisis, 408, 409-10; attitude to unemployment, 414; exerts constant pressure for economy, 416, 417, 419; action over General Strike, 425-6; against naval parity with U.S.A., 439, 455-6, 511; gets C.I.D. to accept Ten Year Rule in permanence, 462-3; efforts to revive Baldwin's Government, 472-3; in the political wilderness, 531. Mentioned, 37, 56, 74, 126, 127 *note* 1, 131, 139, 156, 170, 270, 315 *note* 2, 378, 465, 519, 533-4, 561, 574, 575

Churchill Committee, appointed to adjudicate on Geddes Report, 259-60

C.I.D. (Committee of Imperial Defence) H's early connection with (as Secretary), 33, 61, 64-5, 74, 105, 112, 125; H's successful efforts to revive on pre-war basis, 155-7, 173-4, 204, 230, 280, 322-3, with Dominion co-operation, 195, 431-432, and institution of C.O.S. subcommittee, 340. Mentioned, 127, 133, 134, 135, 205, 235, 260, 290, 299, 306-7, 310, 311, 313, 315, 330, 336 *et seq.*, 344-5, 347, 353-4, 359-60, 361, 363-4, 365, 379, 390-3, 394, 396, 400 *et seq.*, 405-6, 409-10, 415, 418-20, 426, 427-8, 433-4, 436, 437, 445, 448-9, 450-1, 453, 458, 460, 463-4, 465, 466, 467, 468, 472, 475-6, 479, 480, 493, 494, 496, 498-9, 500-1, 521, 522, 524-6, 528, 531, 535-8, 540, 574, for Sub-Committees of, *see* Balfour, Birkenhead, Bonar Law, Churchill and Salisbury.

Clemenceau, Georges, Prime Minister of France, 25, 28-9, 43, 45, 50, 52, 56, 58, 61, 63, 69, 73, 81, 85, 86, 90-1, 94, 97-8, 99, 100, 116, 118-19, 137, 138, 143, 144, 145, 146, 147, 152, 573

Clémentel, Etienne, 372 (and *note* 4)

Clerk, Sir George, 138, 183

Club, The, H's membership of, 212

Clynes, Rt. Hon. J. R., Lord Privy Seal, 360, 365, 380, 546 *note* 1

Coates, J. G., Prime Minister of New Zealand, 428

Collins, Michael, death of, 266

Colwyn, 1st Baron (Colwyn Committee), 417 (and *note* 1), 418

Committee of Civil Research (C.C.R.), 391-2, 427-8

Connaught, Duke of, 28

Constantine, King of the Hellenes, restored, 199-200; policy of, 213; defeat and deposition of, 283, 288, 289

Constantinople, problems of, 72, 115, 118, 138, 142-3, 147; Turkish nationalist threat to, 173-4, 200; still in Sultan's possession, 219; renewed threat to, 230; Indian reaction to, 263; Chanak Crisis, 282 *et seq.*; renewed difficulties over, 318; settled at Lausanne, 326, 334

Cook, Sir Joseph, 401 (and *note* 1)

Coolidge, Calvin C., Vice-President, then President, of U.S.A., 239 (and *note* 1), 343, 438

Coontz, Admiral Robert, U.S. Chief of Naval Operations, 240 (and *note* 2), 245

Copeman, Able Seaman, 558
Corbett, Sir Julian, 126
C.O.S. (Chiefs of Staff Sub-Committee of C.I.D.), 344-6, 390, 426, 446-7, 448, 449, 468, 479, 498, 499, 520, 522, 524, 535-7, 538, 541-2, 574
Cosgrave, William, President of Irish Free State, 359
Council of Five, 73, 100
Council of Four, meetings of, 58, 69, 73, 75, 76, 77; H becomes Secretary of, 80, 82; Italian withdrawal from, 83, and return to, 87; further meetings of, 94, 95 *note* 1, 96-8, 100; leakage of minutes of, 103-4, 257. Mentioned, 250
Council of Ten, 43-5, 46, 48, 50, 52, 53, 55, 61, 62, 64, 70; replaced by Council of Four, 73; temporarily revived, 96
Council of Three (i.e. Council of Four after Italian withdrawal), 84-7, 88, 250
Cowdray, 1st Viscount, 280
Cox, Major-General Sir Percy Z., 203 (and *note* 1)
Craig, Sir James (later 1st Viscount Craigavon), 205 (and *note* 4), 359
Craigie, R. L. (later Sir Robert), 494, 495 (and *note* 2)
Cramp, Concemore T., 121 (and *note* 3)
Creedy, Sir Herbert, 337
Crichton-Stuart, Lord Colum, 183 *note* 3
Cromer, 2nd Earl of, Lord Chamberlain, 471 *note* 3
Crowe, Sir Edward, 464 (and *note* 2)
Crowe, Sir Eyre, 119 *note* 1, 139 (and *note* 1), 158, 235, 304, 331, 332, 369, 383, 396, 405
Cunliffe, 1st Baron, Governor of Bank of England, 62 *note* 2; (Hughes-Cunliffe Committee on Reparations), 168, 175
Cunliffe-Lister, *see* Lloyd-Greame and Swinton
Curtis, Lionel, 307 (and *note* 1), 420, 421, 422
Curtius, Julius, 488 (and *note* 1)
Curzon, 1st Marquess, member of War Cabinet, 31, 33; policy in Mesopotamia, 37; advises H against accepting post with League of Nations, 65-6; praises H for work at Paris Peace Conference, 109; work on Turkish Treaty, 137; becomes Foreign Secretary, 142; his views on Near East, 143, 149; at San Remo Conference, 172, 173; at Spa, 175; relations with Derby, 180, 182; chairman of meeting of B.E.D. for first League Assembly, 195; against revision of Treaty of Sèvres, 200; regards mandates as Foreign Office responsibility, 202; opposed to alliance with France, 209-10; relations with Lloyd George, 210, 214-15; attitude to Greek question, 223, 233; opposed to trade agreement with Russia, 224; opinion of Auckland Geddes, 228; at Imperial Conference of 1921, 232; expresses satisfaction that H will be at Washington Conference, 236; quarrel with Montagu, 263-4; opposed to recognition of U.S.S.R., 267; not at Genoa Conference, 268, 277; attitude to Chanak Crisis and behaviour during last days of Coalition Ministry, 284-5, 287, 288, 289, 290, 291-2, 293, 294, 295, 300, 301, 302; attitude to Cabinet Secretariat and subsequent apology to H, 320-1; position in Bonar Law's Ministry, 323; Birkenhead's manœuvres against, 324-5; at Lausanne Conferences, 326, 334; and at Paris Reparations Conference, 330 (where pays tribute to H), 331; member of Salisbury Committee, 336; fails to become Prime Minister, 341-3; at Imperial Conference of 1923, 348, 349-50; pays tribute to H on leaving Foreign Office, 357; general relief at his departure from Foreign Office, 367; becomes Lord President of Council and Chairman of C.I.D., 390-1, 394;

Curzon, 1st Marquess [*contd.*]
opposed to Four Power Pact, 396; his death and H's views on, 399-400. Mentioned, 39-40, 42, 74, 119, 127 *note* 1, 138, 139, 147, 150, 152, 168, 170, 171, 185, 196, 221, 259, 402, 433
Curzon Line, 187
Cushendun, 1st Baron, Chancellor of Duchy with responsibility for League of Nations (after Cecil's resignation), 451 (and *note* 3), 453 *note* 1, 454, 457

D'Abernon, 1st Baron (later 1st Viscount), British Ambassador to Germany, 180 (and *note* 2), 181, 182, 183 *note* 3, 185, 186, 217, 221, 229, 258, 274, 552
Dalmatia, *see* Adriatic question
Dalton, Rt. Hon. Hugh (later 1st Baron), 475 *note* 1
Daniels, Josephus, U.S. Secretary of Navy, 75
Davidson, J. C. C. (later 1st Viscount), 227, 306, 310, 333, 342, 356, 409
Davidson, Randall, Archbishop of Canterbury, 40
Davies, J. T. (later Sir John), Private Secretary to Lloyd George, 28, 124, 158, 188, 224, 287
Davis, John W., U.S. Ambassador in London, 147 *note* 2
Dawes, General Charles G., 372 (and *note* 1), 458, 490, 511
Dawes Plan (on Reparations), 332, 372, 374, 480 *note* 2
Dawson, Geoffrey, Editor of *Times*, 103 *note* 4, 307 *note* 1, 422, 494, 570
Dawson of Penn, 1st Viscount, 470
Delacroix, L., 175 (and *note* 4)
De La Warr, 9th Earl, 570 (and *note* 2)
Deleuze, Captain, 468
Denby, Edwin, U.S. Secretary of Navy, 240 (and *note* 1)
Denikin, General A. I., 138, 170
Derby, Rt. Hon., 17th Earl of, Ambassador to France, congratulates H on services at Peace Conference, 109; solicits a G.C.B., 167 and *note* 2; quarrels with Curzon, 180, 182; refuses India Office, 264; becomes War Secretary, 301 *note* 2, 323, 324, 336, 337, 338. Mentioned, 299
Deschanel, Paul, President of France, 145 (and *note* 4)
De Valera, Eamon, 219 *note* 1
Devonshire, 9th Duke of, refuses India Office, 264; becomes Colonial Secretary, 323 (and *note* 2), 334, 351
Disarmament, of Germany, 68, 69, 150-1, 163, 166, 171-2, 173, 176-7, 179, 209, 216, 459-60, 465, 508 (general), 196, 415-16, 418, 433-5, 438-41, 441-4, 466, 468, 537 *et seq.*, *see* also Geneva Conference, London Naval Conference and Washington Conference.
Disraeli, Benjamin, 31, 32
Divine, Mr., 555 *note* 2
Dreyer, Vice-Admiral F. C. (later Admiral Sir Frederic), 535 *note* 3
Drummond, Sir Eric (later 16th Earl of Perth), Secretary-General to League of Nations, 87, 164, 165, 171, 193, 234, 263, 328
Duff, C. P. (later Sir Patrick), MacDonald's Private Secretary, 497 (and *note* 4), 498
Duncan, A. R. (later Sir Andrew), 190 (and *note* 5)
Dupré, Maurice, 528
Dutasta, Paul, 50, 51, 52, 53, 82, 95
Dyne, Mrs. A. M. Bradley, 384 (and *note* 3), 461

Eagles, Mr., 183 *note* 3
Ebert, Gustav, President of Germany, 150-1, 177 *note* 1
Edward VII, 24, 104 *note* 1
Egypt, British position in, 112, 115, 117, 126, 138, 140, 144, 169, 193, 202, 209, 213, 214, 260, 286, 349, 350, 360; murder of Stack and replacement of Allenby by Lloyd, 407-8; defence problems concerning, 450, 469; dismissal of Lloyd

and beginning of a new British status in, 478-80, 544
Elliot, Air Chief-Marshal Sir William, 575
Emma, Queen Mother of the Netherlands, 504 (and *note* 2)
Esher, Rt. Hon. 2nd Viscount, letters to and from H, 26, 27, 32, 34, 58, 60, 64-5, 66, 76, 110, 120, 125, 135, 136, 156, 182, 210, 263, 309-10, 312, 314, 338, 428, 430, 444, 445, 452-3
Evans, Ernest (Lloyd George's Private Secretary), 219
Evans, G. M., member of Cabinet Secretariat, 124

Facta, Luigi, Prime Minister of Italy, 258 (and *note* 1), 269, 270
Faisal I, King of Iraq, 116, 118, 119, 121, 203, 204, 213, 223
Farquhar, 1st Earl, 300 (and *note* 3)
Fayle, C. E., 341
Feetham, Mr. Justice, 359 *note* 1
Fehrenbach, Konstantin, German Chancellor, 177 (and *note* 1), 178, 229 *note* 2
Field, Admiral Sir Frederick, First Sea Lord, 499 *note* 6, 509, 554
Fisher, Admiral of Fleet, 1st Baron, 91, 293, 373
Fisher, H. A. L., President of Board of Education, 195, 196, 202, 217, 219 *note* 1, 261, 305
Fisher, Sir Warren, Permanent Secretary to Treasury, his relations with H, 309-20, 327, 329, 338, 345 *note* 1, 358, 364, 366, 419, 472, 481, 501, 550. Mentioned, 154, 201, 216, 235, 408, 559
Fitzmaurice, Commodore (later Admiral Sir) Herbert, 199 (and *note* 6)
Fitzroy, Sir Almeric, 313 (and *note* 1)
Fiume, Italo-Yugoslav dispute over, 78, 80, 82, 91, 143-4, 162 (and *note* 1)
Fletcher, Senator Duncan V., 228 *note* 3
Foch, Ferdinand, Marshal of France, 25, 28, 29, 58, 68, 69, 76, 87, 94, 100, 149, 152, 161, 162, 173, 176, 177, 179, 184, 245, 575
Fontainebleau Talks (1919), 70-3, 76, 271
Forbes, G. W., 526 *note* 3
Fortescue, Hon. (later Sir) John, 126, 393, 475
France, 25 *passim* 30, 37, 43 *passim* 64, 68 *passim* 92, 93 *passim* 100, 116 *passim* 119, 133 *passim* 138, 140, 143-4, 145 *passim* 152, 158, 159 *passim* 163, 165 *passim* 170, 713 *passim* 180, 182, 183, 186, 193, 195, 200, 201, 209-10, 213, 216-17, 219 *passim* 224, 228 *passim* 234, 245, 246, 251, 254, 255, 258-9, 263, 266, 268, 270, 273-6, 281, 284, 285, 288, 291-2, 295, 318, 324, 326-7, 331-3, 334, 343, 348, 368-73, 374, 395-7, 414-15, 436, 437, 467-9, 472, 482, 485-8, 489, 503, 505-7, 508, 512, 513, 514, 515, 516, 517, 520, 539, 541, 545
Franklin-Bouillon, Monsieur Henri, 285 *note* 2, 295
Freedom of Seas, H's pre-occupation with, 23, 38, 42, 76, 84, 451, 459, 494, 511, 522, *see* also Belligerent Rights
French, Field-Marshal Viscount (later 1st Earl of Ypres), Viceroy of Ireland, 126, 153, 235, 564
Fromageot, Monsieur, 162, 229, 274
Fry, G. S. (later Sir Geoffrey), 306 (and *note* 1), 389
Fry, Patrick, 535
Fuller, Admiral C. T. M., 557 (and *note* 3)

Game, Air Vice-Marshal Sir Philip, 495 *note* 1
Garbasso, Monsieur, 162
Garran, Sir Robert, 55
Garrett, John W., U.S. Secretary-General of Washington Conference, 242 (and *note* 2), 257
Garvin, J. L., 146
Gaunt, Admiral (later Sir) Guy R. A., 207 (and *note* 1)
Geddes, Rt. Hon. Sir Auckland (later 1st Baron), member of War Cabinet,

Geddes, Rt. Hon. Sir Auckland [*contd.*] 35, 36, 47; views on Cabinet Secretariat, 63; Ambassador in Washington, 82, 227-8; President of Board of Trade, 107, 111, 123, 127, 130; J. H. Thomas's view of, 124. Mentioned, 103

Geddes, Rt. Hon. Sir Eric, as First Lord of Admiralty seeks H's advice on his career, 22; in charge of demobilisation, 35 *note* 2, 36-7; anti-Russian views of, 47; anti-strike measures, 122, 144, 227; J. H. Thomas's view of, 124; political position of, 127; against Channel Tunnel, 134; maintains mandates are a Colonial Office responsibility, 202; on Naval Inquiry Committee, 208; chairman of Geddes Committee, 259

Geddes Committee (and Report) on National Expenditure, 252, 254, 255, 259, 299, 321, 519

General Elections
- (1918), 21, 33, 35, 39-41
- (1922), 302, 311, 324
- (1923), 351-2
- (1924), 382, 385-6
- (1929), 474
- (1931), 569-70, 570 *note* 4

General Strike (1926), 424-6, 444, 460, 461, 573

Geneva Conference (1927), 249, 393, 438-41, 467, 472, 508, 509, 513

Geneva Protocol (1924), 381, 393-9, 413

Genghis Khan, 437 (and *note* 4)

Genoa Conference (1922), 258-9, 262, 266-77, 483

George II, King of the Hellenes, 200 *note* 3

George V, concerned at Asquith's exclusion from Peace Conference, 23, 25; entertains President Wilson, 36, 39; attitude to proposed trial of Kaiser, 99, 110; offers Balfour a peerage, 129; interest in Unknown Soldier, 192; signs emergency proclamation over coal strike, 226; receives resignation of Lloyd George, 293, 296, and sends for Bonar Law, 297; sends for Baldwin in preference to Curzon, 341-2; insists Baldwin faces Parliament after electoral defeat in 1923, 353; asks MacDonald to form Government, 355; entertains overseas visitors to Wembley Exhibition, 375; agrees to dissolve Parliament, 382; accepts Allenby's recall from Egypt, 407; concern over Shanghai, 436; attitude to Belligerent Rights, 454-5, 456, 494-5; his illness, 470-1; makes Margaret Bondfield first woman Privy Counsellor, 477; supports abolition of submarines, 491; his actions during 1931 crisis, 546, 547, 548; receives report of Invergordon Mutiny, 557; signs Bank Holiday Proclamations, 559; his attitude to Samuel, 566, 567; firm supporter of idea of a National Government, 569-70.
His relations with H and Cabinet Secretariat, 22-4, 27-8, 109, 131 *note* 4, 132, 183, 262, 279-80, 352, 388, (Baldwin resumes 'King's Letters'), 445, 504. Mentioned, 31, 212, 364, 411, 425, 441, 443

Germany, presented with Peace Treaty, 88 and forced to accept it, 94-6; failure of Kapp Putsch, 150-2; suffers further occupation because of default in reparations, 221-2; loses part of Silesia, 233-4; signs Treaty of Rapallo, 271; Ruhr occupied by France, 333; French agree to withdraw from Ruhr, 374; Locarno Pact signed, 414-15; end of Rhineland occupation and beginnings of National Socialism, 506-8, *see* also Disarmament and Reparations

Gessler, Otto, 176 (and *note* 3), 177

Gibbon, Edward, 413

Gibson, Hugh, 511

Gilligan, P., 526 *note* 3

Giolitti, Giovanni, Prime Minister of

Italy, 188 (and *note* 1), 212, 217, 258 *note* 1
Gladstone, W. H., 279
Glenconner, Lady (later Viscountess Grey of Fallodon), 25 (and *note* 1)
Glyn, Major Ralph (later 1st Baron), 570 (and *note* 3)
Gold Standard, return to (1925), 410-11; abandonment of (1931), 561
Gosling, Harry, 122 (and *note* 3)
Gounaris, Demetrius, 222 (and *note* 2), 324-5
Grabski, Stanislaw, 186 (and *note* 3)
Grabski, Wladislaw, 186 (and *note* 3)
Graham, William, President of Board of Trade, 502 (and *note* 1), 546 *note* 1
Graham-Harrison, W. M. (later Sir William), 548 (and *note* 1)
Grandi, Count Dino, 514 (and *note* 2), 517
Greece, her position and claims at Paris Peace Conference, 49, 79, 88-9, 100; ambitions of Venizelos, 143, 149; and his attendance at First Lympne Conference, 174; defeat of Venizelos and return of King Constantine, 198-200; growing threat from Kemalist troops, 213; attends Third London Conference, 219, but rejects all compromise with Turkey, 220-1; likelihood of Greek defeat, 230, realized with fall of Smyrna, 282-3; abdication of Constantine and visit to England by Venizelos for help, 288-90; Anglo-Turkish negotiations at Mudania, 291, 294-5; the Gounaris letter 324-5; peace restored by Treaty of Lausanne, 326; Italian aggression against Corfu, 348
Greenwood, Sir Hamar, Chief Secretary for Ireland, 114, 153, 188, 190, 196, 197, 253 *note* 5
Greenwood, Rt. Hon. Arthur, 546 *note* 1
Gregory, J. D., 383-4, 461
Gregory, Maundy, 282
*Greville Memoirs*, 281
Grey of Fallodon, 1st Viscount, discusses with H League of Nations and Freedom of Seas, 25; agrees to lead mission to U.S. but is unable to proceed, 112-13; discusses Ireland with Lloyd George and declines to join B.E.D. to First League Assembly, 194, 196; writes to *Times* supporting Curzon's peace-making efforts during Chanak Crisis, 288. Mentioned, 483
Griffith, Arthur, President of Provisional Government of Ireland, death of, 266
Griffith-Boscawen, Sir Arthur, 298 (and *note* 1), 325, 335-6
Grigg, Sir Edward (later 1st Baron Altrincham), Private Secretary to Lloyd George, 255 (and *note* 3), 267, 277, 282, 288, 292, 307, 309
Grigg, P. J. (later Sir Percy), 455
Guest, M. L., Chief Government Whip, 114, 120, 188; Secretary of State for Air, 261, 285 *note* 1, 289
Gwyer, M. L. (later Sir Maurice), 454 (and *note* 3)

Haddad Pasha, General, 223
Hague Conferences on Reparations, First (1929), 480, 481-90, 496, 545; Second (1930), 480, 501, 502-8, 532, 545
Haig, Field-Marshal Sir Douglas (later 1st Earl), 31, 37, 108
Hailsham, *see* Hogg, Sir Douglas
Haldane, General Sir J. Aylmer L., 203 (and *note* 2)
Haldane, Rt. Hon. 1st Viscount, proposals on machinery of government (1918), 127; ideas on Naval Inquiry, 206; gives evidence before Salisbury Committee, 338; helps negotiate Trenchard-Keyes agreement, 339, 418; acting Chairman of C.I.D., 359, 365; his services to MacDonald's Government on defence issues, 374; exemplary behaviour over custody of Cabinet minutes, 378, 380; C.I.D. activities, 391, 406; death and H's warm tribute to, 471-2. Mentioned, 208

Hall, Admiral Sir Reginald, 261
Hamilton, Nina, Duchess of, 91 (and *note* 2)
Hankey, Adeline (wife), convalesces at Torquay, 31-2; health of, 34, 107-8, 277, 401 (and *note* 3); in Paris with H, 62, 77, 91; H's concern for future of, 108; attends debate in Parliament over grant to H, 109; at Hunstanton, 113; at Cliveden, 146; alone with H, 148; in Lucerne with H, 187; spends Christmas of 1920 in London with H, 208; in Paris with H, 216-17; visits Italy with H, 217-18; her thoughtfulness, 236-7; keeps scrap-book, 241, 387 *note* 1; joins H in Genoa, 273; at Frinton, 279; at St. David's, 370, 374; with H in Venice, 386; family life of, 389-90; in Paris, 441; on holiday in Switzerland, 469; with H in Vienna, 523; good management of, 553; letters from H, 44, 46, 47, 49-50, 51, 52, 53-4, 55, 56-7, 58-9, 61-2, 77-8, 80, 83, 87-8, 90, 114, 145 *note* 5, 158 *note* 3, 162, 173 *note* 2, 174, 175-6, 177, 178-80, 184, 187, 217 *note* 1, 233 *note* 3, 236, 237 *note* 3, 238 *note* 2, 239, 241, 242-3, 246, 248, 250, 251, 253 *note* 4, 254, 255, 265-6, 266, 268 *note* 4, 269, 270 *note* 1, 271, 272 *note* 3, 279, 281 *note* 4, 282, 331 *notes* 3 and 4, 336, 355 *note* 2, 357 *note* 1, 370 *note* 2, 371 *note* 3, 373 *notes* 1 and 2, 424-5, 461 *note* 1, 482, 485-6, 488 *note* 2, 489, 504, 505, 506 *note* 2, 532. Mentioned, 431
Hankey, Clement (brother), 373
Hankey, Christopher (son), 389, 441, 543
Hankey, Donald (brother), 91
Hankey, Henry (son), 279, 389, 441, 543
Hankey, Hilda (sister), 318, 441
Hankey, Maurice,
1. *Career*
A. *Under Lloyd George* (1918-22), 19-303; returns to work and starts preparations for Peace Conference, 19 *et seq.*; with wife in Torquay, 31-2; occupied with problems of post-war reconstruction of Cabinet, 32-4; and with peace terms, 35 *et seq.*; at State Banquet to President Wilson, 39-40; expresses regret to Asquith on his electoral defeat, 41; at Criccieth with Lloyd George, 41-2; arrives in Paris where makes secretarial arrangements for Council of Ten and B.E.D., 43 *et seq.*; becomes British secretary to Peace Conference, 47 *et seq.*; visits battlefields with Smuts, 53; his views on difficulties, secretarial and political, at Paris, 53 *et seq.*; consults Esher and Curzon on taking a post with League of Nations, 64-7; further difficulties in Paris, 68-9; sends Lloyd George a memo on issues involved and attends Fontainebleau Talks, 70-2; present at meetings of new Council of Four, 73; sends Smuts and Cecil a sketch plan of organisation for League of Nations, 74-5; briefs Smuts on his Hungarian mission and opposes Freedom of Seas, 75-6; concerned over procedure of Council of Four and other problems, pays visit to London and decides against working for League of Nations, 77-80; becomes Secretary of Council of Four and encounters further political problems (mainly with Italy), 81-7; his views on offer of peerage, 87-8; final problems sorted out and the German Treaty ready for signing, 88 *et seq.*; receives thanks from Borden and Lloyd George for his work, 92; Treaty signed, 96; H records his impressions of whole Conference and of Treaty, 96-101; back in London becomes concerned with leakage of minutes of Council of Four and prepares for return to pre-war cabinet system,

103 *et seq.*; at Hunstanton with family, 107; given K.C.B. and grant of £25,000, 108-9; again immersed in immediate post-war problems, 110-13; at Riddell's house at Hennequeville with Lloyd George and other members of Cabinet to discuss situation in Middle East, 114-20; closes his Paris office, 121; attitude to railwaymen's strike, 121-4; still preoccupied with problems of Cabinet re-organisation and Middle East issue, 125-6; War Cabinet abolished and H accommodates himself to new situation and its attendant difficulties, 127-32; attitude to Channel Tunnel, 133-4; his views on League and other problems, 135-9; his review of international situation, 140-2; at Paris Conference, 142 *et seq.*; at Cliveden, 146; again at Paris, 146 *et seq.*; disquieted by Lloyd George's diplomatic methods, 149; and disturbed by events in Germany, 150-2; his views on Ireland, 152-4; attempts to revive C.I.D., 154-7; at San Remo Conference, 157-63; beginning of preparations for Spa Conference, 164 *et seq.*; at First Lympne Conference, 166-8; Middle East problems, 168-9; Russian trade negotiations, 170-3; at Second Lympne Conference, and Boulogne Conference, 173-4; at Spa Conference, 175-80; goes on special mission with D'Abernon to Poland, 180-7; at Third Lympne and Lucerne Conferences, 187-9; comments on Ireland and coal strike, 190-1; presses for Foreign Office official to supervise League affairs, 192-3; his view of mandates, 193-4; delivers lecture on 'Diplomacy by Conference' to Institute of International Affairs, 194-5; organises B.E.D. for first League Assembly, 195-6; further views on Ireland, 196-8; problems in Asia Minor, Mesopotamia and Palestine, 198-204; helps arrange Naval Inquiry, 204-8; views on Anglo-French relations and Lloyd George's behaviour to his colleagues, 210; receives Honorary Degree of Doctor of Laws, 211; and becomes member of 'The Club', 212; further concern over problems facing Government, 213-216; at Paris Conference, 216-18; at Third London Conference, 219-224; reaction to resignation of Bonar Law, 224-5; industrial troubles, 225-8; at Fourth Lympne Conference and inter-Allied Meeting in London, 228-30; activities at Imperial Conference of 1921, 230-3; further meeting in Paris, 233-4; views on unemployment, 235-6; leaves for Washington, 236-7; at Washington Conference, 238-58 (visits President Wilson, 245-6); opinion of Geddes Report and involvement in Admiralty-Air Ministry quarrel, 259-62; at Anglo-French meeting at Boulogne, 262-263; view of Montagu's resignation, 264; and reaction to Henry Wilson's murder, 264-6; makes preparations for Genoa Conference, 266 *et seq.*; at Genoa Conference, 269-76; again worried about Cabinet Secretariat, 277; for which he does battle, 279-81, 282; involvement in Chanak Crisis, 282-95; activity and opinions during last days of Coalition Government, 296-301; tribute to Lloyd George, 302-3

B. *Under Bonar Law* (1922-3), 304-42; renewed struggle (with Bonar Law and Warren Fisher) to preserve Cabinet Secretariat, 304-20; Curzon apologises for criticism of Secretariat, 320-1; and H receives support from Lord Lee, Grey and Birdwood, 322; attempts to revive

Hankey, Maurice [*contd.*]
C.I.D., 322-3; opinion of Bonar Law's ministry, 323, 325-6; action over Gounaris-Curzon letters, 324-325; not at Lausanne Conference but at London Reparations Conference, where records impressions of Mussolini, 326-8; contact with Lloyd George, 328-9; goes to Paris for further talks on Reparations, 330-4; observations on American debt and conduct of Baldwin, 333-5; determination to preserve Cabinet secrets, 335; work for Salisbury and Balfour Committees, 336-41; resignation of Bonar Law and H's view of situation thus created, 341 *et seq.*
C. *Baldwin's First Ministry* (1923-4), 342-52; supplanted by Jones as P.M.'s principal adviser, 343-4; helps establish C.O.S., 344-6; organises Imperial Conference of 1923, 346-51; reaction to Baldwin's defeat, 351-2
D. *MacDonald's First Ministry* (1924), 353-86; instructs P.M. in functions of C.I.D., 353-4; receives tributes from Curzon and Hoare, 357-8; relations with MacDonald, 358-9; immersed in defence problems, 359-65; secures Treasury minute on departmental co-operation, 366; sends Smuts a review of government and its problems, 366-7; at London Reparations Conference, 368-74; and is concerned about Campbell Case and custody of Cabinet minutes, 375-82; believes Zinoviev letter to be genuine, 385; takes holiday in Venice, 386
E. *Baldwin's Second Ministry* (1924-9), 387-474; relations with Prime Minister, 387-9; his family life, 389-90; occupied in C.I.D. affairs and formation of C.C.R., 390-3; attitude to Geneva Protocol and Four Power Pact, and his relations with Cecil, 395-9; opinion of Curzon, 399-400; efforts to secure closer links with Dominions, 400-401; again pre-occupied in defence matters, and becomes member of A.R.P. sub-committee, 402-5; presses for action over War Book and Anti-Aircraft Defence sub-committee, 405-6; views on Egypt, 408; agrees with Beatty over Shanghai crisis, 409-10; attitude to economic affairs at home, 410-12; exchange of views with Cecil, 413; congratulates Chamberlain on Locarno, 414-15; views on disarmament, 415-16; neutrality over naval aviation dispute, 417-18; but still in favour of Singapore Base and against a Ministry of Defence, 418-20; reaction to Chilcott affair, 421-4; attitude to General Strike, 424-6; work for Imperial Conference of 1926, 426-33; lack of enthusiasm for Cecil's ideas, 433-4; firm but balanced attitude to Shanghai crisis, 435-6; further deterioration in relations with Cecil, 437-41; on holiday in Norway, 441; reaction to Cecil's resignation, 441-4; question of future raised, 444-5; beneficial influence on Air Staff thinking, 445-9; work on C.O.S. and Overseas Defence Sub-Committee, 449-50; defends Belligerent Rights, 451-9; gives warning about German rearmament, 460; sorrow on death of Balfour, 460; disinterested in Trade Disputes Bill, but disquieted about Russian activities in England, 460-2; sends Smuts a general review of situation, 462; concern over naval programme, 463; helps prepare industrial mobilisation in event of a future war, 463-7; supports Anglo-French Compromise, 467-8; attitude to Kellogg-Briand Pact, 469; takes holiday in Switzerland, 469; relations with Royal Household, 470-1;

pays tribute to Haldane, 471-2; writes to Birkenhead on retirement, 472; last days of Baldwin's ministry and marriage of his daughter, 472-4
F. *MacDonald's Second Ministry* (1929-1931), 475-546; receives G.C.M.G., 475; produces 'Instructions to the Secretary on Cabinet procedure', 475-7; profound interest in Egypt and its problems, 478-9; prepares for First Hague Conference, 480-1; which he attends, 482-90; concerned over MacDonald's visit to U.S.A. and Anglo-American relations, 491-6; fights for Singapore Base, 496-8; attitude to League and disarmament, 498-500; resists idea of Ministry of Defence, 500-1; at Second Hague Conference, 502-8; keeps watchful eye on naval strength and negotiations with U.S.A., 502-8; at London Naval Conference, where earns thanks of MacDonald, 513-18; continued concern over naval strength and Ten Year Rule, 519-22; stays with Phipps in Vienna, 523; prepares for Imperial Conference of 1930, 524-5; which he attends, 526-30; contemplates writing memoirs, 532; reaction to publication of Lloyd George's *War Memoirs*, 533-4; once again immersed in defence, disarmament and C.I.D. affairs, 535-42; on holiday in France, 543; views on national crisis, 544-5
G. *National Government* (1931) and aftermath, 546-76; H's activities during formation of National Government, 546-53; approves of its measures and prepares for general election, 553-72; review of his position, 572-6
2. *Characteristics*
Family Life, happiness in, 34, 62, 114, 148, 225, 389-90, 441, 469, 473-4, 503, 518
Loyalty (in friendship) *see* Asquith, 23, 41, 42, 400; Balfour, 400, 459, 460; Haldane, 359, 374, 471-2; Lloyd George, 302-3, 308, 400, 534
Military and Strategic Ideas, 112, 138, 169, 181, 193, 207-8, 260 *et seq.*, 437-8, 447-8, 450 *et seq.*, 463 *et seq.*, *see* also Belligerent Rights, Channel Tunnel, Freedom of Seas and Ten Year Rule
Organising Ability, 43-4, 50-1, 54, 57-8, 80, 96-8, 122, 125, 129, 324, 368-9, 480-1, 506
Phil-Hellenism, 72, 143, 149, 198, 200, 224, 283
Tact (and discretion), 39, 162, 252, 258, 339, 373, 446, 483, 503
Work, dedication to, 19, 20, 24, 45-6, 52, 128, 141, 228, 267, 268, 281, 366, 532
3. *Tributes from* Albert of the Belgians, 176; Amery, 430; Baldwin, 444; Balfour, 281; Borden, 92; Burgis, 430-1; Clemenceau, 97, 146, 573; Curzon, 109, 236, 321, 357; Derby, 109; Sir William Elliot, 575; Esher, 430; George V, 23, 183; Harding, Sir Edward, 430; Hoare, 357; Hodsoll, 575; Hughes, C. E., 250; Jones, Tom, 572; Lloyd George, 92, 109; MacDonald, 488-9, 518, 574; Riddell, 88, 388; Stevenson, Frances, 97, 573; Wilson, Henry, 109
Hankey, Robin (later 2nd Baron) (son), at Rugby School, 90; with H at Lucerne Conference, 187; Lloyd George's favourable view of, 216; with H at Genoa Conference, 268, 273; at Oxford, 386; prepares for Diplomatic Service, 441; is accepted, 462; Third Secretary at Berlin, then Paris, 473; engaged to be married, 474; temporarily seconded for Second Hague Conference, 502, 503. H's letters to, 481, 483, 484, 486-8, 490, 573 *note* 1. Mentioned, 87
Hankey, Ursula (Lady Benn) (daughter), early years of, 53, 96, 389, 441;

Hankey, Ursula (Lady Benn) [*contd.*] presentation at Court and marriage, 473; birth of a daughter, 518
Harcourt, Sir William, 279
Harding, Sir Edward, 429 (and *note* 4), 430, 566, 574
Harding, Warren G., President of U.S.A., 166 (and *note* 1), 204, 234, 238, 239, 258, 333
Hardinge of Penshurst, 1st Baron, Permanent Under-Secretary at Foreign Office, 22, 24, 25, 47, 48, 49, 182, 183, 192, 284
Hardinge of Penshurst, 2nd Baron, 566 *note* 1
Harington, General Sir Charles, 286, 290, 291, 318, 321
Harmsworth, Cecil B. H. (later 1st Baron), 170 (and *note* 1)
Harmsworth, Esmond (later 2nd Viscount Rothermere), 311
Hartington, Marquess of (later 8th Duke of Devonshire), 279 (and *note* 1)
Hartshorn, Vernon, 190 (and *note* 4), 380
Harvey, Sir Ernest, 559 (and *note* 1), 561
Hastings, Sir Patrick, Attorney-General, 366 (and *note* 2), 375-7
Headlam-Morley, J. W., *quoted*, 49
Henderson, Rt. Hon. Arthur, early position in Labour movement, 35, 122, 124; Home Secretary in First Labour Government, 356, 366, 370, 381; appointed Minister Plenipotentiary at Cairo, 407; Foreign Secretary in Second Labour Government, 475; recalls Lloyd from Egypt, 478-9; at First Hague Conference, 481-2, 483, 484, 488; defence policy of, 499; visits Rome and Paris after London Naval Conference, 521; Chairman of sub-committee (of C.I.D.) on disarmament, 526; warned by H not to raise Belligerent Rights issue at Imperial Conference of 1930, 527-528; opposed to cut in Unemployment Relief, 546 *note* 1; attitude to National Government, 552-3; becomes Leader of Opposition, 553, 561, 566. Mentioned, 493
Henry, Prince Consort of the Netherlands, 503, 504
Hermon-Hodge, Commander the Hon. C.P., 453 *note* 1
Herriot, Edouard, Prime Minister of France, 318 (and *note* 1), 369, 370, 372, 373, 396
Hertzog, General James B. M., 349 (and *note* 2), 428-9, 431, 432, 526 *note* 3
Hewart, 1st Viscount, 130 (and *note* 3)
Hilferding, Rudolf, German Minister of Finance, 485, 486 (and *note* 1)
Hill, Major J. W., 336 *note* 1
Hill, T. St. Q. (later Sir St. Quintin), 227, 308 (and *note* 2), 312
Hindenburg, Paul von, President of Germany, 507
Hitler Adolf, 333, 344, 465, 519, 537
Hoare, Rt. Hon. Sir Samuel (later 1st Viscount Templewood), Secretary for Air, 262 (and Member of Salisbury Committee, 336, 339), 347, 348; pays tribute to H on quitting office (1924), 357-8; Secretary for India, 562-3. Mentioned, 103, 538 *note* 6
Hodges, Frank, 103 (and *note* 2), 190, 191, 227
Hodges, Admiral Sir Michael, 554 (and *note* 2)
Hodsoll, Wing Commander E. J. (later Sir John), 477 (and *note* 2), 512, 575
Hogg, Sir Douglas (later 1st Viscount Hailsham), 453 *note* 1, 461, 538 *note* 6
Hoover, Herbert C., U.S. Food Controller, 26 (and *note* 2), President of U.S.A., 458, 491-2, 494, 495, 510-11, 521; Hoover moratorium, 545
Horne, Rt. Hon. Sir Robert (later 1st Viscount), Minister of Labour, 47, 107, 111, 115, 127; President of Board of Trade, 120, 173, 190, 202, 208; Chancellor of Exchequer, 215, 267 *note* 2, 268, 288, 289, 335

Horwood, Brigadier-General Sir William T., 265 (and *note* 3)
Houghton, Alanson B., 468 *note* 2
House, Colonel E. M. (President Wilson's special emissary), 30, 36, 58, 62, 67, 166, 452, 494
Howard, Sir Esmé (later 1st Baron Howard of Penrith), British Ambassador in Washington, 440 (and *note* 6), 454, 470, 494
Howorth, R. B. (later Sir Rupert), Deputy Secretary of Cabinet, 131 *note* 4, 205, 308, 312, 314, 477 (and *note* 1), 523, 543-4, 546, 553
Hughes, Charles Evans, U.S. Secretary of State, 228; at Washington Conference, 239, 241, 249, 250-1, 256, 258
Hughes, W. M., Prime Minister of Australia, at Paris Peace Conference, 30, 37, 38, 51, 52, 54, 55, 62 *note* 2, 77-8; unrepresented at Boulogne and Spa Conferences, 175; at Imperial Conference of 1921, 230, 232; offers help during Chanak Crisis, 285. Mentioned, 276
Humphreys, Sir Travers, 376
Hurd, Archibald, 205
Hurley, Edward N., 26 (and *note* 3)
Hurst, Sir Cecil, Legal Adviser to Foreign Office, 48 *note* 4, 77, 267, 273, 393, 427, 453
Hutchison, General Sir Robert (later 1st Baron), 420 *note* 2
Hymans, Monsieur, 85, 86, 373
Hythe, *see* Lympne

Illingworth, 1st Baron, 216 (and *note* 1)
Imperial Conferences (1921), 230-3; (1923), 343, 346-51, 427; (1926), 403, 426-33; (1930), 497, 501, 522, 524-30, 532
Imperial War Cabinet, 20, 21-2, 24, 28, 29, 31, 32-3, 34, 35-7, 38, 39, 43; H's ideas on reconstruction of, 105-6, 110; last days of, 121 *et seq.*; replaced by pre-war Cabinet, 127 *et seq.*
Imperial War Conference (1919), 20
India, British position in, 112, 140, 144; effect of Turkish Treaty upon Moslem opinion in, 142-3; claim of India Office for representation at San Remo Conference, 157; military and political difficulties concerning, 169, 193, 213, 260; resignation of Montagu from India Office over future of Constantinople, 263-4; demand for equal representation at Imperial Conference of 1923, 348; opposed to Geneva Protocol, 395; the Chilcott affair, 420-4; question of Indian representation at Imperial Conference of 1926 raised, 426; defence problems over, 448, 450; Round Table Conference summoned, 529, 565 (and *note* 1); consulted over disarmament issues, 538; H critical of British policy in, 544; difficulties with London over value of rupee (1931), 561-2
Inskip, Sir Thomas (later 1st Viscount Caldecote), 346 (and *note* 2)
Invergordon Mutiny (1931), 509, 554-8
Ireland, problem of, 112, 133; Home Rule Bill and continued civil strife, 137, 140, 152-4, 169, 189; Lloyd George's policy towards and passing of Government of Ireland Bill, 190, 194, 196-8; further difficulties, 218-19, 224, 235, 239; Treaty with Britain signed, 253, but renewed troubles, 260, culminating in murder of Wilson and Collins, 264-6; cabinet committee on, 325; boundary with Ulster settled, 359, 370; indifferent to Singapore Base, 360; but hostile to Geneva Protocol, 395; represented at Imperial Conference of 1926, 428; but not sent C.I.D. papers, 480; represented at Imperial Conference of 1930, 526
Irwin, Baron (later 1st Earl of Halifax), Viceroy of India, 436 (and *note* 7), 473
Ismay, Colonel (later General 1st Baron), 499 (and *note* 3), 531, 575

Ismet Pasha, 326
Italy, claims and behaviour at Paris Peace Conference, 28, 30, 45, 51, 58, 60, 61, 64, 69, 73, 78-9, 80-2, 83-4, 85-6, 87, 89, 91, 96, 97, 100; continued friction with Allies over Adriatic question, 135, 138, 142, 143-4, 146-8; attends San Remo Conference, 160-2, and Conferences at Boulogne and Spa, 174, 175; H's visit to, 217-18; attitude to Reparations, 220, 222, 223, 229; not included in Four Power Pact at Washington Conference, 252; at Conference of Cannes, 258; and Genoa, 266 *et seq.*; London Conference on Reparations attended by Mussolini, 324, 326, 327-8; attack on Corfu, 348; H's views on Fascist régime in, 386, 462; attends London Naval Conference, 512; where clashes with France, 514, 517; British efforts to mitigate quarrel with France, 521

Japan, claims at Paris Peace Conference, 37, 45, 82-3, 95 *note* 1, 227-8; H's view of, 112; naval programme of, 205; attitude to Reparations, 220; at Washington Conference, where signs Four Power Pact, 249-51, 254-5, 256 *note* 1, 257; at Genoa Conference, 268; H's fears of, 367, 399; Churchill's attitude towards, 403; Beatty's views on, 408-9; position over Shanghai, 435-6; negotiations with Britain over naval parity at Geneva Conference, 439-40; attitude at London Naval Conference, 512, 514-16, 520; occupation of Manchuria, 536, 563
Jaspar, Henri, Belgian Foreign Minister, then Prime Minister, 327, 330, 485 (and *note* 2), 486, 487, 503, 505-6
Jellicoe, Admiral of Fleet, 1st Earl, 508, 521
Jenkinson, Sir Mark, 543 *note* 2
Joffé, Adolf, 274
Johnson, Robert U., U.S. Ambassador in Rome, 163 (and *note* 1)
Johnson, Dr. Samuel, 212, 504 *note* 6
Johnston, Rt. Hon. T., Lord Privy Seal, 546 *note* 1
Jones, Captain (later Sir) Clement, 47 *note* 3, 48, 51, 52
Jones, Colonel Dally, 19, 106
Jones, Thomas, position in Cabinet Secretariat, 22, 23; acting Secretary whilst H in Paris, 42, 47, 58-60, 63, 68-9, 73, 74; discusses Secretariat with H, 105; views on naval building programme, 112; skill in handling industrial disputes, 123, 144, 152, 191, 226; attitude to Cabinet leakages, 131; interest in Irish problem, 154, 198; again in charge when H away at Washington Conference, 234; attitude to unemployment, 235-6; plays leading part in negotiating Irish Treaty, 253, 256, 260, 264; reports on London Reparations Conference, 255; deputises for H at Cannes Conference, 258; H's desire to retain, 307-9, 311, 312, 314; supplants H in Baldwin's favour, 344, 351, 352; positions reversed under MacDonald, 358; negotiations over Ulster Boundary, 359; connection with Campbell Case, 377-8, 379; opposed to dissolution of Parliament (1924), 382; again replaces H as Baldwin's principal adviser, 387-8; secretary of C.C.R., 391; continued friendship with Baldwin, 404, 411; attitude to General Strike, 424, 425-6; assists Canada in study of cabinet organisation, 431; considered by H to be satisfactory as his deputy, 445; shows Baldwin H's letter on Belligerent Rights, 452; advocate of appeasement, 466, 469-70; goes to U.S.A. with MacDonald, 490, 491, 493-4; becomes Secretary of Pilgrim Trust, 523; tribute to H, 572. Mentioned, 151, 155, 182, 189, 217,

218, 267, 299-300, 330, 333, 400, 469, 481, 515
Jowitt, Sir William A. (later 1st Earl), 568 (and *note* 1)
Joynson Hicks, William (later 1st Viscount Brentford), Home Secretary, 380 (and *note* 1) 472
Juliana, Crown Princess (later Queen) of the Netherlands, 504 (and *note* 2)
Jusserand, Jules, 183 (and *note* 2), 186

Kaiser (Wilhelm II, German Emperor and King of Prussia), proposed trial of, 20, 29, 72, 96, 99, 110, 144
Kakovsky, C., 381 *note* 3
Kalogeropoulos, M., Prime Minister of Greece, 222 (and *note* 1)
Kamenev, L. B. R., 172 (and *note* 3), 187, 188, 271
Kapp, Wolfgang ('Kapp Putsch'), 150-1, 163
Kaptanzoglu, Monsieur, 223
Kato, Baron Tomosaburo, 250
Keith, Professor A. B., 419 *note* 1
Kellogg-Briand Pact, 349, 469, 520
Kelly, Vice-Admiral W. H. (later Sir William), 468
Kemal Pasha, 126, 163, 173, 200, 213, 219, 222, 223, 225, 285, 289, 290, 291
Kennedy Jones, 78 (and *note* 3)
Kenworthy, Commander J. M. (later 10th Baron Strabolgi), 495 *note* 1, 556
Kenyon, F. G. (later Sir Frederic), 320 (and *note* 2)
Kerr, Philip (later 11th Marquess of Lothian), Private Secretary to Lloyd George, 36, 39, 41, 54 *note* 2, 62, 70, 72, 99, 137, 138, 139, 142, 147, 158, 166, 199, 207, 223, 224, 225, 255, 277, 307 *note* 1, 455, 530, 532, 538 *note* 6, *see* also Lothian
Keyes, Admiral Roger (later 1st Baron), 508-9, 519, *see* also Trenchard-Keyes Agreement
Keynes, J. M. (later 1st Baron), 84, 96, 552
Kiep, M., 370 *note* 3
Kisch, Colonel (later Brigadier-General), F. H., 78 (and *note* 2)
Kitchener, Field-Marshal, 1st Earl, 197, 571
Klishko, N., 170 (and *note* 2)
Klotz, Monsieur, 86
Kolchak, Admiral Alexander, 110
Krassin, Leonid B., Commissar for Trade and Industry, later first U.S.S.R. Ambassador in London, 169 (and *note* 3), 170-2, 188, 270
Kruger, S. J. P., President of Boer Republic, 101
Kun, Bela, 70, 75

Lampson, Sir Miles (later 1st Baron Killearn), 368 (and *note* 4), 371; Minister to China, 385, 461; High Commissioner for Egypt, 479
Lansbury, Edgar, 131
Lansbury, George, 131, 546 *note* 1
Lansing, Robert, U.S. Secretary of State, 45 (and *note* 3), 58, 147 *note* 2
Latham, Charles (later 1st Baron), 543 *note* 2
Latham, J. G. (later Sir John), 54 (and *note* 1)
Lausanne Conferences and Treaty (1923), 324, 326-8, 330, 331, 334
Lawrence, T. E., 116-17, 119, 128
Leadbitter, E. (later Sir Eric), 314 *note* 1
League of Nations, first proposals about, 25, 26, 27, 36, 38, 39, 54; H flirts with idea of becoming its first Secretary-General, 57-8; but after advice from Esher and Curzon turns it down, 60-1, 64-7, 73, 79-80; U.S. Senate opposed to, 69, 99, 152; First Assembly of (1920), 195-6; Silesian problem referred to, 233-4; fails to cope with Italian aggression against Greece, 348; drafts a Treaty of Mutual Assistance, 363; and the Geneva Protocol, 381 *note* 1; initiates disarmament talks, 415-16, 433-4; renews attempts to gain acceptance for 'Model Treaty to strengthen the

League of Nations [*contd.*]
means of Preventing War', 498 *et seq.*; produces Draft Disarmament Convention, 539-40; H's views on, 71, 232-3, 263, 348, 371, 398-9, 414, 462
Lee of Fareham, 1st Viscount, First Lord of Admiralty, 202, 212, 237, 240, 252, 261, 285 *note* 1, 289, 294, 301 *note* 2, 322
Leith-Ross, Sir Frederick, 330 (and *note* 1), 502, 559
Lenin, V. I., 185
Leslie, Sir Norman, 447 (and *note* 3)
Leveson, Admiral (later Sir) Arthur C., 207 (and *note* 2)
Lewis, Sir George, 104 (and *note* 1)
Leygues, G., Prime Minister of France, 200, 216
Liddell, F. F. (later Sir Frederick), 308 (and *note* 4)
Liddell Hart, Sir Basil, 117, 533 *note* 2, 541
Lindemann, Professor F. A. (later 1st Baron Cherwell), 406 (and *note* 4)
Lindsay, Sir Ronald C., 478 (and *note* 3), 479 *note* 5, 502
Litvinov, M., Russian Foreign Minister 266 *note* 3, 270-1, 272
Llewellyn Smith, H. (later Sir Hubert), 111 (and *note* 2)
Lloyd, 1st Baron, High Commissioner in Egypt, 407 (and *note* 7), 408, 478-80
Lloyd George, Rt. Hon. David (later 1st Earl), Prime Minister 1916-22, (19-303), 19 *passim* 42, 43 *passim* 52, 54 *passim* 58, 60 *passim* 66, 68 *passim* 71, 73 *passim* 92, 94, 96, 101, 103 *passim* 113, 114, 115, 118 *passim* 125, 127 *passim* 130, 132, 133, 134, 137, 138, 139, 141, 142, 144 *passim* 162, 164 *passim* 181, 186 *passim* 194, 196 *passim* 203, 205 *passim* 212, 214 *passim* 236, 239, 241, 244 *passim* 249, 251 *passim* 262, 264 *passim* 278, 279 *passim* 284, 287, 288, 289, 293-303. In Opposition (304-571); his political position, 343; attends C.I.D. meeting over Channel Tunnel, 364; attitude to MacDonald's Government (1924), 367; MacDonald's dislike of, 371; raises issue of a Ministry of Defence, 467; criticises MacDonald's American visit (1929), 494; tentative approach to made by MacDonald, 430-1; consulted by H about writing his (H's) Memoirs of World War I, 532; his own *War Memoirs*, 533-4; represented by Samuel in negotiations for formation of National Government, 547, 550, 565; visited by MacDonald, 568. Relations with H, 23, 38-9, 41, 61, 87-8, 92, 106, 108-9, 121, 181, 210, 214, 220, 225, 230, 244-6, 288-9, 299-300, 325, 331, 358, 397. H's observations on, 69, 98, 103, 121, 148-9, 166, 188, 197, 221, 248, 343, 349, 366, 371, 374, 397, 400, 573. Observations on Cabinet Colleagues – on Addison, 210; Baldwin, 329; Bonar Law, 329; Birkenhead, 124; Curzon, 210, 214-15, 294, 295, 300, 329; Griffith-Boscawen, 298; Milner, 156; Runciman, 571. Mentioned, 277, 304, 305, 306, 307, 308, 310, 315 and *note* 2, 320, 321, 323-4, 327, 330, 333, 335, 336, 342, 346, 352, 364, 369, 378, 387, 388, 451, 473, 484, 486, 495 *note* 1, 544, 561 *note* 1, 562, 570
Lloyd-Greame, Sir Philip (later Sir Philip Cunliffe-Lister and finally 1st Earl of Swinton), Secretary to Department of Overseas Trade, 268 (and *note* 1), 276; President of Board of Trade, 323, 330, 331, 332, 352, 453 *note* 1, 561 – as Swinton, *see* 276, 297, 466
Locarno Pact (1925), 374, 396-7, 414, 415, 507
Locker-Lampson, Commander Oliver S., 188 (and *note* 4)
Lodge, Senator Henry Cabot, 240 (and *note* 5), 244

London Conferences, First (1918), 28-31; Second (1920), 146-8; Third (1921), 219-24
London Naval Conference (1930), 491, 495, 497, 501, 504, 508-20, 521, 522, 524, 532, 545
London Reparations Conference (1921), 255; (1924), 368-75, 382
London, Secret Treaty of (1915), 57 *note* 1, 78, 81, 89, 99, 135, 142, 292
Long, Rt. Hon. Walter (later 1st Viscount), Colonial Secretary and then First Lord of Admiralty, 113, 127 *note* 1, 130, 137, 154, 173, 205, 208
Long-Béranger Agreement (1919), 145 *note* 2
Longhurst, Cyril, member of C.I.D. Secretariat, 31, 106, 308, 312
Loraine (later Sir), Percy, 138 (and *note* 3)
Lothian, Marquess of, *see* Kerr, Philip
Loucheur, Monsieur, 221, 229, 487, 488
Lucerne Conference (1920), 187-9
Luttwitz, General von, 150 *note* 1
Lyautey, Louis-Hubert, Marshal of France, 321
Lympne Conferences (First) – May 1920 – 166-8; (Second) – June 1920 – 171, 173-4, 198; (Third) – August 1920 – 187; (Fourth) – April 1921 – 228

MacDonald, Rt. Hon. J. Ramsay, Prime Minister 1924 (Jan. to Oct.), 353-86; briefed by H on position and work of C.I.D., 353-4; appoints Haldane Chairman of C.I.D. when he himself absent, 359, 365-6; cancels work on Singapore Base, but allows Navy more cruisers, 360-2; rejects Treaty of Mutual Assistance, 363; revives, then (at H's prompting) abandons idea of Channel Tunnel, 364-5; calls Reparations Conference which leads to acceptance of Dawes Plan and French evacuation of Ruhr, 368-74; involved in Campbell Case, 375 *et seq.*; attitude to Geneva Protocol, 381; negotiates with U.S.S.R., 381, but is defeated at election following Zinoviev Letter, 382-5. Prime Minister (1929-31), again becomes Prime Minister, 474; antipathy to Snowden and Henderson, 475; policy towards Egypt, 478-80; not easy to work with, 481; attitude to British delegation at First Hague Conference, 484, 486-7; thanks H for his services at Hague, 488-9; visits U.S. for talks with Hoover and discusses Belligerent Rights and West Indian bases, 490, 491-5, 511; attitude to Singapore Base, 496-8; and to League of Nations and disarmament, 499-500; insists on H going to Second Hague Conference and reporting on its progress, 504 *et seq.*; involved in preparations for London Naval Conference (1930), 509 *et seq.*; his policy as its Chairman, 513-14, 516; his exaggerated claims of its achievements, and again thanks H for his help, 517-19, 520, 521; finally rejects idea of Channel Tunnel, 522-3; his part in preparations for Imperial Conference of 1930, 524-5; agrees to allow Chiefs of Staff's Annual Review to be sent to Dominions, 528; summons Indian Round Table Conference, 529; makes tentative approach to Lloyd George, 530-1; warned by H on defence problems, 537-8; establishes Three Party Sub-Committee on Disarmament, 538-540; adopts May Report, 542-3; faced with monetary crisis, 544-5; forms National Government, and wins election of 1931, 546-53, 558-572. Relations with H, 354, 358, 361-2, 366, 370, 371, 373, 375, 376-8, 380, 481, 484, 486, 488-9, 490, 495, 518, 520, 562-3, 569, 573-4. Mentioned, 131 *note* 4, 391, 393

Mackenzie King, W. L., Prime Minister of Canada, 347 (and *note* 2), 349-50, 428, 429, 431, 432
Maclean, Sir Donald, 277 *note* 6, 280, 571 (and *note* 2)
Macmillan, Rt. Hon. Harold, 532
Macmillan, H. P. (later Lord), 412 *note* 3
Macnamara, Rt. Hon. Dr. Thomas J., 202, 205
Macready, General Sir Nevil, 153, 154, 196
McSwiney, Terence, Lord Mayor of Cork, 189 (and *note* 4)
Madden, Admiral (later Admiral of Fleet), Sir Charles, First Sea Lord, 445 (and *note* 3), 446, 453, 492, 508, 509, 510
Makino, Baron, 95 *note* 1
Malkin, H. W. (later Sir William), 77 (and *note* 3), 149, 229
Mandel, Georges (Chef de Cabinet to Clemenceau), 99
Mantoux, Paul, 50, 73, 76, 81, 98, 369
Markham, Violet R. (Mrs. Carruthers), 151 (and *note* 4)
Marsal, François, 167
Marx, Wilhelm, German Chancellor, 369 (and *note* 3), 373
Masaryk, Jan, 183 (and *note* 5)
Masaryk, T. G., 183 (and *note* 5)
Massey, W. F., Prime Minister of New Zealand, 52, 54, 55, 231, 232, 347, 348, 350
Massigli, René, 276
Masterton Smith, Sir James, 282, 297, 298, 309, 314, 349
Maund, Commander (later Rear-Admiral), Loben E. H., 512 (and *note* 3)
Maxse, Lieutenant-Commander H. F. B., 384
Maxton, James, 375 (and *note* 4)
May, Sir George, 500 (and *note* 5)
May Committee (of 1931) and Report (Minority Report, 543 *note* 2), 500-1, 542, 543, 554
Maynard, Major-General C. C. M. (later Sir Charles), 35 (and *note* 4)
Meighen, Arthur, Prime Minister of Canada, 231, 232, 349 (and *note* 1)
Mesopotamia, British interest in, 28, 37, 90, 112, 116-20, 125, 126, 135, 138, 140, 145, 169, 174, 194, 200-4, 205, 213, 214, 216, 223, 325
Millerand, Etienne A., President of France, 147, 149, 150, 152, 159, 160, 161, 162, 165, 167, 173, 175, 176, 177, 178, 182, 216, 333
Milligan, Sir William, 178 (and *note* 2)
Milne, General (later Field-Marshal 1st Baron), Chief of Imperial General Staff, 437, 449 (and *note* 1), 460, 528, 540
Milner, Rt. Hon. 1st Viscount, Secretary of State for War, 21, 26-7, 32, 37, 43-4, 46; Colonial Secretary, 55, 61, 127 *note* 1, 138 and *note* 1, 156, 158, 173, 202, 203, 214, 307 *note* 1, 312
Ministry of Defence, proposals for and H's opposition to, 32, 110, 154, 255, 259, 336, 337, 339-40, 346, 420, 448, 467, 500-1
Mola, Admiral, 30 *note* 1
Mond-Weir Committee (1922), 419
Monro, Robert (later 1st Baron Alness), 202 (and *note* 2)
Montagu, Rt. Hon. Edwin S., Secretary of State for India, concern over fate of Constantinople, 142-3; considers Indian Delegation should be at San Remo Conference, 157; believes any agreement with Russia should include non co-operation with Kemal, 173; policy over mandates and position of Feisal in Mesopotamia, 202, 203; policy on Tariff Reform, 215; at Imperial Conference of 1921, 232; quarrel with Curzon and resignation over Turkish question, 263-4. Mentioned, 127 *note* 1, 280
Morgan, Brigadier-General Sir John H., 460 (and *note* 1)
Morley, 1st Viscount, 371
Morrison, Rt. Hon. Herbert (later 1st Baron), 475 *note* 1, 546 *note* 1
Morrow, Dwight, 517 (and *note* 6)

Morton, Major D. (later Sir Desmond), 464 (and *note* 4), 465, 466
Mosley, Leonard, 350
Mosley, Sir Oswald, 400 *note* 2, 475 *note* 1
Mosul, British claim to accepted, 28-9, 90, 116, 119, 201, 334
Mudania Conference (1922), 291, 294, 318
Mudros, armistice with Turkey at (1918), 140
Müller, Hermann, German Chancellor, 151 *note* 1, 507 *note* 2
Mussolini, Benito, 258 *note* 1, 324, 326, 327
Mutual Assistance, draft Treaty of, rejected, 363

Nawanagar, Jam Sahib of, 421
New Zealand, attitude at Paris Peace Conference, 45, 52; represented at Conferences of Boulogne and Spa, 175 *note* 2; at Imperial Conference of 1921 where favours renewal of Anglo-Japanese alliance, 231; at Washington Conference, 240; offers help during Chanak Crisis, 285; supports Imperial Preference, 347; at Imperial Conference of 1923, 347; where supports Singapore Base, 348; regrets MacDonald's decision to halt this, 360, 361; opposed to Geneva Protocol, 395; at Imperial Conference of 1926, 428; High Commissioner in London takes part in work of C.I.D., 431, 450; H suggested as Governor-General of, 495; dislike of Labour Government, 513; attitude at Imperial Conference of 1930, 526, 528; cool reception to disarmament Draft Resolutions, 538
Newbold, J. Walton, 383 *note* 1
Newfoundland, 49, 285, 360
Newman, Sir George, 189
Newnham (Lloyd George's valet), 81, 158
Nicolson, Sir Harold, 44, 50, 83, 89, 96, 100, 152, 165, 234, 291, 326, 342, 350
Niemeyer, O. E. (later Sir Otto), 130, 205 (and *note* 2), 410
Nitti, Francesco, Prime Minister of Italy, 91, 143 (and *note* 3), 147, 148, 160, 161-2
Noel-Baker, Philip, 193, 195, 263
Nollet, General, 209, 373
Norman, H. C., 48 *note* 4
Norman, Montagu (later 1st Baron), Governor of Bank of England, 546 (and *note* 3), 547
Northcliffe, 1st Viscount, 25, 103 *note* 4, 104, 191
Noske, Gustav, 151 *note* 1
Novar, 1st Viscount, 334 (and *note* 1)
Nutting, Rt. Hon. Anthony, 131

O'Connor, Rory, 266, 517, 519
Official Secrets Act (1920), 131, 335
O'Flannagan, Father, Vice-President of Sinn Fein, 197
Olga, Queen of the Hellenes, 199
Oliver, F. S., 29
Olivier, 1st Baron, 365 (and *note* 4), 380
O'Malley, Owen, 384
Orlando, Vittore, Prime Minister of Italy, 25, 28, 58, 69, 73, 78, 81, 83, 85, 98, 143, 162
Owen, F. W. (H's stenographer), 166, 226
Owen Committee on Reparations, 484-5
Paderewski, Ignace, Prime Minister of Poland, 182 (and *note* 4), 183
Paléologue, Maurice, 182 (and *note* 2)
Palestine, British position in, 28-9, 37, 38, 71, 90, 112, 116, 117, 119, 126, 135, 144, 163, 169, 194, 200-4, 213, 216; Balfour's visit to, 397
Paris Peace Conference (1919), preparations for, 21 *et seq.*, 36 *et seq.*; in session, 43-64, 68-92, 94-101; closing of, 108, 121; resumption of, 142-6. Mentioned, 104, 114, 140, 141, 211, 232, 250, 257, 271, 483, 505, 533

Paris, Second Conference of (Jan. 1921), 216-18
Paris, Third Conference of (Aug. 1921), 233-4
Paris, Fourth Conference of (1923) – on Reparations – 330-3
Parmoor, 1st Baron, 381 (and *note* 2)
Pasitch, N., 143 *note* 4
Passfield, 1st Baron (Sidney Webb), 380, (Colonial and Dominions Secretary), 493
Patek, Stanislaw, 171 (and *note* 1), 176
Paul, Prince (later King) of Greece, 200 *note* 3
Peacock, E. R. (later Sir Edward), 559 (and *note* 2), 561
Pearce, Senator (later Sir) George, 240 (and *note* 7)
Peel, 2nd Viscount (later 1st Earl), Secretary of State for India, 264, 285 *note* 1; member of Salisbury Committee, 336, 337, 338, 393; and Belligerent Rights Sub-Committee, 453 *note* 1
Perley, Sir George, 175 *note* 2
Pershing, General John H., 245
Persia, British (oil) interests in, 140, 145, 168, 170, 171, 174, 194, 201, 202, 203, 209, 210, 213; Persian Gulf, 469
Phipps, E. (later Sir Eric), 48 *note* 4, 483 (and *note* 2), 502, 507, 523
Pichon, Etienne, 28, 29, 44
Pilsudski, Jozef, 181 (and *note* 2)
Poincaré, Raymond, President of France, 98, 133, 145, Prime Minister, 255, 258; intransigent attitude of, 259, 263, 266, 269, 273-4, 281; conduct during Chanak Crisis, 288, 291, 292, 318; at London Reparations Conference, 324, 326-7; at Paris Conference on Reparations where decides to occupy the Ruhr, 331-3. Mentioned, 216, 367
Poland, discussed at Paris Peace Conference, 69, 72; H's view of, 138; Curzon uninterested in, 142; relations with Russia, 170, 171, 176, 179; H accompanies D'Abernon on special mission to, 180-1, 183 *et seq.*; settlement of her frontier with Russia, 187, 189, 194; Anglo-French friction over, 209; secures Upper Silesia, 233-4
Polk, Frank L., 118 (and *note* 2)
Ponsonby, Rt. Hon. Arthur (later 1st Baron), 381 *note* 3, 463 (and *note* 3)
Power, Sir John, 420 (and *note* 4), 421, 422
Pugh, Arthur, 543 *note* 2
Pursey, Commander H., 555 *note* 2

Radcliffe, General Sir Percy de B., 181, 182, 185, 186
Radek, Karl, 274
Rakovsky, Christian, 383
Rapallo, Russo-German Treaty of (1922), 271-3, 275, 275
Rawlins, Major (chief clerk to H.), 43, 312
Reading, 1st Marquess of, Lord Chief Justice, accepts post of High Commissioner in charge of relief and revictualling allied, enemy and neutral countries, 20-1, 25-6; Viceroy of India, 263-4; joins National Government, 550, 565, 567, 568, 569. Mentioned, 206
Redmond, John Edward, 197
Reed, Sir Stanley, 422 (and *note* 1), 423-4
Reparations, Permanent Commission established, 68, and H's views on, 71-2; Australian view of, 77; Belgian view of, 85-7; Keynes's view of, 96; problems of, 140, 142, 161, 162, 164; discussed at First Lympne Conference, 167-8; and at Spa, 175, 178-80; at Paris, 216-17, and at London, 220; negotiations with Germany broken off and Allied troops sent into three more Rhineland towns, 221-2; continued failure to solve problem of, 326-7; again unsuccessfully discussed in Paris, 330-2; French occupation of Ruhr, 333; London Conference secures acceptance of Dawes Plan and evacuation of

Ruhr, 367-74; again dealt with by First Hague Conference, where Germany secures a reduction of, 480-90; and Second Hague Conference where Young Plan adopted, 502-7
Revelstoke, 2nd Baron, 480 *note* 3
Reynolds, Sir Joshua, 212
Rhallis, Demetrios, Prime Minister of Greece, 149 (and *note* 2)
Rhineland, discussed before and during Paris Peace Conference, 29, 72, 142; occupation of, 151-2; extended, 221-2; Germany secures evacuation of, 485, 489, 505, 506-7
Richmond, Sir Herbert, 207, 453, 457, 525
Riddell, 1st Baron, 81, 88, 107, 113, 114, 132, 148, 158, 159, 219, 242, 284, 387, 414, 475, 564
Riga, Treaty of (1921), 187
Rizo-Rangabé, Alexander, 221 *note* 1
Roberts, Field-Marshal 1st Earl, 27
Robertson, Field-Marshal Sir William, 108, 109, 153, 321
Ronaldshay, Earl of (later 2nd Marquess of Zetland), 325, 350
Roosevelt (Jr.), Colonel Theodore, 244 (and *note* 4), 245
Root, Senator, Elihu, 240 (and *note* 4), 244
Rothermere, 1st Viscount, 159, 310-11
Ruhr, French designs on, 150-1, 158, 159, 161, 228-9, 281, 326, 332; French occupation of, 333, 334; French agree to evacuate, 370, 372, 374
Rumbold, Sir Horace, British Minister in Poland, 184, 186; High Commissioner and Ambassador at Constantinople, 286, 290, 291; Ambassador at Berlin, 507, 508
Runciman, Rt. Hon. Walter (later 1st Viscount), 568, 571, 572
Russell, Sir Odo, 483 (and *note* 1)
Russia, British military intervention in, 35; exclusion from Peace Conference, 45; Lloyd George's view of, 47, 69, 75; Esher's view of, 77; collapse of Kolchak, 110; H's views on, 111-12; Churchill's views on, 115; British policy towards, 133, 138, 140, 144; visit of Krassin to Britain to establish trade relations, 170-1, 172-3; relations with Poland, 176, 180-7; Krassin and Kamenev expelled from Britain, 188-9; attitude of Cannes Conference towards, 258; attends Genoa Conference, 267 *et seq.*; and concludes Treaty of Rapallo with Germany, 276; relations with MacDonald's First Government, 331; and affair of Zinoviev letter, 382 *et seq.*; relations with Baldwin's Second Ministry, 461; and rupture of diplomatic (but not trade) relations with Britain, 462
Ryle, Dr. Herbert E., Dean of Westminster, 192

Sackville-West, Major-General Sir Charles (later 4th Baron Sackville), 176 (and *note* 2)
Sakarya, battle of (1921), 282 and *note* 4
Salisbury, 4th Marquess of, successively Lord President of Council, Chancellor of Duchy of Lancaster and Lord Privy Seal, 156, 301, 322 (and *note* 4), 336, 338, 349, 393, 438, 468, 498
Salisbury Committee, Sub-Committee of C.I.D. to inquire into co-operation between the Services, 336-41, 344, 347, 362, 393, 419, 498; to examine Belligerent Rights, 453-4
Salmond, Sir John, 240 (and *note* 8), 244
Salter, Sir Arthur, 26
Samuel, Rt. Hon. Sir Herbert (later 1st Viscount), Chairman of Royal Commission on Coal Industry, 412, 424; approaches to by MacDonald, in 1930, 530; member of Three Party Committee on Disarmament, 538 *note* 6; actions during crisis of 1931, 546, 547, 550, 552,

Samuel, Rt. Hon. Sir Herbert [*contd.*] 560, 561, 563, 565, 566, 567, 568, 569, 570
Samuel, Marcus (later 1st Viscount Bearsted), 145 (and *note* 3)
San Remo, Conference at (1920), 146, 157, 159-63
Sankey, 1st Viscount, 74 *note* 1, 528, 529, 550, 560, 563
Sapieha, Prince Eustache, 186 (and *note* 2)
Sargent, Sir Orme, 507 (and *note* 4)
Sassoon, Sir Philip, 153, 166, 173, 190, 228, 288, 289, 567
Schacht, Dr. Hjalmar, 488 *note* 1, 505 (and *note* 2)
Schanzer, Carlo, Italian Foreign Minister, 266 (and *note* 4), 270, 272
Schubert, Carl von, 370 (and *note* 4)
Schuster, Sir Claud (later 1st Baron), 474 (and *note* 1), 569
Schuster, Sir George, 562 (and *note* 7)
Scialoja, Vittorio, Italian Foreign Minister, 138 (and *note* 2)
Scullin, J. H., 526 *note* 3
Seely, J. E. B. (later 1st Baron Mottistone), 115, 120, 298
Selborne, 2nd Earl of, 208
Selby, Sir Walford, 320 (and *note* 2)
Sèvres, Treaty of (1920), 163, 198, 200, 219, 263, 283, 292, 295
Sforza, Count Carlo, Italian Foreign Minister, 174 (and *note* 3), 175, 217, 219, 222, 223
Shanghai Crisis (1927), 408-10, 434, 435-7
Shantung, dispute over, 83, 251, 254, 255, 371
Shaw, George Bernard, 374
Shaw, T., 538
Sherwood, W., 412 *note* 2
Shortt, Rt. Hon. Edward, Home Secretary, 127 *note* 1, 197 (and *note* 1), 202, 265
Siegfried, André, 545
Silesian Plebiscite (1920), 233-4
Simon, Rt. Hon. Sir John (later 1st Viscount), joins National Government, 567 (and *note* 2), 568, 571, 572
Simons, Walther, German Foreign Minister, 177 (and *note* 3), 179, 219-20
Sinclair, Admiral H. F. P. ('Queux') (later Sir Hugh), 189 *note* 2
Singapore Base, construction of decided upon, 231, 254, 347, 348, 350; halted by Labour Government, 360-2, 367; work on resumed, 402-3, 418, 426, 434, 446, 449-50, 480; agreed to by Labour Government, 496-8, 510, 513, 522, 524, 536
Sirianni, Admiral Giuseppi, 513 *note* 3
Slesser, Sir Henry, Solicitor-General, 366 (and *note* 2)
Smartt, Sir Thomas W., 232 (and *note* 2)
Smillie, Robert, 103, 120, 190, 191
Smith, Colin, 314 *note* 1, 444
Smith, Herbert, 191
Smith-Dorrien, General Sir H. L., Governor of Gibraltar, 158 (and *note* 6)
Smuts, General (later Field-Marshal) Jan Christiaan, close association with Hoover Peace Conference, 22, 31, 33, 35, 38, 46, 52, 53, 54, 57 *note* 2, 60, 70, 74; goes on mission to Hungary, 75; opinion of Treaty of Versailles, 94; leaves Paris, 101; H keeps in touch with, 121, 136; views on League of Nations, 135, 195; at Imperial Conference of 1921, 231-2; at Imperial Conference of 1923, where defends League and helps mediate between Curzon and Mackenzie King, 347, 348, 349, 350; receives H's impression of MacDonald, 358; opposed to Singapore Base, 360-1, 362, 367; receives from H report of Imperial Conference of 1926, 433; further letter from H, 482; their close connection, 532. Mentioned, 354, 366, 427, 429, 529
Smyrna, assigned to Greece, 72, 79, 89, 149, 198, 200, 213, 219, 220-1, 223-4, 230, 263; taken by Turks, 283, 288, 437, 500, 533
Snowden, Rt. Hon. Philip (later 1st

Viscount), Chancellor of Exchequer in first MacDonald Cabinet, 365; produces orthodox budget, 367; behaviour at London Reparations Conference, 369, 371 *et seq.*; critical of MacDonald's behaviour over Campbell Case, 377; announces breakdown of Anglo-Soviet Conference, 381; again Chancellor of Exchequer in second MacDonald Ministry, and again unable to get on with Prime Minister, 475; policy and behaviour at First Hague Conference, 481-90; action over West Indian bases and Belligerent Rights, 492-3; at Second Hague Conference, 502, 503, where adopts Young Plan, 505; at Imperial Conference of 1930, 526; and present at MacDonald's meeting with Lloyd George, 530; member of Cabinet Committee on Disarmament, 538; and proposes abolition of all sea-borne aircraft, 541; discusses financial situation with T.U.C., 542; actions during formation of National Government, 546 *note* 1, 550, 551, 552, 560, 563, 565. Mentioned, 380, 492, 545

Snowden, Mrs., 483, 484

Sonnino, Baron Giorgio, Italian Foreign Minister, 28, 30, 58, 61, 162

South Africa, position and claims at Paris Peace Conference, 36, 45, 53, 71, 101; at Imperial Conference of 1921, 231, 232; attitude over Chanak Crisis, 285; at Imperial Conference of 1923, 348, 349, 350; welcomes abandonment of Singapore Base, 360-1; opposed to Geneva Protocol, 395; at Imperial Conference of 1926, 428, 431; Hertzog's policy of neutrality, 432; at Imperial Conference of 1930, 526

Spa Conference (1920), 164, 165, 167, 171, 172, 174, 175-81, 187, 219, 484 *note* 2

Spicer, G. S., 192

Sprague, Oliver M. W., 552 (and *note* 2)

Spring-Rice, Thomas A. (later 3rd Baron Monteagle), 368 (and *note* 5)

Squires, Sir R., 526 *note* 3

Srinivasa-Sastri, Rt. Hon. V. A., 244 *note* 1

Stack, Sir Lee, Sirdar of Egypt, murder of, 407 (and *note* 3)

Stalin, J. V., 185

Stamfordham, 1st Baron, Private Secretary to George V, relations with H, 23, 27-8, 31, 36, 99, 131 *note* 4, 132, 235, 279, 287, 355, 382, 407, 411-12, 425, 436, 443, 445, 470 *note* 6, 477-8, 491, 559

Stamp, Sir Josiah (later 1st Baron), 412 *note* 2, 480 *note* 3, 481 (and *note* 3)

Stanhope, 7th Earl, 510, 544 (and *note* 3)

Stanley, Sir Albert (1st Baron Ashfield), 31

Stanley, Lieutenant-Colonel G. F., 336 *note* 1

Stavridi, Sir John, 199 (and *note* 4), 200, 288 *note* 2

Stern-Rubarth, Dr., 88 *note* 4

Stevenson, Frances (later Countess Lloyd George), 97, 106, 114, 158, 159, 166, 168, 178, 208, 248, 573

Sthamer, Dr. Friedrich, German Ambassador in London, 229-30, 230 *note* 1)

Stimson, Henry L., U.S. Secretary of State, 249 *note* 4, 510 (and *note* 6), 514, 515, 516, 527

Stinnes, Hugo, 178 (and *note* 5), 179, 180

Storr, Lancelot, Military Assistant, Secretary to H, 124, 162, 192, 356

Straker, William, 191

Stresemann, Gustav, German Foreign Minister, 372 (and *note* 3), 414, 483, 488 *note* 1

Stuart-Menteth, Frances (Mrs. Robin Hankey), 474

Sumner, 1st Viscount, 62 (and *note* 1)

Sun Yat Sen, 408

Supreme War Council, 43, 44, 46, 62, 68, 69, 70, 75, 147-8, 165, 194, 196, 229, 315, 332-3, 559

Swift MacNeill, J. G., 287
Swinton, 1st Earl of, 276, 297, 466, *see* also Lloyd-Greame and Cunliffe-Lister
Sykes-Picot Agreement (1916), 37, 78, 90, 116, 119, 204, 292
Sylvester, A. J. (H's Private Secretary), 48, 52, 53, 57, 58, 80, 114, 147, 166, 182, 218, 226, 256, 335, 540
Syria, French control of, 37, 61, 90, 116-20, 135, 138, 147, 163, 202, 223

Takarabe, Admiral Takeshi, 513 *note* 3
Talleyrand-Périgord, Charles Maurice de, 210
Tardieu, André, 25, 513, 514, 515
Ten Year Rule, adopted, 107, 112; H's long struggle against, 346, 403, 416, 463, 521-2, 535-8
Tewfik Pasha, Ahmed, 222 (and *note* 3), 223
Theunis, Georges, Belgian Prime Minister and Minister of Finance, 221 (and *note* 3), 324, 326, 327, 330, 331, 369, 373
Thomas, Rt. Hon. J. H., General Secretary of Railwaymen's Union, 107, 121, 123-4, 190, 298; Colonial Secretary in First MacDonald Ministry, 356, 358, 360, 370; Lord Privy Seal in Second MacDonald Ministry, 475 *note* 1, 493; attitude during formation of National Government, 552, 557, 560, 566-7, 568
Thomson, 1st Baron, 356 (and *note* 4), 448, 538
Thomson, Sir Basil, 235
Thrace, assigned to Greece, 72, 198, 219, 220, 263, 282-3, 288, 289, 292, 295
Tizard, Sir Henry T., 406 (and *note* 3)
Tomkinson, Rear-Admiral Wilfred, 555 (and *note* 1), 557
Toretta, Marchese Pietro della, Italian Ambassador in London, 327 (and *note* 1), 330
Trenchard, Sir Hugh (later 1st Viscount), Chief of Air Staff, 32, 46-7; receives grant for War services, 109; suggests control of Mesopotamia by aircraft, 169; in conflict with Admiralty, 204, 261-2; suggestions during Chanak Crisis, 286; renewed conflict with Admiralty, 337; reaches agreement with Keyes, 339; attitude to C.O.S. and C.I.D., 344-5; continued friction with Admiralty, 403, 446-9, 574; views on role of Air Power, 525. Mentioned, 413, 437
Trenchard-Keyes Agreement (1924), 339, 417
Trevelyan, Sir Charles, 380
Trotha, Admiral von, 95 *note* 2
Trotsky, L. D., 185, 266 *note* 3
Trumbitch, A., 143 *note* 4
Tudor, Major-General H. H. (later Sir Henry), Member of Irish Executive, 197, 253 *note* 5
Tukachevsky, Marshal, 185
Turkey, peace terms discussed at Paris Peace Conference but left unsettled, 37, 68, 72, 79, 114-15; further discussed, 115, 117-20, 126, 135, 136, 137-8, 140, 142-3, 147, 148, 149, 157, 158, 160; Treaty with signed at Sèvres, 163; military revival of, 173, 174, 198, 200, 213, 219, 220-1, 222-4, 230, 263; Chanak Crisis, 282-96; and its aftermath, 318; Conferences and Treaty of Lausanne, 324, 326
Tyrrell, Sir William (later 1st Baron), 287, 330, 408, 453, 473, 494
Tyrwhitt, Admiral (later Admiral of the Fleet, Sir) Reginald, 435 (and *note* 4)

Ullswater, 1st Viscount, 301 (and *note* 1)
Unknown Soldier, Tomb of, 191-2
U.S.A., activities before and during Peace Conference, 19, 25-6, 29; arrival of President Wilson, 30; who comes to London, 36, 38-40, 41-2; Wilson's attitude in Paris, 45, 50, 53-5, 57-9, 60, 62, 64, 67,

68, 69, 71, 73, 75-6, 78, 81-4, 85-6, 87, 89, 91, 95, 96-8, 99, 104; rejection of Treaty of Versailles and breakdown of Wilson's health, 99-100, 118, 126, 152; President Harding summons Washington Conference, 234; Washington Conference and Four Power Pact, 238-58; debt settlement with Britain, 333-5; attitude to Geneva Protocol, 398; President Coolidge suggests another naval conference, 438; naval rivalry with Britain, 439-40; friction with Britain over Belligerent Rights, 451 *et seq.*; reaction to Anglo-French Compromise, 467-8, 472; signs Kellogg-Briand Pact, 469; MacDonald's visit to, 491 *et seq.*; continued naval disagreement with Britain, 509-12; attends London Naval Conference and signs Three Power Treaty, 513-17; dissatisfaction with, 521; question of Belligerent Rights left dormant, 527-8; favours disarmament, 540

Van den Heuvel, J., 85
Vandervelde, Monsieur, 85
Vansittart, Sir Robert (later 1st Baron), 117, 222, 307 (and *note* 2), 400, 457, 479 *note* 5, 492, 494, 506, 508, 521-2, 523, 539, 550
Venizelos, Eleutherios, Prime Minister of Greece, 49, 89, 143, 149, 174, 199, 200, 283, 288, 289
Versailles, Treaty of, presented to Germany, 88; signed 94-6, 105; ratified, 144; rejected by U.S.A., 118, 152, 203. Mentioned, 141, 146, 166, 171, 179, 255, 460, 505, 508
Visconti Venosta, Giovanni Maria (Marchese di Sostegno and Cà del Bosco), 252

Wakatsuki, Reijiro, 514
Wales, Prince of (later Edward VIII), 297, 298, 355
Washington, Conference and Treaty, 104, 218, 234-7, 238-58, 263, 270, 360, 368, 371, 438, 439, 491, 509, 511, 512, 515, 516
Waterhouse, Colonel R. (later Sir Ronald), 341 (and *note* 6), 342, 376, 443, 457
Watt, William A., 175 (and *note* 1)
Webb, Sidney (later 1st Baron Passfield), 380, (Colonial and Dominions Secretary), 493
Wedgwood, Josiah (later 1st Baron), 356, 378, 380
Wedgwood Benn, Rt. Hon. W., 526 *note* 3
Weeks, John, U.S. Secretary of War, 240 (and *note* 3)
Wei hai wei, cession of, 255-6
Weir, 1st Viscount, 47, 336-7, 338, 339
Weizmann, Dr. Chaim, 397 *note* 1
Wells, Ronald, 405 (and *note* 4), 406
Wemyss, Admiral (later 1st Baron Wester Wemyss), 31
Westminster, Statute of (1930), 432, 471, 526, 528 and *note* 4
Weygand, General Maxime, 29, 161, 162, 173, 182, 185, 186
Wheatley, Rt. Hon. John, Minister of Health, 365 (and *note* 5)
Wickham Steed, H., Editor of *Times*, 103 (and *note* 4), 104, 291-2, 316
Wicks, Pembroke, 308 (and *note* 3)
Wiehl, Dr. E., 370 *note* 3
Wigram, Clive (later 1st Baron), 374 (and *note* 2), 559, 566
Wigram, Ralph, F., 368 (and *note* 6)
Wilhelmina, Queen of the Netherlands, 503, 504 (and *note* 2)
Willert, Sir Arthur, 242 (and *note* 3), 374
Williams, Tom, 122
Willingdon, 1st Marquess of, Viceroy of India, 562 (and *note* 2)
Wilson, Sir Arnold, 201 (and *note* 3)
Wilson, General (later Field-Marshal) Sir Henry, Chief of Imperial Staff, at Anglo-French meeting, Dec. 1918, 29, 31; at Fontainebleau talks, 70; comments on procedure of Council of Four, 73, 76; and on German attitude to peace terms,

Wilson, General [*contd.*] 95-6; becomes Field-Marshal, 108; and given a grant, 109; at Criccieth, 110; his military advice to Montagu, 142; concerned over paucity of military strength to cope with industrial strife, 144; informs H of number of French coloured troops in Rhineland, 151; attitude to Irish troubles, 153; at Spa Conference, 175, 176, 179; anxious to evacuate Persia, 203; alarmist views of, 226; assassination of, 264-6. Mentioned, 159, 277, 282, 331, 533
Wilson, Sir Horace, 320 (and *note* 1), 343, 550
Wilson, Leslie, 34, 324
Wilson, Brigadier-General Sir Samuel H., 59, 157 *note* 2
Wilson, Woodrow, President of U.S.A., leaves for Europe, 30; visits London, 36, 38-40, 41-2; attitude and policy at Paris Peace Conference, 45, 50, 52 *passim* 62, 69, 73, 75-6, 78, 80 *passim* 87, 89, 91, 95 *passim* 99; his breakdown, 113, 118, 126, 136; declines to attend London meeting of Lloyd George and Clemenceau, 147; criticised at San Remo Conference, 163; visited by H in Washington, 245-6. Mentioned, 26, 67, 104, 135, 194, 213, 229
Wingate, Sir Reginald, 115
Wirth, Joseph, German Finance Minister, 229 (and *note* 2)
Wise, Edward F., 171 (and *note* 2)
Wiseman, Sir William, 166
Wood, Edward, F. L. President of Board of Education, 317 (and *note* 1), *see* also Irwin, Baron
Worthington-Evans, Sir Laming, Minister of Pensions, then Secretary of State for War, 130 (and *note* 1), 175, 191, 217, 229, 268, 272, 284, 285 *note* 1, 289, 298, 325, 336
Wright, Peter, 309

Yap, dispute over island of, 82-3, 223, 245
Yardley, H. O., 249 *note* 4
Yegorov, General, 185
Young, Owen D. (and Young Report), 332, 480 (and *note* 3), 481, 502, 505, 506, 507
Younger, Sir George (later 1st Viscount), 224 (and *note* 2)

Zinoviev, Grigory (Zinoviev Letter), 382-6, 461